The Last Libertines

The Last Libertines

BENEDETTA CRAVERI

Translated from the Italian by Aaron Kerner

nyrb **New York Review Books** New York

This is a New York Review Book
published by The New York Review of Books
435 Hudson Street, New York, NY 10014
www.nyrb.com

Library of Congress Cataloging-in-Publication Data
    Names: Craveri, Benedetta, 1942– author. | Kerner, Aaron, translator.
Title: The last libertines / Benedetta Craveri ; translated by Aaron Kerner.
Other titles: Gli ultimi libertini. English
Description: New York City : New York Review Books, [2020] | Series: New York
    Review books | Includes bibliographical references and index.
Identifiers: LCCN 2019044362 (print) | LCCN 2019044363 (ebook) |
    ISBN 9781681373409 ; (hbk.) | ISBN 9781681373416 ; (ebook)
Subjects: LCSH: Nobility—France—Biography. | France—History—Louis XVI,
    1774–1793—Biography. | France—History—Louis XV, 1715–1774—Biography.
Classification: LCC DC137.5.A1 C7313 2020 (print) | LCC DC137.5.A1 (ebook) |
    DDC 944/.0340922—dc23
LC record available at https://lccn.loc.gov/2019044362
LC ebook record available at https://lccn.loc.gov/2019044363

ISBN 978-1-68137-340-9
Available as an electronic book; ISBN 978-1-68137-341-6

Printed in the United States of America on acid-free paper.

10 9 8 7 6 5 4 3 2 1

for Bernard Minoret

Contents

Preface

THIS BOOK TELLS THE STORY of seven aristocrats whose youth coincided with the French monarchy's final moment of grace—a moment when it seemed to the nation's elite that a style of life based on privilege and the spirit of caste might acknowledge the widespread demand for change, and in doing so reconcile itself with Enlightenment ideals of justice, tolerance, and citizenship.

"It is always a beautiful thing to be twenty years old," Sainte-Beuve wrote of that generation of nobles. But never was it more so than in 1774, when Louis XVI's ascension to the throne seemed to herald the beginning of a new age, one that would allow these "princes of youth" (as Louis-Marcelin de Fontanes described them) to "advance step by step" with their era, in perfect harmony with the world around them.[1] "We mocked the old customs, the feudal pride of our fathers and the solemnity of their ways, so as to continue to enjoy all of our privileges," the Comte de Ségur would write many years later.[2] "Freedom, royalty, aristocracy, democracy, prejudice, reason, novelty, philosophy—all combined to make our days delightful; and never was so terrible an awakening preceded by so sweet a sleep and by dreams so seductive."[3]

But could matters really have been so simple? Could the liberal nobility (which welcomed the summoning of the Estates General as an opportunity to put in place those institutional reforms that the country sorely needed, and to establish a constitutional monarchy along English lines) truly have lacked a sense of reality? Did they realize only belatedly, after toying with philosophical theories whose consequences they wholly failed to grasp,[4] just how much they had contributed to their own ruin?

This is not the impression one has when retracing the lives and political choices of the Duc de Lauzun, the Comte and Vicomte de Ségur, the Duc de Brissac, the Comte de Narbonne, the Comte de Vaudreuil, and the Chevalier de Boufflers, the protagonists of this book. In making my selection of precisely these seven from among the many brilliant and representative figures of the era, I was driven, of course, by the romantic character of their exploits and amours—but also by the keenness with which they experienced this crisis in

I

the civilization of the ancien régime, of which they themselves were the emblem, all while keeping their gaze fixed on the new world that was in the process of being born. Each of them belonged to the ancient feudal nobility and possessed those prerogatives that their class took the most pride in: dignity, courage, refinement of manners, culture, wit, and the art of pleasing. Aware of their advantages and determined to make themselves felt in the world, they responded with all they had to the demands of a profoundly theatrical society, in which one was obliged to know how to hold one's place at center stage. They were also past masters of the art of seduction, and their many successes with the *dames du grand monde* did not prevent them from practicing libertinism in its broadest sense. This is why I have called them "the last libertines"—even if each of them eventually met the woman capable of binding him to her for the rest of their days.

They were all tied to one another by long friendships or social acquaintance. They frequented the same milieus, shared the same interests, pursued the same ambitions, and often the same women, as well. Not only do their stories share numerous similarities, shedding light on one another, but they gesture toward the stories of many others. Their behavior and their choices were influenced by family ties, matrimonial alliances, love affairs, and social relations but also by rivalries, resentments, and the desire for revenge. And in these pages the reader will cross paths with Marie-Antoinette, Catherine II of Russia, the Duc de Choiseul and Talleyrand, the Baron de Besenval and the Polignac clan, the Duc d'Orléans and Laclos, Chamfort and Mirabeau, Princesse Izabela Czartoryska and Lady Sarah Lennox, the Prince de Ligne (an inexhaustible chronicler of this cosmopolitan elite), the painter Élisabeth Vigée Le Brun (who captured that era's "sweetness of life" on canvas), and various other illustrious personalities essential to the understanding of our seven gentlemen. After all, if we know a good deal about them today, it is not only because they poured forth their impressions of themselves and their world in memoirs, letters, and poems but also because they figured powerfully in the diaries and correspondence of their contemporaries.

And yet though they emerged from the same mold, products of that same "perfected civilization"[5] that produced a seemingly endless amount of commentary upon itself, the seven protagonists of this book were irreducible individualists. Each of them sought to forge a destiny true to his image of himself. Sons of the Enlightenment, endowed with a surprising capacity for work, they possessed an unlimited faith in their own abilities to range at will through politics and economics, literature and art, all while maintaining military careers. Curious about everything, at ease wherever they happened to find themselves, Lauzun, Boufflers, the elder of the Ségurs, Narbonne, and Vaudreuil were great travelers as well, and we will find their traces in Africa, America, England, Italy, Germany, Poland, and Russia. Still, convinced as they were of their worth, many were forced to acknowledge that personal merit gave no assurance of serving their sovereign in posts of command. Subjects of an absolute monarchy, they may have bowed their heads before the arbitrariness of royal favor, but they were unwilling to simply let court intrigue or the excessive power of the King's ministers decide their fates. The reasons that led them to keep their distance from the politics of Versailles, however, were more than merely personal. "A regiment, an ambassadorship, a military commission, everything nowadays depends on royal favor or the whims of society," as the Duc de Lauzun wrote indignantly to a friend.[6] Their experiences of military service, government administration, and diplomacy, as well as their encounters with the systems prevailing in other lands, had convinced them that the French monarchy needed to change its methods of governance and provide itself with new institutions in order to be able to respond to the political, economic, and social crises then devastating the country. England served as a model: in London, where they mixed with fashionable society and took a keen interest in horse racing, they envied the positions held in public life by a nobility engaged in both politics and business. The American War of Independence proved no less decisive for the Duc de Lauzun and the Comte de Ségur, showing them that a democratic country governed by free citizens was not merely a utopia to be found in books.

With the exception of the Comte de Vaudreuil—the only one who, having staked everything on royal favor, was forced to flee after the fall of the Bastille—all of our protagonists hailed with enthusiasm the summoning of the Estates General, and only during the course of the revolution that followed did their respective paths diverge.

Elected as a deputy to the National Constituent Assembly, the Chevalier de Boufflers would yield to the entreaties of his beloved, an intransigent royalist, and side with the monarchy. A mediocre orator, and fully aware that he was fighting for a lost cause, the Chevalier was far from brilliant when it came to institutional debate, but in his passion for nature and love of beauty he strove to protect confiscated forests and Church properties from speculators and to defend the work of artists and artisans newly deprived of support. Once the assembly had fulfilled its duty, he opted to emigrate, repelled by the violence of political struggle.

The first of our seven to die, a victim of popular fury, was the Duc de Brissac, the faithful and chivalrous lover of Mme du Barry, Louis XV's last favorite. Obedient to the imperatives of honor—"I merely pay what I owe to the ancestors of the King, and to my own"[7]—the Duc accepted the command of the sovereign's personal guard, knowing full well that in doing so he was resigning himself to certain death.

A convinced constitutionalist, the Comte de Narbonne was the last minister of war appointed by Louis XVI, thanks to the campaign waged in his favor by Mme de Staël, who was madly in love with him. But his scheme to restore the King's prestige by way of a brief war against the electorate of Trèves, the headquarters of the emigration, fell apart at the seams. On August 10, after the storming of the Tuileries and the fall of the monarchy, he was accused of high treason by the Jacobins, but made an extraordinary escape to England.

A constitutionalist like Narbonne, the Comte de Ségur chose to remain in France with his family, including his brother, who had long since shed his illusions about the possibility of reform. During the Terror, they would attempt to keep a low profile, but both the Maréchal de Ségur and the Vicomte wound up in prison, and only the fall of Robespierre saved them from the guillotine.

For all seven, the trial and execution of the King represented an irremediable trauma and sanctioned their definitive alienation from the Revolution.

The only one of them to swear loyalty to the Republic was the Duc de Lauzun, who would become a general under the old family name of Biron. But in spite of his deep resentment toward the royal family, he too came to detest the violence of the Jacobins, and was well aware that his aristocratic origins had never been forgiven. A professional soldier in a nation at war, he felt duty-bound to defend his homeland against foreign invasion. In contrast to Lafayette and General Dumouriez, he remained at his post and commanded successively the Army of the Rhine, the Army of Italy, and the troops charged with putting down the uprising in the Vendée. This final commission was a question of civil war, Frenchman against Frenchman, and Lauzun was unprepared to see it through. He did his best to avoid direct confrontations and worked toward compromise until, having become suspect in the eyes of the Committee of Public Safety, he resigned, thereby signing his own death warrant.

With the Revolution behind them, Boufflers, Narbonne, the Ségur brothers, and Vaudreuil found themselves facing new choices: some opted for Napoleon, and only one of them returned to France in the wake of Louis XVIII. Each carried grief in his heart for parents, friends, and acquaintances killed on the scaffold, the consciousness of having fallen short of his proper destiny, and a sense of guilt for having survived the disappearance of a world that he had loved intensely and whose end his own actions had helped precipitate. But all—no matter their convictions, responsibilities, or weaknesses—confronted danger, poverty, and exile with heads held high, maintaining their caste's tradition of courage and stoicism. And now, resuming their lives in a new society, they turned their minds to finding new places for themselves, making it a point of honor to demonstrate by way of their exquisite courtesy, the elegance of their manners, and their unremitting geniality their fidelity to an aristocratic civilization of which they themselves were the last representatives.

The Duc de Lauzun

It was there, passing by me, in hussar's garb, going full gallop on a Barbary steed, that I saw one of those men in whom a whole world came to an end: the Duc de Lauzun.

—CHATEAUBRIAND[1]

IN 1811, RESPONDING TO WIDESPREAD CONCERN, Napoleon ordered the police to seize and destroy the manuscript of the memoirs of the Duc de Lauzun.[2] Evidence of a past at odds with the exigencies of the moment, the recollections of the last famous libertine of France's ancien régime had begun to circulate surreptitiously,[3] alarming Paris's beau monde. Luckily, however, Queen Hortense, eager to read the manuscript, had a copy of it made in secret for herself,[4] and it is thanks to this transcription that ten years later, in the midst of the Restoration, the memoirs of the Duc de Lauzun were finally published, triggering a genuine scandal.

But why, exactly, would the youthful recollections of one of the innumerable victims of the guillotine kindle so much outrage? And why had a similar uproar been caused only a few years earlier by the publication of the memoirs of the Baron de Besenval, who, for his part, had had the good fortune to die in his bed shortly before the fall of the Bastille? The Baron's memoirs had also appeared posthumously in 1805, thanks to the efforts of a good friend of the Duc, the Vicomte Joseph-Alexandre de Ségur.

Evoking the customs and traditions of the French aristocracy by following the thread of one's own personal experience was, of course, nothing new. For at least three centuries numerous nobles had left written traces of their own affairs and decisions, both in the public sphere and on the battlefield. Moreover, beginning in the early years of the nineteenth century, the desire to bear witness would spread among those who, having survived the Revolution, had been intimate with the society of the ancien régime, and felt the need to fix their recollections in print. Many of these memoirists—the Prince de Ligne, the

Comte de Ségur, the Marquise de La Tour du Pin, Mme de Genlis, Élisabeth Vigée Le Brun, to name only a few—had been friends or acquaintances of Besenval and Lauzun, and would also describe, with the same milieu and cast of characters, the aristocratic way of life at its apogee.

What made the testimonies of Lauzun and Besenval so different, dangerous, and, for we modern readers, particularly interesting, was the moment at which they were written. Both men had set down their memories before the coming of the Terror—that is, while still oblivious to the tragic end awaiting the society whose glorious recklessness they so delighted in describing. Both had been part of Marie-Antoinette's circle of favorites, and their portraits of the beautiful, frivolous Queen and her entourage were difficult to reconcile with the image of the Christian martyr that had been established in the wake of the Revolution. Moreover, when their memoirs were published, a significant number of the gentlewomen whose amorous pasts they recounted were still among the living and had long since adopted the role of respectable matrons.[5] Nor were the families of those who had perished—often quite violently—pleased to learn that the conduct of their noble grandmothers clashed so violently with the bourgeois morality of the new century. Besenval and Lauzun, killed during the Revolution, lacked the opportunity to revise their writings, to temper the irreverent license of their memories, which now risked appearing as an implicit denunciation of the moral failings that had weakened the court from within—a denunciation particularly embarrassing since both men had played leading roles there.

Faced with a pair of witnesses whose testimony was difficult to confute, the eulogists of the old regime's best available strategy was to deny the authenticity of their work. This was Mme de Genlis's approach to the memoirs of Besenval;[6] and in 1818, when copies of Lauzun's manuscript began to circulate, Talleyrand declared in *Le Moniteur*[7] that it was a vulgar fraud.[8] This was a brazen lie— Talleyrand had known Lauzun too well to be able to deny the veracity of his youthful friend's love affairs.[9] However, having passed into the service of the Restoration, the former Bishop of Autun now presented himself (for political reasons) as a white knight defending the respectability of the survivors of the ancien régime, that world whose destruction he himself had helped hasten. "All those who knew the Duc de Lauzun know that to lend his tales charm he needed nothing but those graces native to his intellect; that he was eminently a man of good form and fine taste, and that never was anyone less capable of voluntarily doing harm than he," Talleyrand wrote. "And yet it is to this man that they dare attribute the most odious satires of women both French and foreign, and the grossest calumnies against an august figure [the Queen] who displayed as much kindness as she did greatness of soul amid the excesses of her misfortune. Such are the most prominent features of the so-called *Memoirs* of the Duc de Lauzun which have been circulating for some time in manuscript, and of which I have a copy in my hands."[10]

Thirty years later, addressing the persistence of the controversy, Sainte-Beuve would finally make clear the political significance of Lauzun's *Memoirs*, which, he affirmed, "though they strike one as frivolous at first glance, have a serious side far more enduring...history records them as evidence for the prosecution in the great trial of the eighteenth century."[11] This certainly was not the spirit in which Lauzun had first taken up his pen in the autumn of 1782. The idea of retracing the first thirty-five years of his life occurred to him at the end of his second military expedition to the United States, while waiting to embark on the ship that would return him to France. Leaving behind him the successes of his American adventure, uncertain as to the prospects that awaited him in his homeland, suspended between two worlds, the Duc amused himself by reviewing those experiences and encounters that had meant the most to him.[12] "You shall see me successively take on the roles of *galant*, gambler, politician, soldier, hunter, philosopher, and occasionally more than one of these at the same time," he announces at the beginning of his memoirs.[13] And since the narrative was addressed to his paramour of the moment, the beautiful and free-spirited Marquise de Coigny, it was inevitable that his love life would constitute a central theme.

There was nothing so odd about any of this. Hadn't the Comte de Bussy-Rabutin written, more than a century earlier, during the lulls of a military campaign, his *Amorous History of the Gauls* for the amusement of a distant lover? In that case, too, it had been a question of a private divertissement, a work intended for a handful of friends, which only by chance wound up in the hands of unscrupulous publishers. But unlike Bussy-Rabutin's amorous tales of life in the court of the Sun King, there was not a trace of satire to be found in Lauzun's memoirs, wherein even the loosest of women were described with respect. By the Duc's era, sexual freedom had become customary among the nobility, both male and female. Stendhal likened Lauzun's memoirs to the best of the libertine novels,[14] but for the Duc, the nature of "libertinism" was altogether different: Lauzun, unlike the heroes of Crébillon fils, was no systematic seducer, driven by a blind will to dominate—in him the pursuit of pleasure was always circumscribed by sentiment. Modern readers might liken his memoirs to a bildungsroman rather than a libertine novel—the story of an individual struggling since birth against a future dictated to him by others, striving to choose freely what form to give his own life.

On April 13, 1747, it was as though the fairies had gathered around the cradle of Armand-Louis de Gontaut de Biron to shower him with blessings. Aside from having an illustrious name and a grand inheritance, the future Duc de Lauzun would be handsome, daring, generous, and brilliant.[15] First and foremost, however, he was the scion of a singular family.

His father, Charles-Antoine-Armand, Marquis (and later Duc) de Gontaut, had been a courageous soldier until, gravely wounded in 1743 at the Battle of Dettingen, he was obliged to abandon the army. The following year, notwithstanding a cruel nickname—"the White Eunuch"—with which he was saddled in the wake of his injury, the Marquis married Antoinette-Eustachie Crozat du Châtel, a wealthy heiress, aged sixteen. It was whispered that he had "*most probably*"[16] delegated to his wife's lover, and his own best friend, the Duc de Choiseul, the task of making her a mother—but the means were justified by the ends, since what truly mattered to him was securing the continuation of his line. Yet the family's joy at the birth of an heir was dampened by the sudden demise of the Marquise, carried away in a matter of days by a puerperal fever. The young woman's final thoughts were not about the child that had cost her her life but rather for the man she loved: Choiseul lacked the means to make a successful career for himself, and so, in order to secure his future, on her deathbed Antoinette-Eustachie extorted from her ten-year-old sister a promise that she would become his wife. The immense inheritance brought to Choiseul by the young Louise-Honorine's dowry, as well as the support of Gontaut, an intimate friend of Louis XV and the Marquise de Pompadour, would guarantee Choiseul a splendid future: after serving as an ambassador to Rome and to Vienna, he would govern France as de facto prime minister for nearly twenty years.

Having become brothers-in-law, and quite attached to each other, Gontaut and Choiseul decided to share the same house, the elegant Hôtel du Châtel in the rue de Richelieu,[17] where the two men displayed an equal indifference when it came to little Armand-Louis. The only one to take any interest in the orphan was his aunt, the sweet and charitable Mme de Choiseul, who would never know the joys of motherhood herself. However, "the predominant passion" of the young Duchesse was her unrequited love for her husband, and it induced her to relegate all other ties of affection to second place, and to subject her will in every respect to that of her lord and master. And this would not always prove favorable to the young Armand-Louis.

Choiseul did not limit himself to being an impenitent Don Juan and squandering his spouse's fortune (destined to pass by inheritance to his nephew) on a princely lifestyle; he also saddled the Duchesse with the presence of his favorite sister, Mme de Gramont. Until she was nearly forty, Béatrix de Choiseul-Stainville had been forced to content herself with the position of canoness at Remiremont Abbey, but as soon as he became minister, Choiseul wanted her by his side. Introduced into the innermost circle surrounding Mme de Pompadour, elevated to the rank of Duchesse thanks to a marriage of convenience, Mme de Gramont wasn't particularly concerned about disguising the influence she exerted on her brother—with whom she maintained a rapport so symbiotic that it led the malicious to speak of incest. Soon enough relations between the two sisters-in-law erupted into open conflict, one in which it was not the wife but rather the sister who had the upper hand.

Armand-Louis would soon be forced to reckon with this domestic strife, but his earliest household was the royal court. During the period in which Choiseul represented the King of France in Rome and then in Vienna, the Duc de Gontaut brought the boy along with him to Versailles, where he maintained a residence. And Lauzun himself recalls that the earliest years of his childhood were passed, "so to speak, in the lap of the King's lover,"[18] who kept him perpetually at her side, teaching him to read aloud to her and to serve as her private secretary. The proximity of Mme de Pompadour, the most seductive of the royal favorites, could not have failed to leave its mark on Lauzun's erotic imagination. This precocious initiation into the life of the court, under conditions of exceptional privilege, was determinant in anchoring in him the conviction that he was "destined for an immense fortune, and to occupy the most splendid position in the kingdom"[19] without being obliged to do anything in particular to deserve it. Indeed, when at the age of twelve he was enlisted in the regiment of the Gardes Françaises, the King promised that someday he would become a colonel, like his grandfather and uncle before him. Yet with the passage of time this self-confidence would begin to weaken.

A child of his era, Lauzun was determined above all to be serenely himself, without taking into account the fact that under the French monarchy, favor lid not necessarily go hand in hand, and that membership in the privileged imposed a set of strictures that were difficult to flout.

...e he was obliged to acknowledge this reality was when, at age urteen, he deluded himself into thinking he could propose to his youthful paramour, Mlle de Beauvau. But the Duc de Gontaut had other plans for the young man, and following that logic by which marriage was meant to reinforce the prestige of the line, had already made his choice on Lauzun's behalf: Amélie de Boufflers belonged to an illustrious family, possessed a huge dowry, and was the pedagogical masterpiece of her grandmother, the celebrated Maréchale de Luxembourg, who, having put her libertine youth behind her, had won general acclaim as the supreme arbiter of aristocratic decorum. Jean-Jacques Rousseau, who had known Mlle de Boufflers as an adolescent, has left us a spellbound description of her: "There was nothing more amiable and more interesting than her face, nothing more tender and chaste than the sentiments that she inspired."[20]

Even though the Duc de Gontaut was, by Lauzun's own admission, "a perfectly honest man, with a compassionate and charitable soul,"[21] he remained unmoved by his son's entreaties, and limited himself to allowing the boy two years of freedom in advance of the arranged marriage. So that when, on February 4, 1766, filled with rage at the obligation forced upon him, Armand-Louis led the not yet fifteen-year-old Amélie de Boufflers to the altar,[22] he made it a point of pride not to nurture any sentimental expectations with regard to his wife. This didn't prevent him from initially granting her those attentions demanded by the circumstances—attentions that his young spouse received, whether from timidity or inexperience or pride, with a coldness that drove him to observe, going forward, relations characterized above all by a polite indifference.[23] The enchanting Mme de Lauzun would be, as it turned out, the sole woman destined *not* to exercise on him even the least attraction.

At the time of his marriage, Lauzun was seventeen years old and his *education sentimentale* had been completed, as was customary, by a skilled professional who had spent some fifteen days (as she had with numerous other young men at court) leading him through a series of "*délicieuses leçons.*"[24] Indeed, the pupil showed himself so talented that his instructor refused compensation for her labors. Once he had acquired fluency in the conduct appropriate to the bedroom, Armand-Louis hastened to test its efficacy on the women of high society. But notwithstanding the varied succession of experiences that followed—with married women and girls of marriageable age, with aristocrats and bourgeois women of sundry nationalities, all ready to risk their reputations for his sake—he never forgot his first erotic education, and continued to frequent the *filles* of the gambling dens and bordellos. And it would be one of these who clung to him during the final, tragic months preceding his death, remaining by his side almost to the foot of the guillotine.

But what truly marked Lauzun's entry into adulthood—revealing at a blow the violence that lurked behind the elegance of worldly conventions, the hypocrisy of social comportment, the cruelty of the institution of marriage, and above all the dark side of his own family—was the story of his first true love.

In 1761, having been made the minister of war and determined to forge for himself a clan equal to the height of his ambitions, the Duc de Choiseul summoned to Paris, in addition to his sister the Duchesse de Gramont, his brother, the Comte de Stainville, an impecunious soldier in the service of the Duc de Lorraine, securing him a prestigious post in the French army and arranging a brilliant marriage for him. His intended, Mlle de Clermont-Reynel, was exceptionally beautiful, a mere fifteen years old, and enormously wealthy, while Stainville had reached the age of forty and was by no means a pleasant character. Lauzun saw Mlle de Clermont-Reynel for the first time on the day of her wedding and immediately "fell passionately in love."[25] He was still a boy of fourteen, and even if his naive adoration momentarily touched the young Comtesse, he was forced to resign himself to being treated like a handsome little cherub, and to turning his curiosity about the fair sex elsewhere.

The first member of the family circle to realize that Lauzun had become a terrifically attractive young man was Mme de Gramont, who did not hesitate to let him know it. Herself less than beautiful, with a masculine voice, the Duchesse was daring, arrogant, unscrupulous—a "ferocious Amazon"[26]—but also extremely intelligent and "the most congenial company."[27] With youthful ingratitude, Armand-Louis made no secret of taking her side in the conflict with Mme de Choiseul and prided himself on his conquest of the Duchesse de Gramont, who "had the whole court at her feet."[28] It was the most "glorious" of worldly debuts.[29]

But Mme de Gramont's intentions did not escape her sister-in-law, who, having overcome the shock of finding herself tied for life to a brutal and revolting husband, was making the best of the situation by adopting the ways of high society and taking a fashionable lover. And since nothing was more fashionable than a lover stolen from a highly visible lady, the young Comtesse looked with new eyes at her little admirer of two years earlier and decided to snatch him away from her sister-in-law. After all, there was no love lost between the two women: the Duchesse, jealous of the beauty and success of Mme de Stainville and worried that she might gain influence over the Duc de Choiseul, kept her at a distance; and for her part, the Comtesse was afraid of her, but not to the point of renouncing the temptation of spiting her.

Called on to choose between the two sisters-in-law, Armand-Louis listened to his heart and "sacrificed Mme de Gramont."[30] Thrilled by her victory, the young Stainville was quick to respond to the sentiment she had inspired. Both were little more than adolescents—beautiful, famished for life, impatient with the responsibilities that had been imposed upon them—and too utterly in love with each other to realize how obvious their affair was to others.[31] Naturally none of this escaped the perceptive Duchesse de Gramont, who took care not to reveal her disappointment, while at the same time giving Lauzun the cold shoulder and leveling at her sister-in-law an implacable hate.[32] But the Comte de Stainville could not conceal his own jealousy, and ordered his wife not to fraternize with Lauzun, forcing the two lovers to resort to all the canonical expedients of infidelity (the complicity of servants, a secret loge at the theater, fantastic nocturnal rendezvous) in order to continue their relations.

In the meantime, the Duc de Choiseul had taken a fancy to Mme de Stainville as well—and, being aware of her extramarital affairs, felt confident of obtaining a hearing for himself. After all, he was the one who had engineered her marriage, and he was also the head of the family. Alarmed at the Duc's overtures, and determined to resist him to the bitter end, the Comtesse wanted Lauzun to witness her refusal: like a character in a farce, Armand-Louis eavesdropped on the encounter between the two while concealed in an armoire in Mme de Stainville's chamber. Faced with the failure of his advances, Choiseul quickly moved on to threats, demanding that Mme de Stainville quit "playing at virtue," and warning her that he would no longer stand for her games; otherwise, she and her "young lover" would regret it. "Don't transform a man who loves you to the point of madness," he concluded, "into an implacable enemy... for whom nothing would be easier than destroying a rival unworthy of you."[33]

His tone was too outrageous, and Mme de Stainville too indignant, to sustain the sort of self-control the situation called for. In any case prudence was not her strong suit and, exhilarated by the thought of addressing her lover by proxy, she did not bother to deny the charge, claiming the right to be the mistress of her own emotions. "You are certainly powerful, monsieur, I'm not ignorant of that; but I do not, and cannot, love you. M. de Biron is my lover, I admit, since you force me to it; he is dearer to me than anything; and neither your tyrannical power, nor any ill you can do us, will make us renounce each other."[34]

Choiseul retreated, commanding his sister-in-law not to breathe a word of their conversation, but the tale was too beautiful to remain a secret, and the Duc, apprised that Lauzun had overheard it all, "was in a rage which, though he dissembled it, had terrible repercussions."[35]

In his memoirs, Lauzun reports the scene to us while passing over in silence the emotions it must have roused in him. He could not have been ignorant of the fact that Choiseul had been his mother's lover, and Lauzun had good reason to suppose that he himself was the fruit of their liaison. But his case was far from unusual among the aristocracy: at least two of Armand-Louis's friends—the Comte de Narbonne, nicknamed "Demi-Louis" for his notable resemblance to the image of Louis XV engraved on the eponymous coin, and the Vicomte Joseph-Alexandre de Ségur, who bore an "indecent"[36] resemblance to Baron de Besenval—were not the sons of the men whose names they bore. But in contrast with Joseph-Alexandre, who joked with pleasure about the fact that the Maréchal de Ségur wasn't his father,[37] Lauzun (like Narbonne) treated the subject with the greatest reserve.

Whether natural father or close kin, the image of Choiseul that we find in Armand-Louis's narrative is a dark one. In these pages the consummate minister, the great seducer with all of high society at his beck, the very incarnation of the French aristocracy's art of living, drops his mask to reveal the hideous face of a hypocritical libertine[38] determined to flout every rule and work his will by force as well as guile. Here we find the very archetype of the castrating father—a paterfamilias ready to engage in incest with his sister, seduce the wife of his son, and violently rid himself of a son-nephew, so as to replace him in the bed of the woman he loved.

Soon enough, his threats gave way to action. Lauzun narrowly escaped a nocturnal ambush, but Mme de Stainville was so shaken by the incident that she broke off a relationship that had seemed to have become impossible. Still, she was by no means subdued by the experience. She threw herself back into social life and pursued fresh romances, reassured by the indulgence shown by her husband, who seemed mollified by having obtained satisfaction in the case of Lauzun. But she made an irreparable mistake. She completely lost her head for Clairval, a successful actor, and was incapable of hiding her passion. To take a domestic servant or an actor as a lover was to violate the last sexual taboo still imposed by the morality of the era on women. Lauzun, who had remained quite close to her, tried in vain to divert her from "so unreasonable an inclination,"[39] and spoke to Clairval himself, painting for him "all of the risks you run, and all those that threaten Mme de Stainville."[40] The sole precaution that the young woman took was to entrust Lauzun with the letters she'd received from the actor.

For the Duc de Choiseul and Mme de Gramont, it was the chance they'd dreamed of to put their sister-in-law at their mercy. One night, alerted by a servant, Lauzun surprised a man attempting to force the lock of his desk. But taking advantage of the darkness, the thief fled by means of the passage connecting Lauzun's residence with Choiseul's mansion, pulling the doors shut behind him one after another, until at last he slammed that of the apartment of the Duc de Gontaut. Only then did Armand-Louis—who had pursued the fugitive with pistol in hand—realize how close he had come to killing his own father.

In the end, it was the clumsy attempt of Clairval to protect Mme de Stainville from the slander that led to her downfall. Frightened by the turn events had taken, the actor attempted to cover his tracks by wooing one of his young colleagues in the opera, Mlle Beaumesnil.[41] Like most actresses, she led a rather free life and, as a professional courtesan, enjoyed the generosity of a rich lover. But by a thoroughly unfortunate coincidence, that lover was none other than M. de Stainville, who, duly notified of the fact by the Duchesse de Gramont, could not bear the affront of finding himself in competition with Clairval for a second time. Though it had been a while since he had lavished any attention on his wife, he could not tolerate being deceived by her young protégé. And since he could boast no direct authority over the latter, he decided to revenge himself on Clairval by means of the power he still held over his wife.

He seized the opportunity of a grand Chinese costume ball given by the Maréchal de Mirepoix at the Hôtel de Brancas in January 1767. As Mme du Deffand later reported to Walpole, the "guilty and unfortunate Mme de Stainville" was "along with the Prince d'Hénin"[42] among the most accomplished dancers and always took part in the rehearsals, but two nights before the ball all those present noticed that she was unable to conceal her tears. That same evening her husband, supplied with an order signed by the King, which he had obtained thanks to the intercession of the Duc de Choiseul, forced her into a coach and "had the cruelty"[43] of accompanying her in person to Nancy in order to confine her to a convent without a penny, forbidding her to communicate even with her two daughters. "If she'd only taken a man of her own rank," Choiseul commented, "I would have been ready to lend them my own room."[44]

Perfectly legitimate from a legal point of view, the Comte's action contravened aristocratic decorum in a spectacular fashion, and revealed just how precarious a woman's position, balancing between law and custom, really was. In the face of general indignation, Mlle Beaumesnil broke off all contact with the Comte, fearing that it would be suspected that she herself had played some part in "such an iniquity."[45]

Nobody could have been more touched than Lauzun by the plight of this woman whom he now loved like a sister,[46] and for whose sake he had clashed with his family. But the sorrow now stamped on the features of the young Duc drew the attention of Lady Sarah Bunbury, and formed the point of departure for another great love affair.

Deaf to the jealousy of his mistress of the moment (the imperious Mme de Cambis), Armand-Louis had been courting Lady Sarah since her arrival in the French capitol, accompanied by her husband, Sir Charles Bunbury, in December 1766. This was the young woman's second sojourn in Paris, and to Armand-Louis she seemed the incarnation of English charm. In an era of rampant Anglomania, attempting to win her heart was the sort of challenge that a fashionable young libertine like Lauzun simply had to pursue. He was twenty years old, and she was twenty-two.

Since 1763, when France and England had signed the treaty that put an end to the Seven Years' War, a continuous flood of visitors had crossed the English Channel in both directions. In Paris in 1762, Horace Walpole had borne witness to this reciprocal fascination: "Our passion for everything French is nothing to theirs for everything English."[47] Some thirty years earlier Voltaire's *Lettres philosophiques* had celebrated that nation's respect for individual liberty and its form of government, and now the French elite made pilgrimages to London to observe at close range a parliamentary monarchy that many considered a possible model for the future of France. And while the novels of Samuel

Richardson, adapted in French by the Abbé Prévost, revealed the charms of a puritan and bourgeois sentimentalism that would find a formidable echo in *La Nouvelle Héloïse*, English horses, carriages, dogs, and fabrics conquered the French market as tokens of a simpler and more spontaneous way of life.

Baron Friedrich Melchior de Grimm's *Correspondance littéraire*, addressed to the crowned heads of northern Europe, took note of this phenomenon, not without irony: "Nothing, it seems to me, is more amusing than that peculiar and ridiculous trade established for some time now between France and England.... Today we have as many specimens of English postilions as they do of our poor Huguenots; we have the same taste for their horses, their punch, and their philosophers, as they do for our wines, our liqueurs, and our *filles de théâtre*.... In sum, it seems that we have taken up the task of mutually copying each other, so as to eliminate the least trace of our ancient enmity. If the cost to the two kingdoms was no more than a bit of absurdity, it would be a fine price to pay for eternal peace."[48]

But what fascinated the English above all was the way that etiquette dominated French private life, and the natural skill with which the nobility negotiated hierarchies of rank and privilege. It was a lively and sophisticated theatrical performance in a setting rich with silks, gold, and mirrors, one in which both sexes participated, which demanded self-discipline, consummate theatrical skill, limberness, familiarity with customs, playfulness, wit—in other words, that whole ensemble of typically French attributes that Lord Chesterfield had dubbed "the Graces."[49] And if this way of being in the world entailed certain sacrifices, the result of that collective effort seemed fully to justify them: never had the art of sociability attained to such perfection, and the pleasure it conferred was so intense that it moved Mme de Staël to remark that, in Paris, one could even dispense with being happy.[50]

Rivals in hospitality and courtesy, the two nations were now prepared to explore each other—and they were aided by the fact that, even if English was little used on the other side of the Channel, French had long since been compulsory as the international language of elites.

A fluent speaker of French, capable of quoting Mme de Sévigné and La Rochefoucauld from memory, Lady Sarah possessed all the qualities needed to open the doors of the most prestigious Parisian *hôtels particuliers*. She belonged to one of English high society's most distinguished families: her grandfather, Charles Lennox, First Duke of Richmond, had been an illegitimate son of Charles II and Louise de Kéroualle, a spy in the service of Louis XIV.

Though her parents had died before she was five years old, her two elder sisters, who took great care of her, were the wives of very influential men. Caroline had married Henry Fox, the First Baron Holland; and Emily had married the Duke of Leinster, a senior peer of Ireland. What's more, upon her arrival in Paris, Emily could count on the numerous acquaintances she had made two years earlier during her first sojourn in the company of Holland, beginning with the Prince de Conti and his mistress, the Comtesse de Boufflers. But above all it was the unfortunate affection that she had inspired, while still quite young, in the Prince of Wales—soon to become King George III—that stirred general curiosity about her in France. And in the letters from Mme du Deffand to her close friends in England, describing the social exploits of their young compatriot, we find an echo of the welcome that Paris had in store for her.

No question, Mme du Deffand's initial assessment is glowing: "Your Milady Sarah has had a prodigious success; all of our lovely young men have had their heads turned,"[51] she wrote to her friend Crawford. Still, that didn't prevent her from expressing, in strictly confidential letters addressed to her constant correspondent, Walpole, a number of reservations regarding the reasons for such infatuation—reservations which make clear that, in spite of the elderly Marquise's professed Anglophilia (a mark of respect to the lord of Strawberry Hill), the standards of the "*parfaitement bonne compagnie*" in Paris did not altogether coincide with those of London's high society.

Having received the Bunburys at home on numerous occasions, Mme du Deffand had had the opportunity to submit the two of them to attentive examination. Her blindness did not allow her to judge Sarah's much-vaunted beauty—"No Magdalen by Correggio is so charming and expressive,"[52] Walpole had declared—but, in the French capital, no one thought her "particularly pretty." For her part, hadn't Sarah herself said that "Paris had very few beautiful women," and that those considered so in England would have been described there, at best, as "graceful"?[53] Mme du Deffand found the young lady "amicable," "sweet," "vivacious," and "courteous," but clarified that, by French standards, she indubitably behaved like a "coquette."[54]

What especially worried the Marquise was the attitude of that "poor Sir Charles" when it came to his spouse. Was it affection or naivety that led him to allow the presence at Lady Sarah's side of suitors as assiduous as they were troublesome, like Lord Carlisle—who had followed her from London—and Lauzun? It was only shortly before the couple's departure that the old woman discovered the answer: "I'll be very much surprised if this Sir Charles takes after M. de Stainville, even if Milady should take up with the whole *Opéra-Comique*."[55] A month had been long enough for the unfortunate Mme de Stainville to cease to inspire any pity in her, but with her characteristic psychological acuity, Mme du Deffand had divined the grounds of the drama that would soon put an end to the Bunburys' marriage.

It was Sarah Lennox who had chosen Sir Charles as a husband, after the prospect of marriage to the Prince of Wales had dissolved for political reasons. And yet the young Lennox certainly could have aimed for a much more prestigious match. Unlike her, Bunbury did not belong to the highest ranks of the nobility, nor did he possess a great fortune—but he was handsome, cultivated, elegant, courteous, and, above all, she was in love with him. As was customary among the English nobility, Sarah adored domestic privacy, the countryside, horses—those belonging to Sir Charles were famous—and dogs, and her ambitions were limited to being a good wife, provided that she knew her husband returned her love. But Bunbury, by temperament phlegmatic and sexually indifferent, was unable to measure up to her sentimental expectations and, after two years of vain attempts, Sarah had to acknowledge the failure of her marriage. As fate would have it, this was the moment her path crossed Lauzun's.

It was less the Duc's insistent flirtation with her than the sorrow bred in him by the drama with Mme de Stainville that stirred Sarah's affection. The tale he told her about that "disastrous affair"[56] so affected her that she was moved to arrange a rendezvous with him the very same day, on the occasion of a supper given by Mme du Deffand. It was probably January 25,[57] and, in the course of the evening, Lady Sarah slipped a note into Lauzun's hand that said: "I love you."[58]

Yet this declaration of love left no room for hopes of future happiness. As Lady Sarah informed Lauzun the following day, she couldn't possibly imagine deceiving her husband—in their country, adultery was beyond the pale. "A lover," she explained to him, "is in the common run of things barely an event in the life of a Frenchwoman; for an Englishwoman, it is greater than anything; from that moment on everything changes for her, and the loss of her existence and her peace is generally the issue of a sentiment which, in France, has only pleasant and harmless results.... Since we are free to choose our husbands for ourselves, we're not allowed to dislike them, and the crime of betraying them is never forgiven."[59] If, some twenty-five years later, Mme de Staël would learn to her own cost the exactitude of that analysis, Lauzun now found the perfect phrase with which to persist: "I want you to be happy," he responded, "but no power on earth could prevent me from adoring you."[60] His tenacity would be rewarded, but would ultimately render his humiliation the more profound.

Written on February 6, from Calais, when Sarah was on the point of returning to England, the letter that figures in Lauzun's memoirs clearly shows her increasing involvement: "You have entirely changed my heart, my friend; it is sad and broken; and though you cause me so much pain, I can think of nothing but my love."[61] Fifteen days later Lauzun arrived in London, and, from there, followed the Bunburys to their country house in Suffolk, where he spent what remained for him "the happiest [time] of [his] life."[62] It was during the course of this long, amorous tête-à-tête—the imperturbable Sir Charles quickly made himself scarce—that Sarah gave herself to him, assuming complete responsibility for her act. Its full significance would become clear to Lauzun the following day, when Sarah proposed that he start a new life with her in Jamaica, giving him a week to think it over. Lauzun didn't have the courage to accept, and Sarah decided that the affair was over. In failing to consider her "necessary for his happiness," he had "destroyed the sentiment that bound her to him,"[63] and she had ceased to love him. Lauzun's despair—he wept, fainted, spat blood—was futile. Far stronger than he, Sarah was prepared to face the future, regardless of her new situation. "[My] morals are not spoilt by the French," she wrote seven months later from Barton to her best friend: "they are so totally different from my caracter & from what I was brought up to think right, that it would be having a very mean oppinion of me indeed if you thought 3 months [among them] could undo all that nature & custom had taught me."[64] These weren't just empty phrases. Sarah was destined to lead the life of a romantic heroine, and she lost no time in proving she possessed all the moral qualities—courage, sincerity, consistency—necessary. A year later, unable to imagine a life without love, Lady Bunbury took up with a penniless cousin and, after having given birth to a little girl and declined Sir Charles's offer to keep up appearances, ran away with her lover. Their flight was of short duration but the scandal was enormous, and Sarah, who had requested a divorce, spent the next twelve years alone with her daughter, completely isolated at Goodwood House, the country estate of her brother, the Duke of Richmond. Then, at age thirty-six, still dazzlingly beautiful, she finally found that emotional fulfillment she had always sought by marrying Colonel George Napier, a charming and courageous soldier, and bringing no less than eight of his children into the world. Thereafter, even in puritanical England, there were many who would testify to their admiration of her.

For Lauzun, the return to France was bitter: he had met an extraordinary woman, and her loss was nobody's fault but his own. His old life struck him as charmless: "its whole character has altered."[65]

It took the prospect of leaving to fight in Corsica to restore his joie de vivre. In May 1768, Genoa had yielded the island to France, and Choiseul, the architect of the agreement, had decided to quell the separatists, led by Pascal Paoli, with a by-the-books military intervention. The Duc joined the expedition as aide-de-camp to its commander, the Marquis de Chauvelin. It was Lauzun's first opportunity to see combat after seven years of service in the Gardes Françaises. For three centuries, his ancestors had been honored on the battlefield, and now his own moment had arrived. At first blush, an irregular army of separatists might not have seemed such a glorious foe, but in fact the Corsican conflict would prove to be as tough as it was perilous and, moreover, highly instructive. Lauzun's first experience in the field taught him that "no adversary should be underestimated. The will to fight, combined with knowledge of the terrain, could hold in check trained troops equipped with better arms. It was a lesson he would recall years later when he faced the uprising in the Vendée."[66] The campaign also provided him his first acquaintance with Mirabeau—the beginning of a friendship that would ultimately prove fatal.[67]

Without by any means moderating his erotic exploits—he promptly seduced the wife of the Intendant of Corsica, Mme Chardon, who took it into her head to follow him on horseback as he went into battle—Lauzun was able to win the affection of his soldiers and the respect of his superiors, as much by his brashness as by his ingenuity, his sense of duty, and the tactical intelligence that he deployed in the course of the war. It was with a sincere regret that he left the island and its "boulders" in order to bring news of a definitive victory over the insurgents to the King. In Corsica he had experienced a "successful year," one which had gone some way toward reconciling him with himself.

Lauzun arrived at Versailles on June 24, 1769, then joined Louis XV at his hunting lodge, Saint-Hubert; he was immediately admitted in to the presence of the sovereign, who was in consultation with Choiseul. The King received him with "every graciousness," awarded him the Croix de Saint-Louis, and invited him to stay. Choiseul, too, "wished to patch things up with [him] and greeted him with such good grace" that the young Duc "was quite sensible of it."[68] In short, everything seemed to invite optimism. Louis XV confirmed the favor that he had already shown and Lauzun enthusiastically returned to service with the Gardes Françaises, more confident than ever in his vocation as a soldier. Parisian life had regained its attractiveness for him; what's more, Amélie de Boufflers, his wife, did not appear chagrined by his indifference. Confined to a simple respect for form, their conjugal life left him completely at liberty, and he immediately put this freedom to use, enriching his palette of experiences both in the realm of friendship—the Vicomtesse de Laval, the Comtesse de Dillon, and the Princesse de Guéménée would come to be his particularly tender confidants—and in that of classical libertinism. But his chosen family, and his most stable emotional touchstones, were his two long-time friends, the Duc de Chartres (born the same year as he) and the Prince de Guéménée. Soon enough, the Marquis Marc-René de Voyer would be added to their number.

But Lauzun realized that harder times were on the way. Two months before his return from Corsica, on April 22, 1769, the Comtesse du Barry had been presented at court as the King's favorite, assuming a role left vacant by the death of Mme de Pompadour. Shedding the last of his scruples as his virility waned, the King considered this twenty-five-year-old beauty indispensable to his well-being, and wanted her by his side in spite of her notorious past as a courtesan. The scandal was immense and, urged on by Mme de Choiseul and the Princesse de Beauvau who had made it a point of honor, the Duc de Choiseul openly took sides against the favorite. Drawn into the conflict despite his best efforts, even the Duc de Gontaut, who had always had a talent for staying on good terms with the mistresses of Louis the Well-Beloved, saw the doors of the *petits appartements* closed to him. Lauzun had made the acquaintance of the newly minted Comtesse du Barry back when "l'Ange," as she'd been known, had still exercised her old métier—and even though he had maintained more or less friendly relations with her since then, he was forced by decorum to forbid his wife from associating with her. After that slight, Louis XV refused to address another word to him. It was the end of Lauzun's period of royal favor, upon which his military career depended, and the beginning of a struggle for influence between those on the side of the favorite, led by the Duc d'Aiguillon, and those following the Duc de Choiseul—a struggle that ended with the defeat of the latter.

Did the overconfident Choiseul believe that Louis XV, incapable of doing without his extended ministerial experience, would sacrifice the Comtesse du Barry for his sake? And the King, for his part—was he unable to support the challenge to his authority? Lauzun was too discerning not to realize that the clash between the sovereign and his minister had deeper sources and major implications for the political future of France. Contemporary historians tend to point back to the disastrous outcome of the Seven Years' War (which had cost France its first colonial empire) as the beginning of the downward spiral that would eventually take hold of the state's finances and trigger a crisis of confidence on the part of the French in their system of government, becoming one of the precipitating causes of the Revolution.[69] The first to take full cognizance of the seriousness of the defeat was Louis XV himself, who was determined not to run the risk of a new war: his policies abroad were aimed at maintaining peace in Europe, and on the domestic front at reinforcing royal authority, stabilizing the state's deficit, and boosting the economy. Yet Choiseul's plans were utterly opposed to those of his sovereign: his foreign policy planned for France's military revenge—not only the reconquest of colonial power but preeminence over Europe as well, which meant the inevitable reprise of a war with England. It was for this reason that the Duc pursued an ambitious program of reorganization of the army and reinforcement of the navy, which cut deeply into the royal treasury. In reality, he was little concerned with economic problems, and his domestic policy was secretly in service to a project of modernization of the monarchical system, modeled on the one in place on the other side of the Channel. Far from working to preserve the King's authority at a moment of crisis, Choiseul maintained cordial relations with the parliamentary party and the new aristocratic Fronde, which never lost an opportunity to challenge the monarch. Louis XV was a creature of habit: he loved his Minister, appreciated his great intelligence, his tireless work, his affable manners, and would have liked to retain his service. But when he learned that Choiseul had seized the pretext of an altogether marginal conflict that pitted Spain—tied to France by the Pacte de Famille—against England in the distant Falkland Islands in order to revive hostilities, he decided to dismiss him. On December 24, 1770, the Duc received the order to present his resignation and retire to his country estate of Chanteloup, some thirteen hours by coach from

Paris. In April of the following year, four months after the installation in the Cabinet du Conseil of a triumvirate formed by d'Aiguillon, Terray, and Maupeou, Louis XV abolished venal offices and decided to dissolve the current parliament, which he replaced with another whose powers were entirely redefined. It was the beginning of a veritable political revolution that, if it had been pursued in his turn by Louis XVI, might have forestalled the events of 1789.

Public opinion, however, adroitly manipulated by Choiseul, preferred to attribute the Minister's disgrace to the arbitrariness of an aging despot and the revenge of a prostitute. Indeed, never had an exile departed so triumphantly and full of hope. The Duc was a mere fifty years old, and the state of Louis XV's health suggested that soon enough a new king—the Dauphin whose marriage to Marie-Antoinette had been arranged—would stand in need of his counsel. For a faithful monarchist like the Comte d'Allonville, who wrote his memoirs under the Restoration, it was precisely "to the rebellious spirit of the ex-minister and his friends" that they owed "the origin of that frenzy against the court of which the Revolution was the result."[70]

Whatever his private beliefs may have been, honor impelled Lauzun to show solidarity with his kin, even at the risk of compromising his own future. And since he was "courageous, romantic, generous, witty,"[71] he did not hesitate to share in the fate of his family[72] by following them immediately to Chanteloup. By January 7, however, he was already back in Paris,[73] and soon after standing guard at Versailles. Contrary to his expectations, Louis XV had taken no active measures against him—the King was content to ignore him.

During the months that followed, when he wasn't on guard duty, Lauzun frequently sojourned at Chanteloup, where his wife, a close friend of Mme de Choiseul, was also staying. We find numerous details concerning him in the intense correspondence of that period between Mme du Deffand, the Duchesse de Choiseul, and the Abbé Barthélemy, who, afraid that the ordinary postal routes might expose his letters to the scrutiny of the *cabinet noir*, sent them by means of a private messenger.

The Duc's fall from grace had transformed Chanteloup into a sort of utopia. Forced to coexist beneath a single roof, the members of the Choiseul clan set aside their various jealousies and resentments and began working together to make daily existence at the château as serene and pleasant as possible. The Duchesse de Choiseul set the tone: not content merely to sign a nonaggression pact with her sister-in-law, she even went so far as to graciously welcome her husband's mistress, the charming Comtesse de Brionne.

This display of domestic happiness at Chanteloup allowed the French aristocracy to reaffirm its autonomy in the face of meddlesome royal power, to display once again its talent for curbing emotion and embellishing reality with a consummate *art de vivre*. The beauty of the locale, the unceasing procession of visitors, the luxurious sophistication of the hospitality, the succession of hunts, promenades, performances, billiard parties, games of backgammon and dominoes—none of these on their own would have sufficed to make Chanteloup an "Isle of the Blessed." It took the day-to-day contributions of its inhabitants—and Lauzun's proved to be crucial.

Even though Lauzun, now reconciled with his family, lamented the crowds of visitors disturbing the tranquility of their home in a letter addressed to the Marquis de Voyer two months after the sentence of exile had been imposed on Choiseul,[74] he nevertheless devoted himself to amusing them—proving that he possessed to the highest degree that "esprit" capable of lightening the atmosphere and spreading joy. In that domain, according to the Abbé Barthélemy, he was unrivaled: "To my way of thinking he remains the cleverest, and the most humorous, of any of our visitors."[75] Twenty years later, the Marquise de Coigny, who was known as the wittiest woman in Paris, confirmed the Abbé's judgment: "Your banter maintained the cheerfulness of my character and the intelligence of my mind."[76]

Well aware of his "charms,"[77] Lauzun complemented his natural gaiety with the delicate art of wordplay—an art that, since the era of the Hôtel de Rambouillet, had been one of the main qualities essential to a man of society—and he deployed it in both intimate conversation and other diversions particular to life among the cultured. When it came to composing proverbs and couplets, Barthélemy found him unbeatable. "It would be impossible to find more variety, genuineness, warmth, and fine jests,"[78] wrote Mme du Deffand of him, chronicling the various distractions at Chanteloup. The perfected product of a thoroughly theatrical civilization and alert to all the nuances of the *comedie mondaine*—of which we can gain a good sense from Lauzun's two-act play *Le Ton de Paris, or the Lovers of Good Company*[79]—the young Duc was also an excellent actor. But it was not on the stage of high society that he aspired to take a leading role.

Lauzun was intelligent, fickle, turbulent, and determined to make his mark—to be "good at something,"[80] as he confided to his friend Voyer—but he knew that his hands were tied, at least as long as Louis XV's reign lasted. In December 1772, while waiting for more favorable circumstances—after all, he was only twenty-five years old—he decided to return to London. If his first visit had been dictated by sentimental reasons, the second would let him judge for himself what had allowed England to win the Seven Years' War and seize France's overseas territories. Likewise, in light of his conversations with Choiseul at Chanteloup, he was on the lookout for any flaws in Britain's immense colonial empire and intense maritime trade that might allow France some advantage. During the seven months of his stay in London, Lauzun learned English, frequented high society, was presented to the King, and was tutored by the French ambassador in the English sovereign's diplomatic strategies. It was at this time that he discovered the importance of the newspapers—in France still rare and of little influence—when it came to taking the pulse of the political and economic life of the country.

But this second stay in London also marked the beginning of a new affair for the Duc, one which would push him to broaden his political horizons by drawing his attention to the ongoing drama of the partition of Poland by the forces of northern Europe. The same evening that he arrived in London, at the house of Lady Harrington, where he'd been taken by the French ambassador, the Comte de Guines, Lauzun made the acquaintance of Izabela Czartoryska, who has passed into history as one of the great heroines of the national saga of Poland. Lauzun's memoirs convey an image of the Princesse in which the keen appraisal of the libertine—accustomed to sizing up women according to their physical assets and defects, as if they were horses—seems to give way to that ineffable je ne sais quoi that precedes the crystallization of love: "Of modest proportions, but perfectly formed, with the loveliest eyes, the loveliest hair, the loveliest teeth, a very pretty foot, rather good overall, though strongly marked by the small-pox and lacking freshness, sweetly mannered, and having in her smallest movements an inimitable grace, Mme Czartoryska proved that even without being handsome, a woman can certainly be charming."[81]

The importance of the relationship that the Duc established a few months later with Izabela is evident not only from the place he accorded her at the heart of his memoirs—of which she occupies roughly a fifth—but also in the obvious difficulty he had, years after the fact, in clarifying and interpreting his emotions at the time. He prefers to limit himself to observing that "the two most tender, most ardent hearts in the universe, perhaps, had collided."[82]

Lauzun certainly wasn't a novice when it came to romance. He had already practiced every variety of love *à la française*, whose rules demanded that even the deepest desires of the heart be guided by good taste and attention to social comportment. With Sarah, he had experienced the intransigence of a passion informed by the ethos of puritan England. With the Polish Princesse, he would discover a kind of love inseparable from political drama and, seduced by the allure of the tragic sublime, would let himself be drawn into a complex game of passions and interests in which the very future of Poland was at stake.

Born in Warsaw in 1746, Izabela was the only daughter of Jan Jerzy Flemming, Grand Treasurer of Lithuania, and Antonina Czartoryska, who died in childbirth. Raised by her maternal grandmother, she was promised in marriage at fifteen to Adam Czartoryski, her uncle, who was twice her age. According to the customs of the Polish nobility, this marriage was intended to consolidate the bonds of kinship between different branches of one of the most powerful families in the country. Descendants of the Grand Dukes of Lithuania, the Czartoryskis had seen their political influence grow over the course of the eighteenth century. However, in spite of the dowry and family tree that Izabela could boast, it was not easy to convince her fiancé to lead her to the altar. A handsome man—elegant, intelligent, a polyglot, educated by private French tutors,[83] and exceptionally cultivated—Adam Czartoryski was also in love with the Countess Praskovya Aleksandrovna Bruce, a seductive lady-in-waiting to Catherine of Russia, and felt an authentic aversion to his young relative, who was timid, insignificant, and, physically speaking, small, slender, and scarred by smallpox. He was forced to give in to the demands of his father, the terrible Prince Augustus, but he made no secret of his disappointment, and Izabela was forced to resign herself to the marriage. What's more, she had to endure the open hostility of her sister-in-law—another Izabela, the beautiful and admired Princesse Lubomirska—who was very close to her brother and "nourished for this girl so infinitely his inferior in charms and talents" "an invincible antipathy."[84]

Still, the young Princesse Czartoryska did not admit defeat when it came to marital happiness: she succeeded in getting her husband to accept her and in gaining his friendship, following him on his journeys dressed as a page, appealing to his pedagogical streak, making him her Pygmalion. He shaped her tastes and her intelligence; he directed her reading, roused in her a love of art, and gave her the opportunity to perfect her social skills in the grand salons of Paris. She would recall, not without irony, that even before having read *La Nouvelle Héloïse*, her desire to acquaint herself with the latest novelties had driven her, in November 1762, to pay a visit Jean-Jacques Rousseau at his retreat at Montmorency.[85]

A dozen years after their marriage, the ugly duckling had been transformed into a young woman blessed with every social grace, capable of commanding the admiration even of a famous aristocrat from across the Channel. Indeed, wrote Elizabeth Berkeley (who became, following her divorce from Lord Craven, the Margravine of Ansbach), "Her talents were very superior, and her manners without affectation. She was a perfect musician, and a fine painter; danced inimitably; had knowledge without pedantry, and never displayed her learning with ostentation ... she was grave and gay by turns."[86]

Izabela's metamorphosis was not confined to her personality but extended to her physical appearance as well. In 1765, she gave birth to her first child, Teresa, and if we are to believe her contemporaries, maternity embellished her: nothing compared to the brilliance of her black eyes and the purity of her blush."[87] However, it is quite likely that such changes had more to do with her urgent desire to please. The Princesse herself confirms this in a self-portrait written in 1783 at Puławy, when she was thirty-seven years old, which tallies with the description given by Lauzun: "I have never been beautiful, but have frequently been pretty: I have lovely eyes, and as all the movements of my soul are visible in them, they render my physiognomy interesting.... My face is like my mind, the greatest virtue of the one, as of the other, lies in the skill with which I know how to double their value. In my youth, I was quite the coquette, but am less of one with each passing day, even if my young girl's complexion reminds me from time to time that pleasing others is in itself a great charm."[88]

For her, "pleasing" meant above all avenging the many humiliations she'd suffered—and since her husband continued to prefer other women to her, she went on to exercise her coquetry beyond the sphere of marriage. No one, recalled Jean Fabre, "inspired more tumultuous passions. Friedrich Brühl, Repnin, Franciszek Branicki, Lauzun, twenty other suitors, sometimes turned away, but more often satisfied, were madly in love with her."[89] Happily for her, when it came to adultery, the Polish nobility displayed the same imperturbability as the French aristocracy, and her first husband saw love as something wholly distinct from marriage. Whether out of liberalism or indifference, Adam left Izabela to her own devices, and graciously resigned himself to the fact that Teresa was the only one of his four children born in the course of their marriage whose paternity he could definitively attribute to himself. This did not prevent him from behaving as an affectionate father to all of them, and of appearing to be, "throughout his life, the close friend of his wife, and the happiest of husbands."[90]

Having displayed her talents as an actress in the amateur productions of the Théâtre de Société, one of the shrines of Warsaw high society, and turned the head of its organizer, Count Alois Friedrich von Brühl, Izabela was able to take revenge on her sister-in-law Lubomirska by beginning a relationship with Stanisław Augustus Poniatowski, who, since September 1764, had occupied the Polish throne. A penniless relation of the Czartoryskis—his mother belonged to that illustrious family—Stanisław Augustus had been in love with his cousin Izabela, the future Lubomirska, but her father, Prince Auguste Czartoryski, indifferent to the sentiments of his daughter, had given her in marriage to the far more illustrious Stanisław Lubomirski. For a long time the amorous friendship of the cousins endured despite everything, though ultimately the election of Stanisław Augustus as King of Poland came to poison their relationship. Upon the death of King Augustus III of Saxony, everything seemed to point toward Adam Czartoryski ascending the throne, but Catherine of Russia, in a show of strength, imposed on the parliament the election of Stanisław Augustus Poniatowski, whom she knew well (he had been her lover during the difficult years when she was still a Grand Duchess) and considered more reliable. Poniatowski was part of the *Familia*, and the Czartoryskis were obliged to hide their disappointment. Nevertheless, in spite of the favorable treatment that would be reserved for them during his reign, they never lost an opportunity to do him harm. Her pride wounded by the failed elevation of her brother, Princesse Lubomirska boasted that she would take advantage of the influence she had over Stanisław Augustus in order to punish him for his capricious and childish conduct.

Even though he was the most directly affected, Adam Czartoryski was the only one not to show any disappointment following the election of his cousin—to whom, it must be said, he felt immeasurably superior. Having at quite a young age become general of Podolie and a member of parliament, he had accepted various public offices, more in response to family expectations and a sense of obligation than out of personal conviction, but had thrice refused to present himself as a candidate for election to the throne.[91] His true passion was not politics but scholarship, and if Jean Fabre described him heartlessly as "a dilettante of pedantry," he nonetheless recognized that "a philologist by vocation, he took just as much of an interest in other branches of knowledge: literature, history, the arts and sciences, chemistry, political economy, the art of war,"[92] and that he could boast of counting Goethe and Herder among his correspondents. Passionate when it came to pedagogy, the Prince personally oversaw the education of his children, creating for them at his estate in Puławy a small university destined to equip a generation of Polish aristocrats with a new consciousness of culture.

Up until the day that the partition of his country transformed him into a committed patriot, Prince Adam devoted himself to furthering the cause of the Familia. In safeguarding their economic interests and flexibility in parliament, he showed himself to be a master of double-dealing, just like his father. If he received his official support from Stanisław Augustus, and encouraged him to liberate himself from the supervision of Catherine, he simultaneously strove to win the protection of the Empress, and worked for the popularity of the Familia by displaying sympathy for both the nationalists and the Republicans. And, at least when it came to family interests, his wife displayed an ironclad loyalty to him.

It wasn't just her rivalry with her sister-in-law and the desire, with its trace of coquetry, to retain the attention of the new King—who was, royalty aside, handsome, courteous, and an experienced lover—which drove Izabela into the arms of Poniatowski, but a friendship that dated back to the first days of her marriage, when Stanisław Augustus had been the sole member of the family to give her a decent welcome. "Occupied elsewhere,"[93] and determined to draw some profit from the situation, "her husband," as Stanisław Augustus himself recalled, "was so accustomed to going to view the *stolnik*, and then to see the King, the best friend of his wife, who was not yet twenty-two years old, that often enough he took her along to the château and sent her alone into the King's apartments, taking care to inform himself first whether or not his sister was home. If he found that she was there, he would take his wife elsewhere, then bring her back to the château an hour later, when the King was alone, then leave himself. This gave the King reason to believe that his cousin, who was amusing himself elsewhere, himself wanted his wife to please the King."[94]

Culminating in March 1768 in the birth of Maria-Anna—immediately nicknamed by a malicious public "the little calf," in allusion to the bull that figured on the sovereign's coat of arms—this perfect understanding between husband, wife, and lover was soon taken a step further. Indeed, Stanisław Augustus and Adam requested that Izabela come to the aid of Poland and the

Familia by attracting the goodwill of the all-powerful Russian ambassador, Prince Nikolai Vasilyevich Repnin.

At the end of 1763, still not yet thirty years old, Repnin had been sent to Warsaw by his uncle, Count Panin, minister of foreign affairs to Catherine the Great, in order to prepare the ground for the election of Stanisław and thereafter to remain as ambassador. The enormous power with which he'd been invested as spokesman for Catherine had gone to the head of this intelligent, cultured, bold young man, and his arrogant manners, coupled with his brutal methods, made him universally hated in Warsaw.

Repnin was charged with maintaining Poland as a protectorate of Russia by stifling every hope for independence. To that end he applied himself to weakening the authority of the King, manipulating the rivalries between the great families, sabotaging institutional reforms—beginning with a proposition to abolish the right of veto—which Stanisław and the Czartoryskis were counting on to combat anarchy and modernize the country.

Izabela succeeded in inspiring a passionate love in Repnin and in gaining considerable influence over him—which, however, she used not on behalf of Stanisław but rather for the benefit of the Familia, whose interests were diverging more and more from those of the sovereign. It was, without question, a difficult period, and what with the increasing presence of Russian troops in Polish territory and the continual interference of Repnin with the country's internal affairs, the political situation soon became explosive. In February 1768, the separatist Polish nobility assembled in the Bar Confederation, taking up arms to depose Stanisław and liberate themselves from the Russian yoke. The following April, the Empress Catherine, judging that Repnin was guilty of having neglected the interests of Russia and citing as proof of his weakness in regard to the Familia, recalled him to Moscow and named Mikhail Nikitich Volkonski in his place. This was the end of Repnin's career as an ambassador, but not of his relationship with Izabela, who, on January 14, 1770, gave birth to a son who was his "living portrait"[95] and was baptized Adam Jerzy Czartoryski. Two years later, when Russia, Prussia, and Austria announced their intention to partition Poland, Repnin traveled across Europe in the wake of the Czartoryski family, and at the beginning of 1772 followed Izabela to England. No one in London was ignorant of their relationship, and when, at the end of the year, Lauzun made the acquaintance of Izabela, he was immediately informed that a great Russian lord "loved her and . . . had left everything behind in order to follow her and devote himself to her entirely."[96]

Though their case was not one of love at first sight, the French Duc and the Polish Princesse were drawn together when they came to the aid of a common friend, Lady Craven, who had fallen victim to the jealousy of a husband less accustomed to *moeurs mondaines* than Prince Czartoryski.

Twenty-two at the time, and married for six years to Baron William Craven, Elizabeth Berkeley already had plenty of people talking about her. With a beauty attested to by portraits by Thomas Gainsborough, George Romney, Joshua Reynolds, Angelica Kauffmann, and Élisabeth Vigée Le Brun, she was also—Horace Walpole himself acknowledged it[97]—witty, vivacious, and gifted in numerous arts. An excellent actress, she wrote poetry and "had a passion for *aventures sentimentales*, but, unfortunately, failed to confine such sentiments to her verse."[98] Elegant and always surrounded by suitors, she was far from timid with her admirers, and in the end this imprudence proved disastrous for her. During a ball given at the end of April 1773, her husband caught her behind a locked door in a *petit salon* in the arms of the French ambassador, the Comte de Guines, and the scandal was tremendous. Craven challenged Guines to a duel (the ambassador agreed to give him satisfaction once his diplomatic mission had been completed), and then, while deciding the fate of his adulterous spouse, sent her into seclusion in the country. Hurriedly seeking the best defensive strategy, Guines and Lauzun reckoned that only the Polish Princesse, thanks to her illustrious name and her friendship with Lady Craven, which was above all suspicion, would be able to win permission to see her from the outraged husband. Indeed, Princesse Czartoryska succeeded in paying a visit to the unfortunate woman, and in telling her what she should do. If, as seems probable, the country house in question was Coombe Abbey, not far from Coventry—where at Lord Craven's request the famous Capability Brown had laid out a beautiful park—we can imagine the Princesse drawing great benefit from the visit: always passionate about gardens, Izabela would later endow the estate at Puławy with a renowned park on the lines of the new aesthetic criteria defined by the great English landscaper.

In his memoirs Lauzun affirms that he owed his nearer approach to Izabela to Lady Craven's misadventures. The Princesse's beau geste had struck him, and he emphasizes that he was drawn to her "tenderness and generosity of heart." For her part, Izabela was reassured as to the Duc's own character by the story—by this point legendary—of his passion for Sarah Lennox. If we pay so much attention to the Craven "affair," it is because it provides clear evidence of Lauzun's relationship with Princesse Czartoryska, and, by extension, the authenticity of the memoirs as a whole.

From that perspective, it is worth noting that it would be mainly the descendants of Izabela who waged an all-out war against the Duc's memoirs. Certainly, their publication in 1821 gave rise to a chorus of protests, but thirty-four years later, the eldest son of the Princesse, Adam Jerzy Czartoryski, launched another attack, determined to prevent the publication of a new edition[99] that—scandal heaped upon scandal—restored all of the passages and names omitted from the first.

Born of the relationship between Izabela and Repnin, raised at the Russian Court, minister of foreign affairs under Tsar Alexander the First, and champion of Polish independence, Adam Jerzy was a man of great intelligence and culture. It was he who purchased for his mother Leonardo da Vinci's *Lady with an Ermine*, now the pride of the Czartoryski Museum in Kraków. When it came to the elasticity of morals, his private life rivaled those of his parents—an intimate of Alexander the First, he had also been the Tsarina's lover. However, the times had changed: not only did the new moralism of the 1800s condemn the sexual permissiveness of the preceding century but the unvarnished twists and turns of Izabela's love life clashed with the memory that the Princesse had left in the collective imagination, the woes of Poland having elevated her as an icon of patriotism and national conscience. In 1858, when the new edition of the memoirs came out, Adam Jerzy—now eighty-eight years old and living as an exile in Paris, where he maintained a veritable court in miniature at the Hôtel Lambert, his mansion on the Île Saint-Louis—exerted political influence on a European scale and deployed his intense diplomatic activity on behalf of Poland.

To defend the memory of his mother, Czartoryski filed suit against both Auguste Poulet-Malassis and Eugène-Marie de Broise, the editors of the memoirs, as well as the author of the preface and notes, Louis Lacour. The court found in his favor and ordered the seizure of the work—but this victory was fleeting. A second edition saw the light of day four months later.[100] The memoirs were now in the hands of readers, and the Prince abandoned his attempt to quash it. This was good news for the editors, who had already been convicted the previous year for publishing Baudelaire's *Les Fleurs du mal*.

What should be emphasized is that the tribunal's verdict, far from refuting the authenticity of the memoirs, implicitly confirmed the idea that Lauzun was their author, for it condemned the editors for having rendered public the "intimate recollections" of a man "who would never have wished it and who had not committed the indignity of publishing them himself and thus revealing those intrigues which, to his honor, he had concealed."[101]

Thus, for Izabela's descendants, further precautions were necessary to ensure that in the future those with ill intentions wouldn't be able to rummage around in the past of their celebrated grandmother, and it is probably at this moment that the family decided to proceed with the destruction of part of Izabela's correspondence that was preserved in their private archives at Kraków.[102] Could it be a coincidence that, with the exception of two letters dispatched to her husband in London in March 1772 and April 1773, none of the missives to have escaped the flames dates from earlier than 1805, when her period of affairs and illegitimate births had come to a close? It would be all the more surprising given the fact that during the period when Izabela and Lauzun were involved with each other, she would have had a greater need to write to her spouse, since they were so frequently separated. To judge by the two London letters, it seems clear that husband and wife were in the habit of corresponding frequently and—as was general among the European elite—giving each other the latest news on household affairs, family events, social happenings, political developments.

Two letters, then, no more—but both of them are vital in helping us understand Izabela's personality.

First of all, her systematic betrayals and the presence of Repnin at her side seem not to have compromised Izabela's admiration for her husband, or the central place he occupied in her life. "I've just received your letter from Leipzig, my dear friend," she wrote to him on March 16, 1772, from the English capital where she was preparing to spend more than a year. "You are charming to write to me so often; your smallest details fascinate me, everything in your letters pleases me and my heart returns to you posthaste all those emotions that you express so well." And the final phrases—"Adieu, my dear friend, I love you tenderly, I will always love you just so, it makes me happy"[103]—exceed the simple and courteous formulas commonly used at the time among couples. For that matter, didn't she confide to Lauzun soon enough that she felt for her husband, with whom she had never been in love, "a tender friendship" which he deserved "more with each passing day"?[104]

Written a year later, the next letter shows quite clearly that Izabela's feeling for her husband—"I could never return to you everything you have given to me"—had deep roots. When he returned to Poland (we know that only a month earlier he had been in London where, during a ball given by the French ambassador, he had demonstrated with his wife a Cossack dance),[105] Czartoryski had surprised her by sending her a portrait of little Adam Jerzy, who was staying with him in Warsaw. Not a trace of discomfort is discernable in the maternal pride and the happiness that she shows: "The portrait of my son . . . has made me weep with joy; this keepsake, this kindness, it has left me beside myself."[106] It is clear that for both of them, in accordance with aristocratic custom, the "pacte familial" took precedence over personal inclinations and accidents along the way. But that indubitable understanding was accompanied, in their case, by a knowing and affectionate mutuality. Lady Craven's bad luck offered the proof.

There is no question—facts and dates coincide: the beautiful Elizabeth is precisely that "Lulli" whose tragedy Izabela alludes to in her letter of April 31 [sic], 1773, certain that Czartoryski would share her indignation at the jealous husband and the "cruelty" of secluding his wife in the countryside, barred from everyone except her servants. It was a "barbarous" act, one that "shames humanity and terribly degrades the English"[107]—but also one to which she herself feels in no sense exposed. If the London correspondence from Izabela that has come down to us breaks off at this last piece of news, the reason is easily comprehended: Lauzun has made his sudden entrance into her life, and it was judged necessary by her descendants to remove every trace of him.

But what takes shape in these two letters is above all Izabela's growing awareness of an unswerving loyalty to her native land. "I feel the situation of our homeland," she writes in the first letter, "and it could not affect me more";[108] and in the following letter (that of April 31 [sic], 1773) she makes clear her intention of wedding her own fate to that of her nation. In fact, following the partition of Poland, her husband envisaged establishing himself elsewhere and began the search for a suitable spot. Extremely wealthy, raised in England, as comfortable in France as in Holland or Austria, Czartoryski was a true citizen of Europe and had an embarrassment of choices available to him; nevertheless, he didn't intend to decide without his wife's input. London was one of their options, and he sent Izabela there to reconnoiter. And from London, Izabela responded: "You ask me, my dear friend, if it would be agreeable to me to sell everything we own and establish ourselves here, or in France, or elsewhere. I'll give you my thoughts in all frankness. I have told you before, and will repeat now, that by inclination, or perhaps habit, I cling strongly to Poland, and that it is always there I would prefer to live, as long as there is the least shadow of a possibility…what's more, my sweet friend, we can still do good at home, why deny it. If not to the country as a whole, then to particular individuals. It is a privilege that we have the means to indulge, and one all the more substantial in that it will echo down through the ages."[109]

Czartoryski listened to his wife and, over the years, beyond domestic affections and the interests of the Familia, their love for their homeland became the sentiment that definitively sealed their union. But it would not be until the tragic loss of their daughter, Teresa, burned alive in a chimney fire, that Izabela would turn her back on the freedom of the aristocratic manners of the century of light, in order to become a great heroine of the romantic age.

The portrait of the Princesse that Lauzun has left us reveals, behind the seductive charms of a woman of the world, a nature passionate and tragic. After the episode in which they came to the aid of Lady Craven, their relationship unfolded in line with the canonical rituals of courtship. He lavished on her respectful attention, to which she responded sympathetically, while accepting—in spite of his relations with "Lulli"—the attentions of the Comte de Guînes, himself an intimate friend of the Duc. But the anguish that seized the latter at the idea of Izabela becoming involved with the French ambassador came to change their attitude to each other. Jealousy had revealed to Lauzun the violence of his passion, unnerving him to the point that he demanded the Princesse declare the nature of her feelings for Guînes, and then declared his eternal love for her. Izabela, moved by the Duc's despair, swept aside the codified language of *badinage galant*, and spoke the truth plainly to him. She felt for him "an interest that would last as long as her life," but "insurmountable obstacles" prevented her from taking him as a lover. These initial confidences would soon be followed by others. The obstacles, Izabela told him, were of a moral nature, and concerned her relations with Repnin. She had given herself to the Prince out of gratitude when he had defended the interests of the Czartoryskis by incurring the wrath of Catherine. And now, even more than pity, it was her sense of honor that prevented her "from killing with unkindness that man who had sacrificed all for [her], and for whom, apart from herself, there remained nothing in all the world."[110] Thus, for she and Lauzun to continue to see each other, it was indispensable for them to renounce any hope of erotic intimacy and limit themselves to simple friendship.

Over the following months they strove to do just that. Izabela, always accompanied by Repnin, traveled first to take the waters at Spa and then to Holland. Lauzun met them frequently, proceeding with the greatest discretion, but their bodies spoke for themselves,[111] uncontrollable, conjuring up what words were forbidden to say. Fainting fits, spitting blood, nervous breakdowns, and states of prostration were the tangible signs of the violence of their suffering, and were tantamount to declarations of love. "My body," said Lauzun, "could not support the strain of being apart from her."[112] Again and again, desire, undermining their capacity for resistance, brought them to the point of surrender. At the end of the day, it was Izabela who lay down her arms. But her capitulation was tragic. "I flew into her arms; I was happy, or rather, the crime was consummated. But imagine the horror of my fate; even in possessing the woman I worshiped. She herself had not a moment of pleasure; her cheeks were bathed in tears, she pushed me away: 'It is done,' she said to me, 'there is no limit to my wretchedness, I will be unhappy forever.'"[113]

After being driven by her guilt to attempt suicide, the Princesse decided to tell Repnin everything. "That confession, made by a generous soul, was received by a generous soul," and the Prince left the room, having voiced neither "complaint nor reproach."[114]

Returning to Paris together, without the cumbersome presence of Repnin, Lauzun and Izabela found themselves in a situation that was entirely new to the both of them.

The emotion Izabela was now feeling had no equivalent in her past. She was a sensual woman, accustomed to making love with complete freedom, and the relationships she had entered into before meeting Lauzun had been instrumental in nature, dictated by a desire for revenge, coquetry, and ambition, or else simply by convenience. Unrelated as it was to the Polish drama or the needs of the Familia, her connection to the young French seducer must have seemed to her like passion in its pure state.

For his part, in the company of the great Polish lady who had given herself to him amid an atmosphere of tragedy, Lauzun discovered a dimension of the feminine to which he had been denied access in the past: that of maternal love and domestic intimacy. During the months that they spent together, Lauzun saw just how tenderly the Princesse was tied to her children, who rapidly came to feel like his own. Izabela was moved by this affection, and just before returning to Poland, announced to him that she was pregnant: "You have always wanted one of my children, and so you shall; I'm going to give you the dearest, the best part of myself.... I have the courage to confess everything to my husband, to ensure that the most precious token of our ardent love will be returned to you."[115]

Overwhelmed by emotion, Lauzun fainted, and when he regained consciousness he found that his beloved was no longer by his side. Old Prince Czartoryski, who had come to meet his daughter-in-law, had refused to allow her to wait for Lauzun to come around; bundling her into his coach, he had departed with her for Poland.

It was in Warsaw that Czartoryski received his wife's confession. With his characteristic good-heartedness, he declared himself ready to recognize the child as his own, but in exchange, he demanded that Izabela keep up appearances by breaking with Lauzun. This did not prevent the Duc from paying an incognito visit to the Princesse in Poland, and yet another on the night before the birth. Arriving in secret at the Palais Bleu—the Czartoryski home in Warsaw—and concealing himself for some thirty-six hours in an armoire beside Izabela's bed, Lauzun was present during her labor and for the birth of his son.[116]

Was he thinking, as he hid, of the other armoire in which some ten years earlier he had listened as Choiseul attempted to steal his first love? In any event, he could not have imagined that his relationship with the Princesse was drawing toward its end.

Having returned to her own country, where she was faced with the death throes of her homeland and the uncertainty of the Familia, Izabela was forced to face the fact that her passion for Lauzun was incompatible with her patriotic vocation. Her estrangement from him was accelerated by separations and misunderstandings. So as not to be too far from Poland, and able to visit from time to time, Lauzun had been dividing his time between Dresden and Berlin. But the rumors that reached Izabela of his social successes in those cities undermined their harmony. For the Polish Princesse, giving herself away in the name of an overwhelming emotion had come to seem like an unwarranted luxury.

Comte Branicki, one of the most influential men in Poland at the time, knew exactly how to take advantage of Izabela's return to realism. In every way the opposite of Lauzun, Branicki belonged to the minor nobility and had been a youthful friend of Poniatowski, to whom he owed his social rise. Grasping, opportunistic, a swaggerer, quick to fight (his duel with Casanova over a woman remains famous), but also gifted with genuine political intelligence, Branicki had long urged the sovereign to quell the rebels of the Bar Confederation by force, and to distance himself from Russia. But after being dispatched to Moscow by Stanisław Augustus, where he was tied by friendship to Prince Potemkin, Catherine's new favorite, he underwent a political about-face, abandoning the Polish King to his fate and forming a new pro-Russian party with Adam Czartoryski. Long infatuated with Izabela, Branicki had persisted in paying court to her, though he never succeeded in rousing anything in her but contempt. Yet his new alliance with the Czartoryskis drove the Princesse to change her attitude. And it soon became clear to all that the Polish "daredevil"[117] had replaced the chivalrous French Duc in her affections.

Meanwhile, thanks to Izabela's influence, Lauzun had developed a fascination with Polish politics. Following his beloved's return to her country, he had elaborated an ambitious project of political cooperation between France, Poland, and Russia, in hopes of being named ambassador to Warsaw. His idea was not especially original, since, despite its privileged connections with Poland dating back to the era of de Valois and the commitment made by Mazarin to guarantee its integrity, France had pursued a somewhat contradictory set of policies toward its ancient ally over the course of the eighteenth century. The official diplomacy of Louis XV had not prevented secret machinations manifestly against Poland's interests, feeding internal divisions in the country, weakening Stanisław Augustus, and destroying all possibility of "delivering effective aide to a nation marching toward its own ruin."[118] The partition of Poland between Russia, Prussia, and Austria went ahead behind the back of the French —in spite of the marriage of Marie-Antoinette to the Dauphin, the Austrian Empress Marie-Thérèse hadn't believed it necessary to inform Louis XV—and the King was obliged to admit his powerlessness. "From five hundred leagues away," he wrote in 1773, "it is difficult to come to the aid of Poland; I would have liked her to remain intact, but I can do no more than wish."[119]

Nothing was more in line, then, with the preoccupations of the French than the project of assistance to Poland conceived by Lauzun. The Franco-Russian-Polish alliance he had formulated presented obvious advantages for all three nations. By opposing the dismemberment of Poland with the support of Louis XV, Russia would transform it into a satellite state and stem the growing power of its Prussian ally, while France would regain its influence in northern Europe and Poland would retain its territorial integrity. If we believe the memoirs, Lauzun's project had the support of Adam Czartoryski as well as the Baron de Stackelberg, the Russian ambassador to Warsaw, who communicated it to Catherine. The Empress in turn declared herself interested in this solution and waited for it to be formalized by the French government. It was a mission that Lauzun hoped to carry out on returning to Paris, but it wouldn't take long for him to discover that the death of Louis XV had modified France's policy around Poland. The new Minister of Foreign Affairs, the Comte de Vergennes, decided to abandon their old ally to the goodwill of Russia by renouncing the maintenance of a pro-French movement in Poland.

In departing Warsaw, Lauzun left behind a country that would soon survive only in memory, and it was the woman he'd loved so dearly who first realized the political significance of that state of affairs. Over the following years, Princesse Czartoryska turned her magnificent romantic garden in Puławy into a sort of sanctuary, a memorial to Polish history. An idea well in advance of its time, it was conceived of as a national museum, one capable of transmitting to future generations the living memory of Poland and the hope of seeing it born again. And though we cannot know what trace her passion for Lauzun left on Izabela, there is evidence that the memory of the Polish Princesse would accompany her French lover for a long time to come.

At the end of March 1775, Lauzun was back in Versailles—but even before he arrived at the château, he had claimed the attention of both "court and town." On March 7, his horse had taken first prize at a race held on the plain of Sablons,[120] in the presence of the Queen and the royal family. The Duc was no novice when it came to this sort of competition, which was wildly popular in England, though only a recent arrival in France. In the course of his first stay across the Channel, not content with courting Lady Sarah, Lauzun had also benefited from the advice of Sir Bunbury, a great fancier of horses. During his second London sojourn the Duc had assembled a small stable with which he'd entered the races at Newmarket, with great success. Along with the Comte d'Artois, the Duc de Chartres, the Prince de Guéménée, and the Marquis de Conflans, he had introduced the fashion for horse racing to France—but it was their "mentor,"[121] the Marquis de Voyer, who'd had the inspiration of establishing a large stud farm for English thoroughbreds at his estate at Ormes. Thanks to the combined efforts of these great Anglophile aristocrats, a new kind of horse and a new equestrian culture had made its way across the Channel, altering the habits of the French elites.

The fruit of decades of experimental crossbreeding, the English thoroughbred was characterized by its slender frame, its speed, "its breath, its strength, its sturdiness, and the nimbleness with which it leapt the ditches."[122] But how many people are aware today that the Godolphin Arabian, one of the three legendary stallions of this new and valuable breed, had originally arrived in England from France? Given by the Bey of Tunisia to Louis XV, who had no particular affection for Oriental horses, and soon sold off as a draft animal, this superb but mistreated creature had aroused the pity of a British traveler, who bought it for next to nothing and brought it home to England. Welcomed into the stables of Lord Godolphin in Cambridgeshire and baptized with the name of its owner, it proved an unparalleled stud horse.

If the taste for speed lay at the origins of horse racing, the Marquis de Voyer noted that it was "to the allure of the Golden Cup, to the competition spurred by royal and provincial prizes, and to the general taste for gambling—in sum, to its genius for every sort of commerce—which England owes its studfarms."[123] Driven by the hope of stimulating the French economy and developing that same spirit of competition in their own country, Voyer and his friends introduced horse racing and the English thoroughbred in a single blow, and enthusiasm was quick to follow.

The novelty was not confined to the mounts themselves but extended to the whole fashion of riding. Even beyond the racetrack, where jockeys vied with one another in dieting and purging to shed weight, the new style of riding was concerned first and foremost with burdening the horse as little as possible by reducing the weight of the bit and saddle, as well as of the rider's boots and clothing. Thus, horsemen replaced their rich and sophisticated court apparel with the comfortable English tailcoat that, when worn in the presence of the royal family, would elsewhere have constituted a breach of etiquette. The ambassador from Marie-Thérèse couldn't believe that jockeys dared to appear before the Queen "in boots and a riding habit."[124]

"Likewise, the English style of riding—which had its origin in hunting and cross-country riding, and which demanded of the horseman a loose and much more seated posture, the better to adapt himself to varying terrain—became an allegory of British freedom, as opposed to the conventional and less useful fashion of French riding."[125] The conservatives, Louis XVI chief among them, who had kept faithful to the tastes of their grandparents when it came to horses, disapproved of the gambling and betting that accompanied races, and saw in the adoption of fashions and styles of behavior from across the Channel an insult to tradition, as well as a threat to the national economy[126]—none of which prevented the young Queen and her retinue from fully devoting themselves to these two distractions.

With the swiftest thoroughbreds and finest jockeys at his disposal, Lauzun steadily accumulated victories and communicated his "sad and ruinous"[127] tastes to Princes of the Blood—and this new pastime rendered his return to the court "at least as brilliant as his debut there had been,"[128] rousing the interest of the sovereign's new spouse.

The twenty-year-old Marie-Antoinette had been Queen for several months, and while waiting to consummate her marriage with Louis XVI, enjoyed a brief honeymoon with the French court—a period of calm that would not be repeated. The country, wearied by a long series of royal mistresses, welcomed the sight of a young and innocent queen, while Marie-Antoinette, finally free to choose the style of life that suited her, made up for her lack of experience and her unbridled frivolity with grace, courtesy, and beauty, and the supreme elegance of her manners, to which the memoirs of her contemporaries bear witness. And if her need for distraction, amusement, and personal friendship seemed blameworthy in a queen, it constituted a healthy antidote to her emotional solitude and that conjugal impasse for which—in spite of her mother's reproaches—she was not to blame.

Marie-Antoinette's fondness for Lauzun emerged from this period of playful frivolity. It would last for two years, until the Queen—in a far more compromising choice—decided to take up again with the Polignacs, sacrificing her independence of judgment to the interests of a single clan.

In the spring of 1775, Marie-Antoinette divided her friendship among the Princesse de Lamballe, whom she wanted for superintendent of her house, the Princesse de Guéménée, on whom she hoped to grant the position of Governess of the Children of France (which was the privilege of the princess's maternal aunt), the Comtesse de Marsan, and the Comtesse de Dillon, whom she had called to Versailles as female companions. It was Mme de Guéménée and Mme de Dillon who introduced Lauzun into the small circle surrounding the Queen. The daughter of the Maréchal de Soubise and Lauzun's closest female friend, the Princesse de Guéménée was the doyenne of the group. "Bold, vociferous, mirthful, independent, and devil-may-care, she assembled around her gaming tables the very best of society"[129]—but Victoire-Armande-Josèphe de Rohan-Soubise never forgot that she belonged by birth and marriage to one of the most illustrious families in France, and her grand dame's manners earned her the respect of the Queen. The Princesse was partial to Lauzun, with whom she had carried on a long-standing *amitié amoureuse*, and was the mistress of the Comte de Coigny, whose elder brother, the Duc de Coigny, would become one of Marie-Antoinette's favorites. Furthermore, Guéménée seemed to feel not the least bitterness toward his wife—who, for her part, was intimate friends with her husband's mistress, the Comtesse de Dillon, herself another of Lauzun's lovers. "Sweet, noble, and generous," the Princesse was unmatched when it came to her social graces—"the desire, the means, and the certainty of pleasing"[130]—but, free of coquetry and faithful to the Prince, her relations with the Duc were limited to tender friendship.

Like Lady Sarah before her, Marie-Antoinette discovered through the women in her immediate entourage that adultery was a phenomenon endemic to French high society, where it served as a corrective for a matrimonial institution indifferent to the wishes of its contracting parties.[131] Deferential to patriarchal authority, the French monarchy had never formally adapted the dictates of the Council of Trent—which had confirmed the Church's doctrine of consensuality when it came to marriage, recognizing the right of children to wed without the agreement of the head of the family.[132] The 1556 edict by Henri II de Valois that prohibited boys younger than thirty and girls younger than twenty-five from marrying without the approval of their parents under pain of disinheritance remained in force until the Revolution, perpetuating among the privileged caste an ethic that separated familial interests and the reasoning of the heart. As Chamfort wrote, "marriage, as practiced among the great, is an arranged indecency."[133]

But manners, long since adopted as a "substitute morality,"[134] required that lovers never explicitly reveal the nature of their connection in public, even if in the *parfaitement bonne compagnie* extramarital unions were generally known and had nothing reprehensible about them as such. A strict respect for form was required (albeit with a touch of sarcasm) in even the least well-matched marriages, as one of Chamfort's anecdotes shows. "M. de Lauzun was asked how he would respond to his wife (whom he hadn't seen in six years) if she wrote to him: 'I have discovered that I am pregnant,'" Chamfort recalled. "[Lauzun] reflected on this, and replied: 'I should say: I am charmed to learn that Heaven has finally blessed our union. Look after your health; I'll come to pay court to you this evening.'"[135]

Having received a rigorous moral education, the Queen was aware that her position required her to maintain a reputation above all suspicion—but this didn't prevent her from feeling at her ease and happy among a small and privileged elite determined to enjoy life. A natural coquette, she did not object to respectful gallantry on the part of her male acquaintances at court. But it was always a dangerous game (hadn't it cost Anne of Austria dearly?), even if it was difficult, at the beginning of her reign, to predict the pitfalls.

We should not be surprised by the preference that Marie-Antoinette showed to Lauzun: a nephew of the Minister who had been the architect of her marriage with the Dauphin, intimately tied to her best friends, the "perfected product" of that *civilisation mondaine* whose charms she was in the process of discovering, a man with "a beautiful figure, plenty of wit, grace, bravery, gallantry, and manners as noble as his origin,"[136] the Duc must have seemed an ideal knight-errant. In the pages of his memoirs, Lauzun records the signs—horse rides together, intimate conversations, bantering, exchanges of heron feathers, jealousies, tears, sighs—which made him "a species of favorite" in the eyes of the court. But when the Duc claims that the Queen was on the point of opening her arms to him, is he telling us the truth? We can't rule out the idea that vanity and bitterness at having been cast aside in favor of more skillful courtiers had driven Lauzun to overemphasize a moment of weakness on the part of a young woman who was often forced to mask her emotions. But it should also be remembered that at the time when Lauzun was writing these pages, Marie-Antoinette's reputation was no longer spotless. In 1782, a large portion of the court considered her liaison with the Comte de Fersen as an established fact, and the Duc may have believed that his impressions of the past were more than justified.

What's certain is that for a brief instant Lauzun hoped to use the influence he'd gained over the young Queen to revive the project for a Franco-Russian-Polish accord that had been abruptly dropped by Vergennes. Though in the memoirs he justifies his initiative by affirming that he pursued it for the "glory" of the Queen—"I wanted to make her the governor of a grand empire, to let her enjoy at the age of twenty the most brilliant of roles, one that would cover her in glory. I wanted, in short, for her to become the arbitress of Europe"[137] —the interpretation given by the Comte de Mercy-Argenteau, the Austrian ambassador charged by the Empress to watch over her daughter in France, was rather different. "Among the various numbskulls that the Queen allows far too generous an access to her person," wrote the diplomat, "there is one who is quite dangerous, given his restless mind and mixture of various evil qualities: the Duc de Lauzun, who has spent time in Poland and Russia, and has returned with chimerical plans to set M. le Comte d'Artois on the Polish throne. Having thrown himself into that project once before, Lauzun was roundly ridiculed by the King's ministers, and is now attempting to take his revenge. To that end, he is addressing himself to the Queen.... Once the Queen revealed all of this to me, I demonstrated to Her Majesty that, given the Duc's well-known bad character, the plot into which he was attempting to draw her represented a tremendous danger."[138]

Even if he did mix up Lauzun's plans with those of another favorite aspirant, the Chevalier de Luxembourg—the Duc certainly wasn't the only one keen to play the role of political mentor to Marie-Antoinette—Marie-Thérèse's ambassador was sufficiently informed about Lauzun's growing influence over the Queen to fight it tooth and nail. He had already taken measures against Besenval, who was "neither prudent nor exempt from intrigue enough for the Queen to entrust important information to his care without danger."[139] But it was an exhausting underground war, one destined to last for years, in which Marie-Antoinette's friendships and style of life were at stake. Everything conspired to make Lauzun seem like a danger to the reputation of a queen who was headstrong, certainly, but also quite young, and sensitive to the admonitions of her mother's go-between, as well as the reprimands of her confessor, the Abbé de Vermond. A month later, Mercy was able to claim victory: "We have managed to unmask the Duc de Lauzun, one of the most dangerous characters at court, and the Queen has decided to refuse him any access to her confidences from now on. We have succeeded equally well in undermining her dangerous trust in the Princesse de Guéménée, but the Queen, knowing what this lady is worth, will retain her, so as to be able to pay an occasional evening visit to the aforesaid Princesse's home, where the youth of Versailles gather."[140]

But Mercy and the Abbé de Vermond soon came to see that they had won a pyrrhic victory. Lauzun's disgrace was first and foremost the result of the conjoined efforts of a small group of schemers far tougher and more dangerous than he, and who intended to exercise absolute control over the Queen.

Lauzun may not have imagined that he had been the object of a smear campaign on the part of the Austrian ambassador, but he certainly had not failed to note that his old rivals, like the Baron de Besenval and the Duc de Coigny, were joining forces against him and giving renewed impetus to their actions by bringing together the friends and family of the Queen's new favorite. Marie-Antoinette's veneration of the idea of friendship did not necessarily imply any particular friendship's durability, and the Queen's enthusiasm for the Princesse de Lamballe had not lasted long. "Sweet, good, and complaisant"[141] though she was, the Princesse possessed neither wit nor intellect, and the Queen preferred the company of the charming Comtesse de Polignac. But her former friend would give Marie-Antoinette a lesson in faithfulness during the Revolution: Learning of the royal family's tragic predicament, the Princesse de Lamballe, who had left France following the King's flight to Varennes, returned to Paris to serve her Queen. For the sake of friendship, this woman who, it was said, would have fled in terror at the sight of a crayfish, delivered herself up to one of the most atrocious deaths suffered under the Terror.

Still sensitive to Lauzun's charms, but subdued by the insistent pressures of her mother's ambassador and her inner circle, Marie-Antoinette resigned herself to sacrificing the Duc for the sake of her domestic tranquility. Lauzun had more than one card to play in defense of his position, but he preferred to take refuge behind a disdainful indifference. His decision was more than a matter of pride. The two years he had spent in Marie-Antoinette's circle had been quite instructive. He had seen that it was well within the Queen's power to distribute posts and offices at court—she had already made several offers to him[142]—but he also knew that Louis XVI's indulgence of his young wife stopped at the door to the council chamber. Lauzun, who lacked the vocation of a courtier, had come to realize that in serving the Queen he risked imprisoning himself within the narrow confines of Versailles. Now he found himself stirred by a pressing need to give his talents their full rein, and as his ambitions ran the gamut from politics to diplomacy to warfare, he was eager to try his luck beyond the court.

But how, exactly, to do it? At the beginning of 1777, Fortune had turned her back on him along with the Queen: Lauzun was unpleasantly surprised to find himself in serious financial difficulties. At the time of his marriage, he had come into possession of an inheritance of 5 million livres, a bequest from his mother, to which was added the "modest" income of 150,000 livres brought by his wife's dowry. But, as was commonplace among the offspring of the high nobility, Lauzun led a costlier lifestyle than allowed for by his income. The taste for luxury and contempt for money, de rigueur for a gentleman, combined with a passion for travel and racehorses, had obliged him to borrow. It was an expedient regularly adopted by those, like the Duc, who not only had access to considerable property but were poised to obtain important governmental positions. Moreover, as an only son, he would sooner or later come into possession of the paternal inheritance—in addition to that of the Duchesse de Choiseul on the maternal side. Why, then, should his creditors, who until now had been happy enough to extend the length of their loans, have suddenly united to demand the immediate repayment of a debt that had reached the formidable sum of 1.5 million livres?

In his memoirs, Lauzun clearly suggests that he was the victim of a family plot hatched by the domineering—and to his mind, detestable—Mme de Luxembourg. By making it impossible for him to gather, in the space of a few days, the required amount, they were forcing him to "give up all [his] property and [his] person to [his] family, who would make appropriate arrangements for the one and the other."[143]

What is certain is that his wife did not come to his aid, and that his father limited himself to promising to let him know "if anyone proposed imprisoning or exiling [him],"[144] as had already been threatened by the Maréchale de Luxembourg. Nor could Lauzun count on the indulgence of the Duc de Choiseul, who was busy squandering the fortune that was destined to pass to his son-in-law. After the reconciliation at Chanteloup, it was precisely the position that Lauzun occupied in respect to the Queen that had led to a new and definitive break with the Choiseuls. Mme de Gramont wanted Lauzun to use his influence over Marie-Antoinette to restore her brother to his ministerial position, and, in the face of his fair, reasonable, and graceful objections,[145] "swore [him] eternal hatred,"[146] joining the Polignac cabal against him.

Once again, the solidarity of his friends managed to offset the harshness of his family. While the Princesse de Guéménée hastened to pawn her diamonds to allow the Duc to meet the demands of the first wave of creditors,[147] and Lady Barrymore (a grande dame libertine) returned from England to put her fortune at his disposal,[148] the Marquis de Voyer made his young friend the gift of a considerable estate not far from his own.[149]

Lauzun managed to extricate himself once and for all from this difficult situation by taking out a new loan. Then, "in order to face the situation squarely and restore confidence," on April 17, 1777, he granted power of attorney to a parliamentary lawyer, M. Pays, allowing him to "manage his fortune and compensate his creditors. At the same time, he decided to make an appeal to the King to put an end to the rumors that had ruined his credit."[150]

But, bowing to the influence of the Polignac clan, Marie-Antoinette refused to back his request. And even worse, she never let slip an opportunity to injure his cause. It was she who, on the death of the Maréchal de Biron in 1778, opposed Lauzun's bid to succeed him, as planned, in the position of colonel of the Gardes Françaises—an about-face that her old favorite would never forgive. It was then that Lauzun decided to accept his immensely wealthy friend Guéménée's offer to take on both his properties and debts in exchange for a large annuity. At this point, Lauzun's wife obtained a separation from him, retaining her property. Weary of her husband's disrespectful behavior, she profited from his financial disaster by returning to live with Mme de Luxembourg.[151]

The forty or so letters sent by Lauzun to the Marquis de Voyer between April 1778 and December of the following year allow us to gauge the seriousness of the impasse in which the Duc found himself.[152] Disgraced at court, quarreling with his family, without an estate to cover his back, his sole dependable resource the rather uninspiring command of a regiment of dragoons, the Duc, not yet thirty years old, was at risk of falling far short of his destiny—whence his desperate search for an opportunity that would permit him to regain his footing, to prove his worth, to distinguish himself. He was determined to "serve." It was a key word for the Duc, one that runs through the correspondence between Lauzun and Voyer, and brings his situation closer to those of his friends Narbonne, Ségur, and Boufflers.

French gentlemen saw their true vocation in serving the King, as much on the battlefield as in the ceremony of the court. For certain of them, however, in the years preceding the Revolution, the idea of "service" had taken on new implications. According to those nobles shaped by the Age of Enlightenment, and spurred by the unshakable certainty of being fit for any high responsibility whatsoever, "serving" meant above all demonstrating critical thinking, inventiveness, and personal initiative. But if the idea of service had grown individualized, the identity of its object had grown less and less clear. Of course, they all continued to serve the King, but the ambitions of the ministers, the struggles of different coteries for power, the intrigues at court—all of these had wound up dangerously dimming the royal image. A king who delegated his responsibility for governing risked becoming a disembodied and abstract point of reference for his servants, one that could be replaced by any number of dangerously modern words: country, homeland, and nation, for instance.

Marc-René de Paulmy d'Argenson, Marquis de Voyer, fully embodied the new breed of gentleman. He belonged to a great noble family of the court, renowned for its service to the King. His grandfather had occupied the position of lieutenant of the police under Louis XV and minister of justice during the Regency; his father, the Comte d'Argenson, and his uncle, the Marquis d'Argenson, had been, respectively, minister of war and minister of foreign affairs under Louis XV. Voyer himself had undertaken a brilliant military career: appointed field marshal in 1748, he was named inspector of the cavalry and dragoons three years later, and thereafter director of the royal stud, grand master of artillery, and governor of the Château de Vincennes. But in 1756, for reasons which remain mysterious, he had received the order to resign his post as minister and exile himself to his estate at Ormes, on the border of Touraine and Poitou. Even if his father's disgrace didn't directly shake his own professional position, it had been a traumatic event for Voyer, in the wake of which, though continuing loyally to perform his duties, he began to distance himself from the regime of which he was nominally a servant. But it was not mere indignation in the face of royal arbitrariness that had awakened his critical spirit. In the d'Argenson family, independence of judgment and an interest in philosophy were common: his father, a great friend of Voltaire, had sponsored the early stages of the *Encyclopédie* (which had been dedicated to him), and the Marquis was himself known for his strong mind.

Voyer felt great sympathy for the philosophers of the Enlightenment—he protected Dom Deschamps, the Benedictine monk who preached materialism and atheism, and he had acquired a reputation as a "general metaphysician."[153] His freedom of thought and interest in the most audacious of philosophical speculations had certainly contributed to making Voyer the intellectual touchstone of a small group of young aristocrats—beginning with the Duc de Chartres—attracted to new ideas. But above all, the Marquis was a defender of the urgent need for political reforms in the English mode, on the basis of his high level of technical expertise and direct experience of military life during the disastrous Seven Years' War (when he had paid a high personal price for the lack of preparation and rivalry among the generals), and then as inspector of the cavalry, which had forced him to confront the soldiers' paucity of discipline, the insufficiency of their training, the poverty of their resources, and the absence of a coherent plan for the modernization of the army. Still, Voyer was able to compensate by way of intense economic activity for the bitterness of a military career in which his virtues had been underappreciated, depriving him of the Field Marshal's baton.

Ignoring aristocratic prejudices and the law of *dérogeance*—which prohibited the military nobility from pursuing any trade besides that of arms—Voyer worked to strengthen his familial assets by investing in agriculture, the breeding of horses, and business, all with great success. The testimony of the Abbé Barthélemy, on a visit to Ormes from neighboring Chanteloup, is eloquent: "He builds, he clears, he improves, oversees everything, guides everything: he keeps the workers moving, he educates the artisans; all is accomplished with deliberation, economy, and intelligence."[154] In short, his dynamism and initiative made him a fine example of that *noblesse d'affaires*[155] that would consolidate itself over the course of the century, determined to win a role in the forefront of the economic and political life of the nation.

In his memoirs, Talleyrand accused Voyer of having taken advantage of his intellectual ascendancy to exercise a noxious moral influence over his circle of young adepts, beginning with the Duc d'Orléans—denouncing him as "the leader of corrupt men in that period."[156] This is far from the impression one gets in reading the letters he addressed to Lauzun. If the Duc considered Voyer a guide and adviser, it is not merely that he felt a filial admiration and affection for him: He knew that his interlocutor was more capable than anyone of appreciating his "portion of talent and intelligence"[157] and of recognizing his own experience in Lauzun's need to give proof of his worth.

Their epistolary exchange is a conversation conducted wholly between men, and as such, Lauzun's tone differs markedly from that which he adopts in his memoirs. One finds nary a trace of that self-confidence with which, looking back on this period of uncertainty and anxiety in his written recollections, his older self claims that he was "too à la mode not to be employed in a brilliant manner."[158] Dropping his worldly mask, the Duc implores his friend Voyer to help him find a position that will keep him from moldering away on the sidelines.

In fact, numerous opportunities for serving his country seemed to be visible on the horizon. France had returned to the aggressive military policies desired by Choiseul in his time; determined to defend its colonial interests in India, it was preparing to take its revenge on England by launching a naval invasion of the subcontinent's coasts, in order to fly to the assistance of the insurgents. The government had yet to publicly disclose its plans, but Lauzun, kept in the loop by Voyer, who was in contact with the ministers, knew that he would have to think ahead if he wanted to obtain a command in the eventual expedition.

In his long letter of April 19, 1778, Lauzun opens his heart to Voyer, driven by the urgency of the situation and the fear of failing to meet his ambitions. If aristocratic honor remains the Duc's guiding ethic, he does not hesitate to paraphrase Rousseau in order to lend his gesture solemnity: Whatever the consequences may be, his letter is above all a "profession of faith to the man who can best hear, believe, and understand it."

There Lauzun declares himself ready, in the event of war, to fight on land or sea, in India or in America—since, he says, "I will be valued there more than in Europe, where I'm afraid there are always people who don't want to let me be good at anything." In case of peace, he intends to play the diplomatic card, and begs the Marquis to "request from M. le Comte de Maurepas or M. le Comte de Vergennes, in his name, the Ambassadorship to England."

This request, which might appear "audacious" in light of the importance of the position, rested on solid reasons. "Truly," he hastens to clarify, "I would not pretend to such a post if I didn't believe that at the moment I have tremendous advantages which enable me to accomplish what no other would be able to in my place. I dare to hope that you will believe me; you are the first who has deigned to remark in me some aptitude for business, and the only one who has the courage to speak of it at a time when it is quite out of fashion. If peace is maintained for the moment, we cannot flatter ourselves that it will last for very long—and the interval preceding war will be of the greatest concern. One can't get acquainted with England in a single day, and by all appearances events will succeed each other too quickly to leave the new ambassador time to make the necessary introductions, if he hasn't done so already. That reason alone is, I think, sufficient to exempt me from the rules that require one to pass through various political ranks before becoming ambassador. I might cite various examples of men who made their debuts as ambassadors in places they did not know nearly as well as I do England. And there is every reason to believe I would be an agreeable choice for the King of England, and that he would take steps in my favor with pleasure.... I know I may well be refused, and in that case my amour propre will not be at all wounded. I wish my ambition was as well known to everyone else as it is to you. Its aim is far more to be useful than to play a grand role."[159]

Irrespective of their motivations, Lauzun's ambitions for the ambassadorship to England were by no means new. The previous year, a rumor had circulated that the Duc had presented himself to Maurepas armed with a letter of recommendation from the Queen, and that the elderly minister—who never lost an opportunity to cast discredit on Marie-Antoinette, or to deploy his devastating irony—had replied that "'if the request were permissible, Her Majesty would have *commanded* rather than urged; as the case stands, one can only say no.' He finished by saying: 'The best I can do, Monsieur le Duc, is to recommend the Queen's continued beneficence on your behalf.'"[160] If Lauzun irrefutably filled two of the conditions requisite for appointment to an ambassadorship—bearing an illustrious name and enjoying a personal relationship with the sovereign—he lacked the third: possessing the assets necessary to exercise his duties. Generally speaking, diplomats were required to personally advance, at least in the early stages, the costs of their mission, and the recent financial misadventures of the Duc, "all of [whose] funds were under supervision,"[161] did not speak in favor of his administrative abilities.

Still, Maurepas can't have harbored too ill an opinion of Lauzun, since, several months later, at the beginning of 1778, as the Duc prepared for a new voyage to England, he asked him to play the role of a secret agent.

In Warsaw as well as Berlin, Lauzun had already rubbed shoulders with a vast network of envoys, intermediaries, spies, and informers of all kinds in the service of French foreign policy, and the premier's request should not be surprising. What better opportunity could there be for the Duc to prove his legitimacy as a candidate for the ambassadorship to London and to display his knowledge of English society? But the English diplomatic situation was complicated by the fact that Maurepas (who, in contrast to the majority of the members of the council, was against war) intended to urge Louis XVI to revive the old parallel politics of the Secret du Roi, which had fallen into desuetude since the death of the Well-Beloved. Furthermore, Maurepas, displeased with Lord Stormont, the English ambassador to Paris, had obtained from George III, who had accredited him as "personal envoy to the Court of

Versailles (February 13, 1777),"[162] Sir Nathaniel Parker-Forth, an English gentleman and man of the world, familiar with Paris and as well acquainted with the court as with the city.

Lauzun was forced to act on a number of fronts, playing roles that were not always compatible. His first remit—and also the easiest—consisted in simply being himself: A grand French lord in love with England, who, fortified by the friendship of George III, was in a position to confidentially persuade the British sovereign that his government wished to avoid war at any price. His second role was that of political observer, reporting back to Maurepas of the evolution of the Anglo-American conflict, as is shown by the communiqué he dispatched to the minister and also, for safekeeping, to Voyer.[163] Finally, the third involved an activity very close to espionage. During the lull between two amorous exploits, he would dispatch to Maurepas "a very extensive and detailed report on the state of the English defenses and of all England's possessions through the world."[164] Not only did Lauzun display a terrific capacity for work and a sense of observation far superior to that of the current French ambassador, he also proved that he wasn't lacking when it came to initiative and imagination. Though judged unacceptable by Necker, his plan to bring about the bankruptcy of the Bank of England through the defection of shareholders anticipated methods that have since been proven effective.

Repeatedly summoned to Versailles, Lauzun was sent across the Channel one last time, mid-March, immediately after Vergennes's announcement to the English government that France would recognize the United States. Predicting that "the ridiculous declaration" which "gives England advantageous warning to prepare itself for war"[165] would lead to the swift recall of ambassadors from the two countries, Maurepas and Vergennes asked Lauzun to return to London to study their preparations from up close, and to engage in a final attempt at diplomacy with George III. But the Duc did not intend to lend himself to the sort of double-dealing that would have reflected poorly on a gentleman and, on April 4, after a final official meeting with the sovereign, who expressed to him all his bitterness at the French decision, Lauzun departed England. Before embarking at Dover, he wrote to the Comte de Vergennes to justify his decision: "I quit England with regret, and the orders which you gave me to remain in London as long as possible increase the chagrin I feel at leaving when I might be of some use; but in my own defense, I never believed I had to wait until the point that I became suspicious, and in prolonging my stay I would have risked the confidence and consideration I enjoy here and which will perhaps be useful again one day in the service of the King."[166]

Upon his arrival in France, Lauzun rejoined his regiment, based in Ardes in the Auvergne, where, on April 9, he resumed his correspondence with Voyer. If in London he had believed himself able to rely on the esteem of Maurepas and Vergennes, in the solitude of Ardes he was forced to recognize that his future prospects had dwindled to vague promises. Having lost hope that he would be remembered at Versailles, Lauzun asked Voyer in his letter of April 17 to rally to his aid. Over the four months that followed, in letter after letter, he would push himself forward again and again as a candidate "for the service of the King." The uncertainty that lingered around the government's choice of strategies between peace and war undoubtedly demanded flexibility and an ability to adapt quickly from those who aspired to occupy decisive posts. However, in his anxiety over being forgotten, Lauzun pushed further, declaring himself willing to take on any work whatsoever, so long as it was compatible with his title. The only certainty to be found in that desperate search for a chance to avoid being sidelined was the young Duc's confidence in his ability to tackle whatever task might come his way.

In the event of continued peace, his first objective remained the ambassadorship to London, but for that position he would require the assent of the King, on top of the need to neutralize the hostility of the Queen's circle. Now that he had accumulated evidence of his professional competence when it came to England, what accusations could his detractors use to sour him in the eyes of "a just prince who wishes for the best"?[167] The defensive tone of certain passages of his letters—needless with a friend like Voyer—seems to imply that Lauzun envisaged the possibility that they might be intercepted by the *cabinet noir*, and that a transcription might well reach the King himself. This, at least, is what he confides to his correspondent on May 23, 1778: "There you have my sentiments, my dear General. If they should unseal my letter I should not be angry that they were known—I can acknowledge them without embarrassment, with no false shame."[168]

The "sentiments" of Lauzun that appear in these letters are those of a free spirit who wishes to appear no different from what he is, who does not hesitate to assert without hypocrisy his right to live in accord with his temperament and aspirations, who invokes the necessary distinction between the public sphere and private life, and demands to be judged, not on the basis of the various rumors circulating about him but on his abilities. And indeed, the main rumors from which he had to defend himself involved accusations of financial irresponsibility and libertinism. "They can reproach me with living badly," he wrote, "or rather, with not living alongside my wife, and of having squandered part of my fortune; this may prove that I'm a poor choice for a husband, or that I shouldn't be loaned money, but nobody is asking for that, and anyway it has nothing to do with serving the King, in which, politically and militarily, I am well-versed."[169]

They could also, however, reproach him with a flaw no less serious: the ongoing discord between himself and his family. But then, what about the cynicism and harshness of treatment to which they'd subjected him? "For some years now it has been amusing to note that I have occasionally been indebted to the favor of the court for the fondness of my parents, but never to the fondness of my parents for the favor of the court."[170]

On the other hand, it was impossible for him to take up again his place at court, where he recognized he had been "so often amused,"[171] because, he declared: "I have neither the taste nor the talent for intriguing—the court would bore me, and I wouldn't be a success. As you know, the prevailing opinion runs against me—but that opinion is my enemies' sole advantage. I should try to live someplace where they are less important."[172]

His true vocation, he writes, was not scheming at Versailles but distinguishing himself on the field of battle: "If peace were not as certain as everyone believes, and there was some enterprise in the offing in India, that would suit me perfectly: let me not forget that when there is nothing but glory to be gained, and said glory can be achieved only by searching out danger four thousand leagues from home, one rarely has courtiers for rivals."[173]

In writing these lines, Lauzun could not have known that the previous day, June 17, off the coast of Roscoff, a French frigate, *La Belle Poule*, had come up against an English frigate, the *Arethusa*, unequivocally signaling war. Here France found the long-awaited chance to profit from the critical situation besetting Great Britain since the intensification of the American conflict and the massive mobilization of troops across the Atlantic. Two plans on which Lauzun's hopes had been lately concentrated, in addition to the London ambassadorship, were on the verge of materializing: a mission to India (where, following the Peace of Paris in 1753, the French presence had been reduced to the control of a handful of ports) that would strike at the heart of Great Britain's economic interests; and a large-scale landing on the English coast. It seemed unlikely indeed that England, already engaged militarily on the far side of the ocean, would be capable of withstanding such an offensive.

The first project, smacking of danger, distance, and exoticism, was perfectly in keeping with the Duc's adventurous temperament and seemed to offer the long-sought opportunity to show what he was made of: "The hopes you give me in regard to India are tremendously pleasing. You must be aware that for a long time they have been my castle in the sky. If they come to fruition, I will soon be better known than I am today."[174] But that did not prevent him from waxing enthusiastic at the prospect of an invasion of England—a plan that Voyer was involved in drafting—and from launching himself into the formulation of analyses and the elaboration of future projects, suggesting political, economic, and military stratagems based on the knowledge he had acquired in Great Britain. "Seeing as we are ready," he wrote, "why wait for the English to be so as well? They are preparing to meet us on the coast of Sussex, which is bristling with troops and batteries. The Earl of Kent, however, remains almost defenseless. Why not push forward boldly? Sometimes audacity is the wisest course of action. Why not be brave enough to do as the Dutch dared to, once? Why not sail boldly up the Thames, burn Chatham and all of the vessels anchored there while the troops disembark.... Give me twelve hundred volunteers, and I'll undertake to put them in position to support our landing for four days, if that should be necessary. Believe me, this plan isn't that of a young man who thinks nothing of danger but the result of painstaking calculation."[175]

But the Duc's flights of enthusiasm were regularly followed by fits of despondency. The dithering of the government, the rivalry between ministers, the sluggishness of the administrative apparatus, the intrigues at court, the logic of royal favor—together they had a paralyzing effect. For months the army deployed along the Atlantic coast sat idle, awaiting decisions that grew more improbable every day, until the enemy had had time to prepare their defense. "The moment to seize fame and attain victory with a minimum of danger has passed," he declared to Voyer at the beginning of July, still harping on the landing: "It won't be long now until we're attacked by enemies who a few months ago would not have been able to defend themselves from us ... our criminal circumspection has cost us whatever profit we might have drawn from the situation . . . soon enough England will fully regain its maritime superiority."[176] As he had explained to Vergennes[177] two weeks earlier, Lauzun feared above all that England would finally reach an accord with the American rebels, assuring themselves faithful allies and preferential conditions for international commerce. Yet one particularly sensitive element of that commerce—the traffic in slaves, essential for the development of American plantations—would in fact provide Lauzun "the pleasure of being able to help."[178]

Thanks to their network of African trading posts, the English—along with the Dutch— enjoyed a dominant position in the triangular trade of what was commonly referred to as "black gold."[179] Sold by tribal chiefs to white traffickers along with precious raw materials such as gold, ivory, rubber, and shea nuts in exchange for European trinkets, enslaved Africans were shipped toward America, where they were resold to the highest bidder. The same ships returned to Europe laden with sugar and rum.

In London, Lauzun had studied the ways and means of this particularly lucrative trade, from which France had been for the most part excluded with the loss of Senegal, ceded to Great Britain after the defeat in the Seven Years' War. The sole outpost that remained in the hands of France was Gorée, an island just off the coast of Senegal. The Duc was well aware that the English employed a wide network of fortified towns and trading posts to defend their African interests, which served the double function of cowing the local populations and maintaining systematic trade with the various tribal chiefs.

While reading *London Magazine*, Lauzun had come across the report of a parliamentary debate from March 13, 1778, in the course of which the state of decay and lack of security of English fortresses on the African coast[180] were raised; the Duc had concluded that "the defenses of Saint-Louis in Senegal, to which the English never attached paramount importance, had been neglected."[181] Convinced that this was an excellent opportunity for France to regain a commercial base in Africa, Lauzun informed the minister of the navy, Antoine de Sartine, who during the summer had charged him with leading the operation. In reality, it was a mission *within* a mission, since in mid-July Sartine had announced to him the far more consequential decision to organize the expedition to India, naming him vice commander under the direct orders of Bussy, and trusting him with the task of assembling a body of 600 officers and 4,500 soldiers—the *volontaires étrangers* of the navy, a sort of foreign legion avant la lettre[182]—so as to be in position to defeat the Royal Navy. As part of this ambitious enterprise, it had been decided that a small naval unit, detached from the fleet en route to the Indian subcontinent, would make a detour to Senegal in order to chase the English from Saint-Louis before continuing on toward the final destination.

Having recovered his former aplomb, the Duc returned to Versailles with head held high and, fêted by mistresses old and new, took his revenge on the Queen. It was a plot, if one is to believe the memoirs, with two distinct dimensions.

The first was amour propre. Proud of his new responsibilities, Lauzun informed Marie-Antoinette of them personally. Taken by surprise, she did not know how to hide her distress: "Tears rolled from her eyes; she spent some minutes without saying anything to me apart from: 'Ah! M. de Lauzun! Ah! My God!' Then, having recovered a bit, she continued: 'How! To go so far, to separate yourself for so long from all who love you, and all whom you love!' —'I believe, Madame,'" he replied, "'that in so distant a theater, my zeal, and the few talents I possess, will encounter fewer obstacles, and will be rendered greater justice, having less need to struggle against intrigue and calumny.'—'You are leaving us, M. de Lauzun! You are going to India! Can I do anything to prevent it?'—'No, madame, that is impossible, I shall hold irrevocably to this plan, no matter how much it costs me to execute.'"[183]

At this point, the Duc could have left well enough alone. The victim of her own weakness, the Queen had betrayed their friendship and had thought herself able to toy with his emotions with impunity. That she should weep now at her errors was nothing but justice. Certainly, by leaving a written record of their conversation, Lauzun showed himself to be something less than a true gentleman, but the dialogue he recounts could also stand as a simple confirmation of the emotional unsteadiness and sentimentality to which the young sovereign often yielded. As always, the choice of how to interpret this deftly ambiguous tale is left to the reader.

But Marie-Antoinette's tears were not enough to appease Lauzun's rancor, and rather than fostering a reconciliation, they simply exacerbated his need for revenge. Freed from any sentimental impediment, he was bent on humiliating the one who had humiliated him. Although it is hardly credible—at the time, Marie-Antoinette was finally expecting a child, and Lauzun knew it[184]—the second part of his tale could have been plucked from the pages of a libertine novel.

Up until this point, the Queen and Lauzun had been confronting each other one-on-one—but now the entrance of a third party rekindled the game. Friend and sometime lover of the Duc, and an intimate of Marie-Antoinette, Mme de Guémenée had never hesitated to play the matchmaker for each of them, in order to maintain her control over both.

Well informed of the feelings Marie-Antoinette still cherished for her erstwhile favorite, the Princesse assured Lauzun that she would be able to persuade the Queen to open her arms to him if he renounced his plan to depart. And indeed, behind the scenes she was hatching a plot intended to drive the sovereign's wavering virtue toward the "dangerous seas" of adultery.[185]

Mme de Guémenée was certainly no evil genius like Laclos's terrible Marquise de Merteuil, but still, for her, as for so many among the ranks of the privileged, the operative words of aristocratic civilization—love, friendship, loyalty, honor—no longer corresponded to a shared code of ethics, and their respective meanings varied dangerously according to persons and circumstances. Anticipating the Marquise, the Princesse did not hesitate to enter into a pact with her old lover that was incompatible with the selfless emotions of friendship, and to shamelessly abuse the confidence placed in her by the Queen, in order to keep the latter under her thumb. And Lauzun himself was no better.

He was ready to play along with Mme de Guémenée if that would provide him with a foolproof means of avenging himself on Marie-Antoinette, and when the Queen gave him to understand that she was prepared to surrender herself without conditions in order to keep from losing him, he spurned her. "I resisted all, though I will not hide the grandeur of the sacrifice. My vanity was satisfied; I refused the Queen proudly, I showed her that I wanted nothing from her, and that I too could play a major role."[186]

In thrall to his narcissism, deaf to the promptings of chivalry, Lauzun felt no qualms about sacrificing his feelings for the Queen on the altar of ressentiment.

But the task that awaited Lauzun was not, in fact, the "major role" on which all of his hopes had centered.

Amid tears and sighs, Lauzun had already said his farewells to those closest to him—including Mme de Martainville, his then mistress—with all the solemnity and pathos of someone preparing for a long journey to a distant land, when he was informed that the Indian expedition had once again been postponed. Luckily he still had the African mission—but that was a relatively modest governor's job, one which would last no longer than a few months in barbarous and desolate Senegal, rather than a grand military venture in the kingdom of *The Thousand and One Nights*. Yet even in this unrewarding context, Lauzun gave evidence of his remarkable capacity for work, his political intelligence, his sense of responsibility, and his aptitude for command.

The Duc had not been the only one[187] to advocate the opportunity for chasing the English out of Senegal, but no one had exposed with so much clarity the economic and political consequences that such a move might bring about. In his "Essay on English Trade and Holdings in Africa"—one of a number of ministerial reports he authored during this period—he clearly demonstrated that "the conquest of England's colonial holdings on the African coast should not be regarded merely as a considerable injury inflicted on our enemy's commerce and an augmentation of that of France."[188] A strong policy of economic development on the dark continent would allow France not only to cease its dependence on raw materials from across the Atlantic—cotton, sugar, tobacco—but also to undermine American production by blocking the slave trade.

During his brief mission, Lauzun saw that a good number of the tensions that hindered any stable collaboration with the Africans stemmed from the greed and brutality of the traffickers. In his reports, he insisted on the inadvisability of delegating responsibility for the civil and military organization of the trading posts to the traders of the Compagnie de Guyane (the French commercial firm—these were matters on which the commissioners of the King, and they alone, should have the final word.

Lauzun embarked in great secrecy from Lorient on December 3, aboard the *Fendant*, a ship belonging to the Marquis de Vaudreuil. He was responsible for the small group of ships (two warships, two frigates, three corvettes) that would support the landing forces—and forty-six days later he came in sight of Saint-Louis, a small island strategically located in the vast lagoon at the mouth of the Senegal River.

Although his journal—kept daily from January 28 until April 19, 1779[189]— reports with great accuracy the progress of their expedition (and would later go on to feed a more subjective version in the memoirs), we will not linger here over the many difficulties the Duc encountered in reaching and living on

Saint-Louis. We will return to that "heap of sand that produces nothing good"[190] in the wake of the Chevalier de Boufflers, who, seven years after Lauzun, exercised in turn the office of Governor of Senegal. It is a singular coincidence that two indisputable champions of the art of living in high society—bound by friendship and both driven, even if for different reasons, by the need to serve, should have been confronted within a short stretch of time by the same experience of solitude on a small African island where poverty, sickness, and violence were rampant.

Lauzun succeeded in carrying out his mission in record time. The fortress's English garrison, reduced to a handful of men, surrendered without a fight, and the Duc constructed a new system of fortifications to gain the respect of the chiefs of the African tribes, improved the conditions of life on Saint-Louis, and took care of his prisoners and the ill, before passing the torch to his adjutant, Eyriès, a lieutenant of one of the battleships, who would serve in the interim while awaiting a new governor. During this stretch of time the frigate commanded by the Chevalier Pontevès-Gien neutralized all of the English forts on the coast. With naval operations at an end, Lauzun saw to it that the Marquis de Vaudreuil rejoined the French fleet, commanded by the Comte d'Estaing, which was preparing to face the English fleet off the coast of Martinique. And the Duc, in turn, on March 16 left Saint-Louis to return to France.

Even if Lauzun's expedition had nothing particularly heroic about it—he himself speaks of it in his memoirs as an "easy success"—the goal achieved there was objectively important. Thanks to the Duc's determination, France had assured itself control—this time definitively—over a key position in a land destined to become one of the strong points of its colonial system. But in Paris, where reputations were decided in the salons, Lauzun's popularity, as Mme du Deffand wrote to her English correspondent, was by no means great. Which was unsurprising, since the Duc de Choiseul was the first to turn his nephew's mission into a joke, without deigning to wait for its conclusion. However, it had been he himself who, when he was minister, had laid the groundwork for the political strategy that France was pursuing with this African expedition. "M. de Lauzun," Mme du Deffand wrote, "with two battleships and a very small number of troops, has taken your Senegal, which was your trade in slaves; M. de Choiseul said yesterday that M. de Sartine, while reading the King the details of that expedition, hesitated a bit to tell him all of the particulars; M. de Maurepas compelled him not to omit a single detail: and thus he learned that the English garrison had consisted of four men, three of whom were ill. M. de Choiseul told us that the one who was left apparently gave himself up with good grace, and there is no doubt that he was granted the honors of war. If in the course of that exploit M. de Lauzun had stumbled across a gold mine, that would be about as good for him as the glory he'll be returning to."[191]

At Versailles, too, nobody bothered to praise Lauzun: Maurepas, clashing with Sartine, had an interest in discrediting the Senegalese adventure, while Sartine, who was officially responsible, made no attempt to defend it. As for Louis XVI, he abstained from all comment. Since no one had proposed a promotion for him, Lauzun indignantly refused "a cash reward." But there was worse to come.

Lauzun discovered that the planned expedition to India had been defini-tively abandoned—Sartine, telling him nothing about it, and in spite of all his assurances, had dissolved the body of *volontaires étrangeres* that the Duc had put so much work into assembling. Deprived of the means of "serving properly," Lauzun resigned; but this time the sovereign himself intervened unexpectedly in his favor, naming him the colonel to a legion of 1,800 infantry-men and 600 horsemen, which could not be dissolved.[192] And as it turned out, his expedition was not wholly devoid of celebration: on Sunday, Septem-ber 12, at the demand of Louis XVI, all of the churches in Paris burst into a Te Deum for the victory carried off against the English in Africa. And the victory was judged worthy of an etching: *The Taking of Senegal*, which showed Lauzun receiving the surrender of the fort's English governor.[193]

But the most difficult ordeal for Lauzun was facing the court assembled at Marly: "It is impossible to imagine how I was treated by the Queen, and con-sequently by the rest," he recalls in his memoirs,[194] acknowledging that he hesitated over what sort of posture to adopt toward them. Then, like an actor who, having overcome a fit of stage fright, faces the audience and enthralls them with the power of his interpretation, the Duc rediscovered "[his] assur-ance" and "[his] gaiety": "I grew less gloomy, I spoke with the Queen, made pleasantries, she laughed, I was enjoying myself; she remembered that we were not meeting for the first time, she was as familiar with me as she had been three years before, and the end of my evening was as brilliant as the beginning had been dull."[195] It was a particular young woman who had performed the trick of returning his self-confidence to him—a woman who would come to occupy a central place in his life, dramatically influencing his decisions.

Louise-Marthe de Conflans—beautiful, cultured, and highly intelligent—was the daughter of the Marquis d'Armentières. In 1775, at the age of seventeen, she had married the only son of the Duc de Coigny. Her father was the scion of a family of the military nobility that dated back to the Crusades, and her mother the daughter of a wealthy Parisian magistrate; Louise-Marthe's pride in her family's feudal past was combined with the intellectual and moral values of the parliamentary bourgeoisie. Having long ago decided to live separately, her parents led very different lives: an intimate of the Duc de Chartres and his companion in libertinism, the Marquis de Conflans was a habitué of high society, while the Marquise preferred to stay far from the court, entertaining a small, select group of friends at home. An anecdote from the eve of Louise-Marthe's wedding gives us a good picture of the state of relations between the couple: "The marriage... occasioned numerous family dinners, in which all the gaiety of ancient France was revived. When the prospect of these meals came up, the Duc de Coigny said to M. le Marquis de Conflans: 'Do you know how nervous I am?'—'But why?'—'Never once in my life have I dined with your wife.'—'Well, neither have I! We'll be together, in any case: we can comfort each other.'"[196]

Entrusted to the care of her mother, Louise-Marthe had received a thorough education away from the court, and just three years after her marriage, aged twenty, she was presented at Versailles, where her husband's family enjoyed the favor of the Queen. Not in the least impressed, the Marquise de Coigny—entirely self-confident, sure of her physical and intellectual assets—approached life at court with a critical spirit. Displaying that streak of independence that characterized both the magistracy and the high nobility, Louise-Marthe was not disposed to let anyone intimidate her.

And so, when Lauzun made his entrance at Marly that evening, she had been the first person—fully informed about his past life and current situation—to address a word to him. When she approached him, he warned her that "she would not be doing herself any good at court, nor with her family, by speaking with [him], and that she was rather courageous to do so. She responded that she was well aware."[197] Galvanized by the audacity of this young woman, Lauzun immediately recovered his sangfroid, and went on to confound his adversaries, reasserting his status with his distinctive irony and wit. Indeed, forty years later, in the midst of the Restoration, and despite the *damnatio memoriae* that had been inflicted on him, Louis XVIII would affectionately recall Lauzun's irresistible style of conversation: "It would have been impossible to be more amusing than he was: I tell you, I would have stayed twenty-four hours to hear him talk."[198] But over the following months, the gratitude and admiration that Lauzun felt for Mme de Coigny would be transformed into an unprecedented emotion: "I have never seen such spirit, such grace, so wholly different from the spirit and grace of others. I told myself that it was unreasonable to love her, that it would make me unhappy; but no other happiness so suited me."[199]

The heir of a century of libertinism, Lauzun had suddenly rediscovered the pleasures of *vasselage amoureux*, and was prepared to renounce those of the flesh in order to explore the *Pays du Tendre*. Like a courteous knight-errant, he declared himself ready to give his love without asking anything in return.

But the object of his worship was by no means the distant, idealized woman of chivalrous tradition, once celebrated as the supreme guarantor of social regulations and the established order. Mme de Coigny was a rebellious spirit, struggling against every kind of imposed rule, who cultivated with equal determination all the contradictory aspirations of her age. She detested the monarchy out of loyalty to her family, invited Rousseau to her home to read the *Confessions*, and gave Laclos the cold shoulder because she suspected him of taking her as the model for the Marquise de Merteuil in *Les Liaisons Dangereuses*. Like a true libertine, Mme de Coigny was a master of the art of speaking and knew how to impose herself on her interlocutors with the edge and eloquence of her conversation and the originality of her judgments—but she valued her freedom too greatly to go much further. She quickly distanced herself from a husband whom she did not love, but chose to maintain a strategy of defensive feminism, declaring that she never had "any lovers at all, because to do so would be to capitulate"[200]—though this does not necessarily mean she was cruel to her admirers.

Her extreme individualism did not prevent her from loving life in society, where she brooked no rivals, and if numerous anecdotes have come down to us regarding her ability to win the admiration of both the court and the town, to amuse, and to seduce without giving herself away, we also have plenty of evidence of her arrogance, her vindictiveness, her treacherousness. But it was in friendship that the Marquise gave the best of herself, and if she is remembered today, it is because she was able to convince two of the most celebrated libertines of the age to devote themselves to the delicate pleasures of *l'amitié amoureuse* and to pay homage to her in their writings. Indeed, some years later the Prince de Ligne chose to dedicate to her one of his most beautiful literary texts, the famous letters written during his voyage to Crimea in the retinue of Catherine of Russia.[201] But Ligne was far too convinced that love was inseparable from physical pleasure not to have reservations regarding the Marquise's amorous metaphysics, and in the end he expressed these in the long *portrait à clé* that he consecrated to her: "She reasoned too much about love. From analysis she moved quickly to dissection, and the little cadaver that resulted was not particularly pretty. Love is only charming when you embrace it *sans reflection*. Does she or doesn't she love you? Did she? Will she? It's an enigma. If it happened, it was only out of curiosity…If Carite had happened to find a man who resembled her in this, we would all have seen something amusing."[202]

Yet everything seems to suggest that Louise-Marthe had in fact found that man in Lauzun. They had the same friends (the Guéménées, the Dillons, the Marquis de Voyer, the Duc d'Orléans), they harbored the same resentments (he for the Queen, who had turned her back on him, she for the King, who had refused her father the cordon bleu), they both detested the court and placed their hopes in a politics of reform that could renew the monarchy's institutions. They also shared the same emotional uncertainty, the same "emptiness…at [the] heart."[203] His meeting with Mme de Coigny reawakened Lauzun's hope of having finally found a cure for that emptiness, driving him to renounce the old carousel of seductions, which had long since ceased to intrigue him, and to bet instead on submission and patience. For her part, the Marquise revealed herself as a master of the art of equivocation, dodging Lauzun's affections while leaving open the hope of a very different future. Indeed, as we read in the Duc's memoirs: "She did not tell me that she would never love me."[204] A powerful bond was established between the two of them—one which, without changing their lives, would help them exorcise what had seemed a fated solitude.

It is more than likely that over the course of their "beau jeu,"[205] Lauzun in fact won a place in the Marquise's bed—but this is, in any case, of secondary importance compared to the psychological influence that she exerted on him. It was she who, combining political convictions and personal passions, contributed to transforming the Duc's resentment against Marie-Antoinette into hate, driving him to turn his back on his sovereign and embrace the Revolution.

But her position as an agitator in the salons did not prevent her from emigrating when she finally scented danger—while Lauzun remained behind to face the consequences of his decisions.

It was this change of heart spurred by Mme de Coigny that, on May 12, 1780, sent Lauzun sailing for the United States, to participate in what we can finally describe as a *grande expédition*. At the head of his Deuxième Légion, the Duc had spent the summer and autumn of 1779 in Brittany awaiting the order to attack England, and it was there that Chateaubriand had seen him "gallop past me at full speed, in a hussar's uniform and mounted on a Barbary horse," and had recognized him, as he described much later in the *Mémoires d'outre-tombe*, as "one of those men who marked the end of a world."[206] But the planned invasion of England was instead abandoned once again, and at the beginning of February of the following year, the King decided to send an expedition to the aid of the Americans. The command of the fleet was entrusted to the Chevalier de Ternay, and that of the infantry to the Comte de Rochambeau, a brilliant career soldier. It was at the request of Rochambeau that Lauzun, promoted to brigadier general in charge of the light troops, succeeded in taking part in the mission with his legion.

An attentive observer of the conflict that had exploded between Great Britain and its colony across the Atlantic, Lauzun had seen it from the beginning as an opportunity for France to take advantage of its rival's momentary weakness. Moreover, he was persuaded—as he emphasized in his correspondence with Voyer—that the dispute would never lead to a definitive rupture between two countries so closely tied to each other. Familiar with English political pragmatism, Lauzun rather feared that the two adversaries would sooner or later end up coming to an accord detrimental to France. Even if he hadn't immediately understood the significance and irreversibility of the events in America, the Duc tended for more than one reason to sympathize with the claims of the rebels. One of these—a significant one, no doubt—was his affiliation with Freemasonry.

Introduced to France around 1725 by the English Jacobites, Freemasonry had, after an initial period of enthusiasm, experienced a number of difficult years, at first due to the joint hostility of the government and the Church, then to internal disputes that had torn it apart under the disastrous leadership of that irresponsible debauchee, the Comte de Clermont. The movement had managed to survive thanks to the dedication of its administrator general, the Duc de Montmorency-Luxembourg, who, after the death of Clermont, on May 24, 1771, had elected another Prince of the Blood, the Duc de Chartres, to the post of grand master, while continuing to steer the society himself, imposing internal reforms with a firm hand. Thus, on October 22, 1773, after adopting new statutes that conferred upon it authority over all three hundred French lodges, the Grande Loge nationale de France, or Grand Orient, solemnly assembled for the ceremonial appointment of the Duc de Chartres. On the new organizational chart of the order, Guéménée and Lauzun figured in the first ranks, along with numerous intimates of the Duc: the Coignys, Osmond, Laval, Chabot, Durfort, Fronsac, and the Prince de Ligne.[207]

Inspired by the eighteenth century's rationalist and philosophical ideas, French Freemasonry had nothing particularly subversive about it. Its aim was the "improvement of the lot of mankind. The means that it employed to reach this goal were the propagation of morality and charity." And its status as an "irregular" association meant that it had to assure itself of government tolerance by means of irreproachable conduct. Its choice to name the cousin of the King as its new grand master placed it "almost in the shadow of the throne."[208]

Even if that election was largely a political gesture, as Gabriel de Broglie recalls, "the presence of Louis-Philippe-Joseph at the head of Freemasonry proved a decisive factor for the forces of change."[209] While the prestige of a Prince of the Blood served to attract provincial elites who joined in droves, the lack of interest shown by Chartres in the exercise of the duties associated with his post—which he treated as a sinecure—"allowed the development of initiatives and the decentralization" of the Masonic movement, which gained great popularity within the organization. Over time, as "the recruitment of lodges expanded and democratized...Orléanism and Freemasonry became progressively identified,"[210] both assuming on the eve of 1789 an increasingly political character.

But in the 1770s, French Freemasonry was also spreading as a social phenomenon, shedding its occult character, opening itself to women, and launching a multitude of public initiatives. "They enjoy themselves, and are charitable,"[211] commented Sébastien Mercier. In 1775, the King himself joined, certainly without making too much of a fuss, affiliating himself with his two brothers in the military lodge of the Trois Frères Unis "to the east of the court." Meanwhile the Parisian salons were captivated by the debates between the Grand Orient, the Mother Lodge of the Scottish Rite, the Social Contract (founded in Paris in 1776), and the prestigious Lodge of the Nine Sisters, whose membership consisted entirely of men of letters and savants.

It was on the occasion of the Anglo-American conflict that the French Freemasons proved their influence over public opinion by helping to orient it in favor of the rebels, and by building enduring ties with their brothers on the far side of the Atlantic. Benjamin Franklin—who arrived in Paris in January 1777, first as envoy and then as ambassador for the newborn United States—was admitted to the Lodge of the Nine Sisters on the recommendation of the astronomer Lalande and aroused general enthusiasm there: One of Franklin's letters to Congress announced the coming of the French Freemason Lafayette, who, without requesting the permission of the King, had gone to fight for the American cause. Upon Lafayette's arrival, George Washington immediately welcomed the French officer into the American Union Lodge. It is worth recalling that at the ceremony that followed the swearing in of the first president of the United States (on a Bible provided by St. John's Lodge), the French delegation was among the five lodges invited, and that Washington was clad in a Masonic apron, embroidered by Lafayette's wife in white silk, when he laid the cornerstone of the Capitol Building on September 18, 1793.

In France, Freemasonry spread among the high ranks of the army, and numerous volunteer officers went to fight alongside their American brothers. In the case of Lauzun's expedition, another Duc—as it turns out, his superior in rank—the Vicomte de Rochambeau, was a Mason, as were many of his fellow adventurers, such as the Comte de Ségur, the Vicomte de Noailles, the Chevalier de Chastellux, and Alexandre and Charles de Lameth. As Jacques Brengues writes, those Frenchmen who served in America "may well have helped introduce the emancipatory ideology of enlightened French Masonry into the American lodges." And in turn, the French Freemasons who participated in the War of Independence were ideally placed "to observe at close range the first trials of those grand ideas they had earlier promoted in their respective lodges: America provided them with living historical proof of what might be possible going forward."[212]

This was precisely Lauzun's experience. Having disembarked in Rhode Island on July 11, 1780, after a crossing of seventy-two days, he was forced to wait a year before confronting the enemy on the battlefield. Newport, where the French established their headquarters, was—as Louis-Philippe de Ségur reported when he visited it two years later—a "well-built and well-ordered city, with a large population whose affluence proclaims their happiness; there we enjoyed delightful encounters with modest men and pretty women whose charms were embellished by their talents."[213] Lauzun was quick to avail himself of the delights of the three Hunter girls, whose salon formed the heart of the town's social life.

The English had concentrated their forces in New York and in Yorktown, Virginia, two cities with large, secure bays that provided the Royal Navy with a safe anchorage and allowed them to provision and transport their troops. Washington and Rochambeau were both counting on the French naval unit to hamper the movements of the enemy fleet, but they disagreed when it came to strategy. Washington wanted the Americans and French to launch a joint attack on New York; Rochambeau still did not consider it safe to leave Newport, and awaited reinforcements from France.

During the months of inactivity that followed the fortification of the base at Newport, where Rochambeau had settled the bulk of the army, Lauzun looked after his hussars, first in Rhode Island and then, come winter, at Lebanon, Connecticut, "which consists of nothing but a handful of cabins scattered in immense forests, as in Siberia."[214] Formed chiefly of German and Alsatian mercenaries (many of whom were defectors from the English army), Lauzun's legion, scrappy and undisciplined, was in need of an iron fist. The officers set a poor example for the others, seizing on the least occasion to fight duels—beginning with the Comte Arthur de Dillon, deputy colonel to the Duc. But what really mattered to Lauzun was that his men would ultimately obey him on the battlefield, and it is the Comte de Fersen who bears witness to the hold he maintained on them: "He is adored by his troops; he is like a father to all his officers; they are ready to tear themselves to pieces for his sake."[215] By a singular coincidence, thousands of miles from Versailles, the Duc had become fast friends with this handsome Swedish officer, a Freemason as well, who had come to fight for the American cause in hopes of making the French Court forget the predilection that Marie-Antoinette had displayed for him. And if Fersen could not ignore the fact that Lauzun had preceded him in the favors of the Queen, that didn't prevent him from being sensible of the man's charms: as he wrote to his father, the Duc was "the most noble and honest soul I have met."[216] Apparently the glacial cold of Lebanon did not shake the Duc's good humor: when Chastellux arrived for a visit, he was invited—for lack of anything better—to join them in hunting squirrels. After the hunt, they warmed themselves with the heat of their conversation: "For one has to admit that conversation still remains the particular privilege of the genial French."[217]

But these months of forced inactivity were not without use for Lauzun: They allowed him to familiarize himself with the reality of America, to meet numerous times with Washington (for whom he immediately displayed respect and sympathy), and to grasp the civic character of his allies' patriotism. "Never, my dear General," he wrote to Voyer in January 1781, "has the spectacle of America been, and never will it be again, as interesting as it is this winter. The army dissolves itself, only to return in the spring with even more order, more certitude. Each officer becomes a civil servant, going off to passionately plead the cause of the army in the provincial states. The less-influential junior officers disperse themselves across the whole surface of America, searching for men capable of fighting, signing them up, bringing them together, and training them to serve. M. Washington, greater now than he has ever been, dividing the few troops he has between the most important locations, remains with the body of the army alongside two thousand five hundred [sic] men, and by means of his wise and courageous steps seems to indicate the assistance that he should not be obliged to request from us."[218] It was assistance that, in the Duc's opinion, the overly prudent French general was "indecently" refusing to provide.

In the pages of his memoirs dedicated to the American expedition, Lauzun's remarks on Rochambeau are marginal, and suggest an elegant detachment. Yet in the long, confidential letters he sent to Voyer his judgments of the general are overtly critical: he is "excellent at carrying out orders under the direction of a leader, but incapable of calculation, of negotiation, which is the principal part of his mission here. I'm not afraid to say that he has no sense of affairs, and lacks the art of dealing with people—a useful skill, after all, in a land where everyone has some right to equal treatment."[219] In short, Rochambeau had all the virtues of a good subaltern, but no gift for command. But didn't at least some of Lauzun's acrimony stem from the thought that he himself possessed the qualities his superior lacked, without being in a position to use them? Once again, Lauzun in his letters to the Marquis displays his indignation at a system of government incapable of carrying out coherent policies, and accustomed to sacrificing talent to the arbitrariness of royal favor. Here in America, a land founded on the ideal of individual initiative, Lauzun's frustration was aggravated by Rochambeau's obstinacy in rebuffing all his requests to take action—like his suggestion that they rejoin Lafayette in the south of the country. Still, faithful to the military code of honor, he continued to collaborate loyally with Rochambeau, and even, finally, recognized his good qualities. For his part, the general, while admiring Lauzun's courage, did not intend to run any risks to indulge the Duc's sense of adventure. And the Vicomte de Rochambeau's subsequent verdict on the Duc suggests that the obstacles to the recognition he so desired were not entirely due to bad luck. He was certainly, Rochambeau wrote, "the most amiable man in France, the wittiest, the most generous, the most loyal, sometimes the wisest, often the craziest, the gayest of philosophers . . . but his character was never quite strong enough to let him succeed."[220]

At last, in October 1781, the opportunity so long awaited by Lauzun finally arrived. In mid-August, Washington had learned that the French fleet of Admiral de Grasse had cast off for Chesapeake Bay loaded with men and money, ready to establish a blockade that would prevent the English naval forces concentrated in Yorktown from receiving reinforcements or leaving shore. Immediately Washington changed his strategy and, lifting the siege of New York, ordered the Franco-American army to reach Yorktown as soon as possible. Lacking defenses and supplies, and with high numbers of ill soldiers, the town would not resist for long. After the naval defeat of September 5, the only way for Lord Cornwallis to break the encirclement was to cross the York River, which surrounded the town, and to flee south with his men. To cover his retreat, the English general transformed Gloucester, the village on the opposite bank of the river from Yorktown, into a bastion held by a large detachment of infantry and all of his cavalry.

The honor of launching the first attack, on October 3, against the legion of the feared Colonel Tarleton fell to Lauzun's hussars, who showed the Americans that "they could not only drink, duel, and steal like the rest of them, but fight with the best of them. These French were not, as Colonel Fontaine of the Virginia militia said he had been led to believe, 'people living on frogs and coarse vegetables.'"[221] And despite the double mortification of having to submit to the orders of both a French superior and an American general, the Duc managed to steal the show.

Having learned that Tarleton "very much desired *to shake hand with the French duc*,"[222] [*sic*] Lauzun rushed forth at a gallop to satisfy him. Life had once again become amusing and the war an occasion to prove his courage. "On arriving, I saw that the English cavalry was three times more numerous than my own; I charged without pausing; we met each other. Tarleton recognized me and came at me with his pistol raised. We fought together among our respective troops until his horse was knocked down by one of his own dragoons, in flight from one of my lancers. I raced forward to take him; a troop of English dragoons came between the two of us, covering his retreat: his horse remained with me. He charged me a second time, without taking me; I charged him a third, knocked over some of his cavalry, and pursued him until we were beneath the entrenchments surrounding Gloucester. He lost an officer and around fifty soldiers, and I took a sizable number of prisoners."[223] Lauzun's action had deprived the English of their last opportunity to open a path between the enemy armies, and violent clashes would take place during the days that followed. Measuring the gravity of the situation, Lord Cornwallis surrendered on October 19, 1781. "Lauzun was sent to negotiate the surrender and to draw up the articles. He presented himself alone, *en parlementaire*, waving his white handkerchief. The chivalrous Duc never did anything like anyone else."[224] In recognition of his bravery, he was charged by Rochambeau with carrying "the great news" to Versailles, where he received a warm welcome from the King, who "asked [him] plenty of questions, and said plenty of kind things to [him]."[225] But the Duc was plagued by bad luck, for on November 15, Maurepas died, depriving him of all the protection he had at court. Indeed, from then on, the new minister of war and minister of the navy, the Comte de Ségur and the Marquis de Castries, "treated [him] just as badly as they could."[226]

Lauzun embarked once again for America in May 1782, without having obtained the slightest bonus from Ségur, either for himself or his regiment, and profoundly distressed at having to take his leave again from Mme de Coigny. Over the six months he had spent in France, the increasingly intense *amitié amoureuse* that bound him to the Marquise had grown deliciously ambiguous. A perfect incarnation of the "temptress," Mme de Coigny limited herself to engaging him in a species of erotic play that took for its model the tradition of courtly love, one whose rules the Duc soon proved he knew inside and out. He cut a lock of her hair, and she forced him to return it to her—the whole time pretending she couldn't hold back her tears at the thought of inflicting such a sacrifice on him. At a grand ball in honor of the Queen, held at the Hôtel de Ville to celebrate the birth of the Dauphin, the Marquise had worn a dress embellished with a splendid black heron's feather, and the evening before his departure, Lauzun found the courage to beg the Marquise to give it to him: a gesture perfectly in keeping with the veneration that he felt for her. (Perhaps he recalled that during his period of favor, Marie-Antoinette had asked him for the white feather he sported on his hat, which she afterward wore in her hair.) "Never had a knight-errant desired anyone with greater ardor, or greater purity,"[227] he would later write. For her part, Mme de Coigny seemed to have his number, for, while responding "that it was impossible for her to give herself to [him]; and that one day [he] would learn the reasons," she nevertheless succeeded in making him believe that she was profoundly "regretful" of the fact.[228]

In his memoirs Lauzun recalls that the sadness inspired by his separation from the Marquise, heightened by the suspicion that he was not truly loved, manifested itself in fever and fits of delirium throughout his return trip to the United States. Fearing he might not survive, he sewed the letters he had received from the Marquise into the lining of his clothes, so that they would be buried with him in case of his death. Still, if we're to believe the recollections of his friend Louis-Philippe de Ségur, who also took part in that second American expedition, Lauzun can't have lost *all* his joie de vivre, since during a stopover on Terceira, an island in the Azores, he had stumbled across a convent "worthy of being compared to the ancient temples of Amathus and Knidos."[229] But, as the Duc's memoirs were intended for the eyes of Mme de Coigny, his amnesia regarding this episode is not terribly surprising.

Lauzun spent that last year in America far from the battlefield, frequently receiving grim news from Paris. On September 8, 1782, Mme de Dillon, the beloved mistress of the Prince de Guéménée, and a woman bound to the Duc by a long and tender friendship, was carried away by tuberculosis. A week later, on September 16, the Marquis de Voyer, Lauzun's mentor, also abruptly died. Finally, in October, the Duc received word of the spectacular bankruptcy—thirty-two million in losses—of his friend the Prince de Guéménée, to whom he had ceded all of his property in exchange for a lifetime annuity.

By now, the French mission was drawing to an end. At the beginning of December, Rochambeau received orders to set sail with the bulk of the army, leaving the remainder of the troops under Lauzun's command. And on January 20, France and England signed the preliminary peace treaties at Versailles, which would eventually put an end to the war on September 3. England recognized the independence of the thirteen American colonies, and France obtained recognition of its trading posts in India, Senegal, and Saint Pierre and Miquelon, and exchanged Saint-Domingue for the island of Tobago. On May 11 the rest of the French army set sail, and Lauzun headed for home. Looking ahead to an uncertain future, the Duc took his leave of the past by confiding to his memoirs his recollections of the first thirty-seven years of his life.

Profoundly marked by the American adventure, Lauzun could see how rapidly France was changing, and understood how ineptly the monarchy had adapted itself to the times. He knew that he was persona non grata at court, and that he could not count on anyone as a protector, but he was too much of an individualist to back down without a fight, and intended to continue to serve his country with the military and diplomatic expertise he had acquired over the years. He had crisscrossed Europe, lived in Prussia and Poland, knew England like no one else and spoke the language, had traveled to Africa, earned fame in America, had at his disposal a vast network of relationships, and could furnish precise analyses of any of those countries.

The long letters that he sent to Montmorin, Vergennes's successor as minister of war, testify to the breadth of his interests, tenacity, and inexhaustible energy. For example, drawing on the lessons of Choiseul—and well in advance of Napoleon—Lauzun felt it was vital for the French to outpace the English in the realm of commerce and to assure themselves control of Egypt, at that point still under Ottoman rule. From this sprang the need to maintain their ancient alliance with the Turks—who were retreating before the Empress Catherine's army—and to carry out on their behalf a policy of mediation with Russia. The Egyptian issue played out in St. Petersburg, where Lauzun's friend Ségur had been ambassador, but also in the chancelleries of the great powers of Europe and, of course, in London. It was to the English capital that Lauzun requested, one last time, that the government send him on a mission—not as ambassador but with the task of monitoring "that vital negotiation of which the peaceful possession of Egypt is the fruit."[230] With a view to the same objective, he suggested that Montmorin send to Berlin first his friend Mirabeau, then the Baron de Heyman, but all of these candidacies—including his own—were judged to be too close to the Palais-Royal to appear dependable. Facing the systematic rejection of his proposals, the Duc did not hide his indignation at the minister: "Why should one let oneself hope, when the most important positions are given out for reasons unrelated to individual worth? One can love and respect the King, wish ardently for his glory, even sacrifice much for his sake, and in my heart, such feelings are immutable; but one can no longer serve Monsieur le Comte."[231]

They were the same sentiments he had shared with Voyer a dozen years earlier, but now, like many of his contemporaries, Lauzun had begun to believe that a genuine change was possible. With the American war, politics had become a question of the public interest—had once and for all ceased to be a state secret, the personal business of the King.

The controversy surrounding the Order of Cincinnatus—which Lauzun was awarded, along with Dillon, Ségur, and Lafayette—is a fine example of the contradictions that surrounded the Franco-American alliance. At the end of the war, Congress wished to display its recognition of those foreigners who had fought for the independence of the United States by creating for them and their descendants a society christened, in the spirit of the age, with the name of the Roman hero who, after having saved the Republic, had returned home to plow his fields. In authorizing his subjects to wear a foreign decoration for the first time, Louis XVI seemed not to notice that the Order of Cincinnatus was an unequivocal symbol of that Republican heroism that had led the American rebels to shrug off their "legitimate" sovereign. For his part, the American ambassador in Paris, Benjamin Franklin, urged Mirabeau and Chamfort to point out the incoherence of a young republican nation creating a hereditary appointment, thus opening a path to a denunciation of the sham of "founding the social order on birth."[232]

Lauzun didn't allow himself to be discouraged by the failure that met his attempts to obtain the ear of the King's ministers, and continued to busy himself with politics. As he wrote to Montmorin: "The pointlessness of my zeal has set limits to my personal ambition, but patriotism is a sacred duty which I will always obey."[233] In hopes of one day working for a country that could serve its citizens more justly than a sovereign imprisoned by an obsolete system, Lauzun completed his political education by applying himself to the study of economics.

Since Necker had published his "Report to the King" in February 1781, revealing to the French people the secrets of public finance, and the term "deficit" had entered the common discourse, economics and politics had seemed almost synonymous. From his first visits to London—"the place in the world where the methods, means, and techniques of banking and modern business are being developed"[234]—Lauzun had understood that from now on these two domains would be inseparable. But it was a banker from Geneva, Jean-François-Isaac Panchaud, highly critical of Necker's work, who initiated Lauzun into the general problems of the public management of credit and savings. Plenty of others—Talleyrand, Mirabeau, Narbonne, Vaudreuil, Choiseul-Gouffier, Chamfort—were won over by the financial theories that Panchaud expounded in the meetings he held at his home in the rue de Vivienne, and when he became minister of finance, Calonne called on him for advice.

Even if the trio comprised of Panchaud, Mirabeau, and Talleyrand unquestionably exerted a decisive influence on Lauzun's political evolution during the 1780s, the Duc remained faithful to his old friends and social habits. Still, he could not help realizing that social life itself was becoming a battlefield.

Guéménée's bankruptcy, which had affected an enormous number of people—three thousand mortgagees from all walks of society, who had ceded their patrimonies to him in exchange for lifetime annuities—had also shifted the balance of power at court. The Rohans declared themselves ready to do anything in order to save the honor of their family, to preserve for the Prince the position of grand chamberlain, and for his wife that of governess of the Children of France. Once the initial moment of indignation had passed, Louis XVI—who had been raised by Mme de Marsan, née Rohan-Soubise, and was a personal friend of the Prince de Soubise—may have been inclined toward indulgence, but Marie-Antoinette demanded that they separate themselves from the couple. In insisting on such unusual severity, was the Queen defending her own declining reputation, or simply seizing on a pretext to free herself from a friendship that was becoming a burden? Had she forgotten that Mme de Guéménée had taken on a significant part of her debt in order to keep her house open for the Queen? Or was she simply taking advantage of the Princesse's disgrace to transfer the position of governess to her new friend Mme de Polignac? What is certain is that by allowing the Rohans to "collapse into the ignominy of a bankruptcy, Louis XVI committed an unspeakable imprudence, and himself struck the first blow against the nobility, at this point still intact. The second would not be long in arriving, but this time it would be the royals themselves that would be struck full in the face."[235]

Barely three years later, in fact, the royal family received a death blow. During the summer of 1785, Cardinal Louis de Rohan, Grand Almoner of France,

Bishop of Strasbourg and Prince of the Empire, fell victim to the hostility of Marie-Antoinette and to Louis XVI's growing submission to the will of his wife. On August 15, the Cardinal was arrested at Versailles, accused by two jewelers of having appropriated for himself, in the Queen's name, a fabulous diamond necklace. But in the course of the trial it became clear that the King was convinced of Rohan's guilt without having any real evidence, and that the Cardinal had been the hapless victim of a fraud. Throughout this ordeal, which became known as "the affair of the necklace," it was not merely the Rohan family that objected to the treatment of one of their most prestigious members. Judged hasty and arbitrary, the Cardinal's arrest struck the privileged as a scandalous example of the Crown's rank abuse of power. Not only did the trial end in May 1786 with the full and complete exoneration of Rohan, but it definitively tarnished the reputation of Marie-Antoinette. Uninvolved in the affair itself, the Queen wound up looking like its secret instigator, and the prestige of the monarchy itself suffered greatly from a trial that had revealed the corruption of the court, the lack of trustworthiness of the ministers, and their disagreement with, and desire for revenge upon, the judges.

The resentment of Rohan and his clan toward the royal family triggered an aristocratic revolt that found its focal point in the person of the King's cousin at the Palais-Royal. Traditionally, the Orléanses had been distinguished by their liberal positions, while flaunting their loyalty toward the senior branch of the Bourbon family that occupied the throne. But near the end of the 1770s, for any number of pointless reasons, the Duc de Chartres had encouraged the ostracism of Marie-Antoinette, and at the beginning of the Revolutionary War, after a naval battle fought off the coasts of the island of Ushant (July 27, 1778), he had seen the position of grand admiral of the navy, which he had aspired to, slip away from him. At that point, Chartres abandoned the court, transforming the Palais-Royal—which his father had yielded to him in 1780— into a sort of "anti-Versailles"[236] and adopting a contrarian style of life under the sign of progress and modernity. His admiration for England, its forms of government, its habits and customs, couldn't help but come across as an implicit criticism of French institutions.

Even if Lauzun had not been tied since his earliest youth to the Prince de Guéménée and the Duc de Chartres alike, the influence of Mme de Coigny would have sufficed to rally him to their camp. Not only was the Marquise an intimate of Guéménée's but her youngest sister had married the Duc de Mont-bazon, the elder son of the couple, and the Prince's bankruptcy concerned both of them from the point of view of inheritance. Faced with the hardness of heart that Marie-Antoinette had shown toward the Guéménées, the Mar-quise's general antipathy for her quickly curdled into hate. It was a tenacious and belligerent hatred, one that colored all of her social successes and presented a singular challenge to Marie-Antoinette. Informed of the criticisms addressed to her, the Queen melancholically recognized the defeat that the Marquise had inflicted on her in the capital: "I am Queen of Versailles, but Mme de Coigny is Queen of Paris."[237] In any case, the Marquise was by no means content with this initial victory, and in 1791, in a letter to Lauzun written from London, where she had taken refuge "to enjoy the spectacle of the Revolution in safety,"[238] her desire to humiliate the Queen reveals itself to be stronger than her fear of the path that events were taking. "Truly," she wrote, "Marie-Antoinette is too insolent and too vindictive for me not to be pleased at seeing her put in her place, and removed from the side of the King whose power she was so keen to usurp."[239]

Lauzun's passion for the Marquise did not put an end to his career as a seducer. Among the numerous women's names that fill out the list of his conquests, that of Aimée de Coigny, a cousin of Mme de Coigny, remains famous. The daugh-ter of the Comte de Coigny (the brother of a favorite of Marie-Antoinette's), Aimée had lost her mother at a very young age, and had been raised by her father's mistress, the Princesse de Guéménée. The memory of the happy time she had passed in the company of that great lady—who, fallen into disgrace after her husband's bankruptcy, had retired with stoicism and dignity to the solitude of her château at Vigny—would forever be etched into the adolescent's mind. In 1784, barely fifteen years old, Aimée was married to a boy six months younger than herself, the Marquis de Fleury, who would become Duc in 1788. Destined to fail, the marriage allowed her husband, a career military man not known for his intelligence, to squander her dowry at the gambling table, and Aimée to live according to her own eccentric inclinations. (Then again, the young Duchesse's mother had also shown signs of great peculiarity—passionate about anatomy, she traveled everywhere with a skeleton in her luggage.)

Endowed with a fanciful imagination, and dedicated to the worship of the moon, Aimée was at first nicknamed Zilia, after the heroine of Mme de Graffigny's *Lettres d'une Péruvienne* (Letters of a Peruvian Woman), but unlike that novel's protagonist, she seemed mainly concerned with enjoying life and amusing herself. Most important, Aimée was exceptionally beautiful. For Walpole, who met her in London when she was twenty-two years old, she was "far and away the prettiest Frenchwoman" he had ever encountered: "Fairly petite, her face is perfect, with very fine eyes and nose, a very pretty mouth and teeth."[241] Her hair and eyes were so dark that her family gave her a new pet name, "Nigretta," and the account of Élisabeth Vigée Le Brun, whose portraits set a new standard of feminine beauty for the era, leaves us in no doubt: "In her, nature seemed to have combined all of its gifts. Her face was bewitching, her gaze smoldering, her shape the sort one associates with Venus." But Aimée's charms weren't merely aesthetic—they were the outward tokens of her "superior spirit." Mme Vigée Le Brun, who had made her acquaintance in Rome around 1790, affirms that in the cosmopolitan milieu of the city of the popes, "the taste and wit of the Duchesse de Fleury shone above everyone else's." And the sympathy established between that celebrated artist and the twenty-one-year-old aristocrat who had fled France, both of them equally eager to discover the masterpieces of Italian art, couldn't help but speak favorably about the Duchesse's sensibility: "We felt as if we were meant to find each other; she loved the arts, and was as passionate as I about the beauties of nature; in her I found a companion such as I had always desired."

Even though it was written some forty years after that Roman meeting,[242] in the light of the dramatic and occasionally embarrassing episodes that marked the life of the Duchesse, Mme Vigée Le Brun's portrait remains suffused with a profound empathy. And the indulgence that the artist seems to show for the Duchesse is that which the bourgeois conformism of the Restoration would grant (at least in their books) to those romantic heroines exposed to "those dangers that menace all beings endowed with a vivid imagination and an ardent soul." But Mme Vigée Le Brun knew well enough that it was the Revolution of 1789 that had "menaced" the impunity of the aristocratic lifestyle that allowed Aimée to dispose of her heart according to her wishes: "She was so susceptible to falling in love that, in considering how young she was, how beautiful, I trembled for the peace of her life; I frequently saw her writing to the Duc de Lauzun, a handsome man and very kind, but of great immorality, and I feared for her regarding that liaison, no matter how innocent I might think it."[243]

"Innocent" does not seem like quite the right word, given that the young Duchesse's relationship with Lauzun was her first extramarital adventure. Twenty years her senior, the Duc had first known her as a child at the home of Mme de Guéménée. He met her again, now a young wife, at the Palais-Royal, where, beginning with the Duc de Chartres, who called her "my sister," the Orléans clan had opened its arms to her. And because she was truly charming, Lauzun offered to initiate her into the *vie amoureuse*, finding her a highly gifted pupil. Was the fact that Aimée was the cousin of Mme de Guéménée's husband an additional attraction for him? Was he hoping to make the Marquise de Coigny jealous, or rather looking for a chance to strengthen their complicity? And as for the young woman, did the pleasure of rivaling her famous cousin play any part in the favor she showed to Lauzun? As Adolfo Omodeo wrote in his lovely portrait of Aimée, "the Marquise de Coigny knew it all, and let it be: confident in her power over her knight-errant, she left Nigretta to him as an amusement; with a superior spirit she showed pity for the weakness of her cousin, which merely highlighted her own firmness."[244]

However it may have been, Aimée was enamored of Lauzun, and assiduously frequented the *petite maison* that the Duc kept in Montrouge, until in 1790 her husband found it more prudent to leave France and take refuge in Italy. The young woman never claimed to be loyal, and in Rome she quickly fell in love with a handsome English diplomat, the Earl of Malmesbury, with whom Lauzun had previously been friends in Berlin during his liaison with Princesse Czartoryska. Still, in a letter she sent to the Duc from Naples, the memory of their past intimacy loomed large in her reveries, mingling with the "groaning" of the sea "agitated" by its love for the moon.[245] As Aimée was well aware, it was the press of politics that had drawn Lauzun's attention, and she raged against this change of heart: "That damned Revolution preoccupies you, shapes you, makes you lose your head—I, for my part, simply loathe it, and do my best to forget it."[246] The Revolution, however, would not forget about her.

The Vicomte Joseph-Alexandre de Ségur

The prettiest, the most agreeable women at court, as well as the most popular courtesans, vied for his affections or mourned his infidelities.

—COMTE D'ESPINCHAL[1]

IT WOULD BE DIFFICULT to paint a portrait of the Vicomte de Ségur without also describing his ties to the Baron de Besenval, and the latter's scandalously frank account of life at the French court.

While reading Besenval's memoirs, which were published by the Vicomte de Ségur fifteen years after the death of their author, the Prince de Ligne found the traces of a conversation he had had long ago with his old friend on the subject of Marie-Antoinette's change of attitude toward the Baron. "I have spoken," Ligne wrote, "of the pleasure given me by the recollections of various authors . . . and that pleasure is all the greater when it concerns those men in whose company I have spent my life, as for example the Baron de Besenval, whose style is just as brilliant as he was himself. His portraits are extremely true to life. He doesn't miss a thing. Every trait, even the smallest of nuances, is captured precisely. I find them utterly enchanting. And I understand now that at one point I saw him besotted with the Queen without his even realizing it. What he recounts on the subject of that intrigue, where he quotes me, is sobering."[2]

The Prince had told the Baron he was convinced that the sovereign's recent "chilliness" toward him was due to the "*méchancetés*"[3] that various schemers had used to stem the excessive favor Besenval enjoyed. Well informed as to the sort of stratagems current at court, and the fickleness of Marie-Antoinette herself—"the Queen pays little mind to the people she has brought close to her, and draws away from them with ease"[4]—the Baron received this explanation philosophically.

Nothing could have guaranteed the authenticity of the Swiss Baron's memoirs better than the unconditional approval of a figure like Ligne, who was
then in the process of writing hundreds of pages of his own recounting that
final season of the French monarchy. Nevertheless, the publication of the Baron's recollections was later bitterly opposed by the author's own family,[5] even
if the scandal it raised didn't quite equal that provoked by the memoirs of
Lauzun some fifteen years later. It is true that neither of the two texts leaves
any doubt about the moral corruption of the French nobility or the various
intrigues at court. But Besenval, for whom France had been an adopted homeland, chose to craft his memoirs from the point of view of an onlooker, whereas
Lauzun had imprudently depicted episodes from his own private life. Still, in
both cases, the public found those of their memories that related to the golden
years of Marie-Antoinette simply unbelievable. As ignorant as Lauzun of the
tragic fate that awaited the Queen, Besenval had left behind a portrait of her
from life, one in which admiration was mixed with criticism. In both accounts,
her graciousness, her flights of affection, and her nobility of heart were qualified
by her capriciousness, and a frivolous temperament incompatible with the
duties of a sovereign and the exigencies of friendship. It was against this image,
irreconcilable with that of the "martyr Queen" that had been imposed in the
wake of the Revolution, that Mme Campan protested in a set of memoirs that
appeared after Besenval's.[6]

Having entered the service of Napoleon, and buoyed by the approval of the
Emperor, Marie-Antoinette's old *femme de chambre* made it her business to
defend the honor of her former queen. As the years passed, her recollections—
which from the beginning she had declared she would not publish—took on
an increasingly apologetic character. (For example, in his *Foreign Reminiscences*,
Lord Holland reproached Mme Campan for having concealed the truth about
Marie-Antoinette's relationship with Fersen.[7]) Surely, insofar as she was aware
of Besenval's memoirs, Mme Campan would have wanted to clear the Queen
of the accusations of inconstancy by furnishing a completely different explanation for the sovereign's change of heart toward the Baron. According to
Mme Campan, the coldness noted by Ligne was entirely Besenval's fault—far
from being "besotted with the Queen without his even realizing it," as the
Prince put it, the Baron had just been guilty of making a ridiculous declaration
of his affection to her.[8] But then, hadn't Mme Campan—who had certainly
read Lauzun's memoirs when they were still circulating in manuscript—made
a similar accusation concerning the Duc? In Besenval's case, however, the letters

from the Comte de Mercy-Argenteau to Empress Maria Theresa clearly show that the cause of the Queen's "chilliness" was completely different than that alleged by Mme Campan. Informed by her ambassador that Marie-Antoinette had been somewhat too casual in confiding to Besenval her husband's sexual difficulties,[9] the Empress had ordered her daughter to put an end to her intimacy with the Baron.

Ever since the seventeenth century, the writings of memoirists, whether authentic or apocryphal, had been colored by politics—specifically, denunciations of royal absolutism.[10] Over the course of the eighteenth century, the publication of the memoirs of Cardinal de Retz, La Rochefoucauld, and Mlle de Montpensier had given voice to the leaders of the Fronde, and copies of the memoirs of Saint-Simon (the manuscript of which was preserved by the minister of foreign affairs) with its indictment of the Sun King, found their first discriminating readers among the friends and acquaintances of the Duc de Choiseul.[11] Choiseul himself, while in exile at Chanteloup, wrote his own set of memoirs that were extremely critical of Louis XV.[12] And Voltaire, who considered private writings to be vital historical sources, adopted the genre of the memoir in order to proudly proclaim his own freedom from any dependence on the powerful, as well as his dignity as a free individual. Nevertheless, at the dawn of the Revolution, they became effective instruments of royal propaganda, as in the case of the Maréchal de Richelieu.[13] Before long, the émigrés, too, took up their pens to tell their own side of the story—among the men, d'Espinchal, Lévis, Tilly, d'Allonville, Chateaubriand, and Talleyrand; among the women, Mme Vigée Le Brun, Mme de Genlis, Mme de La Tour du Pin, Mme de Boigne, and Aimée de Coigny. But it was the women above all— stripped as they were by the Revolution and the Empire of the dominant position that they had enjoyed under the ancien régime,[14] and isolated in the domestic sphere—who evoked with an overwhelming nostalgia the world that they had left behind. It was a nostalgia not only for the past but also for "the forms, the spirit, and the manners that belonged to the world of high society."[15]

From now on, memoirs would constitute a battlefield, and intimate descriptions of the past would be increasingly written and interpreted in terms of the exigencies of the present. The Empire, for its part, "threw up a wall of silence around the memories of the Revolution, and came down hard on the rare attempts to vault it"—so much so that with the fall of Napoleon, when the censorship was abolished, "everything came together to make the Restoration a festival and drama of memory."[16] Between 1815 and 1848, France was deluged by a flood of memoirs, which inevitably echoed each other.[17] And this was a cause for celebration—since, according to Chateaubriand in his *Genius of Christianity*, the national character was particularly suited to this type of writing. "Vain, thoughtless, and sociable" from the very beginning, the Frenchman "reflects little upon objects in general," but "he is an inquisitive observer of details, and his eye is quick, penetrating, and accurate. He must always be upon the stage himself, and even in the quality of a historian he cannot make up his mind to keep entirely out of sight."[18] Recent history had given the French permission indulge this propensity: "There was nobody who had not become, for at least twenty-four hours, a character, and who did not feel himself obligated to tell the public about the influence he had exerted on the universe," Chateaubriand noted ironically in 1831, at the height of the "fever"[19] for memoirs, even as he himself was in the midst of composing his *Mémoires d'outre-tombe*. But this groundswell of writing was also bittersweet—regardless of the faction with which each of these memoirists was aligned, none of them had emerged from the Revolution unscathed.

The Vicomte Joseph-Alexandre de Ségur was mindful enough of the controversy that the memories of Besenval were bound to stir up that he felt the need to justify their publication to the nostalgic residents of the Faubourg Saint-Germain with an introductory note in which he carefully set out his reasons for bringing them forward. Having learned, he tells us, that the person to whom he'd entrusted the "precious"[20] manuscript during the Terror had surreptitiously copied it, he wanted to prevent unscrupulous publishers from issuing ersatz editions. But this was not the sole motive for his decision. If Ségur considered it his duty as testamentary executor for the Baron to safeguard the future of his memoirs, he was also aware of their veracity and historical value, and wholly agreed with their judgments. Some believed that he was himself the author. But in fact, Ségur was simply expressing his filial devotion to a father who had never been able to openly proclaim his paternity, though he'd always been unstinting with his love.[21] And then, the Vicomte could sense that his own time was short: death carried him off on July 27, 1805, just as the three volumes of the memoirs were appearing in bookstalls.

Like Lauzun, Joseph-Alexandre de Ségur was an illegitimate child, and the similarities between the two friends do not end there. Like the Duc, the Vicomte bore an illustrious name. Like the Duc, he was rich, handsome, witty, elegant, and drove the women mad. They had known each other since their youth, circulating in the same milieus and, in the years before the Revolution, briefly sharing the same political ideas. Younger than Lauzun by nine years, the Vicomte never hid his admiration for his friend. The fact that when all was said and done they chose different camps did not prevent Ségur from paying homage to Lauzun after his tragic end: "He told his stories with an original grace—it would be impossible to repeat them, since he imparted to them an inimitable je ne sais quoi, something impossible to define."[22]

Still, it would be difficult to find two personalities, two temperaments, so different from each other. Lauzun was chivalrous, sentimental, impulsive; Ségur rational, lucid, calculating. The former had a soldier's vocation and an ambition to serve, and knew nothing of prudence; the latter had undertaken his military career out of a sense of duty, and devoted no more time to it than that strictly necessary to advance in rank. The Duc was constantly writing reports and devising audacious diplomatic and military projects, dreaming of grand initiatives; the Vicomte nourished literary ambitions and celebrated the joy of living in the present with a daily flood of verses. Certainly, both proclaimed themselves libertines, but their conduct was quite different. Lauzun shared his attentions equally among high-society ladies and prostitutes, whom he frequented alone or with friends. Police reports highlighted his participation in orgies organized by the Duc de Chartres,[23] as well as the constant flow of filles in and out of his petite maison in Montrouge. And even if this was all par for the course when it came to the customs of society gentlemen at the time, the Duc's erotic experimentation—the Prince de Conti had once surprised him in the company of two giants[24]—still managed to make people talk. But Lauzun was just as fond of playing the highly codified game of society courtship, throwing himself into the conquest of reputedly inaccessible women in hopes of appeasing, even if only briefly, his sentimental restlessness. He was always ready to give his heart away—because when it came to love (as with the Prince de Ligne), what thrilled him most was the magic of beginnings. Nevertheless, on the rare occasions when that initial charm endured, the Duc did not retreat—in such cases, it would be the woman who abandoned him.

Ségur, on the other hand, found mercenary amours far too simple, and his preferred hunting ground was among the bonne compagnie. An unrepentant seducer, he never ceased collecting trophies and sought (like the libertines that fill the novels of Crébillon) to prove the infallibility of his methods on the greatest possible number of people, even if he was able to conceal it behind a shrewd mastery of social grace. This sort of eternal repetition was perfectly suited to the Vicomte's brand of prudent hedonism, and spared him the need of relying on unknown variables or the whims of others to take his pleasure.

The Vicomte had been born into a family just as free-spirited as that which greeted the Duc—but unlike his friend's, his was affectionate and close-knit. Indeed, the ménage à trois established between the Ségurs and Besenval was so stable and happy that it managed to astonish a society in which the most varied domestic arrangements were commonplace.

Philippe-Henri de Ségur was certainly not the sort of man inclined to compromise. Born in 1724, the Marquis descended from a family of Huguenot origin that had distinguished itself in the service of Henri IV. He had embraced a military career, fighting on the front lines in campaign after campaign during the War of the Austrian Succession (1741–1748), distinguishing himself by his physical strength and exceptional courage. At the bloody Battle of Rocoux (October 11, 1746) the young colonel's chest had been pierced by a bullet, and during the siege of Laweld, in spite of an arm pulverized by an artillery piece, he had remained at the head of his regiment, leading it on to victory. "Men like your father," Louis XV had told his son, "deserve to be invulnerable."[25] The loss of his arm did not prevent him from taking part in the Seven Years' War, from being wounded again at the Battle of Kloster Kampen, and finally being taken prisoner by the Prussians. His conduct on the latter occasion was worthy of a *poème chevaleresque*. Surprised in the middle of the night by an enemy assault and rushing from camp at the head of his men, Ségur found himself facing an enormous Prussian detachment commanded by the Prince of Brunswick himself. Diderot recounted the scene in a letter to Sophie Volland on November 6, 1760: "The two armies were on the point of meeting. M. de Ségur was going to be massacred. The young Prince heard someone mention his [Ségur's] name, and flew to his aid. M. de Ségur, who knew nothing about it, noticed him at his side, recognized him, and cried to him: 'Eh, my prince! What are you doing there? My grenadiers, who are just twenty feet away, are about to fire!'—'Monsieur,' responded the young Prince, 'I heard your name, and rushed over to prevent those fellows there from massacring you.' All the while they were talking, the two armies went on firing at each other. M. de Ségur received two saber blows and was taken prisoner by the young Prince, who was nevertheless forced to retreat. . . . Aren't you astonished by the generosity of these two men, one of whom saw nothing but the peril of the other, and who forgot themselves to such an extent that it's a miracle they weren't both killed in the same instant?"[26] The philosopher was certainly aware that the behavior of the two warriors had taken place under the sign of aristocratic morality—yet it was not to the "grand generosity of the knights of old"[27] that his thoughts immediately turned but rather to the natural generosity of Man, full stop: "No, my dear friend, it isn't nature that has made us wicked; it is ill education, bad examples, bad legislation that corrupts us."[28]

Back in France with the war behind him, the elder Ségur finally reaped the rewards of twenty years of service with a nomination to the post of inspector general of the infantry, first in the Hainaut, then in Alsace and Burgundy.

In February 1749, supplied with a wealth of wounds and the glory that came with them, but only a modest inheritance, he found an answer to his financial difficulties by marrying a fifteen-year-old orphan, the heiress to vast properties on the island of Saint-Domingue and endowed with 120,000 livres. By no means beautiful, but still quite attractive, Louise-Anne-Madeleine de Vernon—even by the admission of someone as little inclined to kindness as Mme de Genlis—possessed "a sweet face, a charming shape, and plenty of elegance as far as her bearing and way of conducting herself,"[29] and was admired by all for her generosity and good nature. She immediately showed herself to be an excellent spouse, and did not hesitate to welcome her widowed mother-in-law into her home, becoming fast friends with her and with her help maintaining a salon frequented by aristocrats, dignitaries, and men of letters. The Marquise also assured the continuation of the family line by giving birth to a pair of boys: the elder, Louis-Philippe, in 1753, and the younger, Joseph-Alexandre, three years later. To the latter, however, the Marquis de Ségur was father in name only.

The actual father of the baby was the Marquis's best friend, the Swiss Baron Pierre-Victor de Besenval, companion-in-arms to the Marquis during the War of the Austrian Succession. Born in 1721 at Soleure and raised in France, Pierre-Victor had embarked on a military career there, serving in the prestigious regiment of the Gardes Suisses, where his father was lieutenant general. Thanks to his mother, a Polish aristocrat related to Queen Marie Leszczyńska, the young officer was quickly initiated into life at court, and adopted the manners and customs of the French nobility. When he first met the Ségurs, he had been part of an inseparable trio of fashionable roués, along with the Comte de Frise (a nephew of the Maréchal de Saxe) and the Duc d'Orléans.[30] Indeed, as the

Duc de Lévis later recalled, Pierre-Victor "was of a fine height, with an agreeable figure, witty and audacious," which earned him "plenty of success with the women, though his manners with them were somewhat too free, and his gallantry in poor form."[31] Did the libertinism of his early years leave a mark on him, or was it, as Sainte-Beuve suspected, "simply a way of distinguishing himself, later to be set aside?"[32]

Born on the battlefield, the friendship between Besenval and Ségur was shaped by preoccupations far removed from the taste for transgression and the strategies of the bedroom. They were bound to each other by their common passion for the profession of arms, respect for the moral codes of war, and contempt for danger. When it came to courage, Besenval was more than a match for Ségur. Himself present at the Battle of Kloster Kampen, he had contributed decisively to the French victory, leading his men in an assault on a seemingly impregnable enemy outpost: "Despite the most terrible fire, he rode right up to the wall and climbed it with great effort, barely clinging to the edges of the stones with bloodied hands. All at once, he turns around and says to his grenadiers, with cheerful zest: 'Hell's teeth! Comrades, this is an unpleasant situation; but you know, if they didn't have a few bullets to throw our way, they'd never hold out!' This was enough to rally his men, who had begun to lose heart; their fervor and dedication were redoubled; soon enough, though a frightful number of brave men fell, the redoubt was taken; M. de Besenval was the first to leap onto the ramparts."[33] Two years later, at Amöneburg, still fighting alongside Ségur, Besenval rushed back to the front lines after carrying out his orders to pull back the Gardes Suisses who had been decimated by Prussian artillery. "What are you doing here, Baron? You're done," someone had objected. "Ah, what choice do I have?" replied the Baron: "It's like an opera ball: you get bored, of course, but you have to stay on till you hear the violins!"[34]

Besenval's cheerful insouciance was in keeping with his unfailing energy. Blessed with good luck, the Baron felt invulnerable. Daring beyond all measure, he had never been wounded in combat nor struck by adversity. "I have no intention of regaling you with my misfortunes; after all, I've never had any,"[35] he declared in a letter to Crébillon fils. But it might have been more precise to say that Besenval had simply never allowed bad luck to rattle his joie de vivre. He was armored by an "entirely French levity" that could "make you forget he had been born in Switzerland"[36] and rendered him utterly charming in spite of his dissolute behavior.

In contrast to the Baron, Philippe-Henri de Ségur did not attend balls at the Opéra. His numerous war wounds did nothing to improve his physical appearance, and he had no ambition to please. Cantankerous, peremptory, strict, he was not content to be a mere soldier, however gallant, but was fascinated by the technical, organizational, and disciplinary questions of military life. His character was the antithesis of Besenval's—so much so that one imagines it was precisely this contrast in their respective visions of life that made them inseparable.

Encouraged by their example, the gentle Mme de Ségur felt that both of these very different men were necessary for her happiness, and made no attempt to hide this from her husband. The seventy years that had separated the confession of the Princesse de Clèves from that of the Comtesse had not passed in vain. The Marquis de Ségur felt it unfair to demand that his wife, who had fulfilled with loyalty and devotion all the familial and social obligations that were required by an aristocratic marriage, should renounce love—an emotion that really had nothing to do with to the nature of their contract. Stronger than love, friendship demanded that jealousy be cast aside, and that the two men find some way of sharing her affection.

This is the key to understanding what Besenval seems to suggest throughout his literary works. In his memoirs, we find the story of a young girl of marrying age who refuses to choose between two men equally dear to her, instead persuading them to share her love with tolerance and mutual respect. The author's approval of this solution could not be more explicit: "What makes me doubt the veracity of this tale is the difficulty of believing that chance could throw together three people so sensible, so deeply knowledgeable of the true value of things, and so wholly free from prejudice."[37] By contrast, in *Spleen*, his novella written in 1757, a year after the birth of Joseph-Alexandre, a young woman's decision to follow her feelings collides with the legal and social reality of the institution of marriage. It is the story of a wife who, finding herself pregnant by her lover, decides to ask her husband—whom she has always shown "the truest friendship, the sincerest respect"—to "adopt" another man's child. Profoundly upset by her confession, the husband balks at the idea of giving their legitimate child a brother "unworthy of him," but ultimately resigns himself—above all because, as his best friend reminds him, everyone will consider him the child's father according to law, and to not recognize him would mean dishonoring his mother, while leaving the boy at risk of legal challenges to his inheritance. And to his ultimate question: "What? Do you really believe...that I can be convinced to submit myself to this?" he receives a response that admits of no reply: "More than that: you *must* submit yourself: and, as your friend, I demand that you do."[38]

If Besenval insists twice over, through the lens of fiction, on the psychological and ethical complexity of his relationship with the Ségurs, paying homage to the courage and responsibility of his beloved, he failed to find any language to defend the infant whose father he knew he was, apart from that of the fait accompli. But then, Joseph-Alexandre de Ségur had the good fortune to be born into a family where the Marquis de Ségur's mother, Philippe-Angélique de Froissy, was herself the illegitimate daughter of Philippe d'Orléans and a celebrated actress, Christine Desmares—and the Regent himself had taken charge of her education. Removed from her mother, the girl had been raised in a convent but refused to take the veil when she came of age. Won over by her sweetness, the Regent had given her to François de Ségur in marriage, deciding to officially recognize her as well. Despite the obvious advantages of allying themselves with the House of Orléans (even if they were doing so via the back door), not all of the Ségurs approved of this choice—but Philippe-Angélique knew how to change their minds. Her marriage with François de Ségur could not have borne better fruit. The Marquise, who had the run of Versailles as well as the Palais-Royal, proved to be "one of the finest mothers and greatest wives of the eighteenth century, providing an example of conjugal devotion that has become historic."[39] And after she was widowed, living in the beautiful residence of her son and daughter-in-law on the rue Saint-Florentin, she remained a sort of tutelary spirit for the whole family. But the Marquise was the illegitimate daughter of a father who had finally recognized her, while Joseph-Alexandre bore the name of a father who was not his own, and the best he could hope for was that nobody would have the bad taste to remind him of the fact. Nevertheless, unlike Lauzun, Joseph-Alexandre would not attempt to conceal it.

His birth reinforced the complicity between the Ségurs and their Swiss friend without altering their habits. The Marquis fulfilled his duties as head of the family, overseeing the education of the children, both of whom he intended for military careers. The Marquise attended to her husband's needs and returned to her position in high society, which she maintained with tremendous grace. And Besenval, while preserving his privileged position in the hearts of the two spouses, continued to reap success after success. "Epicurean by principle and taste,"[40] the Baron neglected none of those pastimes that made life pleasant. He was a sophisticated collector[41] and, even if he was a middling reader, loved to write. He entertained with great elegance in his house on the rue de Grenelle, where he had moved in 1764. The *Correspondance littéraire* records a poem that circulated on the occasion of his purchase of that beautiful mansion (previously inhabited by the Bishop of Rennes), in which Love personified heralds the arrival of a "Swiss Baron" "wholly suited to all my mysteries," and escorted by "Laughter, the Graces, and the Amusements."[42] It was a cheerful declaration of libertinism, one that Besenval accentuated by choosing for an alcove of the *petit salon* adjoining his bedroom one of the best versions of Fragonard's *The Swing*, that masterpiece of eighteenth-century erotic painting.[43] He was equally passionate about botany, and the hothouse in his garden, filled with rare plants, allowed him to send his friends marvelous bouquets of fresh flowers, no matter the season.

We do not know precisely when Joseph-Alexandre became aware of his "scandalous"[44] resemblance to the Baron, and when exactly he understood that he was the Baron's son. Surely, though, the "extreme tenderness" that Besenval showed him would have sufficed to remove any "doubts concerning the obligations which were owed to him in that regard."[45] But we might ask why, having learned of the irregularity of his birth, the young Vicomte did not follow the example of his relations in behaving with the sort of discretion that was required in such cases. The respect that he owed as much to his official father as to his actual progenitor, the affection he felt for his mother, the bond that joined him to his brother, should have imposed it upon him. But the fact is that, unlike his friends Lauzun and Narbonne, who shared his situation, Joseph-Alexandre occasionally yielded to the need to tell the truth.

For instance, in his *Secret Memoirs*, the Comte d'Allonville reports a debate between Joseph-Alexandre, the Comte de Genlis, and M. Decazes on the identity of their age's most amiable man. Each of the participants offered the name of his own illegitimate father: for Decazes, the Marquis d'Entragues; for Genlis, the Comte de Tressan; and for Ségur, Besenval.[46] Had the Vicomte claimed the Baron's paternity because he felt proud of being the son of a much admired man? Or was he trying to exorcise the embarrassment and discomfort of his situation by declaring aloud what others murmured behind his back? And when a woman from Toul tactlessly asked him if he was related to a "Monsieur de Ségur, who is something or other at Versailles," and he responded, "out in the world people will tell you that I'm his son, but I certainly don't believe it,"[47] was he simply amusing himself at the expense of a provincial lady or betraying the uneasiness that his ambiguous position brought him within his own family?

In any event, there is no question that it was the Baron de Besenval who Joseph-Alexandre chose as his role model, rather than the Marquis de Ségur. The Vicomte possessed all the lightness, gaiety, self-conceit, and hedonism of his true father—and from adolescence on, he did his utmost to imitate the latter's style. The description that Alissan de Chazet has left us of a mature Joseph-Alexandre would have suited Besenval as well: "One of the wittiest and most amusing men one could meet. Deft words, tasteful jests, entertaining whims, everything came to him with ease: in him, spontaneity came to the aid of wit."[48]

Like his brother, Louis-Philippe, three years his elder, the Vicomte was steered toward the military early on. The Marquis de Ségur applied himself to furthering his career: enlisting in the *corps de la gendarmerie* as a sub-lieutenant in 1772, at the age of sixteen, the Vicomte succeeded his brother twelve years later as commanding colonel of the Ségur regiment. Lacking neither expertise, nor a sense of responsibility, nor courage, he never neglected his duties, but the peace that followed the Seven Years' War deprived him of the opportunity to prove his mettle.

It was social life that provided his competitive spirit its most fertile ground. In his lovely biography of the Vicomte, Gabriel de Broglie reports that, for the young aristocrats of the era, earning a reputation in society was far more arduous and uncertain a task than winning recognition of their military abilities,[49] and many among them pursued it with great determination, beginning with the Vicomte's own brother and their friends and acquaintances: Lauzun, Boufflers, Vaudreuil, and Narbonne. But for Joseph-Alexandre, social success was more than a game for insiders, or a gratification of amour propre—it was his raison d'être, the "great business" of his life.

In a society where reputations were often decided by women, Ségur dedicated himself to their conquest. In a society fascinated by the theater, he made himself into an actor, author, and musician. In a society whose standards of value were amiability, wit, and irony, he made these qualities his only moral precepts. But the Vicomte did not limit himself to putting into practice with true virtuosity a way of being in the world already consecrated by tradition. He described it, analyzed it, theorized it exhaustively in his poetry, plays, essays, and novels. By offering himself up as the perfect incarnation of the aristocratic way of life both in his theoretical reflections and in practice, he most likely found the legitimacy he had otherwise lacked. Above and beyond being the son of Besenval or Ségur, he was the child of that aristocratic civilization whose stamp—for better or worse—he bore.

The Vicomte de Ségur made his social debut in Paris at the age of twenty-two, by treating with "scandalous openness"[50] his relationship with a dancer at the Opéra. Taking an actress as a mistress was a common custom among fashionable young gentlemen, and there was nothing odd about Ségur doing likewise. But it was the personality of the woman he chose that created an uproar.

When she began her relationship with the Vicomte in 1778, Julie Careau was only twenty-two, but already intensely experienced. She too was an illegitimate child—but, unlike Ségur, she had never been able to boast about her father, whose name she had long kept secret. The story went that, as a child, she had been a terrified onlooker at the famous fire of April 1763 that had reduced the Paris Opéra to ashes, and that a considerate gentleman had saved her from the crowd. After inquiring about her address, he brought her back to her mother, afterward proposing to provide for her education. More recent studies, however, demonstrate that this was not quite how things went.

Julie's "savior" had been one Pierre-Joseph Gueullette, a rich bourgeois who was perfectly well acquainted with the young girl because he was the lover of her mother, Marie-Catherine Careau, or Carotte—also known as "the widow Tristan"—whom he supported with great generosity. Endowed with a remarkable business sense, Mme Carotte managed to secure a large and luxurious home, which she occasionally transformed into a clandestine gambling den, in defiance of the law. Gueullette, who had a passion for the theater, arranged for Julie to be admitted to the Opéra's ballet school. Even if the girl proved to be only a mediocre dancer, it remained a decisive episode for her. She taught herself to move with grace and meet the inquisitive gazes of strangers, gaining the self-confidence necessary to feel at ease anywhere, no matter the company. The Opéra, with its prima donnas, rivalries, cliques, hierarchies, discipline, and *splendeurs et misères*, was her first great school of life. Even if she would ultimately renounce a career for which she felt herself unsuited, Julie always retained a mythical memory of her first official debut on the stage, on January 24, 1772. It was during a performance of *Castor and Pollux* by Jean-Philippe Rameau, attended by the future Louis XVI, in the *nouvelle salle* of the Opéra, rebuilt at the Palais-Royal after the fire; and the young woman played one of the Happy Shades who, in the fourth act, sing and dance in the bliss of the Elysian Fields, where the "fires" of love are "pure" and "everlasting." This dreamlike image of a love founded on the reciprocity and transparency of hearts crystallized in the imagination of this "impure" young woman, and would tenaciously withstand the hard confrontation with reality.[51]

The Opéra served as an excellent springboard for courtesans. Unlike actresses, singers, and dancers, they could not be excommunicated, and like their colleagues at the Comédie-Française, they were free to dispense their favors as they pleased, away from the prying eyes of their families and the police. Mme Carotte took advantage of all this to steer her daughter toward prostitution. As Madeleine Ambrière, who has gone through all of the documents relating to Julie, writes: "The only definite reference [to prostitution] is dated June 12, 1771, the day that Julie, having just turned fifteen, received, thanks to the intervention of a banker from Amsterdam, her first lifetime annuity—without the name of the generous donor being specified, naturally."[52]

It was the first in a series of gratuities and payoffs that, judiciously invested in real estate by Mme Carotte, guaranteed both mother and daughter a comfortable and elegant style of life. Since her position as an illegitimate child deprived her of the possibility of inheritance, Mme Carotte decided to make her daughter her business partner, thus justifying their joint possession of property. Nonetheless, up until her death she discreetly harbored a mysterious tenant in a far-flung room of her mansion—none other than Julie's true father.[53]

"I understand passionate people, for I have been one myself,"[54] Julie Careau confided years later to Benjamin Constant, in a letter written only six months before her death. Even if in the course of her brief existence that passion presented itself in a variety of forms, her fidelity to her own particular way of feeling and loving certainly made her an extraordinary woman. And it was her acquaintance with Joseph-Alexandre de Ségur that first revealed this aspect of her personality to her, and that marked the beginning of her metamorphosis.

At the time, the young courtesan was leaving a relationship with the Chevalier Flandre de Brunville, a wealthy prosecutor for the King, who was sufficiently besotted with her to commission her portrait from Mme Vigée Le

Brun,[55] and to finance her purchase of a lot on the rue des Mathurins as well as the initial construction of a small mansion—though not, as it happens, chivalrous enough to recognize the child produced by their union. For Julie, motherhood was a crucial experience, and the primary anchor of her emotional life. When alone, she was more than happy to busy herself with her child. Now wealthy herself and at liberty, she had the luxury of choosing a lover who suited her taste. The Vicomte de Ségur had much to recommend him: he was young, seductive, and courteous, and he possessed to the highest degree of the art of amusing himself and his friends. He spread joy wherever he went, and gave an absolute priority to the pursuit of love.

Likewise, Julie was well equipped to attract Joseph-Alexandre: small, slim, with blue eyes like his own, delicate features, and golden hair, she combined luminous beauty with an unmistakable elegance. Unlike most actresses and courtesans, and thirty years in advance of Mme de Récamier, Julie used no makeup, wore no jewels, dressed herself only in white, and made refined simplicity her calling card. Naturally proud, she had not allowed herself to be ground down by her mercenary past—she had not renounced the love of love, hadn't ceased to hope for surprises from life. It was more than merely an erotic rapport that cemented her relationship with the Vicomte: They shared a passion for music and the theater, and, struck by Julie's instincts and vivid intelligence, Ségur took pleasure in playing Pygmalion, filling the gaps in her education, shaping her taste, and initiating her into the rituals and traditions of high society. A mutual friend, the journalist Jean-Gabriel Peltier, would recall some twenty years later the transformation that Julie underwent after her acquaintance with Ségur: "Julie is one of those women who belonged both to the common people by birth and to high society by way of their habits and relationships, and who were able to make others forget the source of their wealth by the elegance of their wit and their manners."[56]

Before formalizing his relationship with Julie, the Vicomte demanded that his mistress leave the house where she lived with Mme Carotte, and end the business connections they maintained. It was in her new house on the rue Chantereine where the young woman gave birth to a second child; this time, however, the father hastened to recognize the infant, who was promptly named Alexandre-Félix de Ségur.

Recently built in the vicinity of the Chaussée d'Antin after plans by Perrard de Montreuil, and funded with the Baron de Besenval's money, the mansion on the rue Chantereine was "a *petite folie*, a love nest, in the latest style, resembling [the sort of houses] that Ledoux, Wailly, and Brongniart had erected on the boulevards and in the same neighborhood for financiers, actresses, and young aristocrats."[57] The lovers entertained themselves furnishing it together. Julie had the walls of her boudoir covered with white fabric, and the furnishings, made specially for her, were lacquered with the same color. Joseph-Alexandre's harp presided over the salon, and it was there that (while continuing to reside officially at the Ségur mansion) the Vicomte spent much of his time receiving friends. On the rue Chantereine, gentlemen, dandies, and fashionable writers could mingle with popular actresses and singers in complete freedom, with the sole end of amusing themselves. But the mistress of the house remained the main draw. Constant (who was in the position to compare it to that of Mme de Staël) wrote that the quality of Julie's mature conversation combined grace, "the most piquant gaiety," and "the subtlest witticisms"; she "took care to flatter the talents of others as much as her own; it was as much as for them as for herself that she debated and bantered. Her turns of phrase were never obscure; she seized admirably on the fundamental point of every question, be it serious or flippant. In every case she said what had to be said, and it was clear that, to her way of thinking, an idea's precision was as vital for wit as it was for reason."[58] In her letters as well, Julie displays great intelligence and confidence of judgment—her critique of Staël's novel *Delphine*[59] furnishes a fine example, and with Ségur's help she was able to cement her reputation in high society.

Yet after three idyllic years together, the lovers returned to their old ways: the Vicomte paying court to the ladies of high society, and Julie indulging her admirers. Still, she did not allow herself to be moved by the "terrible fever of love"[60] that she had inadvertently inspired in Nicolas Chamfort. In spite of his genius, that writer, an *"enfant de la nature"* like herself, was too ugly and poor to seduce her. But the letters that Mirabeau wrote to Chamfort to report on the visits of the woman he called "our Aspasia," and the strategies he was employing to convince her to take his friend into her bed, make clear that in the eyes of the regulars at the rue Chantereine, Mlle Careau remained a courtesan.[61]

Not only had Julie taken to visiting solicitors' offices once again—a bequest from the Duc de Chartres and another from a lawyer, both in 1782, leave no doubt that she had returned to her old ways—in 1783 she lost her head over a young Irish gentleman of dubious reputation, the irresistible Antoine-Maurice de Saint-Léger, with whom she had yet another child.[62]

The affair was brief. Saint-Léger recognized the child and brought him back to England, while Ségur continued to frequent the rue Chantereine. Despite Julie's systematic infidelities, the Vicomte felt no need to put an end to their relationship and continued to maintain her, leaving it to her to take the initiative for a definitive break.

It was in 1787, taking advantage of Joseph-Alexandre's frequent absences (he had been forced to follow his regiment to Pont-à-Mousson), that Julie opened her arms to Talma, a penniless but ambitious actor seven years her junior who was destined to revolutionize the French theater.

If Talma found in Julie, her salon, her various society contacts, and her secure financial situation the springboard he needed to make his way in the world, Julie found in the actor's masculine beauty and magnetic gaze the impetus to start her life anew. Like her, Talma had sprung from the common people; like her, he was an artist free from social prejudice and in a position to offer her the sort of relationship between equals she had been denied until now. Ségur had shaped her in his own image, had recognized the child produced by their relationship and shared with her his friendships and amusements, but Julie was well aware that, despite his unquestionable freedom of thought, nothing would ever be able to convince him to make their union legitimate. For, if she remained an outsider among those guests that gathered in her own salon, it wasn't for moral reasons—didn't plenty of women in high society sell their favors?—but because of the inexpungible stain of her birth.[63] Julie was far too proud to submit to the logic of caste that relegated her to the margins of society. She had long since ceased to love Ségur, and had likewise left off playing the role of Aspasia. Her passion for Talma gave her the courage to move on. It was the eve of 1789, and everything—including the conversation of numerous habitués of her salon—combined to fill her with hope that a different future was on the horizon. So Julie dismissed Ségur and formalized her relationship with her new lover by receiving him at the rue Chantereine and decisively contributing to his theatrical success. Talma showed his gratitude by marrying her a month before the birth of their twins, baptized Castor and Pollux in commemoration of that legendary evening when, playing a Happy Shade in Rameau's opera, the little dancer had experienced in her own person the transformative power of the theater.

Providing her with the social legitimacy that she had always lacked, the marriage made of her a mother, a wife, and a citizen—and along with Talma, Julie loudly espoused the ideals of the Revolution. She became a Spartan[64] while retaining all her Athenian grace, and sought her revenge on the society that had humiliated her by taking up arms against the privileged and "every species of prejudice."[65]

But to judge by a pair of missives that she wrote to Talma in the summer of 1788, the rupture with Ségur was in fact anything but straightforward. From the beginning of their relationship, Julie had wanted to give her passion for Talma a virtuous tone, which in practice meant recognizing the importance of the bond that had united her with the Vicomte. "Another man has sacred rights over me," she wrote solemnly to her new lover, "soon he will return; he must see us no more; have the courage to spirit me away before his return: prevent, if you can, the unhappiness of seeing *another* man less beloved yet happier than you. It has been no more than fifteen days since I last assured him of my affection, I would never have the audacity to tell him that in such a short space of time somebody else has been able to please me."[66]

But it didn't take long for Julie to find that audacity. As the summer wore on, Ségur was forced to resign himself to the irrevocable character of their separation. He stopped sending to his military commander "requests for the bonuses needed to maintain Julie's style of life, which had multiplied since February 1786."[67] But when the Vicomte proposed to share her affections with others, was Julie correct to see it as the desperate gesture of a "wretch who no longer has the courage of a man"?[68] Hadn't Ségur (perfectly consistent) simply meant to remind her that fidelity had never been a necessary part of their relationship, and that he was loath to give up their bond? In his eyes, the real betrayal lay elsewhere. He had worked to make Julie a new Ninon de Lenclos, and she, annihilating all his efforts, had lost her head over an actor, and taken herself for one of Jean-Jacques Rousseau's heroines. In his eyes, Mlle Careau had once again become a courtesan like any other.

But even with Julie gone, Ségur's name would continue to be tied to that of a famous courtesan: indeed, he made one the protagonist of an epistolary novel. Published in 1789, shortly after the break, his *Secret Correspondence Between Ninon de Lenclos, the Marquis de Villarceaux, and Madame de Maintenon*[69] was a project that he had long entertained during the relationship with Julie. Should we believe, as an authoritative tradition has it, that the Vicomte used their own correspondence in writing his novel? It is a seductive hypothesis, one that accords with his narcissistic taste for making a spectacle of himself—

but it remains difficult to prove. In any case, Ségur's enterprise had nothing original about it, and was in line with a long-established literary tradition.

Inaugurated by the *Letters of a Portuguese Nun* and cemented by the success of Montesquieu's *Persian Letters*, the vogue for the epistolary novel continued through the first decades of the nineteenth century, and was given a fresh impetus by the publication of Laclos's *Les Liaisons Dangereuses* in 1782.[70] And even the decision to use the epistolary form as a vehicle for a literary pastiche was not particularly unusual.

Ségur's *Secret Correspondence* presents itself to readers as a collection of real letters exchanged circa 1650 between Ninon de Lenclos, the Marquis de Villarceaux, Ninon's "dalliance" of the moment, and the young Françoise d'Aubigné who, then still at the beginning of the social rise that would one day make her the secret spouse of Louis XIV, was uncertain about what sort of direction to take in life. This selection of characters was also nothing especially new. Voltaire, after having inaugurated the myth of the Grand Siècle with his *Century of Louis XIV*, had amused himself by writing an imaginary dialogue between Ninon and Françoise at the height of their careers—there, in keeping with the libertine ethic that ultimately earned her the reputation of an *honnête femme*, Ninon refuses the hospitality that her old friend offers her at Versailles, opting instead for the freedom of private life.[71] Moreover, during the previous half century, numerous collections of letters by Mme de Sévigné had been published, as well as those by Mme de Maintenon in an edition by La Beaumelle (which had also included a number of clever fakes), and finally the correspondence of Ninon de Lenclos with Saint-Évremond, which had fascinated numerous readers. This renewed interest in the emblematic female figures of the Grand Siècle also led to a glut of literary counterfeiting. In 1750, even before Ségur's *Secret Correspondence*, there had appeared a fake edition of letters between Ninon de Lenclos and the Marquis de Sévigné[72]—son of the celebrated correspondent—while Sénac de Meilhan had published the forged *Memoirs of Anne de Gonzague, Princesse Palatine*. Sadly, the *Epistles of Ninon*, in which Chamfort—at the same time that Ségur was at work on his epistolary novel—evoked, according to his friend Pierre-Louis Ginguené, "a picture of the frivolous and corrupted manners...of the whole court of Louis XIV," has been lost.[73]

In its review of Ségur's book, the *Correspondance littéraire* characterizes it as "witty and flamboyant, fluent and graceful"[74] but reproaches it for a lack of historical verisimilitude. However, in choosing Ninon de Lenclos as the centerpiece of his work, Joseph-Alexandre was less interested in accuracy than in using the courtesan as a vehicle to illustrate his own conception of love. Choosing as his mouthpiece the most illustrious of the seventeenth century's *femmes galantes* was, for the novelist, a way of distinguishing himself from his contemporaries, who had made erotic freedom the specific emblem of modernity—it allowed him to assert the permanent relevance of that cheerful epicureanism to which the *honnêteté* of the seventeenth century had granted a social legitimacy. At the same time, he was able to maintain his distance from the domineering and deceitful brand of libertinism that had flourished among the elites since the Regency, and whose perverse stratagems are laid bare in the novels of Crébillon fils. There, the famous lesson imparted by Versac to the young hero of *Les Égarements du coeur et de l'esprit* was unambiguous: to succeed among the *bonne compagnie*, it was necessary to sacrifice the vital instinct of desire to a calculating *libido dominandi* incompatible with amorous delight.

Ségur, for his part, had no intention of giving up the right to indulge himself in a pleasure free from all obligation whenever he so chose—which was why he preferred to turn back to the hedonism of Ninon de Lenclos, to the psychological savvy and formal elegance that had characterized the aristocratic civilization of the preceding century, and to the privileged place that that century's women had held when it came to the game of love.

The *Secret Correspondence* thus represented for Ségur a first manifesto for the art of love that he aspired to master, and to which he would return tirelessly in verse, with the *Essay on the Means of Pleasing in Love*, as well as in prose, with his long essay on *Women, Their Condition, and Their Influence in the Social Orders of Various Peoples, Ancient and Modern*, published posthumously in 1820.

But it was not merely women that Joseph-Alexandre was interested in seducing. A social imperative par excellence, the "need to please"[75] was for him a powerful psychological drive, and a challenge renewed every day. Rarer than esprit, congeniality was for him a faculty inseparable from will, though "laziness of mind ... is the most common tendency in society, so that one is more likely to meet intelligent men who keep silent than congenial men who seek to seduce."[76] Congeniality, on the other hand, implied "an almost continual need to please; that disposition of character is so necessary to congeniality, that it practically *is* congeniality; and the extreme desire to succeed is itself already the seed of success."[77]

And when it came to the collective exertions of a society in love with itself—a society that had made the need and the ability to please its principal preoccupations—it was difficult to draw a firm dividing line between social and erotic seduction, between the salon and the bedroom. A master of both, Ségur knew just how to use that contiguity as an excuse for passing happily from one to the other—establishing it, in fact, as the centerpiece of his amorous strategy. The Vicomte could evoke the classical rules of romantic conquest—"Nous plaire sans céder fut le bonheur des femmes, / Et vaincre leur refus le seul but de nos âmes."*—and then go on to recognize that "L'amour s'est corrompu, nous arrivons trop tard; / Il faut bien, malgré nous, avoir recours à l'art."†[78] If a lady of high society could declare to her admirer, "I don't have time to *consider* whether or not you're able to please me: it would be quicker to *do* it,"[79] perhaps the moment had come for the most free-spirited *bonne compagnie* in Europe to speak openly about desire, describing without shame those forms that would allow it to be lived most fully.

Ever since the Regency, novelists, poets, and painters had grappled with eroticism, but no representative of high society had yet had the temerity of the Vicomte in theorizing the art of seduction on the basis of his own personal experience. In his *Essay on the Means of Pleasing in Love*, Joseph-Alexandre was happy to illustrate for his readers a campaign of conquests, each of them organized into three stages—"On Attraction," "On Avowal," and "On Victory"—in which nothing was left to chance. Only the initial moment, attraction—that "spontaneous, indefinable predilection" whose "secret power controls our fates,"[80] and without which all art would be useless—escapes programming. For the rest, the 597 alexandrines in rhyming couplets that comprise the *Essay* are consecrated to the study of signs, to psychological insight, to selecting the perfect moment and location, all of which constitute the fundamentals of masculine conquest and for whose efficacy the author seems to be personally vouching. Turning his back on the licentious rococo style, which would soon pass out of fashion, the Vicomte takes as his allies delicacy, modesty, and the charm of that neoclassical taste that was currently conquering Paris.

Still, Ségur abandoned his readers at the door of the boudoir: intended as

---

*To please without yielding themselves was women's happiness, / And to vanquish their refusal our souls' sole aim.

†Love is corrupted, we have arrived too late; / Whether we like it or not, we must have recourse to art.

it was for the men and women of high society, the *Essay* respected decorum by avoiding the trivial and all-too egalitarian language of sexuality. Even after having employed a vast repertoire of paraphrases, metaphors, and circumlocutions to evoke desire's powers of persuasion, when the moment of the embrace finally arrived, the Vicomte chose to remain silent. After all, what better than silence to restore a bit of mystery to that "contact between two epidermises" that he himself insisted on calling, simply, "love?"[81]

The Vicomte did not always behave in perfect consistency with his theories, and his cheerful epicureanism could sometimes mask the ferocity of a predator. Two of his exploits—which come down to us thanks to the Duchesse d'Abrantès and the Comtesse de Boigne, both of whom would write their memoirs after the Revolution—would not be out of place in *Les Liaisons Dangereuses*. But as Gabriel de Broglie observes, "It would be a mistake to believe that the Vicomte de Ségur sought to imitate Laclos's protagonists. Rather, if he resembles the Vicomte de Valmont, and surpasses him in deviousness, it is that he epitomized the type of man that Laclos wanted to represent, and stigmatize, in Valmont."[82]

The first incident took place during the period that his relationship with Julie Careau was foundering. In 1780, thanks to the support of the Duchesse de Polignac and the machinations of Besenval ("They say that if you have anything to do with M. de Ségur, you're going to have to speak to the Swiss,"[83] the *Secret Memoirs* note with irony), the elder Ségur had been named minister of war. Meanwhile, the Vicomte and his brother had entered the intimate circle of Marie-Antoinette. Among the ladies preferred by the Queen, it was the Marquise de Bréhan who drew the attention of Joseph-Alexandre. Despite the fact that she was nine years older than him, she was a seductive woman of uncommon beauty and great refinement. But her heart was already spoken for. So in order to win her over, the Vicomte hatched a plot whose villainy would leave a lasting impression: a full thirty years later, the Duchesse d'Abrantès would conjure it up in tremendous detail in the purest style of romantic melodrama.

Mme de B—n loved the Comte Étienne de D., who was known as *le beau Durfort*, with a most *idealized* affection. He loved her as well ... Now, Mme la Marquise de B—n loved too purely not to perceive that she herself was the less admired. She noticed a chilliness and such an alteration in their relations that she understood that M. de D. no longer loved her. She told no one, she shut her secret up inside herself, and wept in silence. The Vicomte de Ségur, a tremendously witty man but also very wicked, had long loved the Marquise de B—n. And after all, what could she do? Forbid him to love her? She cared so little for him that it didn't even occur to her. But Ségur never lost sight of her. As soon as he noticed the puffiness of her eyes, the paleness of her cheeks, he came running, and, taking the Marquise's hand, squeezed it without speaking. Nothing is so moving as these silent tokens of an attachment that, misunderstood though they may be, remains one of the sweetest parts of life. So that as soon as the Vicomte de Ségur raised his eyes and rested them on the Marquise, she burst into tears.

"Whatever is the matter?" he said to her.

She did not answer, but continued to weep and could not respond to him.

"Poor child! You are suffering, aren't you? You don't dare to tell me? My poor little thing, I know the reason for your tears, and my conscience obliges me to say that he is wholly unworthy of you."

Mme de B—n made a gesture of indignation, but the Vicomte ignored it.

"Yes, I insist that he for whom you weep is unworthy."

Mme de B—n gave a harrowing cry.

"What! Has your courage left you?"

"No," she replied, "I don't believe you!"

The Vicomte smiled without responding.

Mme de B—n saw [the judgment] in that smile, she looked at the Vicomte with a pleading expression.

"You want proof of what I say?"

Mme de B—n nodded yes.

"Very well. You shall have it within four days, perhaps by tomorrow!"

In fact, Étienne de Durfort's then mistress was a woman named Adélaïde Filleul—newly married to the Comte de Flahaut, there was no question that she constituted a formidable rival. "Pretty as an angel" and quite fashionable, she was well on the way to making a reputation for herself, proving that she was by no means, as Mme d'Abrantès had claimed of her, "dumb as a basket." After Durfort, the Comtesse would go on to become the mistress of Gouverneur Morris and then of Talleyrand, and to lead one of the most important political salons of the prerevolutionary years. Then, the Revolution past, she would marry a second time, taking as husband the Baron de Sousa, the Portuguese ambassador, and begin a career as a novelist, devising romantic tales of love set against the backdrop of the high society of the ancien régime. But at the time of Ségur's plot, the Comtesse de Flahaut was still cutting her teeth, and the Vicomte, who knew her intimately, easily persuaded her to demand that Durfort definitively break with Mme de Bréhan, returning her letters as well as the portrait and ring that the poor Marquise had given him, thereby contravening all the rules of chivalry. When Ségur learned that all this had been accomplished, he "grinned with that infernal glee that brings a smile to the face of Satan, exclaiming to himself: 'Now she's mine!'"

But Joseph-Alexandre had spoken too soon. His "art of love" had never taken into account the vicissitudes of passion, and now its limits were suddenly revealed. In her retelling, Mme d'Abrantès does not shrink from emphasizing this: "On receiving this proof of betrayal by the only man she had ever loved, so deep was the Marquise de Bréhan suffering that death seemed the only place of refuge." In short, the Marquise withdrew to her bedroom and poisoned herself, and it was a miracle that the doctors were able to save her. Unlike the Présidente in *Les Liaisons Dangereuses*, Mme de Bréhan survived the ordeal, though she was never able to rid herself of the nervous tremor that had come upon her at the moment of the revelation. Still, "the Vicomte understood that this grief, silent and tearless though it might be, was a force before which all of his little intrigues were as nothing. He withdrew without speaking, without the strength to venture a single word to this woman whose mourning was so profoundly deep."[84]

The second and even more disquieting episode comes to us by way of Mme de Boigne, who heard it directly from her mother, the Comtesse d'Osmond, a contemporary of Ségur. This great diarist of the ancien régime concisely lays out for us the logic of a libertinism that turns desire to entirely foreign ends.

As in *Les Liaisons Dangereuses*, the incident had its origin in Ségur's wish to avenge himself on a rival by seducing the woman he loved. But what strikes one most of all in the case of the Vicomte is the utter futility of the dispute.

As was customary, January 1, 1783, saw an abundance of poetry of every description produced in Paris. As the many letters of Mme du Deffand attest, the members of high society had a tradition of celebrating the arrival of the New Year by exchanging amusing little gifts, often accompanied by rhymed messages set to the tune of fashionable songs. On that January 1, Ségur had the idea of offering the ladies he knew little sweets containing verses that he had worked up for the occasion. Gifted with an ear for music, the Vicomte was also a deft versifier and possessed to the highest degree the art of improvisation, which itself constituted one of the most enviable social virtues. (He wasn't alone in this: the Chevalier de Boufflers, for example, boasted of a similar talent, and it made him a tireless commentator on all those events, big and small, out of which society life was woven.)

An essential component of these competitive poetic games was the delicate art of mockery—and Comte Henri-Charles de Thiard, who was known as much for his wit as for his talent as a versifier, made good use of that art in the lines that accompanied his New Year's gift to the Vicomte. In his epigram, *The Very Humble Remonstrances of Fidèle Berger, Confectioner, rue des Lombards, to M. le Vicomte de Ségur,* Thiard—who had probably offered sweets to the ladies himself—jokingly reproaches the Vicomte, younger and luckier in love than he, for competing unfairly:

> *Vous, qui des amants infidels*
> *Présentez à toutes les belles*
> *Et les charmes et le danger*
> *Avez-vous besoin de voler,*
> *Ségur, pour vous faire aimer d'elles,*
> *Les fonds du Fidèle Berger?*
> *Que deviendront mes friandises,*
> *Mes petits coeurs et mes bonbons?*
> *Qui brisera mes macarons*
> *Pour y chercher quelques devises?*[*][85]

Playing off of the hyperbolic celebration of the Vicomte's amorous successes, this friendly ribbing concludes with a request for compensation: "Songez au dédommagement / Que vous devez à ma boutique, / Et donnez-moi votre pratique / Pour le baptême et pour l'enfant."[†][86] But the final point displeased the Vicomte. Had he been irritated by its boldness? Did it herald a possible

---

[*]You who will tell beautiful women / Tales of unfaithful lovers, / Their troubles and delights, / What need have you, Ségur, / To steal the goods of Fidèle Berger / To make them fall in love with you? / What will become of my candies, / My little hearts, my bonbons? / Who will crack open my macaroons / In search of verses?

[†]Just think of the damages / That you owe my shop / And grant me your custom / For the christening and the child.

invasion of his territory? Or was Thiard insinuating that Ségur only deployed his skill at seduction in order to show off? All we know is that the Vicomte decided to respond to words with deeds. And he would supply a practical lesson in his talents by turning them on the mistress of the insolent poetaster.

The lady in question, referred to as Mme de Z. in the Comtesse de Boigne's tale, was in reality the Comtesse de Séran,[87] who happily divided her time between Thiard and her husband, between life in the city and sojourns in the countryside. Ségur found a way to have himself dispatched to a garrison not far from the Séran family's estate in Normandy, and went to work paying elaborate court to the Comtesse. But we'll let Mme de Boigne tell the story:

> He played his part perfectly, feigning a delirious passion, and thanks to this assiduousness, which lasted for several months, managed to woo the lady and secure her affections. Soon enough Mme de Z. found herself pregnant; her husband was away, and M. de Thiard as well. She announced her misfortune to the Vicomte. As recently as the previous evening he had expressed the most ardent devotion to her, but now, having achieved his goal, he replied that he had never cared for her at all. His only desire had been to avenge himself for M. de Thiard's sarcasm, and to demonstrate that his wit was sufficient for something more than the manufacture of confectionary couplets. He politely took his leave, and she heard no more of him. Ségur left immediately for Paris, where he repeated the story to all and sundry.[88]

Once again, it is an act of vengeance carried out via a third party that drives the plot of the Vicomte's second literary work, *The Jealous Woman*, published in 1790. In keeping with aristocratic custom, and as had been the case with the *Secret Correspondence*, Ségur declined to attach his name to this epistolary novel, while making sure that everyone knew he was its author. This time, his literary model was undeniably *Les Liaisons Dangereuses*—in it, as in Laclos's fiction, the perverse strategies of seduction and manipulation that Ségur did not hesitate to put into practice in real life take on a moral sense, and end up leading the guilty to their downfall.

While denouncing the lack of originality in the Vicomte's second work, the *Correspondance littéraire* conscientiously summarizes it for its readers: "The Marquis de Sénanges, under the pretext of helping his friend the Chevalier de Lincour win a young widow with whom he's madly in love, manages to inspire in her the keenest affections for himself. The Baronne de Versac,[89] mistress of the Marquis, observes this intrigue with all the unease and perspicacity that jealousy at its most profound is able to inspire. Without scruples, she decides to use the Chevalier to kill the lover. However this attempt at vengeance spins out of control; thanks to the contrivances of this blackest of plots, the two friends fight each other, but it is the Chevalier who pierces his own heart, having hurled himself onto the sword of his friend, who wished only to defend himself." The lesson would seem to be that male friendship endures better than love among the excesses of libertinism.[90]

The Jealous Woman was Ségur's opportunity to put his thoroughgoing knowledge of the habits and customs of contemporary society on full display. Ever since Mlle de Scudéry, French literature had made the description of the lifestyle of the *bonne compagnie* one of its specialties, and in the wake of the "sociological revolution"[91] of the *Persian Letters*, the novelists of the eighteenth century, schooled by the classical moralists, had devoted themselves to depicting the dialectic between the individual and society.

Even if Ségur was part of this tradition, his perspective differed from that of other professional writers. He was himself the perfected product of a style of life that the novelists, despite their acuity of perception, could apprehend only from without. His approach to the world of the privileged, to which he belonged, was profoundly empathetic, and his aim was not to denounce the ravages of social conformism or the corruption of the elites. On the contrary, he meant to re-create the spectacle of a society infatuated with its own formal virtuosity, one whose sole criteria for judgment was the greater or lesser capacity of each of its members to play with elegance his or her appointed role. Ultimately, the point made by one high-society lady after her reading of *The Jealous Woman* hit the nail on the head: "If M. de Ségur wants to make novels, I recommend that he do so as their protagonist, rather than the author."[92] And indeed, the Vicomte saved the best of himself for real life.

Taking note of the disappointing reception the reading public had given his second novel, and driven by his skill in rendering the profoundly theatrical character of life in high society—after all, the staging of his own public persona had always been the keystone of his identity—the Vicomte ended up concentrating his artistic ambitions on the stage.

Joseph-Alexandre's talent for capturing the attention of demanding audiences by reading his poetry, singing his songs, or simply recounting whatever happened to pass through his head was already well known in social circles. Gouverneur Morris, who attended the reading of one of his short plays, *Le Nouveau Cercle*, found that the Vicomte "read too well"[93] for him to be able to judge the merit of the text. Ségur himself would later emphasize the theatrical nature of the raconteur's art: "A man telling a story in the midst of a group is almost an *actor* on stage, the differences being that the *actor* recites what has been written for him while the *storyteller* is obliged to improvise; and since one sees him up close, his naturalness must be truer to life. The *actor* is veiled by prestige; while the *storyteller* is surrounded by his models. He is a *copy* which must always remain faithful in order to withstand continual comparison with its *original*."[94]

It will surprise no one that, as a member (along with his brother, Louis-Philippe) of the amateur company that performed at the private theater of Mme de Montesson, the Vicomte revealed himself to be an excellent actor.

Ever since the era of the Marquise de Rambouillet's Blue Chamber, the theater had been closely associated with society life, and in the course of the eighteenth century, in Paris as at Versailles, aristocrats and financiers equipped their homes with private auditoriums where they would put on shows for audiences made up of their friends. In 1781, bemoaning the decline of the performances at the Théâtre-Français, the *Secret Correspondence* observed: "They say that theatrical talent has become the exclusive purview of aristocrats. We already knew to what a degree of perfection they possessed that ability; but up until now, they have only deployed it behind the scenes."[95] Indeed, as the Chevalier de Méré had theorized in his time, didn't the man of the world have to interpret his role with the critical distance of an actor?

But Ségur's attraction to the theater was deeper and more personal, far beyond the domain of social conventions. Following the manner established by Carmontelle twenty years earlier,[96] Ségur wrote *proverbes*, short one-act plays that illustrated a proverbial expression well enough known that the audience would easily guess it before its final pronouncement, which was bound to trigger applause. Like charades and riddles, *proverbes* were a social amusement, but Ségur meant to make the form his springboard to a professional career. It was a risky project, the ambition of which was perceived by the venomous Tilly: already blessed by fate, the Vicomte wanted to assure himself "a place among those writers who also belong to high society, and thus pursue two careers at once."[97]

In January 1787, Ségur made his debut with *Le Parti le plus Gai*, in which he played the leading role, while the female lead was entrusted to Mlle Contat, one of the most applauded actresses of the moment. In doing so, not only did the Vicomte contravene the rules that prohibited amateurs from performing side by side with professionals (the precedent of the Duchesse du Maine, who had performed with the celebrated actor Baron, could only be attributed to her extravagance), but—as a first strategic step to get himself closer to the Comédie—he chose to stage the premiere of his *proverbe* "in the presence of the town and of the court," at a private theater with two hundred fifty seats that Mlle Contat had built at her house in Auteuil.[98] It is hard to imagine a better publicity scheme, since the mistress of the house was already a center of attention.

Born to Parisian shopkeepers in 1760, Louise Contat had been thrust into a theatrical career by the great actor Préville and his wife, a renowned actress as well, who—impressed by the poise and intellectual vivacity of the little laundry delivery girl—had provided for her education. Two years after having attended the declamation class given by Lekain and Préville, Louise made her debut at the Comédie-Française, where she became a member in 1778. While she immediately showed a predisposition for leading roles, Louise was forced for a good while to content herself with supporting parts, often ones little suited to her, while awaiting the chance to show what she was made of. Indeed, her first great success was achieved in the foyer of the Comédie, a gathering place for theater enthusiasts, men of letters, and artists, who met there to exchange their impressions of the newest plays and current affairs.

Beautiful as she was, Louise was also intelligent and witty, a keen conversationalist—but, unlike her female colleagues, she rebuffed the advances of regulars in quest of affairs, earning for herself the nickname "the Snob." Well aware of her "price," the young actress did not intend to sell herself short, and would not yield until she judged it was actually worth her trouble. The first to obtain her favors was the wealthy René Ange Augustin de Maupeou, first president of the Parliament of Paris, son of the famous chancellor of Louis XV—cultured, affable, and gallant. Despite the generosity of the magistrate, and the birth of a child who was welcomed with joy and immediately provided for with magnanimity, Louise didn't deny herself the pleasure of being wooed by the younger brother of Louis XVI, the dashing Comte d'Artois, and sacrificed her lover for his sake. The choice was not without risks, since d'Artois was distinguished neither for his prodigality nor his constancy, and Louise, perhaps presuming too much, wished to dictate the terms of her surrender.

She gave him to understand that she was ready to open her arms to him on the condition that he agreed to live publicly with her, drawing the response: "Tell her I don't know how to live."[99]

Beginning around 1780, her relationship with the King's brother lasted long enough for a child to be born, and for Louise to effect her professional ascension at the Comédie-Française. During the year 1782 alone, Mlle Contat managed to appear in at least seven productions, and in 1784 she demonstrated the breadth of her talent and artistic maturity in *Les Courtisanes*, a mediocre moralizing comedy by Palissot, aimed at a social phenomenon of which she herself furnished an example. Forced to grapple with a thankless role, Louise rendered her character captivating by means of her brio and elegant irony, managing to wrest applause even from those *impures* who had come to the theater determined to tear the play down. "I swear to you, I would never have believed it could be so amusing to see oneself hung in effigy,"[100] conceded Marie-Madeleine Guimard, one of the most famous dancers of the era, to the no less celebrated chanteuse Sophie Arnould, at the end of the show. The flattering judgment of two of the Opéra's greatest headliners was ample reward for the tenacious ambition with which Mlle Contat, while stuck in supporting roles, had honed her art and enriched her palette. "Her mind adapts itself to all forms,"[101] said Julie Careau of her, and her memory was so well trained that in only twenty-four hours she could memorize, as she proved upon a request from Marie-Antoinette, no fewer than seven hundred lines of verse. Having accomplished that feat, she declared: "I did not know where the seat of the memory was. Now I realize it is in the heart."[102]

Beaumarchais, that genial adventurer enamored of the theater, was among her admirers: no less ambitious and tenacious than Louise, he observed her for several years before giving her a central role in the incendiary play he was in the process of putting onstage. A masterful choice, as it turned out, since—not content with her creation of the character of Suzanne—Mlle Contat pooled her efforts with those of the Comte de Vaudreuil in order to convince the Comte d'Artois to permit *The Marriage of Figaro* to slip past the censor and play on the stage of the Comédie-Française after a season of private performances. It was April 27, 1784, and "that unparalleled evening, when all of the actors triumphed along with the author, belonged, above all, to Contat. 'The charming girl!' exclaimed Figaro, 'Always laughing, blooming, full of gaiety, of wit, loving, delightful!...' and all of Paris said it with him."[103] Among the audience that evening was the young Antoine-Vincent Arnault, a future playwright to whom we will give the final word: "Mlle Contat brought to her role, already so seductive, an authority that astonished Beaumarchais himself. The wit of the part certainly belonged to Beaumarchais, but not the wit with which the part was conveyed; that belonged entirely to the actress, and she possessed perhaps more than the author himself. In conveying, she created."[104]

When two and a half years later she accepted her old friend Ségur's proposal that she play the role of the faithless wife in *Le Parti le plus Gai*, the actress was at the height of her glory and in an advanced state of pregnancy. She was also besotted with the Comte de Narbonne, a friend of the Vicomte's—the same age as he, and like him, a darling of high-society ladies. A production mounted with Joseph-Alexandre offered an unparalleled occasion for her to revel in her triumph as both artist and woman in the course of a one-of-a-kind evening wherein monde and demimonde would find themselves side by side to applaud her—and what's more, in a private rather than a public theater.

This enterprise was possible thanks to the brazen libertinism of various Princes of the Blood, from the Comte d'Artois to the Ducs of Bourbon and Orléans. With "the solemnity of their affection and the excess of their magnanimity," they had created for courtesans (as Jacques de Norvins later recalled) "a real place in the world among the ladies of high society and the nymphs with a bit of property.... These ladies had beautiful apartments, or even beautiful mansions, where the very best sort of men would flock, married or not—so select a company that it was pretty much the custom to introduce young men there who were just setting out in the world, so that they might have an early chance to get acquainted with the *coryphées* of high society."[105] At the beginning of the 1770s, returning home from Paris, Prince Charles of Sweden had written indignantly to his brother Gustav that he had seen "the Duc de Chartres with the Duc de Lauzun, the Duc d'Aumont, and various other Ducs strolling around with Mme de Mirepoix, Mme de Villeroy, and Mme de Montmorency, settling down to prattle with courtesans, then taking them in their arms, sauntering around with them, going off to dinner with them, while the other women laughed, saying *Where are those scatterbrains headed?*"[106] At the beginning, it took all of Mlle Contat's audacity to dare to bring the ladies of high society and courtesans together in the same auditorium—and events show that there was good reason to worry. To judge by a letter, quivering with indignation, sent by the Comtesse de Sabran to the Chevalier de Boufflers, it seems that the courtesans managed to turn the situation to their advantage. "Here in the midst of the activity surrounding the Assembly of Notables, the Vicomte de Ségur has found a way of making himself the subject of conversation. He has just given a short play of his own making, staged at the home of Mlle Contat in Auteuil, called *Le Parti le plus Gai*. It seems to me as if such publicity is always what he's after, and especially at a moment like this—for he himself performed before more than a hundred people of good breeding. Plenty of well-known ladies had no scruples about going to applaud him, and there occurred, among others, quite a disagreeable incident."[107]

The incident she mentions was due to the altogether unusual seating arrangements. The ladies of high society (who at the public theaters followed the performance from boxes usually protected by a high railing) had been invited to seat themselves in the stalls, while the *filles*—a dozen actresses and notorious courtesans, Julie Careau among them—occupied a large box at the rear of the hall. Unaware of this arrangement, three late-arriving society women inadvertently entered said box, and the actresses hastened to give them the best seats. Less courteous, the audience on the floor of the theater, seeing them seated with the courtesans, "hooted" and "hissed" at them, obliging them to "flee in shame."[108] A number of people even maliciously referred to the incident by the title of a play currently drawing attention at the Theatre des Italiens: *Les Méprisés par ressemblance*. No less maliciously, the Comte d'Espinchal, who also been in attendance that evening, noted in his journal that "plenty of those ladies would have stayed to dine with the *demoiselles*, if only they'd dared."[109]

But the evening had another unpleasant surprise in store for its triumphant author. For in fact it was most likely on this occasion that Talma, who had come to Auteuil with Molé—the professor of dramatic declamation and regular collaborator of Mlle Contat, with whom he was preparing to perform *Rosaline et Floricourt*, the Vicomte's new play[110]—met Julie, whose lover he would become soon afterward.[111]

Along with *Le Parti le plus Sage*, *Le Parti le plus Gai* inaugurated Ségur's career as a playwright, and announced those preoccupations that would guide his theatrical writing.

Delicate and evanescent as the little booklets through which they have come down to us, the Vicomte's plays are generally short and lacking in actual plot. In them Ségur sets out a specific situation, a conjugal crisis, a conflict between characters, a life choice, by bringing onstage a number of characters—or rather, silhouettes, barely sketched—who behave, reason, and speak in accord with the rules of the *bonne compagnie*. The true protagonist of this theater is the dialogue, sometimes spirited and witty, sometimes evasive and distracted, lending credibility to the characters, revealing the emotions hidden behind society games and courteous phrases. In numerous plays the dialogue gains in elegance and musicality thanks to the use of rhymed verse, which Ségur employs tirelessly. But the Vicomte's skill consisted above all in his ability to guarantee the participation of renowned actors in his plays, offering them roles that showcased their particular talents, and privileging subjects to which his audience would immediately respond. Indeed, Ségur did not limit himself to imitating in his plays the habits and customs of high society; he wanted to be the interpreter of the expectations of a new bourgeois public.

Armed with an indulgent moralism and agreeable good sense, the Vicomte in his first two *proverbes* adopted the point of view of a husband—a figure that French theater had traditionally relegated to the background. And in these two plays, this husband did not intend to share his wife with anyone else. It is probably above all the desire to amuse himself that drives the protagonist of *Le Parti le plus Gai*, the Marquis de Fulvil, to systematically insert himself into the encounters between his wife and the Chevalier de Linval, gently mocking them, stymieing all of their plans, and finally forcing his rival to flee—thus illustrating the proverbial expression "to a good cat, a good rat." But in *Le Parti le plus Sage*, which is set in the even more bourgeois milieu of the high magistracy, the president is truly in love with his wife. In their case, it is a difference of character that separates them: while the husband loves to withdraw into solitude, his spouse needs to amuse herself with company. The arrival of a Marquis who hopes to turn her desire for escape to his own advantage incites the husband to ask his wife's pardon for not having understood her needs, and the two are reconciled. The moral of the play—"kindness works better than violence"—advocates for a marital bond based on mutual understanding.[112] Leaving aside his personal convictions, Ségur recognized here that many of his contemporaries no longer considered marriage a simple formality but instead a promise of reciprocal happiness.

The plot of *Rosaline et Floricourt*, the first of Ségur's plays to be staged at the Théâtre-Français, on November 17, 1787, is driven by the obnoxious personality of the heroine, a shrew in the Shakespearean mold, who is finally tamed by the tenacious patience of her suitor, with the help of paternal cunning. The reception of the play, based largely around the couple's quarrels and spats, failed to live up to the Vicomte's hopes, and he was forced to shorten it from three to two acts. According to the *Correspondance littéraire*, the performers' execution left something to be desired: Mlle Contat, for whom the play had been written, "played the role of Rosaline with more affectation and mincing than charm and frivolity," and "nowadays Molé looks much too old to once again play the dupe agreeably."[113] Nevertheless, Ségur had succeeded in making his debut as a professional playwright, and intended to hold his ground. And even if his talent was not so great as to leave behind a lasting memory, his theatrical reputation, fragile though it was, would save him from certain death during the Terror.

Still, Ségur's preferred stage remained that of high society. After the scandal raised by the evening at Auteuil, the Marquis Ximénès had come to his defense with a rather pertinent observation:

> *Quelles sont les moeurs du siècle où nous vivons!*
> *La palme des talents ne peut parer nos fronts,*
> *Sans que de nos aïeux les mânes en colère*
> *Ne nous fassent rougir d'avoir su l'art de plaire*[*][114]

Indeed, how was one to decide on the proper comportment in a society that lacked a common criteria of judgment? In turning over the question, the Vicomte seized the opportunity offered by his friend to insist upon a morality of personal pleasure, precisely in the name of the "tolerance" of a "pleasant and frivolous century" where "all is condemned, all permitted":

> *Chacun établit un système*
> *Sur le plan qu'il veut se former,*
> *Et la raison ne sait plus même*
> *Ce qu'il faut permettre ou blâmer.*
> *Grâce à cette tolérance,*

---

*Look at the manners in this century of ours! / We can no longer deck our brows with the genius's laurels / Without throwing the ghosts of our forebears into a rage / Since we blush for having mastered the art of pleasing!

Je vois s'écouler mes beaux jours,
Et je me fixe avec constance
Près des Grâces et des Amours.
Je m'égare parfois, mais c'est avec ivresse;
Le bandeau du plaisir est toujours sur mes yeux,
Et si quelques remords tourmentent ma vieillesse,
Au moins mes souvenirs pourront me rendre heureux[115]

The French monarchy was among the first to demonstrate tolerance in respect of its subjects' freedom of speech, but it also set limits on that freedom—and sometimes Ségur, a little too sure of himself, stepped over the line. Such had been his experience three years before the evening at Auteuil, in March 1784. The *Correspondance littéraire*—anxious as always to notify its subscribers, which included a significant portion of the crowned heads of Europe, of the growing spirit of insubordination among the French elites—hastened to report on the episode: "When the Queen, they say, requested a number of couplets from M. le Vicomte de Ségur, the latter initially balked; but as Her Majesty insisted, adding: *You need only to tell me the truth about myself,* he sang to her the following lines:

On dit, chanson. Sur l'Air: Mon père était pot, ma mère était broc, etc.

Voulez-vous savoir les on dit
Qui courent sur Thémire?
On dit que parfois son esprit
Parait être en délire.
Quoi! De bonne foi?
Oui; mais, croyez-moi,
Elle sait si bien faire,
Que sa déraison,
Fussiez-vous Caton,
Aurait l'art de vous plaire.

*Everyone establishes a system / Tailored to his own ends / And reason is no longer able to judge / What to permit or condemn. / Thanks to this tolerance, / I watch the lovely days flow past, / And keep constant company / with Graces and Loves. / Sometimes I go astray, but it isn't with drunkenness; / Pleasure's blindfold is always over my eyes, / And if my old age is troubled by a bit of remorse / At least my memories will be pleasant ones.

On dit que le trop de bon sens
Jamais ne la tourmente;
Mais on dit qu'un seul grain d'encens
La ravit et l'enchante.
Quoi! De bonne foi?
Oui; mais, croyez-moi,
Elle sait si bien faire,
Que même les Dieux
Descendraient des cieux
Pour l'encenser sur terre.

Vous donne-t-elle un rendez-vous
De plaisir ou d'affaire;
On dit qu'oublier l'heure et vous
Pour elle c'est une misère.
Quoi! De bonne foi?
Oui; mais croyez-moi,
Se revoit-on près d'elle,
On oublie ses torts,
Le temps même alors
S'envole à tire-d'aile.

Sans l'égoïsme rien n'est bon,
C'est là sa loi suprême:
Aussi s'aime-t-elle, dit-on,
D'une tendresse extrême.
Quoi! De bonne foi?
Oui; mais croyez-moi,
Laissez-lui son système;
Peut-on la blâmer
*De savoir aimer.**

*Hearsay, a song. To the tune of: My father's a pot, my mother's a jug, etc.

You're looking to hear what they say / About she who's succeeded Thémire? / They say that at moments her mind / Seems to be *en délire*. / What! Can it possibly be? / Oh yes; but, believe you me, / She has it so well in hand / That this madness of hers, / Were you Cato himself, / Would be able to please.

Scatterbrained, hungry for adulation, fickle, self-centered, but an expert in the art of pleasing: here were the truths that Marie-Antoinette, determined to exercise a political influence, had absolutely no desire to be reminded of, even in courteous banter. And as if that was not enough, weren't Joseph-Alexandre and his brother, Louis-Philippe, the sons of a minister who was indebted to her for his position? Hadn't the Queen, four years earlier—skillfully maneuvered by Besenval[116] and Mme de Polignac, certainly—demonstrated for the first time her influence over her husband by insisting that the Maréchal de Ségur be made minister of war against the wishes of Maurepas? But it was above all the Vicomte's behavior vis-à-vis her lady-in-waiting, Mme de Bréhan, that had outraged Marie-Antoinette: Joseph-Alexandre had betrayed the confidence she had shown him by welcoming him into her intimate circle, and he no longer deserved to be part of it.

However, the Queen had forgotten that the logic of feeling was not necessarily that of politics, and that banishing Ségur from her entourage meant making an enemy of him. For three generations, the Ségurs had been bound to the Orléanses by ties of blood and friendship, and now, no longer welcome at Versailles, Joseph-Alexandre would naturally find a place waiting for him at the Palais-Royal, center of the new aristocratic Fronde's opposition. When, upon becoming Duc d'Orléans in 1786, the future Philippe Égalité named him first gentleman of the chamber, the Vicomte found himself enlisted in a *guerre d'opinion* that would have fatal consequences for the French monarchy.

In contrast to his brother, Louis-Philippe, who had become Louis XVI's ambassador to Catherine of Russia in 1784, Joseph-Alexandre was not moved

---

They say that she's never tormented / By too much good sense; / But that one single grain of incense / Leaves her ravished, enchanted. / What! Can it possibly be? / Oh yes; but believe you me, / She has it so well in hand / That the Gods themselves / Would descend from the skies / For her sake to perfume this, her land.

Has she granted you an appointment / For business or pleasure? / After a moment, be sure / She'll no longer remember. / What! Can it possibly be? / Oh yes, but believe you me, / When you meet her again face-to-face / All her wrongs are erased / And time itself, scattered by pleasure / Wings off out of sight.

Without selfishness nothing is good, / That's her supreme law: / Therefore, they say, she loves herself / With an extreme fondness. / What! Can it possibly be? / Oh yes, but believe you me, / But let her alone; / Can we possibly blame her / For knowing how to love?

by a specific political vision. He limited himself to sharing the reformist and liberal hopes that were on the agenda in various Parisian salons, beginning with that of his mother. This did not prevent him from closely commenting on the rapid shuffling of ministers and the proliferation of fruitless attempts to repair the public deficit, and amusing the *bonne compagnie* with his taste for paradox and his ironic verve. The Maréchal de Ségur's presence in the royal cabinet had always managed to act as a curb on the Vicomte's caustic wit, but now his decision to resign left that irreverence unchecked.

On May 23, 1787, at the Opéra, as the *Correspondance secrète* faithfully reports, the Vicomte responded to someone asking whether it was true that his father had given up his duties as minister of war by saying: "'I have no idea, but it would not be surprising. After all, the King himself is about ready to give up his own!' This sarcasm was overheard, and the author, seized as he left the performance, was placed under arrest for three days."[117]

His insolence was too great to pass unremarked, and Joseph-Alexandre received the order to depart for the countryside—to Luzancy, the beautiful estate of the Comte de Bercheny, a cousin on his mother's side, not far from La Ferté-sous-Jouarre, about thirty miles east of Paris. Limited to a handful of months, and far from unpleasant, this exile nevertheless had enormous consequences for the House of Orléans and the French monarchy. For it was in fact at Luzancy that the Vicomte made the acquaintance of Choderlos de Laclos, whose regiment was garrisoned in the region, and whom he promised to help find a position at Palais-Royal.

A great admirer of *Les Liaisons Dangereuses* (it is no accident that the title of his scandalous play, *Le Parti le plus Gai*, borrows a phrase from Valmont), the Vicomte must have been thrilled to meet its author. But was he aware that Laclos had been rusticated to this little country village thanks to his own father's severity? Though *Les Liaisons Dangereuses* had been published anonymously, the minister of war had not hidden his displeasure at learning that its author was a career military man, and the esteem of Laclos's superior officers had been the only thing that saved him. But when four years later Laclos had the imprudence to publish and put his name to *Letter to M.M.D. of the Académie Française on the Eulogy of M. le Maréchal de Vauban*, in which he allowed himself to criticize that great man,[118] Ségur demanded that he be made an example of. Laclos was forced to leave the artillery school at La Rochelle where, liked by all, he had made good use of his military expertise, and to rejoin his regiment in the provinces, tearing himself with despair from the arms of his beloved young wife, whom he had managed to marry, after a thousand difficulties, only a few days earlier.

It was then that he decided to leave the army. He was forty-eight years old, and though in twenty-eight years of service he had never stepped out of line, neither had he managed to achieve any advancement other than that which came with seniority. Now the minister's stance left him with no illusions regarding his future. And yet, whose career could have been more blameless than his? He belonged to a family of the cultured minor nobility that had distinguished itself in the service of the King. He was intelligent, energetic, and ambitious, and had enthusiastically embraced his military career by joining the artillery, the most scientific division of the army, requiring as it did great study and technical preparation. There he distinguished himself by his zeal, his spirit of sacrifice, and his respect for discipline, and when Louis XVI had declared war against England, he thought his chance had finally arrived to prove himself in the field. But it was all in vain. For three years he had traveled the coasts of Normandy and Brittany, planning fortifications that would prove useless, inasmuch as the cross-Channel invasion never took place. Laclos certainly was not the only one disappointed—the letters of the Duc de Lauzun and the Chevalier de Boufflers bear witness to the same set of frustrations, despite their varying situations—still, like so many other officers, Laclos had resigned himself to missing out on his destiny. Ultimately, it was in witnessing the triumphal return of those privileged young men who had been granted the opportunity to win glory in America, that "his heart shattered."[19] He remained at his post, but vented his contempt for a system of government founded on royal favor, and with no regard for individual merit, in a caustic novel set in a vain and oblivious aristocratic society, blind to the evil eating it away from within, and ultimately devoted to self-destruction. Ready as always to crown any literary work that put it on trial, so long as it was amusing and adhered to the customary elegance of form, the *bonne compagnie* devoured *Les Liaisons Dangereuses* as a libertine roman à clef. Still, the book's political significance was obvious to all those who had weighed the real issues facing the country and saw the urgent need for moral renewal. On the ships that were carrying them to the rescue of the American rebels, those members of the gilded youth that Laclos so envied amused themselves at the expense of the Baron de Montesquieu, a grandson of the author of *The Spirit of the Laws*—the only one who had not read the novel, and who couldn't understand what "*liaisons dangereuses*" meant. When their ship was broadsided by an enemy and the bench where they had been sitting only a moment before was smashed to pieces, "the Comte de Loménie, who was always by Montesquieu's side, pointed it out to him and coolly remarked: 'You want to know what *liaisons dangereuses* are? Take a good look—there you have it!'"[120]

It was on the strength of the ambiguous success of his novel—midway between "blame and praise, disdain and esteem"[121]—that Laclos began to imagine a new life for himself in the heart of Parisian society, where his status as a man of letters seemed to have wiped away distinctions of class. Nevertheless, the latter was still a tenacious factor in the treatment that the French monarchy accorded its servants. Fifteen years his junior and significantly less competent, the Vicomte had already been made colonel of a regiment that bore his name, and enjoyed the sort of freedom to which a simple officer could never aspire. The Maréchal de Ségur (himself the author of an anachronistic ordinance[122] that reserved access to the higher ranks in the army for the nobility) did not limit himself merely to taking Laclos to task for publishing what was considered an immoral book but also punished him harshly for having aired his doubts on the utility of Vauban's fortifications. Meanwhile the Maréchal's son, who served in the selfsame army, could propound libertinism as an ideal of life, raise scandal by performing in plays, and mock the King and Queen without incurring the least measure of discipline.

Laclos was used to disguising his feelings, and, regardless of his opinion of the Vicomte, knew how to gain his confidence. So it was that, on his return to Paris, Joseph-Alexandre proposed to the Duc d'Orléans that he take the author of *Les Liaisons Dangereuses* into his service in the capacity of *secrétaire des commandements*. In October 1788, Laclos left the army to become the strategist of the secret war that the First Prince of the Blood had declared on Versailles.

For a century and a half, it had been the policy of the ruling French family to forbid the Orléanses any appointment that would allow them to exercise a public role. Still, though removed from the scenes of action and reduced to a luxurious idleness, the younger branch of the Bourbons had not renounced its desire for independence, but had distinguished itself by its patronage of the arts, liberal ideas, and support for parliament. Aiding the opposition was its sole means of forcing its crowned cousins to pay heed to its continued existence. In the wake of the glorious parenthesis of the Regency, the next two generations of the Orléanses—each for its own reasons—had withdrawn from the spotlight, retiring into their palaces, and the repeated attempts of the young Duc de Chartres to gain a reputation for himself had only exposed him to ridicule. But upon becoming Duc d'Orléans on the death of his father in November 1785, the future Philippe Égalité decided to raise his family's profile once again. The monarchy's loss of authority, and its obvious difficulty in resolving the economic crisis, allowed him some hope of revenge.

Many years later, Talleyrand, a master of the art of glossing over embarrassing memories, would write: "I have thought that a picture of the life of the Duc d'Orléans would give the features and the color of the weak and transient reign of Louis XVI; that it would set forth in a tangible manner the general laxity of public and private manners under that reign, as well as the degradation in the form of government and in the habits of the administration."[123] It was the simple truth—though he neglects to mention that there were many (he himself chief among them) who counted on Orléans to weaken that reign and hasten its end.

The habits of the Duc were of a piece with those of numerous other representatives of the high nobility at court, for whom transgression had become the norm. But even if the *filles* of the Opéra mourned his marriage, as was said, only for a rather short time, Chartres—unlike Lauzun—was careful at least not to disregard his wife. The daughter of the Duc de Penthièvre, and an illegitimate descendant of Louis XIV, Louise-Marie-Adélaïde de Bourbon had brought as her dowry in 1769 the promise of an immense fortune and made him a father four times over—and the Duc showed his gratitude. They frequented Versailles together and enjoyed cordial relations with the royal family. They were both young and shared the same desire for amusement. While the Duchesse de Chartres urged Marie-Antoinette to patronize Mme Bertin for her clothing, Chartres and Lauzun—then still in favor at court—launched the fashion for horse racing and Anglomania, and initiated d'Artois into the ways of libertinism. But toward the end of the 1770s things changed, and the Duc suffered a long series of humiliations.

He was refused an admiralty and denied permission to leave to fight in America; and in peacetime, too, the authorization for him to travel to London, to amuse himself with the Prince of Wales, was slow in coming; Louis XVI allowed himself to intervene and lecture the Duc about his personal life; on the occasion of the visit of Maximilian of Habsbourg, the brother of Marie-Antoinette, the royal family broke with etiquette in failing to recognize his right of precedence over foreign princes, and neglected to follow through on the project of marrying his sister to the Duc d'Angoulême. And what to say about Lauzun, his close friend, who had been ousted from his command of the Gardes Françaises, a post for which he had been destined from birth? And what about the brave Marquis de Conflans, to whom the King had refused the cordon bleu because of his unkempt appearance, unleashing the implacable hatred of his daughter, the Marquise de Coigny, an intimate friend of the Orléanses? The list of malcontents who had gathered around the Duc was very long. And if rancor and the spirit of revenge had driven Orléans into the arms of the opposition, ambition played its part as well.

At first glance the Palais-Royal Fronde might seem somewhat anodyne, given that the Duc—vain, superficial, and fickle—was a slave to his own caprices. But in addition to bearing an illustrious name, he was the leader of French Freemasonry, had an immense fortune at his fingertips, and combined a keen business sense with a taste for luxury. His style of life, his lavishness, and his affability ended up winning him popular sympathy when he was so cruelly pilloried, and his princely residence at the heart of Paris became the rallying point for those who no longer identified with Versailles. Building upon its intellectual and social supremacy, the French capital now aimed to achieve political primacy as well. It was in the capital, and no longer at court, where the fate of the country was decided, and the first Prince of the Blood could not have chosen a better springboard.

But Orléans himself did not have a clear political project and, too indolent and inconstant to elaborate one, he delegated this task to a mistress who was lacking in neither tenacity nor imagination. Ever since childhood, Félicité Ducrest de Saint-Aubin's had been a passionate busybody, and as she grew older, pedagogy—that key term of the Enlightenment—became her vocation. An autodidact (her sole instructor had been a music teacher), a methodical and indefatigable reader, and a graphomaniac, Félicité, aided by an unusually strong memory and sense of discipline, had accumulated an encyclopedic knowledge that allowed her to express an opinion on practically everyone and everything. She had honed her powers of persuasion on adults long before having the chance to use it on children. Born into a provincial family of the lesser nobility in 1746, poor and just barely pretty, she managed to convince the Comte Brûlart de Genlis (later the Marquis de Sillery) to marry her without the consent of his clan, going on to win the family over bit by bit, and finally making her entrance into high society. Mme de Montesson, her mother's stepsister, had unintentionally fostered her admission to Palais-Royal by engaging her as an actress and playwright in her theatrical troupe—and the resourceful Comtesse's intellectual vivacity, artistic gifts, and powers of seduction had taken care of the rest. Named a lady-in-waiting to the sweet and guileless Duchesse de Chartres, Mme de Genlis had swiftly become the Duc's mistress, and moved to accommodate her whole family at court: her husband (no less free-spirited than herself) was appointed as captain of the guards, and her brother, the Marquis de Crest, as the Prince's chancellor; later on, she would add to these her two sons-in-law, Valence and La Woestyne. Once she had taken control of the little court, Mme de Genlis managed to convince her lover to entrust to her the education of his children.[124] The success of the four volumes of her *Theatre for the Use of Young People*, published in 1779, and followed three years later by *Adèle and Théodore, or Letters on Education*, certainly constituted a fine testimonial. But until now no one had ever seen a "tutor" to young princes wearing skirts, and still less one using methods like those employed by the Comtesse. The instructress moved her charges to the Pavillon de Bellechasse and, taking advantage of her total authority over them, set about forging their bodies and minds according to a decidedly avant-garde set of pedagogical principles. Half a century later, having become King of France, the eldest of these pupils, Louis-Philippe, would acknowledge that despite her great severity, he had been well served by the experience.[125]

If the Comtesse's methods were inspired by Rousseau, her role model was Mme de Maintenon, who as the governess of the illegitimate children of the Sun King had eventually succeeded in becoming his wife, and his secret inspiration. Yet the influence that Mme de Genlis exercised on the Duc d'Orléans, even when she was no longer sharing his bed, was anything but occult. As ambitious for him as she was for her pupils, she pushed the Prince to take advantage of the difficulties the monarchy was struggling with in order to assure himself a position at the forefront of the country's leadership. It was she and her brother who, in 1787, upon the implementation of the new taxes, drove Orléans to step forward for the first time by opposing in the presence of Louis XVI the legality of two royal edicts he had come to register with parliament. The Duc was immediately exiled to Villers-Cotterêts, and the Vicomte de Ségur, newly appointed as first gentleman, was forced to follow him. However "that latest parliamentary crisis laid bare the weakness of the government. Necker was recalled to service, and the need for money forced the King to summon the Estates General."[126]

Thrilled with her role as political mentor, Mme de Genlis now received at Bellechasse the most uncompromising partisans of radical change, men like Barnave, Camille Desmoulins, Pétion, and Volney, and—setting aside all thoughts of Mme de Maintenon—looked boldly toward the future. How could she have imagined that her influence over the Duc was threatened, and that Laclos—whose entry into Palais-Royal she had tried in vain to prevent—would wind up supplanting her? The time had come for women to step aside: the Revolution would be the business of men.

Laclos had no sympathy whatsoever for the Duc d'Orléans, that vain and indecisive Prince whose choices were dictated by pride of caste, and who seemed to see politics as an internal family struggle. Before long, personal resentment was added to this contempt. Having asked the Duc why the patent of *Gentilhomme Ordinaire* that had been awarded to him was so slow in arriving, Laclos found himself answered with a burst of laughter: "They say that you aren't a *gentilhomme* at all." It was a gratuitous insult, since Laclos did, in fact, possess the requisite nobility for the position—and one he intended to avenge. And to the Comtesse de Bohm—who, hearing about the incident, had declared herself surprised since, "like all Paris," she had believed him to be "getting on very well with the Prince"—Laclos had menacingly replied: "You'll hear more before long. I'm at work on it."[127]

Like the libertines in his novel, the author of *Les Liaisons Dangereuses* possessed the art of dissimulation to the highest degree, and it allowed him to gain the confidence of his master and manipulate him as he wished. Mirabeau put it rather bluntly: "If you find yourself in need of a puppet, this idiot is as good as another."[128] The Duc's ambitions served as a screen for those, so long disappointed, of his secretary. Once Louis XVI's incapacity to rule and Marie-Antoinette's disgrace had become facts taken for granted thanks to a well-orchestrated propaganda campaign, it was the First Prince of the Blood who, fully observing the law and tradition, would assume the position of lieutenant general of the kingdom. This would deliver a hard first blow to royal absolutism, put an end to "ministerial despotism," and open a path toward the constitution, but it also would allow Laclos to take charge and finally exercise undisguised power.

From Lauzun to Sillery, Talleyrand to Liancourt, Mirabeau to Sieyès, there were numerous men who took part in this project, but there is no doubt that it was Laclos who "directed from behind the scenes those maneuvers that the Orléans faction engaged in from the end of 1788 until October 5 and 6." Then each of these plotters went on his respective way, abandoning the Duc to his tragic fate.

But for the Vicomte de Ségur, who, all unknowing, had introduced his own angel of death into the Palais-Royal, politics remained a salon amusement. Too intelligent not to understand the gravity of the crisis, he preferred to distance himself from it by lampooning the increasingly absurd language of good intentions. The *Correspondance littéraire* did not fail to report on his "Harangue," an "extemporaneous performance at a dinner given by M. le Baron de Besenval," where they had been celebrating the beginning of the year 1789: "Sire, your children...the people...the nation...you are their father...the constitution...the executive power in your hands...the legislative power... the balance of finances...the glory of your reign...the love of your people... Sire, the credit...the foundations of the monarchy shaken...everything comes together...everything reassures...and your equity...the eyes of Europe astonished...the spirit of sedition destroyed...the tears of your subjects...posterity...abundance...glory...patriotism...abuse of power...clergy... nobility...Third Estate...sublime effort...virtue...confidence...century of Enlightenment...the administration...the splendor of the throne...such rare beneficence...the centuries to come...wisdom...prosperity...voilà, the proclamations of your kingdom...the massing of a mighty nation...an epoch eternally memorable...the splendor of your crown, your benedictions...the virtues of Louis XII, the kindness of Henri IV...Sire, twelve plus four makes sixteen."[129] Only a few months later, charged as deputy commander of the Army of Paris with preserving order in the capital, the Baron de Besenval would be among the first to reveal himself unequal to the task with which, in a supreme irony, he had been entrusted eight years earlier by his friend, the Marquis de Ségur,[130] when he retreated in the face of the insurgents. But for all that, both he and his son would not cease to display their imperturbable good humor, or to turn tragedy into farce.[131]

The Duc de Brissac

Yes, my final thought will be of you.

—Duc de Brissac[1]

Before crossing the threshold of the Hôtel de Brissac[2] in order to review, room by room, the precious collection of art gathered within, the *Guide des Amateurs et des Étrangers voyageurs à Paris* by Luc-Vincent Thiéry, published in 1787, takes care to introduce its readers to the master of the house. He is a great gentleman, a lover of beauty and ostentation, who retains by family tradition the enviable privilege of carrying out his military duties under the direct command of the sovereign. Indeed, "Messire Louis-Hercule Timoléon de Cossé-Brissac, Duc de Cossé, Peer of France," the guide adds, was "the King's Marshall of Camps and Armies, Captain Colonel of the Hundred Swiss, Governor of the Town, Provost and Vicomté of Paris since the month of February 1775, and Chevalier of the Ordres du Roi since 1776."[3]

The most prestigious post held by the Duc, besides his duties as first baker of France,[4] was that of governor of the town, which his father had occupied as well—a species of *droit de famille*, since it had been a Maréchal de Brissac who had handed the keys of the city to the sovereign on March 22, 1594, at the tumultuous beginning of the reign of Henri IV. Even if the appointment had taken on an essentially honorary character since then, it allowed its bearer to take orders from no one but the King, and conferred upon the governor the right of "entry, attendance, and deciding vote in the Grand Chamber of Parliament, in his hereditary capacity of Honorary Counselor."[5] Moreover, like the Princes of the Blood and lay peers, the governor had the right to attend parliament dressed in "a coat of gold cloth, or of velvet, or a black cloak, a short coat, a toque or cap decorated with feathers, and with a sword at his side," and to be escorted by "guards and pages."[6] The celebrations organized by the Duc in honor of his accession showed the solemnity of the moment: "After a superb ball given on February 25, attended by the whole court, the royal family, and even the Queen, who did not leave until six o'clock in the morning, [the Duc] was received today by parliament, whereupon he enjoyed the precious and remarkable prerogative of distributing money to the people."[7]

However, at least according to Saint-Simon, his "most important and finest" duty, "after those of the royal household,"[8] was without question his command of the Cent Suisses, the King's personal bodyguard.

All of these titles and duties made Louis-Hercule-Timoléon de Cossé—who became the eighth Duc of Brissac upon the death of his father in 1780—a typical example of the old nobility of the court, integrated (like the Duc de Lauzun, the Ségur brothers, the Comte de Narbonne, and so many other members of the second order) into the heart of the monarchical machine. But his loyalty to the Crown was by no means dependent on the favor of the sovereign: regardless of his personal convictions, the Duc, whether in good odor or ill at court, was and would remain a faithful servant to the monarchy. When faced with difficult choices, his maxim was: "I do what I do out of obligation to the ancestors of the King, and to my own."[9]

At the publication of Thiéry's guide in 1787, the Duc de Brissac was fifty-two and had not enjoyed the sovereign's favor for a dozen years. Marie-Antoinette had never forgiven him for his relationship with the Comtesse du Barry, the last mistress of Louis XV, and the Marquis de Bombelles's *Journal* illustrates the indignation of the conformists at court around the issue: "M. le Duc spends all of his time at her [du Barry's] side, and his foolish pride revels in having replaced in the arms of *Mlle l'Ange* the monarch who should never have known her, no, not so much as her name."[10] As we are now aware, that isn't exactly how things happened—but to do the two lovers justice, we will have to turn back the clock and retrace their story.

Born in 1735, the second son of the Maréchal de Brissac, Louis-Hercule-Timoléon had a physique worthy of the mythological hero whose name his father had casually given him, and was trained from an early age in the military arts. The superb portrait of him by François-Hubert Drouais in the museum of Versailles shows him nearing forty and dressed in the sumptuous uniform of a colonel of the Cent Suisses; in a luminous face with regular features, his plump lips wear the hint of a smile beneath a brown musketeer's mustache.

At the death of his brother in 1749, Louis-Hercule-Timoléon found himself in the position of the eldest son, and his parents hastened to find him a wife of appropriate rank. The following year, he wed Adélaïde-Diane-Hortense-Délie

Mancini-Mazarini. It was as prestigious a union socially as it was in terms of inheritance. The bride's father, the Duc de Nivernais—grandnephew of Mazarin, Duc and Peer of France, Grandee of Spain, Prince of the Holy Roman Empire, and ambassador for Louis XV—was a leading figure at court as well as in the capital, and combined a man-of-the-world elegance with vast and solid erudition. A genuine savant and member of various academies, Nivernais was also a talented author whose *Fables*, which he read aloud with incomparable grace, were the delight of high society. In keeping with the sort of strategy common among the aristocracy of the ancien régime, his marriage to Hélène Françoise Angélique Phélypeaux, a daughter of the Comte de Pontchartrain and half sister of the Comte de Maurepas, had helped reinforce and extend his family's network of alliances.

The union of the Duc de Cossé, then aged twenty-five, with the "charming Mancinette"[11] was part of this logic, supplementing the longstanding friendship that already bound the two families. Addressing himself to his son's father-in-law in the ornate style of affected courtesy that had been in vogue during the preceding century, and to which he remained loyal—"you would have thought you were seeing a courtier from the salons of Louis XIV"[12]—the Maréchal de Brissac expressed his affectionate happiness at these new familial bonds: "With these brief preliminaries I speed my son on toward his new father-in-law. That holy emanation of yourself, whose charms throw into relief my own dilapidation, has written me the finest letter imaginable. The dear little thing cannot doubt that my most tender love is hers, along with all my finest feelings."[13]

If the "dear little thing" was not quite a "holy emanation," she was indubitably formed in her father's image. The Comte Louis-Philippe de Ségur—the elder brother of Vicomte Joseph-Alexandre, and like him quite skilled when it came to conversation—testifies to the impact that the Duc had on his interlocutors: "No book could have imparted to me what I learned in the course of a few conversations ... with the Duc de Nivernais on the subject of tact, the nuances of grace, and delicacy of taste."[14] His *Letters on the Use of Wit* provide eloquent proof of his ability. So it is not surprising that the daughter of the Duc, initiated from childhood into the sort of worldly knowledge that was passed from generation to generation, should have assimilated the Duc's essential traits.[15] Aside from the fact that she "resembled her father" and possessed "agreeableness, superiority of character, gaiety, and honesty,"[16] the young Duchesse de Cossé was quite pretty, and in the first years of their marriage, when Walpole knew her, "she was vivacious, seemingly reasonable, and had a very good character."[17] She immediately fell in love with the husband her family had selected for her and made no secret of it. The Comtesse de Roche-fort, "*suitable* friend"[18] of Nivernais, describes her following her return to Saint-Maur, the country estate of the Pontchartrains, after her first customary visit with her husband to Versailles, as "always charming and very lively."[19]

Even though Louis-Hercule-Timoléon was an impenitent Don Juan—according to a contemporary journalist, his gaze lingered on the members of the fair sex even at his father's burial[20]—he was fully attentive to his young spouse, and the couple had several happy years together. Their union produced a son and a daughter, and thirty years later, when it came time to draw up his will, Brissac recalled the affection he had felt for his wife, from whom he had long been separated: "Your mother, whom I have always tenderly loved, will not be upset to speak with you about me; she knows me perfectly, and sym-pathized with me, loved me, and I did the same for her, my child, I assure you."[21]

But if contemporary accounts are to be believed, it was in the autumn of 1771, even as the Cossés were celebrating the birth of a male heir, that the first signs of a marital crisis provoked by the Comtesse du Barry made themselves felt. While the Duchesse broke with aristocratic custom and, following the precepts of Rousseau, threw herself lovingly into the care of her child and nursed him herself, her husband was in thrall to the King's new mistress.

Always au courant with the latest news from Versailles thanks to Choiseul, Mme du Deffand informed Horace Walpole, on September 25, 1771, that the Duchesse de Cossé had replaced the Duchesse de Villars—who had died a week earlier—as lady-in-waiting to the Dauphine, Marie-Antoinette. She hastened to clarify: "She would have refused with all her heart, but her hus-band, who is the darling of the Sultana, requested it of her without his wife's knowledge, and obliged the Duchesse to accept; however, since she is nursing her little girl [in reality the young Jules-Timoléon, then three months old], she will not be permitted to take up her duties until after the infant is weaned. Mme la Dauphine has nothing against her; but she is rather upset that one of her own female companions wasn't selected for the position."[22]

Twenty days after Mme du Deffand's letter, the Comte de Mercy-Argenteau, Maria Theresa's ambassador to Versailles, reported the situation to the Austrian Empress in almost identical terms. The Dauphine had not been informed of the nomination of her new lady-in-waiting until after the fact, by a note from the King. At first sight, the choice of the Duchesse de Cossé seemed unassailable, since the young woman enjoyed a general respect. However, added the ambassador, "the circumstance that gives her pause is that the Duc de Cossé is wholly under the sway of the *favorite*, that the latter has affected the nomination in question, and that, consequently, the Archduchess will be unable to place too much trust in her new lady-in-waiting.... What I fear most is that, in the wake of this first step, the dominant party will seek little by little to surround Mme the Archduchess with those loyal to the cabal."[23]

As a close friend of Louis XV, which guaranteed his personal safety, the Duc de Brissac had had ample opportunity to make the acquaintance of Jeanne Bécu—the young courtesan who had been known as l'Ange in the world of high-class prostitution—since the sovereign called him back to Versailles. After her official presentation to the court on April 22, 1769, under the title of the Comtesse du Barry, the King's new mistress had been installed above the royal bedchamber, in quarters originally intended for Cossé in his capacity as captain of the Cent Suisses. Relocated to the floor above, in the garrets, the Duc found himself in close proximity to the newly made Comtesse, toward whom he almost immediately demonstrated a chivalrous devotion.

We do not know if the Duc's resolute support for the King's favorite stemmed from simple loyalty to his monarch, or whether he was bewitched by the triumphant femininity of this surpassingly beautiful courtesan. We can, however, rule out the possibility that the Duc was driven by ambition to pursue the backing of the new official mistress, since, during the four years of Mme du Barry's "reign," he enjoyed no new appointments or promotions.

Indeed, the sole favor obtained by Cossé thanks to the intercession of the sovereign's mistress was the nomination of his wife as the Dauphine's lady-in-waiting. But did the request come to her from the Duc? Or was it not rather the King's idea, or that of the mistress herself? Had Louis XV wanted a young woman of irreproachable character by the side of the Dauphine and given credit for that choice to his mistress? Or had Mme du Barry herself suggested the candidacy of the wife of an incontestably loyal man, in hopes that the charming Duchesse would temper the hostility that Marie-Antoinette persisted in displaying toward her?

In any event, the enterprise proved disastrous.

Mme de Cossé did not appreciate being forced to assume a role that, while certainly honorable, was also quite constraining. The Duchesse did not enjoy life at court and was, at that time, entirely absorbed by the needs of her new child. Moreover, like the majority of the women of the upper aristocracy, Mme de Cossé considered the installation of a prostitute at Versailles an unacceptable scandal, and no doubt experienced her nomination at the suggestion of the King's mistress as a species of insult. Though she yielded in order to please her husband and out of respect for the Dauphine, things changed for the worse when that resentment was further enflamed by jealousy.

A year after her appointment, having won the confidence of Marie-Antoinette, the Duchesse made clear that she did not intend to play a mediating role in Mme du Barry's favor—indeed, that she would use her position to exacerbate tensions between the King's mistress and the Dauphine. Poor Mercy-Argenteau did not fail to report to Empress Maria Theresa: "Today [October 28, 1772] there was a great annoyance, in which I was obliged to intervene. This evening the Duc de La Vrillière gave a dinner for the Comtesse du Barry; he invited Mme la Dauphine's lady-in-waiting, the Duchesse de Cossé, who refused to come.... That refusal ... raised a great scandal; it resulted in bitter reproaches to the Duc de Cossé; it was demanded that he exert his authority over his wife.... With the aim of reestablishing himself in the favorite's graces, he wrote a letter to his wife in which he insisted in very strong terms that she show all kinds of attentions to the Comtesse du Barry, and not refuse to do anything that might please her. The Duchesse de Cossé responded to her husband that when she had taken on her new role she had gone to pay homage to the Comtesse du Barry, but that now she would do nothing else that might cause anyone to think she was part of the favorite's company, that she would never change her mind about this, and that she preferred to offer her resignation."[24]

But the reason that Mme de Cossé finally left the service of Marie-Antoinette three years later had nothing to do with Mme du Barry, who, after the death of the Well-Beloved, had abandoned the court. From the very beginning little Jules-Timoléon's health had been fragile, and despite the tender care of his mother, his state had worsened. The Duchesse repeatedly asked Marie-Antoinette, who had become Queen in May 1774, to be relieved of her duties, but the Queen, mindful of her good qualities,[25] insisted that she remain. In the spring of 1775, when Mme de Cossé once again presented her resignation so as to be able to accompany her son for a spa cure, Maria Theresa's ambassador succeeded in convincing her, in the Queen's interest, to defer the decision until her return.[26] Mme de Cossé consented to this delay, and her resignation was delivered in July of the same year—though in a rather unusual fashion.

In leaving Marie-Antoinette's service, the Duchesse felt it incumbent upon her to tell the Queen (as Mercy-Argenteau acknowledged despite his concern for protocol) a number of "terribly concerning truths": "She went into detail regarding the behavior of those at court, describing the sort of betrayals of confidence that foment the spirit of intrigue and faction, and the various ways courtiers engineered situations they could then turn to their personal advantage. These reflections were supported by various examples."[27]

We can imagine that these must have included the Duchesse's difficulties during the years in which Mme du Barry was ascendant—but the idea of offering the Queen the reflections that had ripened during the last four years in her service as a *testament* of loyalty"[28] before her departure, was in the purest Nivernais style, and recall those penetrating pages written by her father on "the state of the courtier."[29]

The Duchesse's initial retreat from the life of the court was soon followed, at the death of her son, by an estrangement from her husband. The grief that overwhelmed her left no room for the conjugal love that had graced the early years of their marriage, and soon enough aristocratic custom won out over the sentimental aspirations of the new era. From then on, the Duchesse and her husband would lead separate lives, though they always respected each other, and worked together to defend the brilliance of their family by hosting lavish receptions and safeguarding the future of their sole remaining daughter.[30] Wasn't that what really mattered?

Unlike his wife, Brissac remained committed to his duties at court, and his *saison des amours* showed no sign of ending. We cannot be sure when exactly his relationship with the Comtesse du Barry became a stable emotional bond, but we can certainly say that the Duc did not hesitate to take her side during the difficult years of her disgrace.[31]

Only two years after the death of the Well-Beloved, and showing precious little respect for the memory of his predecessor, Louis XVI dispatched to Mme du Barry—who had taken refuge with the Duc and Duchesse d'Aiguillon at Rueil—a *lettre de cachet* in which he ordered her to retire to the Abbey du Pont-aux-Dames near Meaux. Even if tradition called for the former King's mistresses to abandon the court, the recourse to so coercive a means as the *lettre de cachet*—a symbol par excellence of royal arbitrariness—in order to inflict on Mme du Barry the treatment usually reserved for prostitutes, was not an auspicious beginning for a young sovereign. That the desire for an exemplary punishment had originated with Marie-Antoinette—"the King has limited himself to sending the creature to a convent, and chasing from the court everything tarred with the name of scandal"[32]—gave to the measure a character of personal vengeance that seemed unworthy of the Crown.

Alone in a cell of that dismal, half-ruined building where she was treated like a criminal, Mme du Barry faced the ordeal that had been imposed upon her with dignity and courage. The irregular course of her life—from her beginnings as the illegitimate child of a cook and a monk, to her later position as a courtesan—had taught her to adapt herself to the most varied circumstances. But the harshness of her trade had not shaken her joie de vivre, and in good times as in bad she remained true to her sweet, compassionate, and generous nature.

Having been raised in a religious institution, Mme du Barry was familiar with convent discipline, and at Pont-aux-Dames, she found comfort in the prayers of her childhood. Her humility and resignation gained her the sympathy of the nuns, who worked to make her daily life easier. Faced with her exemplary behavior and pressed by such illustrious personages as the Prince de Ligne, Louis XVI soon showed himself inclined to leniency, allowing the Comtesse the possibility of receiving visitors, and returning to her the management of her own financial affairs. At the end of a year of imprisonment, Mme du Barry regained her freedom, but on the condition of residing at least ten leagues from Paris and Versailles. She seized the opportunity to purchase the château of Saint-Vrain, some thirty miles from Paris, where her nephews and sister-in-law joined her, and where she was once again able to take up her social life. Finally, in the autumn of 1776, thanks to the intervention of Comte de Maurepas, the uncle of the Duc d'Aiguillon, who had returned to his duties as prime minister after twenty years in exile, she was able to establish herself at Louveciennes, the place she loved more than any other. Just at the cusp of her thirties, very rich and still quite beautiful, the former mistress began a new life.

For the first time without a master and unconstrained, Jeanne could put her own pleasure first. Louis XV had given her free rein to indulge her passion for beautiful things—clothes, jewels, precious objects, furniture, porcelain, paintings, statues—and like Pompadour before her, her name was attached to a moment of transition in French art: *le style du Barry*.[33] As official mistress, du Barry had displayed the originality and confidence of her taste at Petit Trianon, that architectural gem built for Pompadour by Ange-Jacques Gabriel at Louis XV's command, on the grounds of Versailles. Mme du Barry had selected the decor, turning her back on the mannered grace of the rococo style and opting instead for a refined simplicity. As for Louis XVI, he had handed the keys to this *locus amoenus,* formerly the preserve of royal mistresses, to his legitimate wife as a haven where she might enjoy the innocent pleasures of private life. And though Marie-Antoinette claimed that she wanted to purify the royal residence of all traces of the former mistresses, those "creatures," she had adopted their aesthetic choices and carried them to their logical conclusions. The apparent rusticity of Petit Trianon rendered its luxury even more scandalous: "Royalty has here endeavored at great expense to conceal itself from its own eye. But the attempt is vain,"[34] wrote Gouverneur Morris in 1789. And if Marie-Antoinette found refuge there in the company of a few close friends from the obligations of the court, those excluded tended to see it as a hotbed of conspiracy and suspect friendships.

Louveciennes, a property of the Crown, had been placed at Mme du Barry's disposal by Louis XV at the beginning of their relationship. It was a veritable Petit Trianon for her alone, a place where she could live as she pleased. Surrounded by a magnificent park, the château stood on a hill overlooking the green, wooded valley of the Seine, while on the horizon the steeples of Paris's churches stood in profile against the sky.

To better enjoy the beauty of the spectacle, the Comtesse had charged Claude-Nicolas Ledoux, a young architect of visionary talent, with constructing a pavilion on an earthen platform in the garden overlooking the river. With its three-columned imitation-Roman peristyle, the building inaugurated a new way of conceiving the relationship between nature and architecture, drawing its inspiration from antiquity. The grandiose oval vestibule (provided with a rostrum for musicians on the rear wall), with its ceiling painted by Boucher and its walls adorned with gray marble, could serve either as a reception hall or a theater. Chased like jewels, the various appurtenances in gilded bronze—chandeliers, door handles, and fire screens—were the work of the finest artisans of the time.

An engraving by Moreau le Jeune, *Le Souper à Louveciennes, 1771,* has immortalized the banquet offered by Louis XV's favorite to celebrate the opening of the pavilion. Dressed in white, the mistress of the house is seated at the side of the sovereign, at the end of an immense oval table, lit as bright as day by the enormous torches reflected in the mirrors and enlivened by a centerpiece of Doric columns fashioned by Ledoux, while the Comtesse's servants in their elegant red-and-gold livery serve the guests under the watchful eye of the King's Cent Suisses.

Was the Duc de Brissac in attendance at Louveciennes that evening? It stands to reason—but he certainly could not have imagined that several years later he would himself be this luxurious pavilion's guest of honor. A descendant of the Duc de Brissac, a historian of the house of Cossé, writes that "[the Duc] was the first to come to Saint-Vrain; he was the first to visit her at Louveciennes; and thus there emerged between these two beings tacitly drawn to each other though they exchanged no vows, a love that would last until their deaths."[35] But the author neglects to tell us the grounds on which this claim rests, and research into the family archives provides no answers. Even if we are inclined to take him at his word, we must wait until 1782 to find the first irrefutable evidence of the existence of a *relation amoureuse* between the Duc and the Comtesse. It comes to us from the Comte d'Allonville, who in that year had made the acquaintance of Mme du Barry in Normandy, where Jeanne had traveled in the company of Brissac. In describing that encounter many years after the fact, the memoirist gives us a full sense of his surprise at meeting the former favorite: "Prejudiced against her beforehand, my first reaction was one of curiosity, but that was soon succeeded by interest: In examining her, I could not reconcile what I had read about her with what her face proclaimed; one searched in vain for any trace of her former state in the dignity of her speech, the nobility of her manners, and that deportment equally removed from both pride and humility, license and prudery; the simple sight of her was enough to refute all that has been published about her. Indeed, she struck me as tremendously agreeable, and I easily believed she had inspired passion in those around her, as she had acquired a number of genuine friends. The one among these that did her the most honor was the Duc de Brissac, in whom uprightness of heart and elevation of character made up for wit, inspiring him during the course of our troubles to words and actions that have become historic. His disgrace, from which he emerged so nobly, he owed to his friendship with Mme du Barry; a friendship whose constancy proved that he had been drawn to her not by the lure of her favor but rather her true feminine qualities, which furthermore seemed to me more seductive than intellectual."[36]

Beginning in 1783, the *Nouvelles à la main*[37] had begun to allude to the relationship between the Duc and Mme du Barry as if it were old news; but while popular opinion continued to hammer away at the former favorite, views at court had changed dramatically. We find the echo of this alteration in the postrevolutionary memoirs of aristocrats. D'Allonville would be joined in his judgment by the Duc de Croÿ,[38] the Comtes Dufort de Cheverny[39] and d'Espinchal,[40] and the Marquis de Belleval,[41] who would go on to make public apologies for their earlier presumptions and testify to their admiration for the erstwhile prostitute who had become a perfect *honnête femme*. Certainly, as the Comte d'Allonville observes, the chivalrous love that Brissac bore for her helped to place her in a new light for others—but she herself was the one who made this metamorphosis possible in the first place.

A daughter of the people, Jeanne possessed a natural elegance as well as aristocratic manners acquired during her school years and perfected over the course of her career as a courtesan. In taking her under his roof in order to make a prostitute of her, Jean-Baptiste du Barry had concerned himself with more than merely her erotic education—he had instructed her in the customs and traditions of high society. Her clientele, composed of lords and gentlemen such as the Maréchal de Richelieu, served her as a school of libertinism, but also of good taste. Talleyrand would observe that unlike Mme de Pompadour, who, in spite of her excellent culture, "had bad form, and a vulgar manner of speaking, which she was unable to correct, even at Versailles ... Mme du Barry succeeded in expressing herself clearly ... and grasped the art of telling stories with gusto."[42] That said, it seems undeniable that her palpable kindness was not dictated by mere politeness but sprang from the heart. In spite of the "*vie infâme*"[43] to which she'd been driven by necessity, Jeanne had never shed her basic goodness.

During her years as the King's mistress, the young woman had tried to avoid the intrigues of the court and never sought to avenge herself for the various slights she received—"she did not even humiliate those she could afford to lose"[44]—and even during her period of disgrace she displayed the greatest deference to the ruling family. And it was well known that the scandalous fortune that she now possessed served not merely to satisfy her expensive tastes but also to relieve the poor and needy and to provide for the well-being of a whole tribe of relatives who for the most part did not deserve her generosity and caused her nothing but embarrassment.

Her passion for luxury was far from ostentatious, and was striking for its originality: in spite of the swarm of servants in her employ and an abode filled to bursting with paintings, statues, and precious objects of all sorts, the former mistress led an extremely simple life.[45] "In summer as in winter, Mme du Barry wore nothing but dressing gowns of percale or white muslin," recalled Mme Vigée Le Brun, who would paint her portrait in that rural setting, "and every day, no matter the weather, she would walk in her park or beyond it, without the exercise giving her the least trouble, since her sojourn in the countryside had rendered her health robust."[46] In her new life at Louveciennes, daily contact with nature answered not merely to an aesthetic concern in line with current fashion but was an essential source of physical well-being.

Mme du Barry's lifestyle commanded the respect of Laclos, who, after having written some insolent verses[47] at her expense during her tenure as official mistress, did not hesitate to pay homage to her, as "Elmire," even at the height of revolutionary fervor: "Since Elmire was forced to leave the King's residence, she has chosen for herself a tranquil retreat, where she has passed her time without intrigues or projects, and without that disquiet that accompanies almost all who play some public role, whatever it may be. . . . Living in obscurity and without dissipation, she opens her enchanting hermitage to a small number of men who believe that chastity is a matter of social decorum rather than the mother of all virtues, and that it is possible to be at once greatly loving and greatly benign."[48]

Brissac was certainly one of those men, but he was by no means the only one. Before being able to take his siesta in the pavilion at Louveciennes,[49] confident in the affection of its mistress, the Duc was forced to demonstrate his patience. In fact, during the summer of 1779, Mme du Barry was besotted with an English gentleman who had recently come to live in her neighborhood. Fifty years old, Henry Seymour, a nephew of the powerful Duke of Somerset and half brother of Lord Sandwich, "was a man who for all his grand connections had never realized his talents."[50] Though by no means lacking in intelligence, his unpalatable character had stymied his political career, and he had left England laden with debt and at odds with his family. Seymour had installed himself in a small country house on the hill at Louveciennes with his second wife—a young French Comtesse who would soon bear him a child—and two daughters from his first marriage, and he maintained neighborly relations with

Mme du Barry. Intrigued by this handsome, haughty Englishman—a "proud prince,"[51] as Horace Walpole called him—Jeanne lavished him with kindnesses. In 1781, proposing that William Beckford visit Louveciennes, Ledoux was sure that Mme du Barry would welcome him there, since she had heard him spoken favorably of by "M. Seymour, who at the moment enjoys the sunshine of her favor; and believe you me, [that favor] is a solar radiance terrifically dazzling when she shows herself inclined to dispense it."[52] Eight brief letters to Seymour from the Comtesse, written most likely over the course of the two years that followed his arrival at Louveciennes, allow us to trace the course of her affections for him from beginning to end.[53]

The first two show us Mme du Barry bent on the conquest of her neighbor. "It has long been said that friendship is maintained by pampering,"[54] she feels the need to emphasize when sending him carefully selected gifts: a puppy for his ill daughter, a rare coin from the epoch of Louis XIV. But with the third letter, in which she declares "The assurance of your tenderness, my sweet friend, would fill my life with happiness. . . . I await your coming on Saturday with all the impatience of a soul that is entirely yours,"[55] no further doubt is possible. Here the writer is clearly a woman in love, and one who knows herself loved in return: it was a moment of grace that would not last. What inspired the reproaches that Seymour soon felt himself entitled to send to Jeanne? Was it the presence of another man in her life that spurred his jealousy? Was the person in question Brissac? Though the Comtesse certainly sought to reassure him ("Adieu, I await you with all the impatience of a soul that is entirely yours, and which, despite your unfairness, feels full well it can belong to no one else"[56]), the effort was wasted. Stern and arrogant, Seymour made demands of her while conceding nothing, and punished his mistress by refusing his presence and leaving her in uncertainty. For her part, after attempting in vain to mollify him, Jeanne, in a letter stamped with dignity, decided to break off a relationship that had called her whole way of life into question: "You have not condescended to reassure me on a matter that touches my soul; thus I believe that my peace and happiness matter little to you; it is with regret that I tell you this, but I do so for the last time. My mind is clear; my heart suffers. But with a great deal of effort and courage, I will master it . . . it is the last sacrifice that remains for me to make; my heart has managed to do so for all the others—in this case, my reason will do what is needed. Adieu, believe that you alone will hold my heart."[57]

The sole sign of a response we have from Seymour is an incensed phrase scrawled on the back of a miniature that Jeanne had offered him, and that he had returned to its sender: "*Leave me alone*."[58]

In the wake of this English asperity, Mme du Barry must have found the French gallantry of Brissac deliciously refreshing. There is no question that the Duc subsequently found a definitive place in her life. The marriage of his beloved daughter[59] freed him to carry on his relationship with the King's former mistress more openly. During this period, his estranged wife was growing more and more absorbed by her ill health. The victim of a powerful hypochondria, she made the rounds of doctors and spas, finally deciding to subject herself to techniques of Mesmer—with disastrous results. "Yet another victim of magnetism," commented Mme de Sabran. "She is in a pitiful state: spitting pus and blood. The doctors have forbidden her to speak a word, so she sits in the middle of her room making signs to whoever turns up, with a face like death warmed over."[60] Yet it was likely that her poor state of health saved her life. When the Revolution erupted, the Duchesse was under treatment in Nice, from whence she traveled on to Italy, not to return to France until 1798.

As in the old tales of chivalry, Brissac had surmounted each of the trials with which he had been faced (for love of Guinevere, hadn't Lancelot, in Chrétien de Troyes's telling, risked dishonor by mounting a filthy cart?[61]), possessed by the certainty that the sentiment of love, noble by nature, would purify its object. For her part, the former courtesan proved worthy of the radiant image that had seized the imagination of the captain of the Cent Suisses during his time at Versailles, now long past. And if the Duc's amorous fixation had come through unscathed, Jeanne found in him a partner who was capable of revealing her to herself.

Both of them enjoyed making love and did so expertly, but they were bound to each other by more than merely an erotic rapport. For both the immensely wealthy lord and the daughter of the people who had been forced to sell herself for money, the pleasure of life, the need for refinement and luxury, were accompanied by a profound kindness and desire for beauty. In spite of the social abyss that separated them, Jeanne proved to her lover that generosity and loyalty were by no means the exclusive appanage of aristocratic ethics. And for his part, Brissac allowed Mme du Barry access to the best part of herself by providing a sounding board for her ideas, feelings, and habits.

A staunch philanthropist, the Duc did not limit himself to theorizing about the principles of *liberté*, *fraternité*, and *egalité* in the Masonic lodge of the Collège de Clermont where, in 1777, he had succeeded the Prince de Conti as the grand master of the Order of the Temple. At the death of his father he had swung into action, undertaking at his own expense and with the most up-to-date methods the improvement of a vast swamp that had menaced the health of the inhabitants of Brissac and its environs for centuries. And since it was well known in the region that the Duc had a soft heart, it wasn't uncommon for a newborn infant to be abandoned in plain sight at the foot of one of the great trees in his park. He would invariably provide for the foundling until the moment when, supplied with a trade, the child was able to meet his own needs. A reader of the *Encyclopédie*, the Duc believed in progress. Like other great landowners of his era—the Marquis de Voyer, the Duc de Penthièvre, the Duc de Nivernais—he wanted to modernize agriculture and make the most of his lands, but not to the detriment of the animals that populated his forests. He did not hunt, giving the cold shoulder to that most exemplary of aristocratic sports because he could not bear the idea of killing the harts, stags, and roebucks whose beauty enchanted him. No one was permitted to indulge in the practice on his lands. He preferred to let the game destroy the crops, even if it meant repaying the peasants for the damage.

Sympathetic to Brissac's philanthropic credo, Mme du Barry also busied herself with transforming Louveciennes into an oasis of happiness untouched by poverty—and as the inventories of her paintings[62] reveal, her interest in children and animals was of long standing. Since her years at Versailles, the Comtesse had purchased numerous works by Drouais and Greuze for her private apartments depicting children playing with puppies or cats: an index of her sensibility that was not reflected in her official collection, which—in keeping with aristocratic canons of taste—consisted of royal portraits, mythological subjects, allegorical scenes, and landscapes.[63]

The interest with which both Brissac and Mme du Barry followed contemporary artistic life reinforced their bond. Now freed from the requirement of maintaining an ostentatious collection that would reflect on her prestige as favorite, the Comtesse found in Brissac a passionate connoisseur with whom to compare her tastes and choices. The Duc taught her to look at paintings with the eye of an expert—which is to say, as someone "fully informed as to the fine qualities of a thing presented for his judgment."[64]

The Duc had given irrefutable evidence of his aesthetic authority by beginning to assemble an important collection of artworks at the end of the 1760s. This enterprise was nothing exceptional in itself, since after the death of Louis XIV, the Princes of the Blood, lords, magistrates, and rich bourgeois had gradually taken over the role formerly occupied by royal patronage, and the private collection had become a distinctive part of the lifestyles of elites. The Duc de Choiseul, the Baron de Besenval, the Maréchal de Ségur, the Comte de Vaudreuil, to name only a handful of figures, are perfect examples. It has been estimated that over the course of the eighteenth century in Paris alone, more than seven hundred private collections were created, and they developed rapidly, often thanks to the breaking up of other, preexisting collections.[65] One thinks of the case (as exemplary as it was famous) of the auction of the collections of the Duc de Choiseul, at which the Prince de Conti acquired seventy-four paintings. But his collection, in turn, would be auctioned off at the time of his own death, a mere four years later. As for Mme du Barry—who, thanks to the enormous sums put at her disposal by Louis XV, had assembled during the brief period of her favor a remarkable collection of artworks, among which were various paintings that had belonged to Choiseul—she had been forced to sell the bulk of her art at the death of the Well-Beloved in order to pay off her creditors.

What distinguished Brissac's initiative and drew the attention of art lovers and connoisseurs was the quality of the paintings and objets d'art that he selected. In contrast to those of Choiseul, Vaudreuil, or Besenval, the Duc's collection has still not yet been studied, but Thiéry's guide and the two inventories of the works confiscated by the Revolutionary authorities from his mansion on the rue de Grenelle leave us in no doubt about its importance. It is particularly the second inventory, executed by Jean-Baptiste-Pierre Le Brun, which confirms the exceptional quality of the paintings. A collector, critic, and dealer, Le Brun was "one of the best art experts of his age"[66] on a European scale, and a great lover of Netherlandish painting. In contrast with his wife, Élisabeth Vigée Le Brun, the official painter of Marie-Antoinette, who had taken the path of exile after 1789, Le Brun remained in France, where he succeeded in having himself entrusted by the Revolutionary government with the delicate task of deciding which works confiscated from the enemies of the people deserved to supplement the royal collections of the brand-new museum (the future Louvre Museum), and which could be sold off. For each painting, Le Brun identified its author, categorized it, and gave the price it would fetch on the market. In assessing the value of the Duc's collection of paintings at 191,638 livres and earmarking the majority of those works[67] for the national holdings, he was rendering posthumous homage to the taste of its former proprietor.[68] Moreover, the confiscation on the rue de Grenelle allowed Le Brun to transfer to the museum numerous paintings of the Netherlandish school condemned by a revolutionary aesthetic that tended to be partial to history painting—depictions of heroism and civic virtue—and that considered the former school symptomatic of a bygone aristocratic taste.

Indeed, since the beginning of the eighteenth century the French elite, for whom refinement and elegance were watchwords, had displayed a curious passion for Dutch painting, with its rustic peasant interiors—indeed, "those bourgeois and moralizing scenes of everyday life popularized by Greuze and imitated by Lépicié and Debucourt were themselves deliberate homages to Netherlandish art of the seventeenth century." Still, though they represented a large part of Brissac's collection, the northern school, with paintings by David Teniers, Gabriel Metsu, Gerard ter Borch, Gerard Dou, Paul Bril, Adriaen van Ostade—as well as two portraits by Rembrandt—did not compromise the eclecticism of the whole.[69] As we know from Thiéry's guide, French art was widely represented as well, by landscape paintings, with two splendid seascapes by Claude Lorrain and canvases by Sébastien Bourdon and Claude-Joseph Vernet, as well as by royal portraits, with a Louis XV by Van Loo and a Louis XVI in coronation attire. Even though Italian painting had fallen out of fashion, the Duc had taken the opportunity to purchase a portrait of Charles-Quint attributed to Titian, as well as works by Annibale Carracci, Veronese, Ricci, and Bassano.

As with most great collectors of the era, Brissac's interests were not limited to painting. His collections included both antique and modern statuary, furniture, and precious objects, as well as porcelain,[70] answering to that classical taste that his familiarity with the splendid collections of art belonging to his father-in-law—Mazarin's successor—had probably contributed to reinforcing.

If the Duc's eclecticism was typical for collectors of his period, and if his choices could sometimes come across as conventional, he nevertheless shared with Mme du Barry a strong taste for the new when it came to contemporary painting. To decorate the half dome above her salon at Louveciennes, the Comtesse had preferred the classically inflected style of Joseph-Marie Vien to Fragonard, then at the height of his artistic powers.[71] The subject of his four large panels was one that had already been treated by Fragonard—*The Progress of Love in the Heart of a Young Girl*—but, since he had been forbidden the use of historical or mythological figures, Vien was "obliged to imagine his four allegorical subjects from scratch and, in order to dignify them, execute them in the Greek manner."[72] The painter's somewhat cold elegance did not prevent Brissac from using these paintings as part of a *jeu amoureux* with Jeanne, based on their shared tastes and interests, and on exchanges of gifts to which they alone possessed the key. In 1778, in homage to the mistress of Louveciennes, the Duc purchased *La Marchande à la toilette* (or *La Marchande d'amours*), the work to which Vien owed his success at the Salon of 1763. Inspired by a Roman painting discovered at Stabiae and preserved at the archaeological museum of Naples, this picture—"Vien's most original and, perhaps, most famous"[73]—depicts three women wearing antique dress in profile, as in a sculpted frieze. A young girl, a commoner, kneels with her right hand resting on a basket filled with cherubs, while with her left hand she holds one by the wing, offering it to a seated young matron. We know that in 1787 *La Marchande d'amours* was Brissac's "delight"[74] in his bedchamber on the rue de Grenelle, and the following year the Duc commissioned a painting entitled *L'Amour fuyant l'esclavage* from Vien to provide a counterpart to his own canvas for the Comtesse.[75] Though "love escaping from bondage" was certainly not *his* emblem, as he quipped to Mme du Barry in September 1789, he agreed with the critics that, in spite of a certain coldness and blandness, "the [canvas's] details and the finish, as well as its colors, are beautiful, and always lend this picture charm."[76] Five years later, on the 29th of Frimaire, Year Two, when, with Mme du Barry dead, Brissac's property was confiscated, *L'Amour fuyant l'esclavage* and *La Marchande d'amours* were both hanging in the bedchamber of the house's former owner.[77]

But the contemporary artist preferred as much by Brissac as by Mme du Barry was Élisabeth Vigée Le Brun. "She was made," wrote the Duc to his mistress on the occasion of the Salon of 1789, "to be generally loved and admired, and appears in public whenever she wishes."[78] Nobody could have captured Jeanne's beauty and understood the modernity of her taste better than Marie-Antoinette's favored painter. The two great portraits of the Comtesse that Vigée Le Brun executed at Brissac's request—the famous likeness in a straw hat from 1781, and another portrait with a rose from 1789—were perfect examples of the new model of femininity that the painter was promulgating to the women of her generation: lessons in the difficult art of simplicity. A straw hat or a headband of knotted gauze from which poured a cascade of curls had replaced the vertiginous coiffures of Léonard; a shift of white muslin barely embellished with a bit of lace trimming or a light dress drawn in beneath the bust by a ribbon had unseated the sophisticated outfits of Mme Bertin. In these portraits the Duc found reflected the cheerful hedonism of the mistress of Louveciennes—the "beauty, generosity, and sweetness, the pleasant and perfect steadiness of humor, that made her company so charming"[79]—and from their almond-shaped eyes with lids ever so slightly lowered there seemed to flow an unconstrained sensuality.

It was surely Mme Vigée Le Brun's skill at celebrating feminine beauty by infusing it with the breath of life that drove Brissac to collect her paintings and to request from her various portraits of his beloved[80]—and to commission from her, in the midst of the tragedy of the Revolution, a portrait of Lady Hamilton.

In Naples between 1790 and 1792, Mme Vigée Le Brun had executed three portraits of the celebrated Emma Hart, the mistress and, later, wife of Lord Hamilton, ambassador of His Britannic Majesty to Ferdinand IV of Bourbon. Like that of Mme du Barry, Emma's life had been like something out of "a novel."[81] Like Jeanne, Emma's origins were humble and, also like her, exceptional beauty had allowed her to leave them behind. In the course of her own career as a courtesan, Emma had cultivated a talent for mime, and soon came to excel at representing those various states of emotion—joy, sorrow, terror, ecstasy—that were in line with the new fashion for the sublime. Ceded by her Pygmalion, the honorable Charles Greville, to the passionate antiquarian Lord Hamilton and installed at the Palazzo Sessa with a view of Vesuvius, Emma expanded her repertoire to include a variety of mythological figures inspired by the frescoes of Pompeii and the Greek vase paintings collected by her new lover.

Now, having transformed herself into a work of art, Emma became a major draw in Naples, and more than one famous traveler—beginning with Goethe—recalled the excitement aroused by her tableaux vivants. The Comte d'Espinchal did not hesitate to admit his infatuation when faced with the spectacle of the beautiful Englishwoman. Reaching Naples at the beginning of the emigration, this severe gentleman had admired her, first while watching her execute a less than innocent tarantella—"Mme Hart infused it with a sensuousness, with a grace, that would have roused even the coldest and most insensible man"—then as she brought to life various "masterpieces of the most celebrated artists of Antiquity,"[82] and he finished by swearing that, if she had been his mistress, he would have demanded that she personify for him all the goddesses of Olympus. Painting a portrait of Emma must have presented a true challenge[83] for Mme Vigée Le Brun, since the young woman had already posed for the greatest painters in England and had served as George Romney's favorite model. It also meant returning to the mythological style of painting—with its Dianas, Minervas, and Hebes—that had dominated the portraits of the eighteenth century, and from which she had been happy to distance herself. After having seen Emma play the part of a "delicious" bacchante, "with vivid eyes and wild hair,"[84] Mme Vigée Le Brun first painted her at the edge of the sea, stretched out on a panther skin, a cup in her hand, then dancing with her hair tumbled by the wind, accompanying herself on a tambourine. But it was the Duc de Brissac's commission that allowed her to seek out the proper inspiration, and to interpret Emma's beauty in full agreement with her own genius.

Ever since Élisabeth Vigée Le Burn had sent a long letter to Mme du Barry relating her impressions of Naples,[85] Brissac was well aware that his favorite painter was hard at work on a series of portraits of the young English adventuress—and he hastened to reserve one of them, "a sibyl,"[86] for his own collection. But this time, it was Mme Vigée Le Brun's own aesthetic vision that ruled the day. Disapproving of Emma's way of dressing herself, and finding her "stage costumes" lacking in taste, she disregarded her model's extraordinary hair and wrapped her head in a shawl, "a kind of turban, one of whose ends descended to form a drapery,"[87] her pose inspired by the Sybil painted by Domenichino. Her later portrait of Mme de Staël as Corinne at Cape Miseno reproduces precisely the same iconography. Two French aristocrats fleeing the Revolution who have already crossed our path were admiring witnesses to this transformation. The first was Lauzun's mistress, the Duchesse de Fleury, and the second the Princesse de Monaco, a distant cousin of the Duc and daughter of that Comtesse de Stainville who had inspired his earliest passion.[88] When the sitting had concluded, and Emma had reappeared in her own clothing, these two French friends "had all the trouble in the world recognizing her,"[89] so ordinary did her appearance seem by comparison.

Mme Vigée Le Brun completed the portrait in Rome, where she returned in April 1792, but Brissac never took possession of the painting he had commissioned—he met his end five months later at Versailles, where he was murdered by a furious mob. One year later, Mme du Barry was executed in her turn in Paris, on the square that had once been known as the Place Louis XV.

Remaining in the hands of its creator, the Sybil accompanied Mme Vigée Le Brun on her travels across Europe, testifying to her talent wherever she went. If Brissac never had the pleasure of discovering Emma Hart's beauty for himself, his commission nonetheless seems to us today proof positive of his instinct as a collector. Universally admired, the English Sybil remains one of the most successful examples of Vigée Le Brun's skill at bodying forth the women of her era.

The Duc de Brissac was an unremarkable conversationalist and his writing was slapdash—in a society where wit and intellectual vivacity abounded, he did not enjoy the reputation of an intellectual.[90] But none of that prevented him from following what was transpiring in the culture around him with great attention. Drafted some two months before the fall of the Bastille, the manuscript catalog[91] of the books in his library in the rue de Grenelle shows the presence of seminal works of the culture of the Enlightenment. Among others, there figure Bayle's *Dictionary*, the Abbé de Saint-Pierre's *Dreams of a Good Man*, *The Spirit of the Laws* by Montesquieu, the twenty folio volumes of the *Encyclopédie*, *A Philosophical and Political History of European Settlements and Commerce* by Abbé Raynal, as well as the works of Voltaire, Helvétius, and Rousseau. The catalog particularly shows the interest that the Duc took in the political and institutional debates of the period. It includes the *Memoirs and Documents Relating to the Current Revolution, which Originally Began with the Assembly of Notables in 1780*; documents concerning the *Parliamentary Troubles—A Collection of Documents, Printed and in Manuscript, Concerning the Administration of Calonne, Brienne, de Lamoignon, and Necker*; and under the rubric of Estates General, the *Comprehensive Collection of All the Writings on that Subject: Collection of all the États Généraux of 1789; Complete and General Collection of Everything Published Relative to the États Généraux*. The list of periodicals and journals present in the library is no less instructive. Alongside such institutional publications as the *Mercure de France* and the *Année littéraire*, overseen by the royal censors, one finds the *Gazette de Leyde* and the *Courrier de l'Europe*, published outside of French territory; the extremely critical *Correspondance secrète et littéraire* (1770–1789) and the scandalous *Mémoires* of

Bachaumont (1766–1789), wherein Mme du Barry is frequently slandered. Two short notes penned by the librarian in the margins of the catalog indicate that on January 11, 1790, the Duc had taken out *The Year 2440* by Mercier and, the following day, Rousseau's *Social Contract*.[92] It would have been just in time for him to observe that the visionary utopia of these two works was rapidly taking its first step into reality.

His long-standing acquaintance with the writers and academicians he had first encountered at the home of the Duc de Nivernais, his affiliation with Freemasonry, and his philanthropic engagements had led Brissac to hope for a better future, and driven him to take part in the reformist efforts by which the monarchy of Louis XVI was attempting to shield itself from economic crisis and respond to the needs stemming from the country's modernization. He shared his convictions with Mme du Barry. We know that the latter had admired Necker,[93] and that in 1780, when Voltaire made his return to Paris after an absence of forty years, she had gone to pay homage to the philosopher. Near the end of the visit, Mme du Barry had bumped into a timid young man at the foot of one of the palace's grand staircases, who requested her advice on obtaining an audience with the old philosopher, ill and already overwhelmed by visitors. With the graciousness and goodwill that had always been her mark, Jeanne retraced her steps and interceded on his behalf with the Marquis de Villette, Voltaire's host, and then accompanied the visitor to the threshold of his apartments. This young stranger was Jacques-Pierre Brissot, the future leader of the Girondins, who describes this encounter in his memoirs. Recalling "her smile, so full of charm and generosity," he couldn't help but defend Mme du Barry in conversation with Mirabeau and Laclos, maintaining that, unlike the favorites that had preceded her, Louis XV's last mistress had never "despotically" abused her position.[94] "You are right," Mirabeau responded, citing a verse by Lingendes: "Even if she was no vestal, 'The fault lies with the Gods who made her so lovely.'"[95]

In the dozen letters from the Duc de Brissac found among Mme du Barry's papers at the time of her arrest,[96] one can feel the intensity of a passion untouched by time. "My impatience to meet you is as great as ever," wrote the Duc to his beloved in August 1786, "yes dear heart, the violent desire to be with you again—not in spirit, for I am always there, but in the flesh—is unflagging. . . . I kiss you thousands and thousands of times, with all my heart, till

Tuesday, or early on Wednesday."[97] And in an undated note, we find the same joyous effusion: "A thousand loves, a thousand thanks, dear heart; this evening I will be beside you, yes, it is my happiness to be loved by you. I kiss you a thousand times.... Farewell. I love you now and always."[98]

But we also observe that as 1789 approached, the political began to occupy a greater and greater place in their lives.

In a letter of August 16, 1787, the Duc confides to Mme du Barry his disappointment at "not having been appointed president of the provincial assembly of Anjou,"[99] and wonders about the reasons behind that exclusion. It was a decision that had come from high places—from the moment that the Duc's name had not even figured in the list of the hundred and fourteen nobles (thirty-six of whom were also ducs, his peers) chosen by the government to form the Assembly of Notables convoked in 1787, and once again in 1788, to debate the reforms needed to deal with the state's deficits and popular discontent.[100] So it was only logical that, fearing his resentment, the government would not want to entrust to Brissac the presidency of a provincial assembly, where he would be able to express to the gathering of nobles his dissatisfaction with the royal administration.[101] Apparently, his relationship with Mme du Barry had never really been forgiven.

Still, this rebuff did nothing to lessen the Duc's good-heartedness. Both he and Mme du Barry welcomed the convocation of the Estates General, convinced that the monarchy needed to take into account the demands of the new age. And the first manifestations of violence that followed the fall of the Bastille did not dampen his optimism.

It was necessary to resign oneself to enduring with good spirit "three or four people who disturb the tranquility that reigns around here," wrote Brissac on August 25, 1789, since "freedom is so precious that it certainly must be accepted in the end."[102] And four days later, in response to a "philosophical and learned" letter from the Comtesse, he admitted that the Estates General had not moved swiftly enough "on the real, principal issues that all France awaits." Yet he declared himself convinced that the nobles were ready to accept the sacrifices—first of all allowing the majority to vote by head, rather than by order—that had been demanded of them: "The nation must be made happy and peaceful at their expense, for they are everywhere unarmed and undefended."[103]

The Duc was correct: the long war of attrition by which the nobility and the clergy had defended their privileges through the systematic sabotage of reforms that seemed to threaten them, would not produce a new armed Fronde. But he did not anticipate that the violence would come from below, and that, powerless before the fury of the Jacobins, the oldest and most courageous aristocracy in Europe would utterly fail to defend itself. "An all-powerful education," insists Hippolyte Taine, "has repressed, mollified, enfeebled instinct itself. About to die, they experience none of the reactions of blood and rage.... If a gentleman is arrested in his own house by a Jacobin we never find him splitting his head open. They allow themselves to be taken, going quietly to prison; to make an uproar would be bad taste; it is necessary, above all things, to remain what they are, well-bred people of society."[104] Such, however, was not the case of the Duc de Brissac, who, when his hour finally came, sold his life dear.

The Comte de Narbonne

Never have I known a finer soul.

—*MEMOIRS OF THE DUCHESSE D'ABRANTÈS*[1]

"I DO NOT BELIEVE that at the end of the last century and during the first years of our own ... there has been a mind more refined and unusual, a heart more generous, a man more pleasant when it came to the business of life, nor one bolder, more sensitive, more capable of great things, than Comte Louis de Narbonne, minister of King Louis XVI since the Legislative Assembly, and aide-de-camp to the Emperor Napoleon in 1812. Luck alone was wanting for this man ... whose merit seemed sufficient for anything."[2]

In 1856, at the height of a brilliant university and literary career that had earned him the portfolio of minister of public education, Abel-François Villemain felt the need to do justice to the memory of the lord, dead for more than forty years, who had initiated him into political thought and to life in society, by dedicating a lovely descriptive passage to him at the beginning of his *Souvenirs Contemporains*. At the same time, the unfortunate fate of Louis de Narbonne offered the illustrious critic the key to understanding an entire epoch. On closer inspection, weren't the Comte's lost opportunities also those of the French monarchy, which had been unable to revive itself; of the Revolution, which had betrayed the liberal dream of 1789; and of Napoleon, who had been unable to maintain himself within bounds?

But it should not be surprising that in tracing the intellectual and moral profile of Narbonne, Villemain conscientiously omitted any mention of his private life.[3] Not only would it have risked compromising the exemplary image that the author intended to give of his hero but it would have shown just how incompatible the aristocratic manners of the past were with the present bourgeois ethic. And yet, to the eyes of the Comte's contemporaries, the connection between his private life and his public career had been obvious—beginning with the mystery of his birth.

"The birth of Comte Louis de Narbonne," acknowledged a nevertheless well-informed Comte d'Espinchal in 1792, "remains an unresolved problem, and so many singular tales have been spread on the subject that it would be difficult to winnow the truth from that heap of contradictory claims."[4] The only thing certain to us today is that he could not have been the son of Comte Jean-François de Narbonne—since well before Louis's birth, during the course of the War of the Austrian Succession in which Jean-François had served with the rank of captain, the latter had been gravely wounded by a gunshot in the lower abdomen that had stripped him of "any hope of posterity."[5] The Comte himself declared as much in person during his petition to Louis XV in February 1747, in which he requested that he be assigned a sedentary post in the army compatible with his disability.

The last descendant of an ancient family of Spanish origin that had been settled since the twelfth century in Aubiac, not far from Agen, the Comte de Narbonne could boast among his ancestors the counts of Castille, but his financial situation was more than precarious, and a military career represented for him—as for so many bankrupt nobles—the sole means of leading a dignified life. His petition was not in vain, and the royal benevolence shown to him exceeded all his hopes.

In fact, two years later, the Comte de Narbonne married Françoise de Châlus, the lady-in-waiting to the Comtesse de Toulouse, and shortly thereafter, without having reentered active service, he was promoted to colonel and almost simultaneously appointed as gentleman-in-waiting to the Infante Philippe, Duc de Parma, the husband of Louis XV's eldest daughter, Louise-Élisabeth. Narbonne immediately left his wife to live at Aubiac, and no longer showed himself at Versailles, without thereby hobbling his ascent: on becoming field marshal in 1762, he received the title of Duc and, two years after, that of Grandee of Spain.

At Versailles, nobody doubted that the reason behind this accumulation of exceptional honors was the Comtesse de Narbonne; and the birth of two children—Philippe-Louis, born in 1750, and Louis-Amalric, in 1755—during the absence of a husband whom everyone knew was incapable of procreating, unleashed the widest speculation. Several possibilities presented themselves.

Soon after her marriage, Mme de Narbonne had settled in Parma in her capacity of lady-in-waiting to the Duchesse—her two sons were born at Colorno—but she returned to France numerous times as part of the Princesse's entourage and, at the time of her death in 1759, had remained behind at Versailles to serve as *dame de palais* to another daughter of Louis XV, Mme Adélaïde, who, like her sister Mme Victoire, had preferred not to marry.

For some, then, Louis de Narbonne (since Philippe-Louis, of fragile health and distinctly less intellectually gifted than his younger brother, interested no one) was the son of Mme de Narbonne and the Dauphin,[6] or of the Duc de Parma. For others, he was the fruit of an incestuous affair between Mme Adélaïde[7] and her brother, the Dauphin, or—a more likely theory—with Louis XV himself. And some refused to rule out the possibility that the woman with whom the sovereign had shared his bed was Mme Victoire.[8] But whichever scenario was under discussion, Mme de Narbonne was understood as having been ready to extricate the royal family from its difficulties by pretending to be the child's mother.

Ultimately, in that barrage of hearsay with which the nobility at court conducted its smear campaign against the royal family, neatly anticipating the prerevolutionary yellow press, the most insistent rumor attributed the paternity of Mme de Narbonne's sons to the Well-Beloved himself.[9] Indeed, their birth coincided with the years between the end of his sexual relationship with Mme de Pompadour and the establishment of the Parc-aux-Cerfs, when Louis XV was on the hunt for discreet and attractive young women who would not overshadow the Marquise, still officially the King's mistress. Moreover, it was whispered that the Comtesse de Toulouse—in whose service Mme de Narbonne found herself at the time—guided her nephew's choice to those within her own circle.

In any case, the inhabitants of Versailles would have observed that, upon their return from Italy, the sons of Mme de Narbonne were baptized in the sovereign's private chapel, according to the tradition reserved for royal bastards: as expected, both emerged from their earliest years with Princes of the Blood as godparents, and it was notable that among the first names they were given, Louis stood out. Nor did it escape the careful notice of the courtiers that the Comte de Narbonne was present for neither of these two ceremonies.

One might ask what had driven that ill-starred Gascon gentleman to accept the thankless role of the cuckolded husband. Financial problems aside, his reasons must have been similar to those which, some years earlier, had encouraged the Duc de Gontaut to willingly accept the relationship between his wife and his friend Choiseul, and to hail with joy the birth of a son that was not, in fact, his own.

Both of them had lost hope of fathering children after being gravely wounded in battle and knew that their family line was at risk of perishing with them. In a society where the general interest of the family came before all personal sentiment, they had most likely resigned themselves to delegating the task of ensuring that line's continuation to a third party. In Narbonne's case, perhaps the proud motto passed down from his Spanish ancestors—"We do not descend from kings, but rather the kings from us"[10]—suggested a path forward. In any event, the Comte's attitude toward his sons did not differ materially from what was common among the nobility of the period: he followed them from a distance, busied himself with ensuring their future, received them periodically at his château in Aubiac, and demanded their respect.

Louis de Narbonne's relationship with his mother unquestionably constituted the focal point of his existence. It was a relationship that was anything but simple: despite all her love for her youngest son, Mme de Narbonne, with her authoritarian, intransigent, domineering temperament, could not tolerate the idea of any woman with the same strength of character as herself (Germaine de Staël, first and foremost) supplanting her in the affections of her favorite son and influencing his decisions.

Raised at Versailles—where the Comtesse de Narbonne directed the "household" of Mme Adélaïde and Mme Victoire[11] with an iron hand—and adored by the two princesses, Louis enjoyed a happy childhood in the bosom of the royal family. The Dauphin took an interest in his studies; the future Louis XVI, the Comte de Provence, and the Comte d'Artois were his playmates; and his mother kept herself busy giving him an extraordinary education, "the education of a young prince."[12] After a humanist schooling at the Collège des Oratoriens de Juilly came his military apprenticeship at the artillery school in Strasbourg. During his Alsatian years the young Narbonne—who already spoke English—learned German, along with mathematics, from the celebrated Guillaume Koch, and dedicated himself to the study of history.

Upon his return to Versailles the minister of foreign affairs himself, the Comte de Vergennes, tutored him in the workings of the ministry and the finer points of protocol, as well as those of treaties and secret correspondence. Nobody, Napoleon remarked later, "had a better sense of the negotiations of the old court."[13] Then, determined to complete an education that would render him suitable for any of the state's higher offices, he served in the various corps of the army—dragoons, troopers, cavalry—and, in August 1778, at the age of twenty-three, was appointed second colonel of the infantry regiment of Angoumois. But in contrast with a number of his friends, he did not allow himself to be tempted by the American campaign. He was well aware that Louis XVI was ill disposed to it, and that taking part would smack of disrespect toward the royal family, to whom he owed everything. Instead, he seized the opportunity to throw himself into the aristocratic tradition of the Grand Tour, and visited Italy, Austria, Germany, and England, meeting the leading figures of the European elite and learning to adjust his manner country by country. The Prince de Ligne would recall that later, when Narbonne was serving as aide-de-camp to Napoleon and passing through Vienna after the terrible Russian campaign, his amiability succeeded in overcoming the general embarrassment and "winning over all those who had raged against France."[14]

Amiability was certainly Narbonne's primary asset, the chief mark of his personality—"he was the most amiable and least disagreeable of men," decreed the generally venomous Mme de Boigne[15]—striking even in an age when it constituted the common quality of an entire elite, and was a basic social obligation. But Narbonne's particular brand of amiability was more than a mere mastery of worldly manners, and more than a product of the "need to please," as in the case of the Vicomte de Ségur. It stemmed from a spontaneous cordiality, and had the pleasant immediacy of a natural gift.

In any event, how could one *not* feel amiable after having grown up in the women's quarters, idolized by one's mother, spoiled and fawned over by two older princesses, treated with affectionate kindness by the other members of the royal family? As the years passed, that certainty of being loved by all would put down roots in Narbonne, and the charming cherub soon developed into a very handsome young man of uncommon intelligence and cultivation, as comfortable at court as in town, in the army as in the university lecture hall or the library. And now it was the women, all of the women, who made him feel so irresistible.

Still, aside from arousing feminine admiration, his physical appearance would prove to be a source of embarrassing questions. As an adult his resemblance to Louis XV became so glaring that he earned the nickname of "Demi-Louis," after the coin that bore the image of the Well-Beloved. The Comte had inherited the sovereign's regular features, amber complexion, dark eyes and hair, and the stately bearing that had so struck Casanova when he met

Louis XV.[16] Can we really believe that Narbonne was unaware of a fact so wholly obvious, that it never occurred to him to question the reasons behind the favor that he and his mother had enjoyed at Versailles? Isn't his silence in the face of the rumors a kind of confirmation? What could he have done but remain silent regarding this secret that touched on the personal life of the sovereign? We know that in light of the disastrous scandals that surrounded the Sun King's legitimate children, Louis XV had been unwilling to recognize the offspring produced by his manifold affairs—the exception being the child he had with Mlle de Romans, who was inscribed in the parochial register of Chaillot under the name of Louis-Aimé de Bourbon, and was destined for the Church.[17] Louis-Amalric de Narbonne could consider himself luckier.

We cannot know what sort of psychological impact the mystery of his birth may have had on the young Comte. Certainly plenty of his friends did not bear the names of their true fathers. Moreover, he could not have helped taking pride in his royal blood, and the privileges it had brought him must have been obvious. Still, Narbonne's position as Demi-Louis meant that his future depended entirely on the goodwill of the ruling family. His response to this ambiguous position seems to have been to attempt to justify his royal favor with personal merit.

But his ambition, his zeal for his studies, and his enormous capacity for work did not prevent Louis from leading the joyful and insouciant style of life appropriate for young nobles of his condition, like the Chevalier de Boufflers, the Duc de Lauzun, and the Ségur brothers, to name just a few. Louis was zestful, a hedonist, a libertine, and (his most alarming tendency) a spendthrift—so much so that in 1782, weary of paying off his debts, Mme de Narbonne and Mme Adélaïde decided to find him a wealthy wife.[18]

They settled on Marie-Adélaïde de Montholon, the only daughter of the president of the Parliament of Rouen, heir to an enormous fortune that included significant property in Saint-Domingue. When Louis married her, Marie-Adélaïde was a shy and graceful adolescent of fourteen years, and it would be another four years before she gave birth to the first of their two daughters—much to the chagrin of her father-in-law, who, having recently risen to the rank of Duc, had broken with his usual routine to travel to Paris and attend a wedding on which all of his hopes for the continuation of his line depended.

The young Comtesse fell madly in love with her husband, but this did not render her interesting enough for Narbonne to change his style of life. In

January 1783, the Marquis de Bombelles referred to him as a "highly fashionable young man, whose wit is recognized by all," even if "opinion is certainly divided when it comes to his morals."[19] Nevertheless, before long he would have to take note of the fact that his future was no longer so assured as he'd earlier assumed, and that royal favor was beginning to turn against him.

He received the first sign of this in 1784 when, the ambassadorship to St. Petersburg having fallen vacant, Mme Adélaïde proposed his candidacy to Louis XVI, shoring it up with solid arguments. Even if the Comte was a mere twenty-nine years old, no one could claim they were better prepared than he for such a position, or so likely to prove appealing to the Empress. But Marie-Antoinette, pressed by the Baron de Besenval and the Polignac clan, mooted the name of the Comte Louis-Philippe de Ségur, a son of the minister of war, whom she had taken under her protection. And Ségur, who was only three years older than Narbonne and considerably less skilled at diplomacy, ultimately obtained the appointment. It turned out to be a fortunate choice, inasmuch as Louis-Philippe would go on to show he possessed all the skill necessary to enter into the good graces of the Semiramis of the North. That same year, another close friend of Narbonne's, the Comte de Choiseul-Gouffier, would be named as the ambassador to Constantinople.

A second sign came the following year. Mme Adélaïde stepped into the breach once more to demand a cavalry regiment for her protégé, but again Marie-Antoinette pressed her own candidate forward. Narbonne was clearly bearing the brunt of an internecine war within the royal family.

Ever since becoming Queen, Marie-Antoinette had distanced herself from husband's paternal aunts—the same aunts who, upon her arrival at the French court fifteen years earlier as an inexperienced young wife, had served as her principal emotional supports. This change in attitude was understandable, since the two princesses had used their ingenuity to implicate her in their personal war against Mme du Barry and, more generally, in their various political intrigues. But for their part—as the Comte de Mercy-Argenteau had immediately revealed to the Empress Maria Theresa—Mme Adélaïde, and Mme Victoire along with her, were "wholly subjugated and governed in everything by their lady-in-waiting, the Comtesse de Narbonne,"[20] who used this influence for her own personal ends. The ambassador hadn't neglected to put the Dauphine on her guard against "that scheming and dangerous woman"[21]— and for once his advice had been heeded. However, after the unexpected death of Louis XV, the really crucial issue for Mercy-Argenteau became the influence of Mme Adélaïde on her nephew, the new King. On the advice of his aunt, Louis XVI had recalled the elderly Comte de Maurepas to take charge of business rather than the Duc de Choiseul—the architect of the alliance with Austria—whose return Marie-Antoinette had pushed for in vain. Moreover, decidedly opposed to the influence of Vienna and faithful to the traditions of the old court, Mme Adélaïde did not conceal her disapproval of the personal behavior of the Queen (whom she referred to as "the Austrian")—her frivolity, her expensive tastes, her contempt for rank, the imprudence of her friendships, and the arbitrariness of her favor. Finally, the irruption of Fersen into her Marie-Antoinette's life had profoundly scandalized her. It is said that one day, having heard Marie-Antoinette exasperated by the recent attacks targeting her and railing against these "unworthy [*indignes*] Frenchmen," Mme Adélaïde had replied: "You mean *indignant* [*indignés*], madame."[22]

Hindering Narbonne's career had become for the Queen a fine means of thwarting Mme Adélaïde, particularly since the aging Princesse would struggle, going forward, to secure the support of her nephew. Indeed, not only was Louis XVI more and more inclined to listen to his wife but he was also highly judgmental of his old playmate's libertinism.

Mme Adélaïde consoled herself by making the Comte her *chevalier d'honneur* in 1785, and the following year securing for him the command of the Piémont-Infanterie Regiment. However, Marie-Antoinette's hostile and vindictive attitude undermined Narbonne's relations with the royal family just as it had with the Duc de Lauzun a dozen years earlier, and drove him to keep his distance from Versailles. For their part, Mme Adélaïde, Mme Victoire, and Narbonne's mother, Mme de Narbonne, highly conscious of being sidelined in a court that had never shown particular consideration for the elderly, had abandoned Versailles for the Château de Bellevue, the former estate of Mme de Pompadour.

Incomparably more interesting and entertaining than Versailles, the Paris of the 1780s left Narbonne little time to regret his lost opportunities at court. It was here in the capital that the future of the country was being shaped. Of course, forward-looking though it was, Paris still provided a fertile field for the enjoyment of aristocratic privilege, and Narbonne, open-minded and always elegant, threw himself into a style of life that combined the play of ideas with the quest for pleasure. And when the actress Louise Contat appeared on his horizon, he knew he had found the perfect accomplice. Antoine-Vincent Arnault, the author of plays and fables and a well-known academician, has left us an eloquent portrait of her in his *Memoirs of a Sexagenarian*: "Her intellect, so vivid and incisive, came into its own in conversation. As steel will strike fire from a stone, she drew wit from men who possessed the least of it; but when she met an interlocutor of her own caliber, she surpassed herself, and then her conversation abounded with barbs and sallies, like that of the liveliest characters she portrayed on stage." She surprised with the profundity of her observations: "She expressed herself with clarity, but never pedantry, elegance, never affectation, and she wrote just the way she spoke, as spiritedly and naturally as possible." Arnault recalled her "singular ability to seize on the ridiculous [qualities of a person] and to turn them back [on him]. Thus she was dangerous to have as an enemy," while it was lucky "to have her as a friend. There was no sacrifice of which she was not capable in the name of friendship."[23] Thus, put to the test of fashionable conversation, Mlle Contat proved herself a masterful interpreter of both the spirit and the letter of aristocratic conduct. Indeed, what was the theater of her era if not an inexhaustible repertoire of characters and social situations, a critical review of the mores, virtues, vices, fashions, and absurdities of the *parfaitement bonne compagnie*?

Narbonne first met Mlle Contat in 1786, at the home of Julie Careau, where he had been introduced by his friend Joseph-Alexandre de Ségur. Twenty-six years old, quite beautiful, endowed with "the most enchanting of smiles,"[24] the actress, then at the height of her success, immediately attracted the Comte's attention, and he lost no time in replacing the Comte d'Artois in her "expensive favors."[25] But in contrast to Julie, with whom she was closely linked, Mlle Contat was no simple courtesan. She was a great artist, universally acclaimed, and the theater was her primary raison d'être. If she expected her lovers to spend lavish sums on her behalf, it was because she saw in such prodigality a recognition of her deserts. The Comte d'Artois knew this firsthand: early on in their relationship, she had spurned a financial gift that she judged too modest. Finding himself obliged to modify his tactics in light of that rejection, he took to calling her "the backstage princess."[26] But Mlle Contat experienced her time with the handsome Narbonne as a great love story, and everything seems to suggest that this passion was shared.

Even though he had been married for scarcely four years, Louis never made any secret of his relationship with the actress: he took her along with him on a study tour to England, and in September 1788 he officially recognized the daughter born from their union. Narbonne's brother served as her godfather and she was christened Louise-Amalrique-Bathilde-Isidore, simultaneously revealing her identity and assuring her a steady income.

In Paris, plenty of dandies, whether married or bachelors, considered it indispensable to their social status to have an actress as a mistress and to maintain her in style. But this did not relieve them of their duty to pay court to the ladies of high society. And indeed, Narbonne's relationship with Mlle Contat did not prevent him from turning his attention to women of his own rank as well, beginning with those that his friends were also busy wooing.

Though he had no more success than Lauzun (who had devoted a veritable cult to her) in convincing the Marquise de Coigny to step down from her pedestal and welcome him into her bed, he nevertheless risked death in the attempt. One day Comte d'Houdetot, himself enamored of the Marquise, spotted Narbonne leaving the beautiful Marquise's apartments with a rose in his hand, and fell upon him with sword drawn. Narbonne took the flower between his lips so as to draw his own weapon, but in the heat of the duel it fell to the ground—in bending to gather it up he dodged his enemy's blade by a breath, and a moment later ran him through.

If he failed to seduce Mme de Flahaut away from Talleyrand, he did manage to best the great man in winning the affections of Catherine-Jeanne Tavernier de Boulogne, Vicomtesse de Montmorency-Laval, who was seven years his senior and had a life of passionate affairs behind her. In his memoirs,[27] Lauzun boldly relates that the Vicomtesse made vain advances upon him before turning her attention to her brother-in-law, the Duc de Laval. When a dozen years later Narbonne took her from Talleyrand, he was unaware—as we shall see— how much this encounter with Mme de Laval would mark him.

Narbonne, Lauzun, Talleyrand, and the brothers Ségur did not confine themselves to exchanging mistresses—they frequented the same milieus, shared the same ideas, nourished the same ambitions, and belonged to the same circle of friends.

Narbonne was part of an inseparable trio with the Comte de Choiseul-Gouffier and Talleyrand (who was at that time the Abbé de Périgord)—and, decades afterward, the latter would recall the social frenzy of the 1780s. All of these young men knew that their futures depended on their ability to create personal relationships, but the choices that awaited them were far from simple. From birth they had belonged to the ranks of the privileged, but each was forced to prove himself capable of combining social brio with economic and administrative ability. The power of high society had never been so great, but there was also tremendous "confusion among its ranks," and its "general spirit was undergoing all sorts of changes. People wanted to know everything, to fathom everything, to judge everything. Sentiments were replaced by philosophical ideas; passions by analysis of the human heart; the desire to please by opinions; amusements by plans, projects, etc. Everything was becoming unnatural. I pause, for fear that I might make the reader feel too strongly the coming of the French Revolution, from which several years and many events still separate us."[28]

But all this upheaval, which in retrospect would seem to have presaged the Revolution, at the time constituted for the "triumvirate"[29]—and for many of their friends and acquaintances—an opportunity to live out an unforgettable experience. First and foremost, they chose to ignore differences of rank, to highlight individual virtue, and to tie themselves "to men distinguished most by the lives they had led, or by their works, or by their ambition, or by the future promised by their birth, their relationships, their talent."[30]

Among those who gathered each evening at his home, Talleyrand mentions in no particular order "the Duc de Lauzun, Barthez, the Abbé Delille, Mirabeau, Chamfort, Lauraguais, Rulhière, Choiseul-Gouffier, and Louis de Narbonne." The conversation was freewheeling, and they spoke a bit about everything, but "questions of politics, business, administration, and finance"[31] predominated. The economic lessons of Panchaud, along with the physiocratic theories of Dupont de Nemours, were their guides. English institutions and trade were constant points of reference, and like Mirabeau and Lauzun, the triumvirate were conscious of the pressing need to find solutions adequate to their nation's economic and financial woes. Narbonne, who had spent time with Turgot—to his mind "the finest intellect among thinkers, and among philosophers the one true sage"[32]—was already profoundly marked by the minister's ideas.

In the wake of these reflective evenings, they devoted themselves to the exploration of the Parisian social life, visiting the most influential salons: "All who sought office frequented some of the chief houses of Paris, whose opinions and language they molded."[33] Talleyrand and Narbonne ran into each other at the home of Mme de Montesson, morganatic wife of the Duc d'Orléans, and in the liberal and constitutional salons of the Comtesse de Brionne or the Duc de Beauvau, of Mme Devaines or the Duc de Liancourt. Talleyrand kept his distance from the partisans of Necker, declaring that he was "neither a good minister of finance nor a statesman,"[34] and refrained from visiting his house. Narbonne, by contrast, immediately aligned himself with the Genevan banker and, mixing with the liberal *jeunesse dorée*—Lafayette, the brothers Lameth, Mathieu de Montmorency—became a regular at the salon held by his wife. Having considered the advantages that he would draw by being there, Talleyrand was not long in following their example. And it was there that, in 1788, Necker's daughter, who had been married for barely two years to the Swedish Baron de Staël, Gustav III's ambassador to Versailles, fell in love with "Comte Louis"[35]—preferring him to her old worshipper the Comte de Guibert, to the young Mathieu de Montmorency (son of that Mme de Laval who might have asserted her own right to Narbonne's affections), and even to Talleyrand, who, despite his distaste for Necker, had finally decided to seize an opportunity to advance his career.

Profoundly disappointed by her cold, Nordic husband, Mme de Staël had not abandoned her hopes of experiencing a great love—and the fact that her choice fell on Narbonne is unsurprising. Intelligence, culture, elegance, wit: the Comte embodied all of those qualities she adored about the only society in which she desired to live, and—reassuringly—he was famed for his success with women.

For his part, Narbonne was caught up by the fascination that Germaine exerted on all who believed, along with her, that abstract play of ideas could be translated into political action. Overwhelmed by her vivacity and eloquence, he soon found himself drawn into a torrid—and exceedingly complicated—relationship. But even if Mme de Staël was not—as she demanded—the great love of Narbonne's life, she did have a dramatic effect on his political choices, and would ultimately spur him to take up the cause of the Revolution by her side.

The Chevalier de Boufflers

M. de Boufflers had been, successively, a priest, a soldier, a writer, a civil servant, a parliamentarian, and a philosopher—and, in each of these capacities, he inevitably found himself in the front ranks.

—PRINCE DE LIGNE[1]

"IT WAS A GREAT GIFT that you made to me in 1738; I know not how I could have merited such magnanimity on your part, nor which generous mortal it was that pleaded my case to you in those days, at last convincing you to direct to me those attentions that I scarcely deserved."[2]

Thus ended the letter in which Stanislas-Jean de Boufflers, writing in 1762, gave thanks to his mother (and to her lover of the moment) for having been kind enough to conceive him twenty-four years earlier. It is a note that perfectly illustrates the sort of irreverence that reigned among the Boufflers clan. And Marie-Françoise-Catherine de Beauvau-Craon, Marquise de Boufflers, led the way—a woman who had recognized herself and her style of life in the epitaph composed years earlier by the Comtesse de Verrue for her own tomb: "Here lies, in profound peace, / That *Dame de volupté* / Who, hedging her bets, / Made a Paradise in this world."[3]

For Mme de Boufflers, that earthly paradise was the court that Stanisław Leszczyński—the former king of Poland, now living in exile in Lorraine[4]—maintained at Lunéville between 1737 and 1766, and of which she was the uncontested "queen." That she should find herself in such a position was no surprise, because the Marquise belonged by birth to one of the country's most illustrious families. Her father, Marc de Beauvau-Craon, Prince of the Holy Roman Empire, had been the right-hand man of Duc Leopold de Lorraine—whose son, François III, had wed Maria Theresa of Austria in 1736, seizing the imperial crown—and her mother, Anne-Marguerite de Ligniville, had been the chief mistress of the Duc. This had not prevented the Princes of Beauvau-Craon, who were preparing themselves to depart for Tuscany to represent

François III, from giving a warm welcome to the stepfather of Louis XV. Stanisław bore witness to his gratitude by lavishing honors, appointments, and gratuities upon the various members of their enormous clan. Thus Marie-Françoise-Catherine, who had married the Marquis de Boufflers in 1735, was immediately appointed lady-in-waiting to the Polish Queen, and her husband as a captain of the King's Guard. But it was not until a dozen years later, after having brought three children into the world and filled her lungs with the air of Paris and Versailles, that the young Marquise returned to live at Lunéville. She was pretty, intelligent, witty, and determined to amuse herself, and she did not hesitate to take advantage of the passion she had inspired in Stanisław, as well as the void left by the Queen—Catherine Opalińska, who had died in 1747—to establish an absolute dominance over the little court. A respect for forms and the great difference in their ages (the King was sixty-five, the Marquise thirty-six) might suggest that the relationship was platonic, but there were plenty who suspected the opposite—Voltaire chief among them. Whatever the nature of the relationship between them, Stanisław clearly did not pretend that their tie was exclusive. He even ended up putting a good face—perhaps begrudgingly—on the Marquise's affairs with one of his ministers, even more influential than himself. Antoine-Martin Chaumont de La Galaizière, who served as his chancellor and keeper of the seals, had also received the full powers of Louis XV to administer the Lorraine as conquered territory and to prepare its definitive annexation to France. The extreme respect shown by the impeccable Marquis and imperturbable amiability of the mistress allowed Stanisław to turn a blind eye to their affair, but the elderly sovereign had not been able to resist the temptation to deliver one of his proverbial witticisms. It was said that one day, during a *tête-à-tête galant* with Mme de Boufflers, Stanisław perceived that he would be unable to carry the act through to its conclusion, and "withdrawing with dignity," announced to her: "Madame, my chancellor will tell you the rest."[5] The anecdote almost immediately made its way to Versailles, where it thrilled Louis XV.

Mme de Boufflers's husband, Louis-François de Boufflers-Remiencourt, seems not to have suffered from jealousy. We do not know if his son had good reasons to suspect his paternity, but, as a professional soldier (on top of his position as the captain of Stanisław's guard, the Marquis served in the French army), he could not have spent very much time with his family, and died in a traveling mishap while Stanislas-Jean was still a child. The Chevalier was in any case very proud to bear his name. The Boufflers belonged to the ancient military nobility. The father of Stanislas-Jean's maternal grandmother, the celebrated Maréchal Louis-François de Boufflers—of whom Saint-Simon admitted that "no man ever deserved his triumphs more"[6]—had been one of the great generals of Louis XIV, and the Sun King had rewarded him by raising him to the rank of Duc and peer of France.

As if an omen of his vocation of knight-errant, Stanislas-Jean was born while his parents were traveling. Indeed, Mme de Boufflers's water broke on the road to Nancy and, having forced the carriage to stop, she brought her son into the world with the assistance of the coachman. She was madly fond of this child who had been in such a great hurry to plunge into life and enjoy it with all his might—and she was adored by him in turn.

In 1747, after having spent his childhood in the company of his brother Charles-Marc-Jean-François-Régis, his elder by a year, at the château of their grandparents on the Beauvau-Craon side in Haroué, a splendid residence some twelve miles from Nancy, he rejoined his mother at Lunéville where, along with his brother, he was introduced to their little sister, Marie-Stanislas-Catherine, born in Paris in 1744. Breaking with the custom in aristocratic families, the Marquise kept her children by her side so as to personally oversee their education. And if Charles-Marc-Jean-François-Régis soon had to leave for Versailles where, thanks to the good offices of Stanisław, he had obtained the prestigious post of Page, Stanislas-Jean completed his training at Lunéville and remained there for twenty years.

Marked from the beginning with ephemerality, Stanisław's court was a world apart, midway between opera buffa and utopia. The Polish King had wanted to make his land of exile a happy refuge, and he had been able to win the love of his new subjects who had initially mourned the departure of the former rulers of Lorraine. Having no power over administrative, fiscal, and political decisions, which were made at Versailles, and confined to a purely representative role, Stanisław took advantage of the rich appanage that Louis XV had granted him, and of the numerous appointments, jobs, and benefices that he had full latitude to distribute in order to leave behind a durable memory of himself, and of the kingdom that he knew was destined to end along with him. A fervent philanthropist and patron, the sovereign built schools and hospitals, and launched a number of initiatives for charity and good works. Moreover, with his passion for architecture, gardens, the decorative arts, and automatons and mechanical toys,[7] he had turned Nancy, capital of the duchy, into one of the most beautiful baroque towns in Europe. He also occupied himself with renovating and beautifying the Château de Lunéville, built by the Lorraines around twenty miles from Nancy, transforming it into a miniature Versailles. But what made Stanisław's little court unique in Europe was its joyful hedonism, its intellectual vivacity, and its air of liberty and tolerance. It was a fortunate alchemy that stemmed less from conscious choice than from the sovereign's need to live in peace with his own contradictions.

A practicing Catholic, Stanisław intended to sacrifice to his faith neither his freedom of thought nor the lure of his sensuality: he entrusted the care of his soul to his confessor, Père de Ménoux, and that of his heart and mind to the worldly Mme de Boufflers. After an extended period of strife, the confessor and the mistress finally resigned themselves to tolerating one another—and really the learned Jesuit had no choice, since the Marquise was far from the only enemy that he had to hold at bay. Stanisław was a committed apostle of the Enlightenment, and his court welcomed, in addition to local writers from Lorraine,[8] such illustrious personalities as Montesquieu—who drafted "several of the most beautiful chapters of his *Spirit of the Laws*" while in residence— Helvétius, the Président Hénault, and, most important, the Marquise du Châtelet and Voltaire, the latter of whom composed "some of his tragedies and *contes philosophiques*"[9] there, and whose formidable sarcasms the Père de Ménoux was forced to endure for years. And yet, if we are to believe the philosopher, it was the Jesuit himself who had first encouraged Voltaire's coming to Lunéville along with his mistress, in hopes that the charm of the Divine Émilie would undermine the prestige of Mme de Boufflers. An old friend of Mme de Boufflers, Mme du Châtelet arrived at Lunéville in the company of Voltaire in February 1747 for a stay that was to decide her fate. But the hopes of Père de Ménoux were swiftly dashed, for rather than concentrating her attentions on Stanisław, the visitor threw herself into the conquest of the Marquis de Saint-Lambert, grand master of the sovereign's wardrobe and Mme de Boufflers's current lover. Mme de Boufflers took no pains to retain the Marquis, instead enjoying the comic spectacle of one of the most intelligent women in Europe surrendering to her *amour fou* for an ambitious young poet who was decidedly lukewarm toward her. Fortified by her determination and indifferent to ridicule, Mme du Châtelet overcame every obstacle: the reticence of her beloved, the indignation of Voltaire, and a pregnancy that she was forced to attribute to a husband with whom she had not shared a bed for years. So it was that, in the summer of 1749, still escorted by Voltaire, Émilie returned to Lunéville to give birth to a child. Stanisław and Mme de Boufflers had been sure to offer the two visitors the château's finest apartments and to welcome them with all their usual cordiality. Everything went well. In the lulls between meals, and without losing sight of her lover, Mme du Châtelet continued her translation of Newton's *Philosophiae naturalis principia mathematica*, while Saint-Lambert seized the opportunity to read Voltaire the first lines of *Seasons*, his epic poem in progress, which he hoped would make him known in Paris. Meanwhile Voltaire, his thoughts already turning toward the court of Frederick II of Prussia, prepared to "deliver"[10] himself of a new tragedy, *Catilina*. With great gallantry, the Marquis du Châtelet expressed his pleasure at such an unexpected paternity. But this pleasant farce, which amused and scandalized not just Lorraine but all of France, ended in tragedy. A fortnight after easily giving birth to a little girl, Mme du Châtelet died at the age of forty-three, carried away by an embolism. Not until Mme de Staël would French high society see a woman as devotedly intellectual, or as ready to flout convention.

The year before the arrival of Voltaire and the Divine Émilie at Lunéville, Stanislas-Jean de Boufflers had been permitted to return to court so as to prepare himself to take his place in society. His position as the youngest child had meant he was destined for the Church, but for a long period of time no one had seemed to remember this. The Abbé Pierre-Charles Porquet, the private tutor who had been chosen for him, was cultured, amiable, and witty—and, it must be said, utterly lacking in piety. His religious knowledge left something to be desired as well—appointed as the chaplain to Stanisław at the insistence of Mme de Boufflers, and invited by the King to say grace before lunch, he found himself unable to recall the words. Chamfort recalls that Stanisław granted the man a year in which to attempt to bring himself around to believing in the existence of God.[11] In any case, the Abbé neatly laid out the precepts by which he lived in a witty epigram: "*M'amuser, n'importe comment, / voilà toute ma philosophie, / je crois ne perdre aucun moment, / hors le moment où je m'ennuie.*"*[12] Porquet was greatly admired by his pupil, and supplied the young man with a solid humanist education, sharpening his intelligence and imparting

---

*To amuse myself, no matter how, / there you have the whole of my philosophy; / I don't believe I've lost a moment, / aside from those in which I've been bored.

to him his love of poetry. From his mother Stanislas-Jean learned the art of living; for her, as he later recalled, constant gaiety "was like a perpetual springtime in her soul, never ceasing to produce fresh flowers until her final day."[13] Indeed, her personal behavior did not prevent Mme de Boufflers from being a perfect *honnête femme*. Above and beyond her aristocratic manners, she shared the capacious views, the distinctive manner of expressing herself, and the sense of humor that characterized her whole family. As with the Mortemarts, one could speak of a "Beauvau-Craon spirit." Intelligent and cultivated, the Marquise was also an accomplished musician, painted with great taste, and never showed off her knowledge. She spoke with supreme elegance but preferred not to make a spectacle of herself, and when she happened to be at the center of attention she held to the classical ideal of conversation sans pedantry, responsive to others and based on a principle of *brevitas*: "*Il faut dire en deux mots / Ce qu'on veut dire; / Les longs propos / Sont sots. / Il faut savoir lire / Avant que d'écrire, / Et puis dire en deux mots / Ce qu'on veut dire; / Les longs propos / Sont sots. / Il ne faut pas toujours conter / Citer, / Dater, / Mais écouter. / Il faut éviter l'emploi / Du moi, / Du moi; / Voici pourquoi: / Il est tyrannique, / Trop académique; / L'ennui, L'ennui / Marche avec lui.*"*[14]

Though fickle when it came to love, the Marquise was a loyal and faithful friend. Always ready to use her influence over Stanisław for the benefit of her protégés, she never did so for her own personal advantage. Generous, hospitable, and blessed with a rare talent for making life pleasant for herself and others, she had found in the extravagant, debonair, and amiable Polish sovereign a perfect accomplice. During their reign, the little court at Lunéville—sumptuous but free from the constraints of etiquette and the trappings of politics, at the crossroads of France and the lands of the Holy Roman Empire, not far from the popular spa resort of Plombières—became a favorite meeting place of cosmopolitan high society. After a day punctuated by the nobility's preferred amusements—hunting, promenades, concerts, theatrical performances—the guests would return to the Marquise's quarters to converse on the most varied subjects with a freedom that was encouraged and extended by poetic license. Translating reality into verse, stripping it of its drama, transforming it into a game was indeed the preferred pastime of the Marquise and

---

*Say in two words / what you mean to say; / long-winded speech / is dull. / You must read / before you can write, / then say what you must / in two words; / long-winded speech / is dull. / Don't forever be rambling on, / giving names, / giving dates; / And here's why: / It's tyrannical, / too academic; / boredom, boredom / is the result.

her circle. It was a pastime that the *belle compagnie* had cultivated since the era of the Hôtel de Rambouillet, surviving—as is shown by the success enjoyed in 1737 by Alexis Piron's play *La Métromanie*—various changes in taste and the vagaries of fashion. Even more than conversation, the use of verse required fine timing and conciseness, linguistic expertise and a musical ear, ingeniousness and a respect for the rules, and answered to the social imperative for playfulness: it contributed to the lightening and enlivening of existence, and helped, if only briefly, to banish fear and suffering. Soon enough, Stanislas-Jean himself entered that collective arena in which the sovereign and his favorite vied with their guests for wit and finesse, and showed an undeniable talent for making poetry his passport to society.

The Marquise's other, more costly passion was for gambling, a family vice that exposed her to the loss of enormous sums of money which she had no idea how to meet, and which she also passed on to Stanislas-Jean, as well as to her daughter, Marie-Stanislas-Catherine. It was a vice practiced in defiance of the law at every level of society, up to and including Versailles: the virtuous Marie Leszczyńska herself was an inveterate gambler, and Marie-Antoinette would be as well. A year before her visit to Lunéville, Mme du Châtelet had lost almost a thousand louis in the Queen's apartments at Fontainebleau, and Voltaire had ordered her to renounce gaming because all of her fellow players were cheats. The chronicles of the era[15] relate that—following the example of the numerous professional frauds of the time, masters of rigged dice and cards—even the Princes of the Blood and ladies of the highest rank were in the habit of cheating each other with "an audacious tranquility,"[16] taking advantage of the impunity that came with their social positions. Should we believe Mme du Deffand when, many years later, she writes to Walpole that even the Chevalier and his sister, Mme de Boisgelin, left themselves open to suspicion?[17] The frequency of their losses and their despairing search for money with which to cover their debts would lead us to suppose the opposite—but in any event, following the death of King Stanisław, life would certainly become less easy for the Boufflers family.

During the course of his happy youth in the Lorraine, Stanislas-Jean had no duties to distract him from freely following his own inclinations. He loved the outdoor life and was passionate when it came to horses. Perfectly at ease in society, where he had made a triumphant debut, the young Boufflers cultivated other interests as well. Gifted like his mother with an assuredly artistic temperament, he painted, played music, took part in the theater, and improvised verse with an aristocratic nonchalance that masked with its grace and ease the seriousness, authority, and *labor limae* of a man of letters schooled on the study of the rhetoric of the classical authors (as the verse translation of a comedy of Seneca, produced during his early youth, attests). Moreover, the philosophical and reformist ideas laid out by King Stanisław in his *Charitable Philosopher*[18] had been for his godson the point of departure for a fervent embrace of the Enlightenment. At the age of only nineteen, he was already in a position to contribute an article—"Generous, Generosity"—to the *Encyclopédie*.[19]

In 1760, it became clear to all that it was high time for Stanislas-Jean to think of his future, and enter the seminary to prepare himself for ecclesiastic life. His despair at the prospect was fruitless. Stanisław, who had baptized him and still felt a great affection for him, was disposed to yield to his wishes, but the *dame de volupté* remained inflexible. Unlike the Polish King, she possessed no religious scruples, and the fact that her son felt no vocation whatsoever struck her as quite beside the point. He didn't need to believe in God in order to become a Prince of the Church, and it was Stanislas-Jean's duty to maintain the prestige of the Boufflers and Beauvau-Craons in this, the highest of the three orders of society. Besides, the family's financial position left them no alternative. And so, in December 1760—having assumed the title of Abbé de Longeville—the gates of the austere seminary of Saint-Sulpice shut behind him. But he would not remain there—before long, and quite unexpectedly, his passion for literature came to his aid. Thanks to the intercession of Leszczyński, Stanislas-Jean had obtained permission to pay visits to his numerous relations. One evening, invited by the Comtesse de Boufflers-Rouverel to L'Isle-Adam, the sumptuous estate of the Prince de Conti, and under the influence of champagne, Boufflers forgot his new position and improvised a number of extremely libertine verses that were soon making the rounds of Paris. And once he was back in the solitude of the monastery, his literary recreations maintained their resolutely profane orientation. The situation was exacerbated in 1761, with the circulation in Paris society of a story titled "Aline, Queen of Golconde"—a copy of which Grimm sent immediately to his correspondents[20]—and its publication in the *Mercure*, albeit in a censored version.[21] It was a tale of some fifteen pages, composed in the lively, pared-down style of the Voltairean *conte philosophique*, celebrating the easy morals of Aline, a young peasant girl who, becoming a courtesan by necessity, moves from adventure to adventure while climbing the social ladder, until, in her old age, she meets once again her first seducer. Having remained faithful, through all the vicissitudes of life, to the man who initiated her into the ways of love, she repays him in the end by revealing to him the secret of perfect wisdom. In order to "stabilize"[22] one's pleasure over time and be happy, one must divest oneself of all ambition, transform love into friendship, and live in direct contact with nature.

Published in the summer of 1761, "Aline, Queen of Golconde," which marked Stanislas-Jean's literary debut, was a great success. After reading the description of the little country hamlet modeled on the farm where she was born that Aline, having become Queen, has constructed in a secret corner of her royal park, the Marquise de Pompadour wanted one just like it at Petit Trianon,[23] and Marie-Antoinette would also follow her example. But the tale's greatest triumph was that it put an end to the ecclesiastic career of its author. Indeed, not everybody shared the indulgence of Voltaire, who wrote to his friend Devaux: "I haven't seen the Queen of Golconde, but I have seen some of [Stanislas-Jean's] charming verses, and perhaps he won't be a bishop; he should be made Canon of Strasbourg as quickly as possible, Primate of Lorraine, a cardinal, something where he won't be in charge of souls; it seems to me his vocation is, rather, to give men a great deal of pleasure."[24] The first to take notice of the gravity of the scandal that he had stirred up was Stanislas-Jean himself, who finally found the courage to override the desires of his family by leaving the Seminary of Saint-Sulpice. From then on, he referred to himself as the Chevalier de Boufflers, even when, at the death of his brother in 1774, the title of Marquis passed to him.

Correspondance littéraire didn't fail to publish a detailed account of the affair.[25] For the two editors in chief—the anticlerical and atheist Diderot and the German Protestant Grimm—the case of Boufflers was emblematic of the hypocrisy and moral laxity of a Catholic Church prepared to welcome into its ranks even the most unsuitable characters. But the letter written by the Chevalier to his old tutor, the Abbé Porquet, just as he left Saint-Sulpice—and which the *Correspondance* reproduced in its entirety—had nothing frivolous or cynical about it: "It is no small thing to begin, so to speak, a new life at the age of twenty-four years,"[26] Boufflers admitted, going on to deliver a lucid examination of the conscience of a free man unwilling to trade the right simply to be himself for a brilliant future. He knew well enough that a little skill would have sufficed to profit from his position, and to one day become a high prelate. But he was also aware that his "boiling blood," his "reckless mind," and his "independent humor" were incompatible with the obligations of the ecclesiastic condition: a man of the Church is obliged to "hide all that he desires, disguise all that he thinks, be wary of all he does."[27] Others, more ambitious or realistic than he—after all, mustn't Charles-Maurice de Talleyrand, Abbé de Périgord, have confronted the same dilemma a dozen years later, likewise at the Seminary of Saint-Sulpice?—might have resigned themselves to following the path that their family had chosen for them, but Boufflers was incapable of it. Despite the respect and the love that he had for his mother and the gratitude he owed to Stanisław, he felt it was too much to sacrifice his happiness to ambition and knew he could count on their indulgence.

Meanwhile, he openly celebrated in verse the joy of his rediscovered freedom:

J'ai quitté ma soutane
Malgré tous mes parents;
Je veux que Dieu me damne
Si jamais je la prends.
Eh! mais oui da,
Comment peut-on trouver de mal à ça?
Eh! mais oui da,
Se fera prêtre qui voudra.

J'aime mieux mon Annette
Que mon bonnet carré,
Que ma noire jaquette
Et mon rabat moiré.
Eh! mais oui da,
Comment peut-on trouver du mal à ça?
Eh! mais oui da,
Se fera prêtre qui voudra.[*28]

---

*I have shed my soutane / In spite of my parents; / May God damn me if ever / I don it again. / Ah! Yes, indeed— / How on earth could one find fault with that? / Ah! Yes, indeed— / Let others be priests if they like.

I love my Annette far more / Than my clerical cap, / Than my black jacket / And silken collar. / Ah! Yes, indeed— / How on earth could one find fault with that? / Ah! Yes, indeed— / Let others be priests if they like.

But this freedom came at a price, one that Boufflers would soon perceive.

Aside from the clergy, a military career was the sole option available to a penniless younger son of the nobility. The choice of the Order of Malta, with its religious and military overtones, represented for the Chevalier an honorable compromise. It allowed him, as the *Correspondance* ironically highlights, to preserve without taking the cloth those ecclesiastical advantages that Stanisław had procured for him, while leaving him free to earn a reputation on the battlefield. Thus he prepared himself to take on military life with all that joyful and ferocious energy with which the French nobility had always marched against the enemy:

> *Faisons l'amour, faisons la guerre,*
> *Ces deux métiers sont pleins d'attraits:*
> *La guerre au monde est un peu chère;*
> *L'amour en rembourse les frais.*
> *Que l'ennemi, que la bergère,*
> *Soient tour à tour serrés de près...*
> *Eh! Mes amis, peut-on mieux faire,*
> *Quand on a dépeuplé la terre,*
> *Que de la repeupler après?**29

The Chevalier had the chance to serve under the command of the Maréchal de Soubise in Hesse, and to distinguish himself for his courage at the battle at Amöneburg during the last months of the Seven Years' War. But by February 1763, France had resigned itself to paying a humiliatingly high price for peace, and in the years that followed, Boufflers would distinguish himself instead in the arena of romance.

He returned to Lunéville, but the days of Stanisław's kingdom were numbered. Before dying a horrible death in February 1766—his dressing gown went up in flames while he was alone in his chamber, kindling the fire—the elderly sovereign made an effort to entrust the young man with a number of

---

*Making love, making war, / Both trades have their attractions: / For the world, war is a bit expensive; / Love will repay the costs. / Ah, that the enemy, that the shepherdess, / Should follow each other turn and turn about . . . / Ah! My friends, after having / Emptied the earth, shouldn't / One repopulate it?

ephemeral diplomatic responsibilities. But upon his death, the Lorraine was definitively annexed by France: the royal palace was turned into a barracks, the little court of servants and friends of the sovereign dispersed, the collections sold off, and the utopia of Lunéville was no more than a memory.

Finally appointed in 1767 (thanks to the good offices of the Duchesse de Gramont)[30] as *maître de camp* of the Esterházy Hussars, Boufflers was keen to support the Polish cause and flew to the aid of the Bar Confederation, which had risen up in 1770 against the Russian occupation, making himself, as Catherine of Russia would write contemptuously to Voltaire, "an incognito knight-errant for those supposed confederates."[31] The godson of Stanisław could not have remained indifferent to the drama surrounding the partition of Poland—and on top of that, the Russo-Polish conflict offered him an excellent opportunity to display his skills as a soldier. But the Chevalier threw himself into the escapade in ignorance of the rivalries between the Polish generals, the state of semianarchy in which the confederate government reposed, and the difficulty of obtaining the approval of the French minister of war, on whom he depended. It was only after a series of extended and fruitless negotiations that he resigned himself to renouncing the enterprise. "It taught me," he commented, "that the Poles are knaves—something I already knew—and that I myself was a fool—which I hadn't yet known well enough."[32] And even if he had not been "chopped to bits or hung,"[33] as his friends had feared, nor dispatched to Siberia, as Catherine of Russia[34] had threatened, the results were bitter: "Deprived of that field where my education, my reputation, and my furtherance awaited me...I have sunk back into the obscurity I sought to escape."[35]

Luckily, there were plenty of ways for French gentlemen to demonstrate their worth beyond the sphere of war: in peacetime, the art of living nobly in idleness was one of them. Boufflers had been schooled in that art from his youth in the court of King Stanisław, and even if he now found himself in a milieu far removed from the utopia of Lunéville, his education had by no means been forgotten. "What man combined to so high a degree the talent for brilliance, the gift of pleasing, the deep attractiveness...of that amiable and famous Chevalier de Boufflers?"[36] as the Comte de Ségur would phrase it in his funeral oration for the Chevalier. Ségur had his own brother, Joseph-Alexandre, as a point of comparison; and the Vicomte will be useful in helping us see the Chevalier's singularity.

Unlike the Vicomte, the Chevalier lacked an inheritance, could not rely on a minister father to advance his career, was not well known in Versailles, had no home of his own in Paris, and did not see life in high society as an end in itself. He wasn't as handsome or elegant as Joseph-Alexandre, nor did he possess the Vicomte's perfect manners. He could be "wild," "distracted and surly," with the "manners of a Huron"[37]—nevertheless he was quite fond of women. His features were so lively that, in two literary descriptions of him which have come down to us,[38] the Prince de Ligne found himself obliged to enumerate his impressions in piecemeal fashion: "Childhood is in his laugh, awkwardness in all his movements. He carries his head a little bent; he twirls his thumbs before him like Harlequin; keeps his hands behind his back as if he were warming them, or pulling off his gloves; his eyes are small but agreeable and always smiling; there is something *good* in his countenance: simple, gay, and naive in his grace; though heaviness is apparent in his figure, and his person is ill cared for."[39] Yet this appearance of indolent bonhomie quickly gives way to an extreme physical and intellectual agility. In order to describe it, Ligne has recourse to a string of contradictory attributes: the Chevalier has about him "a bit of the monkey and a bit of the will-'o-the-wisp, frivolousness and depth, restlessness and recklessness."[40] Boufflers himself admitted that he was often tempted to give himself over to idleness, but insisted that this "would make me miss out on everything, while compensating me with nothing."[41] For him, laziness was "the opium of the soul: she brings it troubled sleep and sad dreams."[42] However, this continual alteration of attitudes and moods revolved around one constant, which the Prince de Ligne did not even feel it necessary to mention: Boufflers's interest in women. The Chevalier himself informs us that for him love was a pure pleasure of the senses—"when it comes to love, I am entirely physical"[43]—and not a social game. Moreover, unlike Joseph-Alexandre de Ségur and other fashionable libertines, he felt no need to flaunt his successes with the fair sex.

Likewise, in the exercise of arms, the disparity between the Vicomte and the Chevalier was clear: whereas the former obtained his appointment as colonel in his youth, and without great effort, the latter, in spite of his dreams of glory, would struggle to advance.

Yet when it came to the world of society, Ségur, in spite of all the advantages he enjoyed, was a prisoner of his own worldly role, while Boufflers was free to forge fresh identities for himself to suit the changing needs of his own personal genius. Eternally in debt and itinerant, he spent a good portion of his time on horseback, alone, sans entourage or baggage, free to stop wherever he wished. The Comte de Tressan, a devoted follower of King Stanisław, happening to encounter Boufflers on the road, greeted him with the cry, "I'm charmed to find you at home!"[44] Ever since his childhood stays at his maternal grand-parents' château at Haroué, the Chevalier had adored plants and animals. Traveling with his horse across the length and breadth of France, with the horizon his only frontier, he found both physical well-being and aesthetic pleasure. It was an opportunity for him to experience to the fullest his profound empathy with nature: "One comes to feel maternal sentiments for the trees, the plants, the flowers."[45] The sheep parading by behind a fence seemed to him little different from men, "who believe themselves free because they cannot see their chains, and in following the common course of things think they are pursuing their wills."[46] He was among the first to conceive of nature as an inheritance that needed to be preserved. In 1790, in the midst of the Revolution, he urged the National Assembly to pass a law that would safeguard the forests expropriated from the nobility and the clergy, which were in danger of falling before the axes of unscrupulous speculators.[47] And earlier, in 1768, he had described his emotions as a traveler en route to the south of the country in a letter to the Duchesse de Choiseul: "It is truly a great pleasure, moving south during the winter. It seems as if nature, which appeared all but dead in the country one left behind, begins to awaken moment by moment; with each step you take, the process proceeds; each hour of the journey is another day won. It is as if the spring is coming to meet you; where yesterday you marched through ice, today you tread among flowers."[48] Wherever he went, he carried his paintbrushes, and paused to set down what struck him on canvas; driven by an insatiable curiosity, he visited all of the villages, churches, and châteaus that crossed his path. The Comte de Cheverny gives us a description of him in action on the occasion of the Chevalier's unexpected visit in the mid-1760s: "It was at about this time that a chevalier, in hussar's costume and traveling over hill and dale, happened across the château. He had come from Chante-loup, and was on his way to Lorraine. They came to inform me that this stranger was wandering through the park; it was suppertime, and I invited him to come see the château. We knew each other by sight, without having ever spoken. It was the amiable Chevalier de Boufflers. Not only did he dine with us but he stayed on for four or five days, and for some years he would be a regular visitor. After the Abbé Barthélemy, I find him the most eloquent conversationalist in

France. The proper word springs all but unbidden, without strain, to his lips, and his wit delivers the most delicate turns of phrase. Lazy even when it comes to study, he does not have the learning of others; he knows how to skim a book, but his chief merit is that everything he says has been drawn from the depths of himself."[49]

Still, Boufflers's taste for solitude and direct contact with nature did not preclude an attraction to life in society, and the society he frequented was certainly the best in Paris.

In the French capital, the Chevalier could count on the affectionate solidarity of the vast Beauvau-Craon clan, beginning with the paternal solicitude of his maternal brother, the Prince de Beauvau, who, as a product of the Age of Enlightenment, had cultivated the respect of all and sundry as much by his moral integrity as by his vast learning. He in his turn introduced Boufflers into the intimate circle of his very good friend—also a son of the Lorraine—the Duc de Choiseul, and it was in the course of his frequent visits to Chanteloup during its master's years of disgrace that the Chevalier found once again the sort of carefree utopia that he had known in his youth at the court of Stanisław.

Then there were his maternal aunts, Mme de Bassompierre and Mme de Montrevel, and, above all, the Maréchale de Mirepoix, whose charm was irresistible. "She possessed," said the Prince de Ligne, "that enchantress's spirit that enabled her to please everyone. You would have sworn she had thought of you alone all her life. Where will we find such a society again?"[50]

The cordial welcome given to him by his relatives on the Boufflers side was no less precious to the Chevalier. Indeed, the two most exclusive centers of Parisian society of the age were sustained by his father's cousins by marriage.

The eldest of the two, Madeleine-Angélique de Neufville—the widow of the Duc de Boufflers, who had remarried Charles-François-Frédéric de Montmorency-Luxembourg, Duc de Luxembourg, Maréchal de France—was considered a supreme authority when it came to questions good taste and social comportment, and her judgment was unquestioned in making or breaking reputations.

After having distinguished herself in her youth by "black" wickedness and "unbridled" libertinism—to which the Baron de Besenval bears witness with the vitriolic portrait he paints of her in his memoirs[51]—Mme de Luxembourg managed to pull off a spectacular metamorphosis. Having reached middle age—rather than embracing religion and, like the grandes dames of the past, radically changing her mode of life by renouncing the vain shows of the world—the Maréchale remained resolutely at the center of the social scene, taking up as the weapon of her own redemption the morality of appearances. She showed that she knew the rules like no one else. "She is penetrating enough to make you tremble: the tiniest pretension, the lightest affectation, a tone, a gesture that isn't exactly natural, she will seize upon and judge with the greatest rigor; the subtlety of her wit, the delicacy of her taste allow nothing to escape,"[52] wrote her friend Mme du Deffand. For his part, the Duc de Lévis, who knew her in her old age, recalled that "her influence over the youth of both sexes was absolute; she contained the giddiness of the young women, enforced on them a genial coquetry, obliged the young men to practice continence and respect; finally, she maintained the sacred fire of French urbanity: it was with her that the tradition of noble and confident manners was preserved intact, so that all Europe came to Paris to admire them, and sought in vain to imitate."[53]

Cultivated, intelligent, witty, endowed with a solid experience of the world, and more than capable of changing his tone as needed, Stanislas-Jean was made to please the Maréchale, who opened the doors of her salon to him and treated him like a son. It was there that the Chevalier began a sincere friendship with his young, timid cousin, Amélie de Boufflers, the daughter of the Mme de Luxembourg's son by her first marriage, educated to perfection by the Maréchale, and destined before long to marry the Duc de Lauzun.

The only great social circle comparable to Mme de Luxembourg's was that of the Temple. At its head was Marie-Charlotte Hippolyte Campet de Saujon, the widow of the Comte de Boufflers-Rouverel and official mistress to the Prince de Conti, grand prior of the Order of Malta. In the ancient enclave of the Templars at the heart of Paris, the main subjects of talk tended to be intellectual and political in nature. After having long been the political adviser to Louis XV, Conti had fallen into disgrace and, abandoning the court, openly offered protection to the philosophes, setting himself in opposition to royal absolutism and coming to the defense of parliament in 1770. For her part, the Comtesse de Boufflers combined curiosity and erudition, and had a passion for traveling. She spoke three languages and was one of the first in Paris society to receive foreign visitors, while her voyage to England in 1763 was a historical milestone—"they said that she was the only Frenchwoman of quality to have come as a traveler in two hundred years"[54]—and launched the fashion for

Anglomania. Her social ambition—which Mme du Deffand mocked incessantly in her letters—did not prevent her from passionately sharing in the reformist hopes of the Enlightenment. Her correspondence with David Hume and Gustav III of Sweden, and the protection she extended to Rousseau, bear witness to the seriousness of her interests.

At the Temple—as well as at L'Isle-Adam, Conti's summer residence—Boufflers was introduced to the currents of thought that were driving the emergence of the new Fronde. In 1770, the disgrace of the Duc de Choiseul, and the courageous stand that the Prince de Beauvau-Craon had taken on his behalf, gave the Chevalier an indication of the nature of the field on which he might fight, going forward. But while waiting to see exactly what form his new life would take, Boufflers reveled in his rediscovered freedom, enjoying a Paris then at its intellectual and artistic apogee, and repaying the warm welcome afforded him by the heights of high society with the originality, invariable gaiety, and abundant brio he possessed as a writer of verse.

The feverishness with which Mme du Deffand—who disliked the Chevalier as much as she disliked his mother and sister, whom she had nicknamed the "Steinkerque birds"[55]—sought to keep herself informed regarding Stanislas-Jean's exploits stands as an index of his social success. "Did the Chevalier de Boufflers keep you well entertained? If he's written you any couplets, I humbly ask that you send them my way,"[56] she wrote to the Duchesse de Choiseul in July 1766, and, years later, she inquired anew: "Is the Chevalier de Boufflers staying with you at the moment? Don't you find him almost as intelligent as he is pleasant?"[57] The question was double-edged, since Mme du Deffand thought that Boufflers had "more talent than discernment, more elegance and finesse than aptitude."[58] But in coming to his defense, the Duchesse de Choiseul revealed herself as a more penetrating observer than her friend, giving us a key insight that the Chevalier himself would surely have approved: "I believe that he has wisdom in his heart, and that is sufficient for him, if not for us—it isn't the aegis of Minerva that one flaunts in society, but rather whatever silly fad is current."[59]

The Chevalier's skill at raillery was attested to by no less an authority on the subject than Voltaire. In December 1764, Boufflers paid a call on Stanisław's old friend at Ferney, and took advantage of the opportunity to visit nearby Switzerland. As *Correspondance littéraire* hastened to inform its subscribers, "he decided to give himself out as a painter; and in all of the villages he passed through executed portraits of the principal inhabitants, especially the prettiest women. These sessions were certainly far from dull; songs, poems, and a hundred humorous stories brightened the faces of his sitters as the artist set them down on canvas, earning him the reputation of a singular man, and he took no more than a single ecu for his work; but when he arrived in Geneva he decided to resume his real name, and aroused a fair bit of suspicion among the locals."[60] Voltaire could not have given him a warmer welcome. As the Chevalier would inform the Marquise, "He received me as your son, and bestowed on me all the signs of friendship that he would have on yourself."[61] And Voltaire in turn hastened to communicate his enthusiasm to his old friend: "I currently have the honor, madame, of hosting in my hovel the painter who enjoys your protection. You have good reason to love this young man; he paints with marvelous skill all the ridiculous things of this world—and in truth, the world contains nothing else; in this one might say that he resembles his mother. I believe he will go far. I have seen the young men of Paris and Versailles, but compared to him they are nothing but daubers."[62] Voltaire was always lavish with hyperbolic compliments for his admirers, but he was sincerely entertained by his guest, whom he was ready to describe as "one of the most singular creatures in the world."[63] The Chevalier's visit ended in an explosion of verse, laughter, and salacious jokes, and after having been urged by the old poet to take up his lyre—"*C'est à vous, ô jeune Boufflers, / [...] C'est à vous de chanter Thémire, / et de briller dans les festins, / animé du triple délire / des vers, de l'amour et du vin*"*[64]—Stanislas-Jean returned to Paris, a poet crowned with laurels.

But not all of Boufflers's poems were airy "*méringues* [*sic*]" as Chamfort described them,[65] adapted to the delicate tastes of a society audience. The *honnête raillerie*, that gentle banter whose formula he had almost perfectly mastered, could quickly shed its gloves, becoming a scourge for individuals and institutions alike. The Chevalier allowed himself moments of absolute freedom, counting on the complicity of a few trusted intimates. Like a true *esprit fort*, he celebrated sheer sensual pleasure without euphemisms or metaphors, thumbing his nose at the dogmas and sexual morality of the Church,

*It's your time, oh young Boufflers / [...] Time for you to sing of Thémire, / to shine at every feast, / enlivened by the triple delirium / of verse, love, and wine.

the better to ridicule its beliefs. Each time, it was a question of choosing the language and style most appropriate for the occasion.

Consider the blasphemous verse written on the occasion of the first Mass performed by the Abbé Petit:

> *Petit, Petit,*
> *vous allez faire bonne chère,*
> *Petit, Petit.*
> *Tâchez d'avoir bon appétit.*
> *Le Dieu du ciel et de la terre*
> *pour votre dîner va se faire*
> *petit, petit.*[*66]

Or those verses improvised for an octogenarian Marquise who wanted to put his ingenuity to the test "by requesting a sonnet with the most bizarre rhymes she could find":

> *Enfants de Saint Benoît, sous la guimpe ou le froc*
> *Du calice chrétien savourez l'amertume;*
> *Vous, musulmans, suivez votre triste coutume:*
> *Buvez de l'eau pendant que je vide mon broc.*
> *De vos raisonnements, moins ébranlé qu'un roc,*
> *Je crains peu cette mer de soufre et de bitume*
> *Où vos sots docteurs ont coutume*
> *De noyer les Titus et les rois de Maroc.*
> *Quel que puisse être le maroufle*
> *Que vous nommez pape ou mouphti,*
> *Je ne baiserai point son cul, ni sa pantoufle.*
> *Prêtres noirs qui damnez Marc-Aurèle et Hamti,*
> *Par qui Confucius comme un lièvre est rôti,*
> *Le diable qui les brûle est celui qui vous souffle.*[†67]

*Petit, Petit, / You're going to eat well, / Petit, Petit. / Make sure that your appetite's good. / The God of Heaven and Earth / That you'll be dining on is going to make himself / petit, petit.

†Children of Saint Benoît, wearing wimple or frock, / Enjoy the bitterness of the Christian chalice; / And you, Muslims, follow your drab tradition: / Drink water, while I drain my

Diderot enjoyed these verses for their irreverence, gaiety, and extravagance, and he copied them, along with other texts by the Chevalier, for Sophie Volland.[68]

But sex offered Boufflers the greatest opportunity to mock social conventions—for example, with a facetious apologia for the taboo of incest. In Paris, the Chevalier had once again met up with his sister, Marie-Stanislas-Catherine, who, rather unhappily married to the Comte de Boisgelin, divided her time between her native Lorraine, Versailles—Stanislas had managed to have her appointed as lady-in-waiting to Mme Victoire, one of the daughters of Louis XV—and the French capital, where her aunt Mirepoix hosted her in the Maréchal's grand mansion in the rue d'Artois. As she grew to adulthood, the *divine mignonne* had become hopelessly ugly, but this had not prevented her from enjoying a certain success with men. The siblings were very close and, both having been educated by their mother, had complementary senses of humor, the same familial vocabulary, and a similar sexual freedom.

> *Vivons en famille,*
> *c'est le plaisir le plus doux,*
> *de tous.*
> *Nous sommes, ma fille,*
> *heureux sans sortir de chez nous.*
> *Les honnêtes gens*
> *des premiers temps*
> *avaient des plus douces moeurs,*
> *et sans chercher ailleurs,*
> *ils offraient à leurs soeurs*
> *leurs coeurs.*
> *Sur ce point-là nos aïeux*
> *N'étaient pas scrupuleux.*
> *Nous pourrions faire,*

---

jug. / I fear that sea of sulfur and bitumen / Where your doctors are accustomed to drown / Titus and the Kings of Morocco / Far less than your reasoning, as unshakable as a rock. / Whatever that fraud may be / Whom you call Pope or Mufti, / I certainly won't kiss his ass, or his slipper. / Black priests who damn Marcus Aurelius and Hamti, / In whose eyes Confucius is roasting like a hare, / The devil who burns them is the one that prompts you.

ma chère,
aussi bien qu'eux,
des neveux.[*69]

After all, hadn't the Scripture provided them with an example? The story of Lot's daughters furnished a fine occasion for a laugh. Here, the trump card is the concision of the logical reasoning proposed as an exegesis of the biblical tale:

Il but
il devint tendre
et puis il fut
son gendre.[†70]

Furthermore, some years later, the Chevalier dedicated to his mother a panegyric that openly celebrated her easy morals:

Reniez Dieu, brûlez Jérusalem et Rome,
pour docteurs et pour saints n'ayez que les amours:
s'il est vrai que le Christ soit homme,
il vous pardonnera toujours.[‡71]

According to the Prince de Ligne, Boufflers had once responded to his mother, who lamented not knowing how to love God, that he was certain that if God became a man once again, she would love him just like she did the others.[72]

Finally, Boufflers's cheerfully blasphemous irony assailed the virginity of the Mother of God herself in his quintets recounting the misfortunes of the Duchesse Marie de Durfort, who had given birth to a child of whom her husband could hardly have been the father.

---

*Let's live *en famille,* / It's the sweetest pleasure / Of all. / My girl, we're happy enough / Without leaving the house. / The gentlemen / Of the earliest eras / Had finer manners than we, / And without searching elsewhere / Offered their hearts / To their sisters. / On that point, our ancestors / Were far from scrupulous. / And we, my dear, / Could make nephews / As well as they.

†He drank, / He became tender, / And soon he was / His own *gendre* [son-in-law].

‡Renounce God, burn Jerusalem and Rome, / for theologians and saints have nothing but love: / if it is true that Christ is a man / he will always forgive you.

Votre patronne
Fit un enfant sans son mari.
Bel exemple qu'elle vous donne!
N'imitez donc pas à demi
Votre patronne.

Pour cette affaire,
Savez-vous comme elle s'y prit?
Comme vous, n'en pouvant pas faire,
Elle eut recours au Saint-Esprit
Pour cette affaire.*

These lines, promptly published in the *Mémoires secrets*[73] along with the name of its unfortunate subject, showed just how cruel the Chevalier's irony could be.

Mémoires secrets also reports an episode in which the Chevalier passed from words to deeds. A *belle* Marquise, unidentified and unfaithful, upon whom Boufflers had avenged himself with a "savage epigram," had invited the Chevalier to her home in order to "ratify a sincere reconciliation." "The Chevalier knew women too well to arrive at such a rendezvous unarmed, and he supplied himself with a brace of pistols. No sooner had the two exchanged their first words than four enormous scoundrels burst upon the scene, seized him, stretched him facedown on the bed, stripping him as much as was necessary to execute their plan, and then administered fifty lashes to him at madame's command. This ceremony complete, the Chevalier raised himself coldly, and readjusted his clothing." It was then, threatening the four men with his pistols, that he obliged them not only to whip the Marquise—"The tears of that beauty did not prevent her satin skin from being most pitilessly tattered"—but one another as well. And for good measure, in taking leave of her, he informed the lady that he would regale whoever was interested with the tale of this amusing incident. "They say that the Marquise ran after him, threw herself at his knees, and so begged him to keep the secret that he dined that same evening at her home, in order to conceal their indiscretions; it is further claimed that,

---

*Your patron saint / Made a child without her husband. / What a fine example she gave you! / So don't imitate her by halves, / Your patron saint. // In that affair, / Do you know how she pulled it off? / Like you, unable to do it alone, / She had recourse to the Holy Spirit / In that affair.

the scheme being effective, the evening ended even more merrily than it had begun."[74]

Authentic or not, the episode seems to confirm that Boufflers's reputation as a libertine was seen by those around him to have been earned as much by his conduct as his irreverent verse. But verse was not the Chevalier's only talent.

Following the success of "Queen of Golconde," the letters the Chevalier sent to his mother from Switzerland had cemented his literary reputation. Their collection constituted a sort of travel journal in which his remarks on the habits and customs of the country, its inhabitants, and its natural beauties were presented with the immediacy of conversation, and established themselves as part of a literary tradition which—from Chapelle and Bachaumont's *Voyage through Languedoc and Provence* to La Fontaine's *Journey from Paris to Limousin: Letters to Madame de La Fontaine*—had a number of illustrious precedents. We do not know if the Chevalier had planned the publication of these letters at the time of writing, but certainly he was aware that his mother would show them to her friends and acquaintances, letting them circulate from salon to salon according to a social custom that had been in play since the era of the Hôtel de Rambouillet. The pirated edition of the letters, which was published in Geneva in September 1771, gave evidence of the great curiosity they had aroused. The most attentive of its readers recognized its allusions:[75] the comic virtuosity of Voiture (the Abbé Porquet's wig placed upon "the bald summit of the Alps" so that "his skullcap would become, for the first time, the highest point on earth")[76] and the sovereign irony of Voltaire. But scattered among the witticisms, there were also political reflections: it was easy to make fun of the rusticity of the Swiss, but they had "the pleasure of making their own laws," as well as the right to cultivate their lands "with a free hand" and, exempt from tithing and land taxes, to enjoy the fruits of their labor unmolested.[77] Well aware of the polemical nature of these observations, Boufflers begged his mother to reassure Stanisław that "the sight of free peoples would never make a rebel of him"[78]—thereby demonstrating that he was certainly not taking account of what they might think at Versailles. It was an error for which he would pay a heavy price.

The Duchesse d'Aiguillon hastened to offer the collection to Horace Walpole, that passionate lover of epistolary literature, and he in his turn confided to Mme du Deffand that he had thought the letters enchanting. He found everything that Boufflers put his hand to "quite pretty,"[79] and supported his opinion by noting in his journal a characteristic Boufflers quip: "Only God possesses cheerfulness enough not to grow bored with the praise He receives."[80]

For his part, the Chevalier de Bonnard took note of the warm welcome the work received among a discriminating aristocratic audience, and rightly pegged Boufflers's "fluency" and "cheerful insouciance"[81] as the reasons for its popularity. Rousseau himself was willing to recognize that the Chevalier was "as brilliant as it was possible to be," though, coming from him, this was more a reproach than a compliment: "With his intellect, he might have succeeded in everything; but his total incapacity for steady application and his taste for amusement only permitted him to acquire imperfect accomplishments of every description. By way of compensation, these attainments were extensive; and that is all that is necessary in the great world in which he is anxious to shine. He can compose pretty little poems, write pretty little notes, can play a little on the cithern, and daub a little in pastels."[82] In Rousseau's eyes, Boufflers was the symbol of a vain and artificial aristocratic civilization whose fundamental duplicity he was preparing to denounce in *La Nouvelle Héloïse*. And a tremendous amount of resentment against the Chevalier must have accumulated when Rousseau had seen the former flitting around at Montmorency under the satisfied gaze of the Maréchale de Luxembourg while, paralyzed by timidity, Jean-Jacques himself had not dared to join the conversation, since, as he recalls lugubriously in the *Confessions*, "so dull and heavy did my clumsy blunders appear by the side of [Boufflers's] graceful and refined wit." The "mere presence" of the Chevalier had "crushed him beyond hope of recovery."[83] Indeed, Rousseau's judgment on Boufflers's literary talent would be difficult to contest—were it not that we know what the philosopher could not have known. The worldly aristocrat, whose *petites lettres* from Switzerland were written for his own diversion and that of his friends, was one day to become a true master of the epistolary art. But that metamorphosis would require a genuine emotional revolution.

In the spring of 1777, during one of his frequent sojourns in Paris, the Prince de Ligne took Boufflers to the home of one of his young friends, someone he had known years earlier at Versailles: the Comtesse de Sabran. Following a period of mourning for the death of her husband, which she had spent in the country, the Comtesse had returned to Paris, buying a sumptuous *hôtel particulier*[84]—bordering on one side the Faubourg Saint-Honoré and on the other a magnificent garden that extended as far as the Champs-Élysées—wherein she received a small and select circle of visitors. It was the first time that Mme de Sabran and Boufflers had met, but each had certainly heard tell of the other. Celebrated for his literary successes, the Chevalier was the spoiled child of Parisian high society, and Mme de Sabran could not have been unaware of him. She, however, had also stirred talk—against her own wishes—for the singularity of her behavior and style of life.

In contrast to Boufflers, Françoise-Éléonore Jean de Manville, born in 1749 in Paris to a wealthy family that had distinguished itself in the magistracy and administration, had suffered an unhappy childhood and adolescence. Her mother had died giving birth to her, her father had remarried the most odious of stepmothers, and her maternal grandmother, who was charged with her education, had subjected her to all manner of humiliations. The years she'd spent at school would have been more serene if Éléonore had not been forced to protect her elder sister, very beautiful but mentally deficient, from the mockery of their fellow students. The death of her stepmother had not improved the situation—her father continued to abdicate his responsibilities.

However, when it came time for her to marry, Éléonore, who had submitted with sweetness and resignation to an uninterrupted series of aggravations and injustices, was inflexible. The only man she was disposed to wed, she declared, was an old friend of the family: Joseph de Sabran, Comte de Grammont. Her choice was forty-seven years older than her, and poor, but he descended from Marguerite de Provence and Saint Louis and was considered a hero. Among the various exploits that had contributed to his fame during his naval service, one episode involving the ship he had commanded, the *Centaur*, had become legendary. In 1759, during the Seven Years' War, while tearing through the waters off Gibraltar, the *Centaur* had come under fire from four English warships. In an effort to protect the rear of the French fleet, Sabran had resisted the enemy for hours on end, and it was not until he had run through all of his ammunition and charged his cannons with his own silverware for one final broadside that he resigned himself to lowering his flag in order to prevent his sailors going down with the ship. The English who captured him were the first to display their admiration for his bravery. When he returned to Versailles as a result of an exchange of prisoners, Louis XV complimented him for his courage before the assembled court and, recalling the noble ancestors of the Sabrans, presented him to the Dauphin, saying, "He is our relation."

Seventeen years later, on her daughter's wedding day, Éléonore would recall her own emotional expectations when she presented herself at the altar: "I was marrying a sick old man, one for whom I would be less a wife than a nurse-maid...but in the moment, I had no sense of the consequences: everything seemed to me perfectly proper, perfectly good; loving nothing, everything seemed to me worthy of being loved, and I felt for the gentlemen I was marrying the same sentiment as I did for my father and grandfather, a very sweet feeling, and one that was enough for my heart."[85] Indeed, her choice revealed itself to have been a wise one. The Comte de Sabran was an upstanding, intelligent, and sensitive man, and he gave to this young bride, whose dowry allowed him to settle his debts, all the protection, affection, and sweetness that she wanted. He demonstrated an unconditional trust in her, presented her immediately at court, and gave her complete freedom in choosing her friends. During her first few visits to Versailles—as her son would later recall—"her shyness and modesty were so great that she sought to hide herself with all the energy that someone else would have sought to shine. M. de Puységur, who witnessed her social debut, told me that he was forever discovering her hidden behind some-one's basket, of which she made a rampart and a shelter."[86] But, as Ligne wrote, Éléonore had no need to talk to endear herself to others: "Her eyes are the palette of her soul, and of her mind. There you may read all you please of goodness, delicacy, cleverness, sensibility, and radiance. She agrees, disagrees, blames, without speaking. There you will see benevolence, gaiety, profundity, and reason."[87] And when she did decide to speak, she knew how to do so with tact and eloquence, with "sensibility" and "elevation"[88]—but always, also, with an air of apologizing in advance for the thought that she might be correct.

Free of prejudice and well schooled in the art of dissimulation, society at court looked with indulgence on those who arrived at Versailles armed only with their moral integrity. Innocent virtue embellished by grace brought a breath of fresh air into the stale atmosphere of the royal palace, and it was no accident that Éléonore received the nickname of "Rose de Champs." Taken as a protégée by Mme de Marsan, who held the title of Governess to the Children of France, the Comtesse soon joined the carefree group of young followers of the Dauphine, and the Dauphine—soon to become Queen—welcomed her with open arms.

It was with the Trudaines, however, in Paris as well as at their beautiful summer home of Montigny-en-Brie, that Mme de Sabran was initiated into the intellectual life of the capital.

According to the Marquise du Deffand—still so difficult to please—it was with the Trudaines that one encountered "a different world than one found among high society."[89] There, Éléonore became acquainted with (aside from the sons of the family—Louis Trudaine de Montigny, an honest magistrate and protector of the painter Jacques-Louis David, and Michel Trudaine de La Sablière—both of them intimate friends of the poet André Chénier) various prominent figures of the culture of the Enlightenment, such as Turgot and Malesherbes. She befriended the poet Delille, who offered to tutor her in Latin, and profited greatly from "the tremendously serious conversations"[90] in which she had the opportunity to participate.

When, in 1775, after less than six years of marriage, Mme de Sabran lost her husband, she was sorely afflicted but managed to maintain her spirits. She knew exactly what she needed to do. Her absolute priority was loving, protecting, and raising the children that she had had the joy of bringing into the world: Delphine, born in 1770, and Elzéar, born in 1774. She had to uphold the honor of the Sabrans, maintaining in dignity the position that her husband had given her both in town and at court, fostering those relationships that would be necessary for the future of her children, while remaining firmly her own mistress. However, her plans were not founded on renunciation and a spirit of sacrifice but on solid good sense: she was rich, independent, curious about everything, surrounded by friends, and lacked nothing necessary to lead a pleasant life, while respecting the social conventions. In contrast with the women of her generation who had read *La Nouvelle Héloïse*[91] while still adolescents, Éléonore gave nary a thought to the possibility of finding passion. She was completely satisfied with the life she had chosen: "I am persuaded that our happiness resides within us, and that with the assistance of reason and philosophy it should be impossible to be unhappy in this world—or, at least, very difficult."[92] The Chevalier de Boufflers, however, obliged her to reconsider.

Surely the first thing that struck the Chevalier de Boufflers about the young woman who came to welcome him on that day in May 1777, fulfilling her duties as mistress of the house, was her physical appearance. More than just beautiful, the Comtesse de Sabran was irresistibly attractive. Ligne describes her nymph-like profile, and his son her delicate feet and the supreme grace of her movements. Her portrait, painted by Élisabeth Vigée Le Brun,[93] reproduces for us, beneath a halo of curls, her triangular face with its small upturned nose, and two wide eyes in perfect harmony with her smile. The Chevalier, who evokes in his poetry the ebullient mass of her blond hair rebelling against combs and pins—calling her "Sabran, the ill-coiffed"[94]—and who compares her to a "little gazelle,"[95] recalls their first encounter in giving Éléonore's features to the heroine of "Ah, yes...," one of the stories written in his maturity:[96] "Imagine not the most striking thing you have ever seen, but, what is a great deal more, the most fascinating: a visible soul rather than mere beauty; that is what struck me at the first glance, and the physiognomy somehow prevented me from taking in the face; but the face, too, had its turn; and my gaze lingered on that beautiful hair, of which the silvery fairness contrasted so charmingly with the color of the eyebrows and lashes; on that delicate complexion, with its candid whiteness; those blooming cheeks that seemed tinged by innocence..." And he cannot pass over in silence "that expressive mouth, which speaks without opening; those eyes, the color of pansies, that shed more light than they receive; the nose that with its shape, its fineness, could belong to no one else and seemed like the rallying point for all the face's other charms; and even the chin, at which one could not help staring..."[97] As for Éléonore's virtue, it could only have constituted an additional reason for a professional libertine like Boufflers to want to woo her. Love had taken him by surprise: the Comtesse was a chaste version of his own mother, the only woman whom he had ever truly loved up to that point. Like the Marquise de Boufflers, Éléonore had exquisite manners, a lively intelligence, unusual independence of judgment, and a marked artistic sensibility—but she was reserved, modest, delicate, and even the word "sensuality" would have embarrassed her.

Employing one of those military metaphors that libertines had been in the habit of using since the era of Bussy-Rabutin and his *Amorous History of the Gauls*, the Chevalier, as a seasoned strategist, immediately understood that breaching the walls of Mme de Sabran's heart would be no simple matter. It was useless to pin his hopes on female vanity—the Comtesse was neither frivolous nor coquettish—or to attempt a straightforward seduction, in which she was manifestly uninterested. With her, badinage would be able to take him no further than the limits imposed by social uses. Instead, what he needed to do was find some means of introducing himself into her life little by little without alarming her—for instance, by establishing an intellectual rapport based on their common interests. Right away the Chevalier identified three of them: music, painting, and the translation of classical authors. These would serve as his Trojan horse.

When it came to the first of these, things were simple. Both the Chevalier and the Comtesse had fine voices and, when she sang in accompaniment to the guitar, he responded by improvising songs for the harpsichord. With painting, it was if anything even easier. Many women of high society were skilled in the use of pencils and brushes, and the Marquise de Boufflers as well as Mme de Montesson and the charming Marquise de Bréhan—victim of the libertine maneuverings of the Vicomte de Ségur—were famous for the beauty of their depictions of flowers. But we are informed by no less an authority than Élisabeth Vigée Le Brun just how gifted Éléonore was when it came to art: "She copied the old masters perfectly, imitating their color and gusto to the point that, coming into her studio one day, I mistook her copy for the original. She did not conceal the pleasure that my error had caused her; for she was just as unaffected as she was amiable and lovely."[98] Thus, insensible of the danger to which she was exposing herself, the Comtesse could not resist Boufflers's proposition that each of them execute a portrait of the other. What could be more intimate and revealing than a portrait sitting? Wasn't its goal to seize the irreducible singularity of the model? Observing that it was impossible to "fix" Boufflers "even in a painting,"[99] Mme de Sabran came to the same conclusions that Diderot had while observing his own portrait, executed by Michel Van Loo, when it was shown in the Salon of 1757: "In the course of a single day I assumed a hundred different expressions, in accordance with the things that affected me. I was serene, sad, pensive, tender, violent, passionate, enthusiastic; but I was never such as you see me here."[100] But even if a painter was incapable of rendering on canvas no more than a single facet of an *I* as manifold as it was deceptive, the Chevalier had in any case achieved his goal—for in the process of looking, the artist could not help but establish a privileged rapport with her model. The opportunity that Mme de Sabran gave him to play the role of teacher was just as precious. The Comtesse, who herself wrote charming verse, was eager to work on translations of the Latin poets, and the Chevalier volunteered to assist her: it was yet another chance to secure private time with her that would otherwise have been unthinkable, to enter into the sensibility of his student, to encourage and compliment her, but also to display his intellectual superiority. The results were not long in coming. Over the course of the ten months that followed their first meeting, Boufflers conquered the friendship of Mme de Sabran. While continuing to forbid him to speak of love, the young woman had admitted him to the sphere of her familial relationships, the only emotional ties that counted for her and of which she had any experience. She had dubbed him "my brother," and wished him to refer to her as "my sister."

It took Boufflers two additional years to persuade her to the use of a different kind of vocabulary, and that wait might have been indefinitely prolonged if two unforeseeable factors had not come to his aid: their forced separation, and their recourse to written correspondence. The first exposed Éléonore to the void left in her life by the Chevalier, whom she had grown accustomed to seeing every day; the second allowed her to see the full measure of the humanity, intelligence, and verve of her correspondent. For Boufflers, the distance and correspondence represented an opportunity for him to overcome the resistance of his beloved, to reveal her to herself, by suggesting to her in a million different ways the true nature of the sentiment that bound them and of which he had been forbidden to speak.

It was in February 1778 that Boufflers was forced to leave Paris in order to rejoin his regiment, the Chartres infantry, garrisoned at Landerneau. The minister of war, the Prince de Montbarrey, had deployed an imposing military detachment to the coasts of France, while an enormous war fleet was gathered at Brest under the command of the Comte d'Orvilliers. On January 30, France had signed a treaty of friendship and trade with the United States, which was followed some seven days later by an alliance in the event of a Franco-English conflict. Having finally secured the approval of Louis XVI, the minister of foreign affairs, the Comte de Vergennes, was preparing not only to come to the aid of the American rebels but also to carry out an armed landing across the Channel—a double offensive against the English—in addition to increasing pressure for a naval expedition to India, against British colonial interests. For France—strongly allied by a "family pact" with the Spanish Bourbons and the Low Countries—this was a long-awaited chance to avenge their humiliation in the Seven Years' War. And for the numerous French aristocrats disillusioned with the court, it was an opportunity to embrace a new kind of patriotism, one inseparable from the idea of "liberty,"[101] that had recently made its appearance on the far side of the Atlantic.

Like the Duc de Lauzun in his garrison at Ardes, near Calais, like the Comte de Ségur in Brittany, like Choderlos de Laclos inspecting the coasts of Normandy and Brittany in order to improve their fortifications, the Chevalier de Boufflers saw in the war the possibility of displaying his abilities as a soldier.

He had never enjoyed the favor of Versailles: the Consort, Marie Leszczyńska, detested the Marquise de Boufflers; the Well-Beloved had not been pleased that the Chevalier had been the first to make the journey to Chanteloup following the disgrace of the Duc de Choiseul; and Louis XVI deplored his irreverence as much as his libertinism. The Chevalier's satirical poem on Princesse Christine de Saxe, an aunt of the sovereign, could not have been more impertinent,[102] and, in 1776, the King had removed Boufflers's name from his list of promotions, declaring: "I care neither for his epigrams nor his verse."[103] Having finally achieved the rank of colonel, Boufflers obtained from the Duc de Chartres the command of the infantry regiment bearing the latter's name.

On the coasts of Brittany and Normandy, the Chevalier found himself facing the quotidian miseries of military life rather than undertaking any heroic initiatives. Like Lauzun, the freshly minted colonel immediately saw that the plan for an invasion of England was highly uncertain—whereas the indecision of the French ministers and generals, the absence of clear orders, the arbitrariness of appointments, and the "ineptitude"[104] of those superior officials selected for positions due to their favor at court were all fully apparent. To this was added the difficulty of maintaining the discipline of the troops, sorely afflicted by seasonal epidemics and kept on a constant war footing despite the fact that the enemy was nowhere in sight. After two short months in Brittany, Boufflers could not conceal his pessimism: "There is nothing worse than the sort of prelude to war we are carrying out at present. My regiment would suffer less during a campaign. It is exhausted, divided, dilapidated, infected with scurvy, scabies, etc.: all we're lacking is the plague. War itself would be less disagreeable than this; at least it would offer us a little compensation. But I fear that we won't be going to England, and England certainly won't be coming to us. We will spend years in wait for what will never happen, and rather with the air of fearing the war than preparing for it. Instead of having a fever, we'll have the shakes—and there's nothing at all heroic about that."[105] Finally, in July, the Chevalier glimpsed the possibility of taking ship at Brest, under the command of the Duc of Chartres, in the fleet that was leaving to attack the Royal Navy, which would mark the official beginning of the war against England. But Louis XVI blocked his way: "I did all I could to follow my Colonel to sea, but his cousin opposed it," wrote the Chevalier sadly to the Comtesse de Sabran. "I am utterly mad for the love of Glory, but she has no interest in me whatsoever."[106]

The Chevalier's luck was no better when, in January 1780, Louis XVI decided to send a detachment of 5,500 men to the aid of the Americans under the command of the Comte de Rochambeau. Free to select his preferred regiments and officers, the general paid no heed to the Chartres Regiment, and on May 2, the French fleet left the port of Brest and sailed toward America, carrying the Duc de Lauzun, Comte Arthur de Dillon, the Marquis de Chastellux, the Vicomte de Noailles, and the Lameth brothers, but leaving behind the great-grandson of the Maréchal de Boufflers. After two years of commitment and the sacrifices that should have given ample evidence of his ability and disposed of his reputation for frivolity, the Chevalier was forced to admit—like Laclos—that "Glory" was continuing to turn her back on him. But he would not go so far as to renounce the pursuit of her—for the very idea of glory had acquired a new meaning since the beginning of his infatuation with Mme de Sabran.

In the wake of his Polish misadventure, Boufflers—deprived of the protection of Choiseul, in ill odor at Versailles, confined in the army to duties that suited neither his name nor his abilities—had made a virtue of necessity: life was too lovely to squander it on regrets, and he was too confident of his own worth to depend on the whims of others. He was self-sufficient and had no need of a career to be happy. For him, everything was a source of interest, of amusement, of pleasure, and—a son worthy of his mother—the gaiety he emanated was enough to render him irresistible. "Go on, preserve indefinitely for your own ease that pleasant lightness, that happy gaiety that nothing can alter,"[107] wrote Mme de Sabran to him after having been wholly captivated—but she also reminded him that the "blind confidence" that he had in luck might lead to him "losing it": "It encourages your habitual laziness when it comes to thinking, planning, and reckoning. It rids you of all your cares, true, but how it leaves you exposed!"[108]

However, it was precisely his introduction to the Comtesse that had driven him to reassess, as he approached the age of forty, his deliciously vagabond existence, free of all responsibilities and obligations, and to feel once again the stirrings of ambition. Unlike the role it had played in the Polish adventure of his youth, success on the battlefield was no longer an end in itself but rather the sine qua non to win the affection of the woman he loved—the "currency" with which he could "purchase the sole possession" that he found "worthy of desire."[109]

This was certainly nothing new. Ever since the age of chivalry, aristocratic morality had seen in the figure of the beloved woman the inspiration for both

1. Georges Rouget, *Armand-Louis de Gontaut, Duc de Lauzun (later Duc de Biron)*, 1835

2. Joshua Reynolds, *Lady Sarah Bunbury Sacrificing to the Graces*, 1763–1765

3. Kazimierz Wojniakowski, *Princesse Izabela Czartoryska*, 1796

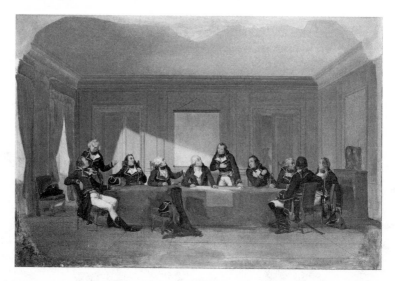

4. Anonymous, *The War Council at Courtrai on June 26, 1792*. Pictured are Berthier, Lameth, Beurnonville, Biron, Luckner, the Duc de Chartres (standing), Valence, Duhoux, d'Aboville, and Lynch as they plan the offensive that will lead to the victory at the Battle of Valmy on September 20, 1792.

5. Pierre Adolphe Hall, *Vicomte de Ségur Contemplating a Portrait of a Lady*

6. Henri-Pierre Danloux, *Baron de Besenval in His Salon de Compagnie*, 1791

7. François-Hubert Drouais, *Louis-Hercule-Timoléon de Cossé, Duc de Brissac*, ca. 1770

8. Élisabeth Vigée Le Brun, *Jeanne Bécu, Madame du Barry,* 1781

9. Herminie Déhérain, *Comte Louis de Narbonne*

heroism and virtue. But the reasons that drove Boufflers to choose Mme de Sabran as the object of his chivalrous quest answered to very specific needs. Indeed, if he succeeded in overcoming her reluctance and winning her love, what form could their relationship take? A practicing Catholic and profoundly virtuous, Éléonore attached great importance to her reputation—there was no reason to believe she was inclined to put it in jeopardy. The sole proposition that the Comtesse might have accepted was that of marriage, but this was not something the Chevalier was in a position to offer. He had no fortune at his disposal: the lion's share of his colonel's appanage had gone to purchasing his equipment and to various other expenses of military life; his only income came from the ecclesiastical benefices that Stanisław had procured for him and that he would have lost in leaving the Order of Malta, where "celibacy" was officially required. And even once his revenues were reduced to his military earnings, honor would not have permitted him to marry a wealthy young widow like Mme de Sabran and be dependent on her, to the detriment of his children's inheritance. Thus, before leaving the Order of Malta, he would have to establish himself with his talents and win for himself some prestigious position.

But in the meantime, nothing prevented Boufflers from indulging the emotion he felt for Mme de Sabran to the full. Correspondence gave him the freedom to do so without allowing the Comtesse an opportunity to escape—unless by the expedient of not reading his letters at all—the increasing intimacy of their relations.

Far from Paris, confined to his outpost in Brittany, the Chevalier focused upon his beloved his proverbial skill as a seducer, rolling out for her in letter after letter "those distinctive qualities of his mind, to which nothing was foreign."[110] And that mind, so different than "the minds of others,"[111] was characterized by "a limitless sagacity, a profound finesse, a nimbleness that never crossed the line into frivolity, and a gift for sharpening ideas by way of wordplay."[112] The Chevalier had already deployed these gifts in correspondence with his friends and relations, and was considered a virtuoso of a form of writing vital to life in society. However, returning from a dinner with the "Steinkerque birds" at which she had heard a dozen letters from the Chevalier to his mother and sister read aloud, Mme du Deffand—who, even before falling in love with Horace Walpole, had been along with Voltaire one of the absolute masters of the genre—denounced the limits of a rhetorical game that aimed only at amusement: "I find [his letters] insupportable. Plenty of witticisms, I'll give you that, some of them natural enough, but more often than not labored—in short, similar to those of Voiture, except that the Chevalier is somewhat sharper."[113] For the Marquise, they were proof that "in the absence of feeling, wit is nothing more than vapor, steam."[114]

Mme du Deffand could not have imagined that ten years later, Boufflers would completely change the register he used to launch himself into correspondence—one in which feeling and intellect would be intimately mixed, mutually clarifying and reinforcing each other. After having himself mocked *la sensibilité* and celebrated inconstancy, the Chevalier now "displayed a profound sensitivity, thereby proving that grace and merit mixed could set him on an even keel."[115]

In his first letters to Mme de Sabran, the Chevalier manipulated the resources of amorous badinage with originality and eloquence—the art of surprise, of amusing allusions, of aptness, of self-pity—and conferred upon them a new sort of charm in the service of an emotion that heretofore he had never admitted. Throughout their correspondence, the Chevalier employed his intellect as a means of making the unspoken more and more explicit, until at last the moment arrived when passion had earned the right to declare itself openly. Meanwhile, in his early letters, he did not hesitate to recount to his beloved his thoughts, dreams, disappointments, and hopes, confident of having found in her an interlocutor perfectly suited to him.

Indeed, as a child, Éléonore, desirous of writing to her father without knowing how exactly to go about it, had taken for her model the letters of Mme de Sévigné, which she had found in the library at school. Realizing that one "could write as one chatted,"[116] simply and naturally, had been a revelation to her. From then on she had taken an authentic pleasure in corresponding with friends. Beginning as a game and quickly becoming a necessity, her exchange of letters with Boufflers turned her into a marvelous *épistolière*, one capable of relating her thoughts with all the sincerity and spontaneity of Mme de Sévigné, and of making the various tonalities of her own emotional life vibrate with the same sort of intensity. For his part, the Chevalier, who from the very beginning of their relationship had taken her literary education in hand, contributed to the maturation of her talent, encouraging her self-confidence and pushing her to give free reign to her feelings.

A correspondence like theirs was duty-bound to free itself from the conventions imposed by society, and in this Boufflers led the way. He did not want to indulge himself in a mere formal virtuosity, but rather to reveal to her the whole truth of himself: "I feel as though you have given me the right not to put on stylistic airs when writing to you, and if it's true that you enjoy my letters, it's far better for me that they be careless, so that it isn't the work invested in an immaculate missive that you enjoy. A man is more easily seen in the errors he makes than in those he corrects, and my goal is to please you with my defects."[117]

A year later, encouraged by their steadily increasing intimacy, the Chevalier could begin to indicate to Mme de Sabran the guiding principles of a new aesthetic of the epistolary form: "Write to me, my dear girl, send me whole volumes, do not reread anything you set down, do not even think of any of the rules of the art of writing, never fear repeating yourself, leaving something out—be sometimes gay, sometimes philosophical, sometimes mad, simply go where your nerves, your reason, your character, your humor take you. You have no need to please me—only love me, and prove it more by what you do than by what you say; for the good of us both, your ideas must pass continually into me, and my own into you, like water that gains in purity and clarity the more it is decanted."[118] Mme de Sabran rose to the challenge, and composed with Boufflers the eighteenth century's most beautiful *correspondance amoureuse* in French literature.

Though having forbidden the Chevalier from openly declaring his passion, Éléonore could not eliminate from their conversations a commonly used word like "love," which served to express all the nuances of the emotional life of the era, from the most ephemeral caprice to the very deepest of sentiments. She herself was obliged to use it to dictate the terms of their arrangement and to attempt to put her own conscience at ease: "Love me with a calm sentiment, pure and constant, the sort that I can share without fear. At our age this is no longer a sort of chimera, and even the most rigid virtue could not condemn a sentiment founded on mutual affection and esteem. That *is* the way you will always love me, is it not, my brother?"[119] But for this "brother," who was becoming more and more "necessary"[120] to her, love was a totalizing emotion, one with no sense of limits. He loved her "with the courage of a lion, the sweetness of a lamb, the tenderness of a mother," loved her "with every sort of love and friendship."[121] And he loved the feelings she inspired in him: "I love being loved by you: it seems to me that thus I seize perfection... and I never think of you without smiling, without tears springing to my eyes."[122] Indeed, "if you love to be loved, who better than I to address yourself to—one who lives only for you, and, so to speak, only *by* you? For to live is to think and to feel, and you are utterly involved in all I feel and think."[123] It was precisely this way of living that Mme de Sabran did not naturally have the courage to pursue. So that occasionally, Boufflers would unsheathe his claws and reproach her for her faintheartedness, reminding her that "with age, the heart grows ever colder. And so be wary of your own. Take care, you who make such protestations of warmth, that you do not become an icicle. Perhaps you will still please, in the manner of an old, well-written book, but you will no longer be loved, because you yourself will never have loved." And he continued, "to preserve some sentiment for the time when your hair is white, you must have shown it when that hair was still blond."[124] And then, given that she was a believer, why not take the son of God made man as a role model? "Do not despise this love, my fine girl, and judge by the Man who loved better than anyone else that, the more we love, the better we become."[125]

It wasn't Boufflers's eloquence that brought Mme de Sabran, after two and half years of dogged resistance, to the point of capitulation, but rather the uncontrollable fear that took her by surprise at Anisy-le-Château, the summer residence of Évêque de Laon, her beloved nephew on the Sabran side of the family. One day, at the beginning of December 1780, the Chevalier, whom she had been expecting before nightfall, had had to change his plans due to a violent snowstorm, and her "terror" that something serious had happened to him had "torn" from her a letter wherein she confessed to him "her heart's secret."[126] That avowal would determine the "fate of her life."[127] Boufflers did not hesitate to write her that, happier than Alexander the Great, he had "conquered what he needed to conquer" and that now he desired nothing more than to "deserve and preserve it."

In reality, five more months would have to pass before the Chevalier could declare victory, for it was only on the evening of May 2, 1781—a date "forever memorable in its splendor"[129]—that Mme de Sabran decided to receive Boufflers in her blue-upholstered bed, thereby inaugurating a new chapter in her life. In the expert arms of her lover, she discovered for the first time that love could possess a physical allure and sensual joy, and she abandoned herself to the pleasure of loving and being loved. It was a veritable metamorphosis.

She who had taken such pains to base her happiness exclusively on herself now thrilled to an absolute symbiosis she had discovered with her beloved: the "dear brother" had become her "husband," her lover, her friend, her whole universe, her soul, her God.[130] And she loved him like a mother, like a sister, like a daughter, like a friend, like a wife—and above all, like a mistress.[131] Thanks to him, she had been born again—"I love you as if I were no more than fifteen years old, and as if the world were in its golden age"[132]—"I love you as they loved in the olden days, as they don't love anymore, and as they'll never love again."[133]

But it did not take Éléonore long to discover that this new happiness would cost her plenty of tears, as well. She suffered from living in sin in the eyes of God, and from compromising her spotless reputation in the eyes of the world. She suffered from her beloved's refusal to legitimate their union through marriage, and the idea that he would subjugate their happiness to a questionable point of social honor. She suffered "torments"[134] of jealousy, fearing that the Chevalier had not broken with his old habits and still engaged in fleeting affairs. She suffered also from the frequent separations required by practical necessity, and at times she sadly apportioned the blame for this to the Chevalier: "Why have you left me? We were so happy, so fine in our cozy domesticity. . . . Your departure has spoiled everything: you've absconded with my gaiety, my rest, and all my happiness."[135]

But above all it was jealousy that drove her mad. Having surprised Boufflers during a voyage through Flanders in the company of a local "Dulcinea del Toboso,"[136] Mme de Sabran ranted at him with such violence that the Chevalier also lost his head, comparing her to Megara and Alecto,[137] before managing to recover his calm and express his consternation: "You have left my heart all but dead. I see no hope of happiness in the future; all my illusions have left me, as one sees the leaves fall in the freezing fogs of autumn, when each day foretells an even grimmer tomorrow. My heart wholly fails me: I feel a sorrow beyond my age, for at forty-five love should almost have lost its name and melted away into a sweet and peaceable friendship. How far we are from that!"[138]

They were far from that precisely because, in spite of their age, both were measuring themselves for the first time against an absolute passion. But ultimately, their conflicts merely augmented that flame. Asking forgiveness became for Mme de Sabran another chance to renew her declarations of love: "Do not hate me, my child, because I love you too much. Have pity on my weakness, laugh at my madness, and never let them disturb the peace of your heart. Today

I am overwhelmed by my shame and remorse." The Chevalier's happiness took priority over her own: "Go, you must be as free as the air, abuse your liberty if you wish, and I will still love you more than I would were you hobbled by too heavy a chain. Your desire alone should guide you toward me, and not mere respect, mere kindness: I could never be happy at your expense." Yet she could not prevent herself from reminding him that her happiness depended entirely on him: "Farewell, my heart. Love me if you wish, or rather if you can, but consider that nobody in the world loves you, cherishes you, like I do, and that I value life only as long as I spend it with you."[139] Boufflers, who hated conflict, did not hesitate to reassure her—"I persist in my good humor and goodwill. I forgive you all your annoyances"[140]—and was anxious to make her smile, because without her, without his "pretty child, pretty love, pretty Sévigné, pretty Deshoulières," he would have been "the unhappiest dog on earth."[141]

Difficulties and misunderstandings did not prevent the lovers from living happily through the last social season of France's ancien régime and actively contributing to its legend. In reconstituting these inimitable years, the Comtesse de Genlis describes Mme de Sabran as "one of the most enchanting creatures I ever knew, thanks to her appearance, elegance, wit, and accomplishments; she danced exquisitely; painted like an angel; wrote pretty verses; and was endowed with boundless sweetness and good nature."[142] Her perfect incarnation of feminine *honnêteté*, and its delicious contrast with the Chevalier's spirit of independence, unpredictability, and whimsicality, allowed the lovers to complement each other wonderfully in that communal exercise "both so superfluous and so necessary" to social life—conversation.[143]

Beginning in 1780, the collected republications of Boufflers's poems and prose writings cemented his literary reputation, while his improvisations continued to delight high society. The private visit made by Prince Henry of Prussia, the brother of Frederick the Great, who arrived in France in 1784, would inspire numerous impromptu witticisms. The Marquis de Bombelles, official spokesman for the court, transcribed with an admiring pen in his journal the verses that the Prince had seen engraved beneath the copy of his bust, sculpted by Houdon in Sèvres porcelain, that presided over the Marquise de Boufflers's salon: "*Dans cette image auguste et chère / Tout héros verra son rival, / Tout sage verra son égal, / Et tout homme verra son frère.*"*[144]

---

*In this august and precious image / Every hero shall see his rival, / Every sage his peer, / And every man his brother.

But Boufflers was able to better this when Mme de Sabran's little Elzéar, who, seated at the Opéra between the Prince and the Chevalier during a performance of Rameau's *Castor and Pollux*, happened to ask what "twins" were. Henry had answered that they were brothers born from the same egg—then asked him in jest whether he, Elzéar, had sprung from an egg himself. Boufflers came to the aid of the child, baffled by this unexpected question, whispering to him: "*Ma naissance n'a rien de neuf; / J'ai suivi la commune règle. / Je me croirais sorti d'un oeuf / Si, comme vous, j'étais un aigle.*"*[145]

But Boufflers's occasional verses were above all an immediate reflection of his moods, habits, and company, and allowed him to respond to each individual knot in his vast network of friendships. His poems, quatrains, couplets, and songs were dedicated to his mother and his sister, to the members of his sizable clan—for instance Mme de Mirepoix,[146] Mme de Luxembourg,[147] the Prince de Beauvau-Craon[148] and his sister, the Vicomtesse de Cambis[149]—as well to their friends the Duc de Choiseul[150] and Mme du Deffand.[151] They were poems that transformed the banality of everyday life into an opportunity for play. A gift, a recovery from illness, an invitation were all pretexts for Boufflers to gratify the amour propre of his friends and relations with elegance and expertise.

If, during the 1780s, certain figures who had accompanied the Chevalier throughout his youth were preparing to leave the stage, others certainly remained present—for instance, the Duc de Nivernais, a long-standing friend of the Marquise de Boufflers, whom the Chevalier sent a gift of a dozen sheep from Lorraine to brighten up the pastures of Saint-Ouen, the Duc's famous château on the outskirts of Paris, where Boufflers and Mme de Sabran were frequently received. Deliciously hyperbolic, the verses accompanying this present went out of their way to emphasize that poetry was the predominating passion of the master of the estate: "*Petits moutons, votre fortune est faite, / Pour vous ce pré vaut le sacré vallon; / N'enviez pas l'heureux troupeau d'Admète, / Car vous paissez sous les yeux d'Apollon.*"†[152] And to the Baron de Besenval, another pillar of Parisian society, the Chevalier demonstrated his admiration by allowing the former to find, pinned to his hat, a card bearing these lines:

---

*My birth was nothing new; / I followed the standard procedure. / I'd believe that I'd hatched from an egg / If, like you, I was an eagle.

†Little sheep, your fortune is made, / For you, this meadow is the equal of the sacred dell; / Envy not the happy herd of Admetus, / For you graze beneath the eyes of Apollo.

"Amour, si tu vois la figure / De ce chapeau, / Tu vas conformer ta coiffure / À ce chapeau; / Mais en vain mon talent s'éprouve / Sur ce chapeau, / Je n'ai pas tout l'esprit qu'on trouve / Sous ce chapeau."[153]

The mischievous verses accompanying a gift from Comte Louis de Ségur to his young wife[154] or those laudatory lines hailing Vicomte Joseph-Alexandre de Ségur's *Essay on the Means of Pleasing in Love*[155] also testify to Boufflers's ties to the foremost personalities of the younger generation. In a letter to the King of Sweden from November 1783, the Comte de Creutz designates the Chevalier, along with the Comte de Choiseul-Gouffier, the Comte de Narbonne, and the Abbé de Périgord, as among those who "give society its tone."[156]

For her part, though constantly declaring that it was contrary to her inclinations,[157] Mme de Sabran led an intensely social life, dividing her time between Paris and Versailles, traveling across Europe, and frequenting various fashionable spa towns. Her best friend, the Comtesse d'Andlau, the paternal aunt of the Duchesse de Polignac, had introduced her into the intimate circle of the royal favorite, where she had gained the sympathies of both the Queen and the Comte d'Artois. Her son recounts that she "acted alongside [the Comte] at Choisy and [that] he attended in disguise a performance at her home in which *The Misanthrope* was staged in the old costumes of the era of Louis XIV."[158] The Comtesse was well aware that the futures of her children—a good marriage for Delphine, a brilliant career for Elzéar—depended first and foremost on royal favor and the extent of her social relations, and so she busied herself in securing both. For example, it was she who introduced Henry of Prussia into Parisian high society, thereby gaining his lasting friendship. An excellent hostess, when the Prince returned a few years later she hastened to offer him a theatrical interlude, in keeping with the fashion of the time, during the course of a grand reception that she gave in his honor. On that occasion, Boufflers adapted several scenes from Molière's *The Bourgeois Gentleman*, to be performed by the Comtesse and her children,[159] who already had a certain amount of experience on the stage.

Indeed, in September 1782, as guests of the Prince de Ligne at Beloeil, the three Sabrans had been drafted by their host for an impromptu staging of *The Barber of Seville*. In the absence of an adult fit for the role—even though he

---

*Love, if you see the face / That wears this hat / You'll surely style your hair / To fit this hat. / But in vain is my talent tested / On this hat, / I haven't the wit that you'll find / Beneath this hat.

was a great lover of the theater, the Prince himself had never felt at ease onstage—it was Elzéar, only nine years old, who had played the part of Figaro. According to his mother, the part fit him like a glove,[160] and the budding actor more than lived up to expectations.

The following year, Ligne chose to stage *The Marriage of Figaro*, which had still never been approved by the censors in France. This time it was Boufflers who triumphed in the role of Figaro, while Mme de Sabran played the Comtesse d'Almaviva; Helena de Ligne (the Prince's ravishing Polish stepdaughter) was Suzanne, and Elzéar appeared as Chérubin.

Informed of the theatrical successes of Delphine and Elzéar, Marie-Antoinette—who was very fond of Éléonore and her children—expressed the desire to see them perform. In the autumn of 1784, the Duchesse de Polignac organized at her home, for the sole enjoyment of the royal family, a *soirée théatrale* that would see the staging of both a tragedy and a comedy. The tragedy selected for the occasion was *Iphigenia in Tauris*: Delphine, "lovely enough to serve as a model for that greatest lover of beauty, Greuze,"[161] performed as Iphigenia, and Elzéar as Orestes. The other actors were the son of the Duchesse de Polignac, the daughters of Mme d'Andlau and Mlle de Montaut-Navailles, the future Duchesse de Gontaut—the latter of whom preserved a vivid memory of that evening when she was acclaimed for her recitation of "The Little White Mouse," a couplet composed for her by Boufflers.[162] Proud of the success that her "poor little children" had enjoyed at court, Mme de Sabran hastened to write to the Chevalier that the Queen had been "moved to tears" by the tragedy and that the King was "'as happy as a king' at the play."[163] When the performances had ended, "a supper was prepared for the young actors; they were made to sit at a table while the King and Queen stood behind them and served them—one behind Orestes, the other behind Iphigenia."[164]

In January 1784, the beginning of an emotionally rich year for Boufflers, the Chevalier received the patent of field marshal, which allowed him to aspire to the military command of a province or a fortress. One rather difficult problem remained: to find a vacant post and to be nominated to fill it. From Nancy, where he had traveled to visit his ailing mother, Boufflers orchestrated a promotional campaign in the grand style. He wrote to his mistress and her sister, indicating the initiatives they should take and the individuals they should solicit. He mobilized friends and acquaintances, entertaining the prospect of a post in Flanders or in the army. In addition to the support of the Prince de Beauvau and the Duc de Nivernais, Boufflers hoped for the aid of Diane de Polignac (an intimate friend of Éléonore) when it came to the Queen, and then the support of the Maréchal de Ségur, his friend's father and at that time minister of war—though as it turned out, the latter would not lift so much as a finger for his sake.[165]

The first opportunity that offered itself up to him was the position of governor of Senegal, and the Chevalier seized on it. The post was disagreeable and carried scant prestige, since it was wrapped up with the slave trade. In order to reinforce the French trading posts on the west coast of Africa, Louis XVI and his minister of the navy, the Maréchal de Castries, had decided to send a new governor to Senegal, one capable of putting an end to the inefficiency and abuses of the administrators who had succeeded one another there since Lauzun's conquest of Saint-Louis in 1779. It should be recalled that the Duc himself had highlighted the essential importance for the future of the colony of "moderate, wise, firm, and stable conduct."[166] Taking a hint from his friend Beauvau, Castries reckoned that Boufflers was the man for the job.

Consulted in secret by the Chevalier, Louis-Philippe de Ségur had attempted to dissuade his friend from applying. But the latter, nearing fifty and deeply in debt,[167] brushed off his advice, and on October 9, 1785, he received his official assignment.

From Moscow, where he had been named ambassador the previous year, replacing the Comte de Narbonne, Louis-Philippe de Ségur took stock of the situation. While he felt obliged to apologize for having obtained a position so much more important than Boufflers's—"which I owe merely to luck and the fervor of my friends"[168]—though fifteen years his junior, Ségur was so suffused by his new role that he did not hesitate to give his old friend diplomatic advice. Paternalism aside, his diagnosis was direct and to the point:

> Your heart will bleed at the state in which you'll find the colony entrusted to you; you will have plenty of oppressed folk to defend and plenty of knavery to put a stop to; you will be the mediator between greedy cruelty of the whites and the deplorable absurdity of the blacks; if you cannot prevent the one from selling and the other from buying, you can at least put a stop to their reciprocal trumpery. Your soul will suffer from that necessary and difficult work, but the precautions that must be taken for the internal security of the country and for its defense in the event of war with England will offer your spirit a larger and

less arid field. You will find all neglected, all in need of creation, in that place: the coastal batteries badly placed, the fortresses badly built, no provision for communicating warnings or calling for aid between one post and another, no attention paid to the quartering of troops or preserving them from the insalubrious climate. Consequently, I foresee that you will do plenty of good there, that you will preserve a good number of men, that you'll send us plenty of fine reports, good projects, excellent maps. Natural history and physics will also have need of your useful observations; but what I desire most of all is that you should carry out that good work as quickly as possible.[169]

One of the small number of intimates informed as to the relationship between the Chevalier and Mme de Sabran, he had no doubt about the motive that had driven his friend to risk this difficult adventure and took leave of him with: "Adieu, Monsieur l'Abbé; put a swift end to that quarrel between the ring and the cross which has so long divided Rome and the Empire; free yourself from the cross and give the ring to that friend of ours."[170]

Conducting that "friend" to the altar was indeed the reason that Boufflers had used to justify his decision to Mme de Sabran. At the news of his departure for Senegal, the Comtesse had sunk into such a state of despair[171] that, in order to give her a bit of courage, he declared himself convinced that "the Being who guides us" would never snatch away from her forever the man she loved and who loved her in return. That "Being" would, in fact, do more: "He will make me more worthy of you, and perhaps when you see your lover again you will be proud to be his, you will love him openly, in full sight of Heaven and of earth, and make a triumph of a love of which you once made a mystery." But wasn't this also a way of reminding her that the need to regularize their union in the eyes of the world came, in fact, from *her*—and that what *he* wanted most of all was to make her happy? "My glory, if ever I acquire any, will be my dowry, and your adornment—it is this that makes me cling to the prospect. If I were handsome, if I were young, if I were rich, if I could offer you all that makes women happy in their own eyes and in those of others, we should long ago have borne the same name and shared the same fortunes."[172]

Mme de Sabran knew Boufflers too well to put her trust in him completely. In her moments of tenderness, she limited herself to comparing him to the imprudent traveling pigeon of La Fontaine's fable, whose "vagabond humor" is "the despair of his sad and faithful companion,"[173] but when the separation became insupportable, she had no more room for indulgence: "My life is over, you ended it on November 22, 1785: Your ambition has destroyed all—*love, happiness, and hope.*"[174]

The Comtesse seemed to forget that in the ethical code of the nobility, love, ambition, and glory were all tightly bound to one another. The cheerful disdain with which the Chevalier had accepted the disappointment of having been kept from the field of battle did not mean that he had given up all hope of distinguishing himself in the service of his country. The triumphal return of friends and acquaintances such as Lauzun and Ségur from the United States, the climate of political effervescence that characterized life in high society during those years, the responsibility of the name that he bore, even the favor that the woman he loved enjoyed at Versailles—none of it could touch his pride, his determination to live to the full his vocation as a gentleman, and to give the last full measure of his valor. Having arrived at the threshold of his fiftieth year, he had no time left to lose.[175]

He formulated this with the greatest clarity in a letter to a friend from Lorraine who had established himself in Saint-Domingue: "I have always wanted to show that if I have remained idle up until now, it has not been for lack of zeal or courage, or even perhaps of capacity, but for lack of opportunities; I have seized the first that has presented itself to be employed according to my rank."

Departing from La Rochelle on December 5, Boufflers reached the French colony of Saint-Louis on January 14, 1786. It was a long, narrow island with scant vegetation and fresh water, provided with a large fortress at its center and populated by around six thousand inhabitants, for the most part blacks and mulattoes. The place was difficult to access. Situated at the delta of the Senegal estuary, which gave its name to the region, the island was separated from the sea by a barrier beach called the Langue de Barbarie (Barbary Tongue). The mouth of the river was obstructed by a sandbar that, placed as it was at the meeting point between maritime currents and the river's flow, continually changed its shape, interfering with the approach of larger vessels. Seven years earlier, after sounding the bar himself, Lauzun had launched his attack on the fort—which, luckily for him, was mostly empty—in a rowboat.[176] Arriving, like the Duc, in January, at a moment when navigation was particularly hazardous, Boufflers was likewise obliged to reach the island by means of pirogue, with his baggage following in a second launch.

The importance of Saint-Louis as a French outpost in Africa was due not only to its "impregnable character"[177] but also to its strategic position, which allowed it to control the river. In the agreements of the Peace of Paris, which concluded the American war, France had been granted a monopoly over commerce on the Senegal River, and England over the Gambia, situated farther to the south. Moving up the Senegal toward the interior, the French attempted to "intercept for their own profit the slave convoys that the African chiefs were delivering to the English,"[178] sending them on to Saint-Louis where they would await a final destination. The other essential component of what was referred to as the "Colony of Senegal" was the island of Gorée. Located sixty-five leagues from Saint-Louis, at the top of the Cape Verde peninsula, Gorée had three thousand inhabitants and was famous for the beauty of its environs and the salubriousness of its climate. A small constellation of trading posts spread among various commercial hot spots filled out the picture of the holdings recovered by France at the end of the war.

The center of government and administration for the whole island, Saint-Louis also served as the seat of the Senegal Company, which managed the triangular trade between France, the African trading posts, and America. In exchange for the state's protection, the company had to pay a significant portion of the colony's expenses and handle its provisioning with their own vessels,[179] while the governor retained supreme authority when it came to civil, military, and judicial administration. It was he who negotiated the agreements with the leaders of the African tribes and maintained their respect—by means of force, if necessary.

As soon as he set foot on the island, the Chevalier understood that the task awaiting him would be a thankless one, but he went to work straightaway, without letting himself lose heart. His house was "hideous, dilapidated," he wrote to Mme de Sabran. Indeed, "not a single door will shut ... none of the floorboards will hold ... all of the walls are crumbling to powder ... the rooms are all furnished with dust-covered rags." He had to repair it all as quickly as possible. He lacked the requisite money, workmen, and wood, yet he somehow made do—"for if the spirit of man is actually the breath of God, he must prove it by showing himself to be a creator." He could hardly have entertained any illusions regarding the several men whom he commanded: "Some of them are dying, others are sick, still others are begging for leave, and the whole lot of them are lazy. Nobody tells me the half of what he should tell me, nobody does the half of what they should do; some of them deceive me, and the rest don't understand me." Nevertheless, he did not despair of "being very useful": "All of these obstacles enliven me rather than knocking me down." A master of the art of change, he reminded his beloved of the cheerful tenacity with which he had wooed her: "If such difficulties had deterred me, you would not be mine: that's what I tell myself to forestall discouragement."[180]

Six weeks after his arrival, in a very long letter to the Maréchal de Beauvau, accompanied by a report intended for the minister of the navy, Boufflers laid out a detailed picture of the disastrous state of the colony. The Chevalier, who harbored a filial devotion and limitless admiration for his mother's brother, also knew that it was to him he owed his position—and this was yet another reason to reassure him of his zeal and confide to him his personal impressions, leaving him free to decide whether or not to communicate these in turn to the Maréchal de Castries. "Your kindness comforts me, dear uncle," Boufflers wrote, "and your advice sustains me, like the invisible voice that Telemachus heard while minding his flock some leagues from here.[181] I do not yet know whether I will surmount the challenges that I have come in search of, but at least they will not kill me. Though at times I am tempted by discouragement (as you seem to suspect), shame follows quickly on that temptation, and I recover my strength before having displayed my weakness. Everything is yet to be done, and even to be *un*done, in this country; never have the task and the means available been so disproportionate . . . but I am determined; I hear all, I read all, I respond to all; I spurn no one, send no one away, I make nobody wait, and since everyone here is under my command, I think it only just that I myself should be at the command of all and sundry."[182]

These were not just empty words. During his two years as governor, Boufflers showed an extraordinary tenacity and energy. He had neither men nor means adequate to his work—he could rely on nothing but his own intelligence, initiative, and good sense. Fortunately for him, as a good reader of the *Encyclopédie*, he took an interest in everything and was a great believer in the circularity of knowledge. Thanks to the "books, scientific instruments, tools of every sort of trade" that he had slipped into the bundles of his "poor possessions,"[183] he was able to transform himself into a city planner, architect, worksite foreman, and craftsman. He had a church erected from plans of his own, shifted the cemetery to a location outside of the city, restored the old fortifications and added new ones, and provided the fortress with a barracks for the soldiers, as well as a decent hospital and jail. While waiting for new small boats that would be able to navigate the sandbar, he had the old ones, which were badly in need of it, repaired. He continually maintained an open table in his quarters where he welcomed the officers, his colleagues, and visiting travelers, doing his best to offer his guests acceptable menus without relinquishing a touch of elegance. He patiently devoted himself to the administration of the colony, settling disputes, conducting trials, striving to put an end to abuse, and training the soldiers of the garrison. He signed an order forbidding the coastal populations from seizing wrecked ships and their cargoes, and organized reprisals against the looters. Responsible not only for Saint-Louis but for all the French trading posts in that region of Africa, he visited them one by one, quite often finding them in a pitiable state. Heading up the Senegal by boat, he ventured into the interior of the country and sealed new alliances as well as commercial treaties with the various kingdoms along the river. He took an interest in the customs and traditions of the Africans, as well as in the land's natural resources, with an eye to the future.

But what could all of his industry do in the face of the death that continually decimated his men? How to protect himself in the almost total absence of medicine, with doctors helpless against insect bites, infections, wounds, and buboes of all sorts, as well as the host of maladies—dysentery, yellow fever, tetanus—that struck every year during the rainy season? And how to prevent the sandbar and its currents from continuing to claim victims?

Even before arriving in Africa, Boufflers had known that in reality the first enemy he would have to combat would be the "infamous"[184] Senegal Company. It was the men of the company who purchased the slaves from the chiefs of the various local tribes in order to resell them to slave traders, who in turn transported them to the far side of the ocean. No doubt he had been put on his guard by his friend Lauzun.

In fact, in the final report on his mission years earlier, the Duc had pointed to the necessity of restricting the company's freedom of initiative to commerce. "For centuries, experience has proven that the companies' troops are always ill governed, and that their policies work to the detriment of politics generally. It is far preferable that they should use the troops of the King, and that their policies should conform to those of the minister."[185] Boufflers in his turn observed all this at first hand. Entirely guided by the logic of profit, the Company paid little respect to its commitments, leaving the colony without supplies for months, employing corrupt and unscrupulous individuals,[186] and rousing the hatred of the population with its inhumane methods. But then, what could be humane about trafficking slaves, the company's main interest? And hadn't the Chevalier been sent to Africa precisely to expand that traffic? The instructions he had been given were very clear: "The importance of the possession of Senegal consists in the aliment it offers to commerce; the objects of trade are of four kinds: slaves for American farming, rubber, gold, and raw ivory."[187] And expand the traffic was exactly what he did—for during the two years of his mandate, the number of slaves sold by the French grew considerably.[188] He was well aware that it was a "barbarous business,"[189] as he confided to his sister, and he was not the only one who thought so. In asking him what "connection" there could be between his "kindness," his "selflessness," and "the harshness and greed of those horrible men who traffic in human blood,"[190] Mme de Sabran expressed an indignation widespread among the cultured elites. In *The Spirit of the Laws*, Montesquieu had denounced the phenomenon with a ferocious irony: "The peoples of Europe have exterminated those of America, and have placed in bondage those of Africa, so as to put them to work there clearing the earth. . . . It is impossible that we should suppose those [slaves] to be men; for if we *did* suppose them to be men, we might begin to believe that we ourselves were not Christians."[191] Few readers were unaffected by the episode in *Candide* where the poor black slave, whose hand and leg had been severed by his Dutch trader, concludes his tale with the celebrated sentence: "This is the price at which you eat sugar in Europe."[192] But these were principled condemnations of what seemed an inevitable evil, and it would not be until 1770 and the (anonymous) publication of *A Philosophical and Political History of European Settlements and Commerce in the Indies*, thanks to the Abbé Raynal, that a detailed indictment was launched against the intolerable atrocities of colonialism and the slave trade. Despite having been condemned to be burned in public, the book aroused "a general enthusiasm"[193]—but, written in haste and by various hands, it lacked unity and presented numerous contradictions. It was in Condorcet that the cause of abolitionism found its first great defender in France. Published under a pseudonym in Switzerland in 1781, his *Reflections on Black Slavery* addressed the subject thoroughly and unambiguously: slavery must be abolished, and if this were not accomplished by the end of the century, posterity would feel nothing but "contempt for those who thought themselves the personification of reason and humanity."[194] Even within the royal administration there were timid attempts to confront the problem, and Daniel

Lescallier, commissioner of the navy and officer in charge of Guyana, declared himself in favor of a gradual manumission of slaves. Still, it would take until 1788—when, along with Condorcet, Brissot, Lafayette, Mirabeau, Kersaint, La Rochefoucauld, the Abbé Grégoire, Sieyès, and other Girondins mobilized themselves—for the cause of enslaved Africans to become a true political movement. Finally, on November 4, 1794, the National Convention decreed the end of slavery in all French territories.

It is not surprising, then, that in his letters from Senegal, Boufflers was rather vague in expressing his indignation at the trade. How could he—a senior official representing the King of France in Africa—openly criticize the policies of his government and cast doubt on the directives he received? Boufflers was a soldier accustomed to following orders, and he was well aware that in Africa, France was conducting a war to defend its economic and colonial interests, whose crux was the commerce in slaves. And even if he had wanted to express his reservations on the subject, it would not have been prudent to reveal them in a correspondence—as he himself explained to Mme de Sabran[195]—that could easily fall into the hands of the indiscreet.

Moreover, Boufflers's comportment coincided perfectly with that theorized two years earlier by Immanuel Kant in his response to the question posed by the *Berlinische Monatsschrift*: "What is Enlightenment?" The philosopher clearly distinguished between the "public use of one's reason, which must be free at all times," and its "private use": the first is the privilege of the scholar who addresses himself to the "reading public"; the second is an obligation of those who serve the public in a position of civic trust. "Thus it would be very dangerous," Kant concludes, "were an officer who receives an order from his superiors to criticize the appropriateness or utility of that directive; he must obey. But as a scholar he could not rightfully be prevented from taking notice of the mistakes in the military service and from submitting his views to his public for its judgment."[196] The Chevalier thus held to his orders, but, setting himself as an example, made it a point of honor to prohibit his officers, soldiers, and all of his employees from profiting off of the slave trade. None of this, it must be said, prevented him from negotiating for the young Comtesse de Ségur the purchase of "around fifty excellent blacks for less than half the price she would have paid."[197] Indeed, the Ségurs owned plantations in the Antilles and, in spite of the liberal ideals they professed, saw nothing unseemly in benefiting from income sustained by the labor of slaves.

Moved by compassion, Boufflers liberated black children destined for the trade, whom he sent as gifts to his friends in France. In his letters, we find more than one allusion to "*la belle* Ourika,"[198] a young slave he offered to his uncle and aunt on the Beauvau side, who welcomed her like a daughter. Decades later, the Duchesse de Duras, daughter of an active abolitionist, told Ourika's story in a celebrated novel. To allow sensitive hearts and kind souls to sleep in peace, the conscience of the Enlightenment salved itself with illusions and forgetfulness—but, as the author of *Ourika* showed, this was a dangerous game.

Boufflers, for his part, did not want to forget what he had seen in Africa, and upon his return to France decided to make it known. He did not join the Society of the Friends of the Blacks—where his past as governor of Senegal would have rendered his presence somewhat incongruous—nor did he take advantage of his election to the Académie Française to launch his *j'accuse* against the government's policies from an institutional platform. In his speech on the occasion of his admission to the Académie, he limited himself to a general allusion to "those simple men, reduced to mere physical needs, confined to ideas that one might call animal," who, rather than receiving from Europeans "the benefits that darkness should expect from light," had been victims of their barbaric greed. Appearing before the Africans like gods, the "vanquishers of the ocean" had soon revealed themselves to be "evil gods, demanding human sacrifice."[199]

In order to raise the awareness of the people and reorient opinion, Boufflers preferred to employ his vast network of social relationships and the brilliance of his conversation.[200] Mme de Staël—married for less than a year to the Swedish ambassador in Paris—did not confine herself to writing to Gustav III that "the details that the Chevalier de Boufflers has related to me regarding the trade in blacks are harrowing,"[201] but chose for the heroine of one of her first novels a young Senegalese woman, Mirza, who delivers herself up to the slave traders in the place of the man she loves, then takes her own life. The wish formulated by Mme de Staël answers to that of Boufflers: "May free trade be established between the two parts of the world!"[202] And throughout her life she would express her "indignation against slavery and the trade in blacks; she would still be advocating in 1814, and her son took up the struggle after her."[203]

Despite the horrors of the slave trade, the innumerable practical and logistical difficulties, and the fruitless expectations of ministerial aides, Boufflers preserved an elevated sense of his mission. In keeping with the spirit of the Enlightenment, his conception of colonialism was bound up with the ideals of progress and civilization.[204] Heretofore, French policy in Africa had been limited to securing possession of simple commercial trading posts. The Chevalier, on the other hand, had his sights set on territorial expansion on a vast scale. With this in mind, he studied the climate, the flora, the fauna, all the natural resources of a land that, in his opinion, represented a formidable potential for the development of the French economy, and an opportunity for salvation for the Africans. In his garden at Gorée he planted "cotton and indigo, which thrived admirably and laid the groundwork for the colony's future prosperity," and buoyed by this success, he could "promise France millions from this part of Africa, whether from commerce or cultivation."[205] Why not imagine that, rather than laboring as slaves on American plantations, the Africans would one day cultivate cotton at liberty in their own land? It was with this in mind that Lafayette would obtain the agreement of Louis XVI and the Maréchal de Castries to launch in Guyana an experiment intended to show that the work of free Africans was more productive than that performed by slaves.[206]

With an eye to the general improvement of colonial conditions, Boufflers tried to produce a model of them at Gorée, where he quickly transferred the seat of government. Easily accessible, healthy, and very fertile, the island could indeed attract numerous settlers; and the Chevalier planned to acquire for the King—and perhaps for himself—"by means of a small treaty and a middling gift," a magnificent province, and to "lay the foundations of the greatest settlement ever established outside of France."[207] At the end of his mission, the Chevalier could proudly announce to his beloved: "The colony has been restored, rebuilt, resuscitated by means of my care, and almost at my own expense; soldiers and officers have never been so well lodged, nor so well maintained, in any colony; the ill are cared for by Mme Necker, and my hospital has become a model clinic.... For its part, trade has never so flourished in the area I have in my keeping, never has there been such freedom, never so effective a defense, never aid so powerful, never so many goods produced."[208]

Still, tormented by the problem of the deficit, and facing an unprecedented political crisis, the King and his ministers had priorities more pressing than the financing of an exemplary colony, and their decisions ran counter to those suggested by Boufflers. When the latter returned definitively to France in December 1787, the minister did not consider it necessary to send a new governor to Senegal, and entrusted all administration of the trading posts to the company.

Had the philanthropic Chevalier lost out by choosing to pursue utopian projects? Had his mission to Africa really ended, as it was whispered, in "defeat"?[209] The colonial policy of the century that followed suggests, rather, that it was the French monarchy that was incapable of imagining the future. No matter how one judges the results of Boufflers's exploits, one thing is certain: it was the African expedition that gave him the opportunity to develop to its fullest potential his talent as a writer.

On the eve of his departure for Senegal, Boufflers and Mme de Sabran had promised to write each other every day, and, to that end, Éléonore had bought for the Chevalier a green leather travel escritoire provided with numbered sheets of paper. Both of them respected their agreement, though they knew that they wouldn't be able to send their missives off as they were written, and that they would have to accumulate while awaiting the next ship to carry them to their destinations. Certainly the lovers already had an extensive habit of correspondence, but the new conditions imposed on them by this separation had a notable influence on their way of communicating. During the long months that passed between the arrival of two packets of letters, they continued day by day to rise to the challenge of this distant dialogue, developing an epistolary strategy capable of saving them from the temptation to withdraw into themselves, transforming their exchanges into painful amorous soliloquies. The most difficult task was Boufflers's: He was the one who had decided to leave, and so had to be forgiven; he had to show that he was at once both satisfied with his choice, and that he deplored its consequences; he had to preserve the intimacy, the complicity, the community of interests that bound him to his beloved even while having undercut the habits, domestic arrangements, and social relationships that had sealed their union; he had to share with her his new life and the difficulties that he was forced to face each day; he was perpetually in search of new words to tell her that he loved her and that he needed her love, and to make palpable to her from a distance of thousands of miles the physical desire he still felt for her. He succeeded by blending these various exigencies into a single, remarkably unified story. He took care to give each of the letters he wrote, day after day, a finished form (emphasized by the valediction) before putting them away in his escritoire to await mailing, while maintaining the feel of an ongoing dialogue. But thanks to its continuity, this epistolary torrent—which, in the absence of replies to which it might react, shaped itself in complete autonomy, moving with freedom between letters of varying length and chains of short notes written in haste—also displayed the distinctive features of a private journal. A journal that, by evading the formal logic of any particular genre, was able to blend with ease the description of day-to-day events and emotional introspection, moral reflection and reverie.

Only a genuine writer could have been able to harmonize so perfectly two stylistic registers as different as the lover's discourse and the travel narrative:[210] the former persuasive, sweeping, musical, rich with general observations; the latter descriptive and informative, swifter and more incisive, quick to seize on the exotic and picturesque. In keeping with the epistolary aesthetics that, since Cicero, had seen in the letter "a conversation between absent individuals,"[211] Boufflers obeyed the imperatives of variety and conciseness, showing himself a master of the art of the transition, moving with terrific grace from one subject to another, playing with surprise, banking on his originality and inventiveness while drawing on a shared sense of culture. The variety of his valedictions is enough to give us a sense of his talent: "Adieu, love. I grant you permission to forget me, if you can find someone who loves you as much from nearby as I do from afar";[212] "Adieu, spare a thought for your poor African. Mention him often in your conversations with our common friends; it's a way of keeping him alive, and even of making him *almost* present, wherever you happen to be";[213] "Adieu, my paradise";[214] "Adieu to the sweetest, the most beloved, the most desired of all God's creatures. Adieu to the dearest and most tender of women, adieu";[215] "Adieu, love; adieu, angel; adieu, of all things between heaven and earth the most charming";[216] "Adieu, my good wife, do not stop loving me";[217] "Adieu, I kiss you and kiss you again with a powerful foretaste of the pleasure with which I will kiss you and kiss you again when I return";[218] "Adieu, love. I have you before my eyes, I carry you in my heart, and my mind contemplates you inwardly every instant of the day";[219] "O my pretty palm, when shall I drink of your wine?";[220] "Adieu, my wife. Your old husband embraces you and grows young again";[221] "Adieu then, you best, you prettiest, you most beloved of women";[222] "Adieu, *fair creature, all my hope, all my comfort.*"[223]

But it was more than stylistic virtuosity that gave unity and coherence to Boufflers's letters. The emotion he felt for Mme de Sabran had various facets, all essential to him. It was a harmony of the heart and the senses, a set of shared interests, an affinity of taste, of admiration, of respect. And for each of these, he knew how to find just the right tone. Writing to his beloved also meant giving a sincere account of himself, expressing his ego in its deepest sense. And for that matter, it was precisely what Mme de Sabran was doing herself. "These are not mere words of the sort one usually finds in letters," Boufflers observed, "rather, it is thought, it is feeling, it is love—it is you yourself that I see in each one of your lines."[224] But then, hadn't he himself already written: "We think the same, we feel the same...we *are* the same, or to phrase it better, we are one"?[225] In the light of that certainty, thinking, feeling, and writing were for him one and the same thing. How could it be surprising that he should ask her not to share with any third party a correspondence so intimate?[226]

Emotions, reflections, and states of mind succeeded one another in Boufflers's letters with all the freedom, urgency, and palpable intensity of life. Allusions to physical desire, of which the "blue bed" is the emblem, are explicit and continual (for "memory, as Locke says, is continuous sensation"); allusions joyful and tender—"once the sea is behind me, I shall enter your bed and never leave again"[228]—but still surprising given the social conventions of the period. Nevertheless, Boufflers was also quick to affirm that, even if it was "a great pleasure to see each other," "true happiness is to love each other, for we see each other, speak to each other, hear each other even when we're absent."[229] And the luminous image that he carried of her could not be tarnished by the passage of time, since "it is only the material part of us that changes, and in you there is so little of that, I feel I have nothing to fear."[230] And when the anguish of a separation that was likely to be a long one, at a time of their lives when neither of them was young anymore, gnawed at Mme de Sabran's heart, Boufflers sought to reassure her with a metaphor that was full of poetry: "The beautiful days of autumn were made for us: they will begin next autumn, and will last through the autumn of life, and just as autumn will have preserved the heat of summer, so winter shall preserve the warmth of autumn. And I like to believe that, after that winter, we will see the birth of an eternal spring, where we will live side by side, and for each other; and *by* each other, perhaps in different forms, but what does that matter, as long as we love each other. Perhaps we shall be gods, perhaps humans once more, perhaps birds, perhaps trees. Perhaps I shall be a plant, and you my flower; I shall arm myself with thorns to protect you, and shade you with my leaves to preserve you. In short, no matter what form you may assume, you will be loved."[231]

Occasionally the Chevalier entrusted the task of making plain what he felt to the poets dearest to him[232]—Virgil, Horace, Ovid, Racine, La Fontaine, and their beloved Milton (whose *Paradise Lost* Mme de Sabran had translated in its entirety in order to teach her son English)[233]—"all those old friends" thanks to whom the two of them had passed "such lovely moments" together.[234] At other times, learned references to mythology—"I love you more than Endymion, or even Acteon, loved the moon"[235]—conferred solemnity on his declarations. In both cases, he knew he could count on the complicity of his reader.

A diary of love, Boufflers's letters are also a war journal—though a very different kind of war than he had hoped to wage at the head of his regiment. He was sufficiently stoic to endure without complaint the climate, harshness, and physical exhaustion of life in Africa, with its procession of insomnia, migraines, fits of diarrhea, fevers, abscesses, and infected wounds. But sometimes, when the "moral and physical energy"[236] on which he had come to depend abandoned him, he faithfully confessed to his beloved the price he was paying for his foolhardy decision: "You cannot imagine, and no one will ever imagine, all of the anguish and contradiction I have suffered in this cursed land that I have sought to render happy, and which is not susceptible to that emotion."[237] Despite all of his efforts, he always ended up "yielding to that interior sorrow, to that secret humiliation which is the other side of zeal."[238] He was also ready to admit to everything she accused him of: the excessive weight he gave to public opinion,[239] his blind trust in chance,[240] his imprudence,[241] his impatience.[242] But he was too proud and stubborn to declare himself defeated—"adversity is the pharmacy of the soul"[243]—too faithful to himself to really want to change. And he knew how to find the decisive argument: "I prefer to remain as I am—odd, choleric, lazy, insignificant, but above all amorous, for that is the way you love me."[244]

Faithful to the teachings of the classical moralists, Boufflers also felt the need to reflect on his contradictions and disappointments from a more general perspective. And he wound up adopting the allegory imagined by La Fontaine in *The Two Pigeons*. In a way, it was coming full circle, since this was the fable in which Mme de Sabran had invited him to "see his reflection"—in the sense indicated by the fabulist[245]—on the eve of his departure for the Senegalese adventure.

"It is a singular thing, those two forces, the one centrifugal and the other that we idiotically designate as centripetal, which act and react continually upon man. The one force launches him beyond himself, his tastes, his most treasured interests, beyond his household, his homeland, and even out of the world itself in pursuit of I don't know what pleasure and I can't say which merit in the eyes of others. The other force soon draws him back toward all that he has left, by means of the most distinct and lifelike imaginary paintings of the happiness he lacks, by a thousand seductive images of home, of his old habits, his family, his friends, a woman he loves, who holds her arms out to him."[246]

On the other hand, confronted with the brutality and rapacity of whites toward the Africans, he was obliged to reevaluate the philosophical optimism of his century, its faith in reason, justice, and social cohesion in the name of shared values, and the civilizing force of commerce:[247] "I begin to see that in the depths of the heart of man there is a germ of aversion for all that is not himself, and that makes him an enemy of the general good, since he finds the piece of it that returns to him always too small. It is true that we are born mean and rapacious, and that nothing apart from philosophy and the habit of right reflection and right action has the power to purify us."[248] Philosophy had to be recognized, however "gloomy" it might be, as "the best remedy for all afflictions, but one of those remedies that never tastes particularly pleasant."[249]

The perpetual confrontation with death—which usually came in the wake of terrible sufferings—drove him to reformulate for himself all those metaphysical questions that he thought he had rid himself of once and for all along with his soutane: "Is the world, as some of us have claimed, a place of punishment, an expiatory vestibule, or is it merely the only place and life that there is, as so many fine minds have maintained? Yet if that is the case, whence have these ideas of justice and perfection descended, so foreign to human weakness? How could man have come to suppose he has a soul?...There are plenty of points that deserve to be cleared up....But in this I would be as mad as if I sought to illuminate the whole huge map of the continent of Africa during the night with a little candle. That night is life itself; the unknown continent, metaphysics; and the little candle is reason."[250]

We will allude here only briefly to the *actual* exploratory journeys under-taken by the Chevalier in Senegal, and his descriptions of them, which bear no trace of the myth of the noble savage. In his writings, men, behavior, and rituals are rendered with an extreme realism, though occasionally with a touch of the comic. It was above all the beauty, the majesty, and the power of the African landscape that fascinated this traveler, for whom nature had been an abiding love, and to which his letters pay abundant homage.

On November 20, 1787, Boufflers left Senegal for the last time. The promises of reinforcements of men and equipment that had been made to him on the occasion of his visit to France between the end of August and the beginning of December 1786 had remained unfulfilled, and he could no longer count on the support of the Maréchal de Castries, who had stepped down from his ministerial post. Facing what seemed like a hopeless situation, sorely tried in both the physical and emotional sense, and pressured by both Mme de Sabran and his friends, he had decided to request a discharge.

Throughout his African adventure, the Chevalier had taken as his "private maxim: Do what you should, come what may."[251] And he would hold to it during the intense years that awaited him back in France, as well. But under-standing just where his obligations lay would not be so simple.

Disembarking at La Rochelle on Christmas Eve, Boufflers was finally able to embrace his "Penelope"[252] as the first days of 1788 arrived, but he found himself facing a France very different from the one he had left behind two years earlier. When it came to his emotional bonds, the Chevalier could no longer depend on the Marquise de Boufflers, who had died during his first sojourn in Senegal—and to whom he would dedicate a splendid if brief literary sketch[253]—nor on the protection of the Maréchale de Luxembourg, whom he thought of as "a second mother."[254] He still had his sister, with whom, despite the little sympathy she felt for Mme de Sabran, he remained very close; Mme de Mirepoix, who at the age of more than eighty still danced at Versailles "with all the lightness and grace of a twenty-year-old";[255] and the Maréchal de Beauvau, who, nearing his seventies, remained the Chevalier's ethical and political lodestar. Mme de Sabran, it is true, had kept him informed in her letters of "the affair of the necklace" and the suit brought by Cardinal de Rohan, of the Assembly of Notables, and the disgrace of Calonne, minister of finance, but since she shared in all points the concerns of her friends the

Polignacs, she never succeeded in grasping the true political implications of these events. Boufflers, on the other hand, immediately understood that the prospect of an imminent convocation of the Estates General, desired by the Assembly of Notables and the parliament, offered him once more the opportunity to play a public role and to fling himself into the fray. For him, 1788 was a thrilling year. Again he took up life in society, where politics fed nearly all conversation; he frequented once more the old liberal and reformist salons of Beauvau, of the Duc de Nivernais—who in 1787 had been appointed a minister without portfolio—and of Mme de Montesson. He could also respond to the more audacious projects that were being discussed in the salon of Mme de Staël. And when Germaine expressed her astonishment that the Chevalier still hadn't entered the Académie, he replied with a gallant improvisation:

Je vois l'académie où vous êtes présente
Si vous m'en admettez, mon sort sera trop beau
Entre nous deux nous ferons les quarante
Vous comme chiffre et moi comme zero.*[256]

Necker's recall to the direction of France's finances on August 26, 1788, filled the Chevalier with hope, for—as Mme de Sabran noted—"Necker loves you with all his being."[257] And when, on September 23, the King announced the assembly of the Estates General for January of the following year, Boufflers set to work. With the help of his sister he managed to transform Malgrange, the country home that they owned together, from a *"vacherie"* into a "fiefdom,"[258] and succeeded that October in getting himself elected as *bailli d'épée* at Nancy. The year ended beautifully with his induction to the Académie Française.[259] The crowd that came to witness the ceremony was so large that the Cent Suisses were forced to intervene to prevent a brawl, and Mme de Sabran attended in the company of Prince Henry of Prussia.[260] By a happy coincidence, it was another native of Lorraine, the Marquis de Saint-Lambert, his mother's old protégé, who had known him since his childhood, who replied to his discourse. After having celebrated the austere virtues of his predecessor,

---

*I see the academy where you hold a place: / If you were to admit me, my fate would be *trop beau*. / Between the two of us, we will make up a forty— / You as the numeral, I as the zero.

M. de Montazet, Archbishop of Lyon, Boufflers focused his remarks on the importance of clarity of style in all genres, from the humblest to the most elevated. A clarity in the service of virtue would also, he claimed, mark the eloquence of the citizen ready to be reborn on the benches of the Estates General. And he himself furnished an example by evoking "the august image of *la patrie*": "That immense multitude, unknown to herself, so to speak, for so many generations; she is France, illuminated by study, by discussion, by wise counsel and long sufferings; these ills have touched the virtuous and tender heart of our King; now he contemplates the cure." His generous proposals surely would be "repaid with more glory than ever a king acquired, with more happiness than ever a king bestowed."[261]

The wishes voiced here were no doubt sincere and widely shared, yet the conclusion of his discourse was less reassuring. Boufflers selected the phoenix as his "emblem" for the process which would allow "the loveliest and most durable of monarchies" to "regenerate itself."[262] But before it could be reborn, wouldn't it have to die?

The Comte Louis-Philippe de Ségur

I tremble that Ségur should be too much a philosopher in a country where it would take an army to destroy philosophy, and too much a man of letters where statesmen are needed.

—PRINCE DE LIGNE TO PRINCE POTEMKIN, letter from Vienna, January 21, 1790[1]

BEGINNING IN 1815, when, with the Napoleonic adventure concluded, "that genial despot quit the stage he had occupied so completely,"[2] numerous Frenchmen felt the need to take stock of the past and leave written records of those events in which and to which they had been both the actors and the privileged witnesses. "It can be established as a rule that the history of a particular individual becomes a public property more quickly the more important the role was that he played on the stage of the world,"[3] declared the Duc de Lévis in 1815, in a new edition of his *Souvenirs-Portraits*, which, only two years earlier, had been subjected to imperial censorship. It is not surprising that Louis-Philippe de Ségur should have been one of these memoirists, for he had succeeded in traversing several political regimes without mishap. Born in 1753[4] and embarking upon a brilliant military and diplomatic career under Louis XVI, Ségur went on to serve as ambassador extraordinary during the Revolution, state councillor under the Consulate, grandmaster of ceremonies under Napoleon, and senator during the first Restoration.[5] He rallied to the Emperor once again during the Hundred Days. It is true he experienced a period of ostracism during the first years of the second Restoration, but ultimately he regained his position as senator.

Unusual though it may have been, his decision to break with convention and publish his *Memoirs, or Recollections and Anecdotes* during his lifetime is far from astonishing. Like Mme de Genlis—who immediately noted the novelty of this enterprise,[6] of which she herself had been the first to set an example[7]—

225

Ségur had never been known for the consistency of his political opinions and wanted to lay them out clearly before he died. But to accomplish this he adopted a strategy that was the very opposite of the Comtesse's. Rather than placing himself at the center of his *Memoirs*, describing himself, his beliefs, and the choices that had marked the crucial years of his youth, Ségur concealed himself behind a sort of collective portrait. His ways of thinking and feeling, he affirmed, had been those common to his whole generation—which in turn implied that whatever errors of judgment he might have been guilty of were in fact the fruit of a general blindness.

It was not merely the need to justify himself that drove Ségur to hypothesize a kind of collective responsibility. He had decided to write his memoirs at the age of seventy after having established his reputation with a vast historical oeuvre, and he was well aware of the difficulty of evoking convincingly, long after the fact, such an important moment of his life, mixed as it had been with the events that marked the end of the ancien régime. It would mean tracing the origins of a conflict that had never been resolved "between his patrimony of aristocratic values and his attachment to progressive ideas"—one which had become for him the source of a "profound sensation of guilt and sin."[8]

Thus Ségur decided to "draw a moral sketch"[9] rather than a "historical tableau"[10] of the era through which he had lived. To the questionable reliability of a belated memoir, tainted by retrospection, he preferred an interpretation more objective—at least in appearance—subordinating his personal memories to the evocation of the social context by which he had been shaped, and whose values and way of life he had shared until 1789.

His approach was far from arbitrary. Indeed, never in the last years of the ancien régime had social convention exercised such a profound influence on the elites, standardizing their conduct in accord with specific models, and, throughout the eighteenth century, numerous voices had been raised in opposition to this tyranny. In his memoirs, Ségur did not fail to recall: "Particularly in high society, through continual blending and friction, the native stamp of every character was effaced; since fashion was all, all was the same. Opinions, expressions, all of them were brought down to the level of common usage; language, behavior, went according to convention; and though each was different internally, everyone displayed to the world the same mask, the same tone, the same appearance."[11] Yet as in any theatrical performance, this social playacting nevertheless allowed its most versatile artists to distinguish themselves by the elegance of their style and the originality of their interpretation.

After his social debut and his presentation at Versailles, Louis-Philippe played to perfection the role that was his thanks to his age, education, and rank, on the double stage of town and court. Though naturally inclined toward reflection and study, he did not neglect the life of society and, thanks to several amorous adventures and two or three notable duels, was forgiven for a certain lack of spontaneity and a style that was a bit too ornate, obtaining credentials sufficient to allow him entry to that merry band of dandies who eventually brought the dangerous game of the Fronde back into fashion.

The eldest son of the Maréchal de Ségur, Louis-Philippe had been raised in the cult of paternal heroism and, as was the custom in his family, took up the profession of arms. Irrespective of his aptitudes and deserts, he rose quickly through the ranks: a cavalry lieutenant at age sixteen, captain at eighteen, the young Ségur obtained the command of the regiment of Orléans Dragoons at twenty-two. And at the tender age of fourteen, before serving his sovereign on the battlefield, Louis-Philippe had the honor, normally reserved only for the greatest in the kingdom, of serving the King at table.

In 1767, Louis XV, who had come to Compiègne to witness the great military maneuvers, had accepted an invitation to dine with the Marquis de Ségur, who was responsible for these exercises. Seeing that, in keeping with etiquette, his host was preparing to remain standing behind his chair in order to serve him, the King declared that Ségur had already served sufficiently in the field, and that now it was time for him to give himself a rest. Having thus invited the Maréchal to sit at his side, the sovereign requested, as an additional sign of his goodwill, that the young Louis-Philippe replace his father in serving. Over the course of the meal, Louis XV spoke to the adolescent several times, predicting among other things that he would have good luck when it came to war. The King recalled that when it came to the Ségurs, fortune and misfortune alternated regularly from one generation to the next—so that his father's many wounds were sure to prevent the young man from being wounded himself.

This precocious encounter with the King made a profound impression on Louis-Philippe, and allowed him to assess at first hand the bond of familiarity between the sovereign and his nobles. It is the first of three personal memories—the only ones relating to his formative years—that he chose to mention in opening his memoirs. The episode allowed him to assert right away the antiquity of his attachment to the House of Bourbon. And the choice of the two other memories, tied as well to the fate of the monarchy, seem no less strategic.

The second memory dates to his eighteenth year, when he had been present at the tremendous fireworks display that had been offered by the city of Paris on the occasion of the Dauphin's marriage to Marie-Antoinette. However, the security measures taken for the event proved insufficient: as the pressure of bodies built, the crowd panicked, and numerous people tumbled into a deep trench left open in a nearby construction site. With more than a thousand dead, the celebration was an enormous disaster. Ségur did not fail to perceive in hindsight a premonitory sign of another terrible event: twenty-four years later, on that same Place Louis XV—rebaptized Place de la Révolution[12] and transformed into a sort of gruesome open-air theater—the heads of "a pair of august spouses"[13] would fall as well. Others would see in that explosion of fireworks that set the Parisian sky alight, and led to the loss of so many human lives, a metaphor dear to the revolutionary imagination: that of an erupting volcano, which rains down destruction in order to clear the way for a better world.[14]

The third episode provided Louis-Philippe with the opportunity to reaffirm his emotional bond with the monarchy, while justifying his not having defended it to the bitter end—it concerns the circumstances following the death of the Well-Beloved, and the moral that might be drawn from them. "Dazzled since [his] childhood by the splendor of the throne, by the extent of royal power," and painfully struck by the final throes and death of the sovereign, Ségur had gone to Versailles to pay his last respects, where he perceived with bewilderment that already the dead man was the subject of general indifference, and that, possessed by "a sort of joy," everyone was forging ahead with their projects and plotting intrigues, their minds turned toward the future. His initial reaction had been indignation at the faithlessness of the courtiers, but the experiences that awaited him would bring him to see in this need for change a pathology common to all human beings: "It is the fate of nations as well as of individuals to live in an almost perpetual state of suffering; thus nations, like sick men, like to vary their position: every movement they make brings them hope of improvement."[15]

Moreover, for that whole generation, the desire for change had taken the form of a collective euphoria: "As for us, the young French nobility, without regret for the past, without anxiety for the future, we walked gaily across a carpet of flowers which concealed the abyss beneath.... The gravity of the ancient doctrines annoyed us. The joyful philosophy of Voltaire attracted and entertained us; and we admired it (without exploring the work of more serious writers) as bearing the stamp of courage and of resistance to arbitrary power.... Enjoying at court and in town the distinctions of our birth, promoted up the ranks in the army thanks to our names alone, and free from that point on to mix without ostentation or restraint among our fellow countrymen and to taste the sweetness of plebeian equality, we saw the brief years of our early lives glide away in the midst of illusions, and in a sort of happiness which, I believe, had never before been enjoyed by any but ourselves."[16]

This general lightness did not prevent Louis-Philippe from taking himself terribly seriously. An ambitious man, he was determined to make a career. In contrast to his brother, Joseph-Alexandre, he saw social success not as an end in itself but as a necessary stage on the path to power. He had neither the physical beauty nor the natural elegance of the Vicomte—which the latter had inherited from the Baron de Besenval—and libertinism was not his strong suit. On the other hand, he was intelligent, willful, and methodical. He completed his education by taking, along with his friend Jean-Balthazar d'Adhémar, the course in international law given by the famous Guillaume Koch (who was also the instructor of Louis de Narbonne) at the University of Strasbourg. Then, with the selfsame seriousness, he set himself to study at the *grande école du monde* that was life in high society.

Beginning with that select circle, refined and open to new ideas, that his mother hosted in the rue Saint-Florentin, the young Comte frequented all of the great salons of the era,[17] befriending men of letters and philosophers,[18] submitting his earliest writings to them and receiving their advice in turn. He even succeeded in extracting from Voltaire himself a cautious "literary benediction."

Having returned to Paris after twenty-eight years of absence, the patriarch of the Enlightenment had twice wished to visit the bedside of the Marquise de Ségur, then at the very end of his life. The encounter between the two old friends, which unfolded among the reverent silence of some fifty curious onlookers, was deeply moving, and Louis-Philippe took advantage of the occasion to give a number of his own verses to the illustrious visitor. After having flattered the amour propre of the young Comte by praising "with grace and delicacy" his "passion for letters" and his first "essays," Voltaire had nonetheless advised him, with all the requisite diplomacy, to distrust his "inclination for poetry," save as practice for writing more elegantly in prose. The formula with which he took leave of the Comte could not have been clearer: "Go, young man; accept the good wishes of an old man who predicts for you a happy fate; but remember that poetry, divine though she may be, is a siren."[19]

While preparing to follow Voltaire's advice and become an indefatigable writer of prose, Louis-Philippe continued to scribble chansons, madrigals, epigrams, and pieces in prose and verse destined for the amusement of high society—and found in his brother, Joseph-Alexandre, three years his junior, a formidable competitor. Yet far from becoming a rivalry, this "metromania"[20] was a shared game that sealed their affinity in spite of all the differences of their chosen lifestyles. Although they were very different, the two young Ségurs appreciated each other, had numerous friends in common, and frequently found themselves in the same places, achieving an equal measure of success. We do not know whether the knowledge that they were not sons of the same father weighed on their relations, but the Vicomte, with his habitual aptness, shielded himself from all conjecture by declaring: "I could be jealous of him, but I prefer to be proud."[21] Mme de Necker, that keen seismograph of social opinion, could affirm that "everyone would have liked to have them as sons, brothers, or friends."[22] The brothers shared a passion for the theater, but there too it was the Vicomte who was at the forefront. Between 1777 and 1780, they were part of a troupe of amateur actors invited to perform in the prestigious private theater of Mme de Montesson, an intimate friend of their mother as well as their paternal grandfather.

Life in society was not merely a springboard for the younger generations; it also offered them a chance to acquire in practice the sort of urbanity and knowledge that could not be found in books. Ségur made the most of this opportunity by frequenting the circles of the previous generation, afterward setting down his recollections of them in pages that have become proverbial. "They displayed," he wrote, "an indescribable mixture of simplicity and elevation, of grace and reason, of criticism and urbanity. From them one might imperceptibly absorb the history and politics of ancient and modern times, a thousand anecdotes of the court, from the time of Louis XIV to the king who then reigned, and thus one wandered a gallery as instructive, as varied in events and portraits, as that which is offered by the inimitable letters of Mme de Sévigné."[23] Philosophy, literature, and poetry were discussed as well, without pedantry and respecting the opinions of all. When it came to subjects like government reforms, the economy, and the political situation generally, Ségur collected the views of a number of great servants of the kingdom, such as President Malesherbes, the Duc de Choiseul, the Prince de Beauvau, and the

Duc de Nivernais. It was a precious experience, for, as he would later theorize: "The conversation of men who have achieved a deserved fame illuminates us even more than their works do. From them we may become acquainted with a thousand rules of tact and taste, which would be almost impossible to convey in writing."[24] Listening to them, the young Ségur was initiated into the art of conversation—essential for a man of society. He had all of the necessary skills—a mastery of the language, an aptness of expression, and the resources of a vast and solid erudition—to cut a fine figure, but he did not sufficiently trust his own instincts. He sought the help of Lekain, the greatest tragic actor of the era, both to perfect the pitch of his voice and to learn to read prose in public like poetry, with the proper modulations and pauses. The results of this zeal were not slow in coming, and it is most likely Ségur's portrait that Ligne paints in his *Alcippe*: "As he enters the company, he has everything necessary to please. One is happy with him, without realizing that before long one *will* be enchanted. If a boisterous and general conversation allows Alcippe the opportunity and strength to slip in a pair of words, you will be astonished by their grace, their authority, their aptness.... He proceeds at his own pace, with calculation: he arrives without laziness or disdain. The delicacy of his voice, of his vision and his views, seem to serve the delicacy of his spirit. Whether it is a tasteful pleasantry, a concise and piquant definition, the composition of verses, or simply holding forth, it is a spectacle for all to see—all the scattered successes of Alcippe, who achieved them so effortlessly, reunite in a general chorus.... How is it that Alcippe agrees with so many people who don't agree with each other?"[25]

Louis-Philippe rapidly proved that he had "everything necessary" to become a deft courtier as well. Like his brother, he had blood ties with the Orléanses and was more at home with them at Palais-Royal than at Versailles. Nonetheless, in 1776 an unexpected bit of good luck allowed him entrée to the intimate circle of Marie-Antoinette. The two young men had been presented to the Comtesse de Polignac by the Baron de Besenval, long before Marie-Antoinette decided that she couldn't live without the lovely Gabrielle-Yolande, and it was the latter, installed at Versailles, who introduced them to the Queen. Marie-Antoinette loved to surround herself with people her own age, and was astonished by the fact that "anyone older than thirty would dare to appear at court."[26] She laughed at decorum and the defenders of tradition, and reserved her warmest welcome for the young friends of her favorite, who brought with them the fashions of the capital.

Along with his brother, Joseph-Alexandre; Lafayette; Noailles; Lauzun; Narbonne; the Lameth brothers; and the Chevalier de Coigny, Louis-Philippe was part of that band of young aristocrats whose gleeful irreverence and passion for novelty went hand in hand with the most ancient vocation of their caste: war. If the disastrous results of the Seven Years' War had inspired Louis XV to a policy of peace, the French nobility's desire for revenge had grown with time. Choiseul, during the term of his ministry, had reinforced the navy and modernized the army with an eye toward a new policy of colonial expansion, which would lead inexorably to armed conflict with England. The minister's disgrace saved the country from a war whose issue would have been far from certain, but allowed the nobility to manifest their displeasure with great insolence. The flower of the French aristocracy never ceased to express their solidarity with the illustrious exile, and the Marquis de Ségur was among them: he too made the journey to Chanteloup in the company of his eldest son. It was the beginning of a new Fronde, and the elegant obelisk raised in the château's park, upon which were engraved the names of visitors, served as its "monument."[27] From then on, the nobility's spirit of opposition would bear down upon the monarchy, during its last fifteen years, like a river in spate. After a happy start to Louis XVI's reign, the younger generation would also find reason for discontent in his cautious and hesitant policies. Deprived as they were of the chance to devote their youth to the single end of "redressing the affront"[28] of the Seven Years' War, Ségur and his friends felt authorized to amuse themselves at the expense of parliament and the government, to fight duels, to costume themselves in the style of Henri IV or dress up as English jockeys.

But finally, with the coming of the American Revolution,[29] these young men were given the chance to pursue the redress they craved. Louis-Philippe received news of the rebellion in Boston while at the highly social resort town of Spa, where the "bold audacity" of the American colonists "electrified every spirit, and excited general admiration."[30] The Comte was amazed to see all of his fellow visitors, subjects of the various European monarchies, so caught up in the enthusiasm for "the revolt of a people against a king": clearly he was not the only one "whose heart beat faster at the sound of liberty awakening, and seeking to shrug off the yoke of arbitrary power."[31] Along with the Marquis de Lafayette and the Vicomte de Noailles, they were "the first three Frenchmen, distinguished by their ranking at court, who offered their martial aid to the Americans."[32] The three friends spoke at length with Silas Deane and Arthur Lee, who had been sent to Paris by the American Congress in 1766, in the company of Benjamin Franklin, in order to solicit the aid of France.[33] When they learned that the advice of qualified officers would be useful in making up for the rebels' lack of experience and technical knowledge, they proposed themselves as volunteers.

Their plan was a perfect combination of the love of glory and independence, the ancient spirit of chivalry that demanded one fly to the aid of a just and noble cause, and the new concepts of liberty and equality. And it had illustrious precedents. A century earlier, the cousins of the Sun King himself[34] had defied the sovereign's ire in order to join the imperial forces in combating the Turks in Hungary. Nevertheless, as Ségur would recall in his memoirs,[35] their primary motivation was the desire for revenge on the English. And Lafayette's battle cry—"To injure England is to serve my country"[36]—left no doubt on the subject. *Liberté, fraternité, egalité* "played no part in it whatsoever, and when the motto did eventually materialize, it disconcerted him."[37]

But the three friends had not taken the court and their families into account. The Comte de Maurepas ordered them to give up their plans, since the government, which was secretly negotiating with the Americans, did not want to risk alerting the English by appearing to condone their departure. As for their families, indignant at not having been consulted, they refused the financial support necessary for the venture and placed their unruly sons under surveillance. Lafayette was the only one of them who refused to resign himself to the situation. In his memoirs, Ségur recounts that two months after that call to order, at seven o'clock in the morning, his friend "burst into his room, sealed the door behind him, and, seating himself at his bedside, said: 'I'm leaving for America; nobody knows, but I love you too much have disappeared without letting you in on my secret.'"[38]

The orphan of a father killed at an early age by English artillery, and heir to a considerable fortune, the Marquis had purchased a ship unbeknownst to his family and outfitted it with arms, victuals, and a sturdy crew, also managing to secure the support of twelve officers determined to participate in the enterprise. His departure took his relations by surprise, but while he was still in France, an order from the King resulted in Lafayette's arrest. Refusing to admit defeat, he managed to escape and boldly set out to rendezvous with his ship, which was awaiting him in Spain. In the autumn of 1777, he weighed anchor for America. The news caused such an uproar that his uncle, the Marquis de Noailles, then ambassador to London, asked Versailles if he was obliged to resign his commission.[39] Lafayette was nineteen years old and was about to pass into history as "the Hero of Two Worlds."

In January 1778, France's decision to side openly with the United States gave Louis-Philippe reason to hope that he would not remain merely "an idle observer of the war."[40] This was the desire of most of the nobles in the army, who vied with one another to be dispatched to the coasts of Brittany and Normandy in anticipation of an invasion of England. With the support of Marie-Antoinette, Ségur obtained the position of assistant quartermaster general to the troops stationed in Brittany[41] under the command of the Maréchal de Castries. For him, as for Lauzun and Boufflers, the months passed "in exercises, in evolutions, in sham attacks, defenses, marine landings, and military reconnaissances,"[42] while they waited in vain to try themselves against the enemy. Hopes for an invasion were revived the following spring, when thirty-two French warships departed Brest and thirty-eight Spanish ships left Cadiz heading in the direction of Plymouth. It seemed as though the moment had finally come for the army to cross the Channel, but a terrible storm scattered the allied fleet, the same ill luck that had overwhelmed the "invincible" Spanish Armada three centuries earlier. The ships returned to their respective ports, and the plan for an invasion of England was definitively abandoned. After so much waiting the disappointment was enormous, and a heavy barrage of pamphlets, satires, and epigrams were aimed at the "ineptitude of power"— with Ségur himself contributing a number of blithely irreverent couplets. By suppressing their liberty—the memoirist would recall—France's absolute monarchy had left its subjects with ridicule as their only weapon, one whose effects would reveal themselves to be far deadlier than anyone had supposed. "Lacking access to the tribune," Ségur notes, "the salons were our battlefields, and unable to engage in direct combat, it was by means of light skirmishes that our compromised liberty made clear that its fire was concealed rather than extinguished."[43]

Before long, though, Louis-Philippe would be faced with an even greater disappointment. In January 1780, the French government finally decided to send to the aid of the Americans an expedition commanded by the Comte de Rochambeau. Ségur used every means at his disposal to join it, but met with the firm opposition of his father—and this time, he lacked the backing of Marie-Antoinette. The Vicomte de Noailles, on the other hand, benefiting from the strong support of his family, succeeded in departing. "Thus, of the three friends who before anyone else in France had had the idea of fighting for the American cause,"[44] Ségur was the only one forced to remain behind. But soon enough the sudden reversal of the political situation would rekindle his enthusiasm. The Marquis de Castries and the Marquis de Ségur were respectively appointed minister of the navy and minister of war—and both of them got along swimmingly with the minister of foreign affairs, the Comte de Vergennes. Eager to see France regain its prestige and triumph on both land and sea, the three ministers were keen on the idea of war. All hope was not yet lost.

Meanwhile, waiting for a propitious moment to make his name, Louis-Philippe had found love—and, almost unheard of among the nobility, he had found it in marriage. It was an old friend of the family, the Marquis de Chastellux, who in 1777 arranged the union of Louis-Philippe and his cousin Antoinette-Élisabeth d'Aguesseau. By way of that network of kinships that essentially made the French nobility a single immense family, Ségur was similarly related to his best friends, Lafayette and the Vicomte de Noailles. The bride was three years younger than her spouse, and, to judge by the portrait of her painted by Mme Vigée Le Brun in 1785,[45] a true beauty. Dark-haired, with perfect features and enormous, searching black eyes, the young woman whose image the painter has captured already possessed, in spite of her shy smile, a deeply romantic aura. Daughter of the Marquis d'Aguesseau, Antoinette joined to her sensibility and greatness of soul the moral integrity of her illustrious grandfather, the Chancellor d'Aguesseau, an ardent defender of Gallican freedoms. She was convinced that happiness had to be sought above all in the sphere of domestic relations—and not only did Louis-Philippe fall in love with his pretty wife but he placed her at the center of his emotional life. For him, the marriage marked his passage into full maturity. In wedding Antoinette, he was also joining himself to the parliamentary tradition of her family, and took her grandfather the chancellor as a model to aspire toward in his own life, in hopes of "elevating himself to the height of the immortal principles of virtue, justice, and love for his homeland."[46] What better political lesson could there be than d'Aguesseau's discourses, which showed that, even as minister to an absolute monarch, he "never lost sight of the public interest, the rights of the citizens, and the limits prescribed to power by eternal reason and the fundamental laws of the State"?[47]

An aristocratic forerunner to the bourgeois marriage of the following century, the Ségurs' domestic idyll did not pass unnoticed. Despite his penchant for libertinism, Gouverneur Morris noted in his Parisian journal that, married now for eleven years, Louis-Philippe had no difficulty in declaring himself faithful to his wife: in the opinion of Washington's envoy, the Comtesse de Ségur fully deserved such loyalty.[48] Invited to their house, the American visitor had served as the audience for a *proverbe* penned by the Comte[49] on the occasion of the birth of the couple's third child, Laure, and performed by their first two children, whom Antoinette had swiftly brought into the world following their marriage. "A little Comedy is acted here by the Children," Morris wrote, "the Subject of which is the Pleasure derived to the whole Family by an Infant of which the Countess was lately delivered. The Play is written by the Father, to whom I address in the Course of it these lines:

For perfecting the comic Art
Let others take a single Part
While you my friend, with nobler Soul
Embrace at once the mighty Whole;
For here we see arise from you
The Subject, Play, and Actors too."[50]

In the spring of 1782, eight months after the surrender at Yorktown, Louis-Philippe finally received the permission he had so long awaited, and at the head of two regiments of reinforcements destined for Rochambeau's army,[51] was able to set sail on the frigate *La Gloire*, armed with thirty-two cannons. At Rochefort, he joined up with another gunboat, also bound for America.[52]

Before the two ships could get underway, however, rumors of an imminent peace arrived, dampening Ségur's enthusiasm. "It is a difficult thing," he wrote to his wife, "to leave all that one loves and travel two thousand leagues, only to learn that one has made a pointless journey."[53] In fact, France and England would not sign their preliminary peace agreements for another seven months,[54] and even if Louis-Philippe arrived too late to fight against the English, the American expedition represented an extraordinary adventure for him. This becomes clear in the extended description of the adventure that he provides in his memoirs, as well as in the letters dispatched to his wife over the course of his mission, which bear witness to the excitement kindled in him by the discovery of a new style of life and thought on the far side of the Atlantic. And even if, a century later, the editor of the critical edition of his letters felt it necessary to sacrifice their most intimate passages for the sake of the family's dignity, there can be no doubt regarding the success of the Ségurs' marriage. Infatuated with and proud of his young wife, Louis-Philippe never lost an opportunity to express his feelings for her, from the moment *La Gloire* finally left the coasts of France: "Adieu, my love . . . I am leaving you behind, my heart is so very sad, so very heavy. Adieu, I can say no more, I love you and I am leaving. Adieu."[55]

Among the officers who set out with him on *La Gloire* and *L'Aigle*, Ségur had a number of friends: the Duc de Lauzun, who had already fought bravely at Yorktown and was making his second voyage to America; Prince Victor de Broglie, eldest son of the Maréchal, who, like Louis-Philippe, after having vainly solicited his family for their blessing, had finally obtained permission to leave; the Baron de Montesquieu, grandson of the author of *The Spirit of the Laws*; the Marquis de Vauban, the Comte Loménie de Brienne, the Comte de Talleyrand-Périgord (who had already distinguished himself at Yorktown), the Vicomte de Fleury, the Vicomte de Vaudreuil, and the Chevalier Alexandre de Lameth. All of them bore illustrious names and shared a common courage and gaiety—they were all, "depending on the time and place, moralizing or lighthearted, serious or scatterbrained, carefree or enthusiastic."[56] They had all left for America seeking the chance to fight in the service of the oldest monarchy in Europe, and were universally impassioned on behalf of the republic struggling to be born.

But none could possibly have guessed the fate that awaited them. Lauzun and Broglie embraced the cause of the Revolution and died by the guillotine; Loménie would suffer the same end; remaining loyal to the Bourbons, the Baron de Montesquieu and the Marquis de Vauban would take part in the disastrous invasion of Quiberon; after becoming one of the principal leaders of the French Patriot Party in 1789, Alexandre de Lameth would be obliged, in 1792, along with Lafayette, to flee to Austria, where he spent years in prison. In a letter written at the time of his departure and quoted in his memoirs, Louis-Philippe showed that even a spoiled child of the high nobility of the court, one who owed everything to the reigning system of privileges, felt himself authorized to affirm that, under an absolute monarchy, "wherein a small number of persons, precariously elevated to the highest positions by the whim of a master, are alone responsible for the laws and the administration," and where "advancement has nothing to do with talent but depends on favor," the "love of glory" was dictated by vanity, rather than love of country. For his part, suffocated by the weight of "arbitrary power," he had abandoned his family and everything he loved in order to seize the opportunity to fight on behalf of liberty and for "a just cause."[57]

The crossing was arduous and risky. The two ships had barely left the French coast when they found themselves beset by horrendous weather, and more than once came close to foundering. Broglie and Lauzun suffered so badly from seasickness that when Ségur announced that they were all going to die, they replied that it did not matter.[58]

They managed to recover their spirits upon reaching the Azores. Aside from the beauty of the scenery, there would have been nothing notable about the stopover at Terceira if Lauzun hadn't taken it as an opportunity to display his sense of savoir vivre. Six years older than Louis-Philippe, the most elegant and original of Don Juans, crowned with the fame he had won at Yorktown, he was the idol of his young friends. "It would have been difficult to find a more pleasant traveling companion," recalled Ségur: "his character was easy-going, his spirit generous, his charm wholly original."[59] No sooner had they disembarked at Terceira than the Duc befriended not only the French consul but his English counterpart as well—that is, the representative of his national enemy—who had at his disposal the most hospitable of homes, the best of chefs, and the most amusing of guests, and who wasted no time in introducing them all to the pleasures of the island. With his full support, Lauzun took Ségur, Broglie, and the Vicomte de Fleury to visit a convent whose Mother Superior proved tremendously welcoming. With the aid of the consul—who acted as interpreter—the four friends engaged in a *galante* back-and-forth with the ladies in residence, who, though they remained virtuously on the far side of a metal grate throughout, did not hide the pleasure they took in this diversion. One *senhorita* from an illustrious family set an example for the rest: "Struck by the fine looks, animated features, and dress of Lauzun, who was wearing his hussar's uniform, she tossed a rose to him through the grate with a smile, asked him his name, and presented him with a corner of her hand-kerchief, which he held tightly while she attempted to tug it back, producing a sweet vibration that seemed to pass from hands to heart."[60] There followed a general exchange of handkerchiefs, flowers, blown kisses, and compliments. The following day, the French travelers presented themselves once again in the visiting room, the Mother Superior receiving them with the same courtesy, and the residents showing themselves even more indulgent than before. Songs were improvised, notes and gifts were exchanged—locks of hair, portraits, rings, and scapulars. Lauzun, Ségur, Broglie, and Fleury performed a sort of dance with their ladies, separated though they were by the grate—and there was already talk of eliminating the latter obstacle when the four friends received orders to return in haste, as the ships were about to cast off.

During the second part of the crossing, *La Gloire* and *L'Aigle* enjoyed magnificent weather and favorable winds, but ran afoul of the enemy's fleet.

The English, who had resigned themselves by this point to recognizing the independence of their former colony and to negotiating with France and Spain, had adopted a purely defensive strategy in regard to the United States, without, however, ending their war on the high seas. Within sight of the American coast, the two French frigates were attacked by the Royal Navy, and wound up running aground in an attempt to find shelter. Forced to abandon their ships, Ségur and his companions succeeded in disembarking in lifeboats under enemy fire, salvaging as they did 2.5 million livres destined for the American government. In the thick of the British bombardment, convinced that his hour had come, Louis-Philippe kissed the portrait of his wife, which he always carried near his breast. Moved by his friend's gesture, Broglie asked to kiss it as well.[61] And perhaps it was this gesture that brought them good luck.

Arriving in Philadelphia in mid-September after various adventures, Ségur had immediately thought of his brother. "Tell him," he wrote to his wife, "that it is from the *City of Brothers* that I tell him I love him with all of my heart."[62] The young colonel was welcomed by the French military staff with all the respect due to the son of the minister of war, and he had the honor of being presented to Washington, with whom he spoke at length. He felt the same amazement at the discipline, order, and expertise of the American army, the same admiration for Washington and the patriotic spirit of the populace that Lauzun had experienced during his first visit.[63] "[Washington's] exterior announced, as it were, his history: simplicity, grandeur, dignity, calmness, goodness, and firmness were stamped upon his features, his whole bearing, and likewise upon his character. ... He displayed none of the pomp or splendor of a general from one of our monarchies; rather, everything proclaimed him a hero of a republic."[64]

The Marquis de Chastellux, beloved uncle of Ségur's wife, whom he met once again in Philadelphia, initiated him into the habits, customs, and laws of the United States. Louis-Philippe could not have dreamed of a better mentor: a disciple of the philosophes, a fervent Freemason, and an intimate friend of Washington, the Marquis had been among the first to cross the Atlantic in order to fight—with the rank of general—at the side of the rebels, and, as he showed in his *Travels in America in 1780, 1781, and 1782*,[65] he knew the country very well indeed. And when, at the end of December 1782, after a stay of three months in the United States, Ségur boarded a ship in Boston at the orders of General de Vioménil to fight the English in Jamaica, the utopian vision of the best of all possible worlds had become a reality for him. He carried in his heart a longing for the land he was leaving, "a country where people are as they should be—frank, loyal, honest, and free." A country where "they...think... say...and do what they wish," and where "by holding to a small number of simple laws, by respecting their traditions, they...are happy and peaceful: whereas in Paris, one is only fashionable by flouting them."[66] It was a country where he would have liked to live along with his wife, since both of them "loved virtue."[67] But he departed with the hope that one day, not too far distant, France would herself follow the example of the United States, becoming a free and virtuous land.

Ségur had as little opportunity to distinguish himself on the battlefield in South America as he had in the United States. The Spanish arrived in Venezuela, where the Comte d'Estaing's fleet and the elite corps led by Vioménil were waiting, too late to join the attack launched against the English on land and sea. But the preliminary peace treaties between France and England, signed in Paris in January 1783, put an end to his hopes. Still, none of this prevented Ségur's career from advancing. While he was still at Puerto Cabello in Venezuela, he received a letter in which his father communicated his promotion to the rank of colonel, commanding a regiment of dragoons bearing his name.

During his journey back to France, Louis-Philippe was able to make a stopover in Saint-Domingue, a colony that "gave annually to France, thanks to its rich productions, an advantage of sixty million francs in the balance of her trade,"[68] and to visit the plantations inherited by his mother. In his memoirs he censures the barbarous practices of slavery that he witnessed on his own family properties, even if his initial reaction had been very different. "I am utterly astonished to feel so at home here," he wrote at the time to his wife, "in the midst of a mass of slaves who take a knee whenever they address me, and whose lives and deaths are wholly in my hands."[69] But nevertheless, he was in a hurry to return to France. Even if he had not achieved glory, his appraisal of his American adventure was distinctly positive. In less than a year, he had toured an entire continent: "I had encountered battles, storms, shipwrecks, camps seized by the enemy, two-month treks through the snow, and southern climes of a savagery that no European had seen before."[70]

After a grueling homeward journey—during which he penned *Coriolane*, a tragedy centered on the struggle between rich and poor, inspired by Washington and the heroic spirit of the American Revolution—Louis-Philippe arrived in Paris at the end of June 1783. The Marquis de Bombelles, who was a guest of the Maréchal de Ségur at that time, witnessed the joy of the young Comtesse at being able to embrace her husband once again.[71]

Various events had conspired to restore their confidence in the future of France: the signing of the Treaty of Versailles,[72] which marked the independence of the United States; the appointment of Calonne to the position of controller-general of finances; a sequence of scientific discoveries; and increasing freedom of speech. In his memoirs, Ségur recalls that he found "the court and Parisian society more brilliant than ever, France proud of her victories, satisfied with the peace, and the kingdom ... flourishing."[73] The word "impossible" seemed to have disappeared from the French language,[74] and Calonne's "magic wand" inspired hope that the public debt crisis would soon be a thing of the past.

Though he was fêted at court, where he wore the American Order of Cincinnatus, and was invited along with his friends to join in the political debates held by the various English-style clubs then flourishing in Paris, Louis-Philippe had little time to wallow in this collective euphoria, since a mere seventeen months after his return from the United States he was once again forced to travel abroad. At the recommendation of Vergennes, Louis XVI had named him the ambassador to Empress Catherine of Russia. The minister of foreign affairs had had the chance to read the letters sent by Louis-Philippe to his father from America and, struck by the cogency of his political analysis, had requested that he be brought on board. But in proposing his name for the ambassadorship to St. Petersburg, Vergennes also intended to appease the ill humor of the Maréchal de Ségur, with whom he had recently, and repeatedly, clashed—and also to please Marie-Antoinette by supporting the candidacy of one of her protégés against that of the Comte de Narbonne, who was championed by

Mme Adélaïde, the sovereign's aunt.[75] Louis-Philippe hesitated to abandon his military career, to which he was tied by family tradition, in order to embrace diplomacy, but his father urged him to accept. In the Marquis's eyes, this was far from a desertion—it was the sort of experience that might well open the path to other ministerial duties for his son. Meanwhile, the command of the family regiment would pass to his brother, the Vicomte de Ségur.[76] The Marquis de Bombelles, as a diplomat sensitive to the logic of royal favor, also saw in Ségur's nomination to the ambassadorship the beginning of a great career: "With wit, and a bit of education, he will be able to make himself indispensable by the political service he renders, and, taking the roundabout path, will be more certain of achieving the position of minister at an age when respect for him has had time to be firmly established.... His service during the American war will furnish his friends with pretexts to show how capable he would be as minister of the navy; and his work in foreign affairs could lead him to the head of that fine department.... The young man should be seen as someone destined for great things in this country."[77] All that remained was for Louis-Philippe to prepare for his new mission. He immersed himself in the correspondence of the French ambassadors who had preceded him at St. Petersburg, and spent two weeks in London in order to learn about Anglo-Russian relations from his friend Adhémar, an old classmate from Strasbourg, who thanks to Polignac had become ambassador to the Court of St. James's. During his short stay across the Channel, Ségur found confirmation of his political convictions in observing "the superiority that long-established customs of public reason and liberty give to that constitutional monarchy over our own, which is almost absolute."[78]

In Paris, Louis-Philippe also received a lesson in political Machiavellianism from the Spanish ambassador to Versailles, the famous Comte d'Aranda. A diplomat's task, the latter explained, is by nature political. Its objective is "to grow acquainted with the strengths, the means, the interests, the laws, the fears, and the hopes of the various powers ... and to be able to reconcile them, divide them, fight them, or bind them together, according to our own needs, our own security." It was sufficient to look at a map of Europe to understand: "all of the powers desire to preserve their various holdings, and to swell themselves whenever the opportunity presents itself."[79] If one took the case of Russia, the first partition of Poland and the annexation of Crimea were blatant examples, and foreshadowed even greater appetites to come.

But the most useful observations came from the Baron Grimm. A habitual correspondent of Catherine and "informer" for the Russian ambassador in Paris,[80] Grimm had a perfect knowledge of the Empress's habits and furnished Ségur with precious advice on the way to make himself agreeable to her. He himself took care to address to the Empress a thousand praises of the new ambassador, in order to predispose her in his favor.

Armed with this support, and having taking leave of his dragoons and all those dear to him, Ségur departed for Russia on Christmas Eve in 1784, without imagining that the France he would return to five years later would be quite a different country from the one he was leaving.

En route to St. Petersburg he stopped in Berlin, where he was presented to members of the royal family and once again saw Henry of Prussia, whose acquaintance he had made in Paris. He had the particular honor of being received at Potsdam by Frederick the Great, who spoke with him at length, declaring that he had always admired France and reassuring him about Catherine. Though on bad terms himself with the Empress, Frederick knew from a trusted source that she was not, in fact, responsible for the death of her husband, and that it was the Orlovs who had hatched the plot to assassinate Peter III behind her back. Furthermore, Frederick intended to recommend Ségur to his representative in St. Petersburg, Comte de Görtz, who would give him all the support he needed. He was by no means ignorant of the goals of Louis-Philippe's diplomatic mission, and hoped in the interest of Prussia that the French influence in Russia would counterbalance that of Austria.[81] And since Ségur's journey would include a stop in Poland, the Philosopher King expressed his perplexity at the contradictions of "a free land where the nation is enslaved, a republic with a king, a vast region hardly populated ... perpetually divided into factions, confederations, and so enthusiastic about a freedom without rules that, in their assemblies, the veto of a single Pole suffices to paralyze the general will."[82] Of course, he neglected to mention that it was precisely because of these contradictions that Prussia had been able to "swell" its own borders at the expense of Poland.

In Warsaw, Ségur was disconcerted when King Stanisław Augustus gave him a warm embrace and declared himself happy to "see him again." Amused by Ségur's stupefaction, the sovereign recounted the friendship that had bound him to Ségur's parents some thirty years earlier, when he was no more than a simple Polish count on a visit to Paris. The day of his departure for Poland, wishing to bid the couple adieu, Stanisław Augustus had found their doors closed: the lady of the house was giving birth to a child, and her husband was with her. Poniatowski was not discouraged and, forcing his way in, had been able to kiss not only the happy parents but the newborn Louis-Philippe as well.

In evoking in his memoirs the warm welcome the sovereign gave him, and in tracing his portrait, Ségur takes care to observe that his good character, and even that art of pleasing that Stanisław Augustus exercised so fully in France, revealed themselves, once he became King, as a species of weakness—and "the source of his misfortunes."[83]

As for Ségur, having arrived in St. Petersburg, he could rely on nothing but his personal ability to appeal to the Semiramis of the North in order to fulfill the mission entrusted to him by Vergennes: "To effect in the Empress's mind and manner of judging France and the French a decisive change."[84]

For many years, diplomatic relations between the two countries had been tempestuous. Catherine courted the philosophers, openly carried on an intense correspondence with Voltaire, and purchased French works of art, but nursed a profound aversion to Louis XV and detested Choiseul; for their part, the King and his minister did not hide the fact that they considered her an unscrupulous adventuress. Having decided that Catherine's aggressive policies toward Poland constituted a challenge to French interests, the Duc de Choiseul had pushed Turkey to declare war on Russia, but the Sublime Porte—the Turkish government—had been defeated, and Catherine had helped herself to Crimea in 1783, thereby securing access to the Black Sea. Forced to resign themselves to this fait accompli, Versailles nevertheless feared that in the long term the Empress aimed at the dissolution of the Ottoman Empire, an outcome that would shatter the European equilibrium. The Empress, on the other hand, was hopeful that the House of Austria would not thwart her plans for expansion at the expense of the Turks, in spite of Vienna's interest in extending its territories to the detriment of its old enemy. Moreover, Russia, Austria, and Prussia were united when it came to the partition of Poland, which Louis XV had shown himself incapable of preventing. Versailles, by way of its new ambassador to Constantinople, the Comte de Choiseul-Gouffier, had persisted in quietly urging the Turks to be vigilant, sending them arms, engineers, and experienced officers. The English in turn had profited by Catherine's irritation with French policy to obtain, along with the Austrians, a monopoly on trade in the Russian port cities of the Black Sea—not to mention the benefits they enjoyed from the support of the Tsarina's powerful protégé, Prince Grigori Alexandrovitch Potemkin, who detested France. But with the death of the Well-Beloved, the Empress had adopted a friendlier attitude, professing her respect for the new sovereign, and Vergennes had opted for a policy of reconciliation, inviting Catherine to distance herself from Prussia.[85] In the spring of 1782, as the Russian army was invading Crimea, the Grand Duke Paul and his wife, having arrived in France incognito under the name of the Comte and Comtesse du Nord, were welcomed with all respect and ceremony at Versailles. Among the various entertainments prepared for them was a musical adaptation of "Aline, Queen of Golconde" by the Chevalier de Boufflers. Even if the Tsarina forced her daughter-in-law to discard all of the clothing from the Queen's dressmaker that she had brought back from Paris, one can still admire today at Tsarskoye Selo a magnificent *service de toilette* in Sèvres porcelain, a gift from Marie-Antoinette. And the Empress could not have been unaware of the popularity that she herself enjoyed in Paris, thanks to the propaganda conducted in her favor for some twenty years by Voltaire, Diderot, Grimm, and other writers and agents in her pay, so much so that "the theaters [were] constantly featuring subjects drawn from Russian history, and studies of Muscovite manners... and Paris was filled with signs: 'To the Empress of Russia.' There were 'Hôtels de Russie' and 'Cafés du Nord' on every street corner."[86] Though the Empress herself declared that it was all mere fashion, it did represent a pleasant sort of revenge on a government that had always been hostile to her.

The task that awaited Ségur in St. Petersburg consisted of taking advantage of this apparent thaw to rekindle relations still marked by a divergence of views and objective interests. But he had little room to maneuver, for Catherine's expansionist projects at the expense of Turkey and Poland remained unacceptable to Versailles. Moreover, unlike his predecessors, he had not been provided with the sort of secret funds needed to assure the sympathy of Russian courtiers. The first to cast doubt on the prospects of the enterprise was Vergennes,[87] but Ségur was not about to give up. Though in Philadelphia he had admired the republican dignity and frank cordiality of the generous Americans, so preferable to the mask required by French courtliness,[88] Louis-Philippe understood that in St. Petersburg he would have to stake his hand on a pair of trump cards: the masterful eloquence that had rendered French diplomacy all but unstoppable, and the delicate art of flattery in which the emissaries of

Versailles were so well versed. In evoking, during the years that followed the Revolution, the virtues and vices of the society of the ancien régime, Mme de Staël would explain the historical reasons for that double supremacy. The first quality was, in her view, tied to the "spirit of conversation," which had "developed so remarkably in the French the more serious spirit of political negotiation,"[89] and made them masters of that particular art. "No foreign ambassador can compete with them on that account, unless he wholly sets aside every pretension to finesse and leaps straight to the heart of affairs, like one who engages in swordplay without having trained as a fencer."[90] The second quality—the art of gratifying the self-regard of others—also called for an adroit deployment of eloquence, but M. de Staël located its origins in the pact of reciprocal respect that subsisted between the King of France and his nobles. Indeed, their sense of honor encouraged those among the ranks of the privileged to behave as if their obedience to the sovereign were, in fact, freely chosen, thus conveying on the court, Mme de Staël tells us, that "piquant gaiety" which, "even more than polished grace, seemed to efface all distance without however destroying it." And for his part, whether complimenting or punishing it, the sovereign could not afford to ignore a sort of public consensus that did not always depend on his goodwill. For this reason, in France, "the flattery that serves the ends of ambition requires far more wit and skill than that addressed merely to women: all the passions of mankind and all the different sorts of vanity must be taken into account, where the combination of government and manners is such that successful intercourse between men depends on their mutual ability to please, and where that talent is the only way of obtaining eminent positions of power."[91]

Ségur's strategy turned out to be a winning one. Accustomed to ruling as an autocratic sovereign over a court completely subjugated to her wishes, Catherine was quick to appreciate the elegant fawning and shrewd worldliness of the new French ambassador, who presented his *lettres de créance* to her on March 25, 1785. "He seemed the spirit of Louis XIV's court made young again,"[92] she would recall years afterward. Indeed, Grimm had not been the only one to sing Ségur's praises since his departure from Paris. The irresistible Prince de Ligne himself had written from Vienna, enthusiastically heralding the Comte's arrival and extolling his "wit and heart."[93] Given the testaments of these two friends, she could hope that Ségur might be capable of amusing her as nobody else had since the loss of Voltaire, that cleverest and most brazen of flatterers.

If, in order to please the Empress, Ségur was able to capitalize on her feminine coquetry (cheerfully disregarding her fifty-six years) and her interest in the social, artistic, and intellectual life of France, he quickly realized that it would be more difficult to enter into the good graces of Grigori Alexandrovitch Potemkin, Prince of the Russian and Holy Roman Empires, minister of war, and chief of the navy and armed forces. Yet this would be a necessity, since for two decades he had exerted over Catherine—whose lover and, perhaps, morganatic husband he had been—an unparalleled influence. "My dear darling, sweetest of lips, my life, my happiness, my adored, my dove, my golden pheasant, I love you with all my heart,"[94] he had written to the Empress during the season of their passion, and once that passion subsided, it had been he who had selected the lovers who filed one by one into the Tsarina's bed. He had also been the one to successfully spearhead Russia's economic and territorial expansion southward, colonizing the northern coasts of the Black Sea and creating within the structure of imperial Russia what was, essentially, a "new nation," of which he became the governor-general. It was he who was "the true inventor of that mixture of Cossack freedom and bureaucratic rationality, magnanimity and strictness, tolerance and violence, that would leave an indelible mark on Russia's colonies there at the border between Europe and Asia."[95]

His most recent exploit had been the annexation of Crimea, for which he was awarded the title of Prince of Tauride. Not content with this success, Potemkin wanted to push Catherine to realize their shared dream: the conquest of Constantinople. He knew that he could count on both the complicity of Austria and the neutrality of the English, and he did not intend to allow the French ambassador to champion an opinion contrary to his plans.

Of an enormous height, his face scarred by a sword blow delivered by Count Orlov that had deprived him of one of his eyes, Potemkin was an elusive figure. Both Ségur and Ligne have left us portraits of him that emphasize the contradictions in his character but that view him from differing perspectives. In his memoirs, Ségur evokes the public figure who would become known to history: "Never, perhaps, had a court, a council, or an army camp seen so sumptuous and savage a courtier, so dynamic and nonchalant a minister, a general so audacious and indecisive; his whole person displayed the most original of ensembles, combining as it did grandeur and pettiness, idleness and activity, audacity and timidity, ambition and insouciance."[96] Ligne, for his part, amused himself by composing a virtuoso portrait that plumbed the intimate life of the Prince, and described for his friend Ségur (who also knew him quite well) the private Potemkin, a man at the mercy of his own psychological and moral fluctuations: "Fearful at the prospect of danger, gay when it finally appears; sad in the midst of pleasures. Made unhappy by his happiness, blasé in the face of the world and easily disgusted: either a sublime politician or a child of ten...believing that he loves God, while fearing the Devil...with one hand gesturing toward the ladies who suit his fancy, and crossing himself with the other; spreading his arms like a crucifix at the foot of a statue of the Virgin, or wrapping them around the alabaster necks of those who, thanks to his ministrations, have left their virginity behind...wearing an outward look of hardness while being, in the depths of his heart, truly sweet...avid for everything like a child, and willing, like a great man, to let it all go."[97]

What was it, Ligne asked himself, that allowed this being of a thousand faces to be perpetually different, yet perpetually himself? The answer was simple: "Genius, genius, and yet more genius."[98] Precisely the sort of genius—or, as the French has it, *génie*—that populated the tales of *The Thousand and One Nights*.

With the exception of the Austrian and English ambassadors, Potemkin did not deign to give audiences to the representatives of foreign countries and was insolent enough to keep the King of France's envoy waiting. But when he felt he had waited long enough, Ségur simply left, to the amazement of all, obliging Potemkin to apologize and propose another meeting. Since, despite his Oriental despot's manners, Catherine's favorite appreciated those with the nerve to stand up to him, Ségur was given a friendly welcome when he returned: Potemkin asked various questions about the United States, and admitted his skepticism regarding the potential for success of institutions so diametrically opposed to those of the Russian government. Ségur was preparing to take his leave when the Order of Cincinnatus, which he wore pinned to his chest, suddenly attracted the minister's attention. Potemkin loved decorations, and the American medal was an absolute novelty for him. He perked up, the Comte recalled, "wanting to know whether it was an order, an association, or a confraternity; why it had been established; what were its regulations,"[99] and, skillfully prompted by Ségur, gave himself up to the pleasure of speaking passionately on the subject, going over the various sorts of Russian decorations and those from all over Europe that he had collected. When after an hour of conversation the ambassador left Potemkin, none of the points of tension in

Franco-Russian relations had been touched upon, but between the two men there had emerged a sympathy that was destined to last. Thanks to a genuine whim of chance, a medal awarded to him by a free and republican country had provided Ségur with the chance to enter the good graces of the all-powerful minister of a despotic regime, and indicated a strategy that might allow him to navigate the latter's positions and temper his terrible rages. Whenever their discussions risked running off the rails, Ségur would know how to divert the Prince's attention, guiding it instead toward those subjects that were dear to him. For example, fascinated by theology, Potemkin was capable of discoursing for hours on the disputes between the Greek and Latin Churches, or the Councils of Nicaea, Chalcedon, and Florence, and his quick and versatile mind could pass with great naturalness from problems of crucial importance to the most eccentric ramblings.

It was not long before Ségur had proof that he had chosen the right line of conduct. In May 1785, only three months after his arrival in St. Petersburg, he was invited with Potemkin and the Austrian and English ambassadors to join Catherine at her summer residence in Tsarskoye Selo, and to accompany her from there on a journey into the interior of the country. It was a sign of great favor, which, as he reported to his minister, had excited the envy of the other diplomats and raised "a good deal of reckless political speculation."[100] But Ségur would still have to parlay this personal success into a political victory for his country.

During this first journey in the Tsarina's suite, Louis-Philippe proposed to Potemkin a commercial treaty between France and Russia analogous to that enjoyed by the English and Austrians, in order to facilitate trade between the two countries. To his great surprise, Catherine immediately gave the idea her blessing—but in reality, as would become clear two years later, she envisaged political agreements of a whole different magnitude. In 1787, her minister of foreign affairs, Alexander Bezborodko, officially suggested the establishment of a coalition against the Turks consisting of Russia, Austria, and France—and the following year, the possibility emerged of also drawing Spain into an alliance against the English. In exchange, St. Petersburg demanded France's tacit approval of the first partition of Poland of 1772. It might have been a means of protecting Poland from further partitions, but Versailles agreed to neither of these two propositions, just as it had disdained the prospect of a Franco-Russo-Polish alliance that the Duc de Lauzun had championed a dozen years earlier for the love of Izabela Czartoryska. Signed on January 11, 1787, a commercial accord regarding the Black Sea was the sole economic negotiation that Ségur was able to bring to fruition over the five years of his Russian mission. On the other hand, he had the privilege of participating in a voyage that would go down in history.

Resolute, pragmatic, methodical, and full of good sense, Catherine II was also animated by a tremendous sense of optimism, and by the need to give her imagination full rein, to build fabulous castles in the air, to let herself be transported by enthusiasm. No one knew better how to set her dreaming than the visionary Potemkin. Their most recent mirage, which the Prince had "set in motion and translated into a sort of adventure novel,"[101] had been the annexation of Crimea, immediately rebaptized with its ancient name, Tauride. It was unquestionably—as history has repeatedly confirmed since—an acquisition of great strategic importance, one that would assure Russia access to the Black Sea. But in Catherine's imagination, this conquest of the bastion of the Tartars was also the first step toward the expulsion of the Turks from Constantinople and the revival of the Greek Empire, the crown of which her grandson—who, not by chance, bore the name of Constantin—would one day wear. It was likewise the dream of Potemkin, who, in order to show the Empress that their goal was within reach and encourage her to push on, had invited her to tour the new province of which he was governor.

Catherine enthusiastically accepted this proposed trip, which would coincide with the twenty-fifth year of her reign and that, apart from providing amusement and gratifying her pride, would also serve a political purpose. Not only would it be in line with the tradition of royal progresses, which allowed direct contact between sovereigns and their subjects, fortifying the bonds between them, it was also a perfect opportunity to display for the representatives of the European monarchies the civilizing power of Russia on its peoples. Finally, it would allow the Tsarina to intimidate Turkey with the spectacle of her military and naval strength.

Catherine departed from Tsarskoye Selo on January 7, 1787, planning to return to St. Petersburg on July 22. The first part of the journey took place under her direction and, with its unheard-of deployment of men and means, illustrated once again both her sense of pomp and the excellence of her organization. The second part, from Kiev to Crimea, would be under the command of Potemkin: it would be up to the Prince of Tauride and governor-general of southern Russia, to guide and receive the Empress. And with him in charge, the spectacle of the empire would give way to the magic of a fairy tale.

Yet nothing could have seemed more extraordinary to Ségur, FitzHerbert, and Cobenzl, the three ambassadors who formed part of Catherine's suite, than the procession of fourteen coaches, each as large and comfortable as a house, each of them mounted on sleighs drawn by eight horses, and followed by a long line of other sleds of more modest dimensions, which glided across the snow like a "fleet of light boats" and "crossed with an incredible swiftness those immense plains that resembled a frozen sea."[102] Five hundred and sixty horses awaited the caravan at each relay station. The Tsarina traveled in the first carriage with her lady-in-waiting, the Comte Alexander Dmitriev-Mamonov (her current favorite); the Austrian ambassador, Cobenzl; the high chamberlain, Shuvalov; and the grand equerry, Narychkin. Ségur followed in the second carriage, accompanied by the English ambassador FitzHerbert, and Count Chernyshev, president of the Council of War. Enormous flaming piles of "fir, cypress, birch, and pine" were arrayed all along their route at brief intervals, "so that we proceeded along a path of fires more brilliant than the rays of daylight: so it was that the proud autocratress [sic] of the North, in the middle of the darkest of nights, willed and decreed *that there should be light*."[103] The travelers visited one another in their respective carriages and spent their nights in lodges prepared for them along the route. Having discarded royal protocol, Catherine joined her guests each evening and spoke with them in a climate of great warmth. Their conversations touched on the most diverse subjects, and each of the participants, beginning with the Empress, would contribute reflections, anecdotes, and stories. Just as in the Parisian salons, they amused each other with riddles, charades, and rhyming competitions. Ségur was able to show off his skills as a versifier, and his improvisations were much applauded.

A month after their departure, the imperial procession reached Kiev, where they spent three months awaiting the thaw so as to continue their journey by river. While Catherine held court in her palace, the three ambassadors held audiences in the luxurious residences placed at their disposal by the Empress, who graciously paid for them. "The whole Orient," Ségur recalls, had converged upon the ancient Russian capital to pay homage to the "modern Semiramis."[104] Princes, local worthies, merchants, military men, Cossacks, Tartars, Georgians, Kalmucks, men and women of the most varied ethnicities and exotic manners, gathered together in a picturesque caravansary that bore witness to the diversity of the empire over which Catherine reigned. But almost every evening, her representative and governmental duties completed, the Empress would retire to her private quarters and take up once again the pleasures of private life along with her traveling companions. When the Prince de Ligne finally joined them, this "little circle"[105] of hers expressed its full potential. Ségur especially was happy to be able to count on the complicity of his friend—for the spirit of French society continued to breathe among the travelers, tempering their various political differences, their resentments, and their suspicions. Indeed, the Belgian Prince was not merely, as Mme de Staël would write, one of the most amiable men in France but also perhaps "the sole foreigner who has become a model for the French, rather than their imitator."[106] The Prince de Ligne had long since won Catherine over. He had arrived in St. Petersburg for the first time in August 1780, sent by Joseph II to work toward a rapprochement between Austria and Russia against Frederick II's Prussia and the Ottoman Empire—a reconciliation inaugurated by the Emperor himself in June, with the historic meeting in Mogilev. It was an auspicious choice, as the English ambassador, James Harris, noted in September of that same year: "He has the talent, under the mask of pleasantry, of conveying to the Empress the most important truths.... His talent for Humour and Ridicule has certainly done both the French and the Prussian Party irreparable harm here."[107] And the Tsarina provoked the jealousy of Baron Grimm by writing to him that Ligne was "one of the most pleasant and easygoing creatures I have ever seen: in him you have an original mind, one that thinks profoundly and yet is as madcap as a child."[108] For his part, Ligne, having a sincere admiration for the Empress, coined for her the moniker Catherine the Great.[109]

At various points in his memoirs, Ségur recalls the qualities that made the Prince irresistible not only at Schönbrunn and St. Petersburg but at Versailles as well: he had "a frank and piquant gaiety, a noble and natural grace, that quickness of humor that only benevolent and witty men possess, that fecund sort of imagination that never allows a conversation to languish, and which, even at court, in spite of all etiquette, leaves no margin for boredom."[110] But the Prince had no need to speak to seduce. "His smile," noted Mme d'Oberkirch, "was worth a whole discourse."[111] In short, this "charmer of Europe" could create wherever he went that atmosphere of playfulness and consensus that was one of the most precious qualities of a man of the world. Yet in him this cheerfulness was not merely a matter of respecting the imperatives of aristocratic sociability—it was, rather, the sign of an authentic joie de vivre.

The child of a century that had placed the aspiration to earthly bliss at the heart of its philosophical and ethical quests, Ligne chose to be happy by staying true to his instincts,[112] convinced that genuine philosophy sprang not from reflection but from pleasure—a pleasure that he snatched without scruple, on the fly, wherever it presented itself to him, though always doing his best to avoid harming his neighbor in the process.[113] His cheerful libertinism had nothing perverse about it. Though he indulged himself, he was always ready to acknowledge his "lapses"[114] without glorifying them. Indeed, he congratulated himself on "not being worse than he was," and on his "great talent for turning everything to the ends of [his] own happiness."[115] What, precisely, constituted that "everything" Ligne would explain over the course of hundreds of pages—pages that do their level best to track the rapid rhythm of his life. For him, writing was truly an existential need, "a way of not ceasing to be."[116]

The Prince was a lover of military life, the splendor of the courts, the intimacy of the great, life in high society, women, literature, the arts, gardens, landscapes, and animals, and passed from one activity to the next with as much naturalness as he did from one country to another (indefatigable traveler that he was), feeling himself at home everywhere. Thus it is not surprising that Ligne should have professed his admiration for his friend Boufflers. The same age as he, the Chevalier was his double in many respects. Like Ligne, Boufflers was forever on the move, curious about everything, ready to savor whatever he found, both lightsome and profound, "too superior to be pretentious," "toeing nobody's line, nor following anyone else's path in the world"; like him, he was always "the happiest and most amiable of men."[117] Like Boufflers, Ligne knew how to draw others into his cheerfulness by communicating his good humor to them: "He told a hundred pleasant tales, and produced madrigals and chansons at the drop of a hat."[118] Like the Chevalier, "he took advantage of the right to say whatever happened to pass through his head, and mixed a bit of politics into his charades, into his portraits; and even if his gaiety occasionally descended into folly, he would manage to tie it all up, at the last moment, with some useful and piquant moral."[119] But, as the rules of sociability demanded, "his pleasantries made everyone laugh, and never wounded."[120]

Ligne and Ségur were friends of long standing as well. Both close to the Polignacs, they had been part of the intimate circle of Marie-Antoinette's favorites during most of the 1770s, and were bound by a strong mutual sympathy. Which did not, however, prevent them from being very, very different. Twenty years Ségur's elder, Ligne was a lucid and disenchanted witness to the cynical realism of the great enlightened despots, but, loyal to the traditional system of European monarchies, he was wary—in contrast to his young French friend—of visions of a better world. His secret desire was above all to see his son Charles, who had married the beautiful Helena Massalska, ascend the Polish throne. While Ligne had gained the admiration of all by following his natural impulses, Ségur had built his success with diligence and tenacity, bending himself to the imperatives of life in high society. The two also differed in their approaches to Catherine. Ségur could not forget that he was bound to protect the interests and prestige of his country, and, like the two other ambassadors in the Empress's retinue, lived in constant fear of committing some faux pas. Ligne, for his part, had no official duties and could allow himself a freedom of speech that amused the Empress and gave all the more charm to his flattery. On the other hand, the Comte had resources at his disposal that the Prince lacked: he was an excellent actor, the author of numerous plays, possessed real skill at versification, and was a master of the art of improvisation. Their dual presence meant that Catherine was equipped with a small, "portable" circle, one that would assure her of all the amusements that had become famous in the salons of Paris. It is not by chance that in the course of the journey, enthused by the experience, the Empress revived her old idea of creating a burlesque knightly order on the model of the Sublime Order of Lanturelus—founded by the Marquise de La Ferté-Imbault, the rebellious daughter of Mme Geoffrin—which had indulged in badinage and mockery at the expense of its members.[121] That enterprise, which had enjoyed a lively success—Catherine herself had been a member by correspondence—had proposed the picture of a world turned upside down, one that "proclaimed a refusal of the spirit of seriousness, and a desire to break with the salons, wherein the world and society were forever being reinvented."[122] Catherine's order was baptized the Société des Ignorants,[123] and Ligne, Ségur, Cobenzl, and Dmitriev-Mamonov presented the Tsarina with a Certificate and a Diploma of Ignorance, finding in this act of parody a new opportunity for adulation. On their return to St. Petersburg, the Société des Ignorants gave way to the Hermitage Circle, which fulfilled Catherine's ambition of having dramatic works specially written for her in French performed in her own personal theater. Between the end of 1787 and the following summer, nineteen works—including comedies and dramatic *proverbes*—were performed there, of which five were by Ségur,[124] one by Ligne, one by Cobenzl, one by Dmitriev-Mamonov, and five by Catherine herself, who, proud of her theatrical tours de force and hoping to encourage the creation of a Russian national theater,[125] wished to have them published straightaway.[126]

With the arrival of spring, the thaw finally rendered the Borysthenes—now the Dnieper—navigable, and on March 1, 1787, Catherine was able to embark on her galley, "followed by the stateliest fleet ever borne by a great river."[127] The extraordinary aquatic procession included seven immense galleys, veritable floating homes furnished with an unheard-of luxuriousness,[128] followed by more than twenty-four vessels carrying three thousand crewmen. The first vessel was occupied by Catherine, her favorite, and her lady-in-waiting; another by Prince Potemkin and his nieces; another still by the Austrian and English ambassadors. Ségur had the opportunity to share his own with Ligne. Their chambers were separated by a mere partition, which allowed them to converse from one room to the next, and each morning Ligne would take advantage of this to wake his friend with a knock and recite to him the verses and chansons he had just composed. And this was only the beginning, as before the day was well advanced Ligne would deliver to him long letters "in which wisdom, folly, politics, gallantry, military anecdotes, and philosophical epigrams were mixed together in the most original manner," demanding an urgent reply.[129] Above all the Belgian Prince and the French diplomat took the opportunity to discuss the incredible expedition on which they found themselves. Both of them have left us records of that expedition—sixty pages from Ligne, and two hundred and thirty from Ségur—as valuable as they are dissimilar. Ligne recounted his experience in nine letters, written over the course of the journey and dispatched to the Marquise de Coigny—the "cruel beauty" beloved by Lauzun, whom the Prince courted as well—which record in real time the rapid succession of the traveler's personal impressions. Like the letters that Boufflers had written to his mother from Switzerland, Ligne's to his Parisian friend were inspired by the epistolary aesthetics of high society, and aimed to surprise and amuse. He knew that the Marquise was an exacting judge of both wit and style, and that her attention could not be abused. For his part, Ségur decided to recount the Crimean expedition forty years later, mobilizing his memories and anything else he could find to fill in the gaps. There is no doubt that he had preserved copies of the reports he sent back to Versailles at the time regarding what he had seen and heard during his journey, and he could also make use of the reports that had been printed by newspapers and magazines throughout Europe. In the meantime, Ligne's letters to the Marquise de Coigny had been published, and these more than any other source helped stimulate his memory.

But unlike his friend, Ségur was writing in the light of the recent past, and he intended to furnish his contemporaries with a precise historical account of what the imperialism of Catherine II had been. For the French who, in 1815, had seen Cossacks watering their horses in the fountains of Paris, Russia was no longer a distant land, charmingly exotic: it was the country that had defeated Napoleon, and Ségur dedicated an entire volume of his memoirs to attempting to understand why. He had been the ambassador to St. Petersburg during an epoch in which, "as the emphatic Diderot phrased it, *Russia was still nothing but a colossus with feet of clay.*" Since then, Ségur wrote with retrospective awareness, "that clay has been allowed to harden, and has now become bronze."[130] Still, too liberal to believe that despotism could have a future, Ségur had perhaps been the first to underestimate its danger. Fascinated like his contemporaries by the great new republican and democratic power on the far side of the Atlantic, he had been slow to realize that, beginning in the 1770s, the despotic Russia of Catherine had pushed aside the old logic of the monarchies of the ancien régime, and that it constituted, along with the United States of America, the other great emergent power Europe would have to reckon with going forward.

A subject of the Austro-Hungarian Empire, and allergic to new ideas, Ligne was infinitely more realistic than Ségur. He had a precise understanding of Catherine's ambitions, personally applauded her all-out war against the Turks, and could not ignore the political importance of the journey to Crimea. But in his letters to Mme de Coigny, he took care to avoid addressing these problems openly, opting once again for the aesthetics of lightness. For that matter, his choice of a correspondent owed nothing to chance. By writing to the Marquise, then at the apogee of her social success, Ligne knew that he was certain to reach a very large circle of Frenchmen. Read aloud, commented on, and copied, his letters circulated from hand to hand, delighting Parisian society. From the heart of Russia, the Prince entertained with all his verve the most demanding social circles in Europe, and invited them to take note of the exorbitant power of Catherine. The Crimean journey, a piece of political propaganda that had as its objective a new equilibrium in central and eastern Europe, seemed reduced by his pen to a pleasure cruise with friends. But the metaphor was clear nonetheless: What other monarchy could possibly have afforded such an entertainment? "Cleopatra's fleet departed from Kiev," he wrote, "while an extended barrage of cannon fire informed us that the Borysthenes's ice was being broken. If we had been asked, as we were climbing aboard our large or little vessels, eighty sails in number, with three thousand crewmen: 'Where the devil are you off to in these galleys?' we might have responded: 'To amuse ourselves; and to sail our ships!' For never before has there been sailing so brilliant, so agreeable."[131]

The Empress was unquestionably pleased by the magnificence of the program prepared for her by Potemkin, and she communicated her contentment to her traveling companions, contributing decisively to the cheerfulness of their little circle. Each one of the members took up his role with renewed ardor: Cobenzl that of the amiable courtier, FitzHerbert that of the caustic and melancholic Englishman, and the grand equerry Narychkin that of the jester. Ségur and Ligne possessed an inexhaustible repertoire of conversational topics, and were continually improvising madrigals, charades, proverbs, and riddles. Catherine was a brilliant conversationalist, and we know by way of Grimm the "eloquence she unspooled, the quips she launched, the sallies that tumbled from her one after another, as one might say, like the limpid waters of a wild cascade."[132] The Empress was also quick to make light of herself. After having been instructed in the principles of prosody by Ségur, she raised general hilarity by seizing up after her second rhyme. Later, carried away by euphoria, she sowed panic among her guests by proposing to address them with *tu*. Why, she asked, should they show more respect to her than they did to God? Ligne partially extricated himself from this predicament by multiplying his uses of "Your Majesty." The others did not know quite what to say, "and Her Majesty went on dispatching her *tu*s with the air of the Autocrat of all the Russias, and almost all the rest of the world besides."[133]

But how could such homely diversions compare with the spectacle that unfolded before their eyes day after day? Ligne,[134] like Ségur,[135] uses the term *féerie* (or "wonderland") to describe it, but it is above all the Comte who lays out for us the sources of that wonder. As the procession of boats gradually made its way into those regions—still uninhabited only a few years earlier— now governed by Potemkin, the travelers saw succeeding each other on the riverbanks "towns, villages, country houses, and sometimes rustic cabins ... so ornamented and disguised by triumphal arches, garlands of flowers, and elegant architectural decorations, that the illusion was complete and they seemed transformed under our eyes into superb cities, palaces suddenly erected, gardens created by magic."[136] Maneuvers performed by Cossack cavalrymen and elite army troops animated those areas of the countryside that were still unsettled. And the impresario of this fairy-tale spectacle was none other than Potemkin himself. "As if by some kind of miracle, he was able to struggle against every obstacle, to vanquish nature, to shorten distances, bedizen poverty, fool the eye as to the dullness of the sandy plains and the mind as to the boredom of the long journey, lending an air of liveliness to the most barren deserts. The stations along the way were placed so as to spare us even the least fatigue, and he was careful that the fleet should pause only at towns or villages picturesquely situated. Enormous flocks of animals traversed the landscape; groups of peasants enlivened the shores of the river; an innumerable crowd of boats that carried young men and girls, singing the rustic airs of their land, surrounded us constantly; nothing had been neglected."[137]

Catherine's minister was not merely a grand *illusioniste*, a magician when it came to trompe l'oeil—to the point that the phrase "Potemkin village" would become a synonym for deceptive construction;[138] his incredible direction would have been impossible without the spectacular work of colonization and commercial development that he had carried out in the enormous conquered territories. Ségur particularly was forced to recognize that Potemkin had quadrupled the population, attracting settlers of the most varied nationalities, who had gone on to develop the area's agriculture and commerce, and that genuine villages were springing up spontaneously almost everywhere. The voyage he had invited Catherine to take was a chance for Potemkin to show her just how far their political path had already taken them and the results it had brought.[139] Certainly much remained to be done, and he had been forced to tidy up the reality, but the spectacle he offered her was not entirely an imposture: it was a model for the future land they were both dreaming of, and also "the creation of a poet who has experienced, at least once, the drunkenness that comes with realizing his dreams."[140]

Similarly, the King of Poland, who appeared before Catherine in Kaniv, a small Ukrainian city on the Borysthenes, had spared no expense to pay homage to her, spending "three months and three millions, in order to see the Empress for three hours."[141] The festivities around his visit culminated with a fireworks display simulating the eruption of Vesuvius. If the spectacle was meant as an allegory for the irresistible power of the Empress, the idea was not an auspicious one: six years later, with the second partition of Poland, Kaniv would become Russian territory.

It had been twenty-eight years since Stanisław Augustus had seen the only woman he had ever loved, and upon whom, now more than ever, his fate and that of his nation depended—and he hoped that Catherine would remember the sentiment that had once bound them. Their meeting took place on the imperial galley. Upon the King's arrival, all in attendance pressed toward him, "curious to see the first emotions and to hear the first words of these two august figures, in circumstances so widely removed from those they had known once upon a time, drawn together by love, separated by jealousy, and pursued by hatred."[142] But their expectations were disappointed—after greeting him "gravely, majestically, and coldly,"[143] Catherine invited Stanisław to follow her into the interior of the boat for a half-hour conversation, with Dmitriev-Mamonov the only auditor. We remain ignorant of what passed between the former lovers.[144] Most likely, Stanisław would have complained of the arrogance with which the Russian ambassador—Comte Branicki, who had supplanted Lauzun in the heart of Izabela Czartoryska—laid down her law in Warsaw, kindling a powerful sense of resentment against Russia, and requested Catherine's aid in implementing the reforms necessary for his country's stability. But judging by the melancholy expression he wore when he finally left their talk, the Empress could not have been very reassuring. What had troubled her was not so much seeing her old lover once more—in any case, as she wrote to Grimm,[145] she found him much changed—but having been present for the jealous scene, as furious as it was improbable, in which Dmitriev-Mamonov had indulged himself. Yet disappointment did not prevent Stanisław from remaining faithful to his own character to the very end. After dinner, as he took his leave of her, he cast about with his eyes for his hat—and when Catherine, having found it first, handed it to him, he gallantly exclaimed: "To have covered my head twice!"—an allusion to the crown that he owed to her. "Ah, madame, you overload me with blessings, with honors!"[146] The Empress did not allow herself to be affected, declined to take part in the ball arranged in her honor by Stanisław, and prepared to depart. "Why did Catherine refuse to linger in Kaniv?" asks the historian Isabel de Madariaga. "Perhaps it was indeed the discomfort provoked by her reunion with a man she had loved, then treated with such cruelty."[147] But the Tsarina was also in a hurry to meet with a sovereign far more important than the King of Poland, one to whom she intended to display her conquests.

Indeed, at Kaydak—a Tartar village near which Potemkin envisaged Ekaterinoslav (now Dnipro), a great city dedicated to the glory of Catherine—she was met by the Austrian Emperor Joseph II, traveling incognito, as was his custom, under the name of Count Falkenstein. The Empress laid the first stone of the church that was being erected there and invited her illustrious guest to lay the second.

Having crossed the steppes and nearly reached Crimea, the travelers made a stopover in Kherson—another city planned by Potemkin and constructed on the ruins of an ancient Greek colony. In record time the Prince had erected its fortifications, barracks, churches, public buildings, and a vast port provided with an imposing fleet of ships. Though it was at this time still an enormous construction site, the new city had drawn many settlers of various nationalities and was already a flourishing commercial center. At Kherson, Catherine and her Austrian counterpart discussed the possibility of a common foreign policy and compared their points of view on issues crucial for both of them: religious tolerance, serfdom in the countryside, the civilizing missions of the countries over which they reigned.[148] However, according to Ségur, rather than positively influencing Joseph II, the journey to Crimea made him realize the unbridgeable gap that separated his own methods of governance from those of the Tsarina of All the Russias. "The strict incognito he maintained was as comfortable for him as it was useful in letting him see and hear,"[149] Ségur noted, and it allowed him to roam at liberty whenever the caravan paused. With a strong personality and a solid education, curious about everything, the Emperor immediately made it plain—as Ligne did not fail to signal to the Marquise de Coigny[150]—that he appreciated the company of the Comte. In the course of their conversations, he let Ségur know that he was not inclined to lend his unconditional support to the projects of his powerful host. He had been favorable toward the annexation of Crimea by Russia because such a move would help shield his own lands from Turkish attack, but Catherine's ambition to proceed with the conquest of Byzantium represented a threat to an already precarious European equilibrium. And if he was disposed to salute Potemkin's economic and urban-development policies, it had also to be remembered that everything was simple when one had unlimited reserves of money and could dispose at will with human life. What was normal in Russia would have been unthinkable in a country like France or Germany: "The master commands; hosts of slaves fall to work. They are paid little or nothing; they are badly fed; and none of them dares to complain."[151]

For his part, Ségur seized the opportunity to defend the pro-Turk policies of France, attempting to convince his interlocutor that "the colossal power of the Russians loomed large, but its foundations were far from sturdy."[152] The unpredictable Potemkin had been known to abandon his projects only halfway complete, and he lacked many of the qualities of a successful administrator. Nevertheless, the Emperor objected, if Catherine's domestic policies presented serious flaws, her enormous power constituted a danger for the rest of Europe: "She commands: immediately troops are raised and ships launched. There is no gap in Russia between the issuing of the order, no matter how capricious, and its execution."[153]

The conversations between the two sovereigns, however, as reported by Ligne to the Marquise de Coigny, were rather different in substance. "They talk about the most interesting things. 'Has no one ever made an attempt on your life? My own has been threatened.'—'I receive anonymous letters, myself.'"[154] Or else: "'I have thirty million subjects,' one of them says, 'and of course they're only counting the males.'—'And twenty-two on my end,' replies the other, 'counting them all.'—'I require,' adds the one, 'an army of at least six hundred thousand men from Kamchatka to Riga, including the Caucasus.'—'With only half of that,' responds the other, 'I have all that I need.'" And on policies of other crowned heads, they both had very clear ideas. "Before cosigning the separation of the thirteen colonies like my brother George [III, of England]," affirmed Catherine, referring to the Treaty of Versailles by which England had recognized the independence of the United States, "I would have dispatched myself with a shot from a pistol." "And before effectively tendering my resignation like my brother and brother-in-law [Louis XVI] by bringing the nation together to talk about abuses," responded Joseph II, referring to the Assembly of Notables, "I don't know what I would do."[155]

But concerning their own plans, the two august travelers remained vague. Even though Ligne had a talent for making light of things, his gaze was penetrating: he had been well schooled in irony by the "divine" Voltaire.[156] "Their Imperial Majesties occasionally attempted to tease out each other's thoughts regarding those poor devils the Turks. They threw out observations, watching each other carefully. As a great lover of the *belle antiquité*, and of novelty as well, I suggested restoring the Greeks; Catherine spoke of bringing new Lycurguses and Solons into the world. I myself favored Alcibiades; but Joseph II, who thinks more of the future than the past, and more of reality than chimeras, said, 'What the devil do we do about Constantinople?'"[157] The *belle antiquité* that the two enlightened despots invoked as a metaphor for their political ambitions was, in the end, less that of Lycurgus and Solon than of Alexander the Great.

Despite the extreme liberty of his correspondence, Ligne was obliged to reserve for his memoirs an anecdote that he could not have told to the Marquise de Coigny, since it would surely have made the rounds of Paris and plunged him into difficulties.

On one of the first stops on their journey, the Prince had been forced to help the Austrian Emperor extricate himself from an embarrassing situation. During the course of a morning stroll, Joseph II had, to hear him tell it, "caressed a young girl—that is to say, did perhaps something more than chuck her under the chin,"[158] provoking the fury of her master, who not only gave her a thrashing but also threatened to complain about the impudent traveler to the regional governor. To prevent word of the incident getting back to Catherine, Ligne, whom the Empress had given the privilege of wearing the uniform of the Russian army, sequestered the girl in a barn; then, insulting the master in various languages, threatened to report the ill treatment he'd inflicted on his servant to the Little Mother (as Catherine was affectionately known to her subjects). As Joseph II had made clear upon his arrival that he did not appreciate seeing an Austrian officer wearing a Russian uniform in his presence, the Prince could not resist taking a little revenge by quipping: "You see now what a Russian uniform can do."[159]

While the two sovereigns were displaying the most affectionate friendship and Ségur and FitzHerbert were observing them uneasily, attempting to understand how far Joseph II was willing to support Catherine's "Greek" ambitions, Potemkin's wonderland was transporting all and sundry to the world of *The Thousand and One Nights*. "I know not where I am, nor in which century,"[160] marveled Ligne. Now that they had left the Don Cossacks behind, Tartar cavalrymen appeared, showing off their audacious horsemanship, while encampments of an Asiatic magnificence sprang up in the desert, ready to welcome the travelers. And then there was the astonishment of Joseph II and Ségur, who, walking one evening in the Tartar desert, beheld a gigantic tent advancing toward them, as it seemed, by itself.[161] For a moment they believed that they were under a spell—and it wasn't until a second or two later that they realized that the tent was being carried along by some thirty Kalmucks hidden inside.

Catherine and her guests finally made their entry into Crimea, escorted by Tartar warriors who, only a few years earlier, had sowed terror in the provinces, so as to show that the Empress had utter confidence in the loyalty of her new subjects and that she was prepared to respect their religion and customs.

The luminous beauty of the peninsula with its hot Mediterranean climate welcomed the travelers from the north with a joyous embrace. Ségur recalls with emotion its valleys, "so rich in flowers, fruits, forests, streams, waterfalls, and crops. Thick trees of every species, pleasant groves, laurels, vines that wind themselves around the trunks of shrubberies, pleasure houses surrounded by lovely gardens."[162]

Their collision with the Muslim world, which came with their arrival in Bakhchysarai, the ancient Tartar capital, was no less charged. The Empress and her guests established themselves in the palace of the Khan, and while Catherine did not conceal her pride as a woman, a Christian, and a sovereign at seating herself on the throne of the Tartars, Ségur and Ligne gave themselves up to voluptuous fantasies. They had been lodged with the other two ambassadors in the seraglio of the last Khan. By chance, Ligne had been given "the room of the prettiest of the sultanas, and Ségur that of the foremost black eunuch."[163] There, Ligne's thoughts dwelled, not without impertinence, on his Parisian correspondent Mme de Coigny: "My cursed imagination is not going to shrivel with age; it remains as fresh, pink, and round as the cheeks of Mme la Marquise."[164] For his part, stretched out on his sofa, "overwhelmed by the extreme heat, and delighting in the murmur of the water, the freshness of the shade, and the perfume of the flowers," Ségur abandoned himself to "Oriental luxury, dreaming and vegetating like a veritable pasha."[165] Not content with dreams alone, the two friends decided that they would not leave the country without seeing a Tartar woman without her veil. After an extended search, they finally managed to surprise three peasant women, all of them decidedly lacking in charm, sitting on the bank of a stream. Becoming aware of the foreigners' presence, the women fled, calling for help, and obliging the two rogues to make their own hasty exit. Rather than leaving well enough alone, the heroes of this misadventure were stupid enough to recount it to the Empress, who, anxious not to offend the sensibilities of the Muslims, was angry rather than amused.

Perfectly at ease in the role of Oriental satrap, Potemkin showed himself more liberal. At the end of their stay in Crimea, leaving the palace where the Empress had been staying, Ségur noticed a young woman, dressed in Oriental fashion, who powerfully resembled his wife, and for an instant—"so quickly does the imagination move . . . in that land of wonders"—believed that it was indeed her. Seeing him standing "as still as a statue," and having learned why, Potemkin had burst into laughter: "Well then! *Batushka* [my little father], that young Circassian belongs to a man who will allow me to do with her what I wish; and as soon as we return to Petersburg, I'll make a present of her to you."[166] The Comte was forced to explain that "such a proof of emotion" might seem very strange to Mme de Ségur.[167] But, so as not to offend, he accepted a Kalmuck child—perhaps the same one that we see seated behind the Comte in a charming gouache that shows Ségur on a sled yoked to two white horses, against the background of a snowy St. Petersburg.[168]

It was in Sebastopol that Potemkin was holding in reserve his most extraordinary coup de théâtre, one that would crown Catherine's triumphal march. At the extreme southeast of the Tauride peninsula, the Prince had in record time constructed an immense port complete with an admiralty, and had also laid the foundations for an imposing city. It was the Empress who had selected its site on a map, choosing its name as well. Lodged on the heights of a hill that commanded the gulf, Catherine and her guests were dining when the windows of the hall were opened wide. "There," recalls Ségur, "the most magnificent spectacle was presented to us: Beyond a line of Tartar horsemen we perceived a deep bay. . . . In the middle of this harbor . . . a formidable fleet, constructed, armed, and equipped in the space of two years, faced us in battle formation. The ships saluted their sovereign by firing all their cannon, the roar of which seemed to proclaim to the Black Sea that it had a ruler whose arms were capable of draping her flags on the very walls of Constantinople."[169]

Prompted by Catherine to give his opinion of what he had seen, Ségur responded that in creating Sebastopol she had completed in the south what Peter the Great had begun in the north with St. Petersburg. There now remained no other "glory to conquer than that of vanquishing nature, by populating and bringing to life these new territories, these vast steppes through which we have just passed."[170] But by this point everyone, beginning with the French ambassador, knew that the glory to which the Empress aspired was that of chasing the Turks from Constantinople. The naval spectacle that they had witnessed was, in effect, a declaration of war.

The imperial caravan returned to St. Petersburg by a route different than that by which they had come, but no less rich in surprises. At Poltava, for instance, Potemkin exhilarated Catherine by offering her a reenactment of the celebrated battle that had marked the victory of Peter the Great over Charles XII. But the general mood was no longer one of euphoria. Discontent raised by Joseph II's reforms had pushed the Netherlands into revolt, obliging the Emperor to return home in haste. For her part, Catherine had to face a terrible famine that had sorely struck a significant number of her provinces. And even graver crises would make themselves felt in the near future.

On August 13 of the same year, driven by Catherine's provocations, the Ottoman Empire took the initiative to declare war on Russia. The following year, it was Gustav III of Sweden's turn to descend into the arena against the Empress, who opposed his ambitions for Norway. And meanwhile the Court of St. James's, the sole ally she could depend on, was interrogating which direction its policies should take and mulling the possibility of a rapprochement with Prussia.

Suddenly, the personal positions of Ligne and Ségur were becoming precarious. In Belgium, Ligne's family had aligned themselves with the uprising, rendering the Prince's relations with the Emperor delicate, to say the least. Ligne could not risk being called to take up arms against his own people, and he found a solution in line with his individualism: he returned to Crimea to combat the Turks at Potemkin's side. And it was there, in perfect solitude at Parthenizza, the "enchanted estate" that Catherine had presented to him as a gift, that Ligne would have the opportunity to "turn inward," and to make "without intending it, a recapitulation of all the inconsistencies of [his] life."[171] It was there that he descended like never before into the depths of his being and he experienced one of those "charming annulments…wherein the mind is wholly at rest, and one's hardly aware of existing."[172]

By now, Ségur understood that the mission he had been entrusted with was obsolete. He had succeeded, not without difficulty, in defusing Catherine's long-standing discontent with the support that France had provided behind the scenes to the Sublime Porte, in order to discourage the Empress's ambitions for conquest, but the beginning of the Russo-Turkish war confirmed the failure of the policy of mediation championed by Vergennes. Moreover, the death of the minister of foreign affairs in February 1787 had deprived Ségur of his support. He attempted in vain to convince his successor, the Comte de Mont-morin, to adopt Catherine's project to form, in opposition to the triple alliance between England, Prussia, and the Netherlands, a quadruple alliance that would include France, Russia, Austria, and Spain.[173] But his proposal was not communicated to Versailles, and Ségur lost all hope of sealing a political agree-ment between his own country and Russia. Thus he decided to request a discharge, and only Catherine's insistence convinced him to postpone his departure. Even more than the discomfort of his position, it was the news arriving from France that called for his return. The convocation of the Estates General thrilled him: the dream of living in a free country was finally within touch. But it was a matter of knowing how to realize that dream, to avoid any false steps, to prevent the forces of reaction from prevailing over the will to renewal, and he burned with the desire to personally take part in this grand adventure. He was convinced that he was perfectly placed to know what needed to be done, and the letter addressed to his friend Boufflers nineteen days after the beginning of the Estates General leaves no doubt about this. The Chevalier was fifteen years his senior, and of a far more illustrious birth—he had been governor of Senegal, he enjoyed an indisputable literary reputation, and was well known for his nonconformism. Still, Ségur could not resist the temptation to give him a lesson in politics, in terms that surely would have surprised the ambassadors and crowned heads who had accompanied him on the journey to Crimea:

At Petersburg, this May 24, 1789. Very well, my dear Chevalier, Catullus, Tibul-lus once upon a time, and today Demosthenes: You are going to mount the rostrum and lend your eloquence, which has been so agreeable in society, to your fatherland.... Preach conciliation, union, what's to follow, wisdom.... Rail against the gravest of errors that one could make in politics, make sure that they feel that if the deputies are not given full power, the Estates General are useless, and that if the minority is not required to submit itself to the plurality on all points without exception, it will all be inconsequential. Make it clear that deputies assembled and presided over by the King embody in themselves all sovereignty... that resistance to the will of the plurality of the Estates is an act of treason against the nation, one which can lead only to anarchy and chaos. Talk of politics as well; open those eyes that have remained so imprudently closed. It is precisely when one is rebuilding one's house that one needs to defend its exterior. Be quick to reinforce executive power: the

French forget about Europe, and I who stand as our homeland's sentinel, I cry to you that she is in danger, that our rivals are gathering to avenge themselves, are forming a menacing compact against us, that they are weakening those who might come to our aid, and that the storm is already upon us.... Adieu, my dear Chevalier. I wish you the most brilliant success; wish me nothing but the pleasure of being at liberty soon enough to bear witness to it in person.[174]

Ségur was not fooling himself when he foresaw the European monarchies coming together to oppose Revolutionary France and attempting to profit by its weakness. Was he thinking of Catherine as well? For now, the response of the Semiramis of the North fluctuated between indignation and fear. The news of the taking of the Bastille roused such enthusiasm in the Russian population that the Empress's first reaction was to prevent the spread of this epidemic of libertarianism with the usual methods of despotism: censorship, control, intimidation. Ségur's position had become objectively unsustainable, and the letter that recalled him to France must have felt to him like a liberation.

At the beginning of October 1789, not without emotion, the Comte took his leave of the Autocrat of All the Russias, who gave him one last sign of her benevolence. Despite her affection and respect for him, she had no illusions regarding his political ideas, and wanted to put him on guard against himself. Her sincerity was the final proof of friendship: "I see you depart with regret; you would do better to remain with me, and to avoid those storms whose full extent perhaps you do not foresee. Your penchant for the new philosophy and for liberty will most likely bring you to support the cause of the people; it pains me, for I remain an aristocrat: it is my métier. Consider that on your return you shall find France feverish, and deeply ill."[175]

The Comte de Vaudreuil

There are only two men who know how to talk to women: Lekain on the stage, and M. de Vaudreuil in town.

—PRINCESSE D'HÉNIN[1]

A FULL FORTY YEARS BEFORE Chateaubriand himself bore the nickname, Joseph-Hyacinthe-François de Paule de Rigaud, Comte de Vaudreuil, was known as "the Enchanter." By contrast with that great writer, Vaudreuil earned the admiration of high society merely by virtue of his splendid parties and personal ability to please. Yet, though it was limited to a small group of privileged individuals, his influence would have fatal consequences for the French monarchy.

A lovely portrait by François-Hubert Drouais from 1758 shows him at the age of eighteen, at the time of his society debut: a slender, supple young aristocrat, dressed with extreme elegance (collar and cuffs of white lace, doublet of blue velour, jacket embroidered in gold, shoes with silver buckles and red heels), his powdered hair tied back at the nape of the neck, and two enormous dark eyes illuminating a face with regular features of an almost feminine beauty—high forehead, straight nose, full red lips, and a gracefully rounded chin. In his right hand the young Comte holds the edge of a large geographical map, his right index finger pointing out his properties in Saint-Domingue, while the armor piled at his feet reminds us that he had embraced a military career and participated in the Seven Years' War under the command of the Prince de Soubise. Like a sumptuous visiting card, the tableau offers up all of the social qualities—nobility, beauty, wealth, elegance—that were destined to assure the young Comte a brilliant future. Discreet though they might have been, his red heels showed that he was quite the dandy.[2] In the decades that followed, Vaudreuil indeed proved that he knew just how to enjoy all of these advantages with a grace that was wholly his own, an indefinable charm that few were able to resist.

*

Born in 1740 in the French colony of Saint-Domingue, Joseph-Hyacinthe-François was descended from one of the oldest families in Languedoc, but none of his ancestors had lent the prestige of his name to any particularly remarkable enterprise, and his grandfather, Philippe de Rigaud, as well as his father, Joseph-Hyacinthe de Rigaud, had sought their fortunes across the Atlantic. The first had been governor of Canada, the second—having become commander in chief of the Leeward Islands—had married Marie-Claire-Françoise Guyot de La Mirande, the widow of a wealthy colonist from Saint-Domingue. It was thanks to his mother's vast sugarcane plantations, built upon slave labor—as well as to the death of his father—that at the age of twenty-four Joseph-Hyacinthe-François found himself in possession of an enormous inheritance, one that would allow him to lead whatever sort of life he pleased. Leaving his cousin, the Marquis de Vaudreuil, the task of bringing honor to the family with a brilliant career in the navy, he dedicated himself to excelling in high society. He possessed all of the qualities necessary to succeed both at court and in town. "Passionate, clever at whatever he put his hand to, and enjoying a strong reputation for loyalty," recalled the Comte de Saint-Priest, "he was a true French character."[3] A sparkling conversationalist, he told stories wonderfully, improvised admirable verses and epigrams, and recited fashionable couplets with delicious skill. Mme Vigée Le Brun saw him as a perfect model of the art of living in high society: "The Comte de Vaudreuil had plenty of wit, but one was tempted to think that he never opened his mouth except to make your own words seem even better, so amiable and gracious was his way of listening to you; whether the talk was serious or frivolous, he would know just how to grasp every tone, every nuance, for he was as learned as he was witty."[4] Even the Comte de Tilly, never particularly known for his benevolence, recognized in him "a good deal of intellect and grace, as well as noble manners; he was happy in his expressions, and in his method of turning a phrase."[5] Moreover, Vaudreuil had an irresistible advantage in a society besotted with the theater. He was an excellent actor and proved it by rivaling Molé himself in the private theaters of the greatest nobles of the era: at Bagnolet with the Duc d'Orléans, at Petit-Bourg with the Duchesse de Bourbon, and at Berny with the Comte de Clermont.[6] *Correspondance littéraire* singled him out to its readers as "perhaps the finest actor that Parisian high society possesses."[7] And it suffices to think of the Vicomte de Ségur, the Chevalier de Boufflers, or the Comte de Ségur to recall that the competition for that particular position was fierce. But Vaudreuil's strongest suit was the influence he enjoyed over the fair sex. And when necessary, he knew just how to put it to work.

We know little about the youthful relationship that produced Marie-Hyacinthe-Albertine de Fierval, whom Vaudreuil never officially recognized but whose education he followed closely, making sure to find her a husband and maintaining affectionate relations with her.[8] On the other hand, nothing could have been less of a secret than the sentimental bond that tied him for more than twenty years to his distant cousin Gabrielle-Yolande de Polastron, who, in 1767, had married the Comte Armand-Jules-François de Polignac. If we are to believe a family legend, a marriage between Vaudreuil and Mlle de Polastron had been planned early on, but the Comte had fleetingly glimpsed the young woman in the parlor of the convent where she had been raised and been less than pleased. When he saw her again years later, by this point married to the Comte de Polignac, she had become so beautiful that he had difficulty recognizing her. Her profile, perhaps, still left something to be desired,[9] but, with a neck like a swan, she was lithe and elegant. A cascade of brown curls framed a finely featured face with a little upturned nose, a vermillion mouth with shining teeth, and enormous blue eyes with a look of sweet astonishment. He fell in love with her, and she, in turn, with him.

As we have already noted, aristocratic morality tended to be indulgent when it came to extramarital love, especially when it was the result of genuine emotion and respected the forms consecrated by gallantry. The duration of such relationships over the course of many years—just think of the Chevalier de Boufflers and Mme de Sabran, or the Duc de Nivernais and the Comtesse de Rochefort—meant that they enjoyed a genuine social legitimacy. "It was quite well understood that Mme de Polignac *had* M. de Vaudreuil. So well understood that a lady inviting Mme la Duchesse de Polignac to dine would have to invite M. de Vaudreuil as well; to do otherwise would have amounted to a failure of politeness and good taste, one that no lady in society would have risked."[10] We do not know what the personal feelings of the Comte de Polignac were on this subject. Tilly affirms that, "more of a friend to his wife than a lover, he was at all times content to possess the former title, and accepted the lack of the latter without ill humor."[11] What we are certain of is that from the early 1780s on, Polignac, his wife, and Vaudreuil formed a sort of intimate trio, sharing habits, amusements, friendships, and interests. The Enchanter refused to marry, and the whole Polastron-Polignac clan welcomed him as a member of the family.

The Polignacs and Polastrons alike could boast respectable family trees, and had faithfully served the monarchy for centuries. Still, like Vaudreuil, they lacked ancestors of particular distinction and did not belong to the high nobility of the court. At the beginning of the eighteenth century, Cardinal de Polignac brought a bit of prestige to the family name, without, however, extracting for them any substantial advantages. A career military man, his nephew Armand-Jules-François was far from wealthy, but neither his wife nor he seemed terribly bothered by this. They generally resided at Claye, a country estate in the neighborhood of Meaux, and spent the winters in a simple apartment at Versailles. The modesty of their resources did not prevent them from living happily in the company of their friends and relatives. The only member of the family who displayed any particular ambition was Diane de Polignac, the sister of Comte Jules, who served as *dame pour accompagner* to the Comtesse d'Artois—but in the end, it was the indolent charm of Gabrielle-Yolande that altered the destiny of the Polignacs.

From the Baron de Besenval to Mme Campan, by way of the Comte de Tilly, the Comtesse de Genlis, and the Baronne d'Oberkirch, the contemporaries of the Comtesse Jules—as Gabrielle-Yolande was commonly called, to distinguish her from her sister-in-law, the Comtesse Diane—have not neglected to describe her in their various memoirs. And all of them, regardless of their judgment of her role as favorite, fully recognized the power exercised by her "celestial gaze and smile,"[12] as well as the "angelic"[13] character of her beauty. "She had one of those faces which in the paintings of Raphael combine an expression of intellect with an infinite sweetness. Others might have been able to excite more surprise and admiration—but from her, one simply could not look away,"[14] the Duc de Lévis would recall.

The first portrait that Mme Vigée Le Brun dedicated to her in 1782 confirms this impression. Not only has the painter given to Gabrielle-Yolande de Polignac, then thirty years old, the face of a charming adolescent, but she appears to have identified with her completely. Resembling strongly the self-portrait executed several months before, the picture of the Comtesse Jules cements the new ideal of feminine beauty to which Mme Vigée Le Brun invited the women of her day, by representing them "as they dreamed of being admired."[15] It was an innocent beauty—without makeup or hair powder, in a simple muslin dress, a beauty that had as its emblem a simple straw hat. On her return from Anvers, where she had admired the play of light on the hat in the famous portrait of Suzanne Fourment by Rubens,[16] the artist had not limited herself to wearing an identical one in her self-portrait: she had proceeded over the following months to crown with this same straw hat two women as different from each other as the Comtesse du Barry and the Comtesse Jules. Apart from their extraordinary beauty, the old official mistress of Louis XV and the bosom friend of Marie-Antoinette shared the same aspiration to live a less mannered life, one in harmony with their most intimate feelings. It would be interesting to know which of the two portraits was painted first: that of the old courtesan, who seduces the viewer with her radiant smile and knowing look, or that of "the most beautiful, the sweetest, the most amiable woman that one could ever see,"[17] who takes refuge behind a shy reserve.

But was the "celestial face"[18] of the lovely Gabrielle-Yolande really, as Mme Vigée Le Brun seems to suggest to us, the faithful reflection of her soul? And need we reach for the language of the angelic to explain that face's charm? Doesn't the fascination of the Comtesse Jules's face spring simply from the aesthetic of the "natural" that from the very beginning of civilization has been tasked with concealing, by way of an art that has become second nature, the gap between essence and appearance? In recalling that when it came to the Comtesse Jules, "nothing at all seemed owed to art, nothing was artificial,"[19] hadn't Tilly forgotten that centuries earlier, Castiglione had used practically the same words to define the supreme art of nonchalance? And rather than being the expression of a *bonne conscience*,[20] as Mme d'Oberkirch supposed when encountering her at the height of her favor at Versailles, weren't the young woman's serenity, her "unfailing calm,"[21] and her sweetness actually the fruit of that nonchalance or, more simply, of indifference? Indeed, nothing beyond the small circle of her close friends and family seemed truly to affect her. And one of her best friends, the Baron de Besenval, who never had need of moral guarantees to decide his sympathies, admitted as much between the lines.[22] In any event, possessed of a mediocre intelligence—as numerous witnesses emphasize[23]—the young woman had a limited range of interests, and was happy to admit as much. "Never was she touched by presumption, and again and again one would hear her respond with great honesty: 'What you've just said is entirely beyond me.'"[24] Enamored of peace and "idleness,"[25] lacking all ambition, she left to her sister-in-law Diane, unattractive but intelligent, the task of intriguing on the family's behalf—and to Vaudreuil, once he became her lover, that of dictating her conduct.

Intellectual gifts were certainly not a priority where Marie-Antoinette was concerned—Mme de Polignac's delicate beauty and natural grace were sufficient to win her over. The Queen's enthusiasm for the Princesse de Lamballe, for whose benefit she had revived the position of superintendent of the royal household, had cooled, and she was in search of a new confidante, someone to whom she could unburden herself. "She went looking for a friend as though seeking to fill a position in her household,"[26] Saint-Priest recalled venomously, and in the Comtesse Jules, the Queen found all of the qualities she desired. She met her for the first time in the spring of 1775 at the home of the Comtesse d'Artois, where Diane de Polignac was then serving, and immediately expressed the desire to see her again soon at the château. The Comtesse having replied with great simplicity that she and her husband were too poor to frequent the court, Marie-Antoinette hurried to remedy the situation. [27]

It is the secret correspondence between the Comte de Mercy-Argenteau and Maria Theresa of Austria that allows us to follow the unstoppable rise of the Polignacs—as well as the uselessness of the combined efforts of the advisers of Marie-Antoinette, her redoubtable mother, and finally of Joseph II to halt it.

As early as August 1775, Mercy-Argenteau informed the Empress that her daughter had "taken a liking to a young Comtesse Polignac, with an affection a good deal livelier" than she had shown for her preceding favorites—the Princesse de Chimay, the Comtesse de Dillon, the Princesse de Lamballe, and the Princesse de Guéménée. And foreseeing the worst, he observed that it was unthinkable that someone so young could be appointed as the Queen's attendant, someone who had never held a position at court and whose family "was not of rank to appear at Versailles."[28] One month later, the ambassador was already confident that he possessed irrefutable evidence that would show Marie-Antoinette "that her favorite the Comtesse de Polignac has neither the intelligence, the judgment, nor even the character necessary to enjoy the confidence of a great princess."[29] And in the following letter, he adds that the young woman has "very little wit" and is "under the influence of dangerous friends."[30]

Though her roster of *dames d'honneur* was full, Marie-Antoinette circumvented this obstacle and assured herself of her favorite's presence at Versailles by appointing, not without scandal, the Comte de Polignac as first equerry.

Since this position was already occupied by the Comte de Tessé, Polignac was granted the "survivance"—that is to say, the right to accompany the Comte in the performance of his duties, so as to be able to take over immediately upon his demise. Not only did this involve doubling the cost of an already onerous position at the precise moment that Malesherbes, recently appointed as secretary of the royal household, was striving to implement draconian budget cuts—it also constituted an insult to the Comte de Tessé, only forty years old and perfectly competent in his duties, and raised the ire of his wife's family, the Noailleses, who considered the post of first equerry a family appanage.

Fully aware of the criticisms to which she had left herself open, and certain that her mother would immediately be informed of her decision, Marie-Antoinette chose to announce the news to her personally. The Comte de Polignac, she assured the Empress, was of an excellent family, and had a wife whom she loved "infinitely." Moreover, her choice was also dictated by the political necessity of containing the pretensions of the Noailleses, "who are a tribe already too powerful here."[31] It was the first occasion that Marie-Antoinette had mentioned to the Empress, though only in passing, the existence of her favorite, unaware that the Comte de Mercy-Argenteau had already provided her with far more detailed information. As the Comte had foreseen right away, Mme de Polignac had revealed herself to be a very bad example for the Queen. The young Comtesse, who now enjoyed "the most unlimited favor," claimed "to set herself above what weak and corrupt minds call prejudices" and shamelessly displayed her lover at court. Moreover, her "behavior touching matters of religious dogma"[32] exercised so pernicious an influence on the Queen that the Abbé de Vermond was ready to renounce his position as her spiritual adviser and abandon Versailles. And what could Mercy-Argenteau say of the "unimaginable mortifications" that he and the Abbé had suffered in the course of the unhappy "affair of the Comte de Tessé," when Marie-Antoinette had remained deaf to their advice—advice that would have "concealed any appearance of frivolity or injustice"[33]—instead allowing herself to be manipulated by the Comtesse de Polignac and her entourage? What's more, the favorite was an obvious schemer: as the niece of the Comte de Maurepas and an associate of what was referred to as "the party of Choiseul," she was patently playing the spy and reporting to the old minister what she overheard in the Queen's circle.

Maria Theresa managed to persuade the Abbé de Vermond not to leave his position, since her daughter "who is striding steadily toward her own ruin, surrounded as she is with base flatterers who prompt her for their own interests,"[34] was now more than ever in need of his aid. The Empress continued to call Marie-Antoinette to order, while the Abbé and the ambassador lavished her with advice. Joseph II himself, while visiting Versailles, warned his sister against her docility in the face of the demands of the Comtesse de Polignac and her clan. But the "looting,"[35] as Mercy-Argenteau phrased it, had only just begun. One early instance presented itself in 1778, when the King established a household for Mme Élisabeth, the elder of his sisters at fourteen years. In spite of her doubtful reputation, Diane de Polignac was appointed as *dame d'honneur* to the young and very virtuous Princesse, the Comte d'Adhémar as first equerry, and the Comte de Coigny as *chevalier d'honneur*. And Vaudreuil in turn profited by securing his protégé Chamfort the position of secretary.[36] The year 1780 would prove even more remunerative. Louis XVI granted a dowry of 800,000 livres to the daughter of the favorite for her marriage to Antoine-Louis de Gramont, Duc de Guiche, to whom he promised the position of captain of the guards. Then he conferred on the Comte de Polignac the hereditary title of Duc,[37] highly coveted, which gave to his wife the *droit au tabouret*—that is to say, permission to sit in the presence of the King and Queen—by financing for her the purchase of the baronage of Fénétrange, which brought with it an income of 70,000 livres. The Comte's father, whose presence was a nuisance to the family, was appointed ambassador to Switzerland. As for Vaudreuil—who the previous year had obtained a pension of 30,000 livres in compensation for the loss of his revenues from Saint-Domingue, due to the cessation of commerce provoked by the American War of Independence—in July he was named inspector of the troops, and, in December, grand falconer. Falconry had long since fallen into desuetude, and the duties of the grand falconer were confined to solemnly taking possession of Icelandic gyrfalcons, a gift of the King of Denmark, or falcons from Malta. Nevertheless, this honorary position was generally reserved for a member of the high nobility who had distinguished himself in the service of the Crown. These two appointments were highly criticized: the Abbé de Véri complained that the Comte lacked the military skills necessary to fulfill the first of his duties,[38] and the Marquis de Bombelles that neither his birth nor his achievements merited the second.[39]

In reporting this awful news, which had outraged public opinion, to Maria Theresa, Mercy-Argenteau mentioned for the first time the name of the Comtesse de Polignac's lover, denouncing the various gifts that the favorite had extorted on his behalf. Reprimanded by her mother, Marie-Antoinette defended herself by maintaining that Vaudreuil had had no need of her recommendations, since he benefited from the protection of his brother-in-law, the Comte d'Artois,[40] and that Mme de Polignac was greatly loved by the King. The latter gave irrefutable proof of his favor on the occasion of the birth of Gabrielle-Yolande's latest child—it was the sole visit made by the sovereign to a private house after his ascension to the throne.[41] That did not prevent venomous tongues from asking whether one should attribute the paternity of the child to the Comte de Vaudreuil, or rather to the Queen.[42] But the crux of the scandal was Marie-Antoinette's unlimited indulgence, rather than the sexual adventures of her favorite—the latter was perfectly in line with the aristocratic attitude toward marriage, which considered it a family matter and left the partners free to dispose of their affections.

Mme de Polignac was fully aware of the opportunities afforded by this conception of marriage. No sooner had she recovered from her delivery than, over the course of the month of July, she celebrated the marriage of her daughter Aglaé-Louise-Françoise, scarcely twelve years old, to the Duc de Guiche, whose personal attractions left much to be desired. But the essential thing for she and her husband was to ensure that their daughter, whom they loved tenderly, was provided with material comfort and an illustrious name. Even more beautiful than Mme de Polignac, the young Guichette was not slow to follow her mother's example by taking a lover. In June,[43] the half brother of Mme de Polignac, Denys-Gabriel-Adhémar, Comte de Polastron—"who did not have particularly great expectations" but "played the violin"[44]—had married a beauty of fifteen years, Mlle d'Esparbès de Lussan, soon nicknamed "Bichette," who increased the influence of the Polignacs by becoming *dame de palais* to the Queen at the age of only sixteen and taking along with her as a lover the flighty Comte d'Artois. In the Polignac family, it was the women who had the talent for pleasing those in high places.

At the end of the year, not content with accumulating honors, positions, and emoluments, the Polignac clan demonstrated that it was fully capable of influencing ministerial nominations as well. Duly instructed by Vaudreuil, Besenval, and Adhémar, the favorite urged Marie-Antoinette to support the Marquis de Ségur's candidacy for minister of war. This was a far from straightforward enterprise, for Maurepas had thrown his support behind a different candidate, and, even though Ségur's valor on the battlefield and moral integrity were indisputable, he seemed far too old to take up an administrative portfolio for which his previous career had not prepared him. But the Polignacs did not let up on Marie-Antoinette, who, on Christmas morning, succeeded in wresting the nomination of their protégé from Louis XVI. Maurepas admitted to a friend that "that particular order had been the sharpest sword-thrust he had ever received in his life":[45] the Queen's "party" had won its first political skirmish.

Carried off by pneumonia at the end of November, Maria Theresa was no longer around to oversee her daughter. If death prevented her from celebrating the birth of the Dauphin,[46] which she had ardently desired, it also spared her the humiliation of seeing Marie-Antoinette delegate to her favorite the task of holding court in her own château. In 1782, following the terrible bankruptcy of her husband, the Princesse de Guéménée had presented her resignation from the position of governess of the Children of France, and Marie-Antoinette wished Mme de Polignac to replace her. The favorite initially attempted to avoid a responsibility so tiring and onerous, but to the pressures imposed by her family (to whom she responded in tears: "I hate all of you; you want to make a sacrifice of me"[47]) were added the explicit requests of the King, always anxious to satisfy the desires of his wife. Obliged to concede, the Duchesse was assigned the most beautiful and vast of the apartments reserved for courtiers at Versailles. Soon the influx of visitors would be so great that a long wooden gallery would have to be added to it. "Is Mme de Polignac receiving the whole of France?" the Prince de Ligne would ask the Chevalier de Lisle, from Brussels. "Indeed," replied the latter, "three times a week: Tuesday, Wednesday, and Thursday. During those seventy-two hours there is a general *ballet*, open to all: anyone who wishes can enter, take lunch, dine. You should see how the place pullulates with the vermin of the court. Over the course of those three days we live—leaving aside the salon, which is always packed—in the hothouse, which has been turned into a sort of gallery, with a billiard table at the end."[48]

But during the other four days, the doors of the salon were open only to intimate friends, and the favorite was free to rediscover the pleasures of private life. "She led a true *vie de château*," wrote the Duc de Lévis, "a dozen individuals, along with her family, formed all her company: a pleasant freedom reigned there . . . they played and made music; they chatted; never was there any question of intriguing or annoyances, no more than if we had all been two hundred leagues from the capital and the court."[49]

Among the standing invitees were the Comtesse Diane, the Comtesse de Polastron, the Comtesse d'Andlau (the favorite's paternal aunt), and her step-daughter (and intimate friend of Mme de Sabran) the lovely Marie-Adélaïde d'Andlau, née Helvétius. There were also the Comte de Guines, Lauzun's friend, who during his years as an ambassador in London had not merely been the subject of gossip for his affair with Lady Craven but had also been at the center of a far-reaching financial scandal[50] from which he had only emerged unscathed thanks to royal favor—and had even been made a Duc upon his return from England. Next, there were the three Coignys: the Duc, a handsome gentleman with white hair for whom, it was whispered, the Queen had a weakness; the Comte, official lover of the Princesse de Guéménée; the Chevalier, nicknamed Mimi,[51] a tireless crafter of anagrams and possessed of "a gay and amiable nature."[52] Finally, it should go without saying that the Prince de Ligne was welcomed with open arms by all and sundry whenever he happened to be at Versailles.

But the three central figures of this little society were the Baron de Besenval, the Comte d'Adhémar, and, naturally, the Comte de Vaudreuil.

A long-standing friend of the Polignacs, Besenval had preceded them at Versailles at the beginning of the 1770s, when, following the disgrace of Choiseul, the regiment of the Gardes Suisses of which the latter had been lieutenant general had come under the command of the Comte d'Artois. Needless to say, the irresistible Baron was immediately assured of the young Prince's favor, and equally of the sympathy of Marie-Antoinette.[53] The arrival of the Polignacs had raised his standing with the Queen after a period of coolness, and Besenval took advantage of the moment to introduce the two young Ségurs at court. For Mme Campan, the Baron was "the most agreeable storyteller of that circle" in which "the freshest chanson, the bon mot of the day, and scandalous little anecdotes formed the sole subjects of conversation."[54]

Intelligent, audacious, and ambitious, the Comte d'Adhémar was also a very attractive man.[55] "He sang pleasantly, acted very well, and composed pretty couplets."[56] Thanks to the combined aid of Besenval, the Marquis de Ségur, and Vaudreuil, he had succeeded in making his noble ancestry generally known and in marrying—and then immediately losing interest in—a wealthy widow much older than he, and being appointed colonel commandant of the regiment of Chartres Infantry. Mme de Polignac, who had a weakness for him, would do the rest by securing him the post of ambassador to London, which the Duc du Lauzun also coveted.

The official lover of the mistress of the house, Vaudreuil was unquestionably the star of the show, deploying all his worldly skills—that "refined gallantry," that "politeness which was all the more flattering in that it came from the heart," that "urbanity," that "graceful assuredness," which Mme Vigée Le Brun would recall constituted the "charm of Parisian society"[57]—and salvaging from mediocrity with his talents as a player those theatrical spectacles of which Marie-Antoinette was such a tireless devotee.[58] The Comte did not merely counterbalance the indolence of Mme de Polignac with his inventiveness and verve; he exercised a powerful influence over the favorite and dictated her behavior with the Queen.

It was he, supported by Besenval and the Comtesse Diane, who decided on the clan's strategies and transmitted them bit by bit to his lover, thence to be passed on to Marie-Antoinette—most of them tied to his own personal financial needs and those of the other members of the Polignac family. But Vaudreuil also gave himself over to pure intrigue as an end in itself—for along with Besenval, he loved working behind the scenes to promote the careers of his friends, to make and unmake ministers. For this reason, he was keen to rid the Queen's circle of his most formidable rivals, beginning with the Duc de Lauzun, encouraging—at least so Saint-Priest believed[59]—the sovereign's amours with Fersen, who, since he was a foreigner, was far preferable to an ambitious Frenchman. In short, they did their very best to make the favorite's household look to Marie-Antoinette like a "happy island" removed from the poisonous atmosphere of the court, a place where friendship reigned supreme.[60]

Thinking back on these distant years, the Prince de Ligne would recall a scene between the Queen and the Comtesse Jules that cannot be bettered in illustrating the playful climate that reigned within the circle and the incredible familiarity of the relationship between the two friends: "One day when I was playing with them at billiards, they began to argue, and then to grapple physically with each other, to find out which of the two was the stronger. The Queen maintained that it was she. 'Because you play the Queen!' her friend exclaimed. 'Come on,' I said, 'quarrel about it!' 'Well, and if we do quarrel,' said the Queen to the Comtesse, 'what would you do?' 'Oh, I would certainly weep,' said the other, 'weep and weep, but I would console myself, because you are a Queen.'"[61] And it was precisely to forget that fact—"When I am with her, I am no longer the Queen; I am myself"[62]—that Marie-Antoinette spent her evenings with the Duchesse. While the sovereign abandoned herself "to delights of a monotonous and tranquil life,"[63] her favorite was busy suavely exposing her to the requests of the clan, using her manifold charms to ensure that her mistress never refused them anything.

But what was Gabrielle-Yolande truly thinking? Did she feel a sincere friendship for Marie-Antoinette, or was she an unscrupulous schemer? Should we see her as a kind of sacrificial victim, or did she fully share in her family's ambitions? There are so many differences of opinion on the subject among those who knew her that, as Simone Bertière observes, it is impossible to say.[64] For us, she remains a genuine enigma. But we know that she was not always prepared to obey the instructions she was given, and, in that case, Vaudreuil had no qualms about employing strong-arm tactics. Dropping his amiable mask, the Enchanter would reveal "his violent, imperious character,"[65] and recall her to order with terrible scenes. Then there remained for the Duchesse no choice but to weep and bow to his wishes. "Never was violence so deeply seated in a man's character as it was in his," recalls Besenval, who was himself known for his hot temper. According to the Baron, Vaudreuil would not tolerate the least irritation, and "his rages were less the product of hot blood than of a measureless amour propre which bristled not merely at the superiority of others but even at presumptions of equality."[66] The grand falconer showed scant respect to the Abbé de Vermond, and treated with terrific priggishness the minister of the royal household, the Baron de Breteuil—both of whom enjoyed the confidence of the Queen. But they certainly were not the only victims. When, scandalized by his imperious tone, the Marquis de Castries reminded him that he was addressing a Maréchal of France and a minister to the King, he was answered: "I have not forgotten, I am the one who created them: *you* are the one who should remember."[67] Marie-Antoinette herself was not immune from his fits of rage. One day, showing Mme Campan a magnificent billiard cue, originally carved in one piece from an elephant's tusk and now broken in half, the Queen told her: "*Voilà*, there you see how M. de Vaudreuil treats my prized possessions. I had set it on the sofa while I spoke to the Duchesse in the salon; he had the presumption to use it himself, and in a fit of rage over a blocked ball he struck the cue so violently against the table that he broke it in two. The noise brought me back to the room; I did not say a single word; but I gave him a look that showed him how deeply unhappy I was."[68] This incident was enough to confirm that Vaudreuil was unfit to take on the post of governor to the Dauphin, which he had coveted.[69] According to Mme Campan, Marie-Antoinette wisely remarked: "It was enough to have looked in my heart to decide whom to choose as governess, and I will not allow the choice of the Governor to the Dauphin to be influenced in the slightest by my friends. If I did, I would be responsible for it to the nation."[70]

Indeed, it was far more in monopolizing positions than in drawing money from the royal coffers that the Polignac clan was doing harm to the French monarchy. As the Comte de La Marck—a friend of and legal executor to Mirabeau—who certainly felt no love for them, observed: "The Comte and Comtesse Polignac have received no more than they needed to maintain at Versailles a house that has, for some time now, become that of the Queen, and where the King often appears . . . but they had to give their friends and relations positions at court, ambassadorships. . . . The evil—and it is a significant evil, I recognize that—is that these positions have not gone to those who deserve them, and who could fill them well."[71]

It was precisely these ministerial nominations, extracted with tears, that would spark the first recriminations against Marie-Antoinette—thereby provoking yet further tears. According to Besenval, one day when the Queen reproached her for having "sacrificed her to personal ends" by urging her to support the Marquis de Ségur's candidacy for minister of war, the favorite did not hesitate to respond that "it was no longer appropriate for her to remain in her service; that she would depart right away, and never set foot in the court again; and that, given her departure, it would not do for her to preserve the various benefits she had received; that she would renounce it all immediately, up to and including the position held by her husband, who would surely not contradict her."[72] Faced with such cold determination, Marie-Antoinette ended up "throwing herself at the knees of Mme de Polignac in order to beg her pardon with all the eloquence that tender friendship and regret at having offended, could inspire."[73] The two friends fell into each other's arms, weeping. And it was perhaps at the sight of this tableau that, happening to step into the Queen's chamber unannounced, the Comte d'Artois apologized for "having disturbed such a *scéne d'amour*,"[74] in a voice loud enough that everyone could hear. Whether it was malicious or a simple gaffe, this exclamation fueled the slanders that circulated regarding a Sapphic relationship between the two friends—and of course, the jealousy that the Queen felt in the face of the influence that Vaudreuil exercised over his lover was lost on no one.[75]

Well aware that he had not succeeded in charming the Queen, the Enchanter busied himself securing the friendship of the Comte d'Artois, whom he accompanied to Spain on an ill-fated military expedition in the summer of 1782.

The Prince had obtained Louis XVI's permission to participate in the Great Siege of Gibraltar; as a result of the American War of Independence, the Spanish and French were attempting to wrest the territory from English control. Surrounded by a "throng of plumed and pompous aides-de-camp who saw in the war an extension not so much of diplomacy, as of *fêtes galantes, petits soupers*, and court intrigues,"[76] Artois and Vaudreuil arrived just in time to be present at the disastrous French naval attack against the citadel. Ships filled with explosives—"floating batteries"[77]—imagined by a French military engineer to crush the English resistance with a storm of fire could not withstand the enemy's artillery and exploded ahead of time, killing the hundreds of sailors and soldiers who were still aboard. Whatever Vaudreuil's emotions may have been when he was faced with that horrific spectacle, he would surely have been surprised to read what the manservant who had accompanied him to Spain confided to his diary: "How many tears are spread by the councils of kings! It is from the bosom of pleasure and softness, sometimes according to the caprices of a mistress, that such bloody orders are dispatched, sending so many thousands of victims to their deaths.... If the frightful spectacle of such carnage was before their eyes, if they could hear the cries of the dying, the lamentations of fathers and wives who have lost their children and husbands, they would not sign so lightly on the death warrants of such a multitude of brave men ... but God gave us kings in anger...happy are those nations who have freed themselves from tyranny, and who are so wise as to govern themselves."[78]

By November 21, Artois and his suite were back in Versailles, and Vaudreuil launched himself into the play of subterranean influences that would oust the partisans of Necker the following year and secure for his good friend, the Comte Charles-Alexandre de Calonne, the position of controller-general of finances. It was not an incongruous choice, for beneath his appearance of frivolity, Calonne intended to rectify the deficit by fighting against the venality of offices and sharing out the burden of taxes in a more equitable manner. Among the projects under consideration was a tax on land rents, possessions of the Crown and the Church included, called the *subvention territoriale*, which would eventually be adopted by the Revolution. And if the Assembly of Notables, which he convened to overcome the resistance of parliament in supporting fiscal reform, did not succeed in reaching an accord, its attempt to do so made a significant impression. The representatives of the three orders summoned by the King to debate the economic reforms necessary for the good of the nation, even if they were "allotted the role of a dumb chorus ... suddenly found that, individually and collectively, they had a powerful voice—and that France was paying attention. This abrupt self-discovery of politics was intoxicating and there are signs that though they are usually dismissed as the tail end of the old regime, with respect to political self-consciousness the Notables were the first revolutionaries."[79]

The Enchanter's privileged connection to the man who held the keys of the public purse proved highly useful. The minister's "magic wand" was able to draw loans and subsidies from the half-empty coffers of the state, allowing Vaudreuil to keep his creditors, at least provisionally, at arm's length. On the other hand, it only intensified the "distance," not to say the "repugnance,"[80] that Marie-Antoinette felt for him. The Queen hated the minister, even though the latter had done all in his power to insinuate himself into her good graces, and she considered Vaudreuil responsible for having worked for his success and for introducing him into the home of her favorite. In 1790, the Queen recounted to the Comte de La Marck that she had one day "ventur[ed]" to "express to Mme de Polignac the displeasure inspired in her by numerous persons that she had encountered when visiting with her."[81] Aside from Calonne, did those "numerous persons" include Vaudreuil? It is quite likely, seeing that "Mme de Polignac, submissive to those who domineered over her, and despite her habitual sweetness, was not ashamed to answer the Queen: 'I do not think that because Your Majesty is pleased to visit my salon, you have any right to exclude my friends.'"[82]

From the time of the Marquise de Rambouillet's salon, the French nobility had asserted the right to live however—and with whomever—they pleased in their own homes. But Mme de Polignac had now shown the unheard-of presumption of doing so in an *appartement de fonction* within the very sanctuary of the absolute monarchy. It was "the world turned upside down," and the main responsibility lay with Marie-Antoinette herself. Hadn't she stubbornly brought into reality her dream of living a private life incompatible with the formality of Versailles? Hadn't she wanted to adopt the lifestyle of her favorite? Hadn't she shown herself incapable of calling the latter back to order, preferring to find excuses for her rather than risking their friendship? That is precisely what Marie-Antoinette declared to La Marck: "I do not blame Mme de Polignac; deep down she is good, and loves me; but she is completely under the control of those who surround her."[83] Her disappointment was no less bitter for all that, and from 1785 on, the Polignacs lost their absolute monopoly over the Queen's favor. Moreover, Marie-Antoinette was no longer the young "scatterbrain" that Joseph II had been forced to reprimand. The joys of mother-hood, her relationship with Fersen, the growing love and respect of her hus-band—all had enriched her emotional life, bringing her psychological independence and maturity of judgment. While maintaining intimate ties to those to whom she had entrusted the education of her children, the Queen drew closer to the Princesse de Lamballe[84] and established a friendship with the Comtesse d'Ossun, her new *dame d'atours*. The Comtesse was not partic-ularly brilliant, nor intelligent, but "perfectly good and sweet, blessed with great virtue,"[85] and profoundly unselfish. "Devoted heart and soul to the Queen," she wished above all that the latter should be "happy at home, and content with her."[86] And, indeed, she was. Marie-Antoinette began to spend her evenings in her own chambers, provoking the resentment of the Polignacs. It was in vain that Mme d'Ossun, whose brother was married to the daughter of Mme de Polignac, proved herself discreet and loyal toward them and refused to take part in any intriguing. The clan of the favorite revenged themselves by spreading tendentious rumors about their benefactress—"Mme de Polignac, in her intimate conversations, sometimes called her a perverse woman"[87]— feeding into a black legend whose consequences they themselves would be the first to feel.

The most brazen and irresponsible of them all was without doubt the Enchanter. In 1783—and we will return to this later—the Comte worked to secure permission for *The Marriage of Figaro* to be performed at the Comédie-Française. The enthusiasm of the public for that satire of titled society was such that even Marie-Antoinette—who had wanted to stage *The Barber of Seville* at the Trianon theater, inviting Beaumarchais to the performance[88]— came to understand the gravity of the provocation. The following year, when the scandal of "the affair of the necklace" broke out, Vaudreuil showed the measure of his ingratitude by taking the side of the Cardinal de Rohan. But he could not prevent the fall of his friend Calonne in April 1787, nor avoid being touched by his disgrace. The inquiry opened into the machinations of the minister of finance—who had taken refuge in London—revealed that Vaudreuil had abused his credit and "obtained nearly a million from the public coffers without justification."[89] Moreover, the suppression of the position of grand falconer for the sake of the economy, and the bankruptcy of the Baron de Saint-James, his trusted banker,[90] left him stripped of resources and exposed to his creditors. With the assistance of the Polignacs, the Comte once again sought the aid of the monarchy, but this time Louis XVI was content to declare: "They must go ahead and pay, I do not intend to be responsible for their follies any longer."[91] And for her part, Marie-Antoinette remained inflexible.

A rapacious and intriguing courtesan at Versailles, Vaudreuil revealed himself in Paris to be an enlightened patron and an authentic connoisseur. The way that he spent the large sums extorted from royal favor as well as his personal fortune seemed to absolve him of any suspicion of venality. Faithful to noble tradition, the Comte made it a point of honor to lead a life of luxury, to have magnificent dwellings at his disposal, to provide financial support for writers and artists, and to collect works of art. His friends the Baron de Besenval, the Comte d'Adhémar, and the Comte de Calonne were collectors as well, but possessed neither his artistic expertise nor his breadth of outlook. His first guide to the artistic landscape of the capital had been a cousin on his father's side, ten years his junior, the Comte de Paroy, who had been able to reconcile the needs of a military career with his more authentic vocation. Blessed with a vast artistic knowledge, Paroy was a deft miniaturist and engraver, a skillful draftsman, and he combined a tireless imagination with remarkable talent as an artisan. From his workshop there flowed a steady stream of engravings, emblems, festival decorations, magic lanterns, and spyglasses, according to the inspiration of the moment.[92] Not only did Paroy initiate Vaudreuil into the problems of artistic practice and to his varying techniques but, as a tenant of an apartment in the Hôtel Lubert in the rue de Cléry, he introduced him to his landlords. Jean-Baptiste-Pierre Le Brun—who had installed his gallery at the same address—was one of the most important and best informed of Parisian art dealers, and his wife, who had her studio there, was the well-known painter Élisabeth Vigée Le Brun. In 1778, at the age of only twenty-three, she had been asked to Versailles to paint a portrait of the Queen. But other artists had also found refuge at the Hôtel Lubert, which had become a veritable "hub": "During the day the studios are abuzz, pictures are moving in and out of storage. In the evening, everyone comes together, enthusiastic after a day of successful work. And what do they talk about? Painting."[93] It was there that, around 1780, having become a regular at the Le Brun soirees, Vaudreuil became passionate about contemporary painting, its various aesthetic tendencies and the underlying theoretical debates, making friends with the artists, listening to their concerns and buying their works. And even if, as is most likely, he did not begin his collection of modern art until after his return from Gibraltar with Artois, all the evidence indicates that he had already been the lover of the mistress of the house for months.

It seems[94] that the Enchanter was the only man that Élisabeth Vigée Le Brun permitted herself to love—in contravention of her strict working discipline and the solid good sense that guided her over the course of her long career. And even in her *Souvenirs*, the product of an advanced age in which she abstains from any allusion to her emotional life, the luminous image of Vaudreuil—"one of the most amiable men imaginable"[95]—and her remembrance of his generosity, of "his noble and pure soul,"[96] are positively vibrant with emotion. Even if the letters that the Comte wrote to her from Spain, and that she jealously preserved, have not come down to us, we know that Mme Vigée Le Brun—whose reputation was immensely important to her—was not afraid to expose herself to gossip by appearing in his company.[97] As early as 1784, summoned to redesign the park of the country home that the Comte had purchased at Gennevilliers, Thomas Blaikie—the fashionable Scottish gardener, nicknamed the "French Capability Brown," whom the Comte d'Artois had already used for the Château de Bagatelle—had run into Élisabeth and without hesitation deduced from her comportment that she was the mistress of the property.[98] Two years later, writing to the King of Sweden, Mme de Staël referred to the relationship between Vaudreuil and Mme Vigée Le Brun as being a matter of public knowledge.[99] Indeed, it was so public that the poet Écouchard-Lebrun, known as Lebrun-Pindare, celebrated the two of them, referring to them by name, in a poem titled "L'Enchanteur et la Fée."[100]

Mme de Polignac seemed to take no umbrage and, when she was in Paris, did not fail to honor the soirees at the Hôtel Lubert with her presence. Their relationship had never prevented the Comte from enjoying a solid reputation as a libertine, and Chamfort celebrated his "amorous exploits"[101] in frankly sacrilegious verse. For that matter, it was unlikely that a Duchesse would display any jealousy over a mere painter. In any case, it is in the *Souvenirs* of the latter that we find echoes of their "leisure time" at Gennevilliers. The Comte had first rented and then purchased that estate, less than ten miles from the capital, from the Duc de Fronsac, the son of the famous Maréchal de Richelieu, in order to invite the Comte d'Artois to hunt with him there, and he had "embellished it as far as possible,"[102] naturally providing it with a theater constructed from "rosewood."[103] Élisabeth performed there, along with her brother and sister-in-law, both of them excellent amateur players, in the company of such professional singers and actors as Mme Dugazon and Garat, for an audience that included the Comte d'Artois and his retinue.[104] "The last show to be performed in the hall at Gennevilliers," the artist recalls, "was a production of *The Marriage of Figaro*."[105]

Indeed, after numerous private readings at Paris and Versailles, the play had been struck by Louis XVI's veto—"It is detestable, it will never be performed"[106]—and seemed destined never to be staged, when the Enchanter took it into his head to "give the public a masterpiece for which they have been waiting with impatience."[107] With the help of the Comte d'Artois and the Polignac clan, he managed to wrangle permission to perform it in his private theater with actors from the Comédie-Française, after certain amendments to the script by the censor. On September 26, 1783, with a cry of "Outside of *The Marriage of Figaro*, there is no salvation!"[108] the play was indeed performed for the first time at Gennevilliers in the presence of the Comte d'Artois, the Duchesse de Polignac, and the cream of the court. At the last moment, an indisposition had prevented Marie-Antoinette from joining them. Contrary to what Mme Vigée Le Brun would write after the fact,[109] the guests displayed no embarrassment at Figaro's tirades denouncing their vices and privileges, and the play was "an enormous success."[110] After all, what could it matter to the *parfaitement bonne compagnie*—so deeply convinced of their own superiority that they could luxuriate in the scorn of their inferiors—that they were being accused of immorality and abuse of power, so long as justice was done to their elegance?

"Intoxicated with happiness" by the applause he received, Beaumarchais "ran back and forth like a man beside himself; and, when someone complained of the heat, he did not wait for the windows to be opened, but shattered the panes himself with his cane—which led them to say that, after the play, he had broken the windows twice over."[111] Seven months later, on April 23, 1784, *The Mad Day, or The Marriage of Figaro* (to give it its full title) was finally performed at the Comédie-Française, and remained on stage for nine months.

Vaudreuil could rightly pride himself on this personal triumph: he had displayed a spirit of independence, once again imposing his choice on Versailles as well as on Paris. Yet he certainly had not intended to support the cause of the Third Estate. If, in Beaumarchais's play, Figaro prevents the Comte Almaviva from claiming his "droit du seigneur"[112] by preceding him in his new wife's bed, it cannot be said that the peasants of Gennevilliers had a similar success when it came to hunting rights, which Vaudreuil exercised on his lands in the company of d'Artois. In 1789, the lists of grievances drawn up by the residents would denounce the ravages that the wild game (which they were not permitted to cull) systematically visited upon their vineyards and crops, reducing no fewer than three hundred families to beggary—complaints that neither Vaudreuil nor d'Artois had taken the trouble to hear. "The flatterers of princes have said that hunting is an image of war," wrote Chamfort. "Indeed, the peasants whose fields they have ravaged must find the likeness quite striking."[113] And if the Comte had taken lightly the subversive irreverence of the play he so ardently defended, Beaumarchais did not seem to understand that his protector, free-spirited as he was, followed a code of honor very different from his own. Mme Vigée Le Brun tells that one day the writer came to see Vaudreuil, in order to ask him to support a financial project of his own devising, offering him a large sum of money in return if it should succeed. "The Comte listened to everything very calmly, and when Beaumarchais had finished, replied: 'Monsieur de Beaumarchais, you could not have come at a luckier moment; for I have passed a good night; my digestion is fine; and I could not possibly feel better than I do today; if you had come to me yesterday with a proposition like that, I would have thrown you out of the window.'"[114] Surprising though it may be, the genial author of plays who had practiced numerous trades and frequented numerous social circles had simply not understood what it meant to be a great lord.

The support provided to Beaumarchais was not an isolated gesture. From the beginning of the 1780s, Vaudreuil demonstrated a growing interest in the world of arts and letters, and showed himself to be a generous and perspicacious patron. Patronage was a distinctive feature of the high nobility, and was encouraged by the esteem enjoyed by writers and philosophers in social circles. From Talleyrand to Norvins, memoirists of the period emphasize the surprising sort of familiarity that was sometimes established, in the name of intellectual prestige, between the different social classes. But Vaudreuil's preference for frequenting "the society of the most distinguished artists and men of letters"[115] was dictated, so it seems, by an authentic respect and a profound admiration.

The proud and wrathful courtier, capable of arrogance toward the King's ministers, was prepared to treat his protégés on an equal footing, to invite them to dine and offer them his friendship. "He finds it very fine, very natural, that one should have talent, merit, even superiority, and that one should be honored for these titles,"[116] observed the cantankerous Chamfort, seeing in this attitude the promise of a new world.

In the domain of the arts, an essay by Colin B. Bailey allows us to judge the importance of the patronage exercised by Vaudreuil and the singularity of his career as a collector.[117] It was a brief career, lasting less than a decade, and marked by two important auctions. The first took place in November 1784, when the Comte decided to remove the old masters from his collection and sell them—the sort of paintings that in that era constituted (recall the Duc de Brissac) the foundation of any collection worthy of interest. Entrusted to the expert hands of Jean-Baptiste-Pierre Le Brun, the paintings put up for auction reached considerable sums of money, thanks, among others, to the Comte d'Angiviller, superintendent of the Bâtiments du Roi, who on behalf of the Crown purchased thirty-six works of Dutch and Flemish masters from the seventeenth century, laying out 300,000 livres. We do not know whether the money from this sale was destined to quiet Vaudreuil's creditors or if it went to fund the repair and embellishment of the sumptuous private mansion that the Comte had purchased two months earlier in the rue de la Chaise. For Bailey, the best explanation is rather the one that Le Brun suggests in the auction catalog, where he emphasizes what Vaudreuil has *not* put up for sale: "The *amateur* could not refuse himself the pleasure of preserving his works of the French school. The species of tribute he pays to our artists, and to those who have preceded them, compensates him in some sort for the privation he has imposed upon himself."[118]

In short, from the beginning of the 1780s, the Comte had directed his ambitions as a collector toward French artists. By covering himself with debt, he bought at a steady rate and for high prices more than eighty canvases of the French school, *ancienne* and *moderne*. After having acquired through the intermediary of Le Brun such masterpieces as *Bacchanal Before a Statue of Pan* by Poussin—of which the Comte de Paroy had executed an engraving displayed in the Salon of 1787—and *The Pleasures of the Dance* by Watteau, Vaudreuil accumulated between 1784 and 1787 the works of the principal painters of the seventeenth and eighteenth centuries. In keeping with the directions of criticism, the Enchanter intended to furnish concrete proof of the existence of a grand French pictorial tradition, which, having rivaled the Italians thanks to the masters of the Grand Siècle, would now assert its supremacy on a European scale. For this, he needed to overcome the widespread idea that the French manner had declined during the eighteenth century—imputable to the decorative hypertrophy of Boucher—and to explain the excellence of French painting in the light of an uninterrupted fidelity to national taste. And in order to show the diversity and wealth of experiences from which, over time, that taste had drawn nourishment, the Comte had recourse to a strict eclecticism, hanging side by side pictures as different from one another in style as Boucher's *Hercules and Omphale* (1734) and the *Oath of the Horatii* (1784) by David.

Naturally, Vaudreuil began his campaign to acquire contemporary works with those by Mme Vigée Le Brun, and allowed himself to be guided by her advice and that of her husband. After the Queen, the Comte was the painter's most important client: he commissioned at least five portraits and his collection includes *Venus Tying the Wings of Apollo*, the magnificent *Self-Portrait with Straw Hat*, two portraits of the Duchesse de Polignac and one of the Duchesse de Guiche, and a sensual *Bacchante*. He also commissioned numerous pictures from painters like Hubert Robert and Claude-Joseph Vernet, whom Élisabeth Vigée Le Brun admired tremendously. He supported several artists who frequented the Hôtel Lubert, from François-Guillaume Ménageot to Jean-Germain Drouais, the son of François-Hubert Drouais and already famous in his own right. And he supplemented the pension of the young neoclassical sculptor Antoine-Denis Chaudet, which allowed this promising artist to spend five years at the French Academy in Rome. And it was most likely at the Le Brun home that he made the acquaintance of David. Thiéry's *Guide des Amateurs et des Étrangers voyageurs à Paris*, published in January 1787, provides us with evidence of the success of the Enchanter's project. Before beginning his tour of the mansion in the rue de la Chaise and describing, room by room, the paintings and sculptures, as well as the profusion of Boulle furnishings, ormolu, cut-crystal lamps, and precious objects mostly of French manufacture, Thiéry takes care to point out to the reader the guiding principle behind the owner's choices. "Love for the motherland and for the talents that she has produced, steered by an exquisite taste," he wrote, "seems to have driven M. le Comte de Vaudreuil to assemble a collection composed of paintings by the best masters of the French school, paintings capable of sustaining comparison to those of other schools and bringing honor to the nation."[119]

Vaudreuil's patronage was of a resolutely patriotic hue. A quarter of a century later, even a fervent revolutionary like Pierre-Louis Ginguené would pay homage to the Comte's passion "for all that did honor to the name of France."[120] Indeed, for the Comte, France could not only pride itself on possessing the most luxurious court in Europe and a superior way of life; it was also the home of the Enlightenment, a land in the avant-garde of civilization. The arts and literature seemed to him essential strong points of national identity. Vaudreuil remained faithful, with like conviction, to all of his country's customs and traditions. Anglomania struck him as a pernicious fashion, and he continued to dress and ride in the French manner. As he did not fail to remind the Comte d'Artois, who, led astray by Lauzun, had adopted the equestrian style from across the Channel, "he believed that a Frenchman had no need to take up the habits of other countries... and that a man of his station should never show any preference for foreign things, but rather lead by example."[121] For him, the ancients remained the sole models in which the French genius could fully recognize itself, as was attested by the masterpieces of the Grand Siècle. Consequently, he granted plenty of space in his collection to paintings inspired by mythology, historical subjects, and landscapes. Also in keeping with the neoclassical taste then triumphant was the copy of the *Oath of the Horatii* he procured, which the Comte d'Angiviller had commissioned from David for the royal collections, and his last purchase was a view of an antique villa by Pierre-Henri de Valenciennes, a theorist and precursor of modern landscape painting.

Vaudreuil also encouraged Artois to follow his example in supporting the painting of an avant-garde that used ancient history as a metaphor for an artistic and moral rebirth that was hardly compatible with the reigning order of things. Was Vaudreuil, as in the case of *The Marriage of Figaro*, simply misjudging the political implications of the works he defended? He certainly would not have been alone in this. His preferences as a collector were shared by a small elite of art lovers who opposed the Revolution in 1789, despite figuring among the best clients of those artists who embraced the Republican credo. But the collectors of the 1780s could hardly have predicted that the celebration of the antique virtues would become a revolutionary battle cry. In the end, the meaning of a painting could vary according to where it was destined to hang and the point of view from which it was regarded. Indeed, Bailey writes, "in the patrician's home at least, fashion, enlightenment and patriotic preference attenuated the radical resonances of historicizing subject matter and classicizing style."[122] Moreover, we can use this as a key to explain more generally the schizophrenia of a society ready to applaud those threatening its very existence. In the climate of the salons, the most audacious ideas of the writers, philosophers, and moralists arrived filtered through respect for a shared aesthetic code, and wound up being reduced to pure *jeux de l'esprit*. Far from disquieting by their possible impact on reality, they amused by their measure of intellectual provocation.

The hope of succeeding the Comte d'Angiviller as director of the Bâtiments du Roi may have played a role in the patriotic character of Vaudreuil's patronage. Prestigious and well remunerated, that position (which we might consider the equivalent of minister of culture today) coincided with the Comte's interests and would have allowed him to restore his finances. But there, too, as with the position of governor to the Dauphin, his hopes were undercut: not only did he lose his nomination and his position as grand falconer but, with the resignation of Calonne, his access to credit from the royal coffers was barred. Crushed by debt, deprived of the aid of Louis XVI, the Comte was obliged to dispose of his assets. During 1787, he sold his estate at Gennevilliers as well as the office of steward of the hunting lodge, while waiting to do the same for the mansion on the rue de la Chaise, which had been placed under seal at the request of his creditors. On November 26, at Le Brun's gallery, he auctioned his furnishings, porcelains, and collection of paintings. But not all of them: those by Mme Vigée Le Brun, for instance, do not figure among the list of works on sale.

The Comte was not present in Paris for the dispersal of his collection. In September—having charged the Duc de Polignac with paying off his creditors—he had left for Rome with his cousin Paroy, his protégé Ménageot (who had been summoned to direct the French Academy there), and his godson Auguste-Jules-François de Polignac, a child of seven years. Welcomed with all ceremony by Louis XVI's ambassador to Rome, the elderly and charming Cardinal de Bernis, Vaudreuil forgot his financial worries while visiting the city of the popes, with its museums, its celebrated archaeological collections, and its antiquarians, accompanied by two expert guides. He continued to be a passionate advocate for the prestige of French art, commissioning for the Palazzo Mancini a cast of the Farnese Hercules belonging to the Bourbons of

Naples. On his return to Paris, where he no longer had a home of his own, in June 1788, Vaudreuil found accommodation at the Tuileries, in a small outbuilding of the Orangerie, thanks to the Comte d'Angiviller. Once again he made the rounds of court and town, as gay and brilliant as ever: after all, money was made for spending, and, as he confidently waited to find it again, he could quite peacefully live the life of an artist.

In order to celebrate his return, Mme Vigée Le Brun hosted a party *à la grecque*. She had been inspired by her reading of *The Travels of Anacharsis the Younger in Greece*, by the Abbé Barthélemy—faithful friend of the Comtesse de Choiseul—with its erudite and picturesque evocation of antiquity, a book that was enjoying great success, having been published earlier that year. After reading the detailed description of a Greek feast, Mme Vigée Le Brun decided to offer something similar to the guests she had invited that evening. The scene deserves to be quoted at length from the hostess's memory of it in her *Souvenirs*, in a passage that has become famous:

> Since I was expecting some very pretty women, I conceived the idea that we should all dress ourselves up as Greeks, so as to surprise M. de Vaudreuil and M. Boutin,[123] who I knew would not arrive until ten o'clock. My studio, filled with everything I used to drape my models, could furnish me with the garments, and the Comte de Paroy, who was living in my house on the rue de Cléry, had a superb collection of Etruscan vases. . . . I cleaned all of these items myself, and set them on a mahogany table without a cloth. That done, I placed an enormous screen behind the chairs, which I took care to hide by covering it with a drapery here and there, as one sees in certain of Poussin's paintings. A hanging lamp shed a strong light on the table; at last all was ready, down to my costumes, when the daughter of Joseph Vernet, the charming Mme Chalgrin, was the first to arrive. I coiffed and dressed her right away. Then came Mme de Bonneuil, so remarkable for her beauty; Mme Vigée, my sister-in-law, who, though she was not so pretty, had the most beautiful eyes in the world, and *voilà*! There you had all three of them transformed into veritable Athenians. Lebrun-Pindare came in; we removed his powder, stripped him of his side curls, and I set on his head a wreath of laurels which I had brought with me to paint young Prince Henry Lubomirski. . . . The Comte de Parois had a large purple mantle with which I draped my poet, and before you knew it Pindare had been transformed into Anacreon. Then came the Marquis de Cubières. While they went to his house to look for a guitar that he had had mounted as a golden lyre, I dressed

him up; I also costumed M. de Rivière (brother of my sister-in-law), Ginguené, and Chaudet, the famous sculptor. It was getting later: I had little time to think of my own costume; but since I always wore white tunic-shaped dresses, it was enough to arrange a veil and set a crown of flowers on my head. I took particular care over my daughter, that charming child, and Mlle de Bonneuil, who was lovely as a little angel. Both of them were ravishing, holding light antique vases, as if about to serve us something to drink.... At ten o'clock we heard the coach drive up with the Comte de Vaudreuil and Boutin, and when these two gentlemen reached the entrance to the dining room, whose doors I had had drawn open, they found us singing the chorus from Gluck's *The God of Paphos and Knidos*, while M. de Cubières accompanied us on his lyre. In all my days I have never seen two faces so astonished, so stupefied, as those of M. de Vaudreuil and his companion.[124]

The sale of the mansion on the rue de la Chaise also finally put an end to a cohabitation that risked becoming embarrassing. For at least four years, Vaudreuil had played host to Chamfort, whose political ideas were revealing themselves day by day to be more and more irreconcilable with his own. And "perhaps feeling that they would each be more confident that their friendship would be a lasting one if they were no longer under the same roof,"[125] Chamfort went on to install himself in a small apartment in the arcades of Palais-Royal. It was there that he would meet with others who wished like him to make France a land of freedom. In literature as in painting, the sole imperative that had guided the choices of Vaudreuil until now was that of taste. For him, elegance, intellectual audacity, and mastery of style took precedence over ideological content. Nothing is more significant in this regard than the testimony of Pierre-Louis Ginguené. Of admitted Republican convictions, the founder of *La Décade philosophique, littéraire et politique* was as closely tied to Ponce-Denis Écouchard-Lebrun as to Chamfort and, after their deaths, Ginguené was tasked with the publication of their works. In spite of their political ideas, both men received Vaudreuil's protection, Ginguené pointed out, and in both cases the critic did not hesitate to pay homage to the Comte's liberalism during the years when he had been reduced to poverty and exile. Forgotten today, Lebrun was considered the greatest lyric poet of his age, and the young André Chénier—the only poet to truly deserve that title—found his odes sublime. While waiting to put his lyre at the service of the Revolution, Lebrun was saved from the poverty into which he had been thrown by a lawsuit filed by his wife, thanks to the intervention of Vaudreuil, who obtained a pension for him from Calonne and lavished him with attention. It was in thanks that the poet celebrated him in "L'Enchanteur et la Fée"—"To love all of the arts was his glory; to be loved himself was his happiness"[126]—introduced a strophe on Gennevilliers into his ode "Le Triomphe de nos paysages,"[127] and defended Vaudreuil from his detractors by praising him in various other of his poetic compositions.[128] Still, he never made any mystery of his political opinions. Indeed, Ginguené recounts, Lebrun had the habit of reading at the Enchanter's invitation extracts from the poem that he was composing on "Nature, or Philosophical and Rustic Happiness." Never completed, that work marked the beginning of a "new poetics—engaged, civic, pre-romantic," and expounded "the boldest of truths,"[129] though nobody among "the happy few"— the Comte d'Artois included—felt particularly disturbed by them. Still, recalled Ginguené, "when certain ideas seemed a bit too strong, that excellent M. de Vaudreuil would say in an amiable tone that I've never heard other than from him: 'These poets are truly mad! But what lovely verses! Lovely verses!' and he would ask Lebrun to read an elegy, or his "Psyche," which would patch everything up."[130] As Ginguené wrote admiringly, "never before, perhaps, has a great man merited, and inspired, such friendship; and never had Lebrun, who was very susceptible to that noble sentiment, felt so much of it for anyone."[131]

Friendship was also Chamfort's dominant passion—the illusion that, despite multiple disappointments, longest withstood the great moralist's inquisitive fury. He experienced it intensely, and, because it permitted him to "reinvent" human relations in a society that had forgotten them,[132] he celebrated its salvific virtue in numerous writings,[133] including his induction address at the Académie Française.[134] In that "sophisticated civilization" whose imposture he never ceased to denounce, Chamfort counted on the reliability of his friends above all. When, in 1783, having cut his ties with literary life and chosen to live in retirement, he lost the woman whose love had brought him the serenity he had always lacked, Narbonne and Choiseul-Gouffier came to his aid, and after a visit to the Prince de Ligne at Beloeil, took him off to Holland in an attempt to distract him.

His friendship with Vaudreuil occupied a special place in his life. The two men had probably met in 1776, at the time that Chamfort's tragedy, *Mustapha and Zéangir*, had triumphed—"easily, too easily"[135]—at Versailles. At that point the writer had enjoyed the protection of the Choiseul clan, frequenting the triumvirate formed by Narbonne, Talleyrand, and Choiseul-Gouffier, and opportunities to meet the Enchanter would not have been lacking. But the year that definitively marked their relations was 1784, when, after the trip to Holland, Vaudreuil—who "had wooed and loved him longest"[136]—snatched Chamfort from his retreat in the country and brought him home to Paris. And when Noël Aubin, a friend from his years as a literary bohemian, asked him in perplexity how long this odd living arrangement could possibly last, Chamfort responded: "As long as life, and death."[137] In a letter to the Abbé Roman, he was even more explicit: "My bond with the Comte de Vaudreuil has become such that leaving this country is unthinkable. It is the most perfect and tender friendship imaginable.... One often sees shared interests producing steady and durable connections between men of letters and men of the court; but here we are speaking of friendship, and that word says everything, in both your language and mine."[138]

Let us attempt to understand what could have bound these two very different men, who appear at first blush to have no more in common than the year of their birth.

In 1785, Vaudreuil and Chamfort were both forty-five years old, but fortune had smiled on the first throughout his shamelessly privileged existence, while the latter had accumulated a long series of failures, as Claude Arnaud highlights in his remarkable biography.[139]

Born out of wedlock in Clermont-Ferrand to a woman of aristocratic family and an obscure canon, Sébastien-Roch had been adopted by parents of very humble origins—a grocer and a maid—who offered him a peaceful childhood; later, with the help of a scholarship, he was able to study at the renowned Collège des Grassins in Paris.

Handsome, intelligent, strong-willed, and cultivated—he had emerged victorious from a competition meant to determine the best student in the kingdom—the young provincial refused to embrace a career in the Church. The reasons he provided to the head of Grassins recall those expressed by the Chevalier de Boufflers in an analogous situation, and in themselves read like a road map for his life: "I will never be a priest; I am too fond of rest, philosophy, women, honor, and real fame; and care too little for quarrels, hypocrisy, honors, and money."[140] Resolved to shape his own destiny, and following the example of Voltaire, the young man abandoned his family name, Nicolas, and

adopted the more bellicose Chamfort. But the humiliating memory of his illegitimate birth continued to weigh on him, and his aristocratic protectors did
not fail to remind him of it.[141] Then, when Chamfort was only twenty-five,
venereal disease undermined the health of that "Hercules with the shape of
Adonis"[142] renowned for his erotic performances, ruining his physique and putting an end to his pursuit of love and pleasure. His season of optimism was over.

Recovering, Chamfort set himself to work forging a new identity, one consecrated to literature. He patronized writers and salons, and benefited from
the protection of the very influential Duclos, secretary of the Académie
Française since 1755. Endowed with a solid humanistic education and great
skill at the art of imitation, he tried his hand at the various literary genres then
in vogue: comedies, tragedies, tales in verse, academic elegies, and apologues.
If his characters and plots lacked originality and his style was still somewhat
academic, the principal themes of his reflections as a moralist—the critique
of a civilization of masks, the condemnation of the great, the analysis of relations between rich and poor, the praise of friendship, the wariness of love—
were already fully present.[143] Thanks to the paucity of young literary talents
in a culture paralyzed by the cult of Voltaire and Rousseau, Chamfort received
various flattering signs of recognition, but it was the success of his *Mustapha
and Zéangir* at Versailles—the Queen herself expressed her admiration to him,
and gave him a pension—that unleashed the jealousy of his rivals. The tragedy's
Paris premiere was a resounding fiasco. Though it wasn't unusual for audiences
in the capital to contradict the verdicts of Versailles, this time it was the critics,
beginning with his old friend Jean-François de La Harpe, who were the first
to castigate Chamfort. His pride sorely wounded, disgusted by the pettiness
of the literary world, the writer decided to publish nothing more, and even
after his election to the Académie Française in 1781, he refused to change
course. His hopes once again dashed, falling prey to resentment and bitterness,
Chamfort decided to "retire wholly into himself,"[144] à la Rousseau, far from
society's venom. But he was not cut out for solitude—he needed interlocutors,
and he found refuge with Mme Helvétius in Auteuil. In the hospitable home
of the widow of the author of *De l'esprit*, who acted as a bridge between the
last philosophers of the Enlightenment and the new generation of ideologues,
Chamfort rediscovered old friends like the writer Antoine Léonard Thomas,
the editor Charles-Joseph Panckoucke, and the Abbé Morellet. It was at the
home of Panckoucke's daughter Mme Agasse, in Boulogne, that he met Marthe-
Anne Buffon, a widow a dozen years older than he, with whom he would

reopen that chapter of emotions that he had believed definitively closed. What united them even more strongly than love was "a complete correspondence of ideas, feelings, and positions"[145] that rendered them indispensable to each other. At Vaudouleurs, Marie-Anne's country home near Étampes, where they settled, Chamfort returned to life and discovered that he could still be intensely happy. But it was a happiness that would not last, for in the spring of 1783, after six months together, Mme Buffon died, throwing Chamfort into despair. It was at Vaudouleurs, "which had become horrible" to him, that Vaudreuil came for him "riding in a carriage"[146] in order to bring him back to the rue de la Chaise.

The product of a reciprocal fascination, the friendship between Chamfort and the Enchanter was the mirror in which each of the two attempted to resolve his own contradictions by peering narcissistically into the sublime image of the other. Despite their differences in character, ideals, and social stature, their shared values—pride, sense of honor, spirit of independence, generosity—drove them to a continual emulation that sealed their connection. As surprising as it may seem—Mme Vigée Le Brun herself was astonished by it[147]—Vaudreuil had no love for life at court. Could he have been the "M. de…" who, as Chamfort writes, declared: "A genuine emotion is so rare that occasionally I stop in the street to watch a dog gnawing a bone: it is particularly when I am returning from Versailles, Marly, or Fontainebleau that I am most drawn to this spectacle."[148] And after all, could he really have felt fulfilled by his success as a courtier? He wanted to be chivalrous, yet knew that he owed his power to hidden stratagems, to his ability to apply pressure to his mistress, and, through her, to the emotional fragility of the Queen, as well as Louis XVI's weakness when it came to his wife. He loved his country, but used his influence to maintain the power of ministers whose chief merit was that they were his friends. He certainly perceived the crisis that the monarchy was experiencing, but preferred to ignore its gravity and look after his own interests. "You have no mote in your eye, merely a bit of dust on your spectacles,"[149] Chamfort did not hesitate to tell him. Paris allowed him to remove his courtier's mask, to maintain his distance from the intrigues, the meanness, the compromise, and to revel in a demanding audience's admiration of the qualities that marked him out: taste, elegance, wit, and the art of verbal seduction. His interest in artistic life and the possibility of finally rendering a disinterested tribute to talent reconciled him with his pride. For this respectable, decent Vaudreuil, winning the esteem of Chamfort was an affirmation of his own worth. It was not just the latter's marvelously contagious, "electric"[150] intelligence that fascinated the Enchanter but his moral integrity, his freedom of judgment, as much as—rare indeed—his absence of personal ambition and determination not to seek favors. Yet this child of the Third Estate, who called the society of rank and station into question, also cultivated the most exquisite aristocratic manners, deploying them with extraordinary verve. The reciprocal gift of friendship was the only thing that could bring them together beyond all of their opposing qualities, and, to show themselves worthy of it, they rivaled each other in generosity and intelligence. The Comte started with a distinct disadvantage, since the superiority of his social condition exacerbated Chamfort's sensitivity, requiring even more tact and delicacy of him. But overcoming that resistance was, for the arrogant and irascible Comte, a victory in and of itself.

The affinity that the Comte felt for Chamfort was in turn an example of the contradictions that characterized his existence and that the writer was the first to emphasize. "My whole life," we read in a famous passage, "is a tissue of obvious contrasts with my principles. I am no lover of princes, yet I am fond of a princess and a prince.[151] I am renowned for my Republican maxims, yet plenty of my friends sport decorations bestowed on them by the monarchy. I am happy in my poverty, yet hobnob with the rich."[152] In the case of Vaudreuil, the contrast was only skin deep; in the Enchanter, Chamfort had found his double.

When Nietzsche traced his portrait of Chamfort in *The Gay Science*, after the "shock" he experienced at reading his fragments, he found in the "hatred" that the writer felt for "all blood nobility" the only explanation that allowed him to comprehend why "a man who understood men and the masses, like Chamfort, ranged himself on the side of the multitude"—why, that is, rather than remaining "to one side, in reaction and philosophical renunciation,"[153] he took up the banner of the Revolution. And one cannot help thinking of Chamfort when reading Nietzsche's reflections, written years later, on ressentiment.[154]

Yet it was not ressentiment that led Chamfort to rail against the inadequacy of the monarchy, the scandalous anachronism of its social hierarchy, the duplicity of a faithless church, and the inequality of citizens before the law, but rather the hope of a better world. Like so many of his contemporaries, what he wanted was a different nation—and his convictions had been on display since his youth, when, nurtured in the love of virtue by an honest and hardworking family, well aware of his intellectual capacities since his school days, and proud of having come "from the people," he saw a life full of promise stretching before him. Certainly, he could not reasonably have regretted the fact that his mother, in refusing to recognize him, had excluded him from a social class that had lost its senses, and that he held in contempt, but the bitterness raised in him by this rejection remained. Indeed, if his father had also been a member of the nobility—as in the case of Lauzun, Narbonne, or Ségur—his real parents might not have felt obliged to disown him. To this was added his fascination with what the nobility considered the sign that most clearly distinguished it—that is to say, its style. And he was greatly tempted to seize that style for himself. After all, didn't they say that it was hereditary? But he was obliged to note that, in spite of all his mimetic prowess, the operation was perilous. As he reflected in his study of Molière,[155] playing a character of a different rank than one's own meant exposing oneself to the fearsome sanction of ridicule. Thus the role that he took up was not without risks: to be able to achieve success in the world of high society, plenty of writers were ready to renounce their dignity and, like courtesans and coquettes, make the art of pleasing their métier.[156] The only recognition that a *respectable* writer could hope to aspire to was that based on merit, and Chamfort was fully conscious of his own. But how could he not feel bitterness in realizing that in a society founded on inequality, any confirmation of that merit was, of necessity, unevenly distributed and to be won only by means of unequal combat? "It is only with great difficulty, said M. [that is, Chamfort himself], that a man of merit sustains himself in society without the support of a name, a rank, or a fortune: the man who does possess these advantages, on the other hand, is sustained by them in spite of himself. There is, between these two, the difference between an unassisted swimmer and a man in a diving suit."[157] And when he waxed ironic on Boufflers's "*méringues*,"[158] as he called the Chevalier's poems, he could never have imagined that privileged men like Boufflers or like Lauzun might feel the same bitterness as he at not seeing their own merits recognized.

Chamfort's bitterness was powerfully pugnacious, however: determined to take revenge on the social order that had excluded him, he chose conversation as his field of battle—one where nobles and intellectuals could confront each other on equal terms. Certainly the freedom to be enjoyed there was a codified one, no matter what the subject—its objectives were pleasure and amusement, and these were pursued according to elaborate strategies of politeness, wit, gallantry, deference, playfulness, and flattery. If the nobles undoubtedly enjoyed the advantage here, having internalized the rules from childhood, those rules were nonetheless the same for all participants. As the *Maximes* reveal, Chamfort had studied them deeply, to the point that he thoroughly knew all of their nuances and limits, and took advantage of them to vanquish his adversaries. The writer did not resist the aesthetic of variety and lightness that marked the conversation of the time. As for Voltaire, Mme du Deffand, and so many of their contemporaries, amusement was the means, temporary though it may have been, to avoid the tragedies of existence. In its superficiality, this society conversation was false, deliberately deceptive: "To understand things properly, one needs to take words in the opposite sense that they are used in society."[159] This same art of "turning things aside"[160] would be of great use in humiliating those who had humiliated him.

Chamfort was an exceptionally gifted conversationalist, and it was in this domain that, as Claude Arnaud writes, "he was at his best, that he abandoned himself to pleasure."[161] His "weapon"[162] there was the subtle deployment of teasing,[163] which required exquisite tact and constituted a higher kind of adulation.[164] He openly said as much: "Irony is what is required to do justice to all the deformations of men and society. It is thanks to this that one avoids compromising oneself. Thanks to irony, one can put everything in its place, without exceeding one's own. And irony attests to our superiority over the people and things that we make fun of, without thereby offending them—so long as they possess a sense of humor and of the ways of society." Once he was sure of his social success, the daring writer passed on to provocation. He pretended to want to flee the company of important people so that they would seek him out and "he could scold them at his ease."[165] With the assurance he gained from knowing himself to be more intelligent than his conversational partners, he did not hesitate "to say and think aloud what no one else dared to or could, and for which they will always be grateful to you for having been bold enough. The surest means of amusing and being fashionable is this: to bestow wit on those who would never have it without us."[166] Didn't the success of his friend Beaumarchais's *The Marriage of Figaro*—it was Chamfort who had introduced him to Vaudreuil—correspond to this logic?

According to Ginguené, Chamfort's verbal superiority rendered him more indulgent toward the nobles whose company he kept: "He found their faults and absurdities less unbearable since he had acquired the privilege, and it even came to be an honor among them to be provoked by him."[167] But his literary friends were indignant: "At the same time that he was telling us in twenty piquant ways that all the folk at court were sots, insolent oppressors, base knaves, greedy sycophants, and their women natterers and strumpets, he talked about Mme Jules, Mme Diane, the Duc de Polignac, the Bishop of Autun and M. Saisseval, and above all about M. de Vaudreuil, whose dinner companion and entertainer he was, as infinitely worthy people, of the loveliest character, of the best, most profound, and finest wit."[168] The contradiction was obvious, but pride was not the only thing behind it. That society, shiftless and arbitrary, composed of "automatons" and "marionettes" condemned to play out again and again the same comedy, that "performance of madness and vice that they call *le monde*,"[169] outraged him, yet exerted a magnetic attraction. He surprised himself by appreciating, in spite of his best intentions, the fine taste of the actors and the aptness of their repartee—he laughed at their extravagances, and found himself astonished by their limitless freedom of spirit. His encounter with Vaudreuil drove him to live out these contradictions to the very end. Stronger than the "inequality of conditions," their friendship had knocked down "the barrier separating souls that belong together":[170] it allowed him to feel perfectly at ease in the most luxurious of houses, and to admire unreservedly in the Enchanter everything condemned by his ideological program. In Chamfort's eyes, Vaudreuil embodied the quintessence of aristocratic style in its mythical dimension, beyond the reach of the verdict of history. Handsome in spite of the marks left on him by smallpox, he represented in his elegance, brio, contempt for money, and libertine reputation everything that Chamfort had wanted at the age of twenty, when he had earned the nickname "Hercules Adonis." Now that he had reached his forties, he could not help admiring the Comte's enlightened patronage, his quest for aesthetic perfection, and the exquisiteness of his manners. By giving him his friendship, Vaudreuil had worked his most powerful enchantment. Yet, by offering Chamfort an idealized image in which to see himself reflected, Vaudreuil allowed his friend to exorcise his maternal rejection and to see without resentment what he might have become, had fate not decreed otherwise.

For two years the mansion on the rue de la Chaise was the "Abbaye de Thélème"—Rabelais's imaginary cloister, in which the sole law is "Do what you will"—where Chamfort was able to live his double identity with a degree of comfort. Wasn't "complete friendship" the thing that developed "all the qualities of soul and mind"?[171] And the delicate friendship offered to him by the Enchanter—so delicate that it might be "wounded by the wilting of a rose"[172]—shielded him from any suspicion of inferiority. Moreover, Chamfort, always so jealous of his independence, had accepted the honorific position of secretary-interpreter for the Swiss regiment under the command of d'Artois and an increase in the annual pension he had been awarded for *Mustapha*.[173] When Vaudreuil expressed his chagrin that they weren't close enough friends for the writer to ask him for a loan, Chamfort was comfortable enough financially to reply: "I promise to borrow twenty-five louis from you once you've paid your debts."[174]

While continuing to preserve his distinctness from Vaudreuil and his guests, Chamfort sublimated his aggression into playfulness, offering them—and himself—the pleasure of performing with authentic virtuosity. Though he denounced Vaudreuil's guests and the theatrical character of their high-society amusements, he was willing to make a spectacle of himself for their sake. Noël Aubin has left us a description of the mansion on the rue de la Chaise at the height of its splendor: "There [Chamfort] thrived as an original, coming off well in contrast to the men who all resembled each other in their amiability, the graciousness of their wit, and their high-society tone. He was a sort of bear who only becomes tame when onstage. Then one would obtain from him a thousand fine turns of phrase, a thousand witticisms. In that company he read rapid aperçus, stories full of finesse, of lightness, of malice. Every stroke he threw off hit its mark and was immediately jotted down; on that select group of listeners nothing was lost that showed the least trace of the grace and charm of its author. It was for that company that he conceived the idea of composing the Soirées of Ninon, which he recited there, in verse whose loss we cannot regret enough. . . . It had an Attic salt to it, grace united with savoir faire; its facility hid a great deal of art, and gave it the seal of perfection."[175] Unfortunately, these verses, stories, and "striking verbal portraits,"[176] as well as his reinterpretation of the previous century through the letters of Ninon de Lenclos, have not come down to us.

Even if Chamfort had renounced publication after the failure of *Mustapha and Zéangir*, he had by no means ceased to write. On the contrary, the humiliation he had endured liberated him from the literary conventions he had previously been in thrall to. The striving scholarship boy had finally found an authentic voice. He was composing an account of contemporary reality stripped of theatrical or novelistic artifice—neither a philosophical nor a moralistic work, nor even a straightforward journalistic chronicling. He had realized that the form best suited to the "mimetic representation of a worldly society deprived of its senses"[177] was the fragment. From the end of the 1770s, he jotted down hundreds of pages of maxims, reflections, anecdotes, and portraits, illuminating and dissecting the customs of his age. Ginguené was convinced that Chamfort ultimately intended to organize these thousands of pieces into a one-of-a-kind mosaic. And when, at his friend's death, he decided to publish whatever had survived the ransacking of the manuscripts, he took the hint provided by a sheet recovered from among the papers, titling the work *Products of the Perfected Civilization.*

It was a title that reflected Chamfort's varied layers of perception. After all, in the rue de la Chaise he had enjoyed a privileged position—there he had come to understand that the worldliness surrounding him was not necessarily artificial, but that, at its best, with its studied nonchalance (its grace, and exquisite manners), it might be capable of revitalizing a way of life that was now only the vestige of the original ideal that had inspired it. Of course, this wasn't enough to justify the existence of the alienated society they inhabited— but even as he condemned it, Chamfort could not help following its agonies with fascination and, while giving an account of it, "helping it to die."[178]

La Bruyère had observed the lives of the great from a distance imposed by his subaltern position, convinced of the need for a social hierarchy with impassable borders. La Rochefoucauld had taken the virtues and vices of the society to which he had the honor of belonging as the unit of measure for human nature. But Chamfort appropriated the literary form whose extraordinary effectiveness these two great moralists had revealed, reversing their metaphysical conception of man as a prisoner of his natural egotism and the rigidity of the social order. In his view it was absolutism that had made France a country without history. Chamfort's field of inquiry was limited to the society of his own time—it did not encompass humanity as a whole. In focusing on the particular, on the revealing detail, he wanted to capture the influence that social and political institutions exerted on behavior, and show how abuse generated corruption.[179] It was precisely by way of the division, the "deconstruction" of the social body into thousands of fragments, that the "ultimate and integral truth of the monarchy,"[180] all the proof of its inability to govern, could finally be revealed.

We do not know at what point Chamfort told Vaudreuil about the plans for a constitutional monarchy which he had debated at Talleyrand's *petite maison* in the rue de Bellechasse with his friends Narbonne, Choiseul-Gouffier, Lauzun, and Lauraguais; or those plans even more radical that he had been hatching with Mirabeau, with whom he had been fast friends since 1780. Whenever it may have been, Chamfort gave Vaudreuil *On Lettres de Cachet and the State's Prisons*, a pamphlet that Mirabeau had written drawing on his own personal experiences. Vaudreuil in turn communicated it to Louis XVI, who, "impressed at the extent of his own [royal] powers,"[181] ordered the closing of the keep where Mirabeau, among others, had been imprisoned. We can be certain that Chamfort habitually discussed politics with the Enchanter without bothering to conceal his convictions. He himself recalled that they were frequently of opposite opinions, and evoked in particular their "very lively discussion" in the summer of 1786 on Calonne's project of fiscal reform; nonetheless, they never stopped "listening to and loving each other."[182] When Necker convened the Second Assembly of Notables in November 1788 to decide the composition of the Estates General, the Comte asked Chamfort to draft a pamphlet arguing against the Third Estate's aim of doubling the size of its representation to counterbalance those of the clergy and the nobility. (Chamfort had obliged him once already by penning an effective anticlerical bagatelle.)[183] But the moment for theoretical discussions had come to an end— now it was time to choose sides. "Vaudreuil thought and spoke like all the men of his caste,"[184] while Chamfort aligned himself with his own kind in the name of the nation as a whole. The letter that he wrote to his friend to decline the request marked a point of no return in their relationship:

> I assure you it would be impossible for me write anything witty or pleasant on so serious a subject as this. This is not the moment to take up the stylus of Swift or Rabelais, as we approach, perhaps, disaster.... Indeed, what is at stake? A suit pitting twenty-four million men against seven hundred thousand of the privileged.... Don't you see that such a monstrous order of things must be changed, if all of us, clergy, nobility, Third Estate, aren't to perish together?... They talk about the danger of the Third Estate gaining too much influence; they even go so far as to say the word *democracy*. Democracy! In a land where the people possesses not even the smallest scrap of executive power! In a land where the paltriest servant of authority finds nothing but obedience, and often enough abjection, wherever he looks! Where royal power has encountered obstacles only in those bodies whose members are all either recent or long-standing

nobles! Where the most unbridled luxury and monstrous inequality of wealth will always leave too great a gap between man and man!... Why not straightforwardly say, as some do: 'I don't want to pay?' I beg you not to judge others by yourself. I know that if you had five or six hundred thousand livres of income from your lands, you would be the first to tax yourself faithfully and rigorously.... And that's the way they reconcile their conscience to making the oppression of the weak the patrimony of the strong, making the most revolting injustice a sacred right, making tyranny a duty.... And you want me to write! Ah! I would write only to reiterate my contempt and horror for such principles; I would fear that the feeling for humanity that so pervades me would inspire me with a fluency capable of enflaming souls already too heated; I would fear doing evil through excess of love for the good. I am afraid of the future.[185]

Here, in his indignation, Chamfort dramatically changes his register: abandoning his epigrammatic style, the classical moralist—who relies on the critical intelligence of the reader to interpret the often ambiguous data of his "objective" inquiry—gives way to an orator with a genius for distillation, whose conclusions admit no reply. Driven by the urgency of opening the Enchanter's eyes, the writer summarizes the true significance of the divisions that are tearing the country apart. His "suit pitting twenty-four million men against seven hundred thousand of the privileged" armed the Revolution with a battle cry destined to go down in history. But when he attempted one last time to appeal to the most noble part of Vaudreuil's personality, he allowed his feelings to speak with tremendous delicacy:

I beg you, in the name of our tender friendship, not to take too strong a position on this matter. I know the depths of your soul; but I also know the means they will use to draw you to support the anti-popular side. Let me appeal to the noble part of that soul I love—to your sensibility, to your generous humanity. Is it nobler to pledge your fealty to a small group of men, respectable though they may be, than to a whole nation, however long debased? Having won its liberty at last, that nation will bless the names of those who came to its aid, but may well show itself severe, if not unjust, to those who have stood against it.... I cry to you from the depths of my cell, as I would from the tomb... as your most tenderly devoted friend, one who has always loved you for yourself.... In speaking to you so frankly, I am fulfilling a noble duty of friendship;

I hope that you will take it for what it is, the expression and proof of the affection that binds me to all that is lovable and honest in you, and to those virtues I would like others to appreciate as much as I do myself.[186]

But imprudence had always been Vaudreuil's watchword, and it was far too late to shield himself from danger. Chamfort's fears were well founded, and ten months later, the Enchanter would take the path of exile.

1789

THE LETTER THAT CHAMFORT WROTE to Vaudreuil in December 1788 went straight to the heart of the political debate over institutions that had engrossed France for three months, and whose outcome would decide the fate of the nation.

On September 25 the Parliament of Paris registered the convocation of the Estates General decreed by the King for January of the following year, thereby declaring itself in favor of the procedures that had been adopted in 1614. But the Third Estate immediately rose up in opposition, invoking natural rights and the equality of all citizens—the bourgeoisie and the people (Chamfort's "twenty-four million") were determined to obtain representation equal to that of the other two orders combined. Thus, on October 5, Necker—who had been back at the Ministry of Finance since the end of August—once again convened an Assembly of Notables in order to decide the forms according to which the Estates General would carry out their mandate.

If Louis XVI had only resigned himself to convoking "the representation" due to the urgency of the financial crisis, for many Frenchmen the "act of representing"[1] now took on a new political significance—they saw in the reunion of the Estates General the opportunity, so long desired, of proposing necessary structural reforms for the nation. Far from being a purely technical issue, the debate over the rules that would guide the proceedings inflamed public opinion. The Society of Thirty was immediately formed[2] in order to find the best solution. This "conspiracy of honest men,"[3] brought together at the initiative of parliamentary magistrate Adrien-Jean-François Duport, with the assistance of Mirabeau, included numerous magistrates, among them parliamentary authorities like Duval d'Eprémesnil, followers of the Enlightenment like Condorcet, Chamfort, and Sieyès, as well as members of the liberal nobility: Lauzun, who helped Duport and Mirabeau found the society, as well as Lafayette, the Vicomte de Noailles, the Lameth brothers, La Rochefoucauld-Liancourt, and Talleyrand. For all of them, it was a means of continuing the "crusade" that had begun in America: "They were courtiers against the court, aristocrats against privilege, officers who wanted to replace dynastic with national patriotism."[4]

Despite their differences of opinion, the Thirty were all monarchists—but for the most part they admitted that the ancient laws of the kingdom were an absurd anachronism, and were convinced that it would be necessary to draft a constitution and recognize the equal rights of all citizens. Their immediate preoccupation was preparing for elections and establishing a sample petition of grievances that could be distributed as a model to the various bailiwicks. When it came to finance and the economy, it was the guru of the rue de Belle-chasse, the banker Panchaud, who led the way, proposing policies diametrically opposed to Necker's. And if the Duc d'Orléans, who for his part presided over the Club de Valois, did not personally take part in the sessions, he was kept informed by Laclos.

Thanks to the pressure of d'Eprémesnil, on December 5, the parliament adopted a neutral position on the problem of the Third Estate's representation, while the Notables declined to recognize the principle of numerical equality except for deliberation over taxes. "To permit a people to protect its money, and to steal from it the right to influence the laws that will determine its honor and its life, is an insult, a mockery,"[5] fumed Chamfort—but the battle had only just begun.

The writer had thrown himself into the struggle with great enthusiasm, and without a shred of personal ambition, adopting the role of secret adviser. It was Chamfort, for instance, who suggested to the Abbé Sieyès the title of the most famous political pamphlet in French history: *What Is the Third Estate?*[6] Published at the beginning of the following year, the third in a series of dazzling texts composed over the course of three months,[7] this opuscule opened with three fateful questions: "What is the Third Estate? Everything. What has it been up until now in the political order? Nothing. What does it want to be? Something," and went on to define the nation as "a body of associates living under a common law and represented by the same legislature," whose general will had the force of law. With this text, the revolution that Chamfort had evoked in such vague terms to Vaudreuil a few weeks earlier stepped onto the stage with the rhetoric and political program to which it would hold going forward.

Before the end of the year,[8] the Council of Ministers decided to double the representatives of the Third Estate in the Estates General, and announced that the number of deputies would be as far as possible proportional to the population and to the taxes of each bailiwick. "The fact of the matter was, the number of deputies was not in the least decisive so long as each order agreed separately and maintained an equal voice,"[9] but in terms of principles, it was already a resounding victory.

"Ah, Monsieur le Duc!" Mirabeau wrote to his friend Lauzun, mad with joy, "let us join the Estates General, no matter what the cost; we shall lead them, and have such great pleasures there that all the toys of the court will be nothing in comparison."[10]

Lauzun needed nobody's encouragement. He had been initiated at an early age into political thought by Choiseul, and in the course of his numerous voyages had acquired direct experience of the characteristics and methods of government of the various European monarchies. His sojourns in England and the American expedition had definitively turned his sympathies in the direction of a constitutional monarchy founded on the balance of power and the guarantee of equality of civil and political rights for all citizens—a society open to individual initiative and merit. Since his return from the United States, he had discussed with his friends—in his own *petite maison* in Montrouge, at Talleyrand's, or with the Duc d'Orléans at the Palais-Royal, and now with the Society of Thirty—the sort of reforms that France needed. The gravity of the economic, financial, and political crisis that had struck the country, and the government's incapacity to remedy the situation, finally offered him the chance to take action. Thus the Duc entered the realm of politics with the same enthusiasm, ideals, and need for affirmation or revenge as many of his old friends who were now taking the same path as he. But he needed an intellectual mentor with whom to put himself in dialogue—as he had earlier with the Marquis de Voyer d'Argenson—and for this role he chose Mirabeau, who for his part had selected Chamfort as his own mentor. Lauzun had met Mirabeau in 1769 in Corsica, where the two had served together in the army dispatched by Choiseul to suppress Paoli's insurrection. Lauzun had been twenty-two years old, Mirabeau twenty, and though at first glance they could not have seemed more different, they became fast friends. The nephew of a great minister, already promoted to the rank of officer himself, and enjoying general esteem, Lauzun was, as we know, handsome, elegant, a perfect man of the world, while Mirabeau, with his massive body and pockmarked face, had decidedly plebeian manners. At the time, the former envisaged a prestigious career for himself, had an immense fortune at his disposal, and was already famous for his amorous exploits. The latter, treated like a pariah by his tyrannical father, lacked the means to support himself and was given over to debauchery. Still, plenty of things tied them together: they were both in conflict with their families, and if Mirabeau gave himself up unrestrainedly to every excess while Lauzun concealed his strife and vices behind the perfection of his style, the bitterness of their rejections was similarly intense. Mirabeau had been repudiated by his legitimate father, Lauzun had never been recognized by his illegitimate father, and both had been subjected to the violence of their respective parents. Thus they had decided to depend on no one but themselves, to reinvent their existence in their own image—rebels against the rules of a patriarchal society that had abused each of them since their youth.

Lauzun "was immediately fascinated by sublieutenant Pierre Buffière [as Mirabeau was also known], blinded by his passion and ardor,"[11] while Mirabeau admired the audacity and chivalrous spirit with which the Duc threw himself into his first military expedition. Both of them sought to win the favor of the lovely Mme Chardon, the young wife of the Intendant of Corsica, and whether or not it was true, both men—brothers in libertinism—claimed to have succeeded. They met once again in Paris at the beginning of the 1780s, at the home of Panchaud, and undeterred by the scandalous reputation that Mirabeau had acquired, Lauzun presented him to Talleyrand, sang his praises to Orléans, recommended him to Calonne, loaned him money, and covered for his misdeeds. With the Duc's help, Mirabeau, despite his pariah status, was able to meet and exercise a growing influence on those who hoped for reforms capable of saving the monarchy by bringing it into conformity with present needs. After the failure of Calonne's policies, Mirabeau was absolutely certain that, in order to escape from institutional paralysis, it would be necessary to rebuild the state by creating an opposing power capable of sweeping away the intrigues of the court and ministerial "despotism." The convocation of the Estates General was the opportunity he had been waiting for.

Up until now, in the academies, the salons, and the private clubs, there had flowed whole rivers of words; Mirabeau opted instead for action. In order to win his nomination as deputy, which was initially denied him due to his rank, he set all Provence aflame with his eloquence, imposed himself upon local authorities, had himself elected as representative of the people, and returned to Paris in triumph. Jacques de Norvins, twenty years old at the time, never forgot the emotion roused in him by the "sublime and terrible words" that

Mirabeau addressed to the Provençal nobles who resisted adding him to their list: "Thus the last of the Gracchi perished at the hands of the patricians. Yet before he died, he hurled a handful of dust toward the heavens and called for their vengeance, and from that dust was born Marius—Marius, who was greater for having annihilated the aristocracy of Rome than for having exterminated the Cimbri."[12] Lauzun, too, recognized that Mirabeau was a genuine political genius, and was drawn along in the wake of his audacity. He ran as deputy for the nobility of Quercy, and was elected with a strong majority. Thus he began the final chapter of his life bearing the name of Biron, which he had assumed upon the death of his uncle. And it is by that name that we will refer to him from this point on.

Unlike Biron and Mirabeau, the Chevalier de Boufflers had not obtained an assignment to Corsica, but the armed struggle of Pasquale Paoli against the Genevans had filled him with admiration. Unaware that control of the island was about to pass to the French,[13] he had confided to the Duchesse de Choiseul: "I have always dreamed about revolutions; I will be pleased to see that poor people shrug off such a horrible yoke." And a man like Paoli, whose sole ambition was to "secure the freedom of his nation," struck him as "a worthy successor to the Romans, and the greatest of Romans at that."[14] He had always imagined antiquity as a kind of ideal homeland, a haven from the frustrations inflicted on him by a regime that valued favor over merit. In Senegal, at his moments of greatest distress, he liked to imagine that if he'd been born a Roman or an Athenian, he would have been able to show what he was worth. Now that everyone had begun to tout the virtues and freedoms of antiquity as models for a French renaissance, Boufflers could finally hope that his "revolutionary dreams" would become a reality. Early on, the Chevalier had expressed his admiration for those countries that enjoyed "the pleasure of making their own laws," and where the earth was cultivated by "free hands."[15] His independent spirit had been bolstered by the pro-parliamentary and anti-absolutist politics of his uncle Beauvau, and by the challenge to royal authority launched by the Choiseul clan, and his experience in Senegal struck him as definitive proof that the monarchy would not allow its administrators to fulfill their mandate with efficiency and dignity. For that matter, many of his friends shared his opinions and encouraged him to embrace, as they had, a "bourgeois" career, so as to free himself from the arbitrariness of royal favor. When the Chevalier finally took his place among the deputies of the Estates General as representative of the nobility of Lorraine, it seemed as if his "revolutionary dreams" were visible on the horizon.

Detained by his duties in Russia until the autumn of 1789, Louis-Philippe de Ségur was unable to be present for the elections, and delegated to his brother the task of defending their shared liberal faith. In reality, the Vicomte had no other option. *Gentilhomme d'honneur* to the Duc d'Orléans, to whom he was tied by both family and friendship, and patron of Laclos, Joseph-Alexandre found himself at the "epicenter"[16] of the merciless personal war that the First Prince of the Blood had declared on Louis XVI and Marie-Antoinette. By launching his own candidacy first, Orléans aimed to support the election to the assembly of as many of his own partisans as possible, in order to counterbalance those of Versailles. Like other intimates of the Palais-Royal, the Vicomte presented himself as a candidate. The Prince achieved a resounding victory, and Ségur was elected as alternate delegate, with a good chance of taking part, sooner or later, in the work of the Estates General. Joseph-Alexandre lacked his brother's idealism and, profoundly skeptical, devoted the best of himself to irreverent criticism and mockery, political ambition taking second place to his literary aspirations. Yet he was well aware that, beyond its rancor and desire for revenge, the party of Orléans could contribute significantly to the formation of a constitutional monarchy capable of responding to the country's need for renewal. His view was shared by Besenval, who had distanced himself from the Polignacs, but still had to recognize that "it was impossible to take advantage of that prince, or to lead him to play a role that his position and riches would have made so simple for him."[17]

At the time of the convocation of the Estates General, the Comte de Narbonne hoped to take part as well, but all his attempts were fruitless. Still, he was too high-minded to be jealous of his elected friends, and continued assiduously to see Lafayette, Talleyrand, Biron, Mirabeau, and the Lameth brothers, assuring them of his support. Mme de Staël busied herself consoling him for this exclusion, reserving him a place of honor at her salon in the rue du Bac, home of the most influential political coterie in Paris. It is worth noting that Narbonne was the only one among his friends to become a minister under Louis XVI.

Having been wounded by the government's decision two years earlier to loudly exclude him from the Assembly of Notables, the Duc de Brissac did not stand as candidate to represent the nobility of Anjou at the Estates General.

He remained faithful to his sovereign, convinced that the nobles would not cling to an anachronistic defense of their privileges.

For his part, the Comte de Vaudreuil saw the convocation of the Estates General as an attack on royal authority, and a plot by Necker to vanquish the resistance of the court. And in a sense, events would prove him right.

The first months of 1789 were devoted to the preparation for the Estates General in a climate of feverish expectation. France was inundated with hundreds of publications on the great political experiment now underway—opinion was intensely divided, and the future unclear. Tormented by glacial cold and beset by a cruel lack of work, the Parisian population—swelled by an influx of poor from the provinces—was suffering the consequences of the disastrous harvest of the previous year and, despite the efforts of Necker, found itself threatened with famine. And yet, recalled Mme de La Tour du Pin, "never had we [in society] been so disposed to amuse ourselves, with no concern for the misery of the public"[18]—while Norvins would pithily illustrate the unexpected epilogue of that final season of high society: "There was dancing that winter throughout Paris, and the nobility had everything to lose, and the bourgeoisie had everything to gain."[19]

True to form, the Vicomte de Ségur began the year by reciting a set of couplets in praise of the Abbé Barthélemy, the author of *The Travels of Anacharsis the Younger in Greece*, on the occasion of a party given by Mme de La Reynière. "*Grâce à l'auteur on oublie / Tous les malheurs du moment, / Le passé par son génie / Nous console du présent*,"*[20] the poem concluded, even though Joseph-Alexandre was fully aware that, more than a mere consolation, the past had become the key to understanding a present that he himself was tirelessly chronicling in verse. This was demonstrated once again when he invited to his home a dozen or so days later a young playwright, Marie-Joseph Chénier, who gave a reading of his *Charles IX, or, The School of Kings*, a tragedy that had been banned by the censors for the past two years. There was nothing surprising about that, since the play—centering on the massacre of the Huguenots on the eve of St. Bartholomew's Day two centuries earlier—virulently denounced the joint responsibility of king and clergy for the atrocity. And it mattered little that

*Thanks to this author, all / Of the moment's woes are forgotten, / With its genius, the past / Consoles the present.

the reigning dynasty at the time had been that of the Valois, since the accusation was ultimately being leveled against the "unconstrained" power of the absolute monarchy. Still, those in attendance—including such distinguished guests as the Duchesse d'Orléans and Prince Henry of Prussia—found the play "admirable."[21] Eleven months later, driven by a wave of public opinion that Ségur's support had reinforced, *Charles IX* finally arrived on the stage of the Théâtre-Français.[22] The show owed its triumph to Talma, the young actor who had stolen the favors of Julie Careau from the Vicomte. His revolutionary performance as the degenerate and criminal King[23] inaugurated the age of the romantic theater in France. The polemics unleashed by the show led not only to the abolition of the royal censorship but also to the breakup of the theatrical company. On November 4, Camille Desmoulins, present in the auditorium, declared that *Charles IX* would do more to serve the cause of the Revolution than the October Days.

In those first months of 1789, the Vicomte participated in discussions at the Palais-Royal regarding the instructions that the Duc d'Orléans intended to give to the representatives of his bailiwicks. Their drafting was entrusted to Laclos, but the Duc, dissatisfied, asked Sieyès—to whom Biron had introduced him in great secrecy at Montrouge—to revise the text. The Abbé preferred to write an altogether new intervention, and his *Deliberations*, "a genuine political program,"[24] were published at the same time as Laclos's *Instructions*. Taking up once again the theses of his previous writings, Sieyès affirmed that the purpose of the Estates General was to give France a constitution, and that the Third Estate, "sole custodian of the national will," would play a determinant role there.

The success of this pamphlet, which reached a print run of one hundred thousand, only increased Orléans's popularity among Parisians. It is true that in the course of that terrible winter the Prince had distinguished himself by his generosity, distributing supplies, water, and money to the poor, the unemployed, widows, orphans, and the homeless. Moreover, thanks to the real-estate operation that had transformed the Palais-Royal into a vast center of attention, he could consider himself the true King of Paris. On three sides of his gardens the Duc had had long galleries constructed, whose arcades sheltered restaurants, cafés, reading rooms and gaming parlors, and shops selling luxury goods and fashionable knickknacks; there was even a circus on the esplanade in front of the palace. Upstairs, luxurious rooms were available for rent, apartments of all sizes and for all budgets. It was a city within a city, where, depending on the time of day, one ran across placid bourgeois families and common people, laboring men and idlers, intellectuals and students, gamblers, thieves, and prostitutes. Above all, it was a mirror of the populace's mood, a zone of liberty where news—whether true or false—circulated without restraint and where everyone could speak freely. "There one can see all, hear all, learn all," wrote Mercier, not without a certain uneasiness, in 1783: "all day long the cafés brim with men whose only occupation is to deliver or listen to the latest news, which one no longer even recognizes thanks to the excess of color imparted to it by each speaker, depending on his state of mind."[25] At the time of that transformation, Louis XVI had teased his cousin by bemoaning the fact that his new activities as a *boutiquier* prevented him from coming to spend the weekend at Versailles. But soon enough the King perceived that the Palais-Royal was becoming a kind of anti-Versailles,[26] a center of power even more influential than that sanctuary of the monarchy erected by the Sun King a short distance from the capital.

The first six months of 1789 were Orléans's moment of glory. The day of the opening of the Estates General, he chose his side: "The position of deputy, rather than that of prince."[27] "To shield himself against all reproach, he had the applause of his heart, his flatterers, and the philosophical friend of equality [Mirabeau]."[28] In a brief span of time he had fully embraced the role of the enlightened, liberal prince, defender of the rights of the people. It was a role that belonged to him by family tradition,[29] one that he had been called to take up by his circle, and in whose name he set himself up in opposition—as potential regent? as lieutenant general of the kingdom? as substitute king?—against his reigning cousin. But ultimately he lacked the character, the energy, and the moral fiber for the task. The Orléanist faction continued to use him to lead the liberal monarchist fight up until the proclamation of the Republic,[30] but "after the instructions were transmitted to his bailiwicks" he ceased to be for Talleyrand "an active political personage.... He was neither the principal, the object, nor the motive of the Revolution. The impetuous torrent carried him off like the others."[31]

The Vicomte de Ségur was quick to distance himself from a political program that seemed far too risky. The democratic spirit was not his strong suit. He had a horror of populism, and decided to oppose himself to Orléans in the very bosom of the Palais-Royal, on a field where he feared no rival: the conquest of the fair sex.

The Duchesse d'Orléans had always submitted herself to the will of her husband. But from the moment the Duc made public his new relationship with Mme Buffon (meanwhile allowing Mme de Genlis to monopolize the affection of their children and to make decisions about their behavior) and, most important, fully revealed his lack of loyalty to the King, the Duchesse, a direct lineal descendant of Louis XIV, began to distance herself from a man who had once tenderly loved her. Supported by her close friend the Marquise de Chastellux, who, still a widow, had become her lady-in-waiting, the Duchesse d'Orléans hoisted the flag of dynastic and religious tradition, to the applause of those loyal to the House of Orléans who no longer recognized themselves in the Duc's decisions.

Like his father, the Maréchal de Ségur, and his stepsister, the Comtesse de Ségur (beloved niece of the Marquis de Chastellux[32] and now a close friend of his widow), the Vicomte decided to take the Duchesse's side and encourage her to resist. His assiduity was certainly motivated by the hope, though vague, that by taking a strong position the Duchesse d'Orléans would be able to slow her husband's perilous headlong rush. But it is also explained by the Duchesse's feminine charms, still intact despite her numerous pregnancies and her thirty-five years ("she seemed perpetually eighteen," the Duchesse de Chaulnes had declared), as well as by the radiant beauty of Mme de Chastellux. Which of the two women did the Vicomte prefer? It is difficult to say, even if, thanks to the journal of Gouverneur Morris, we are able to follow his visits to Palais-Royal day by day, over the course of two years.

A confidant of George Washington and one of the principal authors of the American Constitution, Morris was thirty-seven years old, with a ruggedly handsome face and a wooden leg, when he arrived in Paris in February 1789, charged by his government with negotiating the terms of reimbursement for the American debt. From March 7, 1789, until November 6, 1789, he incisively recorded his various encounters and impressions, supplying a cool and penetrating chronicle of the "work in progress" of the Revolution. This privileged witness is particularly valuable for our purposes because he was in close contact with Lafayette, Talleyrand, the two Ségur brothers, Narbonne, Mme de Staël, and their friends, and provided forceful judgments on all of them. He will aid us in tracking them through certain key moments in the revolutionary chronology.

On March 27, Morris made the acquaintance of the Vicomte de Ségur at the home of the Baron de Besenval, and they quickly became friends. In the eyes of Joseph-Alexandre, Morris, with his dignity, austere dress, and "air of

Republican equality,"[33] embodied the prototype of the American citizen whose praises his brother, Louis-Philippe, had sung upon his return from the United States. The fascination that Ségur exercised on Morris was of the same nature. The elegance and worldly ease of Joseph-Alexandre were the quintessence of the decadent society whose codes the American diplomat would need to decipher in order to carry out his mission. Beyond that, these two pragmatic, disenchanted libertines understood each other instinctively. At once rivals and accomplices, they assiduously courted—each in his own style—the Duchesse d'Orléans and her lady-in-waiting. But we do not know if, by pretending to be in love with Mme de Chastellux, Ségur's intention was to refute those rumors that claimed he had a relationship with the Duchesse, or if he genuinely hoped to win the Marquise's favors. Likewise, we cannot be sure if Morris's hopes of "consoling"[34] the beautiful widow were ever realized. What is certain is that neither Morris nor Ségur had any illusions about Orléans, and strove to infuse into the Duchesse "a Degree of Understanding and Firmness not natural to her"[35] in regard to her husband.

The time that Morris devoted to the fair sex had ends other than the satisfaction of his robust sexual appetites: he had quickly understood that he had arrived in "the land of women,"[36] and that the ladies of high society represented an inexhaustible source of information on the constantly changing stratagems of the various political factions. For example, nothing was more instructive for him than his relationship with Mme de Flahaut, who was as pretty as she was free-spirited. The Comtesse was the mistress of Talleyrand, with whom she had had a son, and her salon provided one of the best political vantage points in the capital. But the company of the Comtesse de Ségur, Mme de Chastellux, and, naturally, Mme de Staël was no less useful. The judgments we find in the American diplomat's *Diary* are remarkable for their precision, beginning with his characterization of the Bishop of Autun as "a sly, cool, cunning and ambitious Man."[37] The portrait of Necker is ferocious: not only is he presumptuous and devoid of real political intelligence but "he has the Look and Manner of the Counting House and being dress in embroidered Velvet he contrasts strongly with his Habiliments. His Bow, his Address &c. say: I am the Man."[38] On the other hand, Morris somewhat revised his verdict on Mme de Staël (whom he had initially dispatched with the observation that she "has very much the Appearance of a Chambermaid"[39]) in order to receive without too much enthusiasm the more or less explicit advances of Germaine; in the end he admitted that she did not lack genius, but that her conversation was far too "brilliant"[40] for him. His friend Lafayette struck him as terribly vain, "very much below the Business he has undertaken," and incapable of "hold[ing] the helm"[41] in case of a storm. He judged that Mirabeau would "always be powerful in Opposition but never great in Administration."[42] As for Narbonne, who vacillated "between the Dictates of his Duty and of his Conscience," Morris could not help responding that, for his part, he knew of no duty but that dictated *by* his conscience—though he suspected that Narbonne's would "dictate to join the strongest Side."[43]

Indeed, if Morris felt that the representatives of the elites were not up to the responsibilities they had proposed for themselves, his judgment on French society as a whole was hardly more reassuring. Despite his libertinism, Morris was the son of a puritan culture on the far side of the ocean, and for him the political strength of a nation resided above all in its morals. In Paris, the unbelievable corruption of the privileged left him speechless. "This unhappy Country," he wrote, "bewildered in the Pursuit of metaphysical whimsies, presents to our moral View a mighty Ruin. Like the Remnants of ancient Magnificence we admire the Architecture of the Temple, while we detest the false God to whom it was dedicated."[44]

Narbonne was not the only one of his rank to question whether he should hark to the call of duty or follow the voice of his conscience. It was a lose-lose dilemma whose nature the republican Morris could not have understood.

On May 6, the day after the solemn opening of the Estates General at Versailles, the Third Estate had demanded the joint verification of the powers of the deputies and, not having obtained it, the National Assembly was constituted on June 17. After having been sworn in, the deputies declared that they had the right to vote on taxes, and were joined two days later by the delegates of the clergy, who had decided to deliberate with the Third Estate. It was the birth of the counterweight that Mirabeau had desired. On June 20, having found the meeting hall barred against their entry, the deputies occupied a tennis court, vowing not to separate until they had given the country a constitution. On June 23, at the end of the formal sitting at which Louis XVI decreed that the three orders should meet separately, the Third Estate and a large part of the clergy refused to leave the hall. Bailly responded to the master of ceremonies, the young Marquis de Dreux-Brézé, who requested that the deputies follow the royal injunction that the assembled nation could not receive such an order. Pressed by Marie-Antoinette and Artois (and not unreasonably convinced that it was his last opportunity to regain control of the situation), Louis XVI also rejected the plan of reforms proposed to him by Necker: voting by head rather than by order, a bicameral system on the English model, fiscal equality, the right of all men to any kind of employment.

For the representatives of the nobility who had hopes for a constitutional monarchy, the moment had come to take sides. In the case of the Chevalier de Boufflers, it was Mme de Sabran who decided his course. In a letter of June 24, clearly upset by the intentions expressed by her lover at the end of the dramatic session of the day before, the Comtesse issued a tearful appeal.

What would you do, my child, in that abominable assembly, if ever your weakness and your too great deference to the perfidious counsels dictated only in the interest of M. Necker and, at your expense, were to carry you away? How great would your humiliation be if that party suffered the fate of all parties opposed to justice and reason? They will perhaps go so far as to be declared in the eyes of all Europe traitors to their King and country. Then the hypocrisy, the deceit, the perfidy, the infernal threats of this abominable Genevese will be seen in their true light—this man whose vanity desired the whole of France for his pedestal without the wings of genius to place and maintain him there. And even if he were to triumph, are the members of that good and ancient nobility, devoted from time immemorial to the honor and preservation of the throne and monarchy of France, to share in such a shameful victory? Is this the sort of victory the Maréchal de Boufflers would have accepted? What would he have said at such a critical moment, and on which side do you think he would stand? . . . In the name, then, of our first friendship, in the name of your best interests and your peace of mind, consult your conscience and remember the blood that flows in your veins. Goodbye, my child, goodbye. I could die of terror at the thought that the dearest part of myself could ever play a part that would make me blush.[45]

The lovers had always differed when it came to politics. A member by marriage of one of the oldest and most illustrious families in the country, having frequented the court since her youth, Mme de Sabran was determined to defend a social position upon which her children's future depended. Her friendship with the Polignacs and her ties to the royal family had been a source of tension with Boufflers, who, regarded with suspicion at Versailles, had paid a high price for his spirit of independence. He took pride in his ostracism at court up until the moment when, hoping one day to marry the woman he loved, he found himself in need of a prestigious appointment. The difficulties that beset him, along with the insistence of Mme de Sabran, had convinced him to accept the assistance of the Polignacs in an attempt to regain the favor of the sovereign. For her part, the Comtesse had cheered the return of Necker in hopes that the Chevalier, a friend of his detestable daughter, might be able to draw some advantage. But despite these reciprocal concessions, Mme de Sabran remained profoundly conservative, while the Chevalier had never shed his support for an enlightened reformism. Indeed, she had always preferred to regard her beloved's liberal and philanthropic convictions as nothing but pleasant pipe dreams, and felt they should remain so. But now, well aware that she would not be able to overcome Boufflers on the field of politics, the Comtesse had decided to do battle in the name of the sentiments that united them rather than the ideas that pushed them apart. It was love that compelled her to remind her lover what should be most important to him: his honor as a gentleman. How could her knight-errant, who had dreamed of the glory that would stir her pride, betray his king at the moment of danger, soiling the glorious name of his family? Without stating explicitly that she would find it difficult to continue to love a man whom she could no longer respect, Mme de Sabran had deployed in her letter those watchwords that would come to define the aristocratic resistance. Honor, respect for one's ancestors, and fidelity to the sovereign had to be placed before any other consideration, leaving aside any political errors the monarchy may have committed. By invoking honor, the Comtesse put Boufflers's back to the wall. She knew that it was his most precious possession, because she had been the first to pay the price for it. Fearful of being seen as a dowry hunter, the Chevalier had refused to marry her, forcing her to make an arrangement with her conscience at the risk of compromising her reputation. Certainly the Chevalier could have responded to his beloved's *j'accuse* by objecting that for him, honor consisted precisely in fighting for a just cause, but he did not have the courage to disappoint her once again by inflicting a wound that he might not be able to heal. Thus, on June 25, when forty-seven representatives of the high nobility, including a number of his friends,[46] went over to the assembly, Boufflers did not follow their example, and declared himself opposed to the gathering of the three orders.

But two days later, when Louis XVI reversed his decision and directed the first two orders to rejoin the Third Estate, Mme de Sabran attacked once more. In her letter of June 24, she urges Boufflers to remain on his guard and not allow himself to be influenced by his friends, because it was the Duc d'Orléans— far more dangerous than Necker—who "infects all minds by means of the crowd in his pay who say all he wishes them to in the Palais-Royal," with the object of "[making] himself, before long, master of the kingdom." On the other side, having forgotten himself, the King had lost all authority and "if he is defended, it will be in spite of himself." With lucid pessimism, the Comtesse was fully aware that "a single day, a single instant, could upend every system, every arrangement, in a revolution established upon madness on one side and weakness on the other."[47]

It was indeed at the Palais-Royal that the popular revolution began. On June 28, a group of soldiers of the Gardes Françaises—an elite corps of 3,600 men tasked with assuring the security of the capital—declared that they would not fire on the crowd under any circumstances. The mutineers were imprisoned at the Abbaye, but freed by the crowd and carried in triumph to the Palais-Royal, they agreed to return to prison for one night, with the assurance that they would be released in the morning. Might the scenario have been different if the soldiers had been commanded by Biron, whom the soldiers adored, rather than by the detested Marquis du Châtelet, the son of the Divine Émilie? Seeing the insubordination of the premier infantry corps of the King's house, the Duc might perhaps have been tempted to think that it was a good lesson for Marie-Antoinette, who had deprived him by pure caprice of a position that had been rightfully his.

As the price of bread, which had been rising since June, reached dizzying new heights, the progressive deployment of troops around the capital alarmed the populace. Ceding to the pressure of his wife, the Comte d'Artois, and the most conservative of his ministers, Louis XVI was determined to impose his authority by force and, on July 11, dismissed Necker without any warning. When he learned of the sacking, Gouverneur Morris ran to beg the minister to present himself at Versailles immediately, in order to warn the King—obviously badly informed—of the gravity of the situation. And when Necker responded that it was too late, Morris insisted: "It is not too late to warn the King of his Danger which is infinitely greater than he imagines. That his Army will not fight against the Nation, and that if he listens to violent Counsels the

Nation will undoubtedly be against him. That the Sword has fallen imperceptibly from his Hand, and that the Sovereignty of this Nation is in the Assemblée National."[48]

Morris's predictions would soon be confirmed, and the first to see the consequences would be the Baron de Besenval.

Louis XVI had dismissed Necker in order to set in motion a counterrevolution prepared behind his minister's back. Hoping to retake control of Paris, the King had entrusted the general command of his troops and the task of creating a security cordon around the capital to the elderly Maréchal de Broglie; at the Maréchal's orders, Besenval's job was to deploy three regiments to strategic points around the city and to step into action in case of revolt. It was a faulty plan right from the beginning, as the Baron would explain in his memoirs, because instead of dispatching a compact army, equipped with artillery and prepared to occupy Paris, the soldiers had been sent en masse without taking account of the fact that the winding alleyways of the old quartiers would not allow for a coordinated military action.

The Baron did not learn of Necker's dismissal until July 12, when the news arrived in the capital, creating panic. It was the beginning of three crucial days for the fate of the country. The Parisians, who saw the Swiss minister as the only one capable of saving them from bankruptcy and famine, immediately spilled into the streets, while at the Palais-Royal, the young Camille Desmoulins leapt onto a table at the Café de Foy and launched his celebrated appeal: "To arms, to arms, citizens! Take up the green cockade, the color of hope!" Instead of preventing the looting of armories, the Gardes Françaises fraternized with the crowd.

Besenval, who has left us his version of the events in his memoirs, at this point ordered his troops to occupy the Place Louis XV—soon to be rebaptized Place de la Révolution—but the soldiers arrived at the same time as the procession of demonstrators carrying busts of Necker and Orléans. The Prince de Lambesc, a cousin of the Queen, who himself commanded the Royal-Allemand Regiment, saw fit to order a charge, transforming a peaceful protest into a riot. At the cry of "The Germans and Swiss are massacring the people!" the crowd bombarded the soldiers with stones, while the Gardes Françaises confronted Lambesc's men. "It was the first moment that an organized armed force had faced the King's soldiers, determined to counterattack. More astonishing still, the *gardes* were in sufficient force to push the cavalry troopers out of the Tuileries altogether. From that point, battle was joined for sovereignty over Paris."[49] Without instructions from Versailles, "which persisted in regarding three hundred thousand mutineers as a crowd, and the revolution as a riot,"[50] Besenval, who had begun to doubt the loyalty of his own troops, ordered his soldiers to withdraw to the Left Bank and reassemble on the Champ de Mars.

The next day, a standing committee of the capital's electors decided to ensure the safety of all Parisians by forming a militia. The arms usually held by the Garde-Meuble were requisitioned, and a delegation went to ask the Marquis Virot de Sombreuil, who commanded the Invalides garrison, to contribute 32,000 muskets. Sombreuil attempted to buy time: he responded that he needed authorization from Versailles and warned Besenval "that, in a word, he could not depend on the Invalides—that, if he were to give the artillerymen the order to load their pieces, they would turn them against their own commander's apartments."[51] Similar messages arrived from the Marquis de Launay, governor of the Bastille, a fortress that Besenval had judged impregnable, and where he had placed the Invalides' supplies of munitions for safekeeping.

During the night of July 13, the insurgents burned forty of the fifty-four customs *barrières* that controlled the entry of goods into the capital, and plundered the stores of foodstuffs at the monastery of Saint-Lazare. On the morning of July 14, after having vainly called for instructions from Broglie, Besenval met with his general staff in order to decide what course of action to pursue. The general opinion was that "this ferment had become impossible to suppress. All the more so, in that our troops were visibly shaken; that they fraternized with the enemy in spite of our vigilance; and that a colonel assured me, with tears in his eyes, that his regiment was refusing to march."[52]

The same morning, the crowd invaded the Invalides without encountering the least resistance from the garrison and, having seized muskets and cannons, headed toward the Bastille to plunder its stockpile of munitions. Convinced that Launay would be able to defend it, Besenval remained at the Champ de Mars, where a message arrived from Du Puget, the King's lieutenant at the Bastille, demanding that he send to the fortress's governor (who was too inclined to surrender) the formal order to defend it, come what may. Besenval's response, intercepted and read aloud by the enraged mob, confirmed: "M. de Launay will hold to his last breath: I have sent him sufficient reinforcements."[53] It was not until the end of the day that he learned that the Bastille had been taken, and that the crowd now meant to converge on the Champ de Mars in order to chase him and his men from the capital. Under the threat of the cannon that the Gardes Françaises had placed on the opposite bank of the Seine, "weakened by defection and certain to be good for nothing,"[54] Besenval fell back to Sèvres without waiting for the Maréchal de Broglie's orders. Thus ended "that terrible day, which displayed the full force of the people, and the full extent of the court's peril."[55]

The Baron de Besenval was sixty-eight years old and, despite his indisputable courage, ended his career by taking responsibility for ordering the most humiliating of retreats without firing a shot. "Had I engaged the troops in Paris," he justified himself in his memoirs, "I would have ignited a civil war. Precious blood would have been shed, regardless of the side on which it flowed, to no good public end. All things considered, I thought the wisest course of action was to withdraw the troops and leave Paris to herself. This was what I decided to do, around one o'clock in the morning."[56] Malicious tongues didn't fail to insinuate that the reason Besenval hadn't joined the battle during the assault against the Invalides was to avoid the plundering of his beautiful home, nearby in the rue de Grenelle.[57]

It was the Duc de La Rochefoucauld-Liancourt, *grand maître de la garde-robe*, who, arriving at Versailles late in the evening, informed Louis XVI of the fall of the Bastille, and of the terrible fate of the Marquis de Launay and the *prévôt des marchands*, whose severed heads had been carried in triumph on pikes. It was in fact the Duc—to whom the famous retort "Sire, it is not a revolt but a revolution" was attributed—who convinced the King to present himself the following day to the National Assembly, in the company of his brothers, to announce the withdrawal of the troops massed around the capital. And it was he as well who asked his good friend Talleyrand[58] to compose the palinode that the King was obliged to read before the assembly. Drafted by the Bishop of Autun such that it might be adapted as needed, this clever appeal for the deputies to pull together in the greater interests of the nation elated all and sundry. Delivering it with a bare head, Louis XVI acknowledged the fact of the assembly's sovereignty, superior to his own authority. It was a definitive defeat for the most intransigent partisans of the divine right of the monarchy. "I give my opinion," Morris reports in his diary, "that, after what is passed, the Count d'Artois should not be suffered to stay in France."[59] The following day, July 16, the King announced the dismissal of Breteuil, Louis XVI's secret plenipotentiary in Belgium, as well as the recall of Necker to the Ministry of Finance, and, again at the entreaty of La Rochefoucauld-Liancourt, on July 17 he presented himself in person in Paris to reconcile with its inhabitants. In keeping with the tradition of royal "*entrées*," the brand-new mayor, Jean-Sylvain Bailly, awaited him at the Porte de Chaillot in order to offer him the keys to the city—the very same keys, he was careful to specify, that had been handed to Henri IV when he had "reconquered his people." Now, however, it was Paris that had "reconquered its King." After being reminded, even if under the auspices of a tribute, that his visit represented a surrender to the will of the people, Louis approached the town hall beneath the crossed swords of the Garde Nationale, over whom Lafayette had taken command, and allowed Bailly to pin the *cocarde tricolore* to his hat. Only then did the crowd cry out in unison: "*Vive le roi!*" For Louis XVI, Norvins would later recall, that visit to Paris, "when he was forced to leave off his family colors and crown and take up those of the Revolution, was the first station of his cavalry. He returned to Versailles bearing on his hat the symbol of his dynastic death."[60] Morris, for his part, observed that if the King hadn't been so weak, that day would have served as a useful lesson for the rest of his life. Under the sway of bad advisers, however, "it [was] impossible he should not act wrongly."[61]

That same day, Gouverneur Morris notes that "the Count D'Artois, the Duke and Duchess of Polignac, Monsr. de Vaudreuil, and in short the whole Committee Polignac, have decamped last Night in Despair," and adds, not without malice: "Travelling may be useful to the Count D'Artois and therefore it would be well if he visited foreign Countries."[62] It was a timely decision, to say the least. A partisan of strong-arm tactics, and the target of numerous libels, Artois was, along with the Polignacs—as Chamfort had predicted during his days with Vaudreuil[63]—at the head of the *listes de proscription* of enemies of the people that had circulated between July 13 and 14 beneath the arcades of the Palais-Royal. Not only was the King no longer in a position to guarantee the safety of his brother and his wife's friends, but their presence now constituted yet one more threat to Marie-Antoinette herself. For years, the Austrian ambassador had warned in his letters of the danger represented by the presence of the Polignacs at Versailles. "That family," he wrote to Joseph II, "has made itself so hateful by way of its pillaging and abuse, that it has occasioned the odious and unjust frenzy in which the populace obstinately persists in regard to the Queen."⁶⁴ And now that Marie-Antoinette was finally resigned to sacrificing her "favorite coterie" to public opinion, Mercy-Argenteau sorely regretted that "she hadn't decided to do so long ago."⁶⁵

Their goodbyes on the night and early morning of July 16 and 17 were emotional. Those of Vaudreuil marked a sort of return to grace. "Approaching the Queen," he would recall, "I fell to one knee and stammered some words of farewell. She deigned to bend her visage toward my own. I felt her tears rolling down my face: 'Vaudreuil,' she said to me in a choking voice, a voice whose sound has remained in my memory, 'you were right. Necker is a traitor. We are lost.' I lifted my eyes with dread to gaze at her. She already had assumed once again an air of calm, of serenity. The woman revealed herself before no one but I; the rest of the court saw only their sovereign."⁶⁶ At midnight, before leaving Versailles, the Duchesse de Polignac received a final message from Marie-Antoinette: "*Adieu*, my tenderest of friends! What a frightful word! But it is necessary. *Adieu*! I haven't the strength to embrace you."⁶⁷

So as not to draw attention, Artois and the Polignacs had decided to follow two different itineraries: the Comte would head toward the Netherlands, the Polignacs toward Switzerland. Faced with the dilemma of whether to follow his Prince or the woman he loved, Vaudreuil felt that his duty was to escort Artois, since the Comte was in the greatest danger. While his two sons, the Duc d'Angoulême and the Duc de Berry, left the château in a coach, Artois set out on horseback, followed by the captain of his guards, the Prince d'Hénin, his *premier écuyer*, the Marquis de Polignac, and several other gentlemen from his entourage, along with Vaudreuil. Having traversed the forest, the small band arrived at Chantilly, where they found seats in coaches prepared for them by the Prince de Condé (whose coat of arms had been removed in haste), and headed in the direction of Valenciennes and the border at Quiévrain—crossing without incident, they passed into Belgium. It was not until the beginning of August that Vaudreuil would once again meet the Polignacs, who had taken refuge in Switzerland. Their flight had been far more eventful than his, and at numerous points they had run the risk of being recognized. But in the end, the Duc and the Duchesse Jules and their four children, the Comtesse Diane, and the Comtesse de Polastron and her child had reunited at a country villa in Gümlingen, a league from Bern. The only ones missing were the Duc de Guiche and the Comte de Polastron, who had remained in France at the head of their regiments. On the other hand, the exiles soon received a visit from

d'Artois, who came under the strictest of incognitos to embrace Mme de Polastron, with whom he found himself more in love every day. It was from Gümlingen that, on August 16, Vaudreuil sent news of Lady Foster's friends to her:
"I have found everyone healthy, everyone courageous, enduring their bad luck
with all the strength and calm that good conscience gives. . . . Only time can
heal the misfortunes over which we sigh, and courage, friendship, and philosophy will give us the strength needed to wait for that happy age."[68] The Comte
could not have imagined that his wait would last twenty-five years.

The departure of the Comte d'Artois and the Polignacs, soon enough followed
by that of the Princes of Condé and Bourbon, of Conti and Rohan, marked
the official beginning of the emigration. Between that point and the end of
the Terror, close to 150,000 people would leave France to seek refuge throughout Europe and across the Atlantic. The émigré—a neologism of that moment
—became a key figure for the revolutionary age. The emigration was carried
out in successive waves, responding to the radicalization of a "general will"
determined to eliminate all who stood in its path—the partisans of absolutism,
the liberal monarchists, the Girondins—but it was by no means limited to
the aristocracy and the clergy. Under the pressure of the Great Fear, the period
saw the flight of members of the petite bourgeoisie, artisans, workers, and
peasants, along with nobles and rich bourgeois landowners.[69] The prisoner
of an increasingly difficult political situation, Louis XVI adopted an ambiguous
stance in regard to the emigration, which he officially condemned but encouraged in secret. Were the nobility betraying their King by abandoning him to
the hands of his enemies and weakening his position by indulging themselves
in bellicose declarations from beyond France's borders? Or was it the sovereign
who had shown himself incapable of defending his most loyal subjects and
was now cynically losing interest in their fate?[70] And who was it that should
ultimately be set back on the throne—"the Lord's Anointed," or the King who
had signed the constitution? Didn't Louis XVI's conduct lead one to suppose
that he was no longer in possession of all his faculties, and that one should
turn instead to his brothers, Provence and Artois? These were questions, uncer-
tainties, and contradictions that would later reveal their full dramatic dimensions among the émigrés gathered at Koblenz. But the emigration of 1789 was
still "*joyeuse*"—it was imagined that the flight would be brief, and those who

went into exile were able to carry along with them money, jewels, paintings, and other precious objects.

A dozen days after the Polignacs, Besenval too departed for Bern. His thankless military mission in the capital had exposed him to the hatred of the populace, and Louis XVI in person had commanded him to return to Switzerland. Less fortunate than the Polignacs, the Baron was arrested before reaching the border and placed under surveillance in the little town of Villenauxe. He had forgotten to bring with him his official dismissal signed by the King, and the municipal council refused to let him depart without a new passport certified by Versailles and the *mairie* of Paris. He was lucky that, on the morning of July 28, the coach carrying Necker, recalled by Louis XVI five days[71] after his dismissal, was passing by Villenauxe at breakneck speed on its way to Paris. Informed by a friend of Besenval's arrest, the minister wrote while in transit a billet giving the Baron full freedom to return to Switzerland. But the municipal council overruled him and handed Besenval over to *commissaires* who had arrived from Paris, and who promptly returned him to the capital, imprisoning him at the Abbaye to await judgment. Still, Necker did not admit defeat. Fortified by the enthusiastic welcome of the Parisians, his daughter recalls with admiration, "he went into the Hôtel de Ville, reported to the newly elected magistrates the order that he had given to save M. de Besenval; and urging upon them with his accustomed delicacy all that pleaded in favor of those who obeyed their sovereign, and who had defended an order of things that had held sway for centuries, requested that he be granted amnesty for the past, whatever he may have done, and reconciliation for the future."[72] In the wake of Necker's intervention, the *mairie* of Paris decided upon the liberation of Besenval and the pardon of all enemies, but was promptly recalled to order by Mirabeau. Furious at the unexpected return of Necker, which was hampering his ministerial projects, the tribunal decreed that in reality these decisions were in the ambit of the assembly, and immediately confirmed Besenval's order of detention while he awaited his trial. But by declaring the accusations leveled against the Baron illegitimate and pleading in his favor, Necker had "saved his life."[73]

Besenval languished in the fortress of Brie-Comte-Robert for three months, some twenty miles from the capital. In spite of its desire to respect the law, the assembly proceeded with extreme prudence, fearing that the decision to liberate Besenval might provoke a reaction in the streets, driving the people to seek justice on their own. Such had been the case on July 22—the same day the municipality of Paris had ordered the Baron's arrest—of the state councillor Foullon and the steward Bertier de Sauvigny. "Besenval's case had taken on the historic dimension of the first test of revolutionary justice."[74] It was finally decided to entrust the hearing of the trial for *lèse-nation* to the tribunal of Châtelet, made up of judges of the old school—Besenval's case would be tried along with those of four other defendants who had obeyed the King's legitimate orders before the latter had recognized the sovereign authority of the assembly: the old keeper of the seals, Barentin; the minister of war, Puységur; and two military men, the Maréchal de Broglie and the Marquis d'Autichamp.

Transferred to Châtelet during the night of November 7, Besenval felt as though he had been reborn. After four dramatic months spent in isolation and at the mercy of the populace, he benefited from a milder carceral regime, and was able to embrace the Vicomte de Ségur and his old mistress Mme de La Suze, to see his friends again, and to prepare his defense with his lawyers.

A charming little canvas by Hubert Robert[75] shows us his cell at Châtelet. The painter—who certainly could not have imagined that this was only the first of numerous prison interiors he would soon paint, not as a visitor but an inmate—focuses on the large open window that occupies almost the whole of the rear wall; a dog curled up on the window ledge stares back at the viewer. If one can forget the iron bars that frame, without obstructing, the view over the city and the Seine, one might almost believe the painting depicted the studio of a starving artist rather than a "horrible dungeon." Besenval himself does not appear in the painting, but a leather briefcase engraved with his name at the foot of the wall lets us know that its owner is not far away. During the three months that he spent at the Châtelet, the Baron's cell was flooded with visitors, despite the crowd that demonstrated in front of the prison calling for his death. His *valet de chambre* brightened up the room with flowers plucked from the hothouse in the rue de Grenelle and ordered his meals from the finest Parisian caterers. Gouverneur Morris, who was among the first to pay him a visit, and who accompanied him on November 21 (along with the Vicomte de Ségur and his brother, Louis-Philippe, who had returned from Russia) to the first hearing of the tribunal, notes in his diary: "The Charges against him are ridiculous and even contradictory but they are sufficient to have caused his Destruction had he been exposed to the Summary Justice of the People."[76]

And yet the outcome of the trial was anything but certain: the testimony against the Baron was abundant but mostly false, and the atmosphere of the four hearings, which were held between November 21, 1789, and January 21, 1790, was extremely tense. The skill of his lawyer, Raymond de Sèze, was decisive. With courage equal to that shown by his client during a trial conducted before a frenzied audience—one that shouted "A noose for Besenval! To the gallows with Besenval!"—the future defender of Louis XVI at the convention proved in his concluding oration that not only was the Baron, victim of a vile denunciation, innocent, but his actions had been driven by a high sense of his responsibility and were in the interest of all citizens. "His plea, of which the judges themselves have requested a copy," reported the *Journal de Paris*, "is the most beautiful tribute that one could render to the French constitution."[77]

Cleared of all charges, Besenval, escorted by the Garde Nationale, returned to the rue de Grenelle, where his jubilant friends awaited him, and it is with this happy epilogue that his memoirs conclude: "And as everything is for the best, I feel at this moment an emotion that no other circumstance of my life has been able to rouse in me."[78] But even if all these ordeals did not rattle his cheerful hedonism, his proverbial health had suffered gravely. He had already been afflicted by illness when the corporals of the six companies of the Gardes Suisses, each of them flanked by a pair of soldiers, had come on their own initiative to testify on his behalf. Overcome by emotion, he had suffered a heart attack, which was soon followed by others. Back at the rue de Grenelle, the Baron commissioned a portrait of himself in his salon, surrounded by his paintings and precious porcelains: he wished to leave behind a memory of himself as a collector rather than a soldier. Executed at the beginning of 1791 by Henri-Pierre Danloux, *The Baron de Besenval in his Salon de Compagnie*[79] has the same dimensions as Hubert Robert's *View from the Cell of the Baron de Besenval*, with which it seems to be in dialogue. Seated in a large wing chair, his torso slightly inclined and his handsome face capped with white hair, in profile, the Baron smiles, pleased at having regained the refined comfort of his salon. His right elbow braced on the richly sculpted edge of the marble hearth, the Baron supports his cheek with the palm of his right hand, while his left clutches a precious snuffbox. On the wall behind him, one finds precisely reproduced ten or so paintings from his collection, and several more reflected in the tall mirror above the mantelpiece. His eclectic taste—typical of the 1770s, and running from Flemish paintings to those of the Italian school, by way of both old-fashioned and modern French works—was by this point out of fashion, and his canvases lacked the quality of those owned by his friend Choiseul. Still, the portrait commissioned from Danloux is "the sole oil painting executed in the 18th century that belonged to a French private collector and was displayed in his study."[80]

It was in this haven of peace and beauty that, fortunate to the last, Besenval serenely passed away in the midst of the revolutionary drama. On the evening of June 12, 1791, the Baron invited the whole Ségur family to dine with him, as well as his cousin, the Baron de Roll—who had come from Switzerland to see him—and various of his colleagues from the Gardes Suisses. It was one of the latter, Victor de Gibelin, who supplies us with the details of the Baron's end. Not feeling well, the Baron mostly kept to his room but rejoined the company at the end of the meal, draped in a white sheet and proclaiming in a sepulchral voice: "It is the Commander's ghost who visits you." Then, pleased at his joke, he greeted his guests and, accompanied by Gibelin, returned to his bed, where, an hour later, he died.[81]

But now we return to the summer of 1789 and the Great Fear that afflicted France after the fall of the Bastille. "For some time now, terror has gripped our spirits," Mercy-Argenteau wrote to Kaunitz, "due to the violence that the people permit themselves in the towns, and even in the countryside; the least suspicion, the least discontent may cost a man his life."[82] The peasants hastened to burn the châteaus, as well as the archives where the *droits du seigneur* were preserved. Incapable of controlling this popular violence, the assembly attempted to restrain it by accelerating its program of reforms: on August 20, feudal rights were abolished; on August 26, the final articles of the Declaration of the Rights of Man and of the Citizen were approved; on September 10, defeating the monarchist party, the deputies chose a single-chamber legislature, and, on September 11, voted to allow the King a "suspensive" (rather than absolute) veto, while Mirabeau, who had become the assembly's leading figure, supported the principle of inheritance of the throne by birthright. Louis XVI attempted to buy time and refrained from giving his approval. But in Paris, the talk was of nothing but conspiracies—in various quarters it was feared that a government coup would call into question the rights that had already been gained. And meanwhile, bread was growing scarce. In this climate, the news of a banquet offered by the King's Guard to the officers of the Flanders

Regiment, who had been called to Versailles as reinforcements, was incendiary. On October 5, the population of the capital, led by its women, decided to march to the King at Versailles, in order to separate him from the influence of the court and demand that he find a solution to the famine. Lafayette tried to prevent the procession, but the Garde Nationale disobeyed him and left for Versailles as well, dragging him along. At the palace a council was held, and Saint-Priest[83] proposed that the King either take refuge someplace safe along with his family or give battle; but Necker, who found the idea of a fleeing King humiliating, advised him to remain. Mounier, then acting president of the assembly, convinced him to sign that body's edicts, as well as the Declaration of the Rights of Man. But it was too late. The crowd had gathered without incident before the palace, awaiting the answers to its demands—that he return to Paris and guarantee the supply of bread—that the King had put off till the next day. But at dawn on October 6, a group of armed men penetrated the courtyard via a side entry. The King's bodyguard retreated, leaving their dead behind. The enraged mob invaded the palace, and the King—along with the Queen and the Dauphin—was forced to display himself on a balcony and promise to return to the city with his family. Hurrying to Versailles, Mme de Staël was a horrified witness to this humiliation inflicted upon the sovereigns.

Almost immediately the rumor spread that, mixed with the crowd, Biron and Orléans had led the march and the assault on the palace, and an investigation opened against them by the Châtelet seemed to confirm this hypothesis. Mirabeau figured among the accused as well. The whirlwind of rumor and contradictory testimony around the role played by the First Prince of the Blood and the Duc in those crucial days for the monarchy prevents us from knowing precisely what occurred.[84] The overly detailed alibi furnished by Orléans—who had not left the city for Versailles, so he affirmed, until after he'd received news of the invasion of the palace—is unconvincing. And we know that during the months in which he spoke insistently of a royal abdication, Mirabeau had not excluded the possibility of a ducal regency, so as to guarantee the transition to a constitutional monarchy. Even if he did not think much of Orléans, he was keenly aware of his great popularity and used their mutual friend Biron to encourage him to persevere in his role of liberal Prince. On the other hand, Mirabeau dreaded the inordinate ambition and lack of political intelligence of Lafayette, who, after having escorted the royal family to Paris, claimed for himself the double merit of assuring the King his protection and interpreting to him the will of the people. Determined to become both Louis XVI's closest adviser and the protector of the constitution, the Hero of Two Worlds felt that the somewhat suspicious behavior of the Duc d'Orléans provided him with the perfect opportunity to rid himself of a formidable rival, "upon whom he wished to pin the crimes of October 6, which Orléans could have neither foreseen nor prevented."[85] And since the assembly, disturbed by this new demonstration of the strength of the popular movement, had demanded that an inquest be opened into the presumed instigators of the march on Versailles, Lafayette took the opportunity to insist on the existence of an "Orléans conspiracy," in which the Duc himself, Biron, Laclos, and others loyal to the Palais-Royal were mixed up. While the Châtelet collected testimony, Lafayette confronted Orléans at the home of the Marquise de Coigny, urging him to leave for London until such time as the suspicions weighing upon him had dissolved. To encourage him further, Montmorin, the minister of foreign affairs, who happened to be present at this encounter, offered him a diplomatic mission. Leaving would have amounted to an admission of guilt, and Mirabeau and Biron tried to convince the Duc to refuse. But as the Cardinal de Retz had written apropos of one of his ancestors, "M. d'Orléans possessed all the qualities necessary for an honorable man, apart from courage,"[86] and the Duc, distressed by a second, more violent series of threats from Lafayette, took ship for England. The Marquis attempted the same operation against Biron, who responded loftily: "If I am guilty, I will be judged." Mirabeau, who had by now been implicated as well, was delighted by his reply, according to La Marck: "M. de Biron has just left my home; he will by no means flee; a man of honor, he refuses," and he railed against Orléans: "They pretend that I am on his side; I would not want him for my valet."[87] Yet, even if he was disappointed by the Duc's behavior, Biron preserved their friendship. For Lafayette, on the other hand, as we will see, he preserved a tenacious contempt.

Narbonne too found himself at Versailles on the fateful night of the march, but for reasons opposed to those of his friends. Informed of what was happening, the Comte, in his capacity as *chevalier d'honneur* to Mme Adélaïde, hurried to the palace in order to offer his aid to the aunts of the King. The next day, escorting their carriage on horseback in the ominous procession that brought the royal family to Paris, the Comte cleverly managed to divert it, and with the help of the Garde Nationale guided the two princesses and his own mother without incident to the Château de Bellevue. Since 1788, Narbonne had been garrisoned with his regiment at Besançon, where he had managed to impose order and make himself respected: "His energy and frank manner had made him popular throughout the Franche-Comté."[88] Appointed to the command of the Garde Nationale with the support of Talleyrand, he maintained the tranquility of the department with fairness and courage. As evidence of his success, in 1790 Rivarol's *Little Dictionary of Great Men of the Revolution* dedicated to him a portrait as venomous as it was well informed: "This ex-courtier, having seen fit to become a citizen, and wishing to distinguish himself at any cost ... has made of himself a provincial patriot. First he shed a number of vices of the old court, along with the daughter of the great Necker, then departed, much improved, for the Franche-Comté ... and if that province becomes its own little kingdom, as there is reason to hope it will, the worst thing that could happen to M. de Narbonne is that he will rule it."[89] Yet despite his constitutional sympathies and the influence exercised on him by Mme de Staël, Narbonne remained a fervent monarchist, deeply tied to the royal family. He had the chance to prove it when the aunts of Louis XVI decided to emigrate. The two princesses had been mulling the decision for some time, and the Civil Constitution of the Clergy, proposed by Talleyrand, which made them fear that they would no longer be able to openly express their religious faith, hastened their decision. They asked Narbonne, in whom they had absolute trust, to accompany them to Rome, where they intended to settle. Though he had declared his opposition to emigration on numerous occasions, and though he was well aware that it would jeopardize his popularity in Franche-Comté, he accepted without hesitation. The enterprise got off to a rocky start. The municipality of Paris refused to issue visas to the princesses, but Louis XVI personally signed their passports, which he had ratified by the minister of foreign affairs, the Comte de Montmorin. To Bailly, the mayor, who came to challenge the decision regarding the princesses, he simply replied that thanks to the Declaration of the Rights of Man and in light of the laws of the state, all citizens were able to travel and to leave the kingdom, however and whenever they wished. This did not prevent the Jacobin press from raising a cry of alarm.

On February 19, informed by a friend of Narbonne that the people were preparing to march on Bellevue in order to return them to Paris, the two sisters decided to leave that same evening. Mme Adélaïde was accompanied by the Duchesse de Narbonne, and Mme Victoire by the Comtesse and Comte de Chastellux, respectively her *dame de compagnie* and *chevalier d'honneur*. Their traveling suite consisted of eight valets, four pages, a chaplain, two doctors, and two equerries. It seems[90] that Narbonne had attempted in vain to convince Mme Élisabeth, the youngest sister of Louis XVI, to depart with her aunts. At Moret, just beyond Fontainebleau, the Comte de Chastellux ordered the cavalrymen of the Chasseurs du Hainaut, who were escorting them, to charge a crowd that was determined to block their path. The Vicomte de Ségur, the titular colonel of the regiment, was not present but was forced to justify before the assembly the actions of the officer who had commanded the detachment, and this contributed to his decision to leave the army. Things grew even more complicated on the third day of the journey: while they were crossing the Bourgogne, the caravan was obstructed by the people of Arnay-le-Duc, who, standing in for the municipal authorities, declared that they would not allow the aunts of the King to pass without a passport from the National Assembly. Narbonne returned in haste to Paris to submit to his friend Mirabeau, now president of the assembly, the request of the princesses, who asked only that they be treated in accordance with the common rights, like any other citizens. The next day, after a grueling debate of several hours, Mirabeau wrested their approval from the deputies, and Lafayette was forced to intervene with the Garde Nationale in order to disperse the crowd that had assembled in front of the Tuileries in protest. Nevertheless, the assembly's decree was not enough to smooth the situation. Now, to the population of Arnay-le-Duc, clearly radicalized by Jacobin agents, were added demonstrators from throughout the region, and all that Narbonne could do was summon a pair of *commissionaires* from Dijon to inform the assembly that their wishes had been flouted. When on March 3 the delegates of the municipality of Arnay-le-Duc returned from Paris armed with the assembly's injunction to respect its orders, the Comte had already taken the precaution of mollifying the most vociferous of the demonstrators with generous gratuities and the caravan was able to get back on the road and cross the Sardinian border at Pont-de-Beauvoisin. The obstacles encountered by the daughters of Louis XV clearly demonstrated that if the municipalities were prepared to ignore the assembly's decisions, they were also unable to control the violence in the streets.

The two princesses arrived in Rome in mid-April, where they were welcomed with all honors by their old friend the Cardinal de Bernis. It was there that Narbonne learned of the sudden death of Mirabeau on April 2, and the attempted flight to Varennes of June 20—two disturbing pieces of news.

As François Furet has written, with Mirabeau's death the Revolution lost its great symbolic figure—perhaps the only one who might have been able to prevent its downward spiral. Convinced that he had done his duty in establishing on the one hand the sovereignty of the people and on the other the equality of citizens before the law, the tribune was convinced that only a strong monarchical power would be able to secure these victories in the face of the Legislative Assembly. Since 1790, through the intermediary of La Marck, Mirabeau had become a secret councillor to Louis XVI, hoping to reconcile the King with the nation and convince the revolutionaries to compromise with the monarchy.[91] The flight to Varennes buried that hope. His final words—"My heart is filled with grief for the monarchy, whose debris will become the prey of factions"[92]—were prophetic.

At the beginning of July, despite the prayers of his mother and Mme Adélaïde, Narbonne returned to France, driven by a "sincere desire to serve the King,"[93] whose fate was becoming more and more uncertain with every passing day. His wife, on the other hand, decided to join the Duchesse de Narbonne in Rome, bringing with her the eldest of her daughters and leaving the youngest with her nurse at Bellevue. The spouses would never live together again.

At the beginning of September 1791, Narbonne reconnected with Mme de Staël in Paris. Both of them saw in the constitution—which Louis XVI had finally resigned himself to swearing an oath upon[94]—the last chance to salvage the monarchy, and devoted themselves to its support. Germaine, who had found in the "beau Louis" the hero of her dreams, poured all of her energy into propelling Narbonne toward the front of the political stage. Now that her father had left his ministerial posts and retired to Coppet, it was her lover who allowed her to play by proxy a political role forbidden to women. Overpowered by the superior intellect of Mme de Staël, Narbonne allowed himself to be carried away by her passion. For some time, Germaine had hoped that the Comte would succeed Montmorin, the departing minister of foreign affairs, but this plan was foiled by the King's veto and, even more so, by that of the Queen, who cordially detested both Narbonne and Mme de Staël. Instead, the sovereigns turned to Louis-Philippe de Ségur, who, since his return from Russia in January 1790, had been on the lookout for a new position equal to his ambitions.

Just as Catherine of Russia had predicted, the Comte had found France "feverish and very ill,"[95] enough so to shake his political certainties. Returning to Paris after no less than five years abroad, he found himself cruelly deprived of his bearings. Besenval was in prison, his father abhorred the Revolution, and his brother dismissed it as a phenomenon of social envy: "Do you want to know, said the Vicomte, what a revolution is? It can be summed up quite neatly with the words: *Get out, so that I may install myself in your place.*"[96] The scandal surrounding the "Livre Rouge" (or Red Book, which recorded the pensions bestowed by Louis XVI upon his entourage), which had broken out shortly after his arrival, had certainly not improved the family atmosphere. The name of the Maréchal de Ségur had figured on this list when it was made public in April. (Why hadn't the King burned it, a devastated Vaudreuil asked in his exile.)[97] During the course of his ministry, the Maréchal had secured pensions and gratuities for himself, his children, and no fewer than eleven members of his family, in addition to the promise of a hereditary dukedom that would be passed down to his eldest son. The Maréchal defended himself in indignant letters sent to the newspapers, and the Comte flew to his father's aid, extolling his virtues as a soldier and statesman. But the Revolutionary government demanded the restitution of sums undeservedly received.[98]

In Paris, Louis-Philippe had once again taken up with his companions from the American expedition—Lafayette, Biron, Broglie, the Lameth brothers, the Vicomte de Noailles—who invited him to join them in the grand challenge of forging a new country in keeping with the ideas inherited from the Enlightenment. But Ségur quickly took the measure of the reality facing them—a difficult political situation, divided minds, an uncertain future—and he was careful not to throw in his lot with any particular party. Using great diplomacy, he equivocated with Lafayette—"I share your wishes more than I do your hopes"[99]—and forgetting that some months earlier he had preached engagement to Boufflers, adopted a policy of prudence. While awaiting some sort of consequential change, the Comte capitalized on the experience he had acquired as the ambassador to Russia and invented for himself the role of mediator between the court and the assembly, and the partisans of constitutional monarchy. First of all he attempted to smooth over the conflict that had emerged between Lafayette and Mirabeau during the "Orléans conspiracy." But after having promised to withdraw the accusations that Lafayette had leveled at Mirabeau while testifying before the tribunal at Châtelet, the Marquis did not keep his word. At that point, the rupture was inevitable. By contrast, Louis-Philippe became an important intermediary between

Marie-Antoinette, who had heaped him with favors during the Polignac era, and his friends in the assembly. "Your friend," Mirabeau wrote to La Marck, "wholly directs foreign affairs."[100] Indeed, using excellent political arguments, Ségur defended the royal desire to renew the familial pact that sealed the alliance between France and Spain. Even though the assembly ended by making the opposite decision, the Comte had earned enough credit to obtain, on March 29, 1791, his nomination as ambassador to the Holy See. But Pius VI, outraged by the assembly's plan to annex Avignon, which had remained up to this point under the jurisdiction of the pope, refused to receive the French ambassador in his states, and Ségur, who had already disembarked with his family at Civitavecchia, was forced to head back to Paris. For his part, Joseph-Alexandre transformed the episode into one of his characteristic witticisms with the help of a pun: "*Mon frère n'est donc plus ambassadeur à Rome, mais ambassadeur à la Porte*" ["My brother is no longer ambassador to Rome, but ambassador to the Porte"—the Sublime Porte, the Turkish government; or "an ambassador who's been sent packing"].[101]

The conclusion of the National Constituent Assembly's work, and the Legislative Assembly's assumption of duty on October 1 of the same year, led to Montmorin's resignation, and, as in the earlier case of the Russian diplomatic mission, Ségur and Narbonne found themselves in competition for the same post. This time, too, Louis-Philippe carried the day. In reality, Marie-Antoinette had originally selected the Marquis de Moustier, an intransigent royalist, who had declined the proposition; so the Queen resigned herself to Ségur as a fallback solution. For her, the constitutionalists were traitors, and rather than redeeming the Comte in her eyes, the steps he had taken to engage the liberal deputies in order to find some common ground had simply increased her mistrust.[102]

Summoned to the Tuileries, Ségur, while entirely conscious of the difficulties that awaited him, accepted the position. But the next morning, even though the news of his appointment was already circulating, he let it be known that he was giving it up, without any explanation.[103] It seems that at the end of their meeting, the Comte, who was leaving the royal presence walking backward in keeping with protocol, had raised his head after making his third bow and perceived in a mirror the expression of annoyance the Queen's face had assumed as soon as she'd turned her back on him.[104] For him, there was no longer any doubt: given that Marie-Antoinette had entirely lost her confidence in him, his mission was doomed to failure.[105] And indeed, the enterprise seemed so desperate that Gouverneur Morris "congratulate[d]"[106] Mme de Ségur on her husband's decision to resign. The Comte's premonition was confirmed when, five months later, Antoine Valdec de Lessart, the minister called upon to replace him, was forced to depart, having been accused of treason by the Legislative Assembly.

Narbonne and Mme de Staël displayed greater audacity than Ségur. Their hopes were revived when the minister of war, Duportail, resigned and Mme de Staël asked for the help of Barnave, who, along with Duport and Alexandre Lameth, formed the triumvirate in charge of the Feuillants, at that point in the majority in the assembly.[107] The Queen had made clear to Narbonne that she took a dim view of his candidacy, but was convinced to change her mind by the young deputy from Grenoble, who had become her paladin after the flight to Varennes. "As of yesterday, Comte Louis de Narbonne is finally minister of war," she wrote to Fersen on December 7. "What glory for Mme de Staël, to have the whole army... on her side! He could be useful, if he wished, having intelligence enough to rally the constitutionalists, and precisely the tone needed to speak to the army as it stands."[108] And she added: "What happiness, if one day I were able to prove to these beggars that I was not their dupe!"[109] Hostility aside, the Queen's analysis was not lacking in perspicacity.

Narbonne immediately put himself to work establishing his program in concert with Germaine and his friends Talleyrand, Biron, and Lafayette.[110] He threw his support behind the centrist politics of the Feuillants, who wanted to consolidate the achievements of 1789 and establish an order founded on property and equality of opportunity rather than of rights, and to exclude both the extreme right wing and the Jacobins.[111] He felt it was indispensable to take a position against the émigrés, who, in asserting their fidelity to the throne and reviling the Revolution, continued to worsen the position of Louis XVI. His initiative also aimed at gaining the favor of public opinion, for which the émigrés were the declared enemies of the fatherland and were conspiring with foreign powers to restore their lost privileges by force. To assure its own safety, the monarchy could not openly ask for the support of other European princes (as the royal couple themselves did, in great secrecy), but needed to reassert its authority with the sole aid of the French. So Narbonne found himself obliged to take up the reins of the army, restore discipline, fortify the borders, and once more project the image of a courageous and patriotic king, ready to defend the prestige of the nation with force of arms. Narbonne saw in the war the surest means of attaining that objective: it would be a performative war, swift and certain of issue, against the Elector of Trèves, who had welcomed the brothers of Louis XVI at Koblenz, and, in their wake, a large number of émigrés determined eventually to recross the armed border. But in order to avoid Austria coming to the aid of a member state of the empire, he had to assure himself of an alliance with Prussia and the neutrality of England. To that end, the new minister asked for the aid of Talleyrand and Biron, the two people in whom he had the most confidence. Biron's[112] correspondence with Narbonne and Talleyrand reflects that moment of grace in which the three friends joined forces to carry out a political project capable of assuring the future of the monarchy in accord with constitutional principles.

In 1791, Biron was forty-four years old—seven years older than Talleyrand, eight years older than Narbonne—and had an intensely eventful life behind him. Of the three, he was the only one who knew the soldier's trade from the inside; he was the one who had traveled the most, who had established relationships in all of the courts of Europe, who had collected the most mistresses, accumulated the greatest debts, and pursued his dreams most fully. Since the dissolution of the National Constituent Assembly in October, disillusioned by his experience as a deputy, having broken with the royal family thanks to his ties to the Duc d'Orléans, and suffering from ill health, he had returned to active service in Valenciennes. Additionally, in exchange for the settlement of his debts, he had promised his father that he would remain far from Paris. In any case, since Mme de Coigny's departure for London, the capital had lost its principal attraction for him.

Animated like Biron by a profound resentment of the royal family, and like him, an intimate of the Palais-Royal, the Marquise, following the Duc's example, threw herself behind the idea of change, assiduously following the work of the assembly and commenting aloud on the most substantial interventions. One day, tired of Mme de Coigny and her friends' repeated interruptions, the Abbé Maury, an eloquent defender of the rights of both Throne and Altar, showed the full measure of his misogyny by demanding that the president silence "these two *sans-culottes*." The term[113] with which the Abbé intended to tar the women who, lacking self-restraint, brazenly flaunted the sort of behavior reserved for men, soon became a widespread synonym for a revolutionary patriot.[114] And yet it was precisely the sans-culottes that drove Mme de Coigny to emigrate. On the morning that the news of the flight to Varennes was spreading through Paris, the Marquise and a friend set out for the Tuileries to see what was happening. Taking her for a spy, the sans-culottes roughed her up and imprisoned her until Biron came to have her released. A rumor went around that she had been whipped as well: it was a form of violence that had become part of the revolutionary repertoire—Théroigne de Méricourt, another victim of this treatment, wound up in a lunatic asylum—and was all the more humiliating given that women of the era did not wear undergarments. The flippancy with which Ligne commented on the misfortune that had struck his idol is surprising—but then, the revolutionary sympathies of the haughty Marquise must have outraged him, and well aware that she was safe in London, he indulged in a bit of mockery:

> *Régnez en paix sur ces rivages;*
> *Remettez-vous de ces outrages,*
> *Qui pourtant ne menaçaient pas*
> *Votre tête, dit-on, mais vos secrets appas,*
> *Que des gens curieux, prétextant la vengeance,*
> *Voulaient voir et montrer, pour l'honneur de la France.*[*][115]

Mme de Coigny's departure, some ten days after "the outrages," greatly distressed Biron, and the nostalgic letters dispatched to him by the Marquise from London bear witness to the continuing intensity of their relationship.[116]

Narbonne's nomination dispelled the Duc's black humor by giving him reason to hope that he too could occupy an important position and distinguish himself in the service of his country. Both raised at Versailles, Biron and Narbonne had known each other since their earliest youth, sharing the same chivalrous conception of honor, and feeling for each other a sincere affection. The friendship between Biron and Talleyrand was more recent: they had come to know and appreciate each other during the course of their circle's discussions at Panchaud's, and their political views had grown closer over time. The Duc's letters reflect the different degrees of intimacy that he felt with his two correspondents. He addressed Narbonne as *tu* and Talleyrand as *vous*—with the first he was unequivocal, and more cautious with the second—but in both cases, he ended his letters with "I love you, and embrace you with all my heart."[117]

---

*Reign in peace on those shores; / Recover well from those outrages / Which did not, however, threaten / Your head, so they say, but your hidden charms / That curious men, making pretext of vengeance / Wished to see and display, for the honor of France.

Upon his arrival at the ministry, Narbonne established three great armies to defend the borders: the Army of the North, under the command of Rochambeau, charged with holding at bay the Austrians based in Belgium; the Army of the Center, under the orders of Lafayette, which was to lead the offensive against the émigrés; and the Army of the Rhine, led by Luckner, ready for eventual interventions beyond the frontiers.[118] He tasked a fourth—the Army of the Midi—with defending the border between Genoa and Nice. Biron, whom Narbonne had asked to choose his preferred destination, responded that his great desire was to return to Corsica, the island where he had carried out his first military mission—but also that he did not want special treatment and was ready to serve wherever his presence would be useful, with the exception of the Army of the Center. He had not forgiven Lafayette for the Châtelet investigation, and wished to hear no more of "his glory, nor his stupidities."[119] It was decided that for the time being he would remain at Valenciennes, under the command of Rochambeau, who had already been his commander in America.

Setting himself to work with renewed enthusiasm, Biron informed Narbonne of conditions in the army and of its most urgent problems—discipline, the training and payment of soldiers, the criteria used to select senior staff—and suggested that he immediately propose the promotion of Rochambeau and Luckner to the rank of *maréchal*, a promotion that, in case of war, would give them the greatest freedom of action. Narbonne did not limit himself to thanking Biron with aristocratic politeness for his letters—"Continue to send them to me, I beg you, and command forevermore your servant and your friend"[120]— but also followed his advice, and on December 27, Louis XVI signed the decree naming the last two *maréchaux de France* to be appointed under the old monarchy.

Minister Narbonne's energy was unflagging: despite the fact that he faced a complex political situation in which he was not only bound to obtain the approval of the King—whose role as supreme chief of the army had been recognized by the constitution—but also that of the majority of the assembly, he was determined to inspect the borders in person, establish direct contact with the higher ranks, and motivate the soldiers. "Narbonne is truly of an inconceivable perfection," Biron wrote to Talleyrand, "he sees all, and is good for everyone; his journey is having a prodigious and salutary effect on the army; but he would have to be made of iron to hold up under all of it, for he does not sleep and is greatly fatigued."[121] Indeed, his tour electrified the troops and, as General Louis-Alexandre Berthier would declare to Napoleon, put a brake on the emigration of officers.[122]

But Narbonne quickly realized that the idea of a swift war against the principality of Trèves was dangerous. Officially, Louis XVI and Marie-Antoinette had adopted the position of Barnave and Lameth, the leaders of the Feuillants, the party that hoped for Emperor Leopold's help to peacefully resolve the problem of émigrés in Germany. In reality, the sovereigns were counting on a conflict that would drive the European powers to intervene in order to halt the Revolution. At the time of the flight to Varennes, the King had written to Breteuil: "Rather than a civil war, it would be a war between states, and that would be better. The physical and moral state of France makes it impossible that it should sustain even a half campaign."[123] Informed of the King and Queen's secret maneuvering, the Girondins, who also wanted war, called on the assembly to defend the constitution by force of arms. Conversely, the Jacobins, led by Robespierre, virulently opposed a war that in the case of victory would mark the triumph of the Girondins, as well as a resurgence of prestige for the King. And what was worse, the diplomatic attempts made by Ségur in Berlin and by Talleyrand and Biron in London turned out to be a complete failure.

Biron had immediately considered the decision of the minister of foreign affairs, Lessart, to send Ségur to Prussia in accordance with the wishes of the King and Queen a "stupidity"[124] that augured no good. Indeed, the two missions carried out by Mirabeau in Prussia, followed in 1788 by the pirate edition of his *Secret History of the Court of Berlin*, undermined the task that had been given to the Comte. Mirabeau had disloyally used his diplomatic correspondence with Talleyrand in order to expose the corruption of the Prussian court and the moral and intellectual defects of Frederick William, the appointed successor of Frederick the Great. Not only did the *Secret History* tell the truth but, in contrast with the Philosopher King, Frederick William, who was under the influence of his favorite, Bischofswerder, as well as the Illuminati, detested the ideas of the Enlightenment, and had been prejudiced against Ségur by the French court itself and the Baron de Breteuil.[125]

Arriving in Berlin on January 9, 1792, the Comte was received "in the most mortifying manner by the King of Prussia, the royal family, and consequently the court as a whole,"[126] and, subjected to general hostility, he was quick to realize that he was hurtling toward failure. He had been entrusted with the task of diverting Prussia from the anti-French coalition that was being formed.

But the King of France was playing a double game, parading a policy of peace, all while directing Breteuil to push Frederick William into declaring war. On the other hand, the minister of foreign affairs and the minister of war, while they agreed on the necessity of reinforcing the King's prestige and of avoiding foreign intervention, were dead set on opposite outcomes—the one upon peace and the other upon a showpiece war. The only policies they shared were those of mistrust and mutual discredit. Each of them had his agents, and the preferred method remained that which the secret diplomacy of the ancien régime had always used: the corruption of the royal entourage.

Ségur held to the instructions that he had been given and, receiving an audience with the King, deployed all his diplomatic skills. But when Frederick William abruptly asked if France's soldiers continued to "refuse all discipline," the Comte could not help responding: "Sire, our enemies will be the judge of that."[127] A handful of weeks were sufficient for Ségur to realize that France could not count on Prussia's neutrality, and that the latter had negotiated a defensive treaty with Austria. Nor was he helped by the parallel efforts of a close confidant of Biron, sent to Berlin in his turn.[128] So the Comte asked his minister to recall him, and departed again for Paris on March 1, feverish, suffering from a severe pulmonary illness, and the victim of the most vicious slanders.[129] Still, his last dispatch from Berlin—which would also be the last of his diplomatic career—does full justice to his analytical lucidity: "We are in a frightful crisis; the fate of France depends on their conduct. If disorder continues, if the government cannot summon the necessary force, we will be seen as both dangerous neighbors and easy prey, and in that case, all the valor of the French will be unable to save us from the greatest misfortune."[130]

The situation was no better on the English front. Talleyrand had proposed that Lessart send Biron to London on a "secret mission," since no one knew that country better than he did and could count on so wide a circle of relationships. When the minister of foreign affairs objected that "a friend of M. le Duc d'Orléans would have an ill effect at the current moment"—which was a way of saying that he had not obtained the consent of the King and Queen—Talleyrand agreed to take his place. But he asked his friend to come along and help him on that first diplomatic mission to a country he had never visited before: "I ask you, why...don't you make a trip of four days or so to see Mme de Coigny—it would do me a world of good."[131] Biron jumped at the chance, and, on January 18, Talleyrand joined him in Valenciennes, bearing a letter from Narbonne[132] that announced his promotion to lieutenant general and entrusted him with the mission of purchasing in England four thousand horses that were urgently needed by the army. The Duc's great expertise in this area fully justified his selection, but it was difficult to keep a secret in Paris, and on January 10, Gouverneur Morris noted in his diary that the object of the Bishop of Autun's mission to London was to "make an Alliance with England, to counterbalance Austria; and the Offer to England is the Isle of France and Tobago [*sic*]." And he commented: "This is a most wretched Policy."[133]

The two friends set out together from Calais on January 22, and upon their arrival in London went straight to work. In order to prepare Talleyrand for his meeting with Pitt, Biron prepared a memorandum[134] that undertook a comparative analysis of the political and economic situations of the two countries and their mutual interests in reaching some accord. The Duc was convinced that only an Anglo-French concord could guarantee peace in Europe. It was an idea that Talleyrand wholly shared, but that he would only realize some forty years later, when he returned to London as ambassador for Louis-Philippe. The English were uneasy at the form taken by the Revolution they had encouraged from the wings and that now threatened to spread throughout Europe. The Whig government was anxious about the sympathy that English radicals felt for the movement, and were well aware of the propaganda of Thomas Paine and James Mackintosh. Determined to wait and take advantage of the French crisis, which was a godsend for English commerce, as best he could, Pitt confined himself to a general declaration of neutrality. He hardly considered Talleyrand's proposal for an alliance between France and Great Britain, in contrast to the familial pact invoked by the Tuileries. It was just as Biron had foreseen, which was why he had insisted on the necessity of establishing contact with the representatives of the opposition, among whom he had numerous friends, so as to secure support for the French cause in Parliament. But he found himself unable to fulfill this program because he was jailed for his debts only a few days after his arrival.

The trouble had started when he disembarked at Dover and found that all of the newspapers were reporting the reason for his visit. The first consequence of this had been an unreasonable increase in the price of horses, rendering the sum at his disposal insufficient. The second was that a certain Foyard, a horse dealer, learned of his presence and demanded the payment of an old debt, and then, on February 6, had him arrested. In reality, it was a modest sum of money, one that Biron would have been able to settle with no difficulty had it not been followed by an avalanche of other claims, false for the most part, which increased the bill precipitously and landed him in prison, awaiting the arrival of a significant bail. None of this had happened by chance: the Duc had fallen right into a trap. To his mind, it was a revenge plot perpetrated by the ultra-monarchists in collusion with émigrés settled in London;[135] Mme de Coigny saw in it a conspiracy orchestrated from Paris—by the court? by Narbonne himself?—in hopes of putting him out of commission for a while.[136] The Marquise also nursed suspicions of Talleyrand, who, in her opinion, was not fighting hard enough on his friend's behalf and, as lazy as he was stingy, pretended not to have sufficient funds to pay the bail.[137] But it was tricky for the government to come to the Duc's aid, since his trip was not an official one, quite apart from the fact that the scandal raised by his arrest did nothing to help Talleyrand's mission.

Fortunately, Biron had other letters of credit. The debts did nothing to sully his honor as a gentleman nor his chivalrous reputation, and there were many in England, beginning with George III, who had not forgotten the noble gesture of the uncle whose name he bore. During the American war, the latter had paid the debts of Admiral Rodney, then imprisoned in Paris, allowing the British captain to return to the fray and to defeat the French at sea.[138] The Marquise de Coigny also offered him her diamonds "to pawn, to sell, to put up for bail, whatever you please,"[139] and she was far from alone. The Prince of Wales, the Duke of York, and Lord Stormont declared themselves ready to vouch for him, while a Frenchman who was a total stranger to him, along with Lord Rawdon, paid the 4,500 pounds sterling demanded in order to free him. Nevertheless, the outcome of this adventure remained bitter: "The disastrous and useless journey that you made me take to England is finally at an end," he wrote to Narbonne upon his return to France. "I do not reproach you with any of the misfortunes that resulted, nor with the long and intolerable consequences that they will have for me; I will only observe that, if I were less aware of your loyalty and friendship... I would suspect you of the most atrocious treacheries, and feel myself entitled to make those suspicions public.... I am fortunate that the only thing I can fault you for is your levity."[140]

Narbonne showed himself to be sincerely distressed by this misadventure, and Biron returned to the army. The war against Austria that the three friends had sought to prevent by any means possible now seemed inevitable, and was "perhaps the only shadow of hope"[141] that remained to them. The King's procrastination, the weakness of the government, and fresh popular unrest provoked by the unflagging rise in prices all convinced Narbonne to cozy up to the Girondins. Driven by Mme de Staël and strengthened by the popularity enjoyed by the assembly, the Comte asked for a private audience with the Queen in order to lay out his political program based on respect for the constitution and an unconditional loyalty to the King. But when he launched his candidacy for prime minister, he found himself asked by the Queen "if he was crazy."[142] Then, still in concert with Mme de Staël, Narbonne attempted to secure the support of the generals. He invited Rochambeau, Luckner, and Lafayette to inform the assembly of the measures and expenses needed to prepare for war, exciting the patriotic spirit of the deputies. Then, forcing the King's hand, he admitted them to the Council of Ministers. Finally, he went for broke by threatening to resign if his rival, the minister of the navy, Bertrand de Molleville (who was secretly undermining the constitution and financing the emigration) was allowed to retain his portfolio. But was it he, as Molleville claims, who had the letters of solidarity sent to him by the generals published in the *Journal de Paris*? Or else, as Lafayette declares, one of the friends to whom he had shown them? Or indeed, as the *Correspondance politique* reported, did the decision come from Mme de Staël?[143] Was Émile Dard right to claim that it represented a kind of military coup d'etat prefiguring that of 18 Brumaire, but for which France was not yet ready?[144] Or was Narbonne's only intention to clarify his position in the eyes of the public? Understandably annoyed by these leaks, and bolstered by Lafayette's last-minute reversal, the other ministers reacted by calling for the resignation of Molleville and the dismissal of Narbonne. Resigned at this point to the deterioration of politics, on March 10, Louis XVI ordered the Comte to hand his portfolio over to Grave, the new minister of war. Indeed, only fifteen days later, none of his colleagues would remain in their seats.

The die was cast, and on April 20, France declared war on Austria. It was a war for which Narbonne had played sorcerer's apprentice, and one that set Europe on a path of bloodshed that would last for twenty years.

For once, the news was welcomed with the same enthusiasm by revolutionary patriots, die-hard royalists, and constitutional monarchists alike. For some, the war was a sign of recognition from Europe for the France that had emerged from the Revolution; for others, it would return order to the country and save the monarchy, even if that monarchy's future prospects would be vastly different. Those who awaited it with the greatest impatience were the thousands of émigrés who, for months, had flowed into Koblenz from the four corners of France—Chateaubriand would recall that the city's Latin name had, in fact, been Confluentia[145]—to serve in the Army of the Princes. Great lords and the provincial petite noblesse, bourgeois lawyers, refractory priests, merchants, soldiers, and peasants, all of them in flight from Jacobin violence, had decided to liberate France from the revolutionary scourge. All professed an unshakable monarchist faith, all desired the restoration of the ancien régime, and all confidently awaited orders from the Comte d'Artois and the Comte de Provence to throw themselves headlong into this holy war.

Among the numerous testimonies of those who participated in that tragic crusade, the letters of Vaudreuil to the Comte d'Artois shed light on the illusions, inexperience, irresponsibility, and political blindness that led to its failure, delivered a coup de grace to the monarchy and condemned the royal couple to death. The correspondence between Vaudreuil and Artois—only a few letters from which have come down to us—began in September 1789, when, leaving the Prince behind safely in Brussels, the Comte rejoined the Polignacs in Switzerland. From the very first letter, Vaudreuil reaffirms to Artois a devotion from which he would never stray: "I assure you that the proof of devotion I give to my friends by leaving you behind to visit them is just as strong as that which I gave in leaving them behind to stay with you; but you know our conventions, and I remind you: at the least word, I will fly once again to my dear Prince."[146] While waiting for that word, he continued to analyze with Artois the evolution of the political situation and to dispense copious recommendations and advice. Nearly fifty, having lived a life devoted to pleasure and now facing an uncertain future, the moment of contrition had arrived for him as well. But it was not enough to weep "night and day for the degradation of [his] unhappy fatherland and the misfortunes of the royal house,"[147] for whose glory he was prepared to shed his own blood. He also needed to reflect on the reasons that had led to this state of affairs, and the ways in which it might be remedied. It was undoubtedly in hopes of inciting the less meditative Artois to reflection that Vaudreuil systematically laid out his opinions for him in letter after letter. But he quickly realized that he was also writing his own defense for posterity. Thus he begged "his" Prince to preserve their correspondence—since, he affirmed, "it will one day allow me to be judged as I feel I deserve."[148]

Artois had established himself with his family and their suite in Turin, where his father-in-law, Victor Amadeus III of Savoie, had offered him hospitality and support, while Vaudreuil and the Polignacs, regarded disapprovingly by the residents of Bern as responsible for their native land's troubles, had been forced to leave Switzerland and spend the winter in Rome. During his second stay in the Eternal City, the Comte was too preoccupied to renew contact with any artists or antiquarians. Indeed, prudence required that he, like the Polignacs—having become symbols of all the abominations of Versailles—should lead an extremely retired life. Thus they did not mingle with those first, "merry" emigrants whose exile in Italy had an air of the Grand Tour about it, like the beautiful, elegant, and brilliant Duchesse Aimée de Fleury—who despite her successes could not forget Lauzun—the Princesse de Monaco, née Choiseul-Stainville, and Mme Vigée Le Brun, who had fled Paris on October 6 because her position as Marie-Antoinette's favorite painter had rendered her highly suspect. Even if in her *Souvenirs* the artist claims that she avoided frequenting the Polignacs out of prudence—Rome swarmed with spies—and does not mention meeting with Vaudreuil, we know that the Enchanter and the Fairy[149] succeeded in seeing each other numerous times. Didn't the Comte write to Artois that his "good angel" had had the grace to steer to Rome that Mme Le Brun whom he loved so "tenderly"?[150] But the person who most helped him to confront with lucidity and good sense the drama that was playing out for the French monarchy during his stay in Rome was not his guardian angel but, rather, the Cardinal de Bernis.

Hearing the news in Turin of the "frightful day of October 6"[151] and of the King's forced return to the capital, Artois launched his crusade against the Revolution by demanding the aid of the crowned heads of Europe. He began with Emperor Joseph II, writing him from Moncalieri a letter in which naivety vies with insolence. Driven by duty, honor, and patriotism to leave his country, he had lived "in silence and retirement" as long as his brother had enjoyed "an apparent freedom." But now that Louis XVI was a prisoner in the Tuileries, his "silence had become a crime" and his "good sense a sort of cowardice," and he had allowed himself the liberty of writing to His Majesty to say that he could imagine "nothing greater, nothing nobler, nothing, in short, more necessary... than to succor your brother-in-law, save your sister, and give to Your Majesty's most loyal ally the support and strength needed for the tranquility of all Europe."[152] Joseph II, with whom Louis XVI and Marie-Antoinette were already conducting a secret correspondence in which they continually denounced the interference of princes, responded to Artois by sternly reminding him of the first of his duties: obedience. "Neither aristocratic, nor democratic," the Emperor confined himself to mentioning that his brother-in-law did not lack the means necessary to protest the decisions of the assembly, and that up to that point he had showed himself to be "perfectly in accord with the nation" by approving all of its initiatives. Who then could assume the right to "raise his voice against all that has been decided and sanctioned by the most incontestable authority in the world, namely: the King reunited with the nation, legally represented by its deputies?" Artois and the princes who had decided to leave France should, like all the other citizens, submit themselves "to all that the King and the nation have seen fit to decree." After this first affirmation of principles, which stripped Artois's initiative of all legitimacy, the Emperor reminded him of the gloomy role that until now had been played by this aristocratic faction for which—was it really necessary to say?—the Prince had become the main point of reference. That faction which, "weak in itself and unable to accomplish the good it senses and desires, has sufficient firmness only for evil." What stupidity, to imagine "remedying the ills of your homeland and alleviating the situation of the King" by resorting to civil war! The first error of the princes had been to abandon the sovereign and thereby sow division, and there was only one way to rectify this: "to repatriate yourself," and thereby "obliterate any trace of the public's sense that there exists an opposing or so-called aristocratic faction; you must reunite to work for the good of the state, and submit your own way of imagining the latter to that of the greater number, who have the authority."[153] Not by chance, Joseph II neglected to mention that conducting an armed counterrevolution with foreign aid would be the surest way of reinforcing the Revolutionary government and of creating an irremediable split between the émigrés and the rest of the nation.

This was precisely the point upon which, backed by the forty years of experience acquired by Bernis, Vaudreuil insisted in his letters to Artois during that Roman sojourn: "Any foreign influence would only reunite the entire nation.... I am appalled at the dangers that the King and the royal family, prisoners in the capital, would be exposed to if foreign powers, at your instigation, mixed themselves in our domestic affairs.... As for rival powers or enemies of France, it would be dangerous, and would appear criminal, to address oneself to them."[154] Vaudreuil also sought to put Artois on his guard against Calonne,[155] who, from his exile in London, was preparing to take his revenge and become "minister of foreign affairs" for the émigrés in Koblenz. Vaudreuil, who at the time had supported him whether he was in favor or in disgrace, was now obliged to remind Artois that the reputation of the former controller of finances was irreparably compromised, and that the aversion the

Queen felt for him was insurmountable. But the Prince was no longer listening, obsessive and deaf to all advice. Take no action without the agreement of the King and Queen, Vaudreuil insisted, since "serving them in spite of themselves is impossible; then you would be a rebel, and responsible for all of the crimes that such efforts would bring about."[156] The Prince had to acknowledge that it was "opinion that had begun the Revolution," and that it must be "opinion that conducts the counterrevolution"—but for the latter to win, it would be necessary to wait for "the ordeal of misery, of new calamities, new excesses of anarchy, to make themselves felt in all their horror, and to lead the people back to the desire, the need, for authority."[157] Vaudreuil's prognosis would reveal itself to be precisely right, but nine years would still have to pass before Bonaparte restored that authority and put an end to the Revolution with the Coup of 18 Brumaire. Meanwhile, Europe's oldest nobility, the émigrés who had given themselves over to the factitious authority of Artois, endured the most distressing and humiliating of ordeals: the loss of their honor.

Not only did Artois fail to take heed of the Enchanter's advice—he wound up infecting the latter with his own illusions. In November 1790, after having accompanied the Polignacs to Venice, the Comte met up with Artois, the Condés, and Calonne in Turin, and allowed himself to be seduced by their plans. After the failure of the Lyon insurrection—whose "premature and ill-organized plans"[158] Vaudreuil had also denounced—the princes, in open disagreement with Louis XVI, were more determined than ever to lead the counterrevolution by calling for the aid of the new emperor, Leopold II. Now deprived of the advice of Bernis, and appalled by Louis XVI's acquiescence to the assembly's most unacceptable decrees, the Comte persuaded himself of the necessity of ignoring the directions coming from the Tuileries and adopting Calonne's strategies. A radical change of tone is notable in his correspondence with Artois, beginning with his return from Venice in May 1791. Beset by a veritable moral fever, he multiplied his letters, surprised himself by humming the "Ça Ira" as a kind of battle song against the Jacobins, and exclaimed with the accent of a paladin in search of adventure: "I have such contempt for our enemies, I believe I will attack them alone."[159] A letter to his cousin, probably written at the end of that same year, clearly shows that he no longer had any doubts about the fact that all Europe would take up arms against the Revolution: "The moment has arrived when the combined might of the sovereigns will destroy the scaffolding of a constitution presented under the guise of modern philosophy, but actually conceived by greed." It was merely a question of time, he insisted, but "in the end, it will always be necessary to strike." In the meantime, he expressed "the most ardent desire for the reestablishment of order and the public good," and declared himself determined not to set foot in his homeland until "the foundations of the French and monarchical constitution" had been put back in place. Until then, his place was by the side of the princes "whose loyalty and virtues excite and demand admiration."[160]

The flight to Varennes allowed the princes to distance themselves from the policies of the Tuileries and to take autonomous action openly. Unlike the King, the Comte de Provence succeeded in leaving France, and, having met up once again with Artois, decided along with him to accept the hospitality of their maternal uncle, the Elector of Trèves. On July 7, 1791, announced by a salvo of cannon fire and accompanied by their respective suites, the two princes made a solemn entrance into Koblenz, rendering the little German town at the confluence of the Rhine and the Moselle the capital of the emigration.

"My friend, you would think you were at Versailles,"[161] Vaudreuil declared to the Marquis de Clermont-Gallerand upon arriving in Koblenz, where he was invited to join the Council of Princes. The Comte's "enthusiasm" for the place might make us smile, but in its own way, his observation was correct. While thousands of émigrés of the most varied social stations—having abandoned all they held most dear, deprived of money and resources—had flowed into the electorate of Trèves in order to defend the monarchy, only to discover that nothing was waiting to welcome them, Monsieur and his brother, the Comte d'Artois, had organized around themselves a court that harked back to the golden age of Versailles. The "house" shared by the two princes could not have been more grandiose and boasted "pages, numerous men in livery, sentinels guarding their quarters, and places at table for nearly a hundred people each day," notes the Comte d'Espinchal, flabbergasted, at the beginning of his emigrant's diary. He adds that they had re-created all the rituals of Versailles, and "five days a week, the princes host a large dinner and receive both the nobility and those newly arrived," in accordance with the strictest etiquette. "That is to say, here one finds everything necessary to remind one of the abuses of the court and to dispose the provincial nobility against these courtiers and insolent creatures."[162]

The first to express concern about all of this was Calonne, who saw the funds earmarked for the war evaporating. The high nobility that had rushed to Koblenz were living a life of luxury, spending what money remained to them, in the certainty that within a few months they would return to France and retake possession of their former belongings and privileges. As far as the criteria determining the choice of officers for the army that was being formed, the unfortunate preferences introduced by the Maréchal de Ségur had been retained: more than rank and competence, it was a noble bloodline and—sine qua non—an unshakable devotion to the monarchy that counted, a species of "upside-down Jacobinism" with which the constitutional monarchists, whom the Terror had also forced into emigration, and who wished to enroll themselves in the Army of Koblenz, would find themselves butting heads. The case of the Duc de Lévis is exemplary: an ex-captain of Monsieur's guards, guilty of having shared the hopes of the liberal nobility in the assembly, he was rejected by the commission charged with selecting officers. Lévis fell back on the Austrian army, where, thanks to the recommendation of the Prince de Ligne, he succeeded in enlisting as a simple soldier under a false name.[163] It was a practical, social set of worries that drove him reluctantly to take up arms against his own country: the conviction, as he wrote to his wife, that if he did not, it would be difficult when the war ended to return to live in France "with any sort of respect."[164] The fear of seeing a member of one's own family contravene the imperatives of duty and honor also drove the Bishop of Laon to insist to Mme de Sabran that her son, Elzéar, join the Army of the Princes. After a long hesitation, the Comtesse decided to write to the Comte d'Artois to ask whether Elzéar—who lacked a warrior's temperament—might be appointed as an aide-de-camp, and must have been greatly relieved when she learned the young Comte would serve as an attendant to the Duc de Polignac, who represented the brothers of the King at the court of Vienna.[165]

In that operetta kingdom where, imprisoned by the past, the French aristocracy lived out its Indian summer, hatreds, divisions, and conspiracies flourished. Artois, Provence, and Condé each had their faction, and pursued differing stratagems. Incomparably more intelligent than Artois, wily and dissembling, Monsieur bided his time, leaving his younger brother to launch appeals, make impossible promises, and spread optimism with his amiability and chivalrous aplomb, while confidently waiting for Austria and Prussia to decide to enter the war. On at least one point, the three princes were entirely in agreement: the King was no longer in a position to exercise his free will, and it fell to them to defend the interests of the monarchy. For their part,

Provence and Artois shared a total inexperience where military matters were concerned. Condé was the only prince acquainted with the profession of arms, and had shown his mettle during the Seven Years' War. Outraged by the frivolity and thoughtlessness of the others, Condé was quick to distance himself from them and withdraw to Worms, where he raised an army that bore his name for eight years and established a reputation for heroism to which even the Republican officers paid homage.[166] The same could not be said for the Army of Koblenz when its time to fight came around. The casus belli was the Declaration of Pillnitz,[167] published after the flight to Varennes, in which the Emperor of Austria and the King of Prussia limited themselves to communicating that, "having heard the wishes and representations of Monsieur and the Comte d'Artois," they considered "the present situation of the King of France to be an object of common interest to all the sovereigns of Europe."[168] Phrased though it was with the greatest of prudence, this declaration constituted an unwarranted interference in the political life of another country, and France delivered a political response by declaring war on April 20, 1792.

Dragged in spite of themselves into a conflict whose costs and risks seemed greater than its eventual benefits, Austria and Prussia took care to grant the French exiles a role at the forefront of military operations. While they had hoped to march in tight formation at the head of the coalition army and retake their country in the name of the King of France, Brunswick, who held the supreme command of the armed forces and considered the émigrés a needless inconvenience, divided them into three distinct units. The four thousand men led by the Duc de Bourbon would have to join the Austrian troops stationed in the Netherlands, Condé's five thousand met up with Esterházy in Fribourg, and the ten thousand who formed the Army of the Princes, led by the elderly Maréchal de Broglie, were incorporated into the rear guard of Brunswick's forces, to march on Paris under his orders. Among the last-minute volunteers was François-René Chateaubriand, who had joined the Army of the Princes after the start of the war. In 1792, the writer, then twenty-four years old, "did not care in the least about the fate of Louis XVI, whom he held in low esteem, and, in spite of his 'liberal' opinions, even less about the Revolution currently underway,"[169] but he aligned himself with the ideas of Malesherbes, who held that it was necessary for the nobility of the sword to respond to the call to arms launched by the brothers of the King. "My zeal," Chateaubriand would recognize much later, "was in excess of my faith; I felt that the emigration was idiotic, a folly.... My distaste for absolute monarchy left me with no illusions about the side I was taking."[170] Yet the Army of the Princes inspired him to write those celebrated pages in which *pietas* mingle with indignation. Made up of high-ranking lords, the general staff shone by the elegance of their uniforms, the glittering of their weapons, the abundance of their victuals. "One saw nothing but wagons packed with provisions; nothing but cooks, valets, aides-de-camp. What better to represent the court and the province—the monarchy expiring at Versailles, and the monarchy dying in the wilderness of Du Guesclin."[171] The troops, for their part, struck Chateaubriand by their dignified poverty. Indeed, the provincial nobles who had obeyed the imperative of honor like the mythical heroes of the Hundred Years' War, were a "confused assemblage of grown men, the elderly, and children,"[172] who spoke all manner of dialects. Poorly equipped, lacking weapons and money, civilian émigrés served alongside soldiers who had defected from the French army, and there were numerous officers serving as simple soldiers, in a chaos of old uniforms and picturesque outfits. "This hodgepodge, ridiculous as it looked, had something honorable and touching about it, for it was animated by sincere conviction.... That whole poor crowd, who hadn't received a sou from the princes, fought the war at their own expense, while decrees were stripping them of all their possessions and jailing their wives and mothers."[173] Ready to sacrifice themselves for their King, the émigrés had not foreseen that their Austrian allies would treat them with contempt, ordering them around like inferiors, nor that their compatriots would welcome them as "enemies of liberty, aristocrats, satellites of Capet"[174] when they thought of themselves as liberators. They expected to enter Paris in triumph, not to suffer the humiliation of retreating under a deluge of rain and mud after the defeat at Valmy. Still less could they imagine that after the deposition of Louis XVI, with France still in the grips of the Terror and the property of the émigrés being confiscated, Monsieur and Artois would accede to the King of Prussia's request that they dissolve their army. The princes' final order, which on November 23, 1792, demanded that the soldiers withdraw "to wherever they wish," without any compensation, had the air of an ultimate snub. For the most part financially ruined, the émigrés could not return to France, where they had been condemned to death in absentia, and the various other nations of Europe showed little inclination to receive them. The Austrian army was not disposed to welcome into its ranks those who wished to continue the fight.

If the King's brothers, as the Marquis de Marcillac wrote, left their soldiers "no resource save despair,"[175] the Prince of Condé showed himself to be of an entirely different temper. When the Emperor ordered him to discharge his men, he limited himself to responding: "You'll have to kill every last one of them!" Vienna did not dare to insist.[176]

Vaudreuil participated in the princes' campaign as part of Artois's general staff, but in the absence of letters—his correspondence is interrupted during the crucial months of the conflict—we do not know how he faced the failure of a war upon which he had concentrated all of his hopes. In the letters that follow we find nary a word about the humiliations and sufferings of the émigrés whom he had contributed in sending into disaster. His dominant preoccupation remained politics, even if he was obliged to recognize his own errors. In April, he was still convinced that at the moment they reentered France, "the princes and the émigrés [would be] in the vanguard, while the Austrian and Prussian troops [would be] no more than auxiliaries."[177] But, by mid-June, he had begun to harbor serious doubts about the loyalty of the Viennese court,[178] and wound up admitting: "My God, what snakes they are! Vienna truly made us swallow it!"[179] In spite of the strength of Vaudreuil's loyalty to Artois, the latter's "valiant" declarations in the wake of the disaster—"I believe that my soul is precisely as it was before; my pride is as great, and I defy the whole universe to cut me down, or even to discourage me"[180]—had ceased to reassure. "He so deluded me," Vaudreuil confided to the Comte d'Antraigues, "that I have lost the lion's share of my confidence."[181] The news arriving from France—the end of the monarchy, the royal family's detention in the Temple, the victories of the Revolutionary army, the election of the National Convention—hurled Vaudreuil into a state of prostration. Feeling useless after the dissolution of the Koblenz army and the flight of Calonne, who had put his wife's fortune at the disposal of the princes, he took leave of Artois and rejoined the Polignacs, who had meanwhile established themselves in Vienna. Having there heard news of the death of Louis XVI, he responded on March 6, 1793, to Lady Foster, who had inquired about his health: "I have learned of the most harrowing catastrophe, the gruesome death of the best of men and kings, the benefactor of my friends. The details of that death, the bravery of that unfortunate monarch, the atrocious, unbelievable cruelty of his enemies, that sublime testament, the most beautiful monument that a man could leave of his moral and Christian virtues, the dangers to which the Queen, and that whole august family, have been exposed, the shame, the ineffaceable dishonor of my country—all of these mournful objects have lodged themselves so firmly in my heart and spirit that I cannot help but succumb."[182] Did Vaudreuil feel remorse for having contributed to the discredit of the royal family, at having neglected his due obedience to the King by embracing the weak-willed and unrealistic decisions of Artois, which had ultimately delivered the coup de grace to the monarchy? Or was there room in his mourning only for the memory of those happy years when the Polignacs had lived so intimately with Marie-Antoinette? In any event, it was not the Comte who "succumbed" to the news of the death of the royal couple but rather the Duchesse Jules. Having been ill for some time, "victim of her sorrows, her attachment, her gratitude,"[183] this close friend of the sovereign passed away in Vienna on December 5, 1793, at the age of forty-four. Like so many of his companions in misfortune, Vaudreuil, the former skeptic and anticlerical, found comfort in religion. In this he followed his mistress, who in the past had never made a secret of her agnosticism. Swept along by her sister-in-law's example, the Comtesse de Polastron also encouraged the conversion of the Comte d'Artois. Libertinism was now decidedly out of fashion. "She has gone to join her august benefactors, whose martyrdom surely merits them the company of this faithful friend ... forever in the bosom of the Lord himself," the Comte wrote to Lady Foster, announcing the death of his beloved. For him, still among the living, exile became above all a state of soul: "I remain alone in the world, on this odious earth, lacking purpose, lacking hope ... I have nothing now, I am nothing. I was everything to her; and in her I possessed all! I no longer harbor even the faintest desire for the happiness of my country, so barbarous, so ungrateful. What good thing can I desire, when she will never come again!"[184]

In October 1791, with the work of the National Constituent Assembly at an end, the Chevalier de Boufflers made the decision to emigrate. He would have left Paris long before if he had not felt obliged to see through to the end the mandate that had been entrusted to him by the bailiwick of Nancy. His experience as a deputy, which had obliged him to take a position on reforms far more radical than he had been prepared for, had been traumatizing. Naturally tolerant and peace-loving, the Chevalier had banked on a moderate political program, one that would be able to reconcile his loyalty to the monarchy with demands for renewal, and he was painfully struck by the climate of violence that had established itself between the different parties, poisoning the work of the assembly. "My soul," he wrote in 1789 to Mme de Sabran, "feels something like a traveler, naturally healthy and sensitive, who finds himself obliged to pass a long night in a caravansary among the plague-stricken and leprous. I hope to contract neither the plague nor leprosy—but how can one do anything about the disgust?"[185] Boufflers certainly did not lack the courage to defend his opinions, but though he may have been a virtuoso conversationalist, he was only a mediocre orator. Since he did not know how to improvise at the rostrum, he was obliged to read his speeches, and his style was too elegant, his voice too weak, his manners too polished, to hold the attention of an assembly accustomed to the thundering of a Mirabeau.[186] None of this prevented him from fully playing his role as deputy[187] with the sort of moderation and good sense that, unsurprisingly, won the admiration of Gouverneur Morris.[188] Anticlerical and a freethinker, the Chevalier proposed among other things a project of clerical reform that would reject perpetual vows, but he opposed the nationalization of religious property that Talleyrand had been hoping for. Indeed, he maintained that depriving the Church of its means of subsistence was out of keeping with the will of the nation, and that the sale of those holdings would not only hurt the interests of its creditors—was he thinking of his own advantage here?—but would also bring the real-estate market crashing down at the expense of the peasants and agriculture. Following the approval of the decree, he called for measures that would prevent the new owners from cutting down forests for their own profit. Moreover, faithful to the spirit of the *Encyclopédie*, Boufflers encouraged the creation of a national conservatory of arts and crafts, and brought to a vote a decree meant to protect discoveries in the domain of industry and trade with the establishment of patents guaranteed by the state.[189] He also made sure to introduce a system of grants especially for the benefit of artists, intended to encourage the "noble" as well as the "useful arts."[190]

On the strictly political level, the Chevalier defended again and again the exclusive right of Louis XVI to make executive decisions: in his opinion, the assembly must limit itself to legislation. "I picture all of this," he wrote to Mme de Sabran, continuing with his habit of literary allusion, "as a *Thebaid* in which two brothers, *Legislative Power* and *Executive Power*, irreconcilable children of a blind father, *the People*, bloody the earth in the course of their combats."[191] In 1790, he had founded, along with Malouet, La Rochefoucauld-Liancourt, Clermont-Tonnerre, Lally-Tollendal, and other friends, the Club des Impartiaux (Club of the Impartial), which proposed to "bring back order, peace, and security; it is the only way of saving the fatherland, of keeping the faith promised and owed to the creditors of the state, of reviving trade and restoring the collection of public revenues, without which we shall soon see the constitution itself perish, and with it, liberty."[192] This sort of centrist program would soon become obsolete. In any event, the club was long dissolved by the time of the flight to Varennes. And then, how could one speak of a "free monarchy" when "the King was confined to his château and Frenchmen are wholly prevented from leaving France? In any case, God knows where we would go!"[193] Unlike the King, the Chevalier succeeded in crossing the Swiss border without incident at the end of November and, at the beginning of 1793, joined Mme de Sabran in Rheinsberg, the residence of Henry of Prussia. In a letter of January 22, the Graf Maximilian von Lamberg informed Casanova of the Chevalier's arrival at the château, noting that he had heard him declare that France would soon see the end of the crisis, and that "the King [would be] more of a King than ever."[194]

The Comtesse de Sabran had not waited for the flight to Varennes before leaving the country with her son, Elzéar. Moreover, the welcome that the brother of Frederick the Great offered her, as well as the Chevalier, seemed to augur a relatively pleasant exile, "a sufficiently sweet sort of lethargy."[194] Highly cultured and a profound Francophile, Prince Henry was indeed happy to be able to rely on the collaboration of these two virtuosos of social life to infuse his little court with the true Parisian *esprit de société*.[195] In exchange for a deeply considerate hospitality that freed them from any financial worry, the two lovers had simply to persevere in their old customs: conversing, improvising poetry, composing theatrical sketches, performing onstage, and engineering witty diversions. Passing through Rheinsberg, Mme Vigée Le Brun found them in full swing.[196] But it was difficult to maintain an unchanging good humor when the most terrible news kept arriving from France. Mme de Sabran had left her daughter, Delphine, in Paris—she was now imprisoned, after having heroically assisted her father-in-law, General de Custine, and her young husband, both of whom had been sent to the guillotine. Shortly afterward, the Chevalier's beloved sister met the same fate.[197] An old relative of Boufflers, General Dampmartin, passing through Rheinsberg, was struck by the change he saw in him: "The famous Chevalier, with his vivid imagination, his unique talent, his swift sense of humor, his happy character, and his perfect courtesy; that Chevalier possessed the French spirit par excellence; but the spirit that so delighted the court of Lunéville, of Versailles, and the salons of Paris, found it difficult to bear the ordeal of expatriation. He was like one of those flowers that are spangled with the most varied colors when kindled by the sun's light, but whose charms wither away in harsher climes: his habitual silence was interrupted only at long intervals, but then there would flow from him a stream of witticisms, fresh, fine, gay, perhaps sweetly malicious—but always ingenious. In order to truly appreciate them, one must have...*drunk the waters of the Seine*."[198] In the end, Henry of Prussia too began to weary of his guests, and Boufflers and Mme de Sabran must have felt "how bitter is the taste / of foreign bread, and how difficult / to climb and to descend a stranger's stairs."[199]

In recalling the terrible days that had marked the end of the monarchy, Narbonne confided to Villemain "that he would not have let the King wait in the Tuileries for August 10, nor for June 20, but, armed with a title and the remnants of his power, would have found a sanctuary for Louis XVI not abroad but on the border."[200] Indeed, we know that even after his forced retirement from the position of minister of war, the Comte attempted to save the royal family, devising with Mme de Staël an audacious escape plan. After being dismissed by the King and having defended himself against the attacks of the Jacobins by eloquently citing his work as minister before the assembly, the Comte had rejoined Lafayette in Metz and once again taken up his army position. But at the end of May, his friend sent him back to Paris to follow the political developments brought about by the war. As Barnave had predicted, the first defeats suffered by the French army on the Belgian front—at Tournai, General Dillon had been massacred by his own troops, and Biron was forced to fall back to Valenciennes—unleashed a popular reaction and pushed the extreme left into power. Fearing a foreign invasion and the treason of Louis XVI, and exasperated by the veto with which the King had opposed the deportation of refractory priests, an armed mob stormed the Tuileries chanting savage rhymes against "Monsieur and Mme Veto"—they forced the King to don a Phrygian cap, and held the royal family hostage for hours. When, in spite of all this, the King refused to withdraw his veto, the popular movement, roused by Marat, "the Friend of the People," loudly demanded his deposition. Foreseeing the worst, Narbonne and Mme de Staël encouraged the royal couple to flee. Among the numerous more or less practicable plans that were mooted in the wake of Varennes, the one that had sprung from the fertile mind of Germaine was the most ingenious: Mme de Staël would pretend she wished to purchase the estate of Lamotte, offered for sale by the Duc d'Orléans, and strategically located on the coast of Normandy; there she would carry out numerous reconnaissance trips, always traveling in the same coach and according to the same itinerary, stopping at the same places, in the company of a presumed *homme d'affaires*, two ladies-in-waiting, and a child, all having roughly the same measurements as the members of the royal family, and always dressed in the same fashion. Narbonne would accompany them on horseback, disguised as a page. Postilions and soldiers at checkpoints would grow accustomed to their comings and goings, and let down their guard. When the moment arrived, the King, the Queen, Mme Élisabeth, and the Dauphin would climb into the coach dressed like their doubles and, escorted by Mme de Staël and Narbonne, would be able to reach the château of Lamotte without arousing curiosity and set sail from there.[201] This proposal was rejected: Louis XVI was finally persuaded of the Comte's loyalty, but both he and Marie-Antoinette distrusted Mme de Staël and preferred to listen to their advisers, who considered the constitutionalists to be traitors. Nor would they consider the plan conceived by Montmorin, in collaboration with Liancourt, then commanding a garrison of troops at Rouen. A year later, Talleyrand would write to Mme de Staël from London: "After Varennes, the royals were saved by the *parti constitutionnel*; on August 10, they were lost by the *parti aristocratique*, which up to the last moment had opposed the idea that the King should depart for Rouen."[202] The die-hard monarchists retained their hatred for the constitutionalists even after August 10. At the beginning of the month, the Brunswick Manifesto, which threatened Paris with fire and blood if any harm should come to Louis XVI and his family, and the assembly's refusal to proceed with the deposition of the King, unleashed the rage of the people, who again stormed the Tuileries. Narbonne, Mathieu de Montmorency, La Tour du Pin-Gouvernet, Lally-Tollendal, François de Jaucourt, Stanislas de Clermont-Tonnerre, and other constitutionalist gentlemen rushed to the palace to defend the sovereign, but even exposed to this extreme danger, the hard-core royalists refused the aid of their would-be rescuers. Mme de Staël would recall in her *Considerations on the French Revolution* the despair of Narbonne and his liberal friends, faced with their own powerlessness: "Unable to join the opposing side despite the rebuff they had received [from the royalists], they wandered around the palace, exposing themselves to massacre as consolation for being unable to fight."[203] The first to be massacred were in fact the Cent Suisses, while the palace was being looted and the royal family sought refuge with the assembly. Utterly incapable of regaining control of the situation, the deputies suspended Louis XVI's powers of government and imprisoned him in the Temple. Even as the massacres continued, the hunt for suspects began. Left behind at the embassy following her husband's recall to Sweden, and in spite of her advanced state of pregnancy, Mme de Staël went from house to house offering her aid to friends she knew were in danger: Mathieu de Montmorency, La Tour du Pin-Gouvernet, and Beaumetz all concealed themselves at her home in the rue du Bac. But she could do nothing for Stanislas de Clermont-Tonnerre who, that very same evening, was hurled from the window of the house where he had taken refuge.

Narbonne was luckier. Wanted by the Jacobins, he succeeded in reaching Mme de Staël's, where, invoking God and the Holy Virgin, he begged for the aid of the embassy's chaplain, the Protestant pastor Charles-Christian Gambs, who, after Staël's departure, had become Sweden's representative to the French government. Despite his fervent Republican convictions, Gambs hid Narbonne for four days beneath the altar of the chapel.[204] Mme de Staël's courage and sangfroid did the rest. As she herself recounts, she welcomed the officials who had arrived to search her house for suspects, reminding them that they were guests at a diplomatic mission and thus in violation of international law. Taking advantage of their weak understanding of geography, she managed to persuade them that Sweden abutted France and would avenge their trespass with an immediate attack—she even had the presence of mind to joke about the groundlessness of their suspicions. At last, mobilizing all her capacity to charm, Germaine succeeded in convincing them. "I escorted them as far as the door," she remembers, "and blessed God for the strength he had granted me."[205] Now it was necessary to find some way for Narbonne—a warrant for whose arrest had meanwhile been issued—to slip out of the embassy without being seen and leave France. The chaplain, also eager to rid himself of the Comte, introduced Mme de Staël to a twenty-four-year-old German doctor, Justus Erich Bollmann, who had come to France to observe the progress of the Revolution. Won over by the "chivalrous frankness" of Narbonne (who even in the greatest of danger maintained all his characteristic gaiety and society manners), and attracted by the romantic flavor of the situation—"a pregnant woman nearly ready to give birth, lamenting the fate of her lover... her tears, a man in deadly danger, and the hope of saving him... the charm of the extraordinary, all this was quite stirring at the time"[206]—Bollmann agreed to organize the Comte's escape and to accompany him across the English Channel. Thought through to a fare-thee-well, the plan worked perfectly. Narbonne left the embassy disguised as a coachman, spent the night at Bollmann's lodgings, and the next day, furnished with a fake English passport and proceeding with the greatest nonchalance, the two travelers left the capital without incident, passing through numerous checkpoints along the route and arriving safe and sound at Boulogne, where they embarked for Dover. On August 23, the Comte arrived in London.

At only thirty-seven years of age, Narbonne could consider his political career at an end, and his exile had a bitter and defeated flavor. None of his enterprises had borne fruit. He had believed, like Mme de Staël, that the Revolution would lead to a constitutional monarchy with two legislative chambers and executive power entrusted to the King, but had been forced to resign himself to a single chamber and the limitation of royal power. And in gambling on military action for the purpose of restoring the power and prestige of Louis XVI, he had bolstered a war that had proven fatal to the monarchy. Certainly he wasn't the only one to have been fooled: Talleyrand, Biron, and Lafayette had all nursed the same hopes, but none of them had been so intimately tied to the royal family, nor felt so deeply the loss of the monarchy. If his friends were fully responsible for their own decisions, the Comte couldn't help asking himself whether his own would have been quite so dangerous without the influence of Mme de Staël. Now that the political adventure that had bound the two of them so closely had come to nothing, what would remain of their sentimental companionship? The sole certainty that Narbonne had not lost was that of his honor as a gentleman, and it served as his guide on the long desert crossing that awaited him. He would endure forced expatriation, poverty, and the uncertainty of the future with the elegance and insouciance that had been characteristic of him both at court and in town, and that had become second nature. But nothing could protect him from the anguish he felt as the violence of the Revolution reached its crescendo.

During the first few weeks in London, which he spent in the house that Talleyrand had rented in Kensington Square and where Mme de La Châtre had been entrusted with the role of *maîtresse de maison*, Narbonne found a cure for his depression by busying himself with the search for more permanent lodgings for himself and his fellow exiles. On September 15, Talleyrand arrived in London. Having managed to obtain a regular passport from Danton, he did not officially figure on the list of émigrés. He was followed by Mathieu de Montmorency, Pierre-Victor Malouet, and François de Jaucourt, all three saved by Mme de Staël and then, in time, by other deputies of the National Constituent Assembly, such as the Marquis de Lally-Tollendal, the Duc de Liancourt, and the Comte de Beaumetz. The house in Kensington Square became a meeting place for all of them, and Justus Erich Bollmann, who as Narbonne's savior had been welcomed with open arms, was dumbstruck by the freedom, intensity, and brio of their conversation.[207] In contrast to British customs, the women, who espoused the same political convictions as their lovers, participated fully: there was Mme de Flahaut, who had left France after the September Massacres with the help of John Wycombe, the man who had succeeded Talleyrand and Morris in her bed; the beautiful and brilliant Princesse d'Hénin, who lived apart from her husband and was close with Lally-Tollendal; and naturally Mme de La Châtre, who was in love with François de Jaucourt, with whom she had had a child.

Still, despite the relief of finding themselves alive and in a safe place, and despite their recourse to the magical rite of conversation to help exorcise their nostalgia for their lost homeland, Narbonne and his friends were conscious of the numerous dangers that the British capital held for them. Granted, having remained neutral, England had given a far warmer welcome to French expatriates than other countries, sympathizing with their misfortunes and providing aid to the most impoverished among them. And Narbonne enjoyed the advantages—by no means negligible—of having traveled there many times in the past, of speaking the language perfectly, and of counting numerous Londoners among his friends. He was immediately received by prominent representatives of the parliamentary left—Charles James Fox, Lord Grenville, Lord Erskine—who shared the overarching ideals of the French Revolution and supported, in opposition to Pitt, a policy of radical reforms. But if Narbonne and his constitutionalist friends found sympathy from the Whig aristocracy, they were regarded with suspicion by the Tory government, and were particularly kept at a distance by the earlier wave of émigrés. Noailles, Choiseul, Beauvau, Mortemart, Fitz-James, Duras, Osmond, and many other members of the old French nobility—who, since 1789, had chosen England as their place of exile, frequented London's high society, and circulated in the English court—were unanimous in considering the newcomers to have been responsible for the Jacobin dictatorship and the fall of the monarchy. Not only did they do nothing to help the newcomers, but they also subjected the "traitors" to a vicious smear campaign.[208] The proclamation of the Republic, the imprisonment of the King, and the massacres of September 2 did nothing but exacerbate the situation, raising a wave of indignation among the English public, one which only increased with the trial and death sentence of Louis XVI. Miss Berry, the young protégée of Horace Walpole—who had succumbed to the charm of French high society—now denounced all of its intrinsic weaknesses in a ferocious parody of the Credo:

I believe in the French, the makers of all fashions. I acknowledge their superiority in conversation, and their supremacy in dancing. I believe in their fanaticism for what is new, not in their enthusiasm for what is great, and I expect neither consistency in their plans nor constancy in their sentiments. I believe in the King, the weakest and most injured of mortals, and in the Queen, as equal to him in sufferings and surpassing him in understanding; and in the Dauphin, whose kingdom will never come. I believe equally in the folly of the Princes, the baseness of their councillors, and the cruelty and madness of their enemies. I expect neither the resurrection of order, nor the regeneration of morals, and I look neither for the coming of liberty, nor the permanence of their constitution. Amen![209]

Initially a mecca for liberals, as Ghislain de Diesbach described it, London "had become the capital of the most intransigent royalism, the last bastion of that ancien régime which had gathered together more partisans than it counted three years earlier."[210] In order to escape the hostility of the hard-core monarchists and to not increase the government's difficulties, but also for reasons of economy, numerous refugees sought lodgings beyond London. Lally-Tollendal, the Princesse d'Hénin, and Liancourt encountered Mme de Genlis at Bradford Hall, midway between Aylesham and the capital, under the protective wing of the democratic Francophile Arthur Young. For his part, with the money that Mme de Staël had sent him, Narbonne decided to lease Juniper Hall, a vast and comfortable country house near the village of Mickleham, in Surrey, some twenty-five miles from London, and settled there with Mme de La Châtre, Jaucourt, Mathieu de Montmorency, and Charles de Lameth. Soon they were joined by another of Narbonne's good friends, and Lafayette's former chief of staff, General d'Arblay. For her part, the Duchesse de Broglie, who had fled France after the arrest of her husband, General Charles-Louis-Victor de Broglie, rented a modest cottage not far from Juniper Hall. Her son Achille-Léonce-Victor-Charles, seven years old at the time, would one day become Mme de Staël's son-in-law. Arriving last, on January 25 or 26, 1793, Germaine passed "four months of happiness salvaged from the shipwreck of life"[211] at Juniper Hall, finding it "a terrestrial paradise."[212] Yet it was she who would introduce the apple of discord. For nearly a year, Juniper Hall was a laboratory in which all the manifold forms of affective life—passion, love, pity, friendship, honor, duty—were experimented with, and where multiple stories were plaited together into an extraordinary *comédie sentimental*. Here two profoundly different national characters—the puritanical Englishman who would serve as a model for bourgeois Europe in the century to come, and the worldly French aristocrat who had come to the end of his historical path—stood confronting each other. We have retained the written traces of that division in various voices thanks to the epistolary activity of its principal personalities, and we hear its echo as well in the novels of Mme de Staël. But it is the English correspondents who have left us the most detailed chronicle of the period.

From the beginning, the arrival of the French refugees in the peaceful and bucolic Surrey valley had aroused the curiosity of the neighborhood. William Lock and his wife, Frederica Augusta, spent extended periods of the year at Norbury Park, the most beautiful country house in the district, which overlooked Juniper Hall from a hill on the opposite bank of the River Mole. It was said—strange geometries of fate—that Lock was an illegitimate son of Louis XV raised in London, and his wife was a goddaughter of Frederick the Great. Rich, cultured, and generous patrons of the arts, the Locks were fervent liberals and, despite their significant difference in age, enjoyed a conjugal idyll founded on the convergence of their ideals and the openness of their hearts. Both extended a warm welcome to the newcomers, offering them a friendship that would never weaken. Democrats and fervent admirers of Lafayette, the Phillipses—good friends of the Locks who lived in a graceful cottage in Westhumble, an hour's walk from Juniper Hall—were just as welcoming. Molesworth Phillips served in the navy, while his wife, Susanna—who before her marriage had been a promising musician—devoted herself to the education of their three children. They too had married for love, but the husband's extravagances and the financial difficulties that flowed from them had put an end to their initial harmony. On the other hand, Susanna could depend on the unlimited solidarity of her older sister, Fanny Burney, who, unlike her, had not married, and was the author of two novels, *Evelina* and *Cecilia*, whose successes had not, however, improved her style of life. After five grueling years as the Queen's keeper of the robes, a post that had earned her only a modest pension, Fanny had returned to live with her father, the famous musicologist Charles Burney, for whom she cherished a respectful admiration. Very close, the two sisters wrote to each other assiduously. Intelligent, cultured, and curious about everything, their correspondence touched on the most varied subjects, but from the beginning of October, their attention was monopolized by the "interesting details of the French Colony."[213] Brought to Juniper Hall by Mrs. Lock at the beginning of November, Susanna was finally able to make the acquaintance of the new neighbors that so fascinated her. Not only were they intrepid patriots who had risked their lives for their ideals, but they also were the same age as she—none of them were out of their forties—and all were affable, witty, and marvelously exotic. She hastened to describe them, one by one, to her sister, beginning with Mme de La Châtre, the sole woman in the group. Without being a beauty, she was elegant, civilized, full of wit, "lively and charming."[214] She had fled not only the Terror but also an execrable husband whose political ideals were diametrically opposed to her own, and who had gone to join the princes in Koblenz. Deeply impressed by such independence, Mrs. Phillips did not even begin to suspect that Mme de La Châtre was the mistress of the Comte de Jaucourt, also present at Juniper Hall. Eager to meet the latter after having heard of his eloquence as a member of the National Constituent Assembly, Susanna was not disappointed, finding him "comic, entertaining, unaffected, unpretending, and good-humored"—in short, simply "delightful."[215] The youngest member of the group was "M. de Montmorency, a *ci-devant duc*, and one who gave some of the first great examples of sacrificing personal interest to what was then considered the public good,"[216] by proposing to the assembly the abolition of titles. On this subject, Susanna reported to her sister an anecdote that gives a glimpse of the flights of incisive wit with which Talleyrand was soon regaling the gatherings at Juniper Hall. Encountering Montmorency several days after his beau geste before the assembly, Talleyrand had addressed him by his family name, Mathieu Bouchard. "'But I am a Montmorency,' exclaimed the young duke, and he at once mentioned his great ancestors who had fought at Bouvines and Saint-Denis. 'Yes, yes, my dear Mathew,' interrupted the wit, 'you are the first member of your family who has laid down his arms.'"[217]

But the star of this scene was Narbonne, handsome, a grand seigneur, courteous and infinitely melancholy, and his friends did not cease to sing his praises. He had persuaded General d'Arblay to join him, Mme de La Châtre told Susanna, when he learned that his friend, incriminated as Lafayette's right-hand man and reduced to poverty, was seeking sanctuary abroad: he would happily share with him his last piece of silver. A fine figure of a man, broad-minded and virile,[218] d'Arblay was the least sophisticated and witty member of the group, but striking for his delicate kindness, which was extraordinarily moving. After the first few courteous visits, the exchanges between Juniper

Hall, Norbury Park, and Westhumble intensified. Informal invitations and enchanting day trips multiplied, while the astonishment and admiration of the English at a way of life capable of surviving so many misfortunes grew apace. One feels there is enough material for a novel in the letters that Susanna and the Locks send back to London, and in fact they furnished Fanny Burney with the elements that would go to form her most beautiful work of fiction. An intransigent monarchist who had inherited the rigorously Tory positions of her father, who himself saw the French Revolution with the eyes of his friend Edmund Burke, Fanny did not share the progressive enthusiasms of the Phillipses, but the news that Susanna and the Locks sent to her about the residents of Juniper Hall exerted an irresistible attraction on her. She did not meet them herself until January, when she finally joined her sister in West-humble. Less than a year later, in defiance of paternal disapproval and in spite of the most elementary good sense, she married General d'Arblay.

While the two sisters—passionate readers of Mme de Sévigné and faithful to an epistolary aesthetic that saw in the form of the letter "the conversations of those absent"—gave that literary genre a British version in the style of Jane Austen, Mme de Staël maintained an impassioned correspondence with Narbonne. "Burning letters for burning—a fine moral lesson too,"[219] Mme d'Arblay wrote years later on the envelope containing them. Narbonne had most likely entrusted them to d'Arblay when he left England, and they remained with the general's papers, escaping destruction at the hands of Mme de Staël's descendants, who had destroyed Narbonne's letters as well as a large part of Germaine's amorous correspondence. Luckily Fanny did not dare to burn Germaine's letters, and kept them with her own papers and those of her husband in a metal trunk, from which they would emerge a century later.[220]

"Ah! how happy the day when we lay bare our life for the one friend our soul has selected for her own—the day when some act of absolute devotion supplies at least a hint of the emotion that has oppressed our hearts because it was impossible to express!"[221] In evoking the exhilarating moment when she had saved Narbonne's life by risking her own, Mme de Staël's vision of herself was somewhat awry: to judge from the hundred and fifty letters that she sent to her lover following his escape, it was not her ability to express her emotions that was lacking—it was Narbonne who showed himself incapable of responding appropriately to her passion.

Written from Paris, where she remained until September 3 in order to lend her assistance to other friends in danger, the first letters from Germaine are unequivocal: "I can do nothing but love you, miss you, and give birth to your child."[222] For the sake of that child, her second with Narbonne, who would soon be born, she had renounced the idea of following her lover to London and had returned to Switzerland. But the atmosphere in Coppet was grim. Deaf to the pleading of her parents, she had remained in Paris after her husband's departure, but now the relief of the Neckers at having her back with them again was nothing compared to their indignation at her scandalous relationship with Narbonne. Her mother would not speak a word to her, and despite the limitless indulgence that he had always shown her, her father did not spare her his reproaches. But she was ready to subordinate her filial adoration to her love for Narbonne. "I have something horrible to tell you," she admitted to the Comte shortly after her arrival: "I will never be [my father's] with all my soul, so long as he does not share my feelings for you."[223]

But Germaine was soon forced to question her feelings for Narbonne. Why were his letters so few and far between? Did he even know what passion was? Was he inspired enough to feel it?[224] She never let slip an opportunity to remind him of her own—"the sort of passion that consumes my whole being"—with the tone and style of a tragic heroine. But no matter how she appealed to "that purest of hearts, to which [she] entrusted the whole of [her] fate,"[225] no matter how tirelessly she reiterated what he was for her—"*vous, toi*, my angel, spouse, lover, friend...everything"[226]—Narbonne continued to be evasive, prudent, detached.

If he was worried about the future, she was more than ready to reassure him on that front. Passing without embarrassment from the register of the sublime to that of bourgeois pragmatism, Mme de Staël indulged in a bit of math: she expected to receive enough from her father that they would not have to renounce the lifestyle they had become accustomed to, but neither would it be necessary for them to divorce their respective spouses. The only resources that Narbonne could depend on were the properties belonging to his wife, of whom Germaine had no reason to be jealous. And for her part, she was well aware that divorcing M. de Staël would cost her dearly. Fundamentally, there was no sense in marrying Narbonne unless it would benefit the two of them financially.[227] She hoped that a settling of the political situation would allow them to return to France someday, "but if not, America, together; America, if your heart can stand the solitude, would still be paradise with you."[228] Even news as tragic as that of the trial of Louis XVI did not cause her to lose sight of her own interests. For example, the defense of the King[229] that her father had decided to send to the convention seemed to her "quite worthy of respect in many ways," but terribly inconvenient. Driven by his need to take center stage, Necker's intervention could do nothing to change the fate of Louis XVI, and on the contrary furnished the Jacobins with an excellent excuse not to repay the loans he had made to the French government. Sending a copy of the aforementioned text to Narbonne, Germaine admitted, not without embarrassment: "I am quite disturbed by its effect on our fortune. My God, how miserable I would be if I lost it! . . . my father's love of attention and of the King, two very different things, may cost our happiness dearly."[230] Evidently Germaine had still not perceived that Narbonne, who fully shared Necker's views, was preparing even graver worries for her. As surprising as it may seem, Mme de Staël showed that she did not really know the Comte. Love had never been high among his priorities—it was his ambition and his passion for politics that had sealed his union with her. Now that both of these had collapsed like houses of cards, he was entirely absorbed by the tragedy of the monarchy. With the season of heroism drawing to an end, the plans for conjugal bliss that his mistress was proposing, the allusions as insistent as they were indiscreet (and that certainly weren't in keeping with the rules of aristocratic adultery) to the children their relationship had produced, her sentimental exaltation and banker's daughter calculations, all were incompatible with the Comte's way of being in the world and took for granted a level of engagement that did not actually exist on his part. But how to escape the demands of a woman who had saved his life and to whom he owed an enormous debt of gratitude? The physical distance between them allowed him to defer the problem, but not for long. After having given birth on November 20 to a child who, like her, would exist, she claimed, only to love him, and would bind even more closely their two "inseparable destinies,"[231] Mme de Staël seemed more determined than ever to join him in England.

But that November Narbonne's worries were of an entirely different sort. The announcement of the trial of the King, who was accused of treason and held responsible for the defeats at Longwy and Verdun, had thrown Juniper Hall into consternation. The Comte had proposed to the constitutionalist ministers, who found themselves at the time in London, that they draft "a joint declaration in order to claim, under the terms of the constitution of 1791, responsibility for the actions of their ministries, and to obtain permission for each of them to come to the bar of the convention to defend himself, and his deeds, in person during the King's trial."[232] Having failed to convince them, Narbonne asked the convention for safe conduct to return to Paris to witness the trial and take responsibility for all the initiatives that had been approved during his three-month tenure as minister of war. His friends d'Arblay, Lally-Tollendal, Liancourt, and Malouet followed his example. The convention having rebuffed all of their requests, the Comte instead sent a written statement—"The Declaration of Louis de Narbonne, Former Minister of War, in the Trial of the King"[233]—to Tronchet and Malesherbes, who had taken upon themselves the King's defense. It was a testimony that refuted the accusation—the most serious in the trial—of a secret understanding between Louis XVI and the foreign powers. Malesherbes thanked the Comte numerous times, assuring him that he had shown his declaration to the sovereign, who had been "touched, and even moved,"[234] but had recommended not making it public for fear of compromising him. It was a useless precaution, for Narbonne hastened to have it published in both Paris and London, sending copies to the members of the convention. When she learned of the uproar that the Comte's letter had caused in the convention, Mme de Staël saw in her lover's gesture not an act of extreme fidelity to the sovereign who had held him over the baptismal font and with whom he had spent his childhood but rather a cruelty perpetrated against herself. "You have delivered a mortal blow to me M. de Narbonne," she wrote to him on December 2. "I believed that my life was worth more in your eyes than this maddest, most futile, most dangerous of initiatives, both for the King and for yourself. But it must be that the need to make a spectacle of yourself has made you fierce.... What man has the right to tear apart the heart that loves him whenever he wishes, to make that heart undergo, inexorably, all the sufferings, all the anguish of death? The factitious duty to display oneself, to make oneself talked about, even more than being useful—can it be compared to this barbarism? I can do no more; I hate you, I despise you, and I am dying with all the tortures of the damned in hell.... If you set foot in France again, the very same instant I shall blow my brains out."[235]

Before the year ended, Mathieu de Montmorency, Mme de La Châtre, and Jaucourt would reenter France in an attempt to salvage what they could before the convention's decree of October 22, which aimed at the perpetual banishment of the émigrés and the confiscation of their goods, went into effect. The goodbyes with which they took their leave of the Phillipses and the Locks were moving. The evening after their departure, Narbonne and d'Arblay were invited to dine at Norbury Park; now that Mme de La Châtre was gone, her English friends wanted to know if her husband was really a monster, as she had claimed. Not without embarrassment, d'Arblay was attempting to explain that M. de La Châtre's manners were a bit brusque, but that he was really a very fine person, when a servant came to inform Narbonne that someone was asking for him. Several moments later, the Comte returned in the company of a small, oddly dressed man with straightforward manners—none other than M. de La Châtre himself. Dismissed without a sou from the Army of the Princes, La Châtre had arrived in London after a risky voyage and was in search of his wife and child, whom he had not seen in two years. Everyone was astounded by this coup de théâtre, but La Châtre succeeded in astonishing those present still further. He was indeed a brusque gentleman: he did not bat an eye when he heard that he had missed his family by merely a day and, in spite of the most elementary rules of politeness, settled himself in the warmth before the fireplace, paying no attention whatsoever to anyone but Narbonne. "They had not met since the beginning of the Revolution," Susanna Phillips hastened to report to her sister, "and, having been of very different parties, it was curious and pleasant to see them now, in their mutual misfortunes, meet *en bons amis*." La Châtre described his disastrous journey to England, where he had found himself penniless, and added apropos of missing his son, "God knows if I shall see him again for forty years to come," which moved the English; but immediately after, he "went on gaily enough, laughing at *ses amis les constitutionnaires*, and M. de Narbonne, with much more wit and not less good-humor, retorting back his raillery on the *parti de Brunswick*. 'Eh bien,' said M. de la Châtre, 'each in his turn. You were the first to be ruined. You framed a constitution which could not hold water.'—'Pardon me,' cried M. d'Arblay with quickness, 'it was never tried.'—'Well, it was set aside all the same; there is no question about it now,' said M. de La Châtre; 'and there is nothing left for all of us to do but to starve merrily together.'"[236] Whatever wrongs he had done to his wife, the unexpected guest certainly did not lack a sense of humor.

On the other hand, the news of Mme de La Châtre's departure vexed Mme de Staël, who had counted on her friend's presence to justify her visit to Juniper Hall. For all that, she was not deterred in her plan, from which she was dissuaded neither by her parents nor by Narbonne, who had attempted to convince her to at least postpone her trip. But Germaine would listen to no one but herself. "The moment has come," she wrote to her lover, "to choose between you and the rest of the world, and it is toward you that my heart drives me. May the gift of my life embellish your own, may the very same sacrifices I've made to my passion for you not lower me in your eyes, and should they hurt my reputation, remember me as someone whose love for you was her only law."[237] All that Narbonne could do was resign himself.

At Juniper Hall, Mme de Staël found that a rather somber atmosphere reigned: Narbonne and d'Arblay had followed the progress of Louis XVI's trial in anguish, and the news of his death, on January 21, had plunged them into despair. It was then that Fanny Burney, on a visit to her sister, finally made their acquaintance. Having heard plenty of talk about the courage, dignity, and affability of the residents of Juniper Hall, she had ceased to think of them as dangerous revolutionaries, and their grief convinced her of the sincerity of their monarchical faith. "M. de Narbonne and M. d'Arblay have been almost annihilated," Fanny wrote almost immediately to her father: "they are for ever repining that they are French, and, though two of the most accomplished and elegant men I ever saw, they break our hearts with the humiliation they feel for their guiltless birth in that guilty country! '—*Est-ce vrai*,' cries M. de Narbonne, '*que vous conservez encore quelque amitié, M. Lock, pour ceux qui ont la honte et le malheur d'être nés Français?*'* Poor man!—he has all the symptoms upon him of the jaundice; and M. d'Arblay, from a very fine figure and good face, was changed, as if by magic, in one night, by the receipt of this inexpiable news, into an appearance...black...meagre, and...miserable."[238]

In truth, Narbonne had hoped until the very last moment for an English intervention that would save Louis XVI, appealing both to his friends in the opposition and to Pitt; but when Pitt finally decided to receive him, he had declared that "England could not risk interceding in vain in such a matter, and before such men."[239]

Having imposed herself on the place by main strength, Mme de Staël quickly made amends by filling Juniper Hall with the breath of life. Reassured by the proximity of her lover and abandoning the tragic register, she once again gave the best of herself, taking an interest in everything, conversing, debating,

---

*"Is it true that you still feel a measure of goodwill, M. Lock, for those with the shame and misfortune of having been born French?"

writing, reading, and never ceasing to surprise and delight with her indefatigable intellect. "Madame de Staël, daughter of M. Necker, is now at the head of the colony of French noblesse, established near Mickleham," Fanny wrote with enthusiasm to her father. "She is one of the first women I have ever met with, for abilities and extraordinary intellect."[240]

Her arrival attracted various constitutionalist friends to Juniper Hall: the Princesse d'Hénin, Lally-Tollendal, Malouet, the Lameth brothers, and, naturally, Talleyrand, who immediately established himself, with "his [astonishing] powers of entertainment . . . both in information and in raillery," as "one of the first members, and one of the most charming, of this exquisite set," obliging Fanny, who had heard horrible things about him in London, to change her opinion.[241] In the beautiful wood-paneled salon elegantly sculpted in pure Adamesque fashion—which the visitor to Juniper Hill can still admire today[242]—the French exiles entertained each other, reading their writings aloud and commenting on them together, offering their English guests "a marvelous . . . excess of agreeability"[243] and including them in their diversions. Mme de Staël launched herself into the conquest of Fanny, whose novels she admired, writing her letters in English, while General d'Arblay offered to instruct her in French in exchange for English lessons. Fanny and d'Arblay also got into the habit of exchanging compositions written in each other's language every evening, building between them a rapport that would soon transform itself into love.

But the days of this utopia at Juniper Hall were numbered. The indignation aroused by Louis XVI's death sentence and, at the end of January, by England's entry into the war against France, rendered the position of the constitutionalists who had sought refuge in Great Britain even more problematic. A new law, the Aliens Act, now exposed those French émigrés judged dangerous to imprisonment or expulsion without trial, and London became the scene of a veritable witch hunt. It was in this climate that Dr. Burney received a letter from a family friend expressing his great alarm at their dear Fanny's "intimacy" with the "infamous" Mme de Staël, a "Diabolical Democrat" and "Adulterous Demoniac," who had come to England to join her lover, Narbonne, with the sole end of hatching new intrigues.[244] The old musicologist, who had noted his daughter's growing enthusiasm for the residents of Juniper Hall with alarm, now ordered her not to see Mme de Staël again and to return in haste to London. Fanny obeyed the paternal injunction, though not without expressing her "horrour & indignation at this incessant persecution of ruined & desolate individuals,"[245] attempting to clarify the constitutionalists' political positions, which she now in fact saw as wholly legitimate, and insisting on the purely intellectual nature of the relationship between Narbonne and Mme de Staël with arguments—namely that of Mme de Staël's plainness and the beauty of the Comte[246]—that would, perhaps, not have been appreciated by the parties concerned. The arrival of that "atrocious ambassadress"[247] in England had stimulated a flood of hostile commentaries, and Fanny could not risk exposing herself to critiques that might put the pension the Queen had granted her in jeopardy. Moreover—a hard blow for her puritanism—she began to suspect that the relations between Mme de Staël and Narbonne were perhaps not as innocent as she had believed.

In reality, what Fanny feared most was compromising her relationship with d'Arblay, and so, upon her return to London, she gathered her courage and wrote, in French, to confide in him how detrimental Mme de Staël's presence was to Narbonne, and how difficult it was to defend her: "*Elle n'est ni Emigree, ni banni—c'est M. de N[arbonne] qui la séduit de son Mari et de ses Enfans'— C'est vainement que je parle du mœurs de son pais; on ne me réponde jamais que 'Elle est Femme, elle est Mere!'*" [sic]*[248] Pushed to his limits, all the poor d'Arblay could do was swear that, "without being able to say that the liaison between Mme de S. and Mr. de N. had not at some point been of the utmost intimacy," he could nonetheless affirm that "at present [it] consists of nothing but the most respectable friendship."[249] There was now nothing for Fanny to do but maintain a prudent distance from a person she continued to admire but was no longer able to respect. When Mme de Staël finally came to understand the reasons that Fanny had ceased to visit her, she was wounded—but the circles she moved in were too superior for her to be able to hold a grudge for long. Besides, several days spent in London brought home to her that her presence in England was no longer justifiable, and she resigned herself to planning her return journey. In order to buy time and keep up appearances, she wrote to her husband and asked him to come and join her. M. de Staël limited himself to assuring her that he would send someone he trusted to meet her at

---

*"'She is neither an Émigré, nor an exile—it is M. de Narbonne who has seduced her away from her Husband and Children'—It is in vain that I speak of the customs of their country; they always reply that 'She is a Woman, she is a Mother!'"

Ostend and escort her to Switzerland. In spite of everything, Germaine succeeded in prolonging her stay in England until the end of May.

Wholly unintimidated by the accusations aimed at Mme de Staël, Mrs. Phillips continued assiduously to frequent Juniper Hall and to send accounts of her visits to her sister. For her part, Fanny kept a journal intended for Susanna in which she kept her apprised of the development of her love affair with d'Arblay. Now that she knew the Juniperians fairly well, she was able to perceive the signs of crisis in the relationship between Mme de Staël and Narbonne. In spite of his habitual courtesy, the Comte betrayed a certain embarrassment at his mistress's offhandedness, while she was irritated by his apathy and his reluctance to plan for the future.[250] Only the news of the treason of General Dumouriez—who, aware that he would be sent to the guillotine for the French defeat at Neerwinden, had announced that he was marching upon Paris to restore law and order[251]—momentarily revived the Comte's hopes. But, as had already happened with Lafayette, the army did not follow Dumouriez, who was forced to seek refuge abroad, and Narbonne was once again plunged into inertia. On the other hand, the future was more than ever at the center of Germaine's preoccupations, as she busied herself preparing the necessary conditions for Narbonne and Talleyrand—the latter of whom had now been added to the list of exiles—to be able to follow her to Switzerland.

Tensions, reluctances, and fits of melancholy did not prevent the Juniperians from giving the best of themselves in conversation, and Susanna, wholly charmed by them, expressed her admiration to Mme de Staël. "Conversation in France," Germaine had responded, "is not, as elsewhere, merely a means of communicating ideas and sentiments, or of conveying directions concerning the business of life; it is an instrument upon which we love to play, and which cheers and invigorates the mind as music does in some countries or wine in others."[252] This remark prefigures almost to the letter the definition that she would give years later in *On Germany*, and shows with what precision and intelligence Susanna reported to her sister all that she saw and heard. For his part, Bollmann, visiting Juniper Hall in the spring, noted two different varieties of conversation: "Narbonne pleases, but wearies in the long run; one could listen to Talleyrand for years. Narbonne intends to please, and one can hear it; Talleyrand speaks without the least effort, in a constant atmosphere of perfect peace and contentment. Narbonne's language is more brilliant; that of Talleyrand more graceful, more delicate, tidier. Narbonne is not a man for every taste; sensitive people cannot take him; and he cannot hold them.

Talleyrand, without being less morally corrupted than Narbonne, can move even those who despise him to tears. I know of several striking examples."[253]

Mme de Staël left at the end of May, and as she departed from Dover, Narbonne assured her that he would join her in Switzerland as soon as possible. During their four months together at Juniper Hall, the Comte had not dared to put their relationship in question: he detested scenes, and, incapable of standing up to Germaine, had avoided contradicting her, hoping that passive resistance would discourage her in the end. Talleyrand had perhaps been right when he declared that Narbonne lacked the courage necessary to "choose a side," and that "the courage he possessed was [nothing but] bravado."[254] When his mistress decided to leave, he was in no hurry to place himself under her thumb again, and found various pretexts for postponing his own departure.

It was upon her return to Switzerland, once the charm of a cohabitation away from prying eyes in the peace and quiet of the English countryside had dissipated, that Mme de Staël realized she was no longer loved. "I am convinced that your heart no longer loves me, except out of habit and gratitude,"[255] she wrote to him two months after their separation—but resignation was not part of her repertoire. The twenty-four letters that she sent to Narbonne from Switzerland set the pattern that she would replay with the different men she fell for after him. The handsome Louis, whom she had loved with all the passion of a twenty-year-old, had been the first—and, in her extreme attempts to shake his indifference, Mme de Staël did not hesitate to make use of contempt, insults, reproaches, threats, and blackmail. If he did not share her feelings, it was because he was incapable of loving: "You never enter into the situations of others; your mind gives itself over, but your heart remains confined in itself."[256] His behavior showed "to the last degree that frivolousness of the French court."[257] He was not a man at all, but "a baby tiger," and his weakness had made him "atrocious."[258] He had no idea what gratitude was: "Must I be so base as to remind you of everything I have done for your sake, my life exposed and delivered over to you in so many ways?"[259] And then: "Your atrocious ingratitude is even more vile than anything you're able to think up to conceal it. My life, my fortune, my reputation, my peace, all of them have been yours."[260] He had no heart: "You drive me mad, you are the most barbarous of men, even Marat would take pity on me."[261] He was "atrociously cold": "I understand Robespierre better than I do you."[262] He was nothing but a cynical assassin:

"Come and crack jokes at the grave of the unfortunate woman whose blood and tears you have devoured; cruel man, how you have wronged me!"[263] But even when she moved from accusations to supplications, her grief was unbearably melodramatic: "After a night of tears, I prayed to God over the cradle of my son; he awoke, and I entreated him to ask *that his father should have pity on me*; his little voice repeated these words, and he fell asleep once again."[264]

Mme de Staël did not kill herself as she threatened, and her unhappiness in love did not prevent her from continuing to look after the numerous imperatives of her life, as contradictory as they were essential. If, in her letters to her lover, Germaine shamelessly gave herself up to despair, in her *Treatise on the Influence of the Passions upon the Happiness of Individuals and of Nations*, which she began at Juniper Hall, the experience she had lived through became grist for ethical reflection. Still, at the same moment that she was theorizing the necessity of resisting the call of the passions, she gave in to one of the basest by avenging herself on Narbonne in a roman à clef—*Zulma*[265]—wherein the Comte, easily identifiable, certainly does not appear in the best light. In August, she gave the first great proof of her talent as a writer with her magnificent *Reflections on the Trial of the Queen*, which Talleyrand took charge of having published in London. At the same time, Germaine knew well that a woman's sentimental freedom came at a price, and she was ready to pay it with an absolute sangfroid. Even as she begged Narbonne to have pity on her and their children, she proposed to her husband, M. de Staël, that they resume living together in the name of their respective interests, while finding consolation in a brand-new affair. Indeed, since September, Comte Ribbing, the extremely handsome Swede who had fled his country after having participated in the assassination of Gustav III, had monopolized her attention, becoming her lover in February of the following year. But Germaine did not lose interest in the fates of her friends and their families. While the Terror was still in full swing, she mobilized her husband's political network and, paying handsomely, managed to save her dear Jaucourt and Mathieu de Montmorency from prison for the second time, along with Montmorency's mother and some twenty others. She also had the satisfaction of ensuring the safety of the Comte's second daughter, who had remained in France with her nurse. "You may rely on my heart," she wrote to Narbonne in the last letter she addressed to him. "Ah! My Auguste is not dearer to me; does [our daughter] not also possess everything I love in him? My dear little one, I shall have her, and no one *but you* shall take her from me."[266] It was an elegant way of leaving the stage with her head held high, affirming her moral superiority without disavowing the love that she had felt for him.

Among the numerous reasons that Narbonne invoked to delay his voyage to Switzerland was his desire to go and fight at Toulon. At the end of July, the town had risen up against the convention and opened its gates to the English Admiral Hood. It was then that Talleyrand planned along with Narbonne and d'Arblay to reunite all the former deputies of the National Constituent Assembly and form an executive committee in which Narbonne would play the part of minister of war in order to lend political legitimacy to the revolt, guaranteeing free elections so as to ward off the risk of a reactionary drift. The English government refused this proposition, to the great relief of Fanny Burney, who had recently become Mme d'Arblay, and against the backdrop of yet another fit of hysteria on the part of Mme de Staël. Talleyrand had kept his friend informed of the progress of the plan, step by step—now not only did Germaine think that he was out of his mind but she was convinced that "the Bishop" (that depraved man "who toys with life and death"[267]) was plotting behind her back and turning Narbonne against her. She hid these suspicions from the party in question, with whom she maintained an intense correspondence unbeknownst to Narbonne, meanwhile discharging all of her indignation upon her lover. "*If you go to Toulon without coming here first, I swear I will kill myself. Take whichever side you like*, but know that you are the most miserable of men for preferring the maddest of ideas to the most concrete of duties.... All the Bishop can do is drag you along with his treacherous advice."[268]

But for Mme de Staël, Talleyrand was an irresistible siren, and he encouraged her. "It is for the purpose of living with you that I make all my arrangements,"[269] he assured her, and Germaine continued to work on plans for his emigration to Switzerland. On January 25, 1794, he was caught off guard[270] by an order from the English government to leave the country within five days, and faced with the difficulty of finding asylum in Europe, he decided to take ship for the United States. "When one makes a study of political ideas, it is a country that must be seen," he wrote to Mme de Staël, announcing his departure. "At the age of thirty-nine I begin a new life: for it is life that I want; I love my friends too dearly to change my ideas...I must show how much I have loved liberty, how much I love it still, and how much I hate the French."[271] To tell the truth, Talleyrand's friends worried much more about him than he did about them. In hearing the news of his expulsion, Narbonne rushed to inform d'Arblay—"Can you conceive of anything crueler, of a more deplorable situation? What will become of him?"[272]—then hurried to London to plead his friend's case. All of his attempts to meet with Pitt or George III came to nothing, but he succeeded in delaying the Bishop's departure by several weeks. Even though he was himself struggling with serious financial difficulties—in order to survive he had been forced to sell his collection of bronzes—he managed to obtain a loan for Talleyrand (who for his part had put his precious library up for auction), giving as a guarantee his properties in Saint-Domingue, and did all that he could for him, boasting meanwhile of his friend's "calm, his courage, what one might almost call his gaiety."[273] Yet once he had become an adviser to Napoleon, Talleyrand did not lift a finger to help Narbonne rejoin the army, nor to defend Mme de Staël—to whom he owed his return to France and his position as minister of foreign relations—from the Emperor's ire. And when the Restoration came, he would turn his back on d'Arblay, to whom he had once sworn eternal friendship.[274] Narbonne had far too much elegance to mention Talleyrand's ingratitude, and preferred to speak of his "too great sense of resignation when it came to the unhappiness of his friends." His indulgence was always more scathing than indignation: "He habituated himself to their disgrace, as he had to his own position, and ended by finding everything in order. His ingenious mind always provided a thousand reasons why others should be patient."[275] Hadn't La Rochefoucauld said: "We all have enough strength to bear the misfortunes of others"?[276] But to judge by the treacherous portrait that Talleyrand sketched of Narbonne in his memoirs, what was at issue was more than indifference: the weight of gratitude that he owed to the Comte seemed, perhaps, too great for him to do anything but refuse the latter all moral credibility, and to disburden himself by disavowing their friendship. In his youth, Talleyrand wrote, his name had often been associated with those of the Comte de Choiseul-Gouffier and the Comte de Narbonne, but in reality only the former had been his friend. The character of the latter lacked those qualities he looked for: "M. de Narbonne has the sort of intellect that aims only at effect, which is either brilliant or hopeless, and which exhausts itself in the writing of a note or the delivery of a jest. He has politeness without nuance; his wit often crosses the line of good taste, and his character fails to inspire the confidence required by intimate relations. One finds him amusing, but rarely agreeable. A sort of grace, that he knows better than anyone how to impart to his companions, has earned him a fair measure of success, largely among witty and slightly vulgar men. He is less pleasing to those who appreciate what, in our youth, we referred to as *le bon ton*."[277]

It was with great surprise that, several months after Talleyrand's departure, Narbonne received an invitation to lunch with the prime minister, who had until then been careful to maintain his distance. Pitt received him in private with great cordiality at his home in the country, and the Comte soon came to learn the reason why. Contrary to what he had believed, his host was not in the least interested in his opinions on the French political situation but was seeking detailed information of a military nature. He took for granted that the Comte, having taken refuge in England, had ranged himself in opposition to the ferocious dictatorship that had so bloodied France. And who better than the former minister of war to indicate a winning strategy to break the resistance of the Revolutionary armies? What was at stake—Pitt took care to emphasize—was nothing less than "a question of life and death for civilization." Containing his indignation, Narbonne replied that "honor was still in the Republic's camp," that "excess of danger could render it indomitable, and that even as it suffered from internal tyranny in the name of freedom, it jealously guarded the independence of its territories." Certainly, with Dumouriez or Biron, it had lost its great generals, but Pitt could be sure that "even with them gone, tomorrow the virtue of that soil will produce others; and just as those former soldiers had emerged from their palaces, these new men would spring from between the paving stones in the streets. No one will reveal to you the secret of France's strength," he proudly affirmed. "That secret and that strength are everywhere." As for the information that had been demanded of him, he concluded, it was impossible not to consider revealing it as incompatible with his honor as a soldier and a gentleman: "Like you, monsieur, I hate the bloody policies of the Committee of the Convention; I expect from it nothing but proscription and death. But if, from my former administrative duties and the memories I retain of them, I retrieved a single word that was harmful to the military defense of my country, I would consider myself a traitor, and would be one indeed; I prefer to remain a simple refugee, perhaps soon to be chased from his place of exile, just as he was from his homeland."[278]

Grappling with a war that grew more demanding and difficult day by day, Pitt did not appreciate the lesson Narbonne had delivered, and went on to sacrifice him, as he had with Talleyrand, to the hatred of the conservatives and absolutist émigrés. Several weeks later, the Comte received his order to leave the country. After having done his best to protect the interests of his wife in Saint-Domingue, then in the grips of a bloody slave uprising, he bid an emotional farewell to d'Arblay and his friends at Juniper Hall, and, on June 20, 1794, embarked for Holland under a Spanish passport, to which he had a right as the descendant of a grandee of Spain. One month after that, he rejoined Mme de Staël in Mézery, a village not far from Lausanne. They had not seen each other for a year.

"He has come, and I have broken all my ties with him,"[279] Germaine hastened to write to Comte Ribbing, and insisted in the letters that followed that Narbonne had attempted to revive their relations. How far should we believe her? Did the Comte really still care for her, or was he putting on a display of disappointment for the sake of chivalry? Perhaps, in keeping with one of her habitual tactics, Mme de Staël hoped to rouse the jealousy of Ribbing, who was already displaying unsettling signs of weariness. In any case, she had reserved an affectionate welcome for Narbonne. The ties that bound them were still very strong, and after having survived the Revolution, they were able to thrill together during the last days of July at the news of the fall of Robespierre. But the end of the Terror also sounded the death knell for their political alliance. Indeed, under the influence of Benjamin Constant, who had recently burst into her life, Mme de Staël declared herself in favor of a republican France, while Narbonne remained faithful to the monarchy. Nevertheless, the fascination that the Comte exerted upon Mme de Staël remained strong, and Constant—who, in his obstinate and apparently hopeless passion for Germaine, feared a return of her affection for the nobleman (whereas Ribbing, openly in flight, no longer constituted a danger)—did everything in his power to help Mme de Laval prevent such a revival.

Almost twenty years older than Mme de Staël, the Vicomtesse was, as Aimée de Coigny put it, "of all women the most amusing, most cheerful, most intransigent, and least good."[280] Since the 1770s she had been one of the foremost figures of the Parisian beau monde and was distinguished for her open-mindedness even in an era when libertinism was rampant. The list of her lovers included, among others, Lauzun, Talleyrand, Narbonne, and Calonne, and she had maintained excellent relations with each of them. Tenacious in friendship, she was no less so in hate. A "passionate enemy of Mme de Staël,"[281] whether because of the hostility she had shown to the policies of Calonne or the influence she exerted upon her son Mathieu, the Vicomtesse nevertheless owed her rival a debt of gratitude, unpleasant as it might be. Not only had her enemy saved her life but she had also offered her hospitality to her closest friends, and affectionately shared her grief over the death of her youngest son, the Abbé Hippolyte de Montmorency, whom Germaine had not been able to save from the guillotine. But Narbonne's arrival swept away any scruples Mme de Laval might have had. She who, up to that point, had been "so unfortunate, so sad, so sweet... immediately adopted the attitude of an outraged, rather than impassioned, woman claiming what was rightfully hers," and fell upon the Comte like "a dove of prey."[282] She had been the mistress of the handsome Louis before Mme de Staël and, in spite of her fifty years, knew how to reconquer him. Mme de Staël would not forgive Narbonne for this second betrayal, which marked their definitive break. It was by Mme de Laval's side that the Comte would confront the long, difficult years that still awaited him. After his tumultuous relationship with Mme de Staël and his attempts to keep pace with her indefatigable intellect, Narbonne, who had by now renounced politics and all of his old ambitions, must have found the elegant frivolousness of the Vicomtesse, her lively social life and grande dame's manners, infinitely restful, and in harmony with that aristocratic civilization into which he had been born, and which the Revolution had brought to an end. Through all the trials he endured, his loyalty to that vanished way of life became a form of moral resistance. And after Thermidor, he began to hatch new plans. "As for me," he confided to his friend d'Arblay, "as soon as I am removed from the list of exiles, I will go to embrace my old mother and the rest of my family; but then I will find something to turn my hand to, for I must live. I have nothing before me but my health and a number of years, and must work to prepare for old age. What precisely I will do is impossible to say."[283] He counted on Mme de Laval's help to lighten the load.

In February 1791, the same Frenchmen in London who were preparing to hurl their anathemas at Mme de Staël did not hesitate to celebrate Mme du Barry, who, forty-five years earlier, had outraged all Versailles. The simple fact of her having been the favorite of Louis XV now seemed like a solid guarantee of her devotion to the holy cause of the monarchy. In reality, the Comtesse had not crossed the Channel to escape the Jacobins but rather to retrieve the jewelry that had been stolen from her at Louveciennes. The theft had taken place on the night of January 10 of that same year, while Mme du Barry was in Paris for a grand reception given by Brissac to celebrate Epiphany. At the time the capital was relatively tranquil, and the Duc's way of life more or less unchanged. Taking advantage of Mme du Barry's absence and the complicity of the Gardes Suisses charged with the security of the château, the thieves had slipped in through a second-story window and helped themselves to the most precious jewelry that the Comtesse kept under lock and key in her room. Mme du Barry hurried back to Louveciennes as soon as she heard of the theft and an investigation was soon underway, but the culprits appeared to have vanished into thin air. On the advice of Brissac, and with the help of her trusted jeweler, Mme du Barry had drawn up a detailed list of the stolen jewels and had several hundreds of copies printed and distributed, promising a reward of 2,000 louis to whoever recovered them. This information made its way to Baron Lyon de Symons, London's principal diamond merchant, to whom the scoundrels, not daring to peddle their loot in France, had gone shortly after the theft, proposing to sell him a first lot of precious stones. Evaluating them, Symons immediately saw that the diamonds being offered to him at such a derisory price belonged to Mme du Barry, and as he was "one of the rare honest jewelers in the city,"[284] he bought them, asking the sellers to return the next day with the other jewels they had mentioned. But this time, the police were waiting for the thieves, who wound up in prison. Informed right away that her jewels had been found, Mme du Barry left for London to retrieve them, accompanied by her jeweler and four servants. Brissac, unable to leave the Tuileries, had one of his aides-de-camp, d'Escourre, escort her, and insisted on covering the trip's expenses, maintaining with his accustomed chivalrousness that if she had not been so good as to accept his invitation to spend the night in the rue de Grenelle, the theft would never have occurred. Jewels had always been Jeanne's greatest passion. She loved the luminous beauty of precious stones, whose rarity, fineness, and dimensions she was able to judge with absolute confidence, selecting with tremendous taste the mountings that would show them to best advantage. But even beyond the aesthetic pleasure she took in them, she felt a visceral attachment to her gems. All of the precious stones she had amassed with such avidity since first finding favor with the King stood as a testimony to her beauty and seductiveness, as a confirmation of her *"prix,"* as the *précieuses* in the capital would have phrased it a century earlier. And for someone who had known poverty, as she had, they also represented a guarantee that she would not fall back into indigence, that she would be free to live as she wished. She threw herself with great determination into the long and complex legal procedure necessary for her to take back her treasure. Welcomed by the mayor of London in person, she identified the recovered stones with the help of her jeweler, confronted the thieves (only one of whom was ultimately found guilty), and pressed charges against them. Meanwhile, she kept company with the leading lights of the emigration, from the Vicomtesse de Calonne (whose husband was then in Koblenz) to the Baron de Breteuil (who had served as minister for some hundred hours, between the recall of Necker and the fall of the Bastille), as well as Bertrand de Molleville (former minister of the navy and enemy of Narbonne) and the Duc de Rohan-Chabot (a great friend of Brissac). Nor did the English aristocracy fail to give her a warm welcome, beginning with the powerful Duke of Queensberry, who had made her acquaintance in Paris when she was still a high-priced courtesan and wanted to present her to the Prince of Wales—an old *compagnon de libertinage* of the Duc d'Orléans— who was quite curious to meet her. But when Mme du Barry returned to London for the second time between April and May of the same year, the situation had grown more complicated. Given that British law did not provide for the prosecution of those who had committed crimes in other countries— with the exception of those who had confessed, and were English—the thieves were released. Moreover, one of them, a Frenchman named Levet who had not ceased to proclaim his innocence, brought suit against the English jeweler who had denounced them.

Neither Mme du Barry nor Brissac seemed to be worried about the uproar that the theft of the jewels and Jeanne's frequent trips had raised in the revolutionary press. Now, with the departure of Louis XVI's aunts at the end of February, conspiracy theories were spreading wildly and sparing no one. Generous and optimistic, the two lovers had nothing to reproach themselves with: they had enthusiastically welcomed the summoning of the Estates General, and the October Days had done nothing to change their attitude. Like the rest of the liberal nobility, the Duc was convinced that the country was in need of substantial reforms, and took it for granted that the path to bringing them about would be fraught with episodes of violence. But in his opinion, these would be isolated incidents that—as he wrote to his mistress—could have no great influence over "the most important questions that await all of France."[285] And what could Mme du Barry possibly have to fear? After all, well before the Revolution she had given proof of her incontestable civic-mindedness and charity in Louveciennes. The progressive convictions of the two lovers and their agreement with Necker's policies were accompanied, however, by an absolute fidelity to the monarchy. After the march on Versailles and the assault against the château, Mme du Barry had taken in and cared for two wounded guards who had sought refuge at Louveciennes. Marie-Antoinette had expressed her gratitude for this gesture, and, setting aside all her rancor, Mme du Barry had responded that "the wounded young men" regretted nothing "but not having laid down their lives alongside their comrades for the sake of a Princesse as perfect and as worthy of all praises as Your Majesty most assuredly is." And she renewed the offer she had made at the time when the Notables had come together to wrestle with the national debt: "Louveciennes is yours, madame. Is it not your goodness and generosity that has granted it to me at all? All I possess has come to me from the royal family... I offer it to you once more, madame, in haste and with all sincerity: you have so many expenses hanging over you, and so many beneficences to bestow on others. Permit me, I beg you, to render to Caesar what is Caesar's."[286] A grand dame could not have put it better.

On October 6, Brissac had gone to await Louis XVI as he arrived at the Tuileries surrounded by a procession of men with pikes, and, "paying no mind to the vociferations of the populace," knelt before the sovereign and kissed his hand—while the King, "displaying the kind of terror that he never felt for his own person," implored him: "What are you doing! Go away, my friend, they're looking at you, you'll be massacred."[287] From that point on, as a colonel in the Cent Suisses—the King's bodyguard—Brissac served at the Tuileries. The flight to Varennes caught him off guard. It had been decided not to inform him of the plan, out of fear that he would tell Mme du Barry.[288] It was then, facing the forced return of Louis XVI and the monarchy's ultimate humiliation, that he ceased to hope for the future. He disregarded the friends who advised him to emigrate, recalling "that saying of Marie-Antoinette, formerly so august: 'a gentleman is always in his proper place when he stands by his King.'"[289] Besides, nothing on earth would have been able to separate him from Mme du Barry, to whom he constantly repeated: "I send you a single phrase that contains it all: I will love you as long as I live, in spite of the gods and their envy."[290] And when, more and more isolated and vulnerable, Louis XVI asked him to assume the command of his new personal bodyguard, "confident in his valor and experience of arms... and above all in his loyalty and particular affection for Our Person,"[291] the Duc could only accept, seeing that the King's safety was at stake. His task, as prescribed by the new constitution, consisted of creating a body of three thousand men culled from the army or the Garde

Nationale to replace the Cent Suisses. The King had the right to personally select a third of the men, and Brissac took care to recruit officers faithful to the monarchy (many of whom had left their regiments to avoid having to take an oath on the constitution), and succeeded in assembling an elite unit—strong, disciplined, and wholly trustworthy. But the Duc could not accept the King's inertia, given the gravity of the situation, and finally encouraged him to react. Louis XVI responded that he must be patient: it was the people who, weary of disorder, would restore him to his place, and the nobility needed to follow his example. "Sire," Brissac permitted himself to object, "for you, with twenty-five million in revenue, it is simple—but for we nobles who no longer have anything, who have lost and sacrificed all in your service, there remain only two choices: to join with your enemies and remove you from the throne, or to make war and die honorably in the field; and Your Majesty knows well that, if I am to be believed, it is the latter solution that we will choose."[292] He was one of the first to feel the consequences of the King's waiting game. The beginning of the war against Austria, the armed mobilization of the émigrés, the first defeats, and the fear of new attempts to flee on the part of the royal family all contributed to rendering those who had joined what should have been the King's Constitutional Guard highly suspect. Many of the soldiers who had come from the Garde Nationale resigned their commissions, and the clubs and municipality demanded that an investigation be conducted. Finally, on May 29, 1792, the Legislative Assembly decided to dissolve the guard even before it had gone into service. And François Chabot, the terrible defrocked priest who would vote for the death of the King, denounced Brissac for having introduced into his men "an unconstitutional and anti-revolutionary spirit,"[293] and obtained his arrest. Louis XVI, who, faithful to his mandate as a highly Christian king, was planning to employ his veto against the decree for the deportation of refractory priests, did not wish to inflame the conflict with the assembly any further, and preferred not to oppose a decision concerning his own personal security. Consequently—as Saint-Priest would bitterly recall—he abandoned the "generous"[294] Brissac to his fate. As the authenticated copy of the accusation against the Duc in his family archives[295] shows, Louis XVI was forced to sign the decree depriving himself of the man whose job it had been to protect him—but, learning of the convention's decision in the middle of the night, he hastened to send the young Duc de Choiseul, then in service at the château, to inform Brissac, who was staying at the Tuileries, of his imminent arrest, and urge him to flee. The Duc did not heed his King's advice. Flight, shameful in itself, also seemed to him an admission of guilt, when he had nothing with which to reproach himself. He spent the night writing a long letter to Mme du Barry, and asked his orderly, the Chevalier de Maussabré, to take it to her at Louveciennes.[296] Arrested at six o'clock in the morning, Brissac was immediately transferred to Orléans, where the National High Court of Justice, charged with prosecuting all crimes reported to the Legislative Assembly, had been established—and on June 2, Maussabré was able to inform Mme du Barry that the Duc had arrived there without incident.

Conscious of the gravity of the charges against her lover and mindful that their letters would pass through the hands of the censor, the Comtesse reminded him of her "tender and faithful friendship," and festooned her pages with testaments to civic-mindedness: "I know that you have nothing to fear so long as reason and good faith reign in that assembly. . . . Your conduct has been so pure since you have been at the Tuileries that no one can impute the least misconduct to you. You have so many acts of *patriotism* to your credit that, truly, I have no idea what anyone could find fault with."[297] For her part, Mme du Barry received a letter from Brissac's daughter, at that time an émigré living in Spa, who wrote requesting news of her father and asking for advice regarding an eventual return to France. All of the prejudices that the prideful Duchesse de Mortemart had harbored on first encountering l'Ange were swept away by the profound feeling of solidarity that united the two women in their adversity. "Do not take ill," wrote Mme de Mortemart to Mme du Barry, "the fact that your affection for one who is so dear to me has earned for you eternal rights over my heart, and accept, I pray you, the assurance that what I feel for you will last as long as life."[298] While retaining the formally required litotes and euphemisms, Mme de Mortemart was acknowledging the love that Mme du Barry felt for her father, and offering in return a friendship that would never waver.

Even though traveling had become dangerous, Mme du Barry left without hesitation for Orléans, where she managed to secure permission to see her lover, who had been placed in a cell at the old Minim convent. Brissac's morale remained high: he had had installed at his own expense in the ruined refectory a shuttlecock court open to all the prisoners, and passed his time reading and making collages. Mme du Barry's visits filled him with joy. As he faced his trial—which began on June 14—he was buoyed by the certainty that the accusations being leveled against him were baseless. Brissac was an uninspired writer but "spoke with skill," and he responded to his judges with a soldier's pride. When asked to identify himself, he immediately earned the respect of all by replying: "A soldier since birth, having served in every corps."[299] But the news of the taking of the Tuileries on August 10 and of the fall of the monarchy left no doubt regarding what awaited him. On August 11, Brissac drafted his will: He named his daughter as his sole heir, but added a codicil concerning someone very dear to him, someone whom "the misfortunes of the age may place in the greatest distress."[300] This codicil, of course, concerned Mme du Barry, to whom the Duc assured an annual income of 24,000 livres as "a feeble token of my sentiment and gratitude, which I owe all the more in that I was the involuntary cause of the loss of her diamonds."[301] Immediately after, he wrote a final letter to the Comtesse: "Yes, my final thought will be of you. We do not know all the details. Ah, dear heart! If only I could be with you in the desert! But as I have no choice but to be in so incommodious a place as Orléans, I send you a thousand kisses, and a thousand more. Adieu, dear heart."[302] The trial against Brissac and the fifty-nine others awaiting judgment along with him was still far from over when the sections and Jacobin clubs in the capital began to pressure the assembly and commune to have the defendants judged in Paris—as the High Court of Justice in Orléans, guilty of acquitting four men and having allowed a prisoner to escape, had itself become suspect. Thus, on September 2, the day when the prison massacres began, the assembly ordered the transfer of prisoners from Orléans to the château of Saumur. It was Claude Fournier, known as "the American," who had been charged with leading the convoy. This fanatical revolutionary, notorious for his ferocity, had shown from the fall of the Bastille to that of the Tuileries that he was highly skilled at manipulating the violent tendencies of the public. And it was precisely to the people's justice that he intended to deliver up those prisoners entrusted to him. On September 4, after having displayed the prisoners (their numbers reduced to around fifty) in seven open carts escorted by one hundred and eighty of the Garde Nationale, Fournier directed this procession not toward Saumur as he'd been ordered but rather toward Paris, where the Terror was in full swing. But four days later, at Arpajon, he was intercepted by two emissaries from the assembly, who instructed him to divert his course toward Versailles, and informed him that he would be held personally responsible for "whatever might befall the prisoners, who were intended to be judged according to the law."[303] Nevertheless, at Versailles, which the prisoners reached around noon on September 9, the forces of order quickly lost control of the situation. A menacing crowd, inflamed by sans-culottes newly arrived from Paris, had gathered near the palace. Brissac had time enough to pass the house where Mme du Barry had lived when he'd first known her, and even got as far as his own former home before the convoy was attacked by a throng of men armed with sabers, pikes, and bayonets. Fournier and the men of the Garde Nationale vanished, abandoning their prisoners to the hands of the assassins. Brissac was in the third tumbrel, easily identifiable by his light blue outfit with yellow buttons, "his curled hair and pigtail, and the riding boots on his feet, seated as he was on a bit of straw, holding his hat in his hand."[304] Along with the former minister of foreign affairs Lessart, he was the most important prisoner, and the assailants immediately took him captive. One of his descendants described his end as follows, basing the account on the testimony of two servants: "Brissac was facing the prospect of a terrible death. He snatched up a knife, then a staff, and laid into his assailants, who for their part delivered terrible wounds to his nose, his cheek, and his forehead. His blue outfit was torn, his wig transformed into a purple sponge. He was blinded by his own blood, a crimson giant with hollow eyes who, still on his feet, swung wildly around him with his terrible staff. A fatal saber blow finally brought this struggle to an end, and there followed a grim feeding frenzy: they cut out his heart and carried it through Versailles, shouting: 'This heart belonged to Brissac, who fought like a mad dog but died like the rest.'"[305] A rumor circulated that, after having been fixed on a pike and lofted in triumph through the streets of Versailles, Brissac's severed head was thrown over the wall of Mme du Barry's garden at Louveciennes.[306]

The horrible death of the man with whom she had lived the most serene fifteen years of her life was a tremendous ordeal for Mme du Barry. "A fate that should have been so beautiful, so spectacular. What an end! Good God!" she wrote to the Duc's daughter in a letter of condolence, in which she acknowledged: "Your unfortunate father's last wish was that I should cherish you like a sister"; and Mme de Mortemart, in thanking her, assured her that she would, in fact, love her "like a sister"[307] as long as she lived. Still, in spite of the breadth of her despair, Mme du Barry did not cease to love life. "Amidst the horrors that surround me, I am sustained by my health. I will not die of grief,"[308] she wrote to a friend. And she certainly had not forgotten her diamonds, of which she still had not managed to regain possession. Now, in London, the judges were demanding her presence in court: the jeweler who had recovered the gems had entered a suit against her, in order to claim the 2,000 louis she had promised as a reward. Thus, in mid-October, barely a month after the death

10. Firmin Massot, *Madame de Staël with the bust of her father, Jacques Necker*

11. Anonymous, *Comte Louis-Philippe de Ségur Traveling by Sleigh in St. Petersburg*, 1786

12. Ary Scheffer, *Louis-Philippe de Ségur*, ca. 1825

13. Élisabeth Vigée Le Brun, *Antoinette-Élisabeth-Marie d'Aguesseau, Comtesse de Ségur*, 1785

14. François-Hubert Drouais, *Joseph-Hyacinthe-François de Paule de Rigaud, Comte de Vaudreuil*, 1758

15. Élisabeth Vigée Le Brun, *Gabrielle-Yolande de Polastron, Duchesse de Polignac*, 1782

16. Anonymous, *Stanislas-Jean, Chevalier (later Marquis) de Boufflers*

17. Élisabeth Vigée Le Brun, *Françoise-Éléonore de Jean de Manville, Comtesse de Sabran (later Marquise de Boufflers)*, 1786

18. Hubert Robert, *Distributing Milk at Saint-Lazare Prison*, 1794

19. Hubert Robert, *The Prison Cell of Baron de Besenval at the Châtelet*, 1789

Je suis condamné, je mourrai demain dans
des sentiments de Religion dont mon cher papa
m'a toujours donné l'exemple, ce qui sont dignes
de lui. Ma longue agonie reçoit beaucoup
de consolation de la certitude que mon cher
papa n'abandonnera pas à des malheurs de
toutte espèce la Citoyenne Laurent à l'amitié
de qui j'ai de tant de soulagement dans
mes peines; j'ai cher moi à Mousouge
deux femmes anglaises qui sont chez moi
depuis 20 ans, et qui y sont détenues
comme prisonnières depuis le décret sur
les étrangers, elles n'avaient d'autre
ressources que moi, je les recommande
aux secours, et à l'extrême bonté de mon
cher papa; je l'aime, je le respecte
et je l'embrasse pour la dernière fois
de tout mon cœur. Biron

20. Duc de Biron's final letter to his father, written from prison, 1793

of Brissac, Mme du Barry departed once again. She had taken care to comply with all the formalities necessary not to be added to the list of émigrés, and was furnished with a passport issued by the mayor of Louveciennes and approved by the department of Seine-et-Oise and the Directory at Versailles, as well as a letter informing the aforesaid mayor of her journey. She was accompanied by La Bondie, nephew of d'Escourre; her personal chambermaid; and two servants; as well as the Duchesse de Brancas, who also had a valid passport. But Jeanne's prudence stopped there. Installed in a lovely house near Berkeley Square, she once again began to keep company with the émigrés, unmindful of the fact that since her last stay in London the political situation had changed radically. With the promulgation of the decree of November 9, 1791, it had become a crime to maintain contact with émigrés, who were suspected of conspiring against the nation and were subject to the death penalty. Since the beginning of the affair of her jewels, Jeanne had broken with the most elementary rules of caution. And only when she was seated at the defendant's bench before the Revolutionary Tribunal would she finally realize the enormous number of mistakes she had made. How could it be that she had never asked herself what role had really been played by the diligent Irishman who had been the first to inform her of the reappearance of her jewels, and who had advised Symons on how to entrap and arrest the thieves? After having voyaged across the length and breadth of Europe, Nathaniel Parker-Forth had made his fortune in France at the end of the 1770s as an authority on horses, furnishing the Duc de Chartres's equerries with English chargers, hounds, and jockeys. His close ties to the Princes of the Blood and their entourages had made him, during the American war, a perfect spy for the British government, which had entrusted him with diplomatic missions to Versailles. An intimate of the Duc d'Orléans and his host whenever the latter visited London, Parker-Forth was well informed of his political ambitions and maneuvering against the royal family, and was able to transmit this information to Pitt—who in turn used him to foment revolutionary disorder and destabilize France's government, as the French ambassadors to the Court of St. James's were well aware. Now, faced with this new political scenario, Parker-Forth had found a way to enrich himself above and beyond espionage: by helping the French royalists emigrate and transfer their capital to England, for which reason the Revolutionary government kept him under tight surveillance. He had been able to gain the confidence of Mme du Barry, who, having never left France, spoke no English, knew nothing about common law, and placed herself entirely in his hands. It was Parker-Forth who helped du Barry to manage the ongoing trial, as well as organize the practical details of her four journeys—from lodgings, to servants, to the provision of ready money.

Just as Jeanne had never questioned the motives of her amiable London mentor, she had never suspected that, since her first trip across the Channel, all of her movements and contacts had been observed and recorded by a secret agent of the Jacobins, a certain Blache-Dumas, at that time a teacher of French in England. Now, under the equally vigilant eyes of the English spy and his French confrere, Mme du Barry spent even more time with the expatriates than she had on her previous trips, receiving their condolences for the death of Brissac, paying them visits, inviting them to dinner, and playing cards with them late into the evening—just as if they were all still in Paris. Was it merely the need to distract herself that drove her to such imprudent behavior? Or had the tragic death of her lover and the fall of the monarchy brought her into the counterrevolutionary camp? What did she talk about with Narbonne and Talleyrand, whom she met up with upon her arrival in London?[309] And if her courageous gesture of attending the funeral mass celebrated for Louis XVI at the Spanish embassy in full mourning was certainly dictated by her attachment to the royal family, serious doubts remain regarding the enormous sums of money that she had transferred to London. The first payment of 200,000 livres was destined for the Cardinal de La Rochefoucauld, in order to help the refractory priests who had emigrated to England by the thousands; the second, of the same amount, was a contribution to a loan for the Duc Louis-Auguste de Rohan-Chabot, then in London, who was heavily implicated in the Vendée insurrection. Moreover, both of these operations had been executed by the Vendenyvers, bankers who specialized in sending funds to the émigrés. One might well ask whether the money at issue really belonged to Mme du Barry—notoriously in debt at the time—or if she was simply serving as a front for the transfer of funds. Had she consciously chosen to finance the struggle against the Jacobin dictatorship, or was someone abusing her naivety and good-heartedness? One thing is certain: Jeanne did not herself intend to emigrate, and on February 27, 1793, with her suit against Symons finished,[310] she hastily returned to France, without even waiting to reclaim her jewels. She had learned that she had been accused of planning to emigrate, and that Louveciennes had been placed under seal—she now wanted to clear up any suspicion as quickly as possible. Given the uncertainty of the times, she must not have been unhappy that her diamonds remained safe in England. Since England and France had officially been at war since February 1, she requested safe passage from Pitt to embark at Dover, and when the minister attempted to convince her not to leave, responded that she did not want to betray the commitment made when she had received her French passport. "Ah, very well, madame! You shall meet the fate of Regulus,"[311] Pitt cried while taking leave of her, never imagining that in fact it would be an Englishman who would claim her head.

Upon her return home after five months abroad, Jeanne discovered that a stranger who hated her had installed himself at Louveciennes. His name was George Greive, he was a native of Newcastle, and after pursuing a number of trades without success, he had become a professional revolutionary. He had fought in America by the side of the rebels before coming to France, where, embracing the Jacobin cause, he had decided to make a reputation for himself by bringing to the guillotine an exemplary victim, one capable of exciting the imagination and rousing the indignation of the public. Greive, who had never met Jeanne, bore her no personal animosity. Moreover, the former favorite had been living quietly, out of the public eye, for more than twenty years. By now she belonged to the past, and no longer constituted a political target: Marie-Antoinette had long since replaced her in the collective imagination. If the English adventurer nevertheless pursued her with an implacable hatred, subverting her servants, turning the population against her, and bombarding her with accusations, it was because the scandal surrounding the theft of her jewels had transformed her into a perfect trophy of war. "That dazzling catalog of diamonds, rubies, and pearls; that image of numberless gemstones and jewels; those magnificent promises of gold pieces by the thousands; how could they help but arouse attention, stimulate envy, and summon dangerous memories of a still-recent past?"[312] The newspapers took an interest in her, recalling her past as a courtesan, working themselves into a rage over those floods of silver extracted from the state's coffers, and insinuating that the theft itself had been faked, with the sole end of transferring her jewels to England.[313] Greive saw in the last favorite of the ancien régime the opportunity to draw up a vast indictment of the abuses of the French monarchy. He had studied the law in his youth, and possessed undeniable talent as an orator, which he put to use both in his denunciations of Mme du Barry at the *mairie* of Louveciennes, the department of Seine-et-Oise, and to the commune, and in a virulent pamphlet titled *L'Égalité Controuvée* (A Forged Equality), in which he presented himself as "Greive, official defender of the brave sans-culottes of Louveciennes, friend of Franklin and Marat, dissenter and anarchist of the first rank, disrupter of despotism in both hemispheres for the past twenty years."[315] But in spite of his eloquence, his repeated denunciations, and the merits of the evidence he had gathered, the infamous Mme du Barry continued to get away with it: she succeeded in regaining her château; the *mairie*, the department, and the commune expressed themselves in her favor and declined to initiate proceedings against her; the inhabitants of Louveciennes took her side once more, and key witnesses like Salanave, a former chef who had been dismissed, wrote her letters of apology.

For her part, having realized what a dangerous enemy she had in Greive, Mme du Barry strove for discretion: with the help of Morin, her butler, in whom she had complete confidence, she consigned all of her portraits of the royal family to the attic, hid the silverware and jewels that remained to her in the park of her estate in the middle of the night, continued to visit with friends and acquaintances who had not emigrated, and even enjoyed a final love affair with Rohan-Chabot—proof that in spite of her fifty years, Jeanne was still capable of arousing violent passions, as we see in a surviving letter sent to her by the Duc.[316]

Greive was able to reenter the fray thanks to the law promulgated on September 17, 1793, which provided for the immediate arrest of all suspects and created, along with the Revolutionary Tribunal, surveillance committees and groups of sans-culottes charged with tracking down traitors to the nation and enemies of the people. The English vigilante wasted no time: he convinced the Committee of General Security to open an investigation into Mme du Barry, and scarcely five days after the law had gone into effect, armed with an arrest warrant *en règle* and escorted by guards, he burst into the château, taking Mme du Barry completely by surprise. At the sight of her persecutor, the poor woman sought refuge in her bedroom and attempted to burn her letters, but Greive dragged her away by force and, having sealed the château, forced her into a carriage so that he could bring her to jail himself. While imprisoned at Sainte-Pélagie, Jeanne appealed to the Committee of General Security, protesting that she had been "delivered into the hands of a man who had declared himself her enemy,"[317] and who had treated her in a shameful manner—a man who had taken up residence in her château, going through her papers with a fine-toothed comb, thoroughly examining her accounts, and noting down anything that might serve to implicate her in counterrevolutionary activity. To shore up his allegations, he benefited from the precious collaboration of Blache-Dumas, the former London spy who, expelled from England due to the Aliens Act at the beginning of the war, had now become a commissioner in the Committee of General Security on which Jeanne's fate depended. We do not know how long the two men had been acquainted with each other, and it has even been speculated that the pair were responsible for the initial theft of the jewels. In any case, they were made for each other, sharing the same fanaticism, the same desire to revenge themselves on the social order that had excluded them, and the same absence of scruples. Similar sentiments drove Zamor—the Indian servant who had entered Mme du Barry's service while still a child, and who had been her page during the glorious years at Versailles— to lend them his assistance. Uprooted from the land of his birth and with no chance of integrating himself into a country where he had been imported as an exotic amusement, Zamor harbored a keen resentment regarding his marginal position and had embraced the revolutionary cause with enthusiasm. Greive knew how to find the words to convince him to betray Mme du Barry, who had nonetheless showered him with gifts.

When two members of the Committee of General Security finally interrogated her, Jeanne contradicted herself numerous times, taken off guard by the questions prepared by Greive.[318] One of the interrogation's central points concerned her relationship with the Vendenyvers, and when she learned that the bankers had been arrested, she panicked and had difficulty coming up with adequate replies. Convinced of her guilt, the committee referred her to the Revolutionary Tribunal, which convened on November 19. Two months after her arrest, she appeared before the judge for the first time, along with Vendenyver and his two sons. The examination was led by René-François Dumas, the vice president of the Revolutionary Tribunal, in the presence of the representative of the prosecutor's office, Antoine Fouquier-Tinville, who took ten days to draft his indictment. On December 4, the accused was transferred to the Conciergerie, which was considered "the antechamber to the scaffold,"[319] and two days later her trial began. She was accused of having conspired against the Revolution and financing the armed struggle of its enemies by sending to London, where she had emigrated, exorbitant sums of money.[320] After having lied about her age in a final spasm of coquetry—reducing it by eight years— Jeanne listened to the lies and half-truths of the numerous witnesses that had been assembled against her. The declarations of Greive, Blache-Dumas, and Zamor would have been enough on their own to condemn her.[321] On the evening of December 7, it was Fouquier-Tinville's turn to speak. Prepared with the greatest of care, his summation, which he would be sure to have published,[322] gave a certain "symbolic value"[323] to the trial. Only two months after the execution of Marie-Antoinette, the last of the favorites was being called to account. The Revolution, thundered Fouquier-Tinville, made no distinction between the villainous Queen and this "Laïs famous for the dissolution of her morals...whose libertinism has brought her to share the despot's fate"—for their depravity had been equal, and their punishment should be likewise. Jeanne's entire past was remorselessly reiterated in the public prosecutor's speech: "The infamous *conspiratrice* before you today was able to luxuriate in the opulence acquired through her shameful debauchery, to live in the midst of a land which seemed to have buried all memory of her prostitution and rise along with the tyrant whose companion she had been. But in her eyes, the liberty of the people was a crime.... By striking with the sword of Justice this Messalina guilty of conspiring against the nation, not only will you avenge the Republic for her assaults against it—you will uproot a public scandal and affirm the empire of that morality upon which is founded the liberty of peoples."[324]

Mme du Barry's advocate was Chauveau-Lagarde, who had already spoken with skill and courage on behalf of Marie-Antoinette, Charlotte Corday, Mme Roland, and numerous other famous defendants. But the guilt of the accused was a foregone conclusion, and when, at eleven o'clock in the evening on December 7, the judges returned to the chamber and read the sentence that condemned her to be executed at eleven o'clock the next morning, Jeanne was the only one unprepared for what she heard—she emitted a shrill cry and fainted. The next morning at ten o'clock, Mme du Barry demanded to see the judges, and over the course of three hours enumerated for them all of the places her various treasures were hidden.[325] Had she been promised her life would be spared in exchange? Was that why, when she was shown to the tumbrel where the Vendenyvers were waiting for her, she cried that there had been a mistake—why during the whole of her final journey she continued to weep and wail, why she refused to mount the scaffold and was instead hauled up by force, and why she protested her innocence to the very end, begging for mercy? When Louis XV had contracted smallpox, Jeanne had shown that she had no fear of death, staying at his side until the bitter end, heedless of the possibility of contagion—and recently she had aided more than one person at great risk to herself.[326] Still, a daughter of the common people, she had no sense of aristocratic pride—and now, faced with a cruel and unjust death, she appealed to the sentiments of the crowd that had come to witness her punishment. "She was the only woman, among all of the women who perished during those frightful days, who could not support the sight of the scaffold," wrote Élisabeth Vigée Le Brun, a fellow daughter of the Third Estate, who had immortalized her radiant beauty. "She wept, she begged for mercy from the atrocious mob that surrounded her, and that mob was so moved that the executioner made haste to end her torment. This has always persuaded me that if the victims of those execrable times had not possessed the noble pride that allowed them to die courageously, the Terror would have ended far sooner than it did."[327]

During her detention, Mme du Barry certainly had the chance to recall her carefree days of libertinism—in a register rather different than that served up at the trial by Fouquier-Tinville—with an old acquaintance from those bygone times: namely Biron, who had arrived at Sainte-Pélagie two months before Jeanne. Back when she was still selling her charms and he was still called Lauzun, he had been one of her youngest and most attractive clients. The Duc must have maintained his *habitudes de galanterie* even in prison, for Mme Roland, also detained at Sainte-Pélagie, refused to answer her jealous husband when he asked her how frequently General Biron visited the "ladies' quarters."[328] And surely, l'Ange would have greeted him with the selfsame smile he was familiar with from their encounters at Versailles. They would not have been short of things to talk about. But how did Biron come to find himself in prison?

In February 1792, after returning from his unfortunate London expedition in the company of Talleyrand, the Duc had gone back to the general headquarters of the Army of the North at Valenciennes, where he served as a lieutenant under the command of Rochambeau. Less than three weeks later, Narbonne's forced resignation led to the formation of a new government, no longer Feuillant but Girondin, with Dumouriez as minister of foreign affairs and Grave as minister of war. Biron had long been acquainted with Dumouriez, and he soon initiated a correspondence with the minister in order to make his positions clear. The Duc defended a policy of peace—but in order to implement it, it would be necessary to gain the respect of Austria and Prussia and to reinforce the borders, first and foremost that with Belgium: "We will then be in a position to declare to the King of Hungary that we wish to maintain the peace, but that at his first ambiguous response, at the first movement of his troops, we will enter the Brabant."[329] They would need to act likewise with England, placing a fleet of twenty ships at Brest ready to cast off for India. As far as Biron himself was concerned, and as he had already indicated to Narbonne, aside from his wish to return to Corsica, he had "no other ambition than to serve in some position useful to the public."³³⁰ Dumouriez hastened to assure him of his support—"Our feelings have long been in agreement"—adding that he intended to make him "one of the strongest supports of [his] political and military machine."³³¹ But the minister was quickly forced to revise his position. Though for reasons that were certainly opposed to those of the Tuileries, the Girondists were also eager for war; and in Austria, Francis II, who had succeeded Leopold II on the throne of Hungary and Bohemia, was decidedly less of a pacifist than his father. As Francis saw things, not only would a victorious military campaign stop the revolutionary epidemic in its tracks but it would allow him to consolidate his position in Germany by assuring him the imperial crown. As for Prussia, she had offered her support to Austria and was laying the groundwork for a new partition of Poland.

Since France had taken the initiative of declaring war on April 20, Dumouriez was determined to gamble on aggressive military action in hopes of taking the enemy by surprise. Well aware of the difficult situation of the army—formed for the most part of inexperienced volunteers, and with an executive staff decimated by emigration—Rochambeau was a partisan of a defensive strategy but was ultimately compelled to invade Belgium. As he doubted that the operation had any chance of succeeding, he attempted to limit the damage by retaining the bulk of his troops in a defensive position and proceeding with the greatest caution. He limited the offensive to three columns of soldiers under the command of Biron, Dillon, and Carles, who would have to penetrate the enemy's territory by marching on Mons, Tournai, and Furnes, respectively. Dumouriez and Biron himself were convinced that the Belgians, long hostile to Vienna's rule, would welcome the envoys of liberty with open arms, and that they could even count on numerous defections from the ranks of the Austrian army to the French side. But these hopes were soon dashed—it was in fact the French soldiers who disobeyed their officers. With the border behind them and their first military objectives accomplished, Biron's soldiers were seized by panic during the night, after a wholly unjustified alert, and fled. Biron succeeded in retaking control of the situation and holding the positions he had gained, but Dillon was massacred by his own soldiers, who lost their heads during the first salvos exchanged with the enemy's outposts and, thinking they had been betrayed, mutinied.

Facing the failure of a military operation that had been forced upon him by Paris, Rochambeau resigned—to Biron's great regret—and was replaced by Maréchal Luckner. The new commander—to whom the new minister of war had given carte blanche—opted for a defensive strategy: to the disappointment of the assembly, he recalled the troops to their initial positions. The Army of the North's priority was still the defense of Lorraine from the advancing Army of Koblenz. The threat of invasion of the national territory had the immediate effect of radicalizing the political struggle, and Biron would be caught up and finally imprisoned by an onrushing chain of events. In the space of two years, the Duc served successively in five different armies, reporting to at least seven ministers of war, under monarchical as well as republican regimes.[332]

With his nomination to the post of supreme commander of the Army of the Rhine, Biron embarked upon the final adventure of his life.[333] The command of an enormous army was the sort of responsibility to which he did not feel drawn—it was not for nothing that he had refused the leadership of the Army of the Alps, which he had been offered by Narbonne, and that of the Army of the North, which Dumouriez had proposed to him.[334] But the third time, he could not say no. It was no longer a question of proving his mettle on the field of battle but of making strategic decisions, of coordinating the actions of the high-ranking generals under his orders, of organizing a mixed army made up of enthusiastic but inexperienced volunteers and of professionals whose loyalty was by no means certain. Moreover, for him the war had never been an end in itself but a means of diplomacy, and his true passion (which he shared with Mirabeau, Talleyrand, and Narbonne) had always been for politics. But now, the spoiled child of the ancien régime revealed that he was equal to the task.

The events of August 10 and the fall of the monarchy inspired in Biron—like many other officers who had taken an oath on the constitution out of loyalty to the King—a serious crisis of conscience. The Duc did not want to abandon his country and his soldiers, and resigned himself to accepting the Republic as a fait accompli. His priority was the defense of France from the coalition of foreign powers that threatened her sovereignty, and the immediate choice that presented itself to him was not between the monarchy or the Republic but between fighting the invaders or joining them. And given that the constitutional system, based on that of the English, for which he and his men had fought, was not working, he could only hope that the American model would deliver better results.[335] Less coherent than Biron, the republican Lafayette believed he could save the monarchy by marching on Paris with his army, but his soldiers refused to follow, and he was forced to surrender to the Austrians. Biron had no illusions when it came to his personal case. The political methods of the convention were incompatible with his liberal convictions, and he knew that his professional abilities did nothing to erase the stain of his aristocratic birth in the eyes of the Jacobins. More and more he felt like a survivor in a world profoundly foreign to him. His best friends had emigrated, many of them had met terrible deaths, and he had lost all hope of seeing Mme de Coigny again. Indeed, their exchange of letters would soon cease—for in a Europe riven by war, correspondence proved difficult. To judge by the final letter from the Marquise that has come down to us, the fall of Louis XVI drew nary a tear from her. "Apart from the public massacres, as horrible to imagine as to witness, I remain philosophical regarding the King's fall—I do not believe that the kingdom is lost, for a king suspected of conspiring against it is unfit to defend it." It was seeing "civil and foreign war raging at once in that unfortunate land" that anguished her, and drove her to say, even before Mme Roland: "Oh Liberty, how many ills you inflict on us in exchange for your promised benefits." Biron could no longer take comfort in his beloved's political realism, nor allow himself to be lulled by her precious melopoeia. She had bid farewell to him with these words: "Adieu, believe that my heart, my soul, and my mind are wholly yours, and with you."[336]

The sole woman who remained by his side to bring him a little comfort in those rare moments stolen from his grueling work was the sweet and unobtrusive Charlotte Laurent, who, for many years now, had followed him like a shadow. This young actress of middling talent—whose debut at the Comédie in 1785 the *Correspondance littéraire* had greeted with these words: "They say she is less of a cold fish outside of the theater. It is M. le Duc de Lauzun who takes care of her"[337]—had been for Biron an obliging mistress, one with whom he could dispense with all the playacting of worldly seduction. Still, it is surprising that Mlle Laurent possessed neither wit nor beauty; and it is difficult to believe the (rather ungentlemanly) explanation that the Duc provided to a friend who asked the reason for his choice: "If only you knew how foolish she is, and how convenient I find it! In her presence one can discuss the most important matters with complete safety."[338] Indeed, over time, Mlle Laurent would become a necessary presence for Biron. When at the end of the National Constituent Assembly the Duc resumed his duties in Valenciennes, it was she who oversaw the stewardship of his residence and domestic staff, served as a gracious[339] hostess at the daily luncheons and receptions that the general held for his officers, and, above all, looked after him personally. Biron had always been a man of delicate health, but now indigestion, stomachaches, and gout gave him no respite, and Mlle Laurent proved an excellent nurse.

Biron successfully blocked the advance of the Duke of Brunswick, who had crossed the Rhine at Mannheim on August 2 with an army of three thousand men. But he quickly ran up against the ambition of General Custine—the father-in-law of Mme de Sabran's daughter—who, fortified by the popularity he'd won with the surrender of Mainz, intended to take his place at the head of the army. In order to avoid a conflict of authority, Jean-Nicolas Pache, the new minister of war, decided to entrust to Biron the command of the Army of Italy, against the protests of the *commissaires* of the convention, who, having gone on an inspection at Strasbourg, had been overwhelmed by enthusiastic appreciations of his work there.

Before leaving for Paris to be instructed on his new duties, the Duc learned that his wife, whom he had not seen for fifteen years, was at risk of being investigated for having wished to emigrate. Indeed, following August 10, Amélie de Boufflers had sought refuge first in England, then Switzerland, before returning to France to avoid the confiscation of her possessions. At this point, Biron dispatched an open letter to the convention asserting his duties as a husband: "A faithful soldier of the Republic dares to ask the representatives of the people to fix their gaze on the frightful position of a woman, who, thanks to a moment of delirium, for which evidence can be provided, is today exposed to the misfortune of being expelled from the bosom of her homeland. Citizens, this woman is mine. Having been separated from her, our possessions divided, for some fifteen years, I feel, for the first time, with painful remorse, that if it were not for that distance which circumstances have set between us, this woman, more confident, more reassured, perhaps even proud of the patriotism of her husband, and more misfortunate than guilty, would never have attracted the law's severity."[340]

Amélie de Boufflers begged her father-in-law, the Duc de Gontaut, to let her husband know that she had been "deeply touched" by his desire to be useful, but also how ill timed she thought his intervention, which in fact had the effect of bringing her to the attention of the authorities. What's more, the plea for leniency advanced by the Duc amounted to an admission of guilt.[341] No question about it—in good times as in bad, the spouses were destined to misunderstand each other.

In mid-December, Biron returned to Paris, where he had received permission to remain for several weeks in order to recover his health. He stayed with Mlle Laurent at the Hôtel Saint-Marc, on the street of the same name, and paid a visit to his father, who, no less indignant at his debts than his political leanings, received him coldly. His stay in the capital coincided with the trial of Louis XVI, whose death crushed the Duc. Not only did Biron think the judicial proceeding beyond the pale given that the constitution of 1791 had established the inviolability of the King and stipulated that the sole punishment to which he was subject was the forfeiture of his rights, but he asked himself anxiously what the attitude of Orléans would be at the moment of sentencing. He felt a fraternal bond with the Duc, and was very attached to his children. The Duc de Chartres—the future Louis-Philippe—whom he had had as a commander at Valenciennes, testified in his memoirs to the "old, unwavering, and faithful friendship" that Biron had felt for his father until his "last sigh"[342] and, consequently, for his brother Montpensier and himself. Elected to the assembly and rebaptized Philippe Égalité, the cousin of Louis XVI now found himself in an extremely difficult position. As Évelyne Lever writes, "the Revolution was going much further than he had ever foreseen.... He understood this perfectly well during the September Massacres, when the murderers of the Princesse de Lamballe dragged her frightfully mutilated corpse to his very doorstep."[343] Without a party of his own to back him, and buffeted by a constantly shifting political situation, he sat with La Montagne—Robespierre's radical faction, which occupied the highest seats on the left-hand side of the hall—and abstained from speaking. In so doing he hoped to protect himself from the attacks of the extremists, but it was the Girondins who, in order to make difficulties for La Montagne, called for his expulsion from the country along with the rest of the Bourbons. And when, after a raucous debate, the convention decreed that—with the exception of Philippe Égalité—all of the Bourbons-Capets would have one week to leave France, Orléans, who had never had a particularly developed sense of honor, decided that he had no choice but to fight for his own survival. During the King's trial, his children and closest friends, beginning with Biron, well aware of the fragility of his character, sought to convince him not to take the irrevocable step of voting for the death of his cousin. Despite their obvious differences in perspective, the memoirs of the future Louis-Philippe and those of Grace Elliot provide a description of the very same drama. The first—who had distinguished himself for his courage and military know-how under the command of General Kellermann at Valmy and Jemappes, and enjoyed a solid reputation for patriotism—recounts his repeated attempts to convince his father to find an excuse not to participate in the trial. But the result of their conversations was not reassuring. Frightened and disoriented, the Duc was in no state to fight shy of the demands of La Montagne, who had him at their mercy. He did not welcome his son's suggestion that he save his life and honor by emigrating with his whole family to the United States. Chartres departed again for the front in despair, leaving his brother Montpensier the task of wresting from their father at least the promise that he would not vote for the death of the sovereign.[344] Biron, too, hoped to prevent his friend from committing that ignominy—he knew Orléans too well to hope for anything more, and relied on his own influence, as well as that of Miss Elliott. Biron asked the beautiful English courtesan—who, after having been Orléans's mistress, had become his intimate friend—to invite the Duc to her house to speak in private. It was she who reported the substance of that conversation years afterward, in her *Journal of My Life during the French Revolution*. "I hope, Monseigneur, that you will vote for the King's deliverance," the young woman began. "Certainly... and for my own death," Orléans retorted, angrily. At this point Biron intervened in a tone that admitted of no reply: "The Duc will not vote. The King has used him very ill all his life; but he is his cousin, therefore he will feign illness and stay at home on Saturday, the day of the *appel nominal*, which is to decide on the King's fate."[345] Orléans reassured them that he would do just that, and that nothing in the world obliged him to vote against a member of his own family.

But La Montagne decided otherwise. On January 16, the day that the convention was set to pronounce sentence on the King, two of the faction's deputies went to find the Duc at the Palais-Royal, informing him that he could not shirk his responsibilities in the face of so grave a question. That evening, Miss Elliott rejoined Biron at the Hôtel Saint-Marc, where, accompanied by his faithful aide-de-camp Rustan, Mlle Laurent, and Dumouriez, they awaited the results of the vote. The anxiety of those present was soon tinged with dread: the updates that arrived every half hour showed that those voices in favor of capital punishment had the advantage, and the news that the Duc d'Orléans, breaking all of his promises, had presented himself before the convention to cast his own vote for the death of his cousin, left them all speechless. "Even poor Biron, who, alas! was a republican, was almost in a fit," and his aide-de-camp Rustan, who had declined emigration in order to remain at

Biron's side, "tore off his [uniform] coat and flung it into the fire, saying that he should blush ever to wear it again."[346] Orléans waited until he had returned to Palais-Royal to weep in shame. His youngest son found him doubled over in his study: "'Montpensier,' he said, sobbing, 'I don't have the courage to look at you. . . . I can't imagine how I could have been led to do what I did.'"[347]

On January 23, two days after the execution of Louis XVI, Biron departed for Nice to take command of Army of Italy, receiving permission to bring along the young Montpensier[348] and Generals Sheldon and Mieszkowski, who had been by his side since the expedition to Senegal. In anticipation of war with England, his mission was the defense of Corsica, Alpes-Maritimes, and the coast from the Rhône to Var. But for the moment, the most urgent task was protecting Nice from attack by Austro-Piedmontese troops. His correspondence with Paris[349] clearly shows the enormous difficulties he was facing. As in the case of the Army of the Rhine, Biron had not received the promised instructions, the army was sorely lacking in supplies, and only half of its twenty thousand soldiers were in any condition to fight, and even those needed to be trained and disciplined. None of that stopped him from devoting himself to his new task with his characteristic zeal. Far from the horrors of the capital, immersed in the luminous Mediterranean landscape that had always been so dear to him, and called upon to fight once again in the defense of Corsica, Biron had for an instant the sensation of having rediscovered a country worthy of his loyalty. The unexpected French defeat in Sardinia and the assassination of France's representative in Rome were, for him, an opportunity to draw the attention of the minister of foreign affairs, Lebrun, to the "necessity of reinforcing the Army of Italy if we envisage an active French diplomacy on the peninsula."[350]

But the main preoccupation of the Revolutionary government was looking after its own security, and, on April 8, 1793, Biron received the order from the committee to arrest Montpensier and conduct him to Marseille under heavy guard. In tears, Biron informed the Prince, eighteen years old at the time, of his duty and assisted him in destroying all of his potentially compromising documents.[351] The two of them discovered the reasons behind the arrest when they learned that General Dumouriez and the Duc de Chartres had taken refuge abroad in the wake of their abortive attempt to convince the army to march on Paris. Dumouriez had declared that he wished to reestablish the constitution of 1791 and to restore the monarchy, recognizing the young Louis XVII, then imprisoned in the Temple, as King. But many people sensed that the real objective was to install an Orléans on the throne, and the convention immediately gave the order to arrest all the Bourbons who still remained in France's territory. So it was that at Marseille, in the fortress of Notre-Dame de la Garde, Montpensier was able to embrace both his father and Beaujolais, his youngest brother. Transferred shortly afterward to the more secure Fort Saint-Jean, the three Orléanses spent six months of strict imprisonment together until October 23, when the Duc bid an affectionate farewell to his son and was transported to Paris to face the Revolutionary Tribunal and the charge of high treason. Philippe Égalité, who had rigorously kept his distance from the plans of Dumouriez and Chartres, believed until the very end that he would be able to prove that he had been wholly uninvolved in any counter-revolutionary conspiracy, unaware that Fouquier-Tinville had decided his fate even before questioning him. Yet, on November 6, he heard himself condemned to the guillotine "with as much indifference as if he was being told to go to the Opéra"[352] and faced his own death with the determination and courage that he had always lacked in life.

Just after Montpensier's arrest, Biron was forced to contend with a mutiny among his own troops, who were suffering from cold and hunger and alarmed by the treason of Dumouriez. He only succeeded in reestablishing order thanks to his personal influence over the soldiers, but he did not conceal the gravity of the situation from Paris, nor the necessity of taking their needs into account. These ten days of revolt, he wrote to the new minister Bouchotte, "were perhaps those in which I rendered my most essential service to the Republic."[353] But the Republic thanked him by entrusting to him the command of the Army of the Coasts of La Rochelle, then occupied with repressing the insurrection in the Vendée. Biron was dismayed: he was being forced to abandon an army with which, over the course of several weeks, he had already achieved terrific military successes and within which he had numerous trusted collaborators. And he could not "remove himself without pain" from Corsica—"this new fatherland that I have adopted, and that has in turn adopted me"—to which he addressed "his regrets at being unable to further dedicate [his] services."[354] Above all, in the Vendée, it was no longer a question of defending France but of prosecuting a fratricidal war. Biron was probably tempted to tender his resignation, and he immediately declared that the state of his health—indeed more and more troubling—prevented him from taking on a new mission. But he was heavily in debt, and the army gave him something to live on and constituted his final defense, since his friendship with the Duc d'Orléans had rendered him irremediably suspect. One might wonder why the convention had selected him for so delicate a task. The answer given by Clément C. Velay in his fine biography seems convincing: the Revolutionary government, which was in a hurry to resolve the issue of the Vendée and still had not ruled out the possibility of coming to some kind of accord with the insurgents, were relying as much on Biron's skills as a negotiator—of which he had given plentiful evidence in his past positions—as on his military capabilities. But the coup d'etat of June 2 led to a radicalization of the Terror and the decision to simply crush all resistance. The qualities for which Biron had been chosen became suspect: "He would no longer be considered the right man for the situation, but rather a potential traitor."[355]

Having already had the experience of a war of occupation during the period of the Corsican expedition, Biron knew how difficult it was to overcome the resistance of fighters entirely devoted to their cause, supported by the population, and possessing a perfect knowledge of the terrain. Discovering the same situation in the Vendée, with the aggravating factor of the civil war, he opted for a strategy wherein the use of force was accompanied by the search for a compromise acceptable to both parties. He reaffirmed this position in his regular dispatches to the minister of war, denouncing the indiscipline of the soldiers, their lack of experience, and the harassment to which they subjected the populace, as well as the pernicious role played by "the innumerable quantity of agents and subagents of executive power. It is well known that they are everywhere, snatching up horses and carriages and insulting their owners, all without turning any of it to the benefit of the army."[356] These were dangerous demagogues who preached "insubordination, insurrection, and division,"[357] and the defeats suffered at Doué, Saumur, and Angers were the exclusive result of the inadequacy of the Republican army: rather than attempting to face down an elusive enemy on the open field, it would be necessary to circumscribe that enemy and gradually reduce its range of action.

However, the government had come to a different conclusion. To bring the Vendée episode to a close, what was needed was "a plan of massed action,"[358] and Paris demanded that Biron prepare himself accordingly. With great courage, the Duc declared himself ready either to resign or to serve under the orders of some other general. But as long as he was responsible for the army, he would remain "penetrated by the belief that, when a Republican is convinced he is engaged in some necessary task, he must be as prepared to lose his head on the scaffold as on the field of battle."[359] Even before it aroused the censure of the convention, the Duc's stance had gotten in the way of the ambitions of Ronsin, a failed actor who had embraced the Republican cause, developing a passion for military matters. Dispatched to the Vendée by the Executive Committee at the beginning of May with the task of provisioning the army, Ronsin wanted to involve himself in operational aspects as well, and advocated for an offensive of massive scale. Treated as an incompetent by Biron,[360] he decided to avenge himself. Exploiting the discontent of all those against whom Biron had taken disciplinary measures—beginning with a demagogue known as Rossignol—Ronsin spread the rumor that the army's commander in chief was taking refuge behind specious technical arguments in order to support the counterrevolution by way of a pernicious stasis. Ronsin and Rossignol used the Parisian clubs of sans-culottes, with which they were both closely tied, to amplify this message—and Robespierre, who for his part counted on the support of the clubs to rid himself of Danton, listened to their accusations. Conscious of having lost the confidence of the Committee of Public Safety and ceasing to struggle against a perverse logic that placed the concerns of politicians before the interest of the nation, Biron invoked his poor health and asked to be relieved of his duties.[361] On July 26, he was summoned to report on his actions to the Executive Council, and four days later, he arrived in Paris.

Minister of War Bouchotte, as well as Gasparin, Barère, and Hérault de Séchelles, who received him on behalf of the Committee of Public Safety, invited him to draft a report on the initiatives that he had undertaken during his six weeks as commander in the Vendée. He complied, requesting that they acknowledge the fact that he had regularly informed the Executive Committee of the difficulties he had encountered, that he had always acted with their consent, and had, in short, done everything that was within his power to serve the Republic.[362] But Biron's servant, who had gone to the copyist to obtain copies of the report, was arrested as he returned to the Hôtel de la Paix in the Chaussée d'Antin, where the Duc was staying. That same evening, Biron was jailed in Sainte-Pélagie with Mlle Laurent and the faithful Rustan.[363]

While he had held the position of general, the Duc had made it a point of honor to serve his country by respecting the letter of the rules imposed by the military code of ethics, without taking into account the ideas, prejudices, and interests of his various interlocutors. Following his arrest, he once again dispatched letters to the convention, the Committee of Public Safety, and Hérault de Séchelles in which he reaffirmed the rightness of his actions and his non-involvement in any conspiracy whatsoever. Since his youth he had been in the habit of drafting briefs, reports, and political and diplomatic analyses, and he continued to do so up until the moment when, receiving no response, he realized that nobody was interested in his explications and that the charge of treason leveled against him was nothing but a pretext for his elimination. It was clear that France no longer had any use for a general like him, or like his friend and rival Custine, who, in the grip of a similar accusation, preceded him to the guillotine on August 28. In any case, Biron knew the threats facing the country too well not to realize that only the iron fist of the Terror could possibly save the Republic. It would require—as his best biographer writes— "the dictatorship of Robespierre, and above all the efficiency of Carnot, for the army to be properly equipped at last, and for the officers and soldiers to master their new trade."[364] His duty as a military commander at an end, and freed from now on of all responsibility, Biron became once again a man of his own caste, and raised between his enemies and himself an impassible wall of contempt. "These men have bored me for far too long; they're going to cut my throat, but at least it will all be over,"[365] he declared to Beugnot. During the five months he spent at Sainte-Pélagie awaiting his trial, the Duc surrendered himself to the care of Mlle Laurent and his aide-de-camp, conversed genially with the other prisoners, read, drank numerous bottles of wine, and passed the bulk of his time stretched out on his bed, displaying a complete indifference to his own fate.

Finally, on December 29, he appeared before the Revolutionary Tribunal, where, fully aware that the questioning was a pure formality and that his fate had already been decided, he curtly denied having "ever supported by act or intention"[366] any antipatriotic conspiracy. But of course, what he was really guilty of was his own birth. In his closing summation, lacking the least shred of evidence to prop up the charge of treason, Fouquier-Tinville accused him of having been "born into the caste of the formerly privileged; having spent his life in the bosom of a corrupt court groveling before his master, and having only assumed the mask of patriotism, like the traitors Custine, Lafayette, Dumouriez, and so many others, in order to deceive the nation to whose interests he only appeared to devote himself, abusing the confidence she had bestowed on him so as to place her once more in the shackles of despotism."[367]

Pronounced two days later, his death sentence repeated the summation's charges point for point, and found Biron guilty of having behaved in the

Vendée like "a column of the enemy's army," and earlier still, during his command of the Army of Italy, having "as a skilled courtier of a future tyrant" taken "under his orders the son of the traitorous Orléans, who had only voted for the death of the despot so as to take his place"[368]—but also of having been complicit in the treason of Dumouriez. Biron received the sentence with a smile and, upon his return to the Conciergerie, bid farewell to the other prisoners awaiting judgment with: "Well, my friends, it's all over, I'm leaving." Then, taking up pen and paper, he wrote "without corrections, in a firm and confident hand"[369] two letters of farewell. In the first, addressed to "Citizen Laurent" at Sainte-Pélagie, he expressed to the young woman who had remained by his side for so long his worry at leaving her alone and without support: "A few hours more and my fate will be settled; but my dear and unfortunate friend, you will have more to complain of, for your sufferings will not be over so quickly—you will have plenty of time to weep for me. If only I could see some future happiness in store for you, that hope would greatly ease my end."[370] Nevertheless, he did hope that "the sole friend"[371] he had left in the world—a clear allusion to Mme de Coigny and his final declaration of his affection for her—as well as his father, would look after her. We find the same request in the second letter, addressed to his cousin, the Marquis de Gontaut,[372] but in reality meant for his father. Through the intermediary of the Marquis, to whom he was very close (Gontaut had come to his aid before, when he had been imprisoned for debt in London), he intended to make an act of submission to that "old monster"[373] with whom he had been in conflict his whole life. After all those years of estrangement, he chose at the end to express his feelings in the naive and simple language of the child he had been when his father, not knowing what else to do with him, had taken him along to Versailles. "I am condemned, I will die tomorrow with the religious sentiments of which my dear papa has always provided me an example, and which are worthy of him. My long agony receives great consolation from the certainty that my dear papa will never abandon to any sort of misfortune Citizen Laurent, to whose friendship I owe so much of the relief of my suffering. I have at my house in Montrouge two Englishwomen who have lived with me for twenty years and who have been held as prisoners since the decree on foreigners—they have no other support than me, and I commend them to the assistance and extreme generosity of my dear papa. I love him, I respect him, and I embrace him one final time with all my heart. Biron."[374] The ceremony of farewells finished, Biron became himself once more. After having dined with great appetite, he spent the evening reading and slept serenely. The next morning, after dressing with care, he had oysters and Alsatian wine brought to him, and invited the prison guard to drink with him. When the executioner arrived, he asked to be allowed to finish his oysters and offered the man a drink, saying genially: "You must need strength for your trade." Then, as calm and haughty as Baudelaire's Don Juan,[375] he mounted the tumbrel for his final journey.

Up until the autumn of 1793, the Ségur family had managed elude the hunt for suspects, and it was only in October that the Committee of Public Safety decided to take action. Indeed, on October 13 the Vicomte was incarcerated at Saint-Lazare, and a month later the elderly Maréchal sent to La Force prison. The Comte was luckier. In the wake of his disastrous mission to Berlin under Narbonne's ministry, ill and depressed, Louis-Philippe had retired to Fresnes with his wife and children, taking up residence at the country home of his brother-in-law d'Aguesseau some miles from the capital. He was there on August 10 and during the September Massacres, but at the beginning of December, learning that his name had been included on the list of émigrés, he returned to his father's house in Paris. Twice arrested, he managed to escape—first thanks to the intervention of a friend and then by grace of his own courage. Having refused to stand guard over the King, then imprisoned in the Temple, he was immediately denounced and haled before the section's committee, where he boldly defended himself. "I have served," he declared to his judges, "as ambassador to that unfortunate prince; he has lavished me with kindnesses; I could not array myself with his jailers and risk having to fire upon him if he attempted to slip his bonds."[376] Moved by his words, the improvised tribunal applauded. When the King's trial began, Louis-Philippe established contact with the deputies of the convention who he knew were attempting to save the sovereign, but left Paris definitively before the King's execution, taking the Maréchal with him. On the advice of his children's tutor, a native of the place, he purchased a small property at Châtenay, not far from Sceaux, where he settled with his family. When in November the *commissaires* of the convention came looking for the Maréchal, Louis-Philippe asked in vain to be allowed to take his place, and remained at Châtenay under house arrest. The Revolution forgot about him, and he survived the years that followed in extreme poverty, growing potatoes, giving lessons to his children, and writing short stories, light comedies, and plays in hopes of drawing some profit from them one day.

In contrast to his brother, the Vicomte de Ségur continued to mock the Revolution for a long time. After the fall of the Bastille and the misadventures of Besenval, he had ceased to bedevil Versailles, instead putting his satirical verve at the service of the monarchy, in his opinion the sole form of government capable of responding to the country's demands. "Those men still bound to the old system need to take note of the fact that the revolution has been accomplished; and those partisans of the new system must acknowledge that it has gone too far," he wrote in his *Essay on Public Opinion, Considered as One of the Principal Causes of the Revolution of 1789*, proving that he possessed, along with his frivolity, a healthy dose of lucidity and good sense. Public opinion could no longer be guided by "*têtes brûlées*," but rather by capable and responsible men, for one thing was certain: "More than ever, for the next few years, opinion will decide our government, our fate. . . . The freedom to write, the freedom to think, will open an unlimited field for the conflict between opinions. . . . No system is based on truly solid foundations; it will be necessary, however, for the majority to adhere to one of them; and that will be the one which rules our destinies."[377] None of this prevented him from stating that the ideals of the reformers had revealed themselves as chimeras, and that the passion for politics had "ruined his Paris," transforming "the capital of pleasure into a hotbed of disputation and ennui."[378] As it had become more difficult for him to amuse himself in the salons, he decided to take up his pen and craft newspaper columns. Gabriel de Broglie has brought to light the Vicomte's important contributions to *La Feuille du Jour*, a daily paper of eight octavo pages, whose first issue appeared on December 1, 1790. Its founder, Pierre-Germain Parisau, was a colorful character who had practiced a thousand trades but whose dominant passion was for the theater. The editor, Jean-Baptiste Desprès, an intelligent and cultured man of letters who had served as secretary to the Baron de Besenval, had invited the Vicomte to collaborate. Even though it was royalist and conservative, *La Feuille du Jour* was not an ideological paper but rather "a journal whose barbed anecdotes and jokes took aim at all parties,"[379] and its editors expressed their political opinions, seemingly uncensored, on the current events that the journal reported. It was a formula that allowed for great freedom of approach, where "the tone was lively, the polemic biting, but where wit and gallantry were never lacking,"[380] and the Vicomte found himself wholly at ease in its pages. In order to lambaste the Revolution, he employed the same short literary forms—the anecdote, the maxim, the aphorism—that Chamfort, for his part, had used to attack the behavior of Ségur and his fellow nobles. These interventions were anonymous, but Ségur's style was itself a signature. Expressed as nothing more than reported opinion, the seriousness of the political situation was imposed on the reader though the demystifying clarity of irony and paradox: "'What disgusts me,' said a woman of wit, 'is the thought that what happens today will, one day, be history'"; "The great misfortune of our legislature is that everything is premature. Are we really so sure that it isn't necessary to prepare men for liberty and equality, as with inoculation?"[381] At times his texts took on a more personal character, in connection with family events. Others, in the end, simply amounted to a settling of scores. In April 1791, on the occasion of Julie Careau's marriage, he published a rather ungallant announcement: "Monsieur Talma is to wed Mlle Julie, widow of Monsieurs A, B, C, D, etc."[382] And he commented upon the death of the Comte d'Adhémar, an intimate friend of the Duchesse de Polignac and protégé of Besenval and of his father, but guilty of being a constitutionalist, with the following: "That spoiled child of arbitrary power has succumbed to demagoguery."[383]

All the while he continued to pen plays and have them performed at the Théâtre-Français—now the Théâtre de la Nation—where in 1787 he had made his debut as a professional author with *Rosaline et Floricourt*.[384] On January 20, 1790, the premiere of his *proverbe Le Parti le plus Gai, ou À bon chat, bon rat* marked the return to the stage of his good friend Mlle Contat, who had retired to the Aventine in protest against the *coup de force* by which Talma, ignoring the censors' prohibition and the Comédie's regulations, had staged Marie-Joseph Chénier's *Charles IX*. But the reconciliation between those members of the company who had chosen the Revolution and those who had remained faithful to the monarchy did not last. At Easter of the same year, the troupe definitively split. Following the decree of January 13, 1791, which put an end to the old theatrical monopoly, Talma quit the Comédie and, taking along with him Mme Dugazon, Mme Vestris, Mlle Vanhove, and various other actors, installed himself in the new auditorium of the Palais-Royal, in the rue de Richelieu, where they made their debut with *Henri VIII*, also by Chénier. The rivalry between the two troupes soon became a war, with Mlle Contat, Mlle

Raucourt, Dazincourt, and Fleury bearing up at the old Comédie-Française as best they could against the extraordinary dramatic talent of Talma and his theatrical revolution.[385] If in *Le Parti le plus Gai* and (the following year) *Le Detour du mari*,[386] the Vicomte persevered in his exploration of verse comedy, with plays that featured aristocratic couples struggling for the first time with the problems of conjugal love, he also attempted with *Le Fou par amour*,[387] a historical drama in rhyming couplets, to adapt himself to the new tastes of his audience, who were hoping to exorcise the violence of daily life by way of tales of love and death set in convents and ruined châteaus.

Though he had spent his whole life toying with love, and though the society in which he had flitted from conquest to conquest had revealed its fragility, the Vicomte now discovered how sweet a stable relationship could be. On the threshold of his forties, he became involved with Reine-Claude Chartraire de Bourbonne, a wealthy and attractive aristocrat of thirty years, who, married at the age of twelve to the Comte d'Avaux, had long since lived separately from her husband, wholly absorbed in esoteric studies.[388] The Duchesse d'Abrantès, who made her acquaintance under the Directory, describes her in her memoirs as "the most noble of friends, the most dignified of women,"[389] and the elegant discretion with which she carried on her relationship with the Vicomte seems to confirm this. She had divorced[390] without feeling it was necessary to remarry, and rather than moving in with the Vicomte, continued to live in the beautiful residence of the d'Avauxes, the Hotel des Mesmes. In January 1793, the Comtesse gave birth to a child that Ségur officially recognized, and to whom he gave his name. Unlike the two children born during his time with Julie, whom he completely ignored out of hatred of their mother, he took a great interest in the education of little Alexandre-Joseph, and made the boy his sole heir.

After the flight to Varennes, Ségur was forced to cease mocking the Revolution. On August 10, when the sans-culottes burst into Parisau's home and destroyed the typographical equipment used for *La Feuille du Jour*, the Vicomte—who had formerly declared that "When one possesses a hundred thousand livres, one does not emigrate"[391]—contemplated sailing for Saint-Domingue, where he still possessed property inherited from his mother. In the end he did not, in fact, leave, but rather, aware that his collaboration with *La Feuille du Jour* had attracted the ire of the Jacobins, attempted to stay out of the way of the police by hiding himself in the countryside around Paris and frequently changing his lodgings whenever he happened to find himself in town. Yet his precautions were futile, for on October 13, he was arrested and jailed at Saint-Lazare, where, ten days later, he was joined by Desprès. The Comtesse d'Avaux would not listen to reason and was determined to share his detention. The Vicomte did not fail to declare his gratitude in verse:

Ah! Peut-on oublier cette adorable
Qui, contre elle n'ayant ni délit ni soupçon,
Force sans nul effroi les murs de la prison,
Demande, obtient des fers et, méprisant la vie,
Vient soigner un ami, si tendre, si fidèle,
Mourant, non des maux, mais d'être éloigné d'elle?[*][392]

During the first few weeks of his detention, Joseph-Alexandre also found comfort in the echoes that reached him of the great success of a *Romeo and Juliet* based on a libretto of his own creation and set to music by Steibelt, which had been performed on October 19, 1793, at the Théâtre Feydeau. This adaptation, one of the first,[394] was in itself an act of defiance. While the odious Talma, contravening the classical rules of good taste, had proposed to restore a tragic sublimity to Shakespeare's theater,[395] Steibelt and Ségur had chosen to treat *Romeo and Juliet* as a comic opera, alternating singing with recitative and taking a chance on a lively tone. The Vicomte reduced the original text from five to three acts, halved and updated its cast of characters—the Friar became a lawyer, the Nurse, a close friend of Juliet—and opted for a happy ending. For the Vicomte, love was indissolubly bound to joy, and in the libretto we find once again those themes present in almost all of his plays: friendship, filial obedience, the desire to choose one's partner for oneself. Tragedy had never been to Joseph-Alexandre's taste, and it was only in prison that he came to understand how tragic the reality was that now surrounded him. Transformed into a prison during the Terror, the former convent of Saint-Lazare, not far from the Porte Saint-Denis, was an ancient building of three stories that could hold more than seven hundred inmates, and its captives included, alongside real or presumed counterrevolutionaries of all classes—nobles, priests, soldiers, magistrates, doctors, writers, artists, actors[396]—various common-law prisoners. Hubert Robert, who had been arrested like Ségur in October,

---

*Ah! How could we forget this adorable woman, /Who, having against her neither offense nor suspicion, / Fearlessly breaches the walls of our prison, / Demands and obtains her own irons and, despising life, / Heals her friend, so tender, so faithful, / Dying, not from his own ills but rather her absence?

depicted its imposing central stairway, its long corridors that led to the cells, the vast courtyard filled with a crowd of prisoners busy strolling, conversing, and attending to their quotidian activities. In fact, Saint-Lazare was the Parisian prison with the most bearable quality of life: the prisoners had permission to circulate freely, correspondence with those outside had been authorized, and the wealthiest benefited from individual cells that they could furnish themselves and were able to order their meals from outside. The cells on the upper floors featured large windows without bars, and Roucher, the poet, wrote to his wife that the view was magnificent and "the air purer than that out in the fields."[397] But in April 1794, the regime grew stricter. The inmates were no longer allowed to leave their cells or communicate with the outside world, furnishings and personal belongings were confiscated, and meals were taken in common. The everyday life of the prisoners was marred by the presence of "*moutons*," spies who drew up lists of presumed conspirators that were sent on to the Revolutionary Tribunal. "*Un comité secret d'infâmes délateurs, / Jusqu'au fond des prisons, préparait nos supplices,*"*[398] wrote the Vicomte de Ségur, recalling how repugnant that forced cohabitation had been. With deadlines growing shorter and shorter, each morning a *commissaire* would publicly read the list of those detainees called to appear before the Revolutionary Tribunal that same day. Farewells and departures played out under the eyes of all and sundry. The Vicomte de Ségur left Saint-Lazare on May 26 to be transferred to the prison of Port-Libre, but he certainly would have had time—in the refectory or during the *heure de la promenade*—to bump into a young friend from happier times: Aimée de Coigny, Duchesse de Fleury, had arrived at Saint-Lazare on March 15.

Nigretta had suffered various trials and tribulations since we left her in Naples in November 1791, writing to Biron while nonchalantly stretched on a chaise longue and lulled by the sound of the sea. For months she had frequented the court of Ferdinand IV and Marie-Caroline in the company of another young and beautiful French aristocrat, the Princesse de Monaco, daughter of that Comtesse de Choiseul-Stainville who had been Lauzun's first love. Wilhelm Tischbein, a painter and the director of the Accademia di Pittura in Naples,

---

*A secret committee of infamous informers / prepared our tortures in the depths of the prisons.

recalls in his memoirs that "in society and at celebrations, you would always meet them together, arm in arm," and that, "one blond, the other brunette," they made a splendid pair. Tischbein also recounts an expedition to Vesuvius in their company, one destined to take on, in hindsight, a prophetic quality. The goal of the trip was a hermitage on the slopes of the volcano, but when the cheerful and elegant party arrived, they discovered that the hermit who lived there was dying. The Princesse of Monaco, who was very religious, wanted to stay and assist him during his final moments. "Ah!" she said to her companions, "will any of *us* have so tranquil an end, and such company, when our time comes? Surely this man has a lovely soul: what could have driven him to withdraw into solitude with only his soul and his pain! He has abandoned society, and at his last hour, a fine society has come to surround him." Shortly after, Tischbein read in the newspaper that "the Princesse de Monaco had been forced to lay her throat upon the guillotine only the day before that *enragé* [Robespierre] was executed; she cut her lovely hair, begging that they send it to her husband in Germany.... Unfortunate woman, what an end was yours, and what men surrounded you!"[400]

For her part, Aimée had too much desire to live to think of death. An Englishman—as handsome as an antique Hercules—who had participated in the journey to Vesuvius had come to supplant the Duc de Biron in her heart. The son of the "celebrated author of *Hermes* and other works on language and the arts,"[401] Lord James Harris Malmesbury was forty-six years old and a brilliant diplomat. After an ambassadorship in Berlin—where he had been friends with Biron[402]—Malmesbury had represented England at St. Petersburg and, in 1792, found himself in The Hague. While visiting Naples, he had fallen for the charms of the Duchesse de Fleury, who, upon her return to Paris, was pregnant with his child. "As is only right, he loves her passionately, and speaks of her with enthusiasm. She remains in Paris, and he offers her his house in London to come and give birth in, for she is three months pregnant,"[403] the Marquise de Coigny wrote to Biron from London, where Lord Malmesbury had confided in her regarding her cousin. We do not know if and when Nigretta gave birth and, if so, what happened to the child, but we do know, according to Walpole's account, that on August 10, at the time of the sacking of the Tuileries, she was in Paris and living not far from the prison of the Abbaye, for on September 2, she had heard the cries of the priests being massacred.[404] Even so, she succeeded in exchanging a gold watch for a passport, and took refuge in England. In London, where Horace Walpole decreed that she was the "prettiest Frenchwoman" he had ever met[405] and where high society opened its arms to her, she declined to resume her relationship with Lord Malmesbury, but instead lost her head for a compatriot with a scandalous reputation. Aimée must have had a weakness for handsome men, for the Comte Casimir Mouret de Montrond was beauty personified—to the point that this trait was mentioned as a distinguishing feature in his passport[406]—with the exception of a single unattractive detail: the little finger of his right hand, which he kept perpetually gloved, was detached from the palm of the hand to his wrist. This did not prevent him from being a redoubtable swordsman—so good, in fact, that ever since he had killed the Comte de Champagne, who had accused him of cheating, in a duel, no one had dared to challenge his suspiciously easy successes at cards. "He lives on that death," mocked Talleyrand, who referred to him as "the Christ Child of Hell."[407] When Nigretta fell for him in the autumn of 1792, Montrond was no longer the "*âme damnée*"[408] described by the former Bishop of Autun—who had indeed made him "his messmate, counselor, and confidant," and assigned him the "most confidential and convoluted of missions,"[409] which ranged from fraudulent stock-market speculation to political double-dealing to outright espionage—but rather the best friend of the Duc de Fleury. He had been forced to take refuge in London after having campaigned for the Constitutional Party with Théodore de Lameth (whose aide-de-camp he had been), Lafayette, Narbonne, and other members of the liberal *jeunesse dorée*, and he had also entered the fray on the side of the monarchy in *Les Actes des Apôtres*, the newspaper that, up until August 10, had pitted itself against the revolutionary press.[410] When the convention's decree of October 22, which provided for the perpetual banishment of the émigrés and the confiscation of their goods, drove Nigretta like so many other exiles to return to France, Montrond followed her, and the lovers ensconced themselves at Mareuil-en-Brie, a château that she owned in Champagne and which was famous for its splendid gardens. Their presence there did not go unnoticed, and during the winter of 1793 they were both arrested and interrogated, but nevertheless managed to slip through. Aimée got divorced, once again took her maiden name to show that she had nothing to do with a husband who had fought in the counterrevolutionary army, and deployed all of her feminine charms to convince Biron to assist her. She asked him to testify that she had spent with him in Strasbourg those weeks she had in reality passed in England, and to allow her to take shelter, if she felt it was necessary, in the *petite maison* in Montrouge that had once hosted their amours.[411] In the numerous letters that she wrote him, she affirmed with a lovely impudence that her sentiments toward him were unchanged ("I am still your Nigretta. I still love you—and, with or without the moon, you remain as dear to me as you were at Montrouge"[412]), inviting him to love her "without sourness" and "without regrets."[413] Biron, however, was wholly preoccupied with other affairs, and had no desire to play with that "daughter of the Sun," especially given the fact that as a general of the Republic he could not run the risk of giving false testimony or concealing suspects at his home. He preferred to let her believe that he had not appreciated her sentimental frivolity and did not reply to her requests.

Aimée and Montrond succeeded in eluding danger until February 1794. Then, arrested once more in Melun despite their attempts to cover their tracks, they were transferred to Paris and held at Saint-Lazare. Four days later—on March 19—the prison register records the arrival of "André Chénier, aged thirty-one, native of Constantinople, citizen ... by virtue of an order of the Revolutionary Committee of the community of Passy-les-Paris, arrested in the interest of general security":[414] the communards of Passy, who had arrested him on simple suspicion, were unaware that they had a wanted man on their hands. Unlike his brother Marie-Joseph, who had joined the ranks of the Jacobins, André had been a Feuillant, a believer in a Revolution that, under the banner of reason and legality, would ultimately bring about a constitutional monarchy. The relentless press campaign he had led in the name of these principles in the pages of the *Moniteur* and the *Journal de Paris*[415] made him an open enemy of La Montagne. After August 10, reduced to silence, the poet had hidden himself at Versailles until the moment when, while visiting the home of friends at Passy, he was scooped up in a chance raid. His father, deprived of news, discovered while touring the prisons that his son was being held at Saint-Lazare and demanded that Marie-Joseph, closely tied to the leading group of Jacobins, defend the cause of the brother with whom he had fallen out. The latter tried in vain to convince him that any intervention would have the effect of attracting the attention of the Revolutionary Tribunal, which was still unaware of his brother's presence at Saint-Lazare. The wisest strategy was silence and patience. Did Marie-Joseph foresee that the Terror's excesses would lead to the fall of Robespierre? Was he attempting to buy time? Or had he cravenly abandoned his brother to his fate, as his enemies claimed? In any case, his father did not heed his advice, and appealed to Barère—"the idiot, Barère,"[416] as vilified in the *Iambes*—who assured him that his son "would leave" the prison within four days but omitted to mention that this would be for the purpose of execution. It is likely that that the commission instituted to look into the "prison conspiracy" discovered the presence of André Chénier among the large number of inmates waiting to learn their indictments, and alerted the Revolutionary Tribunal.[417] Transferred to the Conciergerie on July 24— 6 Thermidor—the poet was tried and condemned to death as an enemy of the people. He went to the guillotine with Roucher on July 25—7 Thermidor—forty-eight hours before the fall of Robespierre. During the four months that he spent at Saint-Lazare, this poet of innocence, beauty, and harmony dedicated himself to vengeance, and sacrificed the gods of antiquity to a more modern pantheon: "venom, spleen, and horror"[418]—in the process violently revitalizing French poetry. But in his *Iambes* he rages not merely against his executioners—Marat, Collot d'Herbois, Robespierre, Danton[419]—those "wretched criminals," "monsters," "villains," "vampires," "ghouls drunk on human blood, craven executioners of women," and "judges and juries who stamp upon innocence"[420]: the gaze he casts upon his fellow unfortunates could not be more pitiless. The crowds of humanity that fill the "long, somber corridors"[421] of Saint-Lazare are cowardly, egotistical, callous, amoral. The behavior of the nobility in prison, which would soon become legendary, is no less irresponsible than it had been under the ancien régime:

> *On vit; on vit infâme. Eh bien? il fallut l'être;*
> *L'infâme après tout mange et dort.*
> *Ici même, en ses parcs, où la mort nous fait paître,*
> *Où la hache nous tire au sort,*
> *Beaux poulets sont écrits; mari, amants sont dupes;*
> *Caquetage, intrigues de sots.*
> *On y chante; on y joue; on y lève les jupes;*
> *On y fait chansons et bon mots;*
> *L'un pousse et fait bondir sur les toits, sur les vitres,*
> *Un ballon tout gonflé de vent,*
> *Comme sont les discours de sept cents plats béli[tres],*
> *Dont Barère est le plus savant.*
> *L'autre court; l'autre saute; et braillent, boivent, rient*
> *Politiques et raisonneurs;*
> *Et sur les gonds de fer soudain les portes cri[ent].*
> *Des juges tigres nos seigneurs*
> *Le pourvoyeur paraît. Quelle sera la proie*

Que la hache appelle aujourd'hui?
Chacun frissonne, écoute; et chacun avec joie
Voit que ce n'est pas encor lui:
*Ce sera toi demain, insensible imbécile.**[422]

Of them all, only Aimée de Coigny found grace in his eyes and returned him, for the length of an ode, to a world of hope and fertile illusions. And yet she had been the quintessence of the frivolity and moral nonchalance of the privileged caste that Chénier detested. It is not improbable that the poet had had the opportunity to make her acquaintance in the past, for the château of the Coignys at Mareuil was not far from that belonging to his friend François de Pange, where he had frequently been a guest, and he certainly knew enough about her to judge her. But he was overwhelmed by her beauty and her refusal to succumb to despair. Even the year before, when she had found herself briefly in prison,[423] Nigretta's comportment had been astonishing. In a letter to Mary Berry, Walpole mentions "a young scatterbrain who does nothing but sing all day long," asking: "and who, think you, may that be?—only our pretty little wicked Duchesse de Fleury!"[424] And Aimée behaved no differently at Saint-Lazare. Abandoning for a moment the "three-tongued whip, the whip of vengeance,"[425] Chénier answered the young captive's song, which he transformed into a symbol of innocent youth and the right to live life in all its fullness, an allegory of poetic inspiration and of faith in the ideal.[426] Justly celebrated, the verses that he dedicated to her (given as follows in a nineteenth-century translation by Katharine Hillard) provide ample evidence of the poet that Chénier would have become, if only he had had the time to "open his hive to its full extent."[427] As Leconte de Lisle would write, "When he mounted the scaffold, André alone knew what a great poet was going to his death."[428]

---

*We live, live on, in infamy. But how else could it be?: / The infamous, after all, still eat and drink. / Even here, in the pens, where we fatten ourselves / For the axes that dice for our lives, / Little love notes are written; husbands and lovers are duped; / There are gossip and foolish intrigues. / There is singing; and gambling; the lifting of skirts; / Chansons and witticisms flow; / Someone releases a balloon that rises to rebound against the roof, / Against the windowpanes, swollen with wind / Like the breath of those seven hundred dreary imbeciles / Of whom the idiot Barère remains the wisest. / Another runs; another leaps; and quibblers and politicians / Bellow, booze, and laugh; and then / On their iron hinges the cell doors suddenly cry out; / Our tigerish lords' procurer comes to choose. / Who will be called to meet the ax today? / Each of us shivers, listens; each, with joy / Sees that it isn't yet his turn. / Unfeeling fool, tomorrow it will be you.

The corn in peace fills out its golden ear;
Through the long summer days, the flowers without a fear
Drink in the strength of noon.
And I, a flower like them, as young, as fair, as pure,
Though at the present hour some trouble I endure,
I would not die so soon!

No, let the stoic heart call upon Death as kind!
For me, I weep and hope; before the bitter wind
I bend like some lithe palm.
If there be long, sad days, others are bright and fleet;
Alas! what honeyed draught holds nothing but the sweet?
What sea is ever calm?

And still within my breast nestles illusion bright;
In vain these prison walls shut out the noonday light;
Fair Hope has lent me wings.
So from the fowler's net, again set free to fly,
More swift, more joyous, through the summer sky,
Philomel soars and sings.

Is it my lot to die? In peace I lay me down,
In peace awake again, a peace nor care doth drown,
Nor fell remorse destroy.
My welcome shines from every morning face,
And to these downcast souls my presence in this place
Almost restores their joy.

The voyage of life is but begun for me,
And of the landmarks I must pass, I see
So few behind me stand.
At life's long banquet, now before me set,
My lips have hardly touched the cup as yet
Still brimming in my hand.

I only know the spring; I would see autumn brown;
Like the bright sun, that all the seasons crown,

I would round out my year.
A tender flower, the sunny garden's boast,
I have but seen the fires of morning's host;
Would eve might find me here!

O Death, canst thou not wait? Depart from me, and go
To comfort those sad hearts whom pale despair, and woe,
And shame, perchance have wrung.
For me the woods still offer verdant ways,
The Loves their kisses, and the Muses praise:
"I would not die so young!"

Thus, captive too, and sad, my lyre nonetheless
Woke at the plaint of one who breathed its own distress,
Youth in a prison cell;
And throwing off the yoke that weighed upon me too,
I strove in all the sweet and tender words I knew
Her gentle grief to tell.

Melodious witness of my captive days,
These rhymes shall make some lover of my lays
Seek the maid I have sung.
Grace sits upon her brow, and all shall share,
Who see her charms, her grief and her despair:
They too "must die so young"![429]

Aimée, to whom the poet passed the ode he had dedicated to her, could
not have cared much for it if, as seems likely, she offered the manuscript to
one of the *moutons* of Saint-Lazare, the archaeologist Millin de Grandmaison.[430] But in prison, bad companions could prove quite useful. Montrond
succeeded in corrupting Jaubert, a mediocre Belgian actor who was charged
with drawing up the lists of prisoners to be called before the tribunal.[431] For
a hundred louis, he had his own name and that of his mistress erased, and,
indeed, they were forgotten—though they did not leave the prison until October 8, 1794, two and a half months after the end of the Terror. In the memoirs
that she penned at the beginning of the Restoration, Aimée mentions neither

her six months of detention nor Chénier, and limits her comments on the death of Robespierre to a simple "Ouf!"[432]

Joseph-Alexandre de Ségur also owed his salvation to a failed actor, but without having to grease his palm. Transferred to Port-Libre—the former monastery of Port-Royal, which had the reputation of being the most aristocratic prison in Paris—the Vicomte passed the ferocious final months of the Terror within its walls. The law of June 10, 1794, had legalized mass executions, and every day he saw friends and acquaintances depart for the guillotine, without knowing if his own turn would ever come. He certainly could not have imagined that he had a guardian angel among the employees of the Committee of Public Safety. Indeed, it was there, in the Bureau of Prisons, to be precise, that Charles La Bussière began work as a copyist at the beginning of the spring—a figure worthy of a picaresque novel. The youngest son of an impoverished nobleman, he had abandoned the regiment in which he served and, drawn by the world of the theater, had taken to the stage. He specialized in playing simpletons, and dedicated himself to doing just that in the little Théâtre Mareux in the rue Saint-Antoine. But in fact it was at public assemblies that he showed his true talent, giving free rein to his taste for provocation by brazenly playing with revolutionary rhetoric. He amused himself playing the role of the extremist, reaping applause for "a parody of impassioned discourse that ended in farce, and running the risk of being knocked out on the spot."[433] To prevent him from coming to a bad end, his friends managed to find him a job that in itself constituted an unimpeachable sign of patriotism, and soon enough La Bussière found himself at the very heart of the machinery of the Terror. His duty consisted of numbering and entering into the record the documents that the Committee of Public Safety collected on all of the suspects awaiting judgment, so as to communicate them as needed to the Revolutionary Tribunal. He quickly saw that the procedure was wholly chaotic and haphazard: the documents were transmitted without any acknowledgment of receipt, the names of the accused were misspelled, and the accusations were frequently groundless. At the beginning of May, La Bussière appropriated the dossiers concerning those whose names he recognized, and then, realizing that the act had gone unnoticed, discarded all caution and put into play the most audacious and brilliant farce of his life. By day he hid the dossiers that he had chosen in a drawer, then, imitating the zeal of his superiors who worked until dawn, returned to his desk in the evening and plunged the sheets of paper into a bucket of water, so as to ball them up and stick them in his pockets. Early in the morning, he went to the public baths, where he repeated the process, obtaining even smaller balls, which he then tossed into the Seine. Thanks to the complicity of his colleagues, who closed their eyes to his little game, La Bussière saved hundreds of lives, privileging those members of high society whose paths he had crossed in the theaters and the actors he had most admired on the stage. Among them were the Vicomte de Ségur and his father. He knew Ségur well, having frequently encountered him at the Comédie, and had even acted alongside him in the private theater belonging to Mlle Guimard[434]; he was also aware that a great friendship bound the Vicomte to Mlle Contat. He risked it all when he discovered the dossiers of the former members of the Comédie-Française—Dazincourt, Fleury, Raucourt, Mlle Contat and her sister Émilie—guilty of having for the umpteenth time given evidence of their antirevolutionary sentiments by staging a play, *Paméla* by François de Neuf-château, which dared to preach moderation. It was Collot d'Herbois who called for their heads, starting with that of Mlle Contat. Having attempted a career as an actor, he had never forgiven the *sociétaires* for rejecting his candidacy. The file, on which a *G*—for guillotine—was marked in red ink and which was accompanied by a note from Collot d'Herbois to Fouquier-Tinville in which he demanded that they be judged, soon ended up in the Seine. Ten days later, noting that the dossier had not arrived, Fouquier-Tinville wrote a threatening letter to the Committee of Public Safety in which he denounced the shameful inertia of the office in charge of detainees, composed "of *royalists* and *counterrevolutionaries* who hinder the onward march of business."[435] His letter arrived at the Tuileries on 6 Thermidor. La Bussière continued to feign innocence, but soon enough panic was general. Assuredly, without the events of 9 Thermidor, nothing could have saved the actors and their fervent admirer from the guillotine.

We do not know when La Bussière stumbled upon the dossiers concerning Ségur and the old Maréchal, but he certainly did not hesitate to make them vanish as well. Not only was Joseph-Alexandre's life preserved thanks to him but he was able to leave prison at the same time as Mme d'Avaux and his father, immediately after Thermidor. It was only then that he understood that he owed his salvation to his passion for the theater. Free, the Comte felt the need to bear witness for those numerous companions who, less fortunate than he, had not escaped the guillotine. The same year he published a poem of 422 lines, *My Prison*,[436] which he had begun behind bars, and in which he paid homage to the dignity and moral strength of the French nobility as they faced the roughest and most unexpected of ordeals. In addition to the memory of the great Malesherbes mounting the scaffold with his daughter, son-in-law, and grandchildren, Ségur evoked in the notes to his text numerous other beautiful names of the French aristocracy. Female names, mostly—Citizens Stainville de Monaco, Noailles, Périgord, d'Ossun, Luc, Bérenger, Chimay, Ayen, Gramont—all representatives of that "beloved sex" whose "sweet allure" the Vicomte had celebrated and that now became the object of general admiration for its "brilliant courage."[437] The Vicomte did not fail to recall the two poets who had been his companions during his detention at Saint-Lazare: "*Quoi! Chénier, quoi! Roucher, vous périssez ensemble! . . . / Mais l'immortalité tous les deux vous ressemble; / Comment espériez-vous éviter votre sort! / Les talents, les vertus sont des arrêts de mort.*"*[438] Had Ségur had the opportunity to meet André Chénier at Saint-Lazare? Even if Chénier had only published a handful of poems, the Vicomte knew his brother, Marie-Joseph, quite well, and had certainly spoken to him. What is striking, if we limit ourselves to reading the *Iambes* and *My Prison* as simple historical documents, is the difference between the testimonies of the two writers on the same experience. If, in order to stigmatize the Jacobin dictatorship, the skillful worldly versifier frequently resorted to a repertoire of images similar to that of the great poet—"brigands," "tyrants," "tigers," "infamous informers," "ministers of death," "messenger of death," "the ax" that "cut down so many innocent beings"—far from heaping contempt, like Chénier, on a society that had shed all morality, the Vicomte celebrated the heroism of his caste. Going forward, its ordeal would confer upon the French nobility glory and redemption.

Following 9 Thermidor, the guillotine's rhythm slowed, and Paris was able to breathe again. Twenty days after the fall of Robespierre, the *sociétaires* retook possession of their theater—rebaptized the Théâtre de l'Égalité—with Marivaux's play *Les Fausses Confidences*: Mlle Contat's appearance onstage

---

*What! What, Chénier! Roucher, you perish together! . . . / Yet immortality touches both of you; / How could you have hoped to escape your fate! / Your talents and virtues were your death warrants.

was greeted with a standing ovation.[439] It is hard to imagine that the Vicomte de Ségur was not on hand as well to applaud her. The sophisticated verbal acrobatics of the French theater's most aristocratic author proclaimed the end of a long collective nightmare—but everyone knew there was no returning to the past, and that, as far as the future was concerned, they could take nothing for granted.

Turning the Page

WE ARE IGNORANT OF WHAT HAPPENED to Mlle Laurent following the death of Biron, whereas we know that while the Duchesse de Lauzun was incarcerated for a second time in October 1783 following the arrest of her husband, she ultimately managed to escape the guillotine. Having fallen into poverty, she rented a room on the fifth floor of a building in the rue de Bourbon, across from the splendid Hôtel de Boufflers, where she had lived in 1787 after the death of her grandmother, the Duchesse de Luxembourg. Accompanied by her two faithful servants who generously looked after her livelihood, she could sit and contemplate the gardens of her former home from her window. Mme de Genlis, who had come to visit her, wrote in her memoirs[1] that the Duchesse died in 1827, forgotten by all, at the age of seventy-six.

Left a widow in 1785, the Duchesse de Choiseul had used her inheritance to pay her husband's debts, which still amounted to nearly 3 million livres, and then withdrew to a convent. In 1793, she was jailed at Oiseaux, where she discovered her sister-in-law, the Duchesse de Gramont, who on April 17, 1794, after refusing to answer the judges of the Revolutionary Tribunal, went courageously to the guillotine. Mme de Choiseul emerged unscathed from prison after Thermidor, and died in Paris on December 3, 1801.

The Marquise de Coigny returned to France after Thermidor and became a key figure of society life under the Consulate. An enthusiastic admirer of Napoleon, she arranged for her daughter Fanny to marry General Sébastiani and with a heavy heart bore witness to the return of those Bourbons whom she had never ceased to hate. But she remained "thanks to her high intelligence and admirable wit, the queen of *la grande société* of Paris."[2] She died in Paris on September 13, 1832, at the age of seventy-three.

Liberated after Thermidor, Aimée de Coigny married Casimir de Montrond in 1795, and divorced him in 1802, after having squandered with him what remained of his inheritance. Prudence had never been her strong suit, but she swept aside whatever shreds of it she had left by tying herself to an ambitious lawyer, Maillia-Garat (whose uncle had read out the death sentence of

Louis XVI), who turned out to be a failure as well as a brute, and with whom she suffered through years of poverty. She got back on her feet by establishing a *relation sentimentale* with the Marquis Bruno de Boisgelin, and served as an intermediary between he and Talleyrand as they prepared for the fall of Napoleon and the return of the Bourbons. She died in Paris, nearly fifty, on January 17, 1820, at the home of her cousin, the Marquise de Coigny. Two years before her death, she published, in an edition of only twenty-five copies, *Alvare*, a novel about the pathology of amorous passion—one that deserves to be republished—and entrusted to Talleyrand certain passages of her memoirs, which would finally appear in 1902.

With the end of the Terror, Joseph-Alexandre de Ségur recovered all of his good humor and adapted himself handily to the new era. Both he and his brother were now making a living from their literary activities, and it was under the Directory that the Vicomte would have his greatest success in the theater. On March 17, 1795, he made his return to the Théâtre Feydeau with *Le Bon Fermier* (The Good Farmer), which, just as in *Élize dans les bois* (Élize in the Forest) in 1797, showcased the fidelity of those who had not given way to Jacobin propaganda and continued to respect their former lords. He found the form most suited to his talents in vaudeville, a theatrical genre that enjoyed tremendous favor at the time. Not only was the Vicomte able to turn out these light comedies, in which songs were prominently featured, at a steady clip, but he was also one of the shareholders of the Théâtre du Vaudeville, founded in 1792 by Barré, and regularly participated in banquets and poetic competitions staged by the affiliated Société des diners du Vaudeville. He also resumed his activities as a journalist for the *Déjueuner*, a four-page literary journal with a daily circulation whose first issue appeared on January 1, 1797, and that folded some four years later. Ubiquitous wherever high society circulated in the wake of the Terror, unflappable in the face of the vulgarity and political pasts of so many of that new society's parvenus, and careful never to take sides, he continued to curl and powder his hair, to dress in the bygone style, and to be as gay, gallant, and witty as he had been before the Revolution. Irony sufficed for him to hold the insolent and annoying at a distance.

The coup d'etat of September 4, 1797, which drowned an enormous royalist conspiracy in blood, once again left the Ségur brothers exposed—but the beautiful Mme Tallien, an intimate friend of Mme d'Avaux, managed to have their names removed from the lists of deportees. At the fall of the Directory, the Vicomte followed his brother's example and rallied to Bonaparte. Nevertheless, when the First Consul offered him the command of a regiment, he replied that he would never again don the uniform he had worn before the Revolution, and that if *la patrie* needed him, he would serve as a civilian.[3]

He ushered in the new century by translating into verse the text of *The Creation*, the celebrated oratorio completed by Haydn two years earlier, at the request of his friend Steibelt, who had been freshly appointed as the director of the Opéra and was well acquainted with the Vicomte's musical sensibility and experience in the theater. Then, while a new nation was taking shape in Napoleon's iron grip, Ségur, who had always lived in the present, putting his pen at the service of current affairs, felt the need to bear witness to the *mœurs* of a vanished France. He reconstructed the role played by women over the course of the centuries, particularly in France, in *Women, Their Condition, and Their Influence in the Social Orders of Various Peoples, Ancient and Modern*, and developed a series of extremely penetrating reflections on the key concepts of classical worldly aesthetics in "L'homme d'esprit et l'homme amiable," *On Genres, On the Style of Women, On Intellect and Taste, On Storytellers and the Art of Storytelling*, and *On Naturalness in Society and on Stage*. In 1805, he undertook the publication of Besenval's memoirs, before dedicating himself to the composition of his own testament. He died on July 27, 1805, in the Pyrenees, where he had gone to attempt a cure for his tuberculosis, lovingly attended by Mme d'Avaux. He was forty-nine years old.

Julie Careau had preceded him to the grave on May 9, and Félix de Ségur, the illegitimate child of their union, died on February 7, both carried away by the same illness. Ever since Julie had realized her dream of love by marrying Talma, her luck had abandoned her. After having squandered his wife's inheritance, the now famous actor left her, and she was forced to rent her beautiful home on the rue Chantereine to her friend Josephine de Beauharnais, who had become Bonaparte's mistress. Alone now, she saw her five children die one after another, and the passing of Félix, the last of them, delivered the coup de grace. Benjamin Constant, who had been her friend and attended her on her deathbed, rendered posthumous homage to her in his *Lettre sur Julie*.

After the Terror was over, Comte Louis-Philippe de Ségur continued to live in the little village of Châtenay with his wife, their three children, and his father. Having fallen into indigence, he and his family managed to survive thanks to the meager revenue brought in by his literary activities. Far less

fortunate than his brother as an author of plays and songs, he gained a reputation as a historian with two important books on events of which he had a
direct knowledge: *The History of the Principal Events of the Reign of Frederick
William II, King of Prussia, and a Political Tableau of Europe between 1786 and
1796*, which has been called "one of the first great works on the Revolution,"[4]
and *Policies of All the Cabinets of Europe, During the Reigns of Louis XV and
Louis XVI*, in which he took advantage of primary sources such as the correspondence of the Comte de Broglie. Published in 1800 and 1801 respectively,
these works opened to him the doors of a renascent Académie Française.
Napoleon's rise to power changed his life radically, giving fresh impetus to his
ambitions. The recommendations of Talleyrand and Josephine—a good friend
of his brother—had predisposed the First Consul in his favor, as had the whim
of Ségur's eldest son, Philippe-Paul, who, on 18 Brumaire, meeting by chance
a regiment of dragoons marching toward Saint-Cloud, had felt the "warrior
blood"[5] of his ancestors boiling in his veins and enlisted in the army on the
spot, without consulting his family. Philippe-Paul had also been the first to
respond to "Bonaparte's invitation that opened the ranks of the army to young
aristocrats,"[6] just as his father had been among the first representatives of the
former court nobility to put himself at the service of this new arbiter of his
country's destiny. After having served as deputy for the Seine in the Legislative
Corps[7] and as councillor of state under the Consulate,[8] Ségur was charged by
Napoleon with organizing his coronation ceremony. Appointed to the position
of grand master of ceremonies, given the title of Comte de l'Empire, and
endowed with a significant appanage, Louis-Philippe lived for a decade in
close contact with Napoleon, continuously enjoying his favor. This did not
prevent him, after the Battle of Leipzig, from voting for the Emperor's deposition, alongside almost the whole of the senate. "It's all over," he wrote to
his son. "All resistance must now cease. There nothing to do but resign ourselves, to concur, to conform to the general example."[9] Still, upon the advent
of Louis XVIII, he presented himself before the King, convinced that he would
be able to retain his position as grand master of ceremonies. The sovereign
received him coldly, reminding him that the post had already been filled by
someone else and that the appointment was for life.[10] On the other hand, he
did name him a Peer of France. Nevertheless, Ségur greeted the return of
Napoleon with enthusiasm. All of his duties were restored to him, and this
time he was loyal to the bitter end. When the Emperor left for Saint Helena,
he offered to follow him, and, while declining this proposition, Napoleon was

moved. Stripped of his title as a peer, once again reduced to living by his pen, Ségur transformed himself into an indefatigable generalist. To give some sense of the abundance of his production, it is enough to mention the fifteen volumes of his *Abbreviated Universal History, Ancient and Modern, for the Usage of the Young*, the seven volumes of his *History of France*, and the three of his *Memoirs, or Souvenirs and Anecdotes*, his most important work. In 1819, thanks to a liberal turn in the policies of Louis XVIII, Ségur once again joined the other senators seated in the Empire's upper chamber. After vainly preaching moderation during the six disastrous years of the reign of Charles X, he had the pleasure of seeing Louis-Philippe ascend to the throne as King of France. He died eighteen days later, on August 27, 1830, at the age of seventy-seven.

After Thermidor, Louis de Narbonne lived in Germany for ten years, studying and translating Schiller, and in 1798, following the Treaty of Campo Formio, was finally able to visit his mother in Trieste. Mme Victoire was dead, but the Comte was able to be with Mme Adélaïde during her final moments. While remaining a royalist at heart, he had convinced himself that the victor of the Battle of Marengo was the only man capable of pacifying France and returning him to his former prestige—which was reason enough to return to his homeland. Talleyrand and Mathieu de Montmorency signed a petition to have his name removed from the list of émigrés, and Fouché, minister of the police, who had been his professor at the Collège de Juilly, intervened in his favor. At the end of 1800, the Comte was able to return to France, where his right to a general's pension were recognized, and where he accepted the hospitality of Mme de Laval in rue Roquépine, not far from the Faubourg Saint-Honoré. In spite of her now limited means, the Vicomtesse hosted one of the most sought-after and brilliant salons in the capital, frequented by the former liberal aristocracy—the Montmorencys, Choiseul-Gouffier, Jaucourt, the Comte de La Marck, the Marquise de Coigny and her cousin Aimée de Coigny—as well as by prominent foreigners and by Talleyrand, who vied with Narbonne for center stage. In 1806, the Comte married off his eldest daughter, Amable-Rion-Françoise-Louise, to Braamcamp de Sobral, a Portuguese nobleman destined for a brilliant political career in his own country; and two years later, his second daughter married the Comte de Rambuteau, who displayed a son's devotion to his father-in-law.[11] Narbonne, on the other hand, seems to have ignored completely the children born during his relationship with Mme de Staël, and confined himself to showing great courtesy to Auguste whenever they happened to encounter each other. It is impossible to say if the young man actually knew who his father was.[12] With Fouché's assistance, Louis succeeded in having his mother, the Comtesse de Narbonne, removed from the list of émigrés, but the elderly Duchesse, still loyal to the Bourbons, could not bring herself to return to France until 1810.

Nevertheless, his attempts to obtain a position in the army or as a diplomat were fruitless. The requests that he made between 1800 and 1803, like the letter he addressed directly to the First Consul, remained unanswered. Talleyrand, who, thanks to Mme de Staël, had landed the position of minister of foreign affairs, did nothing to help him, and it was not until after his dismissal in May 1809 that Napoleon called Narbonne back into service at the rank of general and with orders to join him in Vienna, where, at the age of fifty-four, he resumed his life in the military with all the energy of a young man—so much so that even the Emperor was astonished at the old minister's attitude: "I think he [Talleyrand] was truly afraid of you,"[13] he subtly observed to Narbonne. Appointed governor of Rába, and later of Trieste, and minister plenipotentiary at Munich—where he participated in negotiations that would result in Napoleon's marriage to Marie-Louise—Narbonne became the Emperor's aide-de-camp and confidant in 1811. He was by his side throughout the Russian campaign, and during the tragic retreat, his courage and cheerful stoicism earned him general admiration. In 1813, he was sent as ambassador to Vienna, then as plenipotentiary to Prague, but his diplomatic skill could not prevent Austria from declaring war on France. The Emperor expressed his dissatisfaction by naming him governor of Torgau, a French bastion in Saxony. Despite the disastrous state of his troops, Narbonne never stopped fighting, but on November 17, 1813, at the age of fifty-eight, worn down by typhus, he died following a fall from a horse.

The Vicomtesse de Laval survived Narbonne along with her son, Mathieu, and continued to regularly receive a small and carefully selected group of guests, becoming a living symbol of the *civilisation mondaine* of the ancien régime. Her relationship with Talleyrand lasted to the very end, and she died in Paris on July 4, 1838, several weeks after him.

Narbonne's best and most faithful friend, General d'Arblay, whom we last encountered at Juniper Hall after his marriage to Fanny Burney—performed on July 31, 1793, at Mickleham—spent nine years in England. He returned to France in 1802 with his wife and their son, but refusing to fight against the country that had been so hospitable to him, he did not resume active service, and was employed as vice director of the Ministry of the Interior, returning to his position in the army with the Restoration. He died in England on May 7, 1818.

With the arrival in Rheinsberg of a new favorite, the Marquis de La Roche-Aymon, the Chevalier de Boufflers and Mme de Sabran ceased to enjoy the friendship of Prince Henry and, wishing neither to seem ungrateful nor to be treated as nuisances, they decided to leave the château. The Chevalier seized the opportunity offered by Frederick William to émigrés to colonize those territories acquired by Prussia in the partition of Poland, and was entrusted with a vast property at Wymysłow in Eastern Silesia. He left for his new home in May 1797, and Mme de Sabran joined him in Wrocław the following month, where they were finally married after a wait of eighteen years. Since the Revolution had reduced both of them to poverty, there was no longer any reason to defer the wedding. But in Poland, too, Boufflers had little luck. He was by no means a man of business, and his optimism, his love of nature, and his enlightened interest in agriculture were not enough to assure his prosperity. He consoled himself by continuing to write, and, on August 9, 1798, delivered his reception speech to the Academy of Berlin, "Discourse on Literature." Yet after three years, he understood that he would rather die of hunger in France than live in Prussia.[14] Delphine de Custine managed to have the names of her mother and the Chevalier removed from the list of émigrés thanks to the intervention of Josephine, with whom she had been close friends during their incarceration at the Carmes prison during the Terror. And on May 15, 1800, after eight years of exile, Boufflers paid his respects in person to the First Consul, who had declared: "Let him come back—he will write *chansons* for us."[15]

The Chevalier followed this program precisely. He regained his academician's seat as a member of the second class of the Institut de France (created in 1795 to bring together the various académies of the ancien régime), where he delivered the eulogy for, among others, his uncle, the Maréchal de Beauvau, who had meant so much to him, and that of the Abbé Barthélemy, whom he had frequented during happier times at Chanteloup. Recalling his studies at the seminary, he published a treatise on free will, wrote numerous *nouvelles*—

La Mode, L'Heureux Accident, Le Dervish, Tamara—and translated Seneca, Ovid, and Dante. But he was conscious of fighting a rear-guard battle when it came to taste and ideas: "The craft of writing, like that of living, would be much more enjoyable if only one found oneself with fewer *enemy* writers than friendly readers," he confided to an old friend of his mother.[16]

In 1803 the Boufflers took up residence at a small country estate in Saint-Léger, not far from Saint-Germain-en-Laye, where, like Philemon and Baucis, they lived in tender symbiosis. Though leading a retired life, the Chevalier had learned how to be a courtier and had secured for himself the goodwill of Élisa Bonaparte. This proved to be highly useful when at dawn on April 13, 1813, his wife's beloved son was arrested and jailed at Vincennes. Elzéar de Sabran had freed himself from his mother's influence only to fall under that of Mme de Staël, to whom he had dedicated a veritable cult. Their correspondence had been intercepted by the police, and Elzéar was only released after Boufflers obtained Élisa's intervention.

Appointed deputy administrator of the Bibliothèque Mazarine, Boufflers died seven months later, on January 18, 1815, at the age of seventy-seven. He was buried at Père Lachaise, between Delille and Saint-Lambert. He had wished to have written on his tomb: "My friends, think that I merely sleep." After all, etymologically, wasn't the word "cemetery" derived from the Greek *koimáo*, "I sleep"?[17] His old friend Ségur delivered his eulogy at the Institut. Like the Ségur brothers, like Narbonne, like his friend Ligne, the Chevalier had been faithful to himself—joyful, gallant, and courtly: wasn't that the surest method of renewing oneself over and over, of distinguishing oneself from all the rest?[18]

His wife, destined to survive him by a dozen years, would do no less. "In spite of her sufferings and her age," recalled Mme Vigée Le Brun, who had painted her portrait in her youth, "Madame de Boufflers—forever good, forever decent—preserved the charm that had pleased and attracted all the world."[19] She could not withstand the sadness brought by the death of her daughter, Delphine de Custine—Chateaubriand's forsaken lover[20]—and died seven months after her, on February 27, 1827.

After Mme de Polignac died in December 1793, the Comte de Vaudreuil remained in Vienna for another two years but declined to follow the Polignacs to Ukraine, where Paul I had granted them property. Instead he decided to settle in England and marry a cousin, the daughter of Admiral Louis-Philippe de Rigaud, Marquis de Vaudreuil, who had emigrated across the English Channel with his family. Even before meeting her, the inconsolable *amant* of Mme de Polignac had fallen in love with his fiancée: "How this Joséphine has transformed me, brought me back to life!" he wrote to his future mother-in-law. "Up until now I have been languishing, dying.... Now I have an object with which to occupy myself day and night—and what an object!" The thirty years that separated them did not bother him in the least, for his soul had remained "very tender and very young."[21] Celebrated in London on September 8, 1795, the marriage made of the Comte a faithful husband and affectionate father. He established himself at Twickenham, accustomed himself to living on very little money, and tolerated the rumors of his young wife's presumed infidelities with a smile. He frequently visited Edinburgh, where Louis XVIII and the Comte d'Artois resided, but he no longer concerned himself with politics and had ceased to call down "divine vengeance" on the "infernal race of atheists and regicides."[22] On the contrary, he preached prudence and moderation, and advised Louis XVIII to encourage the émigré royalists and bishops to return to France in order to preserve the flame of monarchist sentiment. Louis-Philippe d'Orléans, his neighbor in Twickenham, became his closest friend, and he was reported by the French police to be the "most amiable [of the royalists], and the least attached to old ideas."[23] He rediscovered his former haughtiness when, on his return to France in the wake of Louis XVIII, he was showered with honors, appointed lieutenant general, peer of France, member of the Institut, and governor of the Louvre—a position that allowed him to inhabit an official apartment in the former royal palace, now transformed into a museum, and to enjoy once again the daily company of those works of art he had collected in his youth. He became the Enchanter once more—hosting receptions and concerts in the grand style, sparing no expense. He died on April 17, 1817, less than three years after his return to France, leaving behind nothing but debts.[24] He was seventy-seven years old. His eulogy at the Institut was delivered by the same Duc de La Rochefoucauld-Liancourt who had announced the fall of the Bastille to Louis XVI. Vaudreuil died with the sole regret of having failed to obtain from Louis XVIII the title of Duc for his eldest son. Then again, when he ascended the throne under the name of Charles X, d'Artois chose the young Duc de Polignac as prime minister. Luckily for him, Vaudreuil was no longer there to see his best friend, and the son that he had had with the lovely Gabrielle-Yolande, celebrate the *de profundis* of the Bourbons of France.

As for Chamfort, after having broken off all contact with Vaudreuil, he became the secretary of the Club of Jacobins, drafted speeches for Mirabeau and Talleyrand, contributed to the publication of numerous newspapers, and compiled the collection *Revolutionary Tableaux*. In 1792, he was appointed the director of the Bibliothèque Nationale by the minister of the interior, the Girondin Jean-Marie Roland de La Platière. Denounced to the Committee of General Security during the Terror and placed under surveillance by the police, he attempted suicide and died from his wounds on April 13, 1794, the same year that his friend Ginguené brought his *Maxims, Characters, and Anecdotes* to press.

Since the opening of the Estates General, the Prince de Ligne, unlike many of his French friends, had stood in resolute opposition to the Revolution, proclaiming his utter contempt for "the three disordered orders, and for that constitution upon which so many ill-constituted minds are pleased to pronounce,"[25] aligning himself with the Army of the Princes, and lavishing aid on the émigrés. In 1794, chased from his beloved château of Beloeil by the Revolutionary army as well as from his properties in the Austrian Netherlands, he left with his family for Vienna, where, in a small salon with humble straw chairs, he continued to carry the torch of the French spirit. Even the death of his son Charles, whom he loved, on the eve of the Battle of Valmy, could not shake his love for France. Reduced to poverty, or close to it, the Prince survived difficult years in the course of which he devoted himself wholly to writing. But beginning in 1808, fate began to smile on him once more: he was appointed field marshal by Emperor Francis II, recovered Beloeil and his inheritance, and had the pleasure of seeing himself acclaimed as an author. Published in Paris in 1809 with a preface by Mme de Staël, his *Letters and Thoughts of the Maréchal Prince de Ligne* received a triumphal welcome and was translated into numerous languages. Ligne died on December 13, 1814, at the age of seventy-nine, during the Congress of Vienna. His solemn funeral procession, thronged with regiments from all the countries he had served, was likewise the funeral for the Europe of the ancien régime—that vanished world of which the Prince himself had been the emblem.

Acknowledgments

THERE ARE MANY PEOPLE TO whom I would like to express my gratitude for having lavished me with help and advice during the preparation of this book, but I must begin with Teresa Cremisi, who is at the origin of the project of *The Last Libertines* and who, along with Alice d'Andigné, generously expedited my research.

As with my other books, I had the privilege of counting on Giuseppe Galasso as a first reader and sounding board for various historiographical questions. I wish I could express just how precious his encouragement has been to me. Immense thanks are also due to Barbara Piqué for her voluminous advice; to Francesco Scaglione who consulted numerous volumes at the Bibliothèque Nationale de France on my behalf; to Pietro Corsi, for whom the biographical dictionaries hold no secrets; and to Gigliola Fagnito and Francesco Bissoli for their suggestions. And, in recognizing my debt to Sue Carrell for her luminous commentaries on Mme de Sabran and the Chevalier de Boufflers, I would like to tell Anka Begley Muhlstein that the autograph of Boufflers that she offered me has been my talisman.

I am moved by the memory of Roland Mortier and Raymond Trousson, masters and dear friends, whom we have now, alas, lost. I am very grateful for my French friends: Gabriel de Broglie whose *Ségur sans cérémonie 1757–1805, ou la Gaieté libertine* was particularly illuminating, as were our conversations; Geneviève Haroche-Bouzinac, always ready to share her knowledge with a rare generosity; Claude Arnaud, who, in blessing my pages on Vaudreuil and Chamfort—subjects upon which he so magisterially preceded me—gave me confidence in my work when I was most in need of it; and Emmanuel de Waresquiel, who knows everything when it comes to the elusive Talleyrand. And a special thank-you to the Marquis Charles-André de Brissac, to the Comtesse François de Monteynard, and to Yves Guéna for their great kindness.

I would also like to express my gratitude to my friends from Poland: Jean Caillot, Jadwiga Czartoryska, Piotr Kłoczowski, Piotr Salwa, Piotr Ugniewski, and Adam Zamoyski, who helped me in grasping the numerous facets of the personality of Izabela Czartoryska, and to Joanna Borysiak of the National Library of Warsaw and Janusz Nowak, chief of the manuscripts department of the Czartoryski Library of Kraków, who gave me access to the Princesse's papers. And I cannot pass over in silence the emotion that seized me when Serena Vitale informed me that in 1919, in the midst of the Revolution, Marina Tsvetaeva had dedicated a theatrical piece to the Duc de Lauzun.

Three of the characters in my book having been great collectors of art, I was lucky enough to benefit from the advice and aid of Joseph Baillio, Sylvain Bellenger, Jean-Pierre Biron, Anna Ottani Cavina, Serena Gavazzi, Christophe Leribault, Christian Michel, and Xavier Salmon. To them I owe my sincere gratitude, as well as to Laure Depretto, who led me on a first exploration into the Parisian archives; Elena Gretchanaïa, who brought me precious information from the Russian archives; William Stingone and Lee Spilberg of the Department of Manuscripts and Archives of the New York Public Library; Melinda Caron; Anne-Sophie Durozoy, curator of the Collection of Antique Manuscripts at the Library of the University of Poitiers; Élisabeth Verry, director of the Archives Départementales of Maine-et-Loire; and Ali Larbi of the Archives Nationales Françaises.

There is no need to remind my husband, Benoît d'Aboville, of how greatly I am indebted to him.

In regard to the Italian edition, I am happy to be able to thank once again Roberto Calasso, my lifelong editor, who welcomed the book into his *Collana dei casi* at Adelphi; Ena Marchi, who fought with determination to give a more narrative form to my libertines; and Pia Cigala Fulgosi, who supervised the apparatus of notes with her customary expertise.

Last, but not least, I should also like to thank Rea Hederman and Edwin Frank who brought my French *Libertins*, who fought for the independence of America, across the Atlantic once again. My fond memory goes to Bob Silvers and Grace Dudley, who followed and encouraged this book while it was still a work in progress.

Notes

PREFACE

1.   Charles-Augustin Sainte-Beuve, "Le Comte de Ségur," in *Portraits littéraires, Oeuvres*, critical edition by Maxime Leroy (Paris: Gallimard, 1960), vol. II, 367.

2.   Comte de Ségur, *Mémoires ou Souvenirs et Anecdotes par M. le Comte de Ségur*, 3 vol. (Paris: Alexis Eymery, 1824–1826), vol. I, 29.

3.   Ibid., 28.

4.   See François Furet, "La philosophie des Lumières et la culture révolutionnaire," in *L'Europe dans son histoire. La vision d'Alphonse Dupront*, under the direction of François Crouzet and François Furet (Paris: P.U.F., 1998), 153–67.

5.   Sébastien-Roch Nicolas de Chamfort, *Produits de la civilisation perfectionnée. Maximes et pensées—Caractères et anecdotes*, preface by Albert Camus, biographical material and notes by Geneviève Renaux, (Paris: Gallimard, 1970).

6.   Letter from the Duc de Lauzun to the Marquis de Voyer, Paris, September 6, 1779, Université de Poitiers, Archives d'Argenson, 77.

7.   Pierre de Cossé-Brissac, *Histoire des ducs de Brissac. Maison de Cossé* (Paris: Fasquelle, 1952), 309.

THE DUC DE LAUZUN

1.   François-René de Chateaubriand, *Mémoires d'outre-tombe*, critical edition by Jean-Claude Berchet, 2 vol. (Paris: Librarie générale française, 2004–2005), vol. I, 170.

2.   Gaston Maugras, *La Fin d'une société. Le Duc de Lauzun et la cour intime de louis XV* (Paris: Plon, 1909), 10–11.

3.   Jean-Pierre-Jacques-Auguste de Labouïsse-Rochefort noted in his *Souvenirs* that in 1805 he had read the manuscript of the *Mémoires* of Lauzun thanks to the "kindness of M. le Marquis de ***," its possessor, and quoted long extracts conforming in all points to the texts as published by Louis Lacour. *Souvenirs et Mélanges littéraires, politiques et biographiques par M. L. de Rochefort*, 2 vol. (Paris: Bossange Frères, 1826), vol. II, 273.

4. See *Bulletin du bibliophile et du bibliothécaire* (Paris: Techener, 1895), 367; and Geneviève Haroche-Bouzinac, "Madame Campan. L'écriture et la publication de ses Mémoires, 1797–1824," in *Vérité de l'Histoire et vérité du moi. Mélanges offerts à Jean Garapon* (Paris: Honoré Champion, 2016).

5. Labouïsse-Rochefort writes of Lauzun's *Mémoires*: "If they are ever published, there will be *scandal in Landerneau!*," in *Souvenirs et Mélanges*, 273. Likewise, in his *Souvenirs du Prince Clary-et-Aldringen. Trois mois à Paris lors du mariage de l'Empereur Napoléon Ier et de l'ArchiDuchesse Marie-Louise* (Paris: Plon, Nourrit et Cie, 1914), 242, published by the Baron de Mitis and the Comte de Pimodan, the author recounts having read Lauzun's *Mémoires* in manuscript, and reports the anxiety felt by Princesse Czartoryska at the thought of her featuring in them. Concerning the suit brought by the descendants of the Princesse against the French publisher of the *Mémoires*, see also the bibliography. One also finds mention of the affair carried on by a friend of the Princesse, Lady Elizabeth Berkeley—who had married William, Sixth Baron of Craven, in 1767, and then in 1791 Christian, Margrave of Brandenburg-Anspach—with the Comte de Guînes, the French ambassador to London. Lauzun had met her in London in 1773. She authored her own memoirs, *Memoirs of the Margravine of Anspach, Written by Herself*, 2 volumes (London: Henry Colburn, 1826), wherein one finds a lovely portrait of the Princesse Czartoryska. Lacour asserts that among the aristocrats disturbed by the prospect of the publication was the Vicomtesse de Laval, the mistress of Narbonne and friend of Talleyrand, with whom Lauzun had had a brief liaison. See *Mémoires du Duc de Lauzun (1747–1783)*, published entirely in accordance with the manuscript, with a study of the life of the author (Paris: Poulet-Malassis and de Broise, 1858, second edition by Louis Lacour), lxii, 101–3, and 106.

6. *Mémoires inédits de Madame la Comtesse de Genlis, sur le dix-huitième siècle et la Révolution française, depuis 1756 jusqu'à nos jours*, 10 vol. (Paris: Ladvocat, 1825), vol. II, 67n1.

7. *Le Moniteur*, March 27, 1818.

8. The Comte Armand-François d'Allonville claims to have heard Lauzun read them at the home of Mme Buffon, the mistress of the Duc d'Orléans, before the Revolution, in *Mémoires secrets de 1770 à 1830 par le Comte d'Allonville*, 6 vol. (Paris: Werdet, 1838–1845), vol. I, 202–3, furthermore quoting a conversation between the author and Marie-Antoinette, which was not included in Lauzun's memoirs.

9. See also Emmanuel de Waresquiel, "Talleyrand en ses Mémoires," preface to *Mémoires et Correspondances du Prince de Talleyrand*, edited and with notes by Emmanuel de Waresquiel (Paris: Laffont, 2007), viii–ix.

10. Cited in Georges d'Heylli, "Lauzun et ses Mémoires," in *Mémoires du Duc de Lauzun, édition complète précédée d'une étude sur Lauzun et ses Mémoires par Georges d'Heylli* (Paris: Édouard Rouveyre, 1880), xl.

11. Ibid., xli.

12. Charles-Augustin Sainte-Beuve, "Le Duc de Lauzun," in *Causeries du lundi* (Paris: Garnier Frères, [s.d.]), vol. IV, 307. See also: "What a lovely thing they are, the memoirs of an intelligent man who has *seen* things! They are, I believe, the only sort of work that will still have readers in 1850"; letter from Stendhal to Adolphe de Mareste, Grenoble, April 22, 1818, in Stendhal, *Correspondance générale*, critical edition by Vittorio Del Litto, 3 vol. (Paris: Honoré Champion, 1999), vol. III, 114–15.

13. *Mémoires du Duc de Lauzun*, 3–4.

14. Stendhal, *De l'amour*, edited by Henry Martineau (Paris: Garnier, 1959), 5.

15. *Mémoires du Prince de Talleyrand, publiés avec une préface et des notes par le Duc de Broglie*, 5 vol. (Paris: Calmann-Lévy, 1891–1892), vol. I, 159.

16. See Rohan Butler, *Choiseul*, vol. I, *Father and Son, 1719–1754* (Oxford: Clarendon Press, 1980), 684. See also *Mémoires du Prince de Talleyrand*, vol. V, 530, which defines Lauzun as the son of Gontaut or "rather, son of M. de Stainville."

17. Ibid., 961ff.

18. *Mémoires du Duc de Lauzun*, 5.

19. Ibid., 7.

20. Jean-Jacques Rousseau, *Confessions*, in *Oeuvres complètes*, under the direction of Bernard Gagnerin and Marcel Raymond (Paris: Gallimard, 1959), vol. I, 535.

21. *Mémoires du Duc de Lauzun*, 4.

22. Amélie de Boufflers was born on May 5, 1751.

23. *Mémoires du Duc de Lauzun*, 44.

24. Ibid., 25.

25. Ibid., 12.

26. "Amazonian fierce, haughty dame": letter from Horace Walpole to Thomas Gray, January 25, 1766, in *Horace Walpole's Correspondence*, with Thomas Gray, Richard West, and Thomas Ashton, critical edition by W. S. Lewis, George L. Lam, and Charles H. Bennett (New Haven, CT: Yale University Press, 1948), two books in 1 vol.; and *Horace Walpole's Correspondence*, vol. 14, 155.

27. Letter from Mme du Deffand to Horace Walpole, February 13, 1774, in *Horace Walpole's Correspondence with Madame du Deffand and Wiart*, critical edition by W. S. Lewis and Warren Hunting Smith, 6 vol. (New Haven, CT, and London: Yale University Press/ Oxford University Press, 1939, 1962), vol. IV, 18. Walpole's correspondence with Mme du Deffand receives a separate numbering from I to VI and makes up volumes III–VIII of *Horace Walpole's Correspondence*, still available in the edition by W. S. Lewis and Warren Hunting Smith in 48 volumes (New Haven, CT, and London, Yale University Press/Oxford University Press, 1937–1983).

28. *Mémoires du Duc de Lauzun*, 39.

29. Ibid., 37.

30. Ibid., 40.

31. Ibid.

32. Ibid.

33. Ibid., 45.

34. Ibid., 45–46.

35. Ibid., 46.

36. *Mémoires secrets de 1770 à 1830 par le Comte d'Allonville*, vol. I, 173.

37. Ibid.

38. According to Talleyrand, Choiseul had not waited for his fiancée to reach puberty before sleeping with her (in advance of their marriage), thus permanently compromising her health (see *Mémoires du Prince de Talleyrand*, vol. V, 531).

39. *Mémoires du Duc de Lauzun*, 52.

40. Ibid., 53.

41. See Gaston Maugras, *Le Duc et la Duchesse de Choiseul. Leur vie intime, leurs amis et leur temps*, 2 vol. (Paris: Plon, Nourrit et Cie, 1902), vol. I, 292.

42. Letter from Mme du Deffand to Walpole, January 23, 1767, in *Horace Walpole's Correspondence with Madame du Deffand and Wiart*, vol. I, 217 (vol. II of the Yale edition of *Horace Walpole's Correspondence*, critical edition by W. S. Lewis).

43. Jean-Nicolas Dufort, *Mémoires sur les règnes de Louis XV et Louis XVI et sur la Révolution*, introduction and notes by Robert de Crèvecoeur, 2 vol. (Paris: Plon, Nourrit et Cie, 1886), vol. I, 246.

44. *Mémoires secrets de 1770 à 1830 par le Comte d'Allonville*, vol. I, 333.

45. See Lucien Perey, *Histoire d'une grande dame au XVIIIe siècle, Hélène de Ligne* (Paris: Calmann-Lévy, 1887), 135–38.

46. *Mémoires du Duc de Lauzun*, 64.

47. Letter from Horace Walpole to Horace Mann, November 30, 1762, in *Horace Walpole's Correspondence with Sir Horace Mann*, critical edition by W. S. Lewis, Warren Hunting Smith, and George L. Lam, 11 vol. (New Haven, CT, and London: Yale University Press/Oxford University Press [vol. XXII of *Horace Walpole's Correspondence*], 1960), vol. VI, 10.

48. *Correspondance littéraire, philosophique et critique par Grimm, Diderot, Raynal, Meister, etc. revue sur les textes originaux comprenant, outre ce qui a été publié à diverses époques, les fragments supprimés en 1813 par la censure, les parties inédites conservées à la Bibliothèque ducale de Gotha et à l'Arsenal de Paris*, notices, notes, and general index by Maurice Tourneaux, 16 vol. (Paris: Garnier Frères, 1877–1882), vol. X, 415.

49. Letter from Lord Chesterfield to his son, July 9, 1750, in *Letters to His Son: On the Fine Art of Becoming a Man of the World and a Gentleman*, critical edition by Oliver H. G. Leigh, 2 vol. (New York: Dingwall-Rock, Ltd, 1925), vol. I, 331.

50. "A witty woman has said that Paris *is the place in the world where one can best dispense with being happy*," Mme de Staël, *De l'Allemagne*, ed. Simone Balayé, 2 vol. (Paris: Garnier Flammarion, 1968), vol. I, 104.

51. Letter from Mme du Deffand to Crawford, February 13, 1767, in *Correspondance complète de Mme du Deffand avec la Duchesse de Choiseul, l'abbé Barthélemy et M. Craufurt,* introduction by the Marquis de Sainte-Aulaire, 3 vol. (Paris: Michel Lévy Frères, 1866), vol. I, 87.

52. Letter from Horace Walpole to George Montagu, January 22, 1761, in *Horace Walpole's Correspondence with George Montagu,* critical edition by W. S. Lewis and Ralph S. Brown Jr., 2 vol. (New Haven, CT, and London: Yale University Press/Oxford University Press, 1970, [*Horace Walpole's Correspondence,* vol. IX], vol. I, 335.

53. Letter from Lady Sarah Bunbury to Lady Susan O'Brien, June 22, 1765, in *The Life and Letters of Lady Sarah Lennox, 1745–1826,* edited by the Countess of Ilchester and Lord Stavordale, 2 vol. (London: J. Murray, 1902), vol. I, 171.

54. Letter from Mme du Deffand to Crawford, February 13, 1767, in *Correspondance complète de Mme du Deffand avec la Duchesse de Choiseul, l'abbé Barthélemy et M. Craufurt,* vol. I, 87.

55. Letter from Mme du Deffand to Walpole, February 18, 1767, in *Horace Walpole's Correspondence with Madame du Deffand and Wiart,* vol. I, 239.

56. *Mémoires du Duc de Lauzun,* 62.

57. See the letter from Mme du Deffand to Horace Walpole of February 16, 1767, *Horace Walpole's Correspondence with Madame du Deffand and Wiart,* 212.

58. *Mémoires du Duc de Lauzun,* 63.

59. Ibid., 64.

60. Ibid., 65.

61. Ibid., 68.

62. Ibid., 71.

63. Ibid., 75.

64. Letter from Lady Sarah Bunbury to Lady Susan O'Brien, October 23, 1767, in *The Life and Letters of Lady Sarah Lennox,* vol. I, 214.

65. *Mémoires du Duc de Lauzun,* 77.

66. Clément C. Velay, *Le Duc de Lauzun (1747–1793): essai de dialogue entre un homme et son temps* (Paris: Buchet-Chastel, 1983), 56.

67. See Jean-Paul Desprat, *Mirabeau. L'excès et le retrait* (Paris: Perrin, 2008), 68.

68. *Mémoires du Duc de Lauzun,* 94.

69. See Edmond Dziembowski, *La guerre de Sept Ans 1756–1763* (Paris: Perrin, 2015).

70. *Mémoires secrets de 1770 à 1830 par le Comte d'Allonville,* vol. I, 121.

71. *Mémoires du Prince de Talleyrand,* vol. I, 159.

72. "I did not hesitate to devote myself to his fortune," *Mémoires du Duc de Lauzun,* 106.

73. See letter from Mme du Deffand to the Duchesse de Choiseul, January 7, 1771, in *Correspondance complète de Mme du Deffand avec la Duchesse de Choiseul, l'abbé Barthélemy et M. Craufurt,* vol. I, 306.

74. "A few days from now the whole world will be here, I swear I am enraged at the

thought, we were fine [on our own], I had and have no need for more," the Duc de Lauzun to Marc-René de Paulmy d'Argenson, Marquis de Voyer, Chanteloup, February 23, 1771, Université de Poitiers, Archives d'Argenson, 77.

75. Mme du Deffand, *Correspondance croisée avec la Duchesse de Choiseul et l'abbé Barthélemy*, augmented with numerous previously unpublished letters, collected, edited, and annotated by Pierre E. Richard, 2 vol. (Nîmes: Pierre E. Richard, 2011), vol. II, 630.

76. Letter from the Marquise de Coigny to the Duc de Lauzun, [July 27] 1791, in *Lettres de la Marquise de Coigny et de quelques autres personnes appartenant à la société française de la fin du XVIIIe siècle* (Paris: Imprimerie Jouaust et Sigaux, 1884), 66.

77. See *Mémoires du Duc de Lauzun*, 77.

78. Letter from the Abbé Barthélemy to Mme du Deffand, Chanteloup, March 3, 1772, in Mme du Deffand, *Correspondance croisée avec la Duchesse de Choiseul et l'abbé Barthélemy*, vol. I, 338.

79. There exists a modern edition of the theatrical piece written by Lauzun in London in 1787 for the actor Le Texier, prepared by Auguste Ronel and Théodore Lascaris (Paris: Honoré Champion, 1911), and a second edition by Félix Juven (Paris) under the title *Le Ton de Paris, ou les Amants de bonne compagnie. Comédie en prose lue à Londres en 1787 par M. Le Texier*, from 1912, and that of Slatkine Reprints (Genève) in 1973.

80. Quoted in C. C. Velay, *Le Duc de Lauzun*, 65: letter from the Duc de Lauzun to the Marquis de Voyer, May 13, 1778, Université de Poitiers, Archives d'Argenson, 77.

81. *Mémoires du Duc de Lauzun*, 120–21.

82. Ibid., 151.

83. See Piotr Ugniewski, *Relations franco-polonaises de Callières à Vergennes*, in François de Callières, *Mon voyage en Pologne en l'année 1674* (Varsovie-Paris: Polska Akademia Nauk-Société Historique et Littéraire Polonaise, 2009) xiv.

84. *Mémoires du roi Stanislas-Auguste Poniatowski*, 2 vol. (Saint-Pétersbourg: Imprimerie de l'Académie Impériale des Sciences, 1914), vol. I, 364, 528.

85. Raymond Trousson, *Rousseau raconté par ceux qui l'ont vu* (Bruxelles: Le Cri, 2004), 80–82.

86. *Memoirs of the Margravine of Anspach, Written by Herself*, 2 vol. (London: Henry Colburn, 1826), vol. I, 129–30.

87. Julian Ursyn Niemcewicz, *Pamiętniki czasów*, in Gabriela Pauszer-Klonowska, *Pani na Puławach* (Varsovie: Czytelnik, 1978), 22–23.

88. Izabela Czartoryska, "Mon portrait il y a dix ans" (1783), Cracovie, Fondation Czartoryski, Biblioteka XX. Czartoryskich, manuscript 6067, 19–23. Beneath her self-portrait, Izabela explains: "This portrait, composed at the age of thirty-seven years, depicts me as happy and content. The afflictions I have suffered since have altered my character bit by bit."

89. Jean Fabre, *Stanislas-Auguste Poniatowski et l'Europe des Lumières* (Paris: Éditions Ophrys, 1984), 145.

90. Ibid.

91. Adam Zamoyski, *The Last King of Poland* (London: Phoenix Giant, 1998), 89.

92. Jean Fabre, *Stanislas-Auguste Poniatowski*, 146–48.

93. Zamoyski, *The Last King of Poland*, 125.

94. See *Mémoires du roi Stanislas-Auguste Poniatowski*, vol. I, 528.

95. Adam Moszczyński, *Pamiętniki do historyi polskiej w ostanich latach panowania Augusta III I pierwszych Stanislawa Poniatowskiego* (*Memoirs Toward a History of Poland During the Last Years of the Reign of Augustus III and the First of Stanisław Poniatowski*) (Poznań, 1858), 84, in Jean Fabre, *Stanislas-Auguste Poniatowski*, 145.

96. *Mémoires du Duc de Lauzun*, 121.

97. Letter from Horace Walpole to William Mason, May 28, 1780, *Horace Walpole's Correspondence with William Mason*, critical edition by W. S. Lewis, Grover Cronin Jr., and Charles H. Bennett, 2 vol. (Hartford, CT: Yale University Press, 1955, 2 vol. [Yale edition of *Horace Walpole's Correspondence*, vols. 28 and 29]), vol. II (29), 43.

98. A. M. Broadley and Lewis Melville, "Introduction," in *The Beautiful Lady Craven: The Original Memoirs of Elisabeth Baroness Craven afterwards Margravine of Anspach and Bayreuth and Princess Berkeley of the Holy Roman Empire (1750–1828). Edited with Notes and a Biographical and Historical Introduction Containing much Unpublished Matter by A. M. Broadley and Lewis Melville*, 2 vol. (London: John Lane, The Bodley Head, 1914), 48 ill., vol. I, xiv.

99. In the present work we refer to the edition published by Louis Lacour, Auguste Poulet-Malassis, and Eugène-Marie de Broise.

100. May 11 and September 19.

101. Imperial Court of Paris, Chamber of Appeals and Correctional Police, March 14, 1859, Fondation Czartoryski, Bibl. Czartoryskich, manuscript 6067, 5.

102. This is the hypothesis transmitted from generation to generation of librarians at the Czartoryski Library in Kraków.

103. Letter from Izabela Czartoryska to her husband, March 16, 1772, Bibl. Czatoryskich, manuscript 6030.

104. *Mémoires du Duc de Lauzun*, 147.

105. Horace Walpole to Lady Ossory, February 11, 1773, *Horace Walpole's Correspondence with the Countess of Upper Ossory*, critical edition by W. S. Lewis and A. Dayle Wallace, 2 vol. (New Haven, CT: Yale University Press, 1965), Yale edition of *Horace's Walpole Correspondence*, critical editon by W. S. Lewis, 32–34, vol. I, 96.

106. Letter from Izabela Czartoryska to her husband, London, April 31 [*sic*], [1773], Kraków, Fondation Czartoryskich, Biblioteka XX. Czartoryskich, manuscript 6030.

107. Ibid.

108. Letter from Izabela Czartoryska to her husband, March 16, 1772.

109. Ibid.

110. *Mémoires du Duc de Lauzun*, 149.

111. See Michel Delon, "Préface" to Duc de Lauzun, *Mémoires* (Paris: Nouveau Monde, 2006), 12–13.

112. *Mémoires du Duc de Lauzun*, 175.

113. Ibid., 171.

114. Ibid., 175.

115. Ibid., 178.

116. The child, who was given the name of Constantin, was declared to the government a year later, in order to render Adam Czartoryski's paternity credible. See Gabriela Pauszer-Klonowska, *Pani na Puławach*, 47–48.

117. Zamoyski, *The Last King of Poland*, 89.

118. See Renaud Przezdziecki, *Diplomatie et protocole à la cour de Pologne* (Paris: Les Belles Letters, 1934–1937), vol. I, 279.

119. See Piotr Ugniewski, *Relations franco-polonaises*, xxi.

120. It was the Comte de Lauraguais who organized the first race featuring horses mounted by English jockeys, at Sablons. See *Mémoires ou Souvenirs et Anecdotes par M. le Comte de Ségur*, vol. I, 159.

121. See *Mémoires du Prince de Talleyrand*, 152–56.

122. Philippe Salvadori, *La Chasse sous l'Ancien Régime* (Paris: Fayard, 1996), 138, quoted in Nicole de Blomac, *Voyer d'Argenson et le cheval des Lumières* (Paris: Belin, 2004), 200.

123. Marquis de Voyer, *Réflexions sur les courses relativement aux haras* (1776), Bibliothèque Universitaire de Poitiers, Fonds d'Argenson, quoted in N. de Blomac, *Voyer d'Argenson et le cheval des Lumières*, 315.

124. Letter from Mercy-Argenteau to the Empress Maria Theresa, November 15, 1776, in *Correspondance secrète entre Marie-Thérèse et le Cte de Mercy-Argenteau, avec des lettres de Marie-Thérèse et de Marie-Antoinette*, published with an introduction and notes by M. le Chevalier Alfred d'Arneth and M. A. Geffroy, 3 vol. (Paris: Firmin Didot Frères, 1874), vol. II, 525.

125. Daniel Roche, "Les Chevaux au XVIIIe siècle. Économie, utilité, distinction," *Dix-Huitième Siècle*, 42 (2010): 232–46.

126. See *Mémoires ou Souvenirs et Anecdotes par M. le Comte de Ségur*, vol. I, 152–53.

127. *Correspondance secrète inédite sur Louis XVI, Marie-Antoinette, la Cour et la Ville de 1777 à 1792*, preface, notes, and index by M. de Lescure, 2 vol. (Paris: Plon, 1866), vol. I, 152, January 4, 1777.

128. *Mémoires du Duc de Lauzun*, 213.

129. Jean-Christian Petitfils, *Louis XVI* (Paris: Perrin, 2005), 283.

130. *Mémoires du Duc de Lauzun*, 113.

131. See Mathieu Marraud, *La Noblesse de Paris au XVIIIe siècle* (Paris: Seuil, 2000), 147–57.

132. See Daniela Lombardi, *Storia del matrimonio. Dal Medioevo a oggi* (Bologne: Il Mulino, 2008), 41–46, 192–202.

133. S.-R. N. de Chamfort, "Produits de la civilisation perfectionnée," *Maximes et pensées,* no. 396: 117.

134. See Jean Starobinski, "La Rochefoucauld et les Morales substitutives," *Nouvelle Revue française,* no. 163 (1966): 16–34, and no. 164 (1966): 211–29.

135. S.-R. N. de Chamfort, *Maximes et pensées,* no. 721: 201.

136. *Souvenirs-Portraits du Duc de Lévis, suivi de lettres intimes de Monsieur, Comte de Provence, au Duc de Lévis,* introduction and notes by Jacques Dupâquier (Paris: Mercure de France, 1993), 198.

137. *Mémoires du Duc de Lauzun,* 214.

138. Letter from Mercy-Argenteau to Maria Theresa, December 18, 1776, in *Correspondance secrète entre Marie-Thérèse et le Cte de Mercy-Argenteau,* vol. II, 539–40.

139. Letter from Mercy-Argenteau to Maria Theresa, September 18, 1775, ibid., vol. II, 378.

140. Letter from Mercy-Argenteau to Maria Theresa, January 17, 1777, ibid., vol. III, 8.

141. *Mémoires de la Baronne d'Oberkirch sur la cour de Louis XVI et la société française avant 1789* (Paris: Mercure de France, 1970), 362.

142. For the "survivance" of the Duc de Villeroy's bodyguard, and of the first equerry of the Comte de Tessé, see *Mémoires du Duc de Lauzun,* 219, 224.

143. Ibid., 261–62.

144. Ibid., 263.

145. "I assured Madame de Gramont that she could not have been more in error regarding my liaison with the Queen: that I was in no way intriguing or giving advice; and that, even if I *had* possessed an influence over her which, in fact, I did not, I was far too attached to her to push her into meddling with the King's ministers; that everyone knew how devoted I was to M. le Duc de Choiseul, and that, if I had been able to, I would have done him a tremendous disservice at the time by placing him at the head of affairs." Ibid., 229.

146. Ibid., 230.

147. *Correspondance secrète inédite sur Louis XVI, Marie-Antoinette, la Cour et la Ville,* vol. I, 531, October 20, 1782.

148. *Mémoires du Duc de Lauzun,* 269.

149. Ibid., 264.

150. C. C. Velay, *Le Duc de Lauzun,* 90.

151. On the agreement with the Prince de Guéménée and the indignation of Choiseul, see Jean-Pierre-Jacques-Auguste de Labouïsse-Rochefort, *Souvenirs et Mélanges,* vol. I, 286–98.

152. They are part of the sixty-something letters sent by Lauzun to the Marquis de Voyer, written between February 1771 and April 1781, preserved in the Archives d'Argenson, at the Université de Poitiers.

153. Nicole de Blomac, *Voyer d'Argenson et le cheval des Lumières,* 48.

154. Letter from the Abbé Barthélemy to Mme du Deffand, July 30, 1777, in Mme du Deffand, *Correspondance croisée*, vol. II, 1049.

155. See Guy Richard, *Noblesse d'affaires au XVIIIe siècle* (Paris: A. Colin, 1974).

156. *Mémoires du Prince de Talleyrand*, vol. I, 152–56.

157. See the letter from the Duc de Lauzun to the Marquis de Voyer, Ardes, April 19, 1778, Université de Poitiers, Archives d'Argenson, 77.

158. *Mémoires du Duc de Lauzun*, 292.

159. See the letter from the Duc de Lauzun to the Marquis de Voyer, Ardes, April 19, 1778, Université de Poitiers, Archives d'Argenson, 77.

160. *Correspondance secrète inédite sur Louis XVI, Marie-Antoinette, la Cour et la Ville*, vol. I, 40, April 3, 1777.

161. Ibid.

162. See Amédée Britsch, *La Maison d'Orléans à la fin de l'Ancien Régime. La jeunesse de Philippe-Égalité (1747–1785). D'après des documents inédits* (Paris: Payot, 1926), 396.

163. Copy of a report to the minister of February 21, and a letter to Voyer written from Dover the following day, Université de Poitiers, Archives d'Argenson, 77.

164. *Mémoires du Duc de Lauzun*, 290.

165. Ibid., 293.

166. Quoted in Gaston Maugras, *La Fin d'une société. Le Duc de Lauzun et la cour de Marie-Antoinette* (Paris: Plon, Nourrit et Cie, 14e édition, 1913), 161–62.

167. Letter from the Duc de Lauzun to the Marquis de Voyer, Ardes, May 23, 1778, Université de Poitiers, Archives d'Argenson, 77.

168. Ibid.

169. Letter from the Duc de Lauzun to the Marquis de Voyer, Ardes, May 13, 1778, Université de Poitiers, Archives d'Argenson, 77.

170. Ibid.

171. Letter from the Duc de Lauzun to the Marquis de Voyer, Ardes, April 19, 1778, Université de Poitiers, Archives d'Argenson, 77.

172. Letter from Duc de Lauzun au Marquis de Voyer, Ardes, June 18, 1778, Université de Poitiers, Archives d'Argenson, 77.

173. Ibid.

174. Letter from the Duc de Lauzun to the Marquis de Voyer, Ardes, June 23, 1778, Université de Poitiers, Archives d'Argenson, 77.

175. Letter from the Duc de Lauzun to the Marquis de Voyer, Ardes, May 2, 1778, Université de Poitiers, Archives d'Argenson, 77.

176. Letter from the Duc de Lauzun to the Marquis de Voyer, Ardes, July 10, 1778, Université de Poitiers, Archives d'Argenson, 77.

177. Letter from the Duc de Lauzun to the Comte de Vergennes, June 29, 1778, with a copy sent to the Marquis de Voyer, Université de Poitiers, Archives d'Argenson, 77.

178. Letter from the Duc de Lauzun to the Marquis de Voyer, May 23, 1778, Université de Poitiers, Archives d'Argenson, 77.

179. Of the thirty-four European forts dotting the western coast of Africa, seventeen were Dutch, eleven English, three Danish, one belonged to Brandenburg, one to the Portuguese, and one to France. See J. Monteilhet, "Le Duc de Lauzun, Gouverneur du Sénégal. Janvier-mars 1779," *Bulletin du Comité d'Études Historiques et Scientifiques de l'Afrique Occidentale Française* no. 2 (1920): 207, 193–237; no. 4: 515–52.

180. See *Mémoires du Duc de Lauzun*, 303ff.

181. C. C. Velay, *Le Duc de Lauzun*, 123.

182. The creation of this new corps, composed of eight legions and one general company, had been decreed by the minister of the navy, Sartine, on September 1, 1778.

183. See *Mémoires du Duc de Lauzun*, 300.

184. "I am pleased that the Queen is pregnant, it is so important to her," he wrote to Voyer on April 29, 1788 (Université de Poitiers, Archives d'Argenson, 77). The Queen gave birth to Madame Royale on December 20.

185. Madeleine de Scudéry, *La Carte de Tendre*.

186. *Mémoires du Duc de Lauzun*, 301.

187. See J. Monteilhet, "Le Duc de Lauzun," *Bulletin du Comité d'Études Historiques et Scientifiques de l'Afrique Occidentale Française*, no. 2: 207–9.

188. Ibid., 211.

189. The journal was published by J. Monteilhet, "Le Duc de Lauzun," *Bulletin du Comité d'Études Historiques et Scientifiques de l'Afrique Occidentale Française*, no. 4: 515–51. Lauzun sent a copy to the Marquis de Voyer.

190. Duc de Lauzun, *Mémoire sur le commerce et les possessions des Anglais en Afrique*, composed upon his return from Senegal and published on the basis of the manuscript found among Biron's papers seized by the Revolutionary Tribunal by J. Monteilhet in ibid.

191. Mme du Deffand to Horace Walpole, March 21, 1779, in *Horace Walpole's Correspondence with Madame du Deffand and Wiart* (*Horace Walpole's Correspondence*, vol. VII), vol. V, 123.

192. On March 5, 1780, the 2nd Légion des volontaires étrangers de la Marine changed its name to become the 2nd Légion des volontaires étrangers de Lauzun, or the Légion de Lauzun, which followed him to the United States from July 1780 to May 1783. Upon its return to France, it passed into the service of the minister of war as the Régiment des hussards de Lauzun. On January 1, 1791, all regiments were rebaptized on the basis of the branch in which they served, and their seniority in that branch; Lauzun's regiment became the 6th Hussars. In June 1793, in the wake of the mass emigration of hussars, they became the 5th Hussars. See Robert A. Selig, "The Duc de Lauzun and His Legion: Rochambeau's Most Troublesome, Colorful Soldiers," www://americanrevolution.org.

193. *La Prise du Sénégal* was the sixth engraving by the *Recueil d'estampes* to depict the various events of the war that had earned the United States their independence; see J. Monteilhet, "Le Duc de Lauzun," *Bulletin du Comité d'Études Historiques et Scientifiques de l'Afrique Occidentale Française*, no 2: 223.

194. *Mémoires du Duc de Lauzun*, 313.

195. Ibid., 315–16.

196. *Anecdotes échappées à l'Observateur anglais*, vol. I, 233, quoted in *Lettres de la Marquise de Coigny*, 3–4.

197. *Mémoires du Duc de Lauzun*, 315.

198. Letter from Louis XVIII to Decazes, quoted in Ernest Daudet, *Louis XVIII et le duc Decazes* (Paris: Plon, 1899). See also *Mémoires d'Aimée de Coigny*, introduction and notes by Étienne Lamy (Paris: Calmann-Lévy, 1906), 24.

199. *Mémoires du Duc de Lauzun*, 358.

200. See Paul Lacroix, "Notice sur the Marquise de Coigny," in *Lettres de la Marquise de Coigny*, 14. See also Ligne, who found this idea original and profound: Prince Charles-Joseph de Ligne, *Lettres à la Marquise de Coigny*, ed. Jean-Pierre Guicciardi (Paris: Desjonquères, 1986), 36.

201. C.-J. de Ligne, *Lettres à la Marquise de Coigny*, 36.

202. Prince Charles-Joseph de Ligne, "Carite," in *Caractères et portraits*, critical edition under the direction of Daniel Acke, with the collaboration of Raymond Trousson, Jeroom Vercruysse, and Helmut Watzlawick (Paris: Honoré Champion, 2003), 135–36.

203. Ibid., 136.

204. *Mémoires du Duc de Lauzun*, 360.

205. C.-J. de Ligne, "Carite," 135.

206. Chateaubriand, *Mémoires d'outre-tombe*, 170.

207. Organizational chart in *La Jeunesse de Philippe-Égalité*; Prince Adam Czartoryski was listed there as a visitor as well, 239–40.

208. René Héron de Villefosse, *L'Anti-Versailles ou le Palais-Royal de Philippe Égalité* (Paris: Jean Dullis Éditeur, 1974), 133.

209. See Gabriel de Broglie, *L'Orléanisme. La ressource libérale de la France* (Paris: Librairie Académique Perrin, 1981), 114.

210. Ibid., 115.

211. Quoted in R. Héron de Villefosse, *L'Anti-Versailles*, 136.

212. Jacques Brengues, *Les Francs-Maçons français et les États-Unis d'Amérique à la fin du XVIIIe siècle, in De l'Armorique à l'Amérique de l'indépendance. Deuxième partie du colloque du bicentenaire de l'indépendance américaine 1796–1976*, monograph issue of the *Annales de Bretagne et des pays de l'Ouest* 84, no. 3 (1977): 298.

213. *Mémoires ou Souvenirs et Anecdotes, par M. le Comte de Ségur*, vol. I, 394.

214. *Mémoires du Duc de Lauzun*, 333.

215. Quoted in C. C. Velay, *Le Duc de Lauzun*, 165.

216. Ibid.

217. François-Jean de Chastellux, *Voyages dans l'Amérique septentrionale dans les années 1780, 1781 et 1782, présenté par le Duc de Castries* (Paris: Tallandier, 1980), 271.

218. Letter from the Duc de Lauzun to the Marquis de Voyer, January 10, 1781, Université de Poitiers, Archives d'Argenson, 77.

219. Letter from the Duc de Lauzun to the Marquis de Voyer, September 21, 1780, Université de Poitiers, Archives d'Argenson, 77.

220. See Donatien-Marie-Joseph de Vimeur, *Esquisses historiques de la fin du XVIIIe siècle, extraits de documents inédits*, in *Le Cabinet historique*, vol. XV, part I: Documents, 1869, 66.

221. Quoted in R. A. Selig, "The Duc de Lauzun and His Legion," ibid.

222. *Mémoires du Duc de Lauzun*, 354.

223. Ibid., 354–55.

224. G. Maugras, *La Fin d'une société. Le Duc de Lauzun et la cour de Marie-Antoinette*, 245.

225. *Mémoires du Duc de Lauzun*, 356.

226. Ibid.

227. Ibid., 361.

228. Ibid., 363–64.

229. See *Mémoires ou Souvenirs et Anecdotes, par M. le Comte de Ségur*, vol. I, 324.

230. Quoted in C. C. Velay, *Le Duc de Lauzun*, 217.

231. Ibid., 218.

232. See Jean-Paul Desprat, *Mirabeau*, 295.

233. Quoted in C. C. Velay, *Le Duc de Lauzun*, 219.

234. Jean-Paul Desprat, *Mirabeau*, 294.

235. G. Maugras, *La Fin d'une société. Le Duc de Lauzun et la cour de Marie-Antoinette*, 297.

236. See R. Héron de Villefosse, *L'Anti-Versailles*.

237. Quoted in "Notice sur la Marquise de Coigny," in *Lettres de la Marquise de Coigny*, 22.

238. Étienne Lamy, "Introduction," in *Mémoires d'Aimée de Coigny*, 29.

239. Letter from the Marquise de Coigny to Lauzun, September 1, 1791, in *Lettres de la Marquise de Coigny*, 78.

240. Mme de Genlis, *Souvenirs de Félicie suivis des Souvenirs et portraits par M. le Duc de Lévis* (Paris: Firmin Didot, 1857), 61.

241. Letter from Horace Walpole to Lady Ossory, October 8, 1792, in *Horace Walpole's Correspondence with the Countess Upper Ossory*, vol. III, 164.

242. It was around 1829, at the age of seventy-four, that Mme Vigée Le Brun, at the request of the Princesse Natalia Kourakina, wrote the first part of her *Souvenirs*.

243. Élisabeth Vigée Le Brun, *Souvenirs 1755–1842*, text established, presented, and annotated by Geneviève Haroche-Bouzinac (Paris: Honoré Champion, 2008), 384.

244. Adolfo Omodeo, "Introduction," *Aimée de Coigny (La Jeune Captive), La Restaurazione Francese dal 1814, Memorie*, translation by Ada Prospero (Bari: Laterza, 1938), 16.

245. Letter from Aimée de Coigny, Duchesse de Fleury, to Lauzun, Duc de Biron, Naples (1791), in *Lettres de la Marquise de Coigny*, 187–88.

246. Ibid.

THE VICOMTE JOSEPH-ALEXANDRE DE SÉGUR

1. *Journal d'émigration du Comte d'Espinchal*, edited from the original manuscripts by Ernest d'Hauterive (Paris: Perrin, 1912), 311.

2. Prince Charles-Joseph de Ligne, *Fragments de l'histoire de ma vie*, ed. Jeroom Vercruysse (Paris: Honoré Champion, 2008), 264.

3. Ibid., 272.

4. *Mémoires du baron de Besenval sur la cour de France* (Paris: Mercure de France, 1987), 461.

5. See Gabriel de Broglie, *Ségur sans cérémonie 1757–1805, ou la gaieté libertine* (Paris: Perrin, 1977), 268–74. See also Mme de Genlis who disputed the authenticity of the *Mémoires* and attributed them to Ségur (old resentments of the Palais-Royal) before being forced to change her mind (*Mémoires inédits de Madame la Comtesse de Genlis*, vol. II, 67), and the criticisms leveled at them by the Duc de Lévis in "Le baron de Besenval," *Souvenirs-Portraits de Gaston de Lévis (1764–1830), suivis de Lettres intimes de Monsieur, Comte de Provence au Duc de Lévis* (Paris: Mercure de France, 1993), 163–65.

6. Mme Campan had completed a first version of her *Mémoires* in 1799, but, suspect in the eyes of the ultraroyalists for her former Girondin sympathies and afraid of attracting criticism, she declined to publish them and continued to revise and add to her text. It was not until 1813, as can be deduced from a letter she sent to Queen Hortense (the same to whom we owe the survival of the *Mémoires* of Lauzun) that Mme Campan completed a final draft of her memoirs—without, however, deciding to publish them. They would not appear until after her death, in 1822, in the midst of the Restoration, and seemed to Stendhal very different from the pages that he had heard read aloud in a salon after Napoleon's Coup of 18 Brumaire. Obviously rewritten, they had been reduced to a "tearful rhapsody well calculated to stir the emotions of the dames of the Faubourg-Saint-Honoré." See Stendhal, *Vie de Henry Brulard* (Paris: Gallimard, 1973), 407. See Geneviève Haroche-Bouzinac, "Mémoires et temps dans les récits de Mme Campan," *Le Temps des femmes* (Paris: Garnier, 2014), 214. On the question of the reliability of Mme Campan's *Mémoires*, see also *Souvenirs des Cours de France, d'Espagne, de Prusse et de Russie écrits par Henri Richard Lord Holland, publiés par Lord Holland son fils et traduits de l'anglais par E. F., suivis du Journal de Mistress Eliot sur sa vie pendant la Révolution française*, with a preface, notes, and historical elucidations by M. F. Barrière (Paris: Firmin Didot, 1862), 15–16. See also Jules Flammermont, *Études critiques sur les sources de l'histoire du XVIIIe siècle. I. Les Mémoires de Mme Campan* (Paris: Adolphe Richard, 1866), 28–37.

7. See Jean-Christian Petitfils, *Louis XVI*, 292.

8. See *Mémoires de Madame Campan, Première femme de chambre de Marie-Antoinette*, edition presented by Jean Chalon, with notes by Carlos de Angulo (Paris: Mercure de France, 1988), 159–60.

9. Letter from Mercy-Argenteau to Maria Theresa, October 9, 1775, in *Marie-Antoinette, Correspondance secrète*, vol. II, 832.

10. See Marc Fumaroli, "Les Mémoires au carrefour des genres en prose," in *La Diplomatie de l'esprit* (Paris: Hermann, 1998), 214, and *Chateaubriand. Poésie et Terreur* (Paris: Editions de Fallois, 2003), those pages dedicated to the problematic aspects of the *Mémoires*.

11. See the history of Saint-Simon's manuscripts in Saint-Simon, *Mémoires 1691–1701. Additions au Journal de Dangeau*, text established by Yves Coirault (Paris: Gallimard, 1983), vol. I, lxxvl.

12. The Duc de Choiseul's *Mémoires* were printed on the Duc's private press at Chanteloup.

13. For years, the century's most famous libertine had accumulated with fanatical meticulousness a treasury of documents both public and private that would be of use in composing his future autobiography. But, too absorbed by the pleasures of living, he died without having brought about this project, offering others the possibility of doing so in his place. Shortly after his death, two apocryphal autobiographies making free use of the primary documents from his archives were published a year apart: *Mémoires du maréchal de Richelieu* and *La Vie Privée du Maréchal de Richelieu*. See Benedetta Craveri, "Fatti della vita del maresciallo di Richelieu," afterword to *Vita privata del maresciallo di Richelieu* (Milan: Adelphi, 1989); "Préface" to *Vie privée du maréchal de Richelieu* (Paris: Desjonquères, 1993). The *Mémoires du maréchal de Richelieu*, which appeared in five volumes between 1790 and 1793, were the work of one of his former librarians, the Abbé Soulavie, who had abandoned his clerical office and embraced the credo of the Revolution. The former abbé had already demonstrated the extent of his editorial indifference by disfiguring the *Mémoires de Saint-Simon*, which he had been the first to publish, and in his hands, the brilliant myth of the Maréchal was transformed into a dark legend of the ancien régime. Published in 1791, *Vie privée du maréchal de Richelieu*, in three volumes, was probably the fruit of a collaboration between an obscure playwright, Louis-François Faur, who had been in the service of Richelieu, and Jean-Benjamin de La Borde, a wealthy farmer who dabbled in literature. In spite of their obvious imposture, they managed to obtain the backing of the most prominent writers of the moment. For Choderlos de Laclos, who published a critique of it in a Jacobin journal, the *Vie privée* was clear evidence that "the revolution was no less necessary for the restoration of morals as it was for that of liberty"; see *Journal des Amis de la Constitution* (February 8, 1791), and *Oeuvres complètes*, text and notes by Laurent Versini (Paris: Gallimard, 1979), 642–43. According to Chamfort, "they

were enough to give us a sense of the depths of the abyss we have left behind"; S.-R. N. de Chamfort, "Sur la vie privée du maréchal de Richelieu," *Mercure de France* 2, no. 9 (April 16, 1791), and *Oeuvres complètes de Chamfort, réunies et publiées avec une notice historique sur la vie et les écrits de l'auteur par Pierre-René Auguis* (Paris: Chaumerot Jeune, 1824–1825), vol. III, 229–94. For their part, Richelieu's descendants attempted to recover the truth and to defend the family's honor by commissioning a biography of the Maréchal from Sénac de Meilhan. Though they were officially announced in September 1790, in *Journal de Paris*, *Mémoires sur la vie du maréchal Duc de Richelieu, pour servir à l'histoire du XVIIIe siècle* would never actually be published. As the political situation grew more and more extreme, Meilhan, faithful to his moderate reformist convictions, chose to leave France and give voice to the victims of the Revolution in *L'Émigré*, an epistolary novel inspired by real events.

14. See Mona Ozouf, *Les Mots des femmes, essai sur la singularité française* (Paris: Fayard, 1995), 323–65.

15. Henri Rossi, *Mémoires aristocratiques féminins, 1789–1848* (Paris: Honoré Champion, 1998), 65. See also Claudine Giacchetti, *Poétique des lieux. Enquête sur les Mémoires féminins de l'aristocratie française (1789–1848)* (Paris: Honoré Champion, 2009).

16. Pierre Nora, "Les Mémoires d'État: de Commynes à de Gaulle," in *Les Lieux de mémoire. La Nation. II* (Paris: Gallimard, 1986), 360.

17. See Damien Zanone, *Écrire son temps. Les Mémoires en France de 1815 à 1848* (Lyon: Presses Universitaires de Lyon, 2006), 35.

18. F.-R. de Chateaubriand, *Génie du christianisme*, critical edition by M. Regard (Paris: Gallimard 1978), 839, quoted in D. Zanone, *Écrire son temps*, 97.

19. *Mémoires de Madame la Duchesse d'Abrantès, Souvenirs historiques sur Napoléon, la Révolution, le Directoire, le Consulat, l'Empire et la Restauration*, 10 vol. (Paris: Garnier Frères, 1893), vol. I., 181, quoted in D. Zanone, *Écrire son temps*, 23.

20. "Avertissement de M. A. J. de Ségur, Exécuteur Testamentaire de M. le Baron de Besenval," in *Mémoires de M. le baron de Besenval, Lieutenant-Général des Armées du Roi, sous Louis XV et Louis XVI, Grand-Croix de l'Ordre de Saint-Louis, Gouverneur de Haguenau, Commandant des Provinces de l'Intérieur, Lieutenant-Colonel du Régiment des Gardes-Suisses, etc.; écrits par lui-même, imprimés sur son manuscrit original, et publiés par son Exécuteur Testamentaire. Contenant beaucoup de Particularités et d'Anecdotes sur la Cour, sur les Ministres et les Règnes de Louis XV et Louis XVI, et sur les Événements du temps. Précédés d'une Notice sur la Vie de l'Auteur*, 4 vol. (Paris: F. Buisson, 1805), vol. I, iii–iv.

21. "Of course it is also widely known that those attributed to the Baron de Besenval were actually written by the Vicomte de Ségur," *Mémoires secrets de 1770 à 1830 par le Comte d'Allonville*, vol. I, 370.

22. J.-A. de Ségur, "Des conteurs et de l'art de conter," *Morceaux de littérature*, in *Oeuvres Diverses du vicomte J.-A. de Ségur, contenant Ses Morceaux de Littérature, ses Poésies fugitives;*

la Correspondance secrète entre Ninon de Lenclos, le Marquis de Villarceaux, et Mme de Maintenon. Précédées d'une notice sur la Vie de l'Auteur (Paris: Dalibon, 1819), 54 note.

23. See Érica-Marie Benabou, *La Prostitution et la Police des moeurs au XVIIIe siècle* (Paris: Perrin, 1987), 385.

24. S.-R. N. de Chamfort, *Maximes et pensées*, no. 1273: 344.

25. *Mémoires ou Souvenirs et Anecdotes par le Comte de Ségur*, vol. I, 9.

26. Denis Diderot, *Lettres à Sophie Volland*, text largely published for the first time according to the original manuscripts, with introduction, variants, and notes prepared by André Babelon, 3 vols. (Paris: Éditions d'Aujourd'hui, 1978), vol. I, 298–99.

27. Ludovico Ariosto, *Orlando Furioso*, canto I, 22, v. 1.

28. Denis Diderot, *Lettres à Sophie Volland*, 299.

29. *Mémoires inédits de Madame la Comtesse de Genlis*, vol. II, 31.

30. *Lettres et pensées du maréchal Prince de Ligne, publiées par Madame la baronne de Staël Holstein*, Genève, 1809, quoted in Jean-Jacques Fiechter, *Le Baron Pierre-Victor de Besenval* (Lausanne-Paris: Delachaux et Niestlé, 1993), 34.

31. "Le baron de Besenval," in *Souvenirs-Portraits de Gaston de Lévis (1764–1830), suivis de Lettres intimes de Monsieur, Comte de Provence au Duc de Lévis*, 158–59.

32. Sainte-Beuve, "Le baron de Besenval," in *Causeries du lundi*, vol. XII, 497.

33. "Avertissement de M. A. J. de Ségur, Exécuteur Testamentaire de M. le Baron de Besenval," in *Mémoires de M. le baron de Besenval*, vol. I, iii–iv.

34. See *Oeuvres du Prince de Ligne*, introduction by Albert Lacroix, 4 vol. (Bruxelles-Genève: Van Meenen et C.-Cherberliez, 1860), vol. III, 330.

35. Letter to Crébillon, published as an appendix to vol. IV of *Mémoires de M. le baron de Besenval*, vii.

36. *Mémoires ou Souvenirs et Anecdotes par le Comte de Ségur*, vol. I, 56.

37. *Mémoires de M. le baron de Besenval* (edition of 1805), vol. I, 114–15. In an even earlier "Iroquois tale" entitled "The Two Friends," Saint-Lambert had proposed as a model of *sagesse souriante* the sort of ménage à trois adopted by the Marquise du Châtelet and Voltaire.

38. *Spleen*, in *Mémoires de M. le baron de Besenval*, vol. IV, 47–50.

39. Pierre de Ségur, *Le Maréchal de Ségur (1724–1801), ministre de la Guerre sous Louis XVI* (Paris: Plon, Nourrit et Cie, 1895), 25–26.

40. Sainte-Beuve, "Le baron de Besenval," in *Causeries du lundi*, vol. XII, 497.

41. See Colin B. Bailey, "Henri-Pierre Danloux, *The Baron de Besenval in his 'Salon de compagnie,'*" in *An Aspect of Collecting Taste* (New York: Stair Sainty Matthiesen, 1986), 5–6, 48–53.

42. *Correspondance littéraire, philosophique et critique par Grimm, Diderot, Raynal, Meister, etc.*, October 1, 1764, vol. VI, 86.

43. See J.-J. Fiechter, *Le Baron Pierre-Victor de Besenval*, 100.

44. *Mémoires secrets de 1770 à 1830 par le Comte d'Allonville*, 172.

45. *Journal d'émigration du Comte d'Espinchal*, the first months of 1792, 311.

46. *Mémoires secrets de 1770 à 1830 par le Comte d'Allonville*, vol. I, 173.

47. Ibid.

48. *Mémoires, souvenirs, Oeuvres et portraits par René Alissan de Chazet*, 3 vol. (Paris: Chez Postel, 1837), vol. II, 43.

49. G. de Broglie, *Ségur sans cérémonie*, 39ff.

50. *Journal d'émigration du Comte d'Espinchal*, 311.

51. Act IV, scene IV: *Castor*: Abode of eternal peace, / will you not calm my impatient soul? / Even here the face of love pursues me: / Castor sees nothing but his lover, / And all your attractions pale beside her. / Abode of eternal peace, / will you not calm my impatient soul? / How sweet is your murmuring! how cool your shade! / I am enchanted by the voluptuousness of your stirring harmonies: / Everything smiles, everything calls me to linger, / And nevertheless my mind shapes regrets! / Abode of eternal peace.

52. Madeleine and Francis Ambrière, *Talma ou l'Histoire au théâtre* (Paris: Éditions de Fallois, 2007), 91.

53. His name was François Pioch, he was the general clerk for France's cavalry, and in the end he officially recognized Julie. See M. and F. Ambrière, *Talma ou l'Histoire au théâtre*, 100–1.

54. Letter from Julie Talma to Benjamin Constant, Thermidor 18th, Year XII [August 6, 1804], in *Lettres de Julie de Talma à Benjamin Constant, publiées par la baronne Constant de Rebecque* (Paris: Plon, 1966), 214.

55. This lost painting is included on the list of portraits completed by the artist in 1775. There Julie is designated, without her family name, as "Mademoiselle Julie, who married Talma," É. Vigée Le Brun, *Souvenirs*, 332.

56. Quoted in Baronne Constant de Rebecque, "Notes biographiques sur Julie Talma," in *Lettres de Julie Talma à Benjamin Constant*, lxviii.

57. G. de Broglie, *Ségur sans cérémonie*, 63.

58. Benjamin Constant, "Lettre sur Julie," in *Lettres de Julie Talma à Benjamin Constant*, vii–viii.

59. See the letters of January 4 and 6, and February 1 and 24, 1803, dedicated to an analysis of Mme de Staël's novel, ibid., 137–51.

60. *Oeuvres du Comte L. Roederer*, 8 vol. (Paris: Firmin Didot, 1853–1859), vol. V, 202, quoted in Claude Arnaud, *Chamfort* (Paris: Robert Laffont, 1988), 132.

61. See Claude Arnaud, *Chamfort*, 130–33. See also the letters written by Mirabeau to Chamfort between December 1781 and the summer of the following year, in S.-R. N. de Chamfort, *Oeuvres complètes*, edition prepared by Lionel Dax, 2 vol. (Paris: Éditions du Sandre, 2010), vol. II, 591–611.

62. See M. and F. Ambrière, *Talma*, 105.

63. See *Correspondance secrète entre Ninon de Lenclos, le Marquis de Villarceaux et Madame de Maintenon*, letter XXV, in *Oeuvres diverses*, 201–2.

64. "I was born in Sparta," she wrote to Benjamin Constant on January 7, 1799, in *Lettres de Julie Talma à Benjamin Constant*, 11.

65. Benjamin Constant, "Lettre sur Julie," ibid., iii.

66. Quoted in M. and F. Ambrière, *Talma*, 112.

67. Ibid.

68. Ibid.

69. Published in Paris, by the editor Le Jay.

70. See Lucia Omacini, *Le Roman épistolaire français au tournant des Lumières* (Paris: Honoré Champion, 2003).

71. Voltaire, *Madame de Maintenon et Mademoiselle de Lenclos, Mélanges II*, in *Oeuvres complètes de Voltaire*, under the direction of Theodore Besterman, 51 vol. (Oxford: The Voltaire Foundation-University of Oxford, 1968–1977), vol. XXIII, 498–99.

72. Most likely the work of Louis Damours.

73. Preface to *Oeuvres de Chamfort. Recueillies et publiées par un de ses amis*, 4 vol. (Paris: Chez le Directeur de l'Imprimerie des Sciences et des Arts, l'an III de la République), vol. I, ii–iii.

74. *Correspondance littéraire, philosophique et critique par Grimm, Diderot, Raynal, Meister, etc.*, vol. XV, 533, October 1789.

75. See François-Augustin-Paradis de Montcrif, *Essai sur la nécessité et les moyens de plaire* (Paris: Prault, 1738).

76. J.-A. de Ségur, "L'homme d'esprit et l'homme aimable," *Morceaux de littérature*, 12.

77. Ibid., 11.

78. *Essai sur les moyens de plaire en amour par Ségur le jeune* (Paris: Huet, 1797), 15.

79. Ibid., 10.

80. Ibid., verse 97, 6.

81. S.-R. N. de Chamfort, *Maximes et pensées*, no. 259: 110.

82. G. de Broglie, *Ségur sans cérémonie*, 95.

83. See *Correspondance secrète, inédite sur Louis XVI, Marie-Antoinette et la Cour et la Ville*, vol. I, 363.

84. *Histoire des Salons de Paris. Tableaux et Portraits du Grand Monde par la Duchesse d'Abrantès*, 4 vol. (Paris: Garnier Frères, s.d.), vol. I, 183–89.

85. *Très humbles remontrances de Fidèle Berger, confiseur, rue des Lombards, à M. le vicomte de Ségur, qui avait envoyé à toutes les Dames de sa société des pastilles avec des devises de sa composition, par M. le Comte de Thiard*, in *Correspondance littéraire, philosophique et critique, adressée à un souverain d'Allemagne, pendant une partie des années 1775–1776, et pendant les années 1782 à 1790 inclusivement, par le baron de Grimm et par Diderot. Troisième et dernière partie. Tome second* (Paris: F. Buisson libraire, 1813).

86. Quoted in G. de Broglie, *Ségur sans cérémonie*, 102.

87. It is Gabriel de Broglie who reveals to us the identity of Mme de Z., ibid., 103–4.

88. *Récits d'une tante. Mémoires de la Comtesse de Boigne née d'Osmond*, published according to the original manuscripts by M. Charles Nicoulhaud, 4 vol. (Paris: Plon, 1907), vol. I, 63.

89. The name is a clear reference to Versac from Crébillon *fils*, *Égarements du Coeur et de l'esprit*.

90. *Correspondance littéraire, critique et philosophique*, August 1790, vol. XVI, 65.

91. Roger Caillois, "Preface" to Montesquieu, *Oeuvres complètes*, text presented and annotated by Roger Caillois, 2 vol. (Paris: Gallimard, 1949), vol. I, v.

92. *Correspondance littéraire, critique et philosophique*, August 1790, vol. XVI, 488.

93. *Journal de Gouverneur Morris, 1789–1792, ministre plénipotentiaire des États-Unis en France, édition établie par Anne Cary-Morris, traduit de l'anglais par Ernest Pariset, texte présenté et annoté par Antoine de Baecque* (Paris: Mercure de France, 2002), November 30, 1790, 228.

94. J.-A. de Ségur, "Des conteurs et de l'art de conter," 55.

95. *Correspondance secrète inédite sur Louis XVI, Marie-Antoinette, la Cour et la Ville*, vol. I, 369, February 23, 1781.

96. See Clarence Brenner, *Les Développements du proverbe dramatique en France et sa vogue au XVIIIe siècle, avec un proverbe inédit de Carmontelle* (Berkeley, CA: University of California Press, 1937).

97. *Mémoires du Comte Alexandre de Tilly pour servir à l'histoire des moeurs de la fin du XVIIIe siècle* (Paris: Mercure de France, 1986), 241.

98. *Correspondance littéraire, philosophique et critique par Grimm, Diderot, Raynal, Meister, etc.*, vol. XIV, 400, note 1, June 1786.

99. Quoted in *Mémoires secrets pour servir à l'histoire de la République des lettres en France depuis 1762 jusqu'à nos jours, ou Journal d'un observateur*...par feu M. de Bachaumont, 36 vol. (London: John Adamson, 1783–1789), quoted in Béatrix Dussane, *La Célimène de Thermidor. Louise Contat (1760–1813)* (Paris: Charpentier et Fasquelle, 1929), 33.

100. *Mémoires de Fleury, de la Comédie-Française*, published by J. B. Lafitte, 2 vol. (Paris: A. Delahays, Première série, 1757–1789), 301, quoted in B. Dussane, *La Célimène de Thermidor*, 49.

101. Letter from Julie Talma to Benjamin Constant, Thermidor 18th, Year XII [August 6, 1804], in *Lettres de Julie Talma à Benjamin Constant*, 213.

102. J.-P.-J.-A. de Labouïsse-Rochefort, *Souvenirs et Mélanges*, vol. I, 208.

103. B. Dussane, *La Célimène de Thermidor*, 43.

104. Antoine-Vincent Arnault, *Souvenirs d'un sexagénaire*, critical edition by Raymond Trousson (Paris: Honoré Champion, 2003), 102.

105. *Souvenirs d'un historien de Napoléon. Mémorial de Jacques de Norvins*, introduction and

notes by Léon de Lanzac de Laborie, 3 vol. (Paris: Plon, Nourrit et Cie, 1896–1897), vol. I, 191.

106. Letter from Prince Charles to Prince Royal, Frankfurt-am-Main, September 20, 1770, in *Gustave III par ses Lettres*, Édition par Gunner von Proscwitz (Paris: Jean Touzot Libraire, 1986), 91.

107. Letter from Mme de Sabran to the Chevalier de Boufflers, January 9, 1787, in Comtesse de Sabran and the Chevalier de Boufflers, *La Promesse, Correspondance, 1786–1787*, edited and presented by Sue Carrell (Paris: Tallandier, 2010), 287.

108. Ibid.

109. "Derniers préparatifs," *Journal d'émigration du Comte d'Espinchal*, 326.

110. *Rosaline et Floricourt. Comédie en deux actes et en vers libres, par M. le Vicomte de Ségur. Représentée pour la première fois sur le Théâtre Français le 17 novembre 1787* (Paris: Desemme, 1790).

111. See M. and F. Ambrière, *Talma*, 110.

112. Joseph-Alexandre de Ségur, *Le Parti le plus Sage. Proverbe en vers* (London/Paris: Desenne), 1787.

113. *Correspondance littéraire, philosophique et critique par Grimm, Diderot, Raynal, Meister, etc.*, vol. XV, 174, December 1787.

114. Verses by the Marquis de Ximénès to the Vicomte de Ségur, in J.-A. de Ségur, *Poésies fugitives, Oeuvres diverses*, 335.

115. *Response of the Vicomte de Ségur*, 336–37.

116. See *Mémoires de M. le baron de Besenval*, 325.

117. *Correspondance secrète inédite sur Louis XVI, Marie Antoinette, la Cour et la Ville*, vol. II, 144, May 23, 1787.

118. Pierre-Ambroise-François Choderlos de Laclos, *Les Liaisons dangereuses*, second part, letter LXXI.

119. See Émile Dard, *Un acteur caché du drame révolutionnaire. Le général Choderlos de Laclos, auteur des "Liaisons Dangereuses" (1741–1803)* (Paris: Perrin, 1905), 29.

120. *Mémoires ou Souvenirs et Anecdotes par M. le Comte de Ségur*, vol. I, 362.

121. *Mémoires du Comte Alexandre de Tilly*, 244.

122. First requested by Louis XVI and the *cabinet du conseil* and issued by the Maréchal de Ségur on May 22, 1781, this ordinance required proof of nobility for at least four generations for any appointment to the higher military ranks. Violently criticized, the measure was meant to make allowance for the financial difficulties of the impoverished nobility, who, barred from practicing the more lucrative professions, had a military career as their sole resource. See Pierre de Ségur, *Le Maréchal de Ségur*, 256ff.

123. *Mémoires du Prince de Talleyrand*, vol. I, 148.

124. Appointed as the governess to Mademoiselle d'Orléans in 1777, Mme de Genlis was

also charged in 1784 with the education of three young princes known at the time as the Ducs de Chartres, Montpensier, and Beaujolais.

125. *Louis-Philippe duc d'Orléans, Mémoires 1773–1793*, 2 vol. (Paris: Plon, 1973), vol. I, 18.

126. É. Dard, *Un acteur caché du drame révolutionnaire. Le général Choderlos de Laclos*, 145.

127. *Les Prisons en 1793, par Mme la Comtesse de Bohm, née de Girardin* (Paris: Bobée et Hingray, 1830), 188, quoted in G. de Broglie, *Ségur sans cérémonie*, 113–14.

128. Quoted in Émile Dard, *Un acteur caché du drame révolutionnaire. Le général Choderlos de Laclos*, 165.

129. *Correspondance littéraire, philosophique et critique par Grimm, Diderot, Raynal, Meister, etc.*, vol. XV (January 1789): 382–83. See also J.-A. de Ségur, *Morceaux de littérature*, 117–18.

130. See *Correspondance secrète inédite sur Louis XVI, Marie-Antoinette, la Cour et la Ville*, vol. I, 444, October 24, 1781.

131. "The Revolution, the National Assembly, the constitution, the Jacobins, the different parties—for the past two years all of this has been a continual source of good or bad jokes with which he amuses his readership daily in the paper for which he serves as one of the principal collaborators, until such time as it pleases the sans-culottes to make him change his tone." See *Journal d'émigration du Comte d'Espinchal* (February 1792): 312.

THE DUC DE BRISSAC

1. Letter from Brissac to Mme du Barry, August 11, 1792, Orléans, six o'clock, quoted in Charles Vatel, *Histoire de Madame du Barry d'après ses papiers personnels et les documents des archives publiques: précédée d'une introduction sur Madame de Pompadour, le Parc-aux-cerfs et Mademoiselle de Romans*, 3 vol. (Versailles: L. Bernard, 1883), vol. III, 168–69.

2. Erected between 1645 and 1647 by Jacques le Coigneux, *président à mortier* of the Parliament of Paris, the grand mansion—which today houses the *mairie* of the VII arrondissement—at number 116 rue de Grenelle had been purchased in 1710 by the Maréchal de Villars, who installed a celebrated gallery, twenty-four meters long, six meters wide, and eight meters high, with five enormous windows on each side. Finding this structure ideal for his collections of art, the Duc de Cossé bought the house in 1772 and sumptuously furnished it. Moreover, the building possessed a magnificent garden stocked with rare plants. Requisitioned in the wake of Brissac's death, it became the seat of the Ministry of the Interior under the Revolution (see C. L.-L. and M. Th. de T. de L., *Le Faubourg Saint-Germain: La rue de Grenelle*, catalog of the exposition organized by the Délégation à l'action artistique and la Société d'histoire et d'archéologie du VIIe arrondissement, Galerie de la SEITA, November 21–December 20, 1980, 10–13).

3. Luc-Vincent Thiéry, *Guide des Amateurs et des Étrangers voyageurs à Paris. Description raisonnée de cette Ville, de sa Banlieue, et de tout ce qu'elles contiennent de remarquable: par M. Thiéry; Enrichie de Vues perspectives des principaux Monuments modernes*, 2 vol. (Paris: Hardouin et Gattey, 1787), vol. II, 561.

4. The Officer of the Crown who had jurisdiction over the Royal Bakery and who, along with the royal cupbearer, served the sovereign at table during ceremonial meals.

5   *Conseiller en exercice au parlement*; see Émile Littré, *Dictionnaire de la langue française*: "Conseiller-né se disait d'une qualité attribuée à certaines dignités qui donnait à celui qui la possédait entrée au parlement."

6. *Guide des Amateurs et des Étrangers voyageurs à Paris*, vol. II, 561.

7. *Mémoires secrets pour servir à l'histoire de la République des lettres en France*, edition produced under the direction of Christophe Cave and Suzanne Cornaud, 5 vol. (Paris: Honoré Champion, 2009), vol. V, March 4, 1775, 747. Among the sumptuous feasts given by the Duc and the Duchesse, the reception in honor of Gustav III was memorable for the hundred thousand candles that illuminated the garden: "The Prince declared that, apart from that given by the Queen at Trianon, he had never seen anything so beautiful"; *Le Faubourg Saint-Germain. La Rue de Grenelle*, 12.

8. Quoted in de Cossé-Brissac, *Histoire des ducs de Brissac*, 275.

9. Ibid., 309.

10. Marquis Marc de Bombelles, August 17, 1783, *Journal publié sous les auspices de son arrière-petit-fils Georges, Comte Clam Martinic*, text established, presented, and annotated by Jean Grassion and Frans Durif, 8 vol. (Genève: Droz, 1977–2013), vol. I: 1780–1784, 252.

11. *La Fin du XVIIIe siècle. Le Duc de Nivernais 1754–1798 par Lucien Perey* (Paris: Calmann-Lévy, 1891), 19.

12. É. Vigée Le Brun, *Souvenirs*, 137.

13. Letter from the Maréchal de Brissac to the Duc de Nivernais, Brissac, October 1, 1762, in *Oeuvres posthumes du Duc de Nivernais*, published in the wake of his eulogy, by N. François (de Neufchâteau), 2 vol. (Paris: Chez Maradan Libraire, 1808), vol. II, 52–53.

14. *Mémoires ou Souvenirs et Anecdotes par M. le Comte de Ségur*, vol. I, 60–61.

15. In his *Lettres sur l'usage de l'esprit dans la société, la solitude et les affaires*, the Duc de Nivernais has left a number of highly interesting reflections on the importance of conversation as a social bond, and on the rules to follow when conversing; in *Mélanges de littérature, en vers et en prose*, 2 tomes, in *Oeuvres du Duc de Nivernais*, 8 vol. (Paris: Didot Jeune, 1796), vol. III, tome 1, 3–91.

16. Letter from Mercy-Argenteau to Maria Theresa, December 18, 1774, in *Correspondance secrète entre Marie-Thérèse et le Comte de Mercy-Argenteau*, vol. I, 228, and vol. II, 275.

17. Letter from Horace Walpole to Mary Berry, May 19, 1791, in *Horace Walpole's Correspondence with Mary and Agnes Berry and Barbara Cecilie Seton*, critical edition by W. S.

Lewis and A. Dayle Wallace, 2 vol. (New Haven, CT: Yale University Press, 1948, 1970), vol. I, 268 (vol. II of the Yale edition of *Horace Walpole's Correspondence*).

18. Letter from Horace Walpole to Thomas Gray, in *Horace Walpole's Correspondence with Thomas Gray, Richard West and Thomas Ashton*, critical edition by W. S. Lewis, George L. Lam, and Charles H. Bennet, 2 vol. (New Haven, CT: Yale University Press, 1948) (vol. 13–14 of the Yale edition of *Horace Walpole's Correspondence*, critical edition by S. W. Lewis), vol. II, 154. Italics in original.

19. Louis de Loménie, *La Comtesse de Rochefort et ses amis. Études sur les moeurs en France au XVIIIe siècle avec des documents inédits par Louis de Loménie* (Paris: Calmann-Lévy, 1870, 1879), 146.

20. Siméon-Prosper Hardy, *Mes loisirs*, quoted in Charles Vatel, *Histoire de Madame du Barry*, vol. III, 39.

21. See the authenticated copy of September 19, 1811, of the testament of Louis-Hercu-le-Timoléon de Cossé-Brissac, Archives départementales de Maine-et-Loire, Fonds de Brissac, 188 J 121, 5. See also de Cossé-Brissac, *Histoire des ducs de Brissac*, 319–20.

22. Mme du Deffand to Horace Walpole, September 25, 1771, *Horace Walpole's Correspondence with Madame du Deffand*, vol. III, 106–7.

23. Letter from Mercy-Argenteau to Maria Theresa, October 15, 1771, in *Correspondance secrète entre Marie-Thèrese et le Comte de Mercy-Argenteau*, vol. I, 228–29.

24. Letter from Mercy-Argenteau to Maria Theresa, November 14, 1772, ibid., 371–72.

25. Letter from Mercy-Argenteau to Maria Theresa, December 18, 1774, *Correspondance secrète entre Marie-Thérèse et le Comte de Mercy-Argenteau*, vol. II, 275.

26. Letter from Mercy-Argenteau to Maria Theresa, April 20, 1775, ibid., 320.

27. Letter from Mercy-Argenteau to Maria Theresa, July 17, 1775, ibid., 354.

28. Ibid.

29. See Duc de Nivernais, *Essai sur l'État de Courtisan*, in *Mélanges de littérature, en vers et en prose*, vol. I, 127–77.

30. See the letter from Mme de Sabran to the Chevalier de Boufflers of February 7, 1786, in which the Comtesse describes a dinner for sixty guests given by Mme de Brissac, in *Comtesse de Sabran and the Chevalier de Boufflers, La Promesse*, 28.

31. See de Cossé-Brissac, *Histoire des ducs de Brissac*, 299.

32. Letter from Marie-Antoinette to Maria Theresa, May 14, 1774, *Correspondance secrète entre Marie-Thérèse et le Comte de Mercy-Argenteau*, vol. II, 139.

33. On the du Barry "style" or "taste," see *Madame du Barry. De Versailles à Louveciennes*, under the direction of Marie-Amynthe Denis (Paris: Flammarion, 1992).

34. *The Diary of Gouverneur Morris*, May 14, 1789, 58.

35. P. de Cossé-Brissac, *Histoire des ducs de Brissac*, 299.

36. *Mémoires secrets de 1770 à 1830 par le Comte d'Allonville*, vol. I, 153–54.

37. See Charles Vatel, *Histoire de Madame du Barry*, vol. III, 43–44.

38. *Journal inédit du Duc de Croÿ (1718–1784), publié d'après le manuscrit autographe conservé à la bibliothèque de l'Institut avec introduction, notes et index par le Vte de Grouchy et Paul Cottin*, 4 vol. (Paris: Flammarion, 1906), vol. IV, 116ff.

39. Jean-Nicolas Dufort, *Mémoires sur les règnes de Louis XV et Louis XVI et sur la Révolution*, vol. II, 22–24.

40. *Journal d'émigration du Comte d'Espinchal*, August 1790, 146–51.

41. *Souvenirs d'un chevau-léger de la garde du Roi par Louis-René de Belleval, Marquis de Bois-Robin…*, published by René de Belleval (Paris: Aug. Aubry, 1866), 129–35.

42. *Mémoires du Prince de Talleyrand*, vol. V, 584–85.

43. *Journal de Mathieu Marais*, September 27, 1765, quoted in Jacques de Saint-Victor, *Mme du Barry. Un nom de scandale* (Paris: Perrin, 2002), 69.

44. Pierre-Ambroise-François Choderlos de Laclos, "Elmire," in *Galerie des dames françaises*, in *Oeuvres complètes*, 752.

45. *Journal inédit du Duc de Croÿ*, vol. IV, 116.

46. É. Vigée Le Brun, *Souvenirs*, 235.

47. P.-A.-F. Choderlos de Laclos, "Épître à Margot," in *Pièces fugitives*, in *Oeuvres complètes*, 544–46.

48. *Galerie des dames françaises*, 753.

49. See É. Vigée Le Brun, *Souvenirs*, 236–37.

50. Joan Haslip, *Madame du Barry* (London: Weidenfeld & Nicolson, 1991), 119.

51. Letter from Horace Walpole to Henry Seymour Conway, August 20, 1782, in *Horace Walpole's Correspondence with Henry Seymour Conway, Lady Ailesbury, Lord and Lady Hertford, Mrs Harris*, critical edition by W. S. Lewis, Lars E. Troide, Edwin M. Martz et al., 3 vol. (New Haven, CT: Yale University Press, 1974), vol. 3, 390 (Yale edition of *Horace Walpole's Correspondence*, vol. 37–39).

52. Quoted in M. Gallet, "Madame du Barry et Ledoux, histoire d'une amitié," in *Madame du Barry. De Versailles à Louveciennes*, 22.

53. Jean-Paul Palewski, "Voisins de campagne: Henry Seymour et Mme du Barry," in *Revue d'histoire de Versailles*, XXXIX (1937): 159–69.

54. Ibid., 165.

55. Ibid.

56. Ibid., 166.

57. Ibid., 167.

58. See Joan Haslip, *Madame du Barry*, 125.

59. Adélaïde-Pauline-Rosalie de Cossé-Brissac married the Duc de Mortemart in December 1782.

60. Comtesse de Sabran and the Chevalier de Boufflers, *La Promesse*, 416–17.

61. Chrétien de Troyes, *Lancelot ou le Chevalier à la triste charrette*.

62. See M.-C. Sahut, "Le goût de madame du Barry pour la peinture," in *Madame du Barry. De Versailles à Louveciennes*, 106.

63. Ibid.

64. *Dictionnaire de Furetière*, quoted in Patrick Michel, *Peinture et plaisir. Les goûts picturaux des collectionneurs parisiens au XVIIIe siècle* (Rennes: Presses universitaires de Rennes, 2010), 26n2.

65. See Patrick Michel, *Peinture et plaisir*, 29–34.

66. Francis Haskell, *Rediscoveries in Art: Some Aspects of Taste, Fashion and Collecting in England and France* (Ithaca, NY: Cornell University Press, 1976), 18.

67. Thirty-one out of the sixty-one inventoried.

68. See Le Brun's Inventory.

69. C. B. Bailey, "Henri-Pierre Danloux, *The Baron de Besenval in his 'Salon de compagnie,'*" in *An Aspect of Collecting Taste* (New York: Stair Sainty Matthiesen, 1986), 5.

70. In addition to paintings, Le Brun also earmarked for the museum numerous pieces seized from these diverse collections.

71. The four panels by Fragonard declined by Mme du Barry are today preserved in the Frick Collection in New York.

72. Dezallier d'Argenville, quoted in Thomas Gaehtgens and Jacques Lugand, *Joseph-Marie Vien 1716–1809* (Paris: Arthena, 1988), 188.

73. Ibid., 172.

74. Letter from the Duc de Brissac to J.-M. Vien, February 15, 1778, quoted in Charles Vatel, *Histoire de Madame du Barry*, vol. III, 96–97.

75. See L.-V. Thiéry, *Guide des Amateurs et des Étrangers voyageurs à Paris*, vol. II, 572.

76. Letter from the Duc de Brissac to Mme du Barry, in J.-A. Le Roy, *Madame du Barry, 1768–1793*, "Mémoires de la Société des Sciences Morales, des Lettres et des Arts de Seine et Oise," Versailles, 1859, tome V, 87.

77. See Thomas Gaehtgens and Jacques Lugand, *Joseph-Marie Vien*, 207. The *Marchande d'amours* is now held by the Château de Fontainebleau, *L'Amour fuyant l'esclavage* by the Musée des Augustins in Toulouse.

78. Ibid., 88.

79. Ibid., 87–88.

80. See É. Vigée Le Brun, "Liste des Tableaux et Portraits," in *Souvenirs*, 329–42.

81. Ibid., 400.

82. *Journal d'émigration du Comte d'Espinchal*, January 28, 1790, 89.

83. See Geneviève Haroche-Bouzinac, *Louise-Élisabeth Vigée Le Brun, histoire d'un regard* (Paris: Flammarion, 2011), 226–30.

84. É. Vigée Le Brun, *Souvenirs*, 402.

85. See Charles Vatel, *Histoire de Madame du Barry*, vol. III, 80–81.

86. É. Vigée Le Brun, *Souvenirs*, 400.

87. Ibid.

88. See the chapter devoted to Lauzun.

89. É. Vigée Le Brun, *Souvenirs*, 403.

90. See *Mémoires secrets de 1770 à 1830 par le Comte d'Allonville*, vol. I, 154.

91. *Catalogue Des Livres de la Bibliothèque de Monseigneur le Duc de Brissac, mai 1789*, Bibliothèque nationale de France, département des manuscrits, NAF-317. The catalog provided space for 972 titles, but only around 700 are actually listed there.

92. Numbers 603 and 568 of the catalog, respectively.

93. See Charles Vatel, *Histoire de Madame du Barry*, vol. III, 114.

94. Jacques-Pierre Brissot, *Mémoires (1754–1793)*, published with a critical study and notes by Claude Perroud, Paris: Picard, s. d., 2 vol., vol. I, 146–53.

95. Ibid., 148.

96. Archives nationales, liasse W/16 Vaubernier Dubarry Vendenquer D: 9. Title on file folder: "Letters de Brissac avant et depuis la Révolution peu importantes si ce n'est qu'elles prouvent ses liaisons intimes avec elle, ainsi que sa façon de penser sur la Révolution. Il est à remarquer qu'elle a employé toute une nuit à brûler sa correspondance avec lui le jour de sa mort à Versailles." [Letters by Brissac before and after the Revolution, of little importance but for the fact that they establish his intimate relations with [Mme du Barry], and her thoughts and opinions regarding the Revolution. It is notable that she spent a whole night burning her correspondence with him the day of his death at Versailles.]

97. Letter from the Duc de Brissac to Mme du Barry, La Flèche, August 26, 1786, two o'clock in the morning.

98. Letter from the Duc de Brissac to Mme du Barry, s.l., s.d.

99. Letter from the Duc de Brissac to Mme du Barry, Vendosme, August 16, 1787.

100. Desired as far back as Turgot and the Physiocrats, and proposed to the Assembly of Notables, the regional assemblies were instituted in August 1787 by Loménie de Brienne. The regulations dictated that half of the members of the assembly, comprising delegates of the three orders, would be nominated by the King and the other half would be elected.

101. See Charles Vatel, *Histoire de Madame du Barry*, vol. III, 90–92.

102. Letter from the Duc de Brissac to Mme du Barry, August 25, 1789.

103. Letter from the Duc de Brissac to Mme du Barry, Angers, August 29, 1789, noon.

104. Hippolyte Taine, *L'Ancien Régime. La Révolution: L'Anarchie–La Conquête jacobine*, in *Les Origines de La France contemporaine* (Paris: R. Laffont, 1986), 2 vol., vol. I, 128.

THE COMTE DE NARBONNE

1. *Mémoires complets et authentiques de Laure Junot Duchesse d'Abrantès. Souvenirs historiques sur Napoléon, la Révolution, le Directoire, le Consulat, l'Empire, la Restauration, la Révolution de 1830 et les premières années du règne de Louis-Philippe*, first complete edition, 13 vol. (Paris: Jean de Bonnot, 1967–1968), vol. VII, 192.

2. *Souvenirs contemporains d'histoire et de littérature par M. Villemain, membre de l'Institut. M. de Narbonne*, 2 vol. (Paris: Didier, 1854–1855), vol. I, 1.

3. The latter has been painstakingly reconstructed in the excellent biography by Émile Dard, *Un confident de l'Empereur, Le Comte Louis de Narbonne, 1755–1813* (Paris: Plon, 1943), which I have consulted extensively.

4. *Journal d'émigration du Comte d'Espinchal*, 325.

5. É. Dard, *Un confident de l'Empereur*, 31–32.

6. It is the hypothesis held to by Jean-Denis Bredin in *Une singulière famille. Jacques, Suzanne et Germaine de Staël* (Paris: Fayard, 1999), 234.

7. *Récits d'une tante. Mémoires de la Comtesse de Boigne*, vol. I, 58.

8. Victorine de Chastenay, *Deux révolutions pour une seule vie, Mémoires, 1771–1855*, edited and with notes by Raymond Trousson (Paris: Tallandier, 2009), 141.

9. See É. Dard, *Un confident de l'Empereur*, 36–37. For scandalmongering during the build-up to the revolution, see Robert Darnton, *The Forbidden Best-Sellers of Pre-Revolutionary France*, (New York: Norton, 1998).

10. "We do not descend from kings, but the kings descend from us."

11. See *Récits d'une tante. Mémoires de la Comtesse de Boigne*, vol. I, 57–60.

12. É. Dard, *Un confident de l'Empereur*, 45.

13. Ibid.

14. Ch.-J. de Ligne, *Fragments de l'histoire de ma vie*, 421.

15. *Récits d'une tante. Mémoires de la Comtesse de Boigne*, vol. I, 58.

16. Giacomo Casanova, *Storia della mia vita*, introduction by Pietro Chiara, critical edition by Pietro Chiara and Federico Roncoroni, 3 vol. (Milan, Mondadori, 1983), vol. I, 766.

17. See Michel Antoine, *Louis XV* (Paris: Fayard, 1989), 508, 842.

18. "Comte Louis was the first to laugh at this; for in those days, any peculiarity, any vice, any dirty trick, as long as it was openly avowed and accepted according to the presiding standards of wit, would be assured of finding indulgence," *Récits d'une tante. Mémoires de la Comtesse de Boigne*, vol. I, 59.

19. M. de Bombelles, *Journal*, vol. I, 188.

20. Letter from Mercy-Argenteau to Maria Theresa, September 19, 1770, in *Correspondance secrète entre Marie-Thérèse et le Comte de Mercy-Argenteau*, vol. I, 56.

21. Letter from Mercy-Argenteau to Maria Theresa, June 28, 1774, ibid., vol. II, 186.

22. *Diary of Gouverneur Morris*, May 4, 1789, 51.

23. Antoine-Vincent Arnault, *Souvenirs d'un sexagénaire*, critical edition by Raymond Trousson (Paris: Honoré Champion, 2003), 194–95.

24. É. Vigée Le Brun, *Souvenirs*, 219.

25. É. Dard, *Un confident de l'Empereur*, 51.

26. *Correspondance secrète de Louis XVI, Marie Antoinette et la cour et la ville*, September 1, 1780, 306.

27. *Mémoires du Duc de Lauzun*, 115–18.

28. *Mémoires du Prince de Talleyrand*, vol. I, 67.

29. Marie-Antoinette's description.

30. *Mémoires du Prince de Talleyrand*, vol. I, 33.

31. Ibid., 37.

32. Quoted in A.-F. Villemain, *M. de Narbonne*, vol. I, 15. Turgot died in 1781.

33. *Mémoires du Prince de Talleyrand*, vol. I, 59.

34. Ibid., 48.

35. See the letter from Mme de Staël to Clermont-Tonnerre, toward 1789: "I have greatly loved and still tenderly love Comte Louis"; quoted in Georges Solovieff, "Introduction" to Mme de Staël, *Lettres à Narbonne*, preface by the Comtesse Jean de Pange, introduction, notes, and commentary by Georges Solovieff (Paris: Gallimard, 1960), 14.

THE CHEVALIER DE BOUFFLERS

1. Ch.-J. de Ligne, "Portrait de M. de Boufflers," in *Caractères et portraits*, 244.

2. Letter from the Chevalier de Boufflers to the Marquise de Boufflers, toward 1762, quoted in Gaston Maugras, *La Marquise de Boufflers et son fils, le chevalier de Boufflers* (Paris: Plon, Nourrit et Cie, 1907), 85.

3. Quoted in Gaston Maugras, *La Cour de Lunéville au XVIIIe siècle. Les Marquises de Boufflers et du Châtelet, Voltaire, Devau, Saint-Lambert, etc.* (Paris: Plon, Nourrit et Cie, 16th edition 1925), 229.

4. The accords laid out between France and Austria at the end of the War of Succession (1733–1738) anticipated the renunciation of the Polish throne by Stanislas Leszczyński, who was supported by the father-in-law of Louis XV, in favor of Augustus of Saxony, the Austrian candidate, in exchange for the Duchies of Lorraine and Bar—territories which, at the death of Stanislas, would pass under the jurisdiction of France. For their part, the Lorraines obtained the Grand Duchy of Tuscany in compensation.

5. Gaston Maugras, *La Cour de Lunéville au XVIIIe siècle*, 232.

6. Saint-Simon, *Mémoires*, vol. III, 320.

7. Among the many wonders of the château's park, designed by Richard Mique (who would later become the favorite architect of Marie-Antoinette) was a kiosk that rotated to the sound of music, and on a large rock a model of a village inhabited by men and women busily going about their daily affairs.

8. Along with Jean-François de Saint-Lambert, there were Mme de Graffigny and her young protégé, François-Antoine Devaux, also known as Panpan. Receveur particulier des finances [Official Receiver of Finances] for Lorraine and reader for King Stanislas beginning in 1751, Panpan had also become the "tender calf," the "private animal" of the Marquise de Boufflers. See G. Maugras, *La Cour de Lunéville au XVIIIe siècle*, 73ff.

9. *Réponse de M. de Saint-Lambert, Directeur de l'Académie, au Discours de M. le Chevalier de Boufflers. Discours prononcé dans l'Académie française, le mardi 9 December 1788, à la réception de Monsieur de Boufflers* (Paris: Demonville, 1789), 28.

10. Voltaire to René de Voyer de Paulmy, Marquis d'Argenson, Lunéville, September 4 [1749], in Voltaire, *Correspondence and Related Documents*, in *Oeuvres complètes*, vol. XI, 151.

11. S.-R. N. de Chamfort, *Maximes et pensées* no. 938, 263.

12. Quoted in Gaston Maugras, *La Marquise de Boufflers et son fils le chevalier de Boufflers*, 355.

13. "Portrait de Madame de Boufflers," in *Oeuvres posthumes du chevalier de Boufflers* (Paris: Louis, 1816), 195.

14. Quoted in G. Maugras, *La Cour de Lunéville au XVIIIe siècle*, 180–81; see also "Portrait de Madame de Boufflers," in *Oeuvres posthumes du chevalier de Boufflers*, 200.

15. *Correspondance secrète, politique et littéraire ou Mémoires pour servir à l'histoire des cours, des sociétés et de la littérature en France depuis la mort de Louis XV*, 18 vol. (London: John Adamson, 1787–1790), vol. IV, 277–78, quoted in Gustave Desnoiresterres, *Voltaire et la société française au XVIIe siècle*, 8 vol. (Paris: Didier et Cie, 1867–1876), vol. III: *Voltaire à la cour*, 135. The episode of the rigged dice at the Queen's table is cited in *Correspondance secrète inédite sur Louis XVI, Marie-Antoinette, la Cour et la Ville*, vol. I, 330–31, November 1780.

16. Louis-Sébastien Mercier, *Tableau de Paris, édition établie sous la direction de Jean-Claude Bonnet*, 2 vol. (Paris: Mercure de France, 1994), vol. I, 857.

17. Letter from Mme du Deffand to Horace Walpole, March 7, 1770, in *Horace Walpole's Correspondence with Madame du Deffand*, vol. II, 381.

18. Stanislas I, *Oeuvres du philosophe bienfaisant*, 4 vol. (Paris: [s.n.], 1763).

19. Published in 1757, in volume VII of the *Encyclopédie*.

20. "*The Queen of Golconde* is by the Abbé de Boufflers. This tale, which I think you will find quite pretty, seems to show that M. l'Abbé de Boufflers has more of a vocation for the *métier* of wit than for that of the prelate," *Correspondance littéraire, philosophique, critique par Grimm, Diderot, Raynal, Meister, etc.*, vol. IV, July 15, 1761, 443. See Friedrich Melchior Grimm, *Correspondance littéraire*, critical edition by Ulla Kölving, in collaboration with Marie Burkdahl and Mélinda Caron, Ferney-Voltaire, Centre international d'études du XVIIIe siècle, 2006–2013, still in course of publication, volume VIII, 222–31. Ulla Kölving and Jeanne Carriat note that Boufflers's tale appeared not only in the issue of July 15, 1761, but once again in that of May 1, 1766, on the occasion of the opera adaptation of the *Queen of Golconde* by Sedaine and Monsigny; Ulla Kölving and Jeanne Carriat, "Inventaire de la Correspondance littéraire de Grimm et Meister," in *Studies on Voltaire and the Eighteenth Century*, 3 vol. (Oxford: The Voltaire Foundation-University of Oxford, 1984), vol. I, 97.

21. *La Correspondance littéraire, philosophique et critique par Grimm, Diderot, Raynal, Meister, etc.*, denounces "the flatness and insipidity" of that censured version, vol. IV, 471, September 1761.

22. See *Aline, Reine de Golconde. Nouvelle*, in *Oeuvres complètes de Boufflers*, vol. I, 22.

23. See *Mémoires secrets pour servir à l'histoire de la République des lettres en France*, quoted in Octave Uzanne, "Notice sur la vie et les Oeuvres de Boufflers," in *Contes du chevalier de Boufflers* (Paris: A. Quantin, 1878), xvi–vii.

24. Letter from Voltaire to the Lorraine poet François-Étienne Devaux, October 26 [1761], in Voltaire, *Correspondence and Related Documents*, vol. XXIV, in *Oeuvres complètes*, vol. CVIII, 66.

25. *Correspondance littéraire, philosophique et critique par Grimm, Diderot, Raynal, Meister, etc.*, vol. VI, 193–98, February 15, 1765.

26. Letter from M. l'Abbé de Boufflers to M. l'Abbé Porquet, written at the beginning of 1762, ibid., 193.

27. Ibid.

28. Quoted in Gaston Maugras, *Dernières années de la cour de Lunéville* (Paris: Plon, Nourrit et Cie, 1925), 311–12.

29. "Chansons, rondes et couplets," in *Oeuvres complètes de Boufflers*, vol. I, 221.

30. See Letter from the Chevalier de Boufflers to his mother, quoted in G. Maugras, *La Marquise de Boufflers et son fils*, 84.

31. Letter from Catherine of Russia to Voltaire [May 23/June 4, 1771], in Voltaire, *Correspondence and Related Documents*, in *Oeuvres complètes*, vol. XXXVII, 420.

32. Quoted in G. Maugras, *La Marquise de Boufflers et son fils*, 141.

33. Letter from Mme de Lenoncourt, quoted in ibid., 134.

34. Letter from Catherine of Russia to Voltaire, March 30 [April 10] 1772, in Voltaire, *Correspondence and Related Documents*, in *Oeuvres complètes*, vol. XXXVIII, 334.

35. Letter from the Chevalier de Boufflers to the Duc de Beauvau, May 14, 1771, quoted in G. Maugras, *La Marquise de Boufflers et son fils*, 145.

36. *Discours de M. le Comte de Ségur aux Funérailles de M. le Marquis de Boufflers, le 23 January 1815* (Institut royal de France [s.l., s.n., s.d.]), 2.

37. Letter from Mme de Sabran to the Chevalier de Boufflers, 26 [1782?], in Comtesse de Sabran et chevalier de Boufflers, *Le Lit bleu, Correspondance, 1777–1785*, edited by Sue Carrell (Paris: Tallandier, 2009), 228.

38. Ch.-J. de Ligne, "Fleuros" and "Portrait de M. de B.," in *Caractères et portraits*, 229–31, 244–46.

39. *Ibid.*, 229-230.

40. Ibid., 229.

41. Letter from the Chevalier de Boufflers to Mme de Sabran, June 1780, La Comtesse de Sabran et le chevalier de Boufflers, *Le Lit bleu*, 166.

42. Ibid.

43. See *Oeuvres complètes de Boufflers*, vol. I, 44.

44. J.-P.-J.-A. de Labouïsse-Rochefort, *Souvenirs et Mélanges*, vol. II, 127.

45. Letter from the Chevalier de Boufflers to Mme de Sabran, (Nancy, April or May 1779), in *Le Lit bleu*, 105.

46. Ibid.

47. See Nicole Vaget Grangeat, *Le Chevalier de Boufflers et son temps. Étude d'un échec* (Paris: Nizet, 1976), 93.

48. Letter from the Chevalier de Boufflers to the Duchesse de Choiseul, February 8, 1768, in *Oeuvres complètes de Boufflers*, vol. I, 326. See also the letter from the Chevalier de Boufflers to the Duchesse de Choiseul, January 26, 1768, in *Correspondance complète de Mme du Deffand avec la Duchesse de Choiseul, l'abbé Barthélemy et M. Craufurt*, vol. I, 151–52.

49. Jean-Nicolas Dufort, *Mémoires sur les règnes de Louis XV et Louis XVI et sur la Révolution*, vol. I, 522–23.

50. Quoted in Gaston Maugras, *La Marquise de Boufflers et son fils*, 34.

51. See "De la maréchale de L***, petite-fille du maréchal de V***," in *Mémoires de M. le baron de Besenval*, vol. I, 202–21.

52. "Portrait de Madame la Duchesse de Boufflers depuis Mme de Luxembourg, par Madame la Marquise du Deffand," "Portraits de Madame du Deffand," in *Horace Walpole's Correspondence with Madame du Deffand and Wiart* (vol. VIII of *Horace Walpole's Correspondence*), vol. VI, 83.

53. *Souvenirs-portraits de Gaston de Lévis (1764–1830), suivis de Lettres intimes de Monsieur, Comte de Provence, au Duc de Lévis*, introduction and notes by Jacques Dupâquier (Paris: Mercure de France, 1993), 101.

54. Charles-Augustin Sainte-Beuve, *La Comtesse de Boufflers*, in *Nouveaux lundis*, 13 vol. (Paris: Michel Lévy Frères, 1865), vol. IV, 178–79.

55. A celebrated victory by the French under Guillame d'Orange in the war against the Grand Alliance (1692), to which the Maréchal de Boufflers contributed in a decisive fashion.

56. Letter from Mme du Deffand to the Duchesse de Choiseul, July 5, 1766, in *Correspondance croisée avec la Duchesse de Choiseul et l'abbé Barthélemy*, vol. I, 59.

57. Letter from Mme du Deffand to Mme de Choiseul, April 6, 1773, ibid., vol. II, 699.

58. Letter from Mme du Deffand to Horace Walpole, November 19, 1775, in *Horace Walpole's Correspondence with Madame du Deffand and Wiart*, vol. IV, 237 (volume VI of *Horace Walpole's Correspondence*).

59. Letter from Mme de Choiseul to Mme du Deffand, April 13, 1773, ibid., vol. II, 701.

60. *Correspondance littéraire, philosophique et critique par Grimm, Diderot, Raynal, Meister, etc.*, vol. VI, 192–93, February 1765.

61. *Voyage en Suisse. Lettres à sa mère*, in *Oeuvres complètes de Boufflers*, vol. I, 272.

62. Letter from Voltaire to Marie-Françoise-Catherine de Beauvau-Craon, Marquise de Boufflers-Remiencourt, Ferney, December 15, 1764, in Voltaire, *Correspondence and Related Documents*, in *Oeuvres complètes*, vol. XXVIII, 247.

63. Voltaire to Louis-François-Armand du Plessis, Duc de Richelieu, Ferney, January 21, 1765, ibid., vol. XXVIII, 345.

64. "Épître de Voltaire à Boufflers, en réponse à la précédente," reported on February 20, in *Mémoires secrets pour servir à l'histoire de la République des lettres en France, depuis 1762 jusqu'à nos jours*, vol. I, 437; then in *Pièces mêlées*, in *Oeuvres complètes de Boufflers*, vol. I, 50.

65. See J.-P.-J.-A. de Labouïsse-Rochefort, *Souvenirs et Mélanges*, vol. II, 127.

66. *Correspondance littéraire, philosophique et critique par Grimm, Diderot, Raynal, Meister, etc.*, vol. VIII, 411, December 15, 1769.

67. *Correspondance secrète inédite sur Louis XVI, Marie-Antoinette, la Cour et la Ville*, vol. I, 422, August 14, 1781.

68. Letter from Diderot to Sophie Volland, February 3, 1766, in D. Diderot, *Lettres à Sophie Volland*, vol. III, 33–36.

69. *Correspondance littéraire, philosophique et critique par Grimm, Diderot, Raynal, Meister, etc.*, vol. X, 471–72, August 1774.

70. "Histoire de Loth," in *Pièces mêlées*, in *Oeuvres complètes de Boufflers*, vol. I, 92.

71. *Bouquet à sa mère*, ibid., 83.

72. See *Journal et mémoires de Charles Collé sur les hommes de lettres, les ouvrages dramatiques et les événements les plus mémorables du règne de Louis XV (1748–1772)*, new edition enlarged with previously unpublished fragments collected from the manuscripts in the Imperial Library of the Louvre by permission of S. E., Minister of the Household of the Emperor and of the Beaux-Arts, introduction and notes by Honoré Bonhomme, 3 vol. (Paris: Firmin Didot, 1868; Genève, Slatkine Reprints, 1967), vol. II, 304.

73. *Mémoires secrets pour servir à l'histoire de la République des lettres en France depuis 1762 jusqu'à nos jours*, April 28, 1771, vol. III, 1505.

74. Versailles, August 22, 1784, in *Correspondance secrète, politique et littéraire*, vol. XVI, 395–96.

75. See the letter from Mme du Deffand to Horace Walpole, October 23, 1769, in *Horace Walpole's Correspondence with Madame du Deffand*, vol. II, 288.

76. *Voyage en Suisse. Lettres à sa mère*, in *Oeuvres complètes de Boufflers*, vol. I, 267.

77. Ibid., 260–61.

78. Ibid., 268.

79. See the letter from Mme du Deffand to Horace Walpole, September 23, 1771, in *Horace Walpole's Correspondence*, vol. III, 108.

80. Horace Walpole, *Paris Journals*, March 1766, in *Horace Walpole's Correspondence with Madame du Deffand*, vol. V, 307. See Chevalier de Boufflers, *Voyage en Suisse. Lettres à sa Mère*, 266.

81. "Épître du Chevalier de Bonnard à Boufflers," in *Pièces mêlées*, in *Oeuvres complètes de Boufflers*, vol. I, 59.

82. Jean-Jacques Rousseau, *Confessions*, in *Oeuvres complètes*, under the direction of Bernard Gagnerin and Marcel Raymond (Paris: Gallimard), vol. I, 552.

83. Ibid.

84. It was located between the Hôtel de Charost (which today hosts the British Embassy), the Hôtel d'Aguesseau, and the Hôtel d'Évreux (today home of the Élysée).

85. Letter from Mme de Sabran to the Chevalier de Boufflers, July 31, 1787, in *La Promesse*, 438.

86. See Elzéar de Sabran, "Notice sur Madame la Comtesse de Sabran depuis Marquise de Boufflers," in Alex Sokalski and Susan L. Carrell, "Les souvenirs d'un fils: documents inédits sur la Comtesse de Sabran," *Studies on Voltaire and the Eighteenth Century* no. 302 (Oxford: The Voltaire Foundation-University of Oxford, 1992), 258.

87. Ch.-J. de Ligne, "Zirphé," in *Caractères et portraits*, 141–42.

88. Ibid.

89. Letter from Mme du Deffand to Horace Walpole, July 6, 1768, in *Horace Walpole's Correspondence with Madame du Deffand* (vol. IV of *Horace Walpole's Correspondence*), vol. II, 100.

90. E. de Sabran, "Notice sur Madame la Comtesse de Sabran," 258.

91. Ibid., 255.

92. Letter from Mme de Sabran to the Chevalier de Boufflers, May 8 [1778], in *Le Lit bleu*, 64.

93. Executed, according to the painter, in 1786. See É. Vigée Le Brun, "Liste des Tableaux et Portraits," in *Souvenirs*, 339.

94. "À une dame mal peignée," in *Chansons*, in *Oeuvres complètes de Boufflers*, vol. I, 167.

95. Letter from the Chevalier de Boufflers to Mme de Sabran, [July] 13 [1787], in *La Promesse*, 399.

96. See Joseph Callewaert, *La Comtesse de Sabran et le chevalier de Boufflers* (Paris: Perrin, 1990), 101.

97. *Ah! Si*...Nouvelle Allemande, in *Oeuvres complètes de Boufflers*, vol. II, 159.

98. É. Vigée Le Brun, *Souvenirs*, 272.

99. Letter from Mme de Sabran to the Chevalier de Boufflers, [June] 12 [1776], in *La Promesse*, 57.

100. Denis Diderot, *Les Salons*, Michel Van Loo, "Salon de 1767," in *Oeuvres esthétiques*, ed. Paul Vernière (Paris: Garnier, 1959), 510. See also *Ruines et paysages: Salons de 1761/ Diderot*, texts established and presented by Elsa Marie Bukdahl, Mickel Delon, and Annette Lorenceau (Paris: Hermann, 1995). See Jacqueline Lichtenstein, "Qu'est-ce que le moi? Portrait et autoportrait dans les Salons," in *Diderot, la pensée et le corps*, Cahiers de littérature française, tome XIII, directed by Gianni Iotti, December 2013, coédition Bergamo University Press Edizioni Sestante/L'Harmattan, 17–32.

101. See Simon Schama, *Citizens: A Chronicle of the French Revolution* (New York: Vintage Books, 1989), 40.

102. Dispatched by Stanislas to Christina of Saxony in 1764 to announce her nomination as coadjutrix of the Remiremont Abbey, Boufflers revenged himself for the haughty

reception given to him by that "puffed-up Princesse" with a ferocious mocking; see G. Maugras, *Dernières années de la cour de Lunéville*, 360–62.

103. Letter from Mme du Deffand to Horace Walpole, April 19, 1776, in *Horace Walpole's Correspondence with Madame du Deffand and Wiart* (vol. VI of *Horace Walpole's Correspondence*), vol. IV, 305.

104. See the letter from the Chevalier de Boufflers to Mme de Sabran, [July] 25 [1779], in *Le Lit bleu*, 125.

105. Letter from the Chevalier de Boufflers to Mme de Sabran, [Landerneau] This 28 [of April 1778], ibid., 63.

106. Letter from the Chevalier de Boufflers to Mme de Sabran, [Landerneau] July 7, 1778, ibid., 80.

107. Letter from Mme de Sabran to the Chevalier de Boufflers, February 10, 1786, in *La Promesse*, 31.

108. Letter from Mme de Sabran to the Chevalier de Boufflers, August 3, 1786, ibid., 149.

109. Letter from the Chevalier de Boufflers to Mme de Sabran, [Landerneau, April 1778], in *Le Lit bleu*, 56.

110. Ch.-J. de Ligne, "Portrait de M. de Boufflers," in *Caractères et portraits*, 245.

111. *Mémoires du Comte de Cheverny*, vol. I, 523.

112. Ch.-J. de Ligne, "Portrait de M. de Boufflers," in *Caractères et portraits*, 244–45.

113. Letter from Mme du Deffand to Horace Walpole, October 23, 1769, in *Horace Walpole's Correspondence with Madame du Deffand and Wiart* (vol. IV of *Horace Walpole's Correspondence*), vol. II, 289.

114. Ibid.

115. *Mémoires inédits de Madame la Comtesse de Genlis*, vol. II, 354.

116. E. de Sabran, "Notice sur Madame la Comtesse de Sabran depuis Marquise de Boufflers," 254.

117. Letter from the Chevalier de Boufflers to Mme de Sabran, [Boulogne-sur-Mer] in the evening [1779], in *Le Lit bleu*, 131.

118. Letter from the Chevalier de Boufflers to Mme de Sabran, [Paris?] [October] 11 [1780], ibid., 178.

119. Letter from Mme de Sabran to the Chevalier de Boufflers, [Anisy, August 1779], ibid., 135–36.

120. Letter from the Chevalier de Boufflers to Mme de Sabran, [October] 29 [1779], ibid., 178 (italics in original).

121. Letter from the Chevalier de Boufflers to Mme de Sabran, [Paris? October 1780], ibid., 180.

122. Ibid., 147–48.

123. Letter from the Chevalier de Boufflers to Mme de Sabran, [Eu, November 1779], ibid., 153.

124. Letter from the Chevalier de Boufflers to Mme de Sabran, Raismes, July 16, 1779, ibid., 122.

125. Letter from the Chevalier de Boufflers to Mme de Sabran, [Boulogne-sur-Mer], August 3 [1779], ibid., 130.

126. In a letter of April 28, 1787, Mme de Sabran declares to Boufflers that she has loved him "like a madwoman for ten years," in *La Promesse*, 305.

127. See letter from Mme de Sabran to the Chevalier de Boufflers, November 9, 1787, ibid., 534.

128. Letter from the Chevalier de Boufflers to Mme de Sabran, Au Val, près de Saint-Germain, 17 [December 1780], in *Le Lit bleu*, 189.

129. Letter from Mme de Sabran to the Chevalier de Boufflers, May 2, [1787], in *La Promesse*, 353.

130. Letter from Mme de Sabran to the Chevalier de Boufflers, May 31, 1786, ibid., 44.

131. Letter from Mme de Sabran to the Chevalier de Boufflers, Spa, August 1782, in *Le Lit bleu*, 242.

132. Letter from Mme de Sabran to the Chevalier de Boufflers, [Anisy, April 1784], ibid., 279.

133. Letter from Mme de Sabran to the Chevalier de Boufflers, Spa, [August 6, 1783], ibid., 263.

134. Letter from Mme de Sabran to the Chevalier de Boufflers, Spa, [June 14, 1782], ibid., 233.

135. Letter from Mme de Sabran to the Chevalier de Boufflers, September 1, 1781, ibid., 200.

136. Letter from Mme de Sabran to the Chevalier de Boufflers, [Aix-la-Chapelle, July 6, 1783], in *Le Lit bleu*, 254. See also the letter of 12 [May 1787], in *La Promesse*, 364, where Mme de Sabran writes to the Chevalier that she had encountered the woman in question conversing joyously with a number of officers and had felt jealous "not of her success, but of her happiness, and said to myself: She knew that poor African, she loved him, she did even more than that, and she has been able to put him out of her mind, been able to go on and love others. How is such a thing possible? I would love to know her method."

137. Letter from Mme de Sabran to the Chevalier de Boufflers, at Saint-Germain, Thursday at 8 o'clock [1782?], in *Le Lit bleu*, 230.

138. Letter from the Chevalier de Boufflers to Mme de Sabran, evening of the 27 [autumn of 1782], ibid., 245–46.

139. Letter from Mme de Sabran to the Chevalier de Boufflers, at Saint-Germain, Thursday at 8 o'clock [1782?], ibid., 230.

140. Letter from the Chevalier de Boufflers to Mme de Sabran, [Charleroi] 31 in the morning [autumn of 1783], ibid., 248.

141. Letter from the Chevalier de Boufflers to Mme de Sabran, [Raismes], August 1783, ibid., 263.

142. *Mémoires inédits de Madame la Comtesse de Genlis*, vol. II, 346–47.

143. "Pensées en prose et en vers," in *Oeuvres complètes de Boufflers,* vol. I, 121.

144. M. de Bombelles, *Journal*, Feburary 2, 1785, vol. II, 26. See *Oeuvres complètes de Boufflers*, vol. I, 112.

145. *Oeuvres complètes de Boufflers*, vol. I, 71. See *Mémoires ou Souvenirs et Anecdotes par M. le Comte de Ségur*, vol. II, 146.

146. "Couplets pour la convalescence de Madame the Marquise de Mirepoix," ibid., 149.

147. "Couplet impromptu. À Madame la Maréchale de Luxembourg, en lui donnant un exemplaire de la Bibliothèque bleue," ibid., 208.

148. "Vers à M. le Prince de B***, pour l'inviter à venir dans une campagne que sa soeur avait meublée pour le recevoir," ibid., 67.

149. "Couplets. À Madame de Cambis, cousine de l'Auteur," ibid., 204–5.

150. "Quatrain. Pour le portrait de M. le Duc de Choiseul"; "Couplets. Sur le retour de M. de Choiseul à Paris," ibid., 112, 168.

151. "Pour madame du Deffand, de la part de madame de Luxembourg qui lui avait donné pour étrennes une parure de couleur bleu," ibid., 170.

152. "Pour M. de Nivernais, en lui donnant des moutons pour parquer dans une pièce de terre de son parc," ibid., 82.

153. "Couplet, écrit sur une cocarde de papier attachée au chapeau du baron de Besenval," ibid., 217.

154. "À M. le Comte de Ségur, qui avait donné à sa femme une très jolie tasse de porcelaine, mais seule" and "Réponse de M. le Comte de Ségur," ibid., 79.

155. "In these lines where grace allies itself with art / Who could fail to recognize one of Julie's lovers? / In verse as in love I pity all his rivals: / He has spoken of the art of pleasing / As well as Sabran has of paintings, / Or Henri himself spoke of war," ibid., 80. These lines probably date to 1788, when Julie Careau left Ségur for Talma. The *Essay on the Means of Pleasing in Love* was published in Paris (by Huet) in 1797.

156. Letter from the Comte de Creutz to Gustav III, 31 [*sic*] November, 1783, *Gustave III par ses lettres*, 239–40.

157. See the letter from Mme de Sabran to the Chevalier de Boufflers, 31 [July 1786] and 11 [January 1787], in *La Promesse*, 144.

158. E. de Sabran, "Notice sur Madame la Comtesse de Sabran depuis Marquise de Boufflers," 264.

159. See "Épisode ajouté par le Chevalier de Boufflers à la quatrième scène du second acte du Bourgeois gentilhomme," in *Correspondance littéraire, philosophique et critique*, vol. XV, 401–5, February 1799.

160. Letter from Mme de Sabran to the Chevalier de Boufflers, [August 1782], in *Le Lit bleu*, 241.

161. *Mémoires complets et authentiques de Laure Junot Duchesse d'Abrantès*, vol. XIII, 168n3.

162. *Mémoires de madame la Duchesse de Gontaut, gouvernante des enfants de France pendant la Restauration, 1773–1836*, [1885] (Paris: Plon, 1891), 7.

163. Letter from Mme de Sabran to the Chevalier de Boufflers, [Paris, November? 1784], in *Le Lit bleu*, 298.

164. *Mémoires complets et authentiques de Laure Junot Duchesse d'Abrantès*, vol. XIII, 168n3.

165. "He has never treated you better than he would were he your enemy," is Mme de Sabran's assessment at the time of the Maréchal de Ségur's resignation of his portfolio as minister of war; letter from Mme de Sabran to the Chevalier de Boufflers of 4 [September, 1787], in *La Promesse*, 521.

166. Letter from the Duc de Lauzun to M. de Sartines, at Fort Saint-Louis in Senegal, February 15, 1779, quoted in J. Monteilhet, *Le Duc de Lauzun*, 528.

167. The emolument of 6,000 livres he received as Maréchal de Camp and the 45,000 livres of rental income on his abbeys did not prevent the Chevalier from accumulating some 60,000 livres in debts. See O. Uzanne, "Notice sur la vie et les Oeuvres de Boufflers," in *Contes du chevalier de Boufflers*, xlviii.

168. Letter from the Comte Louis de Ségur to the Chevalier de Boufflers, St. Petersburg, November 12, 1785, quoted in Paul Bonnefon, "Le Chevalier de Boufflers au Sénégal. Lettres et documents inédits," *Mercure de France*, vol. 86 (July–August 1910): 68.

169. Ibid.

170. Ibid., 69.

171. "You'll recall what I told you my first reaction was on learning that dismal news . . . I felt I'd been struck by a thunderbolt"; letter from Mme de Sabran to the Chevalier de Boufflers, July 20, 1786, in *La Promesse*, 132.

172. Letter from the Chevalier de Boufflers to Mme de Sabran, [Rochefort, November 27, 1785], in *Le Lit bleu*, 324.

173. Letter from Mme de Sabran to the Chevalier de Boufflers, [November 24, 1786], ibid., 319.

174. Letter from Mme de Sabran to the Chevalier de Boufflers, 6 [June 1786], in *La Promesse*, 52.

175. Letter from the Chevalier de Boufflers to M. d'Haillecourt, January 18, 1783, in Bonnefon, *Le Chevalier de Boufflers au Sénégal*, 78.

176. J. Monteilhet, *Le Duc de Lauzun*, 2, 216.

177. Duc de Lauzun, *Mémoire sur le commerce et les possessions des Anglais en Afrique*, in J. Monteilhet, *Le Duc de Lauzun*.

178. N. Vaget Grangeat, *Le Chevalier de Boufflers*, 65.

179. P. Bonnefon, *Le Chevalier de Boufflers au Sénégal*, 29.

180. Letter from the Chevalier de Boufflers to Mme de Sabran, 21 [January 1786], in *La Promesse*, 88–89.

181. See Fénelon, *Les Aventures de Télémaque*, in *Oeuvres*, critical edition by Jacques Le Brun, 2 vol. (Paris: Gallimard, 1827), vol. I, 20. Boufflers refers here to the episode in which Telemachus, reduced to slavery and obliged to work as a shepherd in the Egyptian desert, hears the voice of the goddess Athena, who encourages him to bear his tribulations with courage.

182. Letter from the Chevalier de Boufflers to the Maréchal de Beauvau, March 6, 1786, in *Correspondance inédite de la Comtesse de Sabran et du chevalier de Boufflers, 1778–1788*, collected and published by E. de Magnieu and Henri Prat (Paris: Plon, 1875), 170.

183. Letter from the Chevalier de Boufflers to Mme de Sabran, 3 [June 1787], in *La Promesse*, 383.

184. Letter from the Chevalier de Boufflers to Mme de Sabran, 6 [October 1787], ibid., 496.

185. Duc de Lauzun, *Mémoire sur le commerce et les possessions des Anglais en Afrique*, in J. Monteilhet, *Le Duc de Lauzun*, 560–61.

186. As Lauzun had already put it in his own denunciation, the men of the Company "offered rather the image of a band of buccaneers fighting each other over the booty than a society guided by laws"; ibid.

187. *Mémoire du Roi pour servir d'instructions à M. le Chevalier de Boufflers, Maréchal de Camp, Gouverneur du Sénégal et Dépendances*, in Chevalier de Boufflers, *Lettres d'Afrique à Madame de Sabran*, preface, notes and dossier by François Bessire (Arles: Actes Sud, 1998), 439.

188. See N. Vaget Grangeat, *Le Chevalier de Boufflers*, 70.

189. "These words relating to captives, slave prisons, slaves, chains, irons, etc., make my heart bleed," unpublished letter, quoted in S. Carrell, "Introduction au premier séjour du chevalier de Boufflers en Afrique," in *La Promesse*, 17.

190. Letter from Mme de Sabran to the Chevalier de Boufflers [June 20, 1786], ibid., 132.

191. Montesquieu, *De l'esprit des lois*, book CV, chapter 5.

192. Voltaire, *Candide* (1759), chapter XIX.

193. *Mémoires ou Souvenirs et Anecdotes par M. le Comte de Ségur*, vol. I, 293.

194. Élisabeth Badinter and Robert Badinter, *Condorcet (1743–1794). Un intellectuel en politique* (Paris: Fayard, 1988), 172.

195. Letter from the Chevalier de Boufflers to Mme de Sabran, May 6, [1787], in *La Promesse*, 371.

196. Emmanuel Kant, *Réponse à la question: Qu'est-ce que les Lumières?*, trans. by Heinz Wismann, in *Oeuvres philosophiques* (Paris: Gallimard, 1985), vol. II, 212.

197. Letter from the Chevalier de Boufflers to Mme de Sabran, 4 [February 1786], in *La Promesse*, 98.

198. Letter from the Chevalier de Boufflers to Mme de Sabran, 19 [July 1786] and 5 [April 1787], ibid., 218–19, 335.

199. *Discours de M. de Boufflers, lors de sa réception à l'Académie française, 9 December 1788*, in *Oeuvres complètes de Boufflers*, vol. I, 335–36.

200. For a paper by Boufflers treating the problem of slavery, read at the Académie Française, see N. Vaget Grangeat, *Le Chevalier de Boufflers*, 72.

201. Auguste Geffroy, *Gustave III et la cour de France* (Paris: Librairie académique Didier et Cie, 1867), vol. II, 440–41, quoted in S. Carrell, in *La Promesse*, 239.

202. Mme de Staël, *Mirza*, in *Oeuvres de jeunesse* (Paris: Desjonquères, 1997), 162.

203. Simone Balayé, "Introduction," in Mme de Staël, *Oeuvres de jeunesse*, 12.

204. See François Bessire, "Préface" to the Chevalier de Boufflers, *Lettres d'Afrique à Madame de Sabran*, 14–15.

205. Letter from the Chevalier de Boufflers to Mme de Sabran, 25 [September 1787], in *La Promesse*, 491–92.

206. See S. Carrell, "Introduction au premier séjour du chevalier de Boufflers en Afrique," in *La Promesse*, 18.

207. Letter from the Chevalier de Boufflers to Mme de Sabran, 9 [May 1786], ibid., 181.

208. Letter from the Chevalier de Boufflers to Mme de Sabran, 8 [November 1787], ibid., 549–50.

209. See N. Vaget Grangeat, *Le Chevalier de Boufflers*, 73.

210. For an analysis of Boufflers's style, see François Bessire's penetrating preface to his edition of *Lettres d'Afrique à Madame de Sabran*, 15–18.

211. Madeleine de Scudéry, "De la manière d'écrire des lettres," in *"De l'air galant" et autres Conversations (1653–1684). Pour une étude de l'archive galante*, edited and with commentary by Delphine Denis (Paris: Honoré Champion, 1998), 154.

212. Letter from the Chevalier de Boufflers to Mme de Sabran 20 [January 1786], in *La Promesse*, 87.

213. Letter from the Chevalier de Boufflers to Mme de Sabran, 22 [January 1786], ibid., 91.

214. Letter from the Chevalier de Boufflers to Mme de Sabran 15 [February 1786], ibid., 105.

215. Letter from the Chevalier de Boufflers to Mme de Sabran 24 [April 1786], ibid., 171.

216. Letter from the Chevalier de Boufflers to Mme de Sabran 30 [April 1786], ibid., 176.

217. Letter from the Chevalier de Boufflers to Mme de Sabran 5 [May 1786], ibid.., 178.

218. Letter from the Chevalier de Boufflers to Mme de Sabran 6 [May 1786], ibid., 180.

219. Letter from the Chevalier de Boufflers to Mme de Sabran 8 [May 1787], ibid., 373.

220. Letter from the Chevalier de Boufflers to Mme de Sabran 16 [May 1786], ibid., 187.

221. Letter from the Chevalier de Boufflers to Mme de Sabran 10 [May 1786], ibid., 182.

222. Letter from the Chevalier de Boufflers to Mme de Sabran 22 [May 1786], ibid., 191.

223. Letter from the Chevalier de Boufflers to Mme de Sabran 20 [June 1786], ibid., 205.

224. Letter from the Chevalier de Boufflers to Mme de Sabran 18 [May 1786], ibid., 187.

225. Letter from the Chevalier de Boufflers to Mme de Sabran 8 [May 1786], ibid., 180.

226. Letter from the Chevalier de Boufflers to Mme de Sabran 24 [April 1787], ibid., 343.

227. Letter from the Chevalier de Boufflers to Mme de Sabran 5 [June,1787], ibid., 384.

228. Letter from the Chevalier de Boufflers to Mme de Sabran 24 [February 1786], ibid., 109.

229. Letter from the Chevalier de Boufflers to Mme de Sabran, 29 [May 1786], ibid., 194.

230. Letter from the Chevalier de Boufflers to Mme de Sabran, 30 [May 1786], ibid., 195.

231. Letter from the Chevalier de Boufflers to Mme de Sabran, 14 [May 1786], ibid., 183–84. Several years later, fleeing the Revolution, Mme de Sabran would echo him: "What do I care if old age should come to chill my senses? It is my soul that loves you. My love will be as immortal as my soul. It is in God that I love you, if there is a God, when that soul is separated from my body; or in the universe, if a universe is all there is. Whatever being I animate afterward will seek out the one you animate with ardor, and perhaps that will make the loveliest novel in the world"; letter from Mme de Sabran to the Chevalier de Boufflers, August 18, 1789, quoted in Pierre de Croze, *Le Chevalier de Boufflers et la Comtesse de Sabran, 1788–1792* (Paris: Calmann-Lévy, 1894), 179–80.

232. Letter from the Chevalier de Boufflers to Mme de Sabran, 29 [August 1787], in *La Promesse*, 475.

233. See E. de Sabran, "Notice sur Madame la Comtesse de Sabran depuis Marquise de Boufflers," 267.

234. Letter from the Chevalier de Boufflers to Mme de Sabran, 29 [August 1787], in *La Promesse*, 475.

235. Letter from the Chevalier de Boufflers to Mme de Sabran, 3 [January 1787], ibid., 257.

236. Letter from the Chevalier de Boufflers to Mme de Sabran, 21 [January 1787], ibid., 267.

237. Letter from the Chevalier de Boufflers to Mme de Sabran, 27 [January 1787], ibid., 271.

238. Letter from the Chevalier de Boufflers to Mme de Sabran, 29 [January 1787], ibid., 272.

239. Letter from the Chevalier de Boufflers to Mme de Sabran, December 30 [1786], ibid., 253.

240. Letter from the Chevalier de Boufflers to Mme de Sabran, 2 [August 1786] and 1 April [1787], ibid., 227, 332.

241. Letter from the Chevalier de Boufflers to Mme de Sabran, 13 [January 1787], ibid., 263.

242. Letter from the Chevalier de Boufflers to Mme de Sabran, 4 [August 1786] and 4 [February 1787], ibid., 228, 308.

243. Letter from the Chevalier de Boufflers to Mme de Sabran, 13 [April 1787], ibid., 338.

244. Ibid.

245. La Fontaine, "L'homme et son image," in *Fables*, book I, fable XI. Where "the literary reflection" serves as "counterweight to the pathological illusions engendered by *amour-propre*"; see Marc Fumaroli, *Notes à La Fontaine, Fables*, ed. Marc Fumaroli (Paris: Imprimerie nationale, 1985), 821.

246. Letter from the Chevalier de Boufflers to Mme de Sabran, 24 [September 1787], in *La Promesse*, 490–91.

247. See Voltaire, "Sur le commerce," letter X, in *Lettres philosophiques ou Lettres anglaises*, ed. Raymond Naves (Paris: Classiques Garnier, 1988), 45–47.

248. Letter from the Chevalier de Boufflers to Mme de Sabran, 4 [April 1787], in *La Promesse*, 334–35.

249. Letter from the Chevalier de Boufflers to Mme de Sabran, 20 [April 1787], ibid., 341.

250. Letter from the Chevalier de Boufflers to Mme de Sabran, 16 [August 1787], ibid., 468–69.

251. Letter from the Chevalier de Boufflers to Mme de Sabran, 5 [April 1786], ibid., 156.

252. Letter from the Chevalier de Boufflers to Mme de Sabran, La Rochelle, 24 [December 1787], ibid., 570.

253. "Portrait de Madame de Boufflers," in *Oeuvres posthumes du chevalier de Boufflers*.

254. Letter from Mme de Sabran to the Chevalier de Boufflers, 24 [January, 1787], 296.

255. Letter of December 3, 1778, in *Correspondance secrète politique et littéraire*, vol. VII, 153–54.

256. M. de Bombelles, *Journal*, vol. II, 197.

257. See the letter from Mme de Sabran to the Chevalier de Boufflers, August 31, 1788, quoted in P. de Croze, *Le Chevalier de Boufflers et la Comtesse de Sabran*, 133.

258. Letter from the Chevalier de Boufflers to Mme de Boisgelin, quoted in de Croze, *Le Chevalier de Boufflers*, 137.

259. The Chevalier had been elected unanimously on June 12.

260. M. de Bombelles, *Journal*, December 29, 1788, vol. II, 267.

261. *Discours de M. de Boufflers lors de la réception à l'Académie française*, in *Oeuvres complètes de Boufflers*, vol. I, 362–63.

262. Ibid., 364.

THE COMTE LOUIS-PHILIPPE DE SÈGUR

1.   Prince Charles-Joseph de Ligne, *Correspondances russes*, texts gathered, introduced, edited and annotated by Alexandre Stroev and Jeroom Vercruysse, 2 vol. (Paris: Honoré Champion, 2013), vol. II, 689.

2.   Benedetto Croce, *Histoire de l'Europe au XIXe siècle*, translation and preface by Henri Bedarida (Paris: Gallimard, 1959), 41.

3. F.-G. de Lévis, "Preface," in *Souvenirs-Portraits de Gaston de Lévis (1764–1830)*, 52.

4. December 10, 1753.

5. See Pierre de Ségur, "Le Comte Louis-Philippe de Ségur (1753–1830)," *Revue des deux mondes*, fifth series, vol. XLIII (1908): 241.

6. *Mémoires inédits de Madame la Comtesse de Genlis*, vol. VII, 342.

7. Her *Mémoires de Félicie* appeared in 1804. The *Souvenirs-Portraits* of the Duc de Lévis were published in 1813.

8. Leon Apt, *Louis-Philippe de Ségur: An Intellectual in a Revolutionary Age* (La Haye: Martinus Nijhoff, 1969), xi–xii.

9. On Ségur the *"moraliste,"* see Charles-Augustin Sainte-Beuve, "Le Comte de Ségur" [1843], in *Portraits littéraires*, edited by Gérald Antoine (Paris: Robert Laffont, 1993), 597–611.

10. *Mémoires ou Souvenirs et Anecdotes par M. le Comte de Ségur*, vol. I, 2.

11. Ibid., 105.

12. Now Place de la Concorde.

13. *Mémoires ou Souvenirs et Anecdotes par M. le Comte de Ségur*, vol. I, 36.

14. See Cyril Le Meur, *Les Moralistes français et la Politique à la fin du XVIIIe siècle* (Paris: Honoré Champion, 2002), 534.

15. *Mémoires ou Souvenirs et Anecdotes par M. le Comte de Ségur*, vol. I, 38.

16. Ibid., 28–30.

17. In his *Mémoires*, Ségur mentions the salons of Mme Geoffrin, the Marquise du Deffand, the Maréchale de Luxembourg, the Duchesse de Choiseul, the Princesse de Beauvau, Mme de Montesson (morganatic wife of the Duc d'Orléans), the Duchesse d'Enville, and the Comtesse de Tessé.

18. Ségur recalls the names of d'Alembert, Raynal, Guibert, Chamfort, Suard, Delille, La Harpe, Marmontel; ibid., 64.

19. Ibid., 198–99.

20. "Our spouses incline a bit too much to *la métromanie*," we read in an affectionate parody in verse of his wife, the Comtesse de Ségur, quoted in Ch.-A. Sainte-Beuve, "Le Comte de Ségur," in *Portraits littéraires*, 600.

21. See G. de Broglie, *Ségur sans cérémonie 1757–1805*, 232.

22. Quoted in P. de Ségur, "Le Comte Louis-Philippe de Ségur (1753–1830)": 245.

23. *Mémoires ou Souvenirs et Anecdotes par M. le Comte de Ségur*, vol. I, 62–63.

24. Ibid., 65.

25. Ch.-J. de Ligne, *Caractères et portraits*, 166–67.

26. Jean-Christian Petitfils, *Louis XVI* (Paris: Perrin, 2005), 298.

27. *Mémoires ou Souvenirs et Anecdotes par M. le Comte de Ségur*, vol. I, 21.

28. Ibid., 117.

29. Ibid., 86.

30. Ibid., 87.

31. Ibid.

32. Ibid., 120.

33. See Stacy Schiff, *A Great Improvisation: Franklin, France, and the Birth of America* (New York: Henry Holt and Company), 2005.

34. Louis-Armand de Bourbon, Prince de Conti, and his brother François-Louis, Prince de La Roche-sur-Yon.

35. *Mémoires ou Souvenirs et Anecdotes par M. le Comte de Ségur*, vol. I, 117–18.

36. "To strike at England is to serve my country."

37. S. Schiff, *A Great Improvisation*, 78.

38. *Mémoires ou Souvenirs et Anecdotes par M. le Comte de Ségur*, vol. I, 124.

39. S. Schiff, *A Great Improvisation*, 78.

40. *Mémoires ou Souvenirs et Anecdotes par M. le Comte de Ségur*, vol. I, 219.

41. The troops in Brittany were gathered at Paramé under the command of the Marquis de Castries; those in Normandy at Vaussieux were under the command of the Maréchal de Broglie.

42. *Mémoires ou Souvenirs et Anecdotes par M. le Comte de Ségur*, vol. I, 222.

43. Ibid., 229.

44. Ibid., 244.

45. Now held in the Musée de Versailles.

46. Ibid., 323.

47. Ibid., 324.

48. *See Diary of Gouverneur Morris*, December 4, 1789, 175.

49. *Le Trésor, ou Contentement passe richesse*, published in 1790.

50. Gouverneur Morris, *A Diary of the French Revolution*, critical edition by Beatrix Cary Davenport, 2 vol. (Boston: H. Mifflin, 1939), November 21, 1790, vol. II, 67.

51. With the rank of *colonel en second* of the Soissons regiment.

52. *Mémoires ou Souvenirs et Anecdotes par M. le Comte de Ségur*, vol. I, 327.

53. Letter from the Comte de Ségur to the Comtesse de Ségur, Rochefort, July 2, 1782, in *Extraits de Lettres écrites d'Amérique par le Comte de Ségur, colonel en second, et la Comtesse de Ségur, dame de Madame Victoire (1782–1783)*, in *Deux Français aux États-Unis et dans la Nouvelle Espagne en 1782, Journal de Voyage du Prince de Broglie et Lettres du Comte de Ségur*, edited by the Duc de Broglie (Paris: Imprimerie Lahure, Société des Bibliophiles français, Pièce no 6, Mélanges, 1903), 56.

54. They were signed at Versailles on January 20, 1783.

55. Letter from the Comte de Ségur to la Comtesse de Ségur, "Aboard *La Gloire*, under sail, July 14, 1782," in *Extraits de Lettres écrites d'Amérique*, 160.

56. Duc de Broglie, "Avant-propos" to *Deux Français aux États-Unis*, 7.

57. *Mémoires ou Souvenirs et Anecdotes par M. le Comte de Ségur*, vol. I, 322–25.

58. Letter from the Comte de Ségur to his wife, Nantes, May 24, 1782, in *Extraits de Lettres écrites d'Amérique par le Comte de Ségur*, 152.

59. *Mémoires ou Souvenirs et Anecdotes par M. le Comte de Ségur*, vol. I, 320.

60. Ibid., 341.

61. Letter from the Comte de Ségur to his wife, Philadelphia, September 16, 1782, in *Extraits de Lettres écrites d'Amérique par le Comte de Ségur*, 164–65.

62. Ibid., 166.

63. See the letters sent from America by the Duc de Lauzun to the Marquis de Voyer, quoted in the chapter on the Duc de Lauzun, [page TK].

64. *Mémoires ou Souvenirs et Anecdotes par M. le Comte de Ségur*, vol. I, 412.

65. Published in two volumes in Paris in 1786. An English translation by George Greive was released the following year: *Travels in North-America, in the years 1780, 1781, and 1782, by the Marquis de Chastellux; translated from the French by an English gentleman, who resided in America at that period; with notes by the translator* (London: Printed for G. G. J. and J. Robinson, 1787).

66. Letter from the Comte de Ségur to his wife, Boston, December 11, 1782, in *Extraits de Lettres écrites d'Amérique par le Comte de Ségur*, 182–83.

67. Letter from the Comte de Ségur to his wife, "*Au camp de Crampont*," October 5, 1782, ibid., 170.

68. *Mémoires ou Souvenirs et Anecdotes par M. le Comte de Ségur*, vol. I, 517.

69. Letter from the Comte de Ségur to his wife, "In my residence at Cul-de-sac, near Port-au-Prince, this 15 April 1783," in *Extraits de Lettres écrites d'Amérique par le Comte de Ségur*, 204. The letter has been cut off after this opening sentence. It would be interesting to know if the omitted passage contained reflections on slavery that the editor judged it wiser to remove.

70. Ibid., 204–5.

71. M. de Bombelles, *Journal*, vol. I, 231–32 (June 22, 1783).

72. Signed at Paris on September 3, 1782.

73. *Mémoires ou Souvenirs et Anecdotes par M. le Comte de Ségur*, vol. II, 28.

74. Ibid., 40.

75. Ibid., 73.

76. Ibid., 72, 104.

77. M. de Bombelles, *Journal*, vol. I, 305–6.

78. *Mémoires ou Souvenirs et Anecdotes par M. le Comte de Ségur*, vol. II, 79.

79. Ibid., 98–101.

80. See M. de Bombelles, *Journal*, vol. I, 250.

81. *Mémoires ou Souvenirs et Anecdotes par M. le Comte de Ségur*, vol. II, 141.

82. Ibid., 140.

83. Ibid., 167.

84. Kazimierz Waliszewski, *Le Roman d'une impératrice, Catherine II de Russie, d'après ses Mémoires, sa Correspondance et les documents inédits des archives d'État* (Paris: Plon, 1908), 390.

85. See Hélène Carrère d'Encausse, *Catherine II. Un âge d'or pour la Russie* (Paris: Fayard, 2002), 397–98.

86. K. Waliszewski, *Le Roman d'une impératrice*, 389.

87. See L. Apt, *Louis-Philippe de Ségur*, 49.

88. *Mémoires ou Souvenirs et Anecdotes par M. le Comte de Ségur*, vol. I, 413.

89. Mme de Staël, *De l'Allemagne*, vol. I, 105.

90. Ibid.

91. Mme de Staël, *De la littérature*, critical edition by Gérard Gengembre and Jean Goldzink (Paris: Garnier-Flammarion, 1991), 273–75.

92. Letter from Catherine of Russia to the Prince de Ligne, Peterhof, June 30, 1791, in Ch.-J. de Ligne, *Correspondances russes*, vol. I, 200.

93. Letter from the Prince de Ligne to Catherine, Vienna, April 14, 1784, ibid., vol. I, 133.

94. *Lettres d'amour de Catherine II à Potemkine*, unpublished correspondence, introduction and notes by Georges Oudard (Paris: Calmann-Lévy, 1934), 177.

95. Franco Venturi, *Settecento riformatore*, 5 vol. (Turin: Einaudi, 1969–1989), vol. IV: *La Caduta dell'Antico Regime (1776–1789)*, book 2, *Il patriottismo repubblicano e gli imperi dell'Est* (1984), 790.

96. *Mémoires ou Souvenirs et Anecdotes par M. le Comte de Ségur*, vol. II, 260.

97. *Portrait. Le Prince Charles-Joseph de Ligne au Comte de Ségur, Au camp sous Oczakow, ce 1er August 1788*, in Ch.-J. de Ligne, *Correspondances russes*, vol. II, 642–43.

98. Ibid., 645.

99. *Mémoires ou Souvenirs et Anecdotes par M. le Comte de Ségur*, vol. II, 282.

100. See K. Waliszewski, *Le Roman d'une impératrice*, 390.

101. Ibid., 239.

102. *Mémoires ou Souvenirs et Anecdotes par M. le Comte de Ségur*, vol. III, 14.

103. Ibid., 12.

104. Ibid., 55.

105. Ibid., 73.

106. Mme de Staël, "Préface" to *Lettres et pensées du Prince de Ligne d'après l'édition de Madame de Staël (1809)*, introduction and notes, chronology and bibliography by Raymond Trousson (Paris: Tallandier, 1989), 69.

107. Quoted in Philippe Mansel, *Le Prince Charles-Joseph de Ligne. Le charmeur de l'Europe (1735–1814)* (Paris: Perrin, 2002), 95.

108. Quoted in Ch.-J. de Ligne, *Correspondances russes*, vol. I, 441.

109. Letter from the Prince de Ligne to Grimm, Moscou, July 3, 1787, ibid., 448.

110. *Mémoires ou Souvenirs et Anecdotes par M. le Comte de Ségur*, vol. III, 5. See also 73.

111. *Mémoires de la baronne d'Oberkirch*, 238.

112. *Lettres et pensées du Prince de Ligne d'après l'édition de Madame de Staël*, 286.

113. Ibid., 262.

114. Prince Charles-Joseph de Ligne, *Mes écarts ou ma tête en liberté et autres pensées et réflex-ions*, critical edition by Jeroom Vercruysse and Daniel Acke (Paris: Honoré Champion, 2007).

115. Ch.-J. de Ligne, letter V, from Parthenizza, in *Lettres à la Marquise de Coigny*, 71.

116. Ibid., 63.

117. Ch.-J. de Ligne, "Fleuros," in *Caractères et portraits*, 229–31.

118. *Mémoires ou Souvenirs et Anecdotes par M. le Comte de Sègur*, vol. III, 73.

119. Ibid.

120. Ibid.

121. See Benedetta Craveri, "Mme de La Ferté-Imbault (1715–1791) et son monde," *Revue d'histoire littéraire de la France* no. 1 (2005): 95–109.

122. Didier Masseau, *Les Ennemis des philosophes. L'antiphilosophie au temps des Lumières* (Paris: Albin Michel, 2000), 89.

123. See Ch.-J. de Ligne, *Correspondances russes*, vol. I, 95–101.

124. *Crispin Duègne, comédie, en trois actes et en prose*; *Caius-Marcius Coriolan, tragédie, en cinq actes et en vers*; *Le Sourd et le Bègue, proverbe en un acte, en prose* (*"À quelque chose malheur est bon"*); *L'Enlèvement, comédie-proverbe en un acte, en prose* (*"Chat échaudé craint l'eau froide"*); *L'Homme inconsidéré, comédie en un acte, en prose.*

125. See Isabel de Madariaga, *La Russie au temps de la grande Catherine*, trans. by Denise Meunier (Paris: Fayard, 1987), 574.

126. *Recueil des pièces de l'Hermitage*, 3 vol. [St. Petersburg, s.n., 1788–1789]. See also *Théâtre de l'Hermitage de Catherine II, Impératrice de Russie, composé par cette Princesse, par plusieurs personnes de sa Société intime, et par quelques Ministres Étrangers*, 2 vol. (Paris: Buisson, l'an VII de la République, 1799).

127. *Mémoires ou Souvenirs et Anecdotes par M. le Comte de Sègur*, vol. III, 110.

128. In addition to bedrooms, each boat was provided with a music room, a salon with a library, and a tent on deck for shelter from the sun.

129. *Mémoires ou Souvenirs et Anecdotes par M. le Comte de Sègur*, vol. III, 136.

130. Ibid., 214.

131. Ch.-J. de Ligne, letter III, from Kherson, in *Lettres à la Marquise de Coigny*, 43.

132. Quoted in K. Waliszewski, *Le Roman d'une impératrice*, 240.

133. Ch.-J. de Ligne, letter III, from Kherson, in *Lettres à la Marquise de Coigny*, 46.

134. Ibid., 44.

135. *Mémoires ou Souvenirs et Anecdotes par M. le Comte de Sègur*, vol. III, 111.

136. Ibid., 112.

137. Ibid., 131–32.

138. H. Carrère d'Encausse, *Catherine II*, 461.

139. See F. Venturi, *Settecento riformatore*, vol. IV, book 2, 801–2.

140. Georges Oudard, Introduction to *Lettres d'amour de Catherine II à Potemkine*, 27.

141. Ch.-J. de Ligne, letter III, from Kherson, in *Lettres à la Marquise de Coigny*, 44–45.

142. *Mémoires ou Souvenirs et Anecdotes par M. le Comte de Ségur*, vol. III, 125.

143. Ibid.

144. See F. Venturi, *Settecento riformatore*, vol. IV, tome 2, 803.

145. See J. Fabre, *Stanislas-Auguste Poniatowski*, 227.

146. Ch.-J. de Ligne, letter III, from Kherson, in *Lettres à la Marquise de Coigny*, 45.

147. Isabel de Madariaga, *La Russie au temps de la grande Catherine*, 405.

148. See F. Venturi, *Settecento riformatore*, vol. IV, book II, 805ff.

149. *Mémoires ou Souvenirs et Anecdotes par M. le Comte de Ségur*, vol. III, 149.

150. Ch.-J. de Ligne, letter III, from Kherson, in *Lettres à la Marquise de Coigny*, 52.

151. *Mémoires ou Souvenirs et Anecdotes par M. le Comte de Ségur*, vol. III, 150.

152. Ibid., 212.

153. Ibid., 214.

154. Ch.-J. de Ligne, letter IV, from Bakhtchissaraï, June 1, 1787, in *Lettres à la Marquise de Coigny*, 54.

155. Ibid., 52–53.

156. See the plaque at the foot of the philosopher's statue that Ligne had erected in his garden at Beloeil, in the exhibition catalog for *Le Prince Charles-Joseph de Ligne et son temps*, Château de Beloeil, May 8–September 19, 1982, by Georges Englebert and Martine Englebert, Ministère de la Communauté Française, Direction Générale de la Culture (Bruxelles, 1982), illustration 15, 60.

157. Ch.-J. de Ligne, letter IV, from Bakhtchissaraï, June 1, 1787, in *Lettres à la Marquise de Coigny*, 54–55.

158. Ch.-J. de Ligne, *Fragments de l'histoire de ma vie*, vol. II, 134.

159. Ibid.

160. Ch.-J. de Ligne, letter IV, from Bakhtchissaraï, June 1, 1787, in *Lettres à la Marquise de Coigny*, 50.

161. *Mémoires ou Souvenirs et Anecdotes par M. le Comte de Ségur*, vol. III, 159–60.

162. Ibid., 163.

163. Ch.-J. de Ligne, letter IV, from Bakhtchissaraï, June 1, 1787, in *Lettres à la Marquise de Coigny*, 49.

164. Ibid.

165. *Mémoires ou Souvenirs et Anecdotes par M. le Comte de Ségur*, vol. III, 176–77.

166. Ibid., 204–5.

167. Ibid., 205.

168. *Catalogue de l'exposition Le Prince Charles-Joseph de Ligne et son temps*, illustration 8.19, 119–20.

169. *Mémoires ou Souvenirs et Anecdotes par M. le Comte de Ségur*, vol. III, 180–81.

170. Ibid., 183–84.

171. Ch.-J. de Ligne, letter V, from Parthenizza, in *Lettres à la Marquise de Coigny*, 58.

172. Ibid., 65–66.

173. See François-Emmanuel Guignard de Saint-Priest, *Mémoires, Règnes de Louis XV et de Louis XVI*, published by the Baron de Barante, 2 vol. (Paris: Calmann-Lévy, 1929), vol. I, 216.

174. Quoted in Bonnefon, *Le Chevalier de Boufflers au Sénégal*, 85–86.

175. *Mémoires ou Souvenirs et Anecdotes par M. le Comte de Ségur*, vol. III, 531.

THE COMTE DE VAUDREUIL

1. Quoted in *Mémoires inédits de Madame la Comtesse de Genlis*, vol. I, 314–15.

2. See Geneviève Haroche-Bouzinac, *Louise Élisabeth Vigée Le Brun, histoire d'un regard*, 120.

3. F.-E. de Saint-Priest, *Mémoires, Règnes de Louis XV et de Louis XVI*, vol. II, 66.

4. É. Vigée Le Brun, *Souvenirs*, 268.

5. *Mémoires du Comte Alexandre de Tilly*, 137.

6. Léonce Pingaud, Introduction to *Correspondance intime du Comte de Vaudreuil et du Comte d'Artois pendant l'émigration (1789–1815)*, introduction, notes, and appendices by M. Léonce Pingaud, 2 vol. (Paris: Plon, Nourrit et Cie, 1889), vol. I, viii.

7. *Correspondance littéraire, philosophique et critique par Grimm, Diderot, Raynal, Meister, etc.*, vol. XII: 428.

8. Mlle de Fierval married Charles d'Avrange de Noiseville in 1778.

9. *Mémoires de la baronne d'Oberkirch*, 210.

10. *Histoire des Salons de Paris... par la Duchesse d'Abrantès*, vol. I, 214.

11. *Mémoires du Comte Alexandre de Tilly*, 132.

12. *Mémoires inédits de Madame la Comtesse de Genlis*, vol. II, 35.

13. "La Duchesse de Polignac," in *Souvenirs-Portraits de Gaston de Lévis*, 156.

14. Ibid.

15. Pierre de Nolhac, *Madame Vigée Le Brun, peintre de la reine Marie-Antoinette* (Paris: Goupil & Cie/Manzi, Joyant & Cie), 1912, 5.

16. É. Vigée Le Brun, *Souvenirs*, 179.

17. Ibid., 284.

18. Ibid.

19. *Mémoires du Comte Alexandre de Tilly*, 210.

20. *Mémoires de la baronne d'Oberkirch*, 210.

21. *Mémoires de M. le baron de Besenval*, 193.

22. Ibid.

23. See *Mémoires inédits de Madame la Comtesse de Genlis*, vol. II, 35; *Mémoires de la Marquise de La Tour du Pin. Journal d'une femme de cinquante ans (1778–1815), suivi d'extraits inédits de sa Correspondance (1815–1846)*, critical edition by Christian de Liedekerke Beaufort (Paris: Mercure de France, 1979, 1982), 40; *Histoire des Salons de Paris... par la Duchesse d'Abrantès*, vol. I, 207.

24. *Mémoires de M. le baron de Besenval,* 192.

25. É. Vigée Le Brun, *Souvenirs,* 284.

26. F.-E. de Saint-Priest, *Mémoires,* vol. II, 66.

27. In a letter to the Comte de Rosenberg on April 17, 1775, Marie-Antoinette mentions the Comte de Polignac as being among the "hommes aimables" allowed to attend those concerts—where "all formality is shunned"—that were held in her private apartments each Monday.

28. Letter from the Comte de Mercy-Argenteau to Maria Theresa, August 16, 1775, in *Correspondance secrète entre Marie-Thérèse et le Comte de Mercy-Argenteau,* vol. II, 367.

29. Letter from the Comte de Mercy-Argenteau to Maria Theresa, September 18, 1775, ibid., 378.

30. Letter from the Comte de Mercy-Argenteau to Maria Theresa, October 19, 1775, ibid., 391.

31. Letter from Marie-Antoinette to Maria Theresa, September 14, 1776, ibid., 486.

32. Letter from the Comte de Mercy-Argenteau to Maria Theresa, September 17, 1776, ibid., 488, 490. On the irreligiosity of Mme de Polignac, see also the *Mémoires du Comte de Saint-Priest.*

33. Ibid., 491.

34. Note from Maria Theresa to the Abbé de Vermond, enclosed with her letter to Mercy-Argenteau of October 1, 1776, in *Maria Theresia und Marie Antoinette, ihr Briefwechsel,* critical edition by Alfred Ritter von Arneth, enlarged second edition, including the letters of the Abbé de Vermond to the Comte de Mercy-Argenteau (Leipzig: K. F. Köhler, 1866), 192.

35. Quoted in J.-Ch. Petitfils, *Louis XVI,* 283.

36. September 12, 1784.

37. September 20, 1780.

38. *Journal de l'abbé de Véri, publié avec une introduction et des notes par le baron Jehan de Witte,* 2 vol. (Paris: Plon, 1933), vol. II, 323.

39. See M. de Bombelles, *Journal,* vol. I, 53–54.

40. Letter from Marie-Antoinette to Maria Theresa, April 13, 1780, *Correspondance secrète,* vol. III, 486.

41. See Antonia Fraser, *Marie Antoinette: The Journey* (New York: Knopf Doubleday), 2002.

42. Hector Fleischmann, *Madame de Polignac et la Cour galante de Marie-Antoinette, d'après les libelles obscènes, suivi de la réédition de plusieurs libelles rares et curieux et d'une bibliographie critique des pamphlets contre Madame de Polignac, avec notes et commentaires* (Paris: Bibliothèque des curieux, 1910), 32.

43. June 5, 1780.

44. *Mémoires du Comte Alexandre de Tilly,* 138.

45. *Mémoires de M. le baron de Besenval,* vol. II, 373.

46. October 22, 1781.

47. *Mémoires de M. le baron de Besenval*, vol. II, 280.

48. See Victor du Bled, "Un client de l'Ancien Régime. De L'Isle, Mme de Choiseul et ses amis—Le Salon de la Duchesse de Polignac," *Revue des deux mondes*, no. 101 (September 13, 1890): 377.

49. *Souvenirs-Portraits du Duc de Lévis*, 156.

50. In April 1771, the Comte had lodged a complaint against his secretary, Barthélemy Tort de la Sonde, accusing him of using his name in order to speculate with public funds. Placed under arrest, Tort declared that he had acted under the Comte's instructions, convincing the Duc d'Aiguillon—at that time the Minister of Foreign Affairs—of his innocence. Protected by Marie-Antoinette, Guînes was tried by a special commission of state councillors expressly appointed by the King and found not guilty by a vote of seven to six; the Duc d'Aiguillon lost his position.

51. *Mémoires inédits de Madame la Comtesse de Genlis*, vol. I, 373.

52. *Mémoires de la Marquise de La Tour du Pin*, 89.

53. F.-E. de Saint-Priest, *Mémoires*, vol. II, 65.

54. *Mémoires de Madame Campan, Première femme de chambre de Marie-Antoinette*, edition presented by Jean Chalon, with notes by Carlos de Angulo (Paris: Mercure de France, 1988), 128.

55. See *Mémoires ou Souvenirs et Anecdotes par M. le Comte de Ségur*, vol. I, 57–58, and for a less kindly judgment, *Mémoires inédits de Madame la Comtesse de Genlis*, vol. III, 82–83n1.

56. Comte de La Marck, quoted in Adolphe de Bacourt, Introduction to *Correspondance entre le Comte de Mirabeau et le Comte de La Marck pendant les années 1789, 1790 et 1791*, collected, arranged, and published by M. Ad. de Bacourt, 2 vol. (Paris: Le Normant, 1851), vol. I, 35.

57. É. Vigée Le Brun, *Souvenirs*, 233.

58. At the Trianon's *petit théâtre*, Vaudreuil played the leading roles in *Les Deux Chasseurs* and *La Laitière, Le Roi et le Fermier, Le Devin du village, Les Fausses Infidélités*, and, on August 19, 1785, he was the Comte d'Almaviva in *Le Barbier de Séville*, with Marie-Antoinette as Rosine.

59. F.-E. de Saint-Priest, *Mémoires*, vol. II, 67–68.

60. In which one player was pitted against two or more others.

61. Ch.-J. de Ligne, *Fragments de l'histoire de ma vie*, vol. I, 84.

62. *Mémoires de la baronne d'Oberkirch*, 210.

63. Joseph-Alexandre de Ségur, *Les Femmes, leur condition et leur influence dans l'ordre social chez différents peuples anciens et modernes*, 3 vol. (Paris: Treuttel et Würtz, 1803), vol. III, 8.

64. See Simone Bertière, *Marie-Antoinette, l'insoumise* (Paris: Éditions de Fallois, 2002), 227.

65. Comte de La Marck, quoted in A. de Bacourt, "Avant-propos," in *Correspondance entre le Comte de Mirabeau et le Comte de La Marck*, 33.

66. *Mémoires de M. le baron de Besenval*, vol. II, 332.

67. *Mémoires secrets pour servir à l'histoire de la République des lettres en France depuis 1762 jusqu'à nos jours*, 36 vol. (London: Adamson, 1783–1789, vol. XXV, 42, January 16, 1784.

68. *Mémoires de Madame Campan*, 232–33.

69. The scene must have taken place in the early months of 1784. See M. de Bombelles, *Journal*, vol. I, 305, February 7, 1784.

70. *Mémoires de Madame Campan*, 233.

71. Comte de La Marck, quoted in A. de Bacourt, Introduction to *Correspondance entre le Comte de Mirabeau et le Comte de La Marck*, vol. I, 37.

72. *Mémoires de M. le baron de Besenval*, vol. II, 364.

73. Ibid., 365.

74 Joan Haslip, *Marie Antoinette* (London: Weidenfeld & Nicolson, 1987); *Maria Antonietta*, trans. by Amina Pandolfi (Milan: Longanesi, 1989; 2nd edition, 2006), 174.

75. See *Mémoires du Comte Alexandre de Tilly*, 138. Comte de La Marck, quoted in A. de Bacourt, Introduction to *Correspondance entre le Comte de Mirabeau et le Comte de La Marck*, vol. I, 57.

76. J.-Ch. Petitfils, *Louis XVI*, 427–28.

77. Ibid., 427.

78. *Voyage en Espagne, à la suite de S. A. Royale Mgr le Comte d'Artois, par Alexandre Ballet, valet de chambre de M. le Comte de Vaudreuil*, 1782, manuscript preserved at the Bibliothèque Nationale de France, Département des manuscrits, FR 14692, 104–18; partially quoted in *Revue rétrospective, ou Bibliothèque historique contenant des mémoires et documents authentiques inédits et originaux, pour servir à l'histoire proprement dite, à la biographie, à l'histoire de la littérature et des arts*, third series, vol. II, 1838, 122.

79. Simon Schama, *Citizens: A Chronicle of the French Revolution* (New York: Vintage Books, 1989, 1990), 244–45.

80. *Mémoires du Comte Alexandre de Tilly*, 138.

81. Comte de La Marck, quoted in A. de Bacourt, Introduction to *Correspondance entre le Comte de Mirabeau et le Comte de La Marck*, vol. I, 57.

82. Ibid., 57–58.

83. Ibid., 58.

84. See the letter from the Comte de Salmour to the Baron de Stutterheim, minister of foreign affairs for Saxony, April 1787, in "La Cour de France en 1787," *Revue de la Révolution*, vol. II, (1886): 166.

85. Comte de La Marck, quoted in A. de Bacourt, Introduction to *Correspondance entre le Comte de Mirabeau et le Comte de La Marck*, vol. I, 59.

86. Ibid.

87. F.-E. de Saint-Priest, *Mémoires*, vol. II, 79.

88. See *Correspondance littéraire, philosophique et critique par Grimm, Diderot, Raynal, Meister, etc.*, vol. XIV, 215, September 1785.

89. L. Pingaud, Introduction to *Correspondance intime du Comte de Vaudreuil et du Comte d'Artois*, vol. I, xxiv.

90. The financier Claude Baudard de Vaudésir, Baron de Saint-James, was ruined by the construction costs of his elaborate garden, the so-called "Folie Saint-James."

91. See *Correspondance secrète inédite sur Louis XVI, Marie-Antoinette, la Cour et la Ville de 1777 à 1792*, vol. II, 107, quoted in L. Pingaud, Introduction to *Correspondance intime du Comte de Vaudreuil et du Comte d'Artois*, xxv.

92. See *Mémoires du Comte de Paroy. Souvenirs d'un défenseur de la famille royale pendant la révolution (1789–1797)* (Paris: Plon, 1895).

93. G. Haroche-Bouzinac, *Louise Élisabeth Vigée Le Brun, histoire d'un regard*, 87.

94. It is the hypothesis of Geneviève Haroche-Bouzinac in her biography of the artist to which we refer (see note 93).

95. É. Vigée Le Brun, *Souvenirs*, 223.

96. Ibid., 268.

97. See G. Haroche-Bouzinac, *Louise Élisabeth Vigée Le Brun, histoire d'un regard*, 125.

98. Thomas Blaikie, *Diary of a Scotch Gardener at the French Court at the End of the Eighteenth Century* (London: G. Routledge, 1931), quoted in G. Haroche-Bouzinac, *Louise Élisabeth Vigée Le Brun, histoire d'un regard*, 122.

99. Mme de Staël, *Correspondance générale*, vol. I, 105, August 9, 1786, quoted in G. Haroche-Bouzinac, *Louise Élisabeth Vigée Le Brun, histoire d'un regard*, 122.

100. "Lavishing him with favor, the heavens / Give him as Friend a charming Fairy, / One well worthy of my Enchanter... / Have the Fairy and the Enchanter passed beyond the black river? / No, my Friends; behold, V*** and Le Brun have changed my fairy tale into a History," in "Poésies diverses," *Oeuvres de Ponce-Denis (Écouchard) Le Brun*, arranged and published by Pierre-Louis Ginguené, and preceded by a Note on his life and works, drafted by the editor, 4 vol. (Paris: Gabriel Warée, 1811), vol. III, 379.

101. *Vers composés à l'occasion de la fête de M. de Vaudreuil*, in *Oeuvres complètes de Chamfort*, collected and published historical note on the life and writings of the author by Pierre-René Auguis, 5 vol. (Paris: Chaumerot Jeune, 1824–1825), vol. V, 229.

102. É. Vigée Le Brun, *Souvenirs*, 223.

103. "A major reconstruction of the house and gardens was undertaken by the architect Alexandre-Louis Delebrière, whom Vaudreuil also subsequently employed for his Parisian *hôtel*, where Robert Barthélemy and Callet executed decorative paintings in the dining room, the backgammon parlor, and the entrance to his private theater. The billiard room was decorated with three large landscapes by Robert with figures by Boucher"; see Colin B. Bailey, "Courtiers as Collectors on the Eve of the Revolution: Joseph-Hyacinthe-François de Paule de Rigaud, Comte de Vaudreuil (1740–1817),"

in *Patriotic Taste: Collecting Modern Art in Pre-Revolutionary Paris* (New Haven, CT: Yale University Press, 2002), 183.

104. É. Vigée Le Brun, *Souvenirs*, 223–24.

105. Ibid., 224.

106. *Mémoires de Madame Campan*, 229.

107. Letter from the Comte de Vaudreuil to Beaumarchais, September 15, 1783, quoted in Louis de Loménie, *Beaumarchais et son temps, Études sur la société en France au XVIIIe siècle, d'après des documents inédits*, 2 vol. (Paris: Michel Lévy Frères, 1856), vol. II, 316.

108. Letter from the Comte de Vaudreuil to the Duc de Fronsac, Versailles, Friday, s.d., quoted in L. de Loménie, *Beaumarchais et son temps*, vol. II, 311.

109. É. Vigée Le Brun, *Souvenirs*, 224.

110. *Mémoires secrets pour servir à l'histoire de la République des lettres, édition Adamson*, vol. XXIII, 206–7, September 27, 1783, quoted in C. B. Bailey, "Courtiers as Collectors on the Eve of the Revolution," 175.

111. É. Vigée Le Brun, *Souvenirs*, 225.

112. The *jus primae noctis*.

113. S.-R.N. de Chamfort, *Maximes et pensées*, no 507.

114. É. Vigée Le Brun, *Souvenirs*, 225.

115. Ibid., 269.

116. Letter from Chamfort to the Abbé Morellet, June 20, 1785, in "Lettres diverses," *Oeuvres complètes de Chamfort*, vol. V, 287.

117. C. B. Bailey, "Courtiers and Collectors on the Eve of the Revolution," 168–205.

118. Quoted in ibid., 185.

119. L.-V. Thiéry, *Guide des Amateurs et des Étrangers voyageurs à Paris*, vol. II, 542.

120. Pierre-Louis Ginguené, "Notice sur la vie et sur les ouvrages du poète Le Brun," in *Oeuvres de Ponce-Denis (Écouchard) Le Brun*, vol. I, xvii.

121. See Roger Portalis, *Henri-Pierre Danloux peintre de portraits et son journal durant l'émigration (1735–1809)* (Paris: E. Rahir, 1910), 297, quoted in C. B. Bailey, "Courtiers as Collectors on the Eve of the Revolution," 196.

122. C. B. Bailey, "Courtiers and Collectors on the Eve of the Revolution," 205.

123. Probably the wealthy financier Simon-Charles Boutin.

124. É. Vigée Le Brun, *Souvenirs*, 193–94.

125. Pierre-Louis Ginguené, "Notice sur la vie de Chamfort," in *Oeuvres de Chamfort. Recueillies et publiées par un de ses Amis*, 4 vol. (Paris: Chez le Directeur de l'Imprimerie des Sciences et des Arts, Year III of the Republic [1794]), vol. I, xliii.

126. *Oeuvres de Ponce-Denis (Écouchard) Le Brun*, vol. III, 379.

127. Ibid., vol. I, 292.

128. "Aux calomniateurs du Comte de V***," ibid., vol. III, 293.

129. Lionello Sozzi, "Il Settecento," *Storia europea del Settecento francese*, under the direction of Lionello Sozzi, 2 vol. (Turin: Einaudi, 2013), vol. I, 82.

130. P.-L. Ginguené, "Notice sur la vie et sur les ouvrages du poète Le Brun," in *Oeuvres de Ponce-Denis (Écouchard) Le Brun*, vol. I, xxx.

131. Ibid.

132. See Sylvain Menant, "Chamfort: naissance d'un moraliste," in *Cahiers de l'Association internationale des études françaises* XXX, no. 1 (1978): 188.

133. See S.-R. N. de Chamfort, *Maximes et pensées*, nos. 13, 183, 222, 242, 310, 316, 317, 334, 363, 370, 821, 1057, respectively, 25, 65, 75, 80, 99, 310, 100, 104, 111, 112, 228–29, 292.

134. See "Discours de réception de Chamfort à l'Académie française," in *Oeuvres complètes de Chamfort*, vol. I, 251–53.

135. Maurice Pellisson, *Chamfort. Étude sur sa vie, son caractère et ses écrits* (Paris: Lecène, Oudin et Cie, 1895), 72.

136. Pierre-Louis Ginguené, "Notice sur la vie de Chamfort," in *Oeuvres de Chamfort*, xxxii.

137. Noël Aubin, "Notice sur la vie de Chamfort," in *Chamfortiana, ou Recueil choisi d'anecdotes piquantes et de traits d'esprit de Chamfort. Précédé d'une notice sur sa vie et ses ouvrages* (Paris: Marchands de Nouveautés, Imprimerie de Delance, Year IX [1800]), xxi.

138. Letter from Chamfort to the Abbé Roman, October 5, [1784], in "Lettres diverses," *Oeuvres complètes de Chamfort*, vol. V, 281.

139. Claude Arnaud, *Chamfort*.

140. Pierre-Louis Ginguené, "Notice sur la vie de Chamfort," in *Oeuvres de Chamfort*, vol. I, xi.

141. It appears that Chamfort confided to his first protector, the Comte d'Angiviller, the secret of his birth, and that it was he who divulged it. See C. Arnaud, *Chamfort*, 57–59.

142. N. Aubin, "Notice sur la vie de Chamfort," in *Chamfortiana*, IX.

143. See S. Menant, *Chamfort: naissance d'un moraliste*, 193.

144. Letter from Chamfort to the Abbé Roman, March 4, 1784, in "Lettres diverses," *Oeuvres complètes de Chamfort*, vol. V, 274.

145. Ibid., 275.

146. Letter from Chamfort to the Abbé Roman, April 4, 1784, ibid., 289.

147. É. Vigée Le Brun, *Souvenirs*, 269.

148. S.-R. N. de Chamfort, *Maximes et pensées*, no. 1019, 282.

149. Ibid., no. 763, 213.

150. P.-L. Ginguené, "Notice sur la vie de Chamfort," in *Oeuvres de Chamfort*, vol. I, xli.

151. Madame Élisabeth and the Prince de Condé.

152. S.-R. N. de Chamfort, *Maximes et pensées*, no. 335, 104–5.

153. Friedrich Nietzsche, *Le Gai Savoir. Fragments posthumes*, texts and variants edited by G. Colli and M. Montinari, trans. by Pierre Klossowski (Paris: Gallimard, 1967), 108.

154. Friedrich Nietzsche, *Par-delà bien et mal. La généalogie de la morale*, texts and variants edited by G. Colli and M. Montinari, trans. by Cornelius Heim, Isabelle Hildenbrand, and Jean Gratien (Paris: Gallimard, 1971), 234ff.

155. See "Éloge de Molière. Discours qui a remporté le prix de l'Académie française en 1769," in *Oeuvres complètes de Chamfort*, vol. I, 1–31.

156. S.-R. N. de Chamfort, *Maximes et pensées*, no. 452, 131.

157. Ibid., no. 671, 187–88.

158. See J.-P.-J.-A. de Labouïsse-Rochefort, *Souvenirs et Mélanges*, vol. II, 127.

159. S.-R. N. de Chamfort, *Maximes et pensées*, no. 258, 84–85.

160. "I want you to know so well the art of conversation that one is able to flirt with the strictest woman in the world; to speak a little foolishness to grave and serious people," Madeleine de Scudéry, from "Rhetorical Dialogues," in *Selected Letters, Orations, and Rhetorical Dialogues*, ed. and trans. by Jane Donawerth and Julie Strongson (Chicago: University of Chicago Press, 2004), 105.

161. Claude Arnaud, *Chamfort*, 125.

162. Ibid.

163. See the "honnête raillerie" of Boufflers, mentioned on 237.

164. S.-R. N. de Chamfort, *Maximes et pensées*, no. 246, 81–82.

165. N. Aubin, "Notice sur la vie de Chamfort," in *Chamfortiana*, xv.

166. Ibid.

167. P.-L. Ginguené, "Notice sur la vie de Chamfort," in *Oeuvres de Chamfort*, vol. I, xxxiv.

168. *Mémoires de l'abbé Morellet, de l'Académie française, sur le Dix-huitième siècle et sur la Révolution*, introduction and notes by Jean-Pierre Guicciardi (Paris: Mercure de France, 1988), 311.

169. Letter from Chamfort to the Abbé Roman, March 4, 1784, in "Lettres diverses," *Oeuvres complètes de Chamfort*, vol. V, 275.

170. S.-R. N. de Chamfort, *Maximes et pensées*, no. 222, 75–76.

171. Ibid., no. 322, 101–2.

172. Ibid., no. 317, 100.

173. See C. Arnaud, *Chamfort*, 169.

174. S.-R. N. de Chamfort, *Maximes et pensées*, no. 1250, 338.

175. N. Aubin, "Notice sur la vie de Chamfort," in *Chamfortiana*, xx–xxii.

176. P.-L. Ginguené, "Notice sur la vie de Chamfort," in *Oeuvres de Chamfort*, vol. I, xxxiii.

177. Laurent Loty, *Forme brève et pessimisme. Le cas de Chamfort*, in *"La Licorne," XXI: Brièveté et écriture, Actes du Colloque international de Poitiers sur la forme brève*, under the direction of Pierre Testud, November 1991, 227, quoted in C. Le Meur, *Les Moralistes français et la Politique à la fin du XVIIIe siècle*, 390.

178. Jean Dagen, "Préface" to *Chamfort, Maximes, Pensées, Caractères* (Paris: G. F. Flammarion, 1968), 23.

179. See Maurice Pellisson, *Chamfort. Étude sur sa vie, son caractère et ses écrits* (Paris: Lecène, Oudin et Cie, 1895), 132.

180. C. Le Meur, *Les Moralistes français et la politique à la fin du XVIIIe siècle*, 393.

181. C. Arnaud, *Chamfort*, 121.

182. Letter from Chamfort to the Comte de Vaudreuil, December 13, 1788, in "Lettres diverses," in *Oeuvres complètes de Chamfort*, vol. V, 299.

183. Ibid., 293. It concerned the daughters' request upon the expulsion of the bishops.

184. M. Pellisson, *Chamfort. Étude sur sa vie, son caractère et ses écrits*, 116.

185. Letter from Chamfort to the Comte de Vaudreuil, December 13, 1788, 293–97.

186. Ibid., 301.

1789

1. See Ran Halévi, "États généraux," in *Dictionnaire critique de la Révolution française*, under the direction of François Furet and Mona Ozouf (Paris: Flammarion, 1988), 76–83.

2. November 10, 1788.

3. Letter from Mirabeau to the Duc de Lauzun, November 10, 1788, quoted in C. C. Velay, *Le Duc de Lauzun*, 248.

4. S. Schama, *Citizens*, 298.

5. Letter from Chamfort to the Comte de Vaudreuil, December 13, 1788, in "Lettres diverses," *Oeuvres complètes de Chamfort*, vol. V, 295.

6. See C. Arnaud, *Chamfort*, 186.

7. The two others are "Essay on Privileges" and "Views of the Executive Means Available to the Representatives of France in 1789."

8. December 27, 1788.

9. F.-E. de Saint-Priest, *Mémoires*, vol. II, 77.

10. Quoted in J.-P. Desprat, *Mirabeau*, 412.

11. Ibid., 68.

12. J. de Norvins, *Souvenirs d'un historien de Napoléon*, vol. I, 248.

13. By the Treaty of Versailles of 1768.

14. Letter from the Chevalier de Boufflers to the Duchesse de Choiseul, January 26, 1768, in *Correspondance complète de Mme du Deffand avec la Duchesse de Choiseul, l'abbé Barthélemy et M. Craufurt*, vol. I, 152–53.

15. Quoted in the chapter on Boufflers, 241.

16. See G. de Broglie, *Ségur sans cérémonie*, 118.

17. *Mémoires de M. le baron de Besenval*, vol. III, 311.

18. *Mémoires de la Marquise de La Tour du Pin*, 97.

19. J. de Norvins, *Souvenirs d'un historien de Napoléon*, vol. I, 208.

20. *Correspondance littéraire, philosophique et critique, adressée à un souverain d'Allemagne, depuis 1753 jusqu'en 1769, par le baron de Grimm et par Diderot* (Paris: Longchamps et Buisson, 1813), vol. V, 21.

21. Jean-Pierre-Louis de Luchet, *Mémoires pour servir à l'histoire de l'année 1789. Par une société de gens de lettres*, 5 vol. (Paris: Lavillette, 1790), vol. II, 28.

22. See *Correspondance littéraire, philosophique et critique*, vol. V, 239–41, 274–75, 509–61.

23. See Mara Fazio, *François-Joseph Talma. Le théâtre et l'histoire de la Révolution à la Restauration*, trans. from the Italian by Jérôme Nicolas (Paris: CNRS, 2011), 32–38.

24. Évelyne Lever, *Philippe Égalité* (Paris: Fayard, 1996), 293.

25. L. S. Mercier, *Tableau de Paris*, vol. II, 937.

26. See R. Héron de Villefosse, *L'anti-Versailles ou le Palais-Royal de Philippe Égalité*, Paris, Jean Dullis Éditeur, 1974, p. 133.

27. J.-P.-L. de Luchet, *Mémoires pour servir à l'histoire de l'année 1789*, 58.

28. Ibid., 59.

29. See Gabriel de Broglie, *L'Orléanisme: la ressource libérale de la France* (Paris: Perrin, 1980).

30. Ibid., 149–55.

31. *Mémoires du Prince de Talleyrand*, vol. I, 214.

32. On the Marquis de Chastellux, see the portrait by the Comte de Ségur, *Mémoires ou Souvenirs*, vol. I, 409–11, and the letter from the Comte de Ségur to the Comtesse de Ségur, December 6, 1782, in *Deux Français aux États-Unis*, 178. Also mentioned in the *Mémoires de Lauzun*, in the pages relating to his first American expedition.

33. Quoted in Antoine de Baecque, "Préface" to *Journal de Gouverneur Morris*, 13.

34. *Journal de Gouverneur Morris*, March 30, 1789, 33.

35. Ibid., October 22, 1789, 136.

36. Ibid., October 8, 1789, 118.

37. Ibid., June 6, 1789, 70.

38. Ibid., March 27, 1789, 31.

39. Ibid.

40. Ibid., October 30, 1789, 144.

41. Ibid., September 18, 1789, 102.

42. Ibid., November 8, 1789, 154.

43. Ibid., July 12, 1789, 81.

44. Ibid., November 19, 1789, 223.

45. Letter from Mme de Sabran to the Chevalier de Boufflers, 24 [June 1789], quoted in P. de Croze, *Le Chevalier de Boufflers et la Comtesse de Sabran*, 158–59.

46. In addition to the Duc d'Orléans, Stanislas Clermont-Tonnerre, Lally-Tollendal, the Duc d'Aiguillon, the Duc de Luynes, La Rochefoucauld-Liancourt, Alexandre de Lameth, and Montmorency-Laval.

47. Letter from Mme de Sabran to the Chevalier de Boufflers, 24 [June 1789], quoted in de Croze, *Le Chevalier de Boufflers and the Comtesse de Sabran*, 162–64.

48. *Journal de Gouverneur Morris*, July 12, 1789, 80–81.

49. S. Schama, *Citizens*, 384.

50. *Mémoires de M. le baron de Besenval*, vol. III, 500.

51. Ibid., 414.

52. Ibid., 416.

53. *La Journée du 14 Juillet 1789. Fragment des mémoires inédits de L. G. Pitra*, introduction and notes by Jules Flammermont (Paris: Société de l'Histoire de la Révolution française, 1892), cxxxii, quoted in J.-J. Fiechter, *Le Baron Pierre-Victor de Besenval*, 145.

54. *Mémoires de M. le baron de Besenval*, vol. III, 417.

55. J. de Norvins, *Souvenirs d'un historien de Napoléon*, vol. I, 217.

56. *Mémoires de M. le baron de Besenval*, vol. III, 412.

57. See F.-E. de Saint-Priest, *Mémoires*, vol. I, 233–34.

58. See *Journal de Gouverneur Morris*, July 15, 1789, 88.

59. Ibid.

60. J. de Norvins, *Souvenirs d'un historien de Napoléon*, vol. I, 22.

61. See *Journal de Gouverneur Morris*, July 17, 1789, 91.

62. Ibid., July 17, 1789, 90.

63. See the chapter on Vaudreuil, 390.

64. Letter from the Comte de Mercy-Argenteau to Joseph II, August 14, 1787, in *Correspondance secrète du Comte de Mercy-Argenteau avec l'empereur Joseph II et le Prince de Kaunitz*, published by the Chevalier Alfred d'Arneth and M. Jules Flammermont, 2 vol. (Paris: Imprimerie nationale, 1891), vol. II, 113.

65. Letter from Comte de Mercy-Argenteau to Joseph II, July 23, 1789, ibid., vol. II, 257.

66. Quoted in L. Pingaud, Introduction to *Correspondance intime du Comte de Vaudreuil et du Comte d'Artois*, vol. I, xxviii.

67. Quoted in *Mémoires sur la vie et le caractère de Mme la Duchesse de Polignac. Avec des anecdotes intéressantes sur la Révolution française, et sur la personne de Marie-Antoinette, reine de France. Par la Comtesse Diane de Polignac* (London: Chez J. Debrett, Piccadilly, vis-à-vis Burlington-House, 1796), 34.

68. Letter from the Comte de Vaudreuil to Lady Elizabeth Foster, Bern, August 16, 1789, in *Correspondance intime du Comte de Vaudreuil et du Comte d'Artois*, vol. I, 2–3.

69. See Massimo Boffa, "Émigrés," in *Dictionnaire critique de la Révolution française*, 346–54.

70. See for example the intransigent position taken by Ghislain de Diesbach in his *Histoire de l'émigration, 1789–1814* (Paris: Grasset, 1975).

71. July 16.

72. *Considérations sur la Révolution française par Madame de Staël*, posthumously published in 1818 by the Duc de Broglie and the Baron de Staël, 2 vol. (Paris: Charpentier, 1862), vol. I, part one, chapter XXIII: "Le retour de Necker," 202.

73. Ibid.

74. Quoted in J.-J. Fiechter, *Le Baron Pierre-Victor de Besenval*, 181.

75. Hubert Robert, *Vue de la cellule du baron de Besenval à la prison du Châtelet*. [View from the Cell of the Baron de Besenval]

76. G. Morris, *A Diary of the French Revolution*, vol. I, 309.

77. Quoted in J.-J. Fiechter, *Le Baron Pierre-Victor de Besenval*, 181.

78. *Mémoires de M. le baron de Besenval*, vol. III, 435.

79. In the National Gallery of London.

80. C. B. Bailey, "Henri-Pierre Danloux, The Baron de Besenval in his 'Salon de compagnie,'" in *An Aspect of Collecting Taste* (New York: Stair Sainty Matthiesen, 1986), 51.

81. See J.-J. Fiechter, *Le Baron Pierre-Victor de Besenval*, 197–98.

82. Letter from the Comte de Mercy-Argenteau to Kaunitz, August 17, 1789, in *Correspondance secrète du Comte de Mercy-Argenteau avec l'empereur Joseph II et le Prince de Kaunitz*, vol. II, 263.

83. See F.-E. de Saint-Priest, *Mémoires*, vol. II, 13–16.

84. On the eventual participation of the Duc d'Orléans in the march on Versailles, see the clarification by Évelyne Lever, in *Philippe Égalité*, 354–57.

85. Comte de La Marck, *Correspondance entre le Comte de Mirabeau et le Comte de La Marck*, vol. I, 127.

86. Cardinal de Retz, *Mémoires, La conjuration du Comte Jean-Louis de Fiesque, Pamphlets*, critical edition by Maurice Allem and Édith Thomas (Paris: Gallimard, 1956), 154.

87. Letter from the Comte de Mirabeau to the Comte de La Marck, October 14, 1789, in *Correspondance entre le Comte de Mirabeau et le Comte de La Marck*, vol. I, 128.

88. É. Dard, *Un confident de l'Empereur*, 66.

89. Antoine de Rivarol, *Petit dictionnaire des grands hommes de la Révolution, par un Citoyen actif, ci-devant "rien,"* introduction by Henri Coulet, edited and with notes by Jacques Grell (Paris: Desjonquères, 1987), 83–84.

90. See A.-F. Villemain, *Souvenirs contemporains d'histoire et de littérature*, vol. I, 22.

91. See François Furet, "Mirabeau," in *Dictionnaire critique de la Révolution française*, 299–305.

92 J. de Norvins, *Souvenirs d'un historien de Napoléon*, vol. I, 254.

93. Aglaé Saulx-Tavannes, *Mémoires de la Duchesse de Saulx-Tavannes, 1791–1806*, introduction and notes by the Marquis de Valous (Paris: Calmann-Lévy, 1934), 169.

94. On September 14, 1791.

95. *Mémoires ou Souvenirs et Anecdotes par M. le Comte de Ségur*, vol. III, 531. See the last page of the chapter dedicated to the Comte de Ségur.

96. Ibid., 591–92.

97. Letter from the Comte de Vaudreuil to the Comte d'Artois, April 30, 1790, in *Correspondance intime du Comte de Vaudreuil et du Comte d'Artois*, vol. I, 179.

98. See L. Apt, *Louis-Philippe de Ségur*, 72–74.

99. *Mémoires ou Souvenirs et Anecdotes par M. le Comte de Ségur*, vol. III, 574.

100. Letter from the Comte de Mirabeau to the Comte de La Marck, December 19, 1789, in *Correspondance entre le Comte de Mirabeau et le Comte de La Marck*, vol. I, 434.

101. *Correspondance secrète inédite sur Louis XVI, Marie-Antoinette, la Cour et la Ville*, vol. II, 524, May 7, 1791.

102. Philippe de Ségur, *Mémoires du général Comte de Ségur*, 3 vol. (Paris: Tallandier, 2010), vol. I: *Un aide de camp de Napoléon 1800–1812*, 28.

103. It was announced on October 20, 1791, by *La Feuille du jour*, the journal with which the Comte de Ségur so assiduously collaborated.

104. Ibid., 16.

105. See P. de Ségur, "Le Comte Louis-Philippe de Ségur (1753–1830)," 258. See also the letter from La Marck to Mercy-Argenteau, September 28, 1791, in *Correspondance entre le Comte de Mirabeau et le Comte de La Marck*, vol. III, 238; the letter from Montmorin to La Marck, October 3, 1791, ibid., 243, and October 15, 1791, ibid., 249–45; the letter from Mercy-Argenteau to La Marck, October 27, 1791, ibid., 257. See also the letter from Mme de Staël to Gouvernet, October 23, 1791, in Mme de Staël, *Correspondance générale*, vol. I, 501–2.

106. *Journal de Gouverneur Morris*, October 30, 1791, 318.

107. The Feuillants at that point counted among their ranks 334 deputies out of a total of 745.

108. Letter from Marie-Antoinette to Fersen, December 7, 1791, in *Le Comte de Fersen et la cour de France. Extraits des papiers du Grand Maréchal de Suède, Comte Jean Axel de Fersen, publiés par son petit-neveu le Baron R. M. de Klinckowström* (Paris: Firmin Didot, 1877), vol. I, 269.

109. Ibid., 270.

110. See Béatrice W. Jasinski, "Les conjonctures: January–August 1792," in Mme de Staël, *Correspondance générale*, vol. II: *Lettres diverses, 1792–15 mai 1794*, vol. 1, 305–58.

111. The words "right" and "left" first made their appearance in modern political parlance at the beginning of the work of the assembly, according to the seats occupied by the deputies. Monarchists were seated to the right of the president and to his left the partisans of the Revolution.

112. *Un duc et pair au service de la Révolution, le Duc de Lauzun (maréchal Biron), 1791–1792. Correspondance intime, publiée par le Comte de Lort de Sérignan* (Paris: Perrin, 1906).

113. Knee-length culottes fitted with silk stockings were reserved for gentlemen and rich bourgeois. Workers wore pants that fell to the ankle.

114. See Georges Touchard-Lafosse, *La Révolution, l'Empire et la Restauration, ou 178 anecdotes historiques dans lesquelles apparaissent, pour des faits peu connus, 221 contemporains français et étrangers* (Paris: L'Huillier, 1828), 58–59, quoted in Lacroix, "Notice sur la Marquise de Coigny," in *Lettres de la Marquise de Coigny*, 34.

115. Quoted in *Lettres de la Marquise de Coigny*, Notice, 40. See also Ch.-J. de Ligne, *Mélanges militaires, littéraires et sentimentaires, À mon refuge sur le Léopolberg près de Vienne, et se vend à Dresde chez les frères Walter, 1795–1811*, 34 vol.

116. See *Lettres de la Marquise de Coigny et de quelques autres personnes appartenant à la société française de la fin du XVIIIe siècle* (Paris: Imprimerie Jouast & Signaux, 1884).

117. See letter from Biron to Narbonne, December 9, 1791; and the letter from Lauzun to Talleyrand, December 11 [1791], in *Un duc et pair au service de la Révolution*, 27, 32.

118. The Army of the North controlled the border between Dunkerque and Maubeuge, the Army of the Center from Philippeville and Givet as far as Bitsch, and the Army of the Rhine from Landau to Huningue.

119. Letter from Biron to Talleyrand, December 20, 1791, in *Un duc et pair au service de la Révolution*, 78.

120. Note by Narbonne in the margin of the letter from Talleyrand to Biron of December 12 [1791], ibid., 36.

121. Letter from Biron to Talleyrand, December 25, 1791, ibid., 87.

122. See É. Dard, *Un confident de l'Empereur*, 95.

123. Quoted in François Furet and Denis Richet, *La Révolution française* (Paris: Hachette, 1965; Librairie Arthème Fayard, 1973), 148.

124. Letter from Biron to Talleyrand, January 7, 1792, in *Un duc et pair au service de la Révolution*, 101.

125. See L. Apt, *Louis-Philippe de Ségur*, 84.

126. *Journal d'émigration du Comte d'Espinchal*, February 1792, 310.

127. P. de Ségur, "Le Comte Louis-Philippe de Ségur (1753–1830)": 260.

128. See the letter from Talleyrand to Biron, January 5, 1792, in *Un duc et pair au service de la Révolution*, 97.

129. Albert Sorel reconstructed the tissue of intrigues of which the Comte de Ségur was a victim: "Mission du Comte de Ségur à Berlin en 1792," in *Le Temps*, October 10, 1878: 3–6; October 12, 1878: 3–7; October 18, 1878: 3–5.

130. Quoted in P. de Ségur, "Le Comte Louis-Philippe de Ségur (1753–1830)": 261.

131. Letter from Talleyrand to Biron, January 5, 1792, in *Un duc et pair au service de la Révolution*, 98–99.

132. Letter from Talleyrand to Biron, January 16, 1792, ibid., 111, and letter from Narbonne to Biron, January 6, 1792, ibid., 112.

133. *Journal de Gouverneur Morris*, January 10, 1792, 333.

134. Letter from Biron to Talleyrand, January 27, 1792, in *Un duc et pair au service de la Révolution*, 116–19.

135. See letter from Biron to Narbonne, February 21, 1792, ibid., 128.

136. Letter from the Marquise de Coigny to the Duc de Biron, London, [end of January 1792?], in *Lettres de la Marquise de Coigny*, 90.

137. Letter from the Marquise de Coigny to the Duc de Biron, London, February 1792, ibid., 101.

138. See *Mémoires de Madame la Duchesse de Gontaut*, 75–76.

139. Letter from the Marquise de Coigny to the Duc de Biron, London, [end of January 1792?], in *Lettres de la Marquise de Coigny*, 91.

140. Letter from Biron to Narbonne, Boulogne, February 21, 1792, in *Un duc et pair au service de la Révolution*, 126.

141. Letter from Narbonne to Biron, February 11, 1792, ibid., 124.

142. See É. Dard, *Un confident de l'Empereur*, 103.

143. See B. W. Jasinski, *Les Conjonctures: January–August 1792*, in Mme de Staël, *Correspondance générale*, vol. II, 337–38.

144. É. Dard, *Un confident de l'Empereur*, 109–10.

145. F.-R. de Chateaubriand, *Mémoires d'outre-tombe*, vol. I, 454.

146. Letter from M. de Vaudreuil to the Comte d'Artois, Berne, September 8, 1789, in *Correspondance intime du Comte de Vaudreuil et du Comte d'Artois*, vol. I, 4.

147. Ibid., 6.

148. Letter from M. de Vaudreuil to the Comte d'Artois, Venice, May 29, 1790, ibid., 194.

149. See Lebrun-Pindare's poem "L'Enchanteur et la Fée," in *Oeuvres de Ponce-Denis (Échouard) Le Brun*, vol. II, 379.

150. Letter from M. de Vaudreuil to the Comte d'Artois, (Rome), April 23, 1790, in *Correspondance intime du Comte de Vaudreuil et du Comte d'Artois*, vol. I, 175.

151. Letter from the Comte d'Artois to Joseph II, Moncalieri, October 12, 1789, in *Correspondance secrète du Comte de Mercy-Argenteau avec l'empereur Joseph II et le Prince de Kaunitz*, vol. II, 276.

152. Ibid., 276–77.

153. Letter from Joseph II to the Comte d'Artois, Vienna, October 30, 1789, ibid., 278–79.

154. Letter from M. de Vaudreuil to the Comte d'Artois, Rome, November 12, 1789, in *Correspondance intime du Comte de Vaudreuil et du Comte d'Artois*, vol. I, 28–29.

155. Letter from M. de Vaudreuil to the Comte d'Artois, Rome, November 28, 1789, ibid., 39–40.

156. Letter from M. de Vaudreuil to the Comte d'Artois, Rome, April 13, 1790, ibid., 164.

157. Letter from M. de Vaudreuil to the Comte d'Artois, Venice, October 9, 1790, ibid., 328.

158. Letter from M. de Vaudreuil to the Comte d'Artois, Venice, October 16, 1790, ibid., 338.

159. L. Pingaud, Introduction to ibid., vol. I, xxxviii–xxxix.

160. Letter from the Comte de Vaudreuil to his cousin [1791?], three and a half pages in quarto. The original in M. de Vaudreuil's script is held by M. Bégis, Archives nationales de la Fédération de Russie (GARF, Moscou), fonds no. 728 (Collection des documents du Palais d'Hiver), inventaire 2 (Émigration française), no. 288, "Lettres du Comte de Vaudreuil," folder 1728.

161. Charles-Georges de Clermont-Gallerand, *Mémoires particuliers pour servir à l'histoire de la révolution qui s'est opérée en France en 1789* (Paris: Dentu, 1826), vol. III, 207.

162. *Journal d'émigration du Comte d'Espinchal*, November 12, 1791, 284–87.

163. See letter from Gaston de Lévis to his wife, Pauline, Brussels, September 4, 1792, in *Écrire la Révolution: 1784–1795, Lettres à Pauline*, edited and annotated by Claudine Pailhès (Cahors: La Louve Éditions, 2011), 469ff.

164. Letter from Gaston de Lévis to his wife, Pauline, July 9, 1792, ibid., 436.

165. See P. de Croze, *Le Chevalier de Boufflers et la Comtesse de Sabran*, 25–28.

166. See G. de Diesbach, *Histoire de l'émigration, 1789–1814*, 157.

167. August 25, 1791.

168. Quoted in F. Furet et D. Richet, *La Révolution française*, 147.

169. Jean-Claude Berchet, *Chateaubriand* (Paris: Gallimard, 2012), 213.

170. F.-R. de Chateaubriand, *Mémoires d'outre-tombe*, vol. I, 454.

171. Ibid., 473.

172. Ibid., 471.

173. Ibid., 471–72.

174. Ibid., 477.

175. *Souvenirs de l'émigration ou Mémoires du Marquis de Marcillac...*, in *Mémoires sur l'émigration (1791–1800)*, with an introduction, bibliography, and notes by M. de Lescure (Paris: Firmin Didot, 1877), 114.

176. G. de Diesbach, *Histoire de l'émigration, 1789–1814*, 213–14.

177. Letter from M. de Vaudreuil to the Comte d'Artois, Vienna, April 19, 1792, in *Correspondance intime du Comte de Vaudreuil et du Comte d'Artois*, vol. I, 82.

178. Ibid.

179. Letter from M. de Vaudreuil to the Comte d'Antraigues, June 24, 1792, ibid., vol. II, 100.

180. Letter from the Comte d'Artois to M. de Vaudreuil, Hamm, June 15, 1793, ibid., 140.

181. Letter from M. de Vaudreuil to the Comte d'Antraigues, Vienna, October 14, 1793, ibid., 153.

182. Letter from M. de Vaudreuil to Lady Elizabeth Foster, Vienna, March 6, 1793, ibid., 123.

183. Letter from M. de Vaudreuil to Lady Elizabeth Foster, Vienna, December 19, 1793, ibid., 171.

184. Ibid., 170–71.

185. Letter from the Chevalier de Boufflers to Mme de Sabran, Paris, August 7, 1789, in P. de Croze, *Le Chevalier de Boufflers et la Comtesse de Sabran*, 175.

186. On the difficulties of the deputies of the nobility in adapting to the new revolutionary eloquence, see Jean-Claude Bonnet, *La "sainte masure," sanctuaire de la parole fondatrice*, in *La Carmagnole des Muses. L'homme de lettres et l'artiste dans la Révolution*, under the direction of Jean-Claude Bonnet (Paris: Armand Colin, 1988), 205.

187. For a detailed account of Boufflers's interventions at the assembly, see N. Vaget Grangeat, *Le Chevalier de Boufflers et son temps*, 86–94.

188. Over the course of the month of November (16, 22, and 24), the American diplomat had numerous discussions with Boufflers regarding his plans. See G. Morris, *A Diary of French Revolution*, vol. II, 61, 68, 70.

189. "Sur les inventions et découvertes en tous genres d'industrie," approved on December 30, 1790.

190. "Sur la distribution des récompenses nationales accordées à l'industrie en tous genres," approved on September 9, 10, and 27, 1791.

191. Letter from the Chevalier de Boufflers to Mme de Sabran, Paris, [September? 1791], in P. de Croze, *Le Chevalier de Boufflers et la Comtesse de Sabran*, 281.

192. *Journal des Impartiaux*, edited by M. Salles de la Salle (Paris: Impr. de la Veuve Valade, 1790), 11, quoted in ibid., 96.

193. Letter from the Chevalier de Boufflers to Mme de Sabran, Paris, August 11, 1791, in Paul Bonnefon, "La fuite de Varennes (lettres inédites du Ch. De Boufflers)," in *Amateur d'autographes* (1904): 109.

194. Gustav Gugitz, *Casanova und Graf Lamberg: unveroffentlichte Briefe des Grafen Max Lamberg an Casanova aus dem Schlossarchiv in Dux* (Leipzig-Wien: Bernina, 1935), 227, quoted in Alex Sokalski, "Repères biographiques," in *Stanislas de Boufflers, Contes*, ed. by Alex Sokalski (Paris: Société des textes français modernes, 1995), 24.

195. Letter from the Chevalier de Boufflers to Mme Durival, Paris, 26 Messidor, Year VIII, in G. Maugras, *La Marquise de Boufflers et son fils*, 538.

196. É. Vigée Le Brun, *Souvenirs*, 500.

197. The Comte and Comtesse de Boisgelin were guillotined on July 7, 1794.

198. *Relation d'un voyage à Bruxelles et à Coblence* (1791), extract from *Mémoires sur divers événements de la révolution et de l'émigration par A. H. Dampmartin, maréchal des camps et armées du roi*, 2 vol. (Paris: Hubert, 1825), in *Mémoires sur l'émigration* (1791–1800), 348.

199. Dante, *Paradiso*, Canto XVII, verses 58–60.

200. A.-F. Villemain, *Souvenirs contemporains d'histoire et de littérature*, vol. I, 40.

201. See *Mémoires de Malouet*, published by his grandson, the Baron Malouet, 2 vol. (Paris: Plon, 1874), vol. II, 211–22.

202. Talleyrand to Mme de Staël, October 8, 1793, see Duc de Broglie, "Lettres de M. de Talleyrand to Mme de Staël, tirées des archives du Château de Broglie," *Revue d'histoire diplomatique*, 4e année, I (1890): 89.

203. Mme de Staël, *Considérations sur la Révolution française*, vol. I, 385–86.

204. See Armand Lods, "Le Dernier chapelain de l'ambassade de Suède à Paris, Charles-Christian Gambs, 1759–1822," in *Bulletin historique et littéraire, Société de l'histoire du protestantisme français*, I, fourth series (1892): 41,145–52, 198–208.

205. Mme de Staël, *Considérations sur la Révolution française*, vol. I, 392.

206. See Erich Bollmann, *Récit du sauvetage de Narbonne*, in Mme de Staël, *Lettres à Narbonne*, 47–51. See Karl Varnhagen von Ense, *Denkwürdigkeiten Justus Erich Bollmanns*, in *Denkwürdigkeiten und vermischte Schriften* (Leipzig: Henrich Hoff Verlag, 1843), 137–308. See also Friederich Kapp, *Justus Erich Bollmann* (Berlin: J. Springer, 1880).

207. See Mme de Staël, ibid., 85–86. On Talleyrand in London, see Emmanuel de Waresquiel, *Talleyrand, le prince immobile* (Paris: Fayard, 2003), 170–71.

208. See Pierre-Louis Roederer, *Des fugitifs français et des émigrés*, in *Oeuvres du Comte L. Roederer*, 8 vol. (Paris: Firmin Didot, 1853–1859), vol. VII, 49–50.

209. Mary Berry, *Extracts from the Journals and Correspondence of Miss Berry, from the year 1783 to 1852*, critical edition by Lady Theresa Lewis, 3 vol. (London: Longmans Green, 1865), vol. I, 381.

210. Ghislain de Diesbach, *Histoire de l'émigration: 1789–1814* (Paris: Bernard Grasset, 1975), 270.

211. Mme de Staël, *Lettres à Narbonne*, 89.

212. Mme de Staël, "Douce image de Norbury," and letter to Mme d'Arblay, Coppet, August 9 [1793], in *Lettres à Narbonne*, 513.

213. Letter from Frances (Fanny) Burney to Mrs. Phillips, [posted October 4, 1792], in *The Journals and Letters of Fanny Burney (Madame d'Arblay)*, critical edition by Joyce Hemlow and Althea Douglas, 12 vol. (Oxford: Clarendon Press, 1972), vol. II, 1.

214. Constance Hill, *Juniper Hall: A Rendez-Vous of Certain Illustrious Personages during the French Revolution, Including Alexandre d'Arblay and Fanny Burney* (London: The Bodley Head, 1904), 25.

215. Ibid., 28.

216. Ibid., 24.

217. Ibid.

218. Ibid., 25.

219. Georges Solovieff, "Introduction" to Mme de Staël, *Lettres à Narbonne*, 33.

220. After a certain number of vicissitudes, the letters have finally appeared in the lovely edition by Georges Solovieff referenced here.

221. Mme de Staël, *De l'influence des passions sur le bonheur des individus et des nations*, in *Lettres sur Rousseau, De l'influence des passions et autres essais moraux*, under the direction of Florence Lotterie, texts established and presented by Florence Lotterie, annotated by Anne Amend-Söchting, Anne Brousteau, Florence Lotterie, Laurence Vanoflen (Paris: Honoré Champion, 2008), 199.

222. Letter from Mme de Staël to Narbonne, [Paris], August 28 [1792], in Mme de Staël, *Lettres à Narbonne*, 71.

223. Letter from Mme de Staël to Narbonne, Coppet, September 8 [1792], ibid., 81.

224. Letter from Mme de Staël to Narbonne, Coppet, September 12 [1792], ibid., 84.

225. Ibid.

226. Letter from Mme de Staël to Narbonne, fragment, undated, ibid., 145.

227. See letter from Mme de Staël to Narbonne, Rolle, October 23 [1792], ibid., 125.

228. Letter from Mme de Staël to Narbonne, Rolle, October 27 [1792], ibid., 128.

229. Jacques Necker, *Réflexions présentées to la nation française sur le procès intenté to Louis XVI* (Paris: Volland, 1792).

230. Letter from Mme de Staël to Narbonne, Rolle, November 15 [1792], in Mme de Staël, *Lettres à Narbonne*, 144.

231. Letter from Mme de Staël to Narbonne, Rolle, [November 22, 1792], ibid., 149.

232. A.-F. Villemain, *Souvenirs contemporains d'histoire et de littérature*, vol. I, 45–46.

233. Ibid., 47.

234. Ibid., 50.

235. Letter from Mme de Staël to Narbonne, [Rolle, December 2, 1793], in Mme de Staël, *Lettres à Narbonne*, 157–58.

236. Letter from Susanna Phillips to her sister Frances (Fanny) Burney, in C. Hill, *Juniper Hall: A Rendez-Vous Of Certain Illustrious Personages*, 40–41.

237. Letter from Mme de Staël to Narbonne, Rolle, December 23, 1792, in Mme de Staël, *Lettres à Narbonne*, 175.

238. Letter from Frances (Fanny) Burney to her father, Charles Burney, Norbury Park, January 28, 1793, in *The Journals and Letters of Fanny Burney*, vol. II, 8–9.

239. A.-F. Villemain, *Souvenirs contemporains d'histoire et de littérature*, vol. I, 51.

240. Letter from Frances (Fanny) Burney to her father, Charles Burney, Norbury Park, Monday February 4, 1793, in *The Journals and Letters of Fanny Burney*, vol. II, 10.

241. See letter from Frances (Fanny) Burney to Mrs. Lock, Mickleham, Thursday [February 14, 1793], ibid., 14.

242. Today Juniper Hall belongs to the National Trust.

243. Letter from Frances (Fanny) Burney to her father, Charles Burney, Mickleham, February 16–17, 1793, in *The Journals and Letters of Fanny Burney*, vol. II, 19.

244. See Linda Kelly, *Juniper Hall: An English Refuge from the French Revolution* (London: Weidenfeld and Nicolson, 1991), 45.

245. Letter from Frances (Fanny) Burney to her father, Charles Burney, Mickleham, February 24 [1793], in *The Journals and Letters of Fanny Burney*, vol. II, 26.

246. Letter from Frances (Fanny) Burney to her father, Charles Burney, Mickleham, February 22 [1793], ibid., 22.

247. "Derniers préparatifs," in *Journal d'émigration du Comte d'Espinchal*, 327.

248. Letter from Frances (Fanny) Burney to M. d'Arblay, written on February 25, 1793, in *The Journals and Letters of Fanny Burney*, vol. II, 31.

249. Letter from M. d'Arblay to Frances (Fanny) Burney, [Mickleham, sent March 6, 1793], ibid., 32.

250. See G. Solovieff, "Introduction" to Mme de Staël, *Lettres à Narbonne*, 218–19.

251. March 16.

252. Letter from Susanna Phillips to Frances (Fanny) Burney, quoted in C. Hill, *Juniper Hall: A Rendez-Vous Of Certain Illustrious Personages*, 53. French translation in G. Solovieff, "Introduction" to Mme de Staël, *Lettres à Narbonne*, 205.

253. Letter from Erich Bollmann to Frau Brauer, October 14, 1793, quoted in Mme de Staël, *Lettres à Narbonne*, 498–99.

254. Letter from Talleyrand to Mathieu de Montmorency, quoted by Mme de Staël in her letter to Narbonne of March 8 [1794], ibid., 386.

255. Letter from Mme de Staël to Narbonne, [Coppet], August 27 [1793], ibid., 287.

256. Letter from Mme de Staël to Narbonne, [Coppet], September 17 [1793], ibid., 290.

257. Letter from Mme de Staël to Narbonne, [Nyon?], January 31 [1794], ibid., 361.

258. Letter from Mme de Staël to Narbonne, Nyon, February 3 [1794], ibid., 364.

259. Letter from Mme de Staël to Narbonne, Coppet, September 21, 1793, ibid., 294.

260. Letter from Mme de Staël to Narbonne, Nyon, October 8 [1793], ibid., 303.

261. Letter from Mme de Staël to Narbonne, Coppet, 21 [September 1793], ibid., 296.

262. Letter from Mme de Staël to Narbonne, Nyon, March 12 [1794], ibid., 392.

263. Letter from Mme de Staël to Narbonne, Nyon, October 19 [1793], ibid., 342.

264. Letter from Mme de Staël to Narbonne, [Nyon], 5 o'clock in the morning, October 16 [1793], ibid., 314.

265. This novella was published in 1794.

266. Letter from Mme de Staël to Narbonne, Mézières, May 16, 1794, quoted in Mme de Staël, *Lettres à Narbonne*, 446.

267. Letter from Mme de Staël to Narbonne, Nyon, October 11 [1793], ibid., 306.

268. Letter from Mme de Staël to Narbonne, Nyon, October 14 [1793], ibid., 309–11.

269. Letter from Talleyrand to Mme de Staël, High Hycombe, November 8 [1793], in Duc de Broglie, "Lettres de M. de Talleyrand to Mme de Staël, tirées des archives du château de Broglie," in *Revue d'histoire diplomatique*, IV, 1 (1890): 89; see also ibid., 79–94; 2, 209–21.

270. See letter from Talleyrand to Mme de Staël, ibid., 1, 90.

271. Ibid., 91.

272. Letter from Narbonne to d'Arblay, January [?] 1774, preserved at the New York Public Library, The Henry W. and Albert A. Berg Collection of English and American Literature, Frances Burney d'Arblay collection of papers, 337 ALS+AL in French, 31 ALS and 64 AL to Gen. d'Arblay, folder 6.

273. Letter from Narbonne to Mrs. Phillips, quoted in L. Kelly, *Juniper Hall*, 119.

274. Letter from Narbonne to d'Arblay, ibid., 120.

275. A.-F. Villemain, *Souvenirs contemporains d'histoire et de littérature*, vol. I, 93.

276. F. de La Rochefoucauld, *Maximes*, no 19.

277. *Mémoires du Prince de Talleyrand*, vol. I, 35–36.

278. A.-F. Villemain, *Souvenirs contemporains d'histoire et de littérature*, vol. I, 65–68.

279. Letter from Mme de Staël to Ribbing, (toward the end of July), quoted in Mme de Staël, *Lettres à Narbonne*, 454.

280. "La jeune captive," in *Journal d'Aimée de Coigny*, presented by André-Marc Grangé (Paris: Perrin, 1981), 205.

281. J. de Norvins, *Souvenirs d'un historien de Napoléon*, vol. II, 93.

282. Ibid., 95–102.

283. Letter from Narbonne to d'Arblay, 17 Frimaire, Year IX, preserved at the New York Public Library, The Henry W. and Albert A. Berg Collection of English and American Literature, Frances Burney d'Arblay collection of papers, 31 ALS, and 64 AL to Gen. d'Arblay, folder 6.

284. Joan Haslip, *Madame du Barry: The Wages of Beauty* (London: Weidenfeld & Nicolson, 1991), 158.

285. See the chapter on Brissac, 195–96.

286. Letter from Mme du Barry to Marie-Antoinette, in Gaspard Louis Lafont d'Aussonne, *Mémoires secrets et universels des malheurs et de la mort de la reine de France* (Paris: Petit, 1824), 398–99, quoted in Ch.-J. Vatel, *Histoire de Madame du Barry*, vol. III, 132. See also *Mémoires secrets de 1770 à 1830 par le Comte d'Allonville*, vol. II, 180–81.

287. Ibid., 241.

288. See *Relation du départ de Louis XVI, le 20 juin 1791, écrite en August 1791, dans la prison de la Haute Cour nationale d'Orléans, par M. le Duc de Choiseul, pair de France, et extraite de ses mémoires inédits* (Paris: Baudouin Frères, 1822), 45, 51–52.

289. P. de Cossé-Brissac, *Histoire des ducs de Brissac*, 308.

290. Ibid.

291. "Brevet de nomination de M. de Cossé-Brissac, comme commandant général de la garde du roi," quoted in Ch.-J. Vatel, *Histoire de Madame du Barry*, vol. III, 158n1.

292. Letter from the Comte d'Antraigues to Don Simon de Las Casas, Spanish minister in Venice, quoted in Jacqueline Chaumié, *Le Réseau d'Antraigues et la contrerévolution, 1791–1793* (Paris: Plon, 1965), 108–9, quoted in Jacques de Saint-Victor, *Madame du Barry: un nom de scandale* (Paris: Perrin, 2002), 263.

293. *Acte du corps législatif, Non sujet à la Sanction du Roi, Relatif au Sieur Cossé-Brissac donné à Paris, le 12 Juin 1792, l'an 4e de la Liberté* (Paris: Imprimerie Royale, 1792), 2. See also J. de Saint-Victor, *Madame du Barry*, 264.

294. See F.-E. de Saint-Priest, *Mémoires*, vol. II, 49.

295. Laid out in four points—having enlisted unqualified persons; having refused to take an oath on the constitution; having instilled in his men an anti-constitutional and counterrevolutionary spirit; and having made the guard officers under his command swear to accompany the King wherever he wished to go—the act accused Brissac of having sullied the constitution and the security of the state; see *Acte du corps législatif, Non sujet à la Sanction du Roi, Relatif au Sieur Cossé-Brissac*, 2.

296. Ch.-J. Vatel, *Histoire de Madame du Barry*, vol. III, 150.

297. Ibid., 161.

298. Letter from Mme de Mortemart to Mme du Barry, June 5, 1792, quoted in ibid., 164.

299. Ibid., 165.

300. See "Copie authentique du 19 septembre 1811 du testament de Louis-Hercule-Timoléon de Cossé-Brissac," Archives départementales de Maine-et-Loire, Fonds de Brissac, 188 J 121, 5.

301. Ibid., 6.

302. Letter from Brissac to Mme du Barry, Orléans, August 11, 1792, six o'clock in the afternoon, quoted in Ch.-J. Vatel, *Histoire de Madame du Barry*, vol. III, 168–69.

303. See J. de Saint-Victor, *Madame du Barry*, 267.

304. See the testimony of two of the Duc's servants who witnessed the massacre, quoted in Ch.-J. Vatel, *Histoire de Madame du Barry*, vol. III, 178–80.

305. P. de Cossé-Brissac, *Histoire des ducs de Brissac*, 326.

306. Ch.-J. Vatel, *Histoire de Madame du Barry*, vol. III, 181–82.

307. The two letters were published in de Cossé-Brissac, *Histoire des ducs de Brissac*, 327–28.

308. Quoted in J. de Saint-Victor, *Madame du Barry*, 268.

309. Ch.-J. Vatel, *Histoire de Madame du Barry*, vol. III, 184.

310. The verdict delivered on February 27, 1793, set the reward she had to pay to her jeweler at 1,000 louis.

311. Ch.-J. Vatel, *Histoire de Madame du Barry*, vol. III, 190.

312. Ibid., 142–43.

313. As maintained by her Indian servant Zamor during her trial; see ibid., 266.

314. George Greive, *Égalité controuvée, ou Petite histoire de la protection, contenant les pièces relatives à l'arrestation de la du Barry ... pour servir d'exemple aux patriotes trop ardents qui veulent sauver la République, et aux modérés qui s'entendent à merveille pour la perdre* (Paris: G.-F. Galletti, [s.d.]).

315. See Ch.-J. Vatel, *Histoire de Madame du Barry*, vol. III, 200n1.

316. Ibid., 201–2.

317. Ibid., 208.

318. See *Convention nationale—Comité de Sureté générale*, "Interrogatoire de Madame du Barry," ibid., 221–32.

319. Ibid., 247.

320. See the "Note" of her defense attorney Chauveau-Lagarde, ibid., 275–76.

321. Charles-Joseph Vatel has published the notes taken during the hearing by Fouquier-Tinville; ibid., 258–76.

322. See J. de Saint-Victor, *Madame du Barry*, 247.

323. Ibid., 283.

324. Quoted in Ch.-J. Vatel, *Histoire de Madame du Barry*, vol. III, 272–74.

325. See "Déclaration de Madame du Barry (Entre deux guichets)," ibid., 282–86.

326. In writing the history of his family, the Duc de Brissac seemed convinced, on the basis of information furnished by Louis Dutens (1730–1812) in his *Mémoires d'un voyageur qui se repose*, that an Irish priest had offered to bribe Mme du Barry's jailers and let her escape—but that Jeanne, seeing as the plan would only allow for a single fugitive, preferred to offer that chance to Mme de Mortemart, then in hiding at Calais; see P. de Cossé-Brissac, *Histoire des ducs de Brissac*, 341–42.

327. É. Vigée Le Brun, *Souvenirs*, 237–38.

328. Letter from Mme Roland to Montané, [Sainte-Pélagie, September 11, 1793], in *Mémoires de Mme Roland*, new critical edition containing unpublished fragments and letters from prison, published by Claude Perroud, 2 vol. (Paris: Plon, Nourrit et Cie, 1905), vol. II, 373–74.

329. Letter from Biron to M. Dumouriez, March 19, 1792, in *Un duc et pair au service de la Révolution*, 155–56.

330. Letter from Biron to M. Dumouriez, Valenciennes, March 31, 1792, ibid., 165.

331. Letter from M. Dumouriez to Biron, Paris, March 27, 1792, ibid., 163–64.

332. From October 1791 to June 1792, he had been posted to the Army of the North; from June 5 to December 16, he commanded the Army of the Rhine; from the beginning of February to May 1793, the Army of the Midi (or of Italy); and from May 14 to July 1793, the Army of the Côtes de La Rochelle.

333. Biron took command of the Army of the Rhine—which he had been nominated to lead on June 5—on July 18 at Wissembourg, where he set up his general headquarters. He had at his disposal some 47,000 men, to which 8,000 more would be added.

334. See "Appendice. Note relative au général Biron," written by Biron in prison, in *Mémoires du Duc de Lauzun*, 380.

335. See C. C. Velay, *Le Duc de Lauzun*, 335–36.

336. Letter from Mme de Coigny to Biron, 17 [August 1792], in *Lettres de la Marquise de Coigny*, 147.

337. *Correspondance littéraire et critique par Grimm, Diderot, Raynal, Meister, etc.*, vol. XIV (December 1785): 282n1. *Les Mémoires secrets* also notes the presence of Mlle Laurent at the Comédie-Française on this date (vol. 29, 113–14).

338. Mme de Genlis, *Souvenirs de Félicie*, 58.

339. See René-Nicolas Dufriche, Baron Desgenettes, *Souvenirs de la fin du XVIIIe siècle et du commencement du XIXe siècle ou Mémoires de R. D. G.*, 2 vol. (Paris: Firmin Didot, 1836), vol. II, 273. A military doctor, Desgenettes served in the Army of the Mediterranean in 1793.

340. Letter from Général Biron to the convention, Strasbourg, November 18 of Year I of the Republic [1792], in *Lettres de la Marquise de Coigny*, 237.

341. Letter from the Duchesse de Lauzun to the Duc de Gontaut, [November 1792], ibid., 235.

342. *Mémoires de Louis-Philippe Duc d'Orléans écrits par lui-même. 1773–1793*, 2 vol. (Paris: Plon, 1973–1974), vol. I, 241.

343. Évelyne Lever, *Philippe Égalité*, 443.

344. *Mémoires de Louis-Philippe Duc d'Orléans*, vol. II, 291–303.

345. Grace Dalrymple Elliott, *Journal of My Life during the French Revolution* (London: R. Bentley, 1859), 91–92. Despite numerous and obvious inexactitudes, Miss Elliott's memoirs are generally considered reliable by historians.

346. Ibid., 93.

347. *Mémoires de Louis-Philippe Duc d'Orléans*, vol. II, 321.

348. This would be one of the main accusations formulated against him by Fouquier-Tinville at his trial before the Revolutionary Tribunal, and a point of evidence retained in the final sentence. See "Jugement qui condamne Armand-Louis Biron à la peine de mort," in "Affaire Biron," première partie, Archives nationales, W 305, no. 370.

349. See the chapter "L'Armée d'Italie," in C. C. Velay, *Le Duc de Lauzun*, 358–72.

350. Ibid., 366.

351. The Prince recalled the affectionate solicitude shown him by Biron in the account he gives of his time in prison. *Mémoires du Duc de Montpensier (Antoine-Philippe d'Orléans) prince du sang* (Paris: Imprimerie Royale, 1837), 1–7.

352. É. Lever, *Philippe Égalité*, 491.

353. Quoted in C. C. Velay, *Le Duc de Lauzun*, 370.

354. "Lettre de congé et de passage des consignes de sa charge de commandant en chef de l'armée des côtes au général Brunet. Aux commissaires de la Convention nationale corse," Nice, May 9, 1793, Year II of the Republic, in "Affaire Biron," third and final part: "Correspondance officielle avec les ministres depuis le 8 Mai 1793 jusqu'à Juillet 1793," Archives nationales, W 305, no. 370.

355. C. C. Velay, *Le Duc de Lauzun*, 375.

356. Letter from Biron to the minister of war (no. 10), Niort, June 16, 1793, Year II of the Republic, in "Affaire Biron," third and final part, op cit.

357. Letter from Biron to the minister of war (no. 14), Niort, June 22 [1793], ibid.

358. C. C. Velay, *Le Duc de Lauzun*, 382–83.

359. Letter from Biron to the minister of war (no. 11), June 21, 1793, Year II of the Republic, ibid.

360. Letter from Biron to the Committee of Public Safety, Niort, July 1, 1793, ibid.

361. Letter from Biron the Committee of Public Safety, Niort, June 29 [1793], ibid.

362. "De la Guerre de Vendée. Compte Rendu au Comité de salut public et au Conseil Exécutif provisoire par le Général Biron," in "Affaire Biron," second part, Archives nationales, W 305, no. 370.

363. Biron had asked to have him as his aide-de-camp in the Vendée. "Full of intelligence and energy," Rustan had declined the position of colonel general offered him by Custine so as not to leave Biron. See the letter from General Biron to the minister of

war, May 8, 1793, Year II of the Republic, in "Affaire Biron," third and final part, "Correspondance officielle avec les ministres depuis le 8 Mai 1793 jusqu'à Juillet 1793," Archives nationales, W 305, no 370.

364. C. C. Velay, *Le Duc de Lauzun*, 387.

365. *Mémoires du Comte de Beugnot, ancien ministre (1783–1815)*, published by the Comte Albert Beugnot, his grandson, 2 vol. (Paris: Édouard Dentu, 1866), vol. I, 173.

366. See the transcript of the interrogation, countersigned by Biron, in "Affaire Biron," first part, op cit.

367. Indictment by Antoine Quentin Fouquier, Public Prosecutor for the Criminal Tribunal, 8 Nivôse, ibid.

368. Sentence condemning Armand-Louis Biron to death, 10 Nivôse, ibid.

369. Yves Guéna, *Moi Duc de Lauzun, citoyen Biron* (Paris: Flammarion, 1997), 421.

370. Archives nationales, W 134, dossier 1, fragment 66.

371. Ibid.

372. The letter was addressed: "To Citizen Gontaut, rue Chantereine, Chaussée d'Antin."

373. Letter from Mme de Coigny to Biron [London], 20 [February, 1792?], in *Lettres de la Marquise de Coigny*, 104.

374. Archives nationales, W 134, dossier 1, fragment 40.

375. See Charles Baudelaire, "Don Juan aux Enfers," XV, *Spleen et idéal*, in *Les Fleurs du mal*.

376. P. de Ségur, "Le Comte Louis-Philippe de Ségur (1753–1830)": 262.

377. Joseph-Alexandre de Ségur, *Essai sur l'opinion considérée comme une des principales causes de la Révolution de 1789* (Paris: Vezard & Le Normant, 1790), 45–46.

378. *Mémoires ou Souvenirs et Anecdotes par M. le Comte de Ségur*, vol. III, 592.

379. *Journal d'émigration du Comte d'Espinchal*, 403.

380. G. de Broglie, *Ségur sans cérémonie*, 146–47.

381. Ibid.

382. Ibid., 154.

383. Ibid., 149.

384. See the chapter on the Vicomte de Ségur, 149.

385. See M. Fazio, *François-Joseph Talma*, 38–53.

386. On January 25, 1792, at the Théâtre de la Nation. Morris went to see the play on February 7 and, though he praised Fleury's acting, found it mediocre; see G. Morris, *A Diary of the French Revolution*, vol. II, 116.

387. January 29, 1792, at the Théâtre de la Nation.

388. The Comte d'Avaux was an important figure in the sect of the Illuminati—bringing together a circle of disciples and collecting a library of rare works that included the famous psalter of Ingeborg; see G. de Broglie, *Ségur sans cérémonie*, 156.

389. *Mémoires complets et authentiques de Laure Junot Duchesse d'Abrantès*, vol. III, 420.

390. The law authorizing divorce went into effect on September 20, 1792.

391. G. de Broglie, *Ségur sans cérémonie*, 142.

392. Joseph-Alexandre de Ségur, *Ma prison depuis le 22 vendémiaire jusqu'au 10 thermidor, l'an III de la République* (Paris: Huet, Year II of the Republic [1795]), vv. 121–28, 8.

393. *Roméo et Juliette, Opéra en trois actes. Paroles du c. J. A. Ségur, musique du c. Steibelt . . .* (Paris: Huet, Year II of the Republic [1794].

394. It was the sixth adaptation, going in chronological order. The first four had been German, and the fifth, set to music by Dalayrac and with a libretto by Boutet and Monvel, was performed in Paris on July 7, 1792, barely a year before that of Steibelt and Ségur. See Francesco Bissoli, *"Fotografare" Romeo and Juliet*, in Vertemus. Prima serie di studi musicali e teatrali veronesi 2001, 125–51, and Winton Dean, "Shakespeare and Opera," in *Shakespeare and Music*, under the direction of Phyllis Hartnoll (London: Macmillan, 1964), 89–175.

395. See M. Fazio, *François-Joseph Talma*, 69–72.

396. See Gérard Walter, *André Chénier, son milieu et son temps* (Paris: Laffont, 1947), 287–88.

397. Jean-Antoine Roucher, *Consolations de ma captivité, ou Correspondance de Roucher, mort victime de la tyrannie décemvirale, le 7 thermidor, an 2 de la République française* (Paris: H. Agasse, Year VI of the Republic [1797]), first part, 253.

398. J.-A. de Ségur, *Ma prison depuis le 22 vendémiaire jusqu'au 10 thermidor*, vv. 39–40, 4.

399. See the chapter on Lauzun, 99.

400. J. H. Wilhelm Tischbein, *Aus meinem Leben, texte et notes de Carl G. W. Schiller*, 2 vol. (Schwetschke: Braunschweig, 1861), vol. II, quoted in Benedetto Croce, "Dalle memorie del pittore Tischbein," in *Aneddoti di varia letteratura*, 4 vol. (Naples: Ricciardi, 1942; Bari: Laterza, 1954, 2nd edition), vol. III, 217–19.

401. B. Croce, "Dalle memorie del pittore Tischbein," 220.

402. See *Mémoires du Duc de Lauzun*, 190.

403. Letter from the Marquise de Coigny to the Duc de Biron, 12 [juin 1792], in *Lettres de la Marquise de Coigny*, 138.

404. Letter from Horace Walpole to Lady Ossory, October 8, 1792, in *Horace Walpole's Correspondence with the Countess of Upper Ossory*, text and notes by W. S. Lewis and A. Dayle Wallace with the assistance of Edwine M. Martz, 3 vol. (New Haven, CT: Yale University Press, 1965), vol. III [vol. XXXIV of *Horace Walpole's Correspondence*], 165.

405. Ibid., 164–65.

406. See Étienne Lamy, "Introduction" to *Mémoires de Aimée de Coigny* (Paris: Calmann-Lévy, 1902), 40.

407. Quoted in André-Marc Grangé, "Introduction" to *Journal d'Aimée de Coigny, "La jeune captive"* (Paris: Librairie Académique Perrin, 1981), 15n1.

408. E. de Waresquiel, *Talleyrand, le prince immobile*, 226.

409. See the portrait of him by E. de Waresquiel, ibid., 226–28.

410. A. Omodeo, "Introduction" to A. de Coigny, *La Restaurazione Francese del 1814, Memorie*, 22.

411. Letter from Aimée de Coigny to Citizen Biron, Mareuil, February 12 [1793], in *Lettres de la Marquise de Coigny*, 198.

412. Letter from Aimée de Coigny to Citizen Biron, London, [December 1792?], ibid., 192.

413. Letter from Aimée de Coigny to Citizen Biron, Mareuil, February 12 [1793], ibid., 199.

414. See Francis Scarfe, *André Chénier: His Life and Work, 1762–1794* (Oxford: Clarendon Press, 1965), 317.

415. From February to July 1792, Chénier published twenty-one articles there.

416. André Chénier, *III, Iambes*, in *Oeuvres complètes*, édition Gérard Walter (Paris: Gallimard, Bibliothèque de la Pléiade, 1958), 189.

417. See Francis Scarfe, *André Chénier: His Life and Work*, 320–23.

418. A. Chénier, *IX, Iambes*, 194.

419. A. Chénier, *II*, ibid., 188.

420. A. Chénier, *IV*, ibid., 190.

421. A. Chénier, *IX*, ibid., 193.

422. A. Chénier, *VIII*, ibid., 192–93.

423. She had been arrested on March 15, 1793.

424. Horace Walpole to Mary Berry, Strawberry Hill, October 15, 1793, *Horace Walpole's Correspondence with Mary and Agnes Berry and Barbara Cecilia Seton*, 2 vol., *Horace Walpole's Correspondence*, vol. 12 of the *General Correspondence* and book two of that with Mary Berry, 30.

425. A. Chénier, *IX, Iambes*, in *Oeuvres complètes*, 195.

426. On this subject, see the beautiful pages by Lionello Sozzi, *Il paese delle chimere* (Palermo: Sellerio, 2007), 363–69.

427. A. Chénier, *I, Iambes*, in *Oeuvres complètes*, 187.

428. Charles Leconte de Lisle, *André Chénier. De la poésie lyrique à la fin du XVIIIe siècle*, "La Variété," August 5, 1840, quoted in Catriona Seth, *André Chénier. Le miracle du siècle* (Paris: PUPS, 2005), 8.

429. André Chénier, "La jeune captive," *Odes, VII*, in *Oeuvres complètes*, 185–86. English translation by Katharine Hillard, from Charles Dudley Warner, ed., *Library of the World's Best Literature* (New York: J. A. Hill & Co., 1902), pg. 3606.

430. Millin de Grandmaison published the ode in *Le Magazine encyclopédique*, the review that he directed, in February 1795, declaring that it had been composed for Aimée at the time when they both found themselves in Saint-Lazare, and that he himself possessed the manuscript. The poem had already been published, six weeks after the death of Chénier, in *La Décade philosophique, littéraire et politique du 20 nivôse, an III* [January 9, 1795]. See A. Omodeo, "Introduction" to A. de Coigny, *La Restaurazione francese del 1814, Memorie*, 30–31.

431. See É. Lamy, "Introduction" to *Mémoires de Aimée de Coigny*, introduction and notes by Étienne Lamy (Paris: Calmann-Lévy, 1902), 41.

432. *Journal d'Aimée de Coigny*, 126.

433. B. Dussane, *La Célimène de Thermidor*, 130.

434. See G. de Broglie, *Ségur sans cérémonie*, 176.

435. B. Dussane, *La Célimène de Thermidor*, 136.

436. J.-A. de Ségur, *Ma prison depuis le 22 vendémiaire jusqu'au 10 thermidor*, op cit.

437. Ibid., vv. 129–32, 8.

438. Ibid., vv. 278–81, 14.

439. "Poor Mlle Contat obtained her freedom on the eve of her scheduled execution, and for the first time since our emigration performed at the Comédie-Française. A woman in the audience told me that no one had ever been applauded like she was," wrote Narbonne, happily, to d'Arblay, from Lausanne, on the 21 [March?] 1794, New York Public Library, The Henry W. and Albert A. Berg Barret Collection, Fonds Burney, 337ALS+AL in French, 31 ALS and 14 AL to Gen. d'Arblay, folder 6.

TURNING THE PAGE

1. *Mémoires inédits de Madame la Comtesse de Genlis*, vol. VII, 375.

2. P. Lacroix, "Notice sur la Marquise de Coigny," in *Lettres de la Marquise de Coigny*, 62.

3. "Notice historique sur le vicomte de Ségur," in *Oeuvres diverses du vicomte J.-A. de Ségur*, 6.

4. G. de Broglie, *Ségur sans cérémonie*, 233.

5. See Philippe-Paul de Ségur, *Histoire et Mémoires par le Général Cte Philippe de Ségur*, 7 vol. (Paris: Firmin Didot, 1877), vol. I, 48.

6. G. de Broglie, *Ségur sans cérémonie*, 227.

7. February 27, 1801.

8. December 25, 1802.

9. P. de Ségur, "Le Comte Louis-Philippe de Ségur (1753–1830)": 274.

10. G. de Broglie, *Ségur sans cérémonie*, 285.

11. See *Mémoires du Comte de Rambuteau, publiés par son petit-fils*, with an introduction and notes by M. Georges Lequin (Paris: Calmann-Lévy, 1909), 21–22.

12. See letters from Auguste de Staël to his mother, December 5, 1805, and February 27, 1809, in Othenin d'Haussonville, "Auguste de Staël et ses parents," in *Cahiers staëliens*, new series, 53 (2002): 148–49.

13. Cited in É. Dard, *Un confident de l'Empereur*, 154.

14. Cited in G. Maugras, *La Marquise de Boufflers et son fils, le chevalier de Boufflers*, 533.

15. Ibid.

16. Letter from the Chevalier de Boufflers to Mme Durival, Plombières, September 24, 1810, ibid., 548.

17. See Florence Delay, *Mes cendriers* (Paris: Gallimard, 2010).

18. See the letter from the Chevalier de Boufflers to Mme Durival, Paris, October 4, 1806, in G. Maugras, *La Marquise de Boufflers et son fils*, 545.

19. É. Vigée Le Brun, *Souvenirs*, 272.

20. Jean-Claude Berchet (Chateaubriand, 480) speaks of her *"déréliction amoureuse."*

21. Letter from M. de Vaudreuil to the Marquise de Vaudreuil, Vienna, July 12, *Correspondance intime du Comte de Vaudreuil et du Comte d'Artois*, II, 235.

22. "Lettre de M. de Vaudreuil justifiant les maisons de Polignac, de Vaudreuil, de Guiche et de Talleyrand, accusés par un journaliste de Vienne d'avoir profité trop largement des générosités royales" [Letter from M. de Vaudreuil justifying the houses of Polignac, Vaudreuil, Guiche, and Talleyrand, accused by a Viennese journalist of having drawn too great a profit from royal magnanimity] (draft, s.d.), [Vienne, 1793]. Archives nationales de la Fédération russe GARF, Moscou. Fonds 728, inventaire 2: 728-2-275-80 and 728-2-275-81.

23. Jean-Claude Méhée, *Alliance des Jacobins de France avec le Ministère anglais, Imprimerie de la République* (Paris: Year XII of the Republic [1803]), 61, quoted in L. Pingaud, "Introduction" to the *Correspondance intime du Comte de Vaudreuil et du Comte d'Artois*, vol. I, xliii.

24. See "Inventaire après décès de Joseph-Hyacinthe François de Paule, Comte Rigaud de Vaudreuil" [Inventory following the death of Joseph-Hyacinthe François de Paule, Comte Rigaud de Vaudreuil," February 24, 1817, preserved at the Archives Nationales, Minutes and reports of the notary Jean Eustache Montaud, November 12, 1797–July 6, 1832 (étude CVIII), Minutier central des notaires de Paris, inventory number MC/RE/CVIII/23.

25. Philip Mansel, "Le Prince de Ligne et les émigrés français, 1789–1814," in *Nouvelles Annales Prince de Ligne*, X (1996): 9.

Bibliography

ON ARMAND-LOUIS DE GONTAUT, THE DUC DE BIRON, AND
THE DUC DE LAUZUN

Manuscripts

Université de Poitiers, Archives d'Argenson, 77:
  Letters from Lauzun to the Marquis de Voyer.
Paris, Archives nationales, "Affaire Biron," W 305/2, no. 370:
  —"Procès-verbal," countersigned by Biron, first part.
  —"Acte d'accusation," [indictment] "Jugement" [verdict].
  —"De la Guerre de Vendée. Compte Rendu au Comité de Salut Public et au Conseil
    Exécutif provisoire par le Général Biron" [On the War in the Vendée: Report Delivered
    to the Committee of Public Safety and to the Executive Council by General Biron],
    second part.
  —"Correspondance Officielle avec les ministres depuis le 8 mai 1793 jusqu'à Juillet 1793"
    [Official Correspondence with the ministers from May 8, 1793, through July 1793],
    third and final part.
Archives nationales, W 134, dossier 1, pièce 66: final letter from Biron to Mlle Laurent.
Archives nationales, W 134, dossier 1, pièce 40: final letter from Biron to his father.

Works

Published in Paris by Barrois l'Aîné Librairie in December 1821, the first edition of the
Mémoires du Duc de Lauzun was confiscated at the demand of the Duc de Choiseul, who
judged it detrimental to the honor of his family. The following year there appeared a
second edition in which numerous passages and the names of individuals were eliminated.
It would not be until 1858 that the *Mémoires du Duc de Lauzun (1747–1783)* were republished
"complete according to the manuscript with a study of the life of the author, second edition,
unabridged, and augmented with a preface and new notes by Louis Lacour (Paris: Poulet
Malasis et de Broise)." This time it was Prince Adam Czartoryski who managed to have it
confiscated to protect the respectability of his mother, Princesse Izabela Czartoryska—but
this did not prevent the book from circulating. In Russia, on the other hand, the Duc's
Mémoires pleased Marina Tsvetaeva, who, in 1919, took them as the inspiration for a

theatrical piece, *Fortuna*, in which Lauzun featured as the protagonist. As Serena Vitale has kindly pointed out to us, this play was part of a cycle entitled "Romanticism," written for the theater of Yuri Zavadsky, and served, in a starving Moscow ravaged by civil war, as a provocative homage to a bygone aristocratic past, and to the Revolution that had swept it all away. In our portrait of Lauzun, we have relied upon Lacour's edition of his works. Among the numerous successive editions, we single out for the interest of its introduction the *Mémoires du Duc de Lauzun*, complete edition preceded by a study of Lauzun and his memoirs by Georges d'Heylli (Paris: É. Rouveyre, 1880).

Le Ton de Paris ou les amants de bonne compagnie, comédie en 2 actes (Paris: Honoré Champion, 1911; Paris: F. Juven, 1912; Geneva: Slatkine Reprints, 1973).

Duc de Lauzun, "Journal du Sénégal, Janvier–mars 1779," in *Bulletin du Comité d'études historiques et scientifiques de l'Afrique occidentale française*, 2 (1920): 515–51.

Duc de Lauzun, *Lettres sur les États Généraux de 1789* (Paris: Bachelin-Deflorenne, 1865).

Un Duc et pair au service de la Révolution, le Duc de Lauzun (maréchal Biron), 1791–1792: Correspondance intime, published for the first time *in extenso* based on the original manuscript in the historical archives of the Ministry of War by the Comte de Lort de Sérignan (Paris: Perrin, 1906).

Bibliographic References

Sainte-Beuve's 1851 portrait (*Le Duc de Lauzun*, in *Causeries du lundi* [Paris: Garnier Frères, s.d.], vol. IV, 287–308), and the two volumes by Gaston Maugras, *La Fin d'une société: Le Duc de Lauzun et la cour intime de Louis XV* (Paris: Plon, 1893) and *La Fin d'une société: Le Duc de Lauzun et la cour de Marie-Antoinette* (Paris: Plon, 1902), are essential preparatory readings for any study of the Duc.

Le Duc de Lauzun. 1747–1793, preface by Général Weygand (Paris: Plon, 1937), by the Comte R. de Gontaut-Biron, reconstructs his military campaigns.

The best biography of Lauzun is the excellently documented work by Clément C. Velay, *Le Duc de Lauzun (1747–1793): Essai de dialogue entre un homme et son temps* (Paris: Buchet-Chastel, 1983).

For his part, Yves Guéna preferred to tell the story of the Duc's life in the form of a novel: *Moi Duc de Lauzun, citoyen Biron* (Paris: Flammarion, 1997).

For the story of the romance between Lauzun and Lady Sarah Bunbury, see *The Life and Letters of Lady Sarah Lennox, 1745–1826, Daughter of Charles, 2nd duke of Richmond, and Successively the Wife of Sir Thomas Charles Bunbury, Bart., and of the Hon. George Napier; Also a Short Political Sketch of the Years 1760 to 1763 by Henry Fox, 1st Lord Holland*, edited by the Countess of Ilchester and Lord Stavordale, 2 vol. (London: John Murray, 1902, reprint Anonymous).

See also Stella Tillyard, *Aristocrats: Caroline, Emily, Louisa and Sarah Lennox, 1740–1832* (London: Chatto & Windus, 1994).

For the relationship between Lauzun and Izabela Czartoryska, see the letters from the Princesse to her husband, as well as her self-portrait, preserved in Kraków at the Fundacja Czartoryskich, Biblioteka XX., Czartoryskich, manuscripts 6030 and 6067; the biography by Gabriela Pauszer-Klonowska, *Pani na Puławach* (Warsaw: Czytelnik, 1978); as well as the *Mémoires du roi Stanislas-Auguste Poniatowski*, 2 vol. (St. Petersburg: Imprimerie de l'Académie impériale des sciences, 1914, vol. I; Leningrad: Académie des sciences en Russie, 1924, vol. II); Jean Fabre, *Stanislas-Auguste Poniatowski et l'Europe des Lumières* (Paris: Éditions Ophrys, 1984); Adam Zamoyski, *The Last King of Poland* (London: Phoenix Giant, [1992] 1998).

See also the description of Puławy in *La Pologne historique, littéraire, monumentale et pittoresque*, drafted by a group of writers under the direction of Léonard Chodzko, édition d'Ignace-Stanislas Grabowski, 3 vol. (Paris: Au bureau central, 1835–1842), vol. I, 5–7.

For the relationship between Lauzun and the Marquise de Coigny, see *Lettres de la Marquise de Coigny et de quelques autres personnes appartenant à la société française de la fin du XVIIIe siècle*, edited by Paul Lacroix (Paris: Jouaust & Sigaux, 1884).

For his relationship with Aimée de Coigny, Duchesse de Fleury, see Étienne Lamy's introduction to the *Mémoires de Aimée de Coigny* (Paris: Calmann-Lévy, 1902), 1–146; the lovely introduction by Adolfo Omodeo to *Aimée de Coigny (La Jeune Captive), La Restaurazione francese del 1814, Memorie*, Italian translation by Ada Prospero (Bari: Laterza, 1938), 5–45; as well as the introduction by André-Marc Grangé to the *Journal d'Aimée de Coigny, "La jeune captive"* (Paris: Perrin, 1981), 9–64. See also *Alvare* (Paris: Firmin Didot, s.d.).

ON THE VICOMTE DE SÉGUR

Works

Correspondance secrète entre Ninon de Lenclos, le Marquis de Villarceaux, et Mme de M... (Paris: Lejav, 1789).

Proverbes dramatiques (Le Parti le plus Sage, Le Parti le plus Gai, ou À bon chat, bon rat) (Paris: Desenne, 1787).

Rosaline et Floricourt: Comédie en deux actes et en vers libres (Paris: Desenne, 1790). Staged for the first time at the Théâtre-Français, November 17, 1787.

La Femme jalouse (Paris: Henry, 1790).

Essai sur l'opinion considérée comme une des principales causes de la révolution de 1789 (Paris: Vezard & Le Normant, 1790).

Le Fou par amour, drame historique en un acte et en vers (Paris: 1791). Théâtre de la Nation, January 19, 1791.

Le Retour du mari, comédie en un acte et en vers (Paris: Galey, 1792). Théâtre de la Nation, January 29, 1792.

Articles printed in the newspaper *La Feuille du Jour* (December 1, 1790–August 10, 1792).

Roméo et Juliette, Opéra en trois actes, text by C. J. A. Ségur, music by C. Steibelt (Paris: Huet, Year II of the Republic). Staged for the first time in Paris, at the Théâtre Feydeau, September 10, in the Second Year of the Republic, whole and indivisible.

Ma prison depuis le 22 vendémiaire jusqu'au 10 thermidor, l'an III de la République, par le Citoyen Alexandre de Ségur, le cadet (Paris: Huet, Year III of the Republic).

Essai sur les moyens de plaire en amour par Ségur le jeune (Paris: Huet, 1797).

La Création du monde, Oratorio in three parts, translated from the German into French verse by Joseph A. Ségur, music by Joseph Haydn, arranged for the piano and for the Théâtre des Arts by D. Steibelt (Paris: Melles Erard [vers 1800]). Performed for the first time at the Théâtre des Arts on 3 Nivôse, Year IX.

Comédies, proverbes et chansons, par Joseph-Alexandre de Ségur (Paris: Colnet, 1802).

Les Femmes, leur condition et leur influence dans l'ordre social chez différents peuples anciens et modernes, 3 vol. (Paris: Treuttel et Würtz, 1803).

Posthumous edition of *Oeuvres Diverses du vicomte J.-A. de Ségur, contenant Ses Morceaux de Littérature, ses Poésies fugitives; la Correspondance secrète entre Ninon de Lenclos, le Marquis de Villarceaux, et Mme de Maintenon,* preceded by a note on the life of the author (Paris: Dalibon, 1819).

Bibliographic References

On his family:

Georges Martin, *Histoire et généalogie de la maison de Ségur* (La Ricamarie: Imprimerie Mathias, 1991).

Pierre de Ségur, *Le Maréchal de Ségur (1724–1801), ministre de la Guerre sous Louis XVI* (Paris: Plon, Nourrit et Cie, 1895).

Essential for an understanding of the Vicomte de Ségur; his brother, Louis-Philippe; and the aristocratic lifestyle of the era is Gabriel de Broglie's lovely volume *Ségur sans cérémonie 1757–1805, ou la Gaieté libertine* (Paris: Perrin, 1977), to which I have also referred for the complete bibliography of the Vicomte's works.

For the Baron de Besenval, whose life was closely involved with that of the Ségurs, I have referred to *Mémoires de M. le baron de Besenval, Lieutenant-Général des Armées du Roi, sous Louis XV et Louis XVI, Grand'Croix de l'Ordre de Saint-Louis, Gouverneur de Haguenau, Commandant des Provinces de l'Intérieur, Lieutenant-Colonel du Régiment des Gardes-Suisses, etc.; écrits par lui-même, imprimés sur son manuscrit original, et publiés par son Exécuteur Testamentaire, Contenant beaucoup de Particularités et d'Anecdotes sur la Cour, sur les Ministres et les Règnes de Louis XV et Louis XVI, et sur les Événements du temps,* preceded by a note on the life of the author by Alexandre-Joseph de Ségur, 4 vol. (Paris: F. Buisson, 1805).

Additionally, I have had recourse to *Contes de M. le baron de Besenval, lieutenant-général des Armées du Roi,* with a bio-bibliographic note by Octave Uzanne (Paris: A. Quantin, 1881).

In addition to the portraits by the Duc de Lévis (*Souvenirs-Portraits de Gaston de Lévis [1764–1830] suivis de Lettres intimes de Monsieur Comte de Provence au Duc de Lévis* [Paris: Mercure de France, 1993], 158–65) and by Sainte-Beuve ("Le baron de Besenval," in *Causeries du lundi,* vol. XII, 492–510), I have used the biographical study by Jean-Jacques Fiechter, *Le Baron Pierre-Victor de Besenval (1721–1791)* (Lausanne and Paris: Delachaux et Niestlé, 1993), and the invaluable essay on the Baron's art collection by Colin B. Bailey, "Henri-Pierre Danloux, the Baron de Besenval in His 'Salon de compagnie'" in *An Aspect of Collecting Taste* (New York: Stair Sainty Matthiesen, 1986), 5–6, 48–53.

For the Vicomte de Ségur's relationship with Julie Careau, see *Lettre sur Julie* by Benjamin

Constant and "Notes biographiques sur Julie Talma" by Mme Constant de Rebecque, which figures as a preface to *Lettres de Julie Talma à Benjamin Constant*, published by the Baronne Constant de Rebecque (Paris: Plon, Nourrit et Cie, 1966).

See also Micheline Boudet, *Julie Talma, l'ombre heureuse* (Paris: Robert Laffont, 1989); Madeleine and Francis Ambrière, *Talma ou l'histoire au théâtre* (Paris: Éditions de Fallois, 2007); and Mara Fazio, *François-Joseph Talma: Le théâtre et l'histoire de la Révolution à la Restauration*, trans. by Jérôme Nicolas (Paris: Éditions du CNRS, 2011).

ON THE DUC DE BRISSAC

Manuscripts

Archives départementales de Maine-et-Loire, Fonds de Brissac, 188 J 121: "Duc de Brissac: testament et autres papiers."

Archives nationales, fasc. W/16 Vaubernier Dubarry Vendenquer D: 9: "Lettres de Brissac avant et depuis la Révolution peu importantes si ce n'est qu'elles prouvent ses liaisons intimes avec elle [Mme du Barry], ainsi que sa façon de penser sur la Révolution. Il est à remarquer qu'elle a employé toute une nuit à brûler sa correspondance avec lui le jour de sa mort à Versailles." [Letters by Brissac before and after the Revolution, of little importance but for the fact that they establish his intimate relations with [Mme du Barry], and her thoughts and opinions regarding the Revolution. It is notable that she spent a whole night burning her correspondence with him the day of his death at Versailles.] Eighth bundle H., containing ten letters.

Bibliographic References

The life of the Duc de Brissac was recounted in the mid-twentieth century by the current Duc de Brissac, within the frame of the history of his family: "Le dernier gouverneur de Paris," in Pierre de Cossé-Brissac, *Histoire des ducs de Brissac: Maison de Cossé* (Paris: Fasquelle, 1952), 271–330. Numerous details and firsthand documents relating to the Duc are also to be found in Charles-Joseph Vatel's meticulous and indispensable investigation into Mme du Barry, *Histoire de Madame du Barry*, 3 vol. (Versailles: L. Bernard, 1883).

In the absence of a study on the Duc's art collection, I will at least mention two documents that attest to his passion as a collector. The first is *Guide des Amateurs et des Étrangers voyageurs à Paris. Description raisonnée de cette ville, de sa banlieue et de tout ce qu'elles contiennent de remarquable: par M. Thiéry; enrichie de vues perspectives des principaux monuments modernes*, 2 vol. (Paris: Hardouin et Gattey, 1787), vol. II, 569–73. The second is the list of works confiscated from the Duc at the time of his arrest, "Rapport fait par Picault et Naigeon à la Commission temporaire des arts, le quitidi floréal, L'an 2d de la République française, une et indivisible, des Tableaux, Meubles, Bronzes, Marbres et Porcelaines retenus, inventoriés et transportés de la maison Brissac rue de Grenelle Germain au dépôt National Rue de Baune le 9.10.11 et 12 floréal" [Report delivered by Picault and Naigeon to the Temporary Commission on the Arts, the *quitidi* of Floréal, 2nd Year of the French Republic, single and indivisible, of Paintings, Furnishings, Bronzes, Marbles, and Porcelains seized, inventoried, and transported from the Brissac house in rue de Grenelle Germain to the National Depot in rue de Baune on the 9th, 10th, 11th, and 12th of Floréal]. To this list is added one drafted by Le Brun, with his appraisals of the paintings and indications of which of them were destined for the "Museum Central" (the Louvre): "Inventaire des Objets provenans de Brissac rue de Grenelle F. B. Germain. Les quelques objets transportés au dépôt de Nesle et au Muséum, ou Inventoriés et Prisés par moi J. B. Le Brun Peintre adjoint à la Commission temporaire des arts le 23 Thermidor et Jours suivans l'an 2d de la République Française une et Indivisible" [Inventory of Objects formerly held by Brissac in the rue de Grenelle F. B. Germain. Said objects having been transported to the depot at Nesle and to the Museum, or inventoried and appraised, by myself, J. B. Le Brun, assistant painter to the Temporary Commission of the Arts, on 23 Thermidor and the following Days, Year 2 of the French Republic, single and Indivisible]. AN. F/17/1267.

His great passion for books is documented in "Catalogue des Livres de la Bibliothèque de Monseigneur le Duc de Brissac, mai 1789," Bibliothèque nationale de France, Département des manuscrits, NAF-317.

ON THE COMTE DE NARBONNE

Manuscripts

Few of the Comte de Narbonne's writings have come down to us, particularly those concerning his private life. We direct the reader to those letters sent to the General d'Arblay and to his English friends (The New York Public Library, The Henry W. and Albert A. Berg Collection of English and American Literature, Frances Burney d'Arblay collection of papers, "Scrapbook: Fanny d'Arblay and friends, England, 1759–1799," no. 100; "Liasse Louis de Narbonne, 1794–1799"), and those sent beginning in 1807 to his cousin Françoise-Catherine de Narbonne-Lara, the wife of the Duc de Fézensac, in order to give her news of their son Raymond-Aymeric-Philippe-Joseph de Fézensac, a young and brilliant officer who had been with him during the Russian campaigns and whose military career he followed with affection ("Lettres à Mme de Fézensac," Collection Berg L.743 no. 1). Among the official documents, I draw attention to those relating to the brief period of his ministry (1791–1792), to which the five letters dispatched to his friend Biron also make reference (in *Un duc et pair au service de la Révolution*), and the letter to the Convention in which he asks to witness the trial of Louis XVI: *Déclaration de Louis de Narbonne, ancien ministre de la Guerre, en France, Dans le procès du Roi envoyée à MM. Trochet et Malesherbes* [Declaration of Louis de Narbonne, former minister of war in France, in the Trial of the King, sent to MM. Trochet and Malesherbes] (an autographed copy is preserved in "Scrapbook: Fanny d'Arblay and friends") (London: Chez les Marchands de Nouveautés, 1793). Additionally, the beautiful letter of December 24, 1803, sent to Bonaparte, who had ignored his request to resume his service (*Mémoires du Comte de Rambuteau, publiés par son petit-fils avec une introduction et des notes de M. Georges Lequin* [Paris: Calmann-Lévy, 1909], 34–39); the twelve letters written to the Emperor upon his return to public life on the occasion of his mission to Berlin (December 1812–January 1813), and the papers relating to his missions in Vienna and Prague (Archives du ministère des Affaires étrangères, Correspondance politique Bavière, vol. CLXXXVI: 16CP/186; Correspondance politique Bavière, supplément, vol. XV: 17CP/15; Correspondance politique Russie, vol. CLIV: 112CP/154; Correspondance politique Autriche, vol. CCCXCIV, CCCXCV et CCCXCVI: 11CP/394, 11CP/395 et 11CP/396).

Bibliographic References

Even though the descendants of Mme de Staël destroyed the letters sent to her by Narbonne, we can hear the echo of his voice in those addressed to him by Germaine between August 1792 and May 1794 (Mme de Staël, *Lettres à Narbonne*, preface by Comtesse Jean de Pange, with introduction, notes, and commentaries by Georges Solovieff [Paris: Gallimard, 1960]). It was with the aid of various confidences received from the Comte that Abel-François Villemain was able to reconstruct his intellectual and political biography (*Souvenirs contemporains d'histoire et de littérature par M. Villemain, membre de l'Institut. M. de Narbonne*, 2 vol. [Paris: Didier, 1854–1855], vol. I). Villemain's testimony is filled out by the particularly interesting testimony of Narbonne's son-in-law (*Mémoires du Comte de Rambuteau*, 20–120). And among the numerous contemporary memoirs that mention him, I should note the affectionate testimony of the Duchesse d'Abrantès, which reports the letter of condolence that the Comte sent to her upon the death of her husband (*Mémoires complets et authentiques de Laure Junot Duchesse d'Abrantès. Souvenirs historiques sur Napoléon, la Révolution, le Directoire, le Consulat, l'Empire, la Restauration, la Révolution de 1830 et les premières années du règne de Louis-Philippe*, 13 vol., first complete edition [Paris: Jean de Bonnot, 1967–1968], vol. IX, 506–7). The lovely biography by Émile Dard (*Un confident de l'Empereur, Le Comte Louis de Narbonne, 1755-1813*, Paris, Plon, 1943) remains an essential reference work on the Comte de Narbonne.

On Narbonne's exile in England, see *The Journals and Letters of Fanny Burney (Madame d'Arblay)*, 12 vol., edited by Joyce Helmow and Althea Douglas (Oxford: Clarendon Press, 1972–1984), in particular vol. II, which contains the correspondence for 1793 relating to Juniper Hall, and to her engagement and marriage to General d'Arblay. Likewise, the letters of Mrs. Phillips preserved in the Burney Collection in New York, cited previously. See also Constance Hill, *Juniper Hall: A Rendezvous of Certain Illustrious Personages During the French Revolution, Including Alexandre d'Arblay and Fanny Burney* (London: The Bodley Head, 1904); and Linda Kelly, *Juniper Hall: An English Refuge from the French Revolution* (London: Weidenfeld and Nicolson, 1991). On the Vicomtesse de Laval and her son Mathieu de Montmorency-Laval, see *L'Histoire et généalogie de la Maison de Montmorency de Georges Martin* (La Ricamaire: Imprimerie Sud Offset, 2000), 65–67, 76–82.

ON THE CHEVALIER DE BOUFFLERS

Works

Boufflers began his career as a man of letters at age eighteen with the entry *"généreux, générosité"* [generous, generosity] in volume VII of the *Encyclopédie* in 1757, and by publishing his *discours de réception* the following year to the Académie royale des sciences et des belles lettres de Nancy; with *La Reine de Golconde, conte* (s.n., s.l., 1761) and *Lettres de Monsieur le chevalier de Boufflers pendant son voyage en Suisse, à Madame sa mère* (Paris: s.n., 1771), he achieved renown. He was an indefatigable versifier and many of his improvisations and poems were reported in *Correspondance littéraire, philosophique et critique par Grimm, Diderot, Raynal, Meister, etc., revue sur les textes originaux comprenant, outre ce qui a été publié à diverses époques, les fragments supprimés en 1813 par la censure, les parties inédites conservées à la Bibliothèque ducale de Gotha et à l'Arsenal de Paris, Notices, notes et table générale de Maurice Tourneux*, 16 vol. (Paris: Garnier Frères, 1877–1882), by the *Almanach des Muses*, and by other chronicles of the period. The first collection of his writings—*Oeuvres du chevalier de Boufflers*—appeared in 1780 (La Haye: Detune), followed over the years by numerous other collections, prose texts as well as poetry, up until the final edition to have been supervised by the author himself (*Oeuvres de Stanislas de Boufflers, membre de l'Institut et de la Légion d'honneur: Édition seule complète, ornée de seize gravures et du portrait de l'auteur*, 2 vol. [Paris: Briand, 1813]).

For a detailed list of Boufflers's works and of the studies dedicated to him, I point the reader to the excellent bibliography by Nicole Vaget Grangeat (*Le Chevalier de Boufflers et son temps: Étude d'un échec* [Paris: Nizet, 1976], 205–20).

In the pages dedicated to Boufflers above, I have made reference to *Oeuvres complètes de Boufflers, de l'Académie française*, new enlarged edition, with a note on Boufflers by J. Taschereau, 2 vol. (Paris: Furne, 1827); to the edition of *Contes du chevalier de Boufflers de l'Académie française*, with a bio-bibliographic note by Octave Uzanne (Paris: A. Quantin, 1878); and to the edition of *Poésies diverses du chevalier de Boufflers*, with a bio-bibliographic note by Octave Uzanne (Paris: A. Quantin, 1886). There exists a very fine modern edition of *Contes*, edited by Alex Sokalski (Paris: Société des textes français modernes, 1995).

For Boufflers's correspondence with Mme de Sabran, I have utilized the first two volumes of the beautiful edition to have appeared to date, rich with numerous previously unpublished letters, by Sue Carrell (*Comtesse de Sabran et chevalier de Boufflers, Le Lit bleu, Correspondance, 1777–1785* [Paris: Tallandier, 2008], and *La Promesse, Correspondance, 1786–1787* [Paris: Tallandier, 2010]). While awaiting a final volume, currently underway, which will bring together the letters written between 1788 and 1827, I have relied for the years of the Revolution on those published by Pierre de Croze-Lemercier in *Le Chevalier de Boufflers et la Comtesse de Sabran, 1788–1792* (Paris: Calmann-Lévy, 1894). For the Chevalier's sojourn in Senegal, see also Léonce Pingaud, "Le chevalier de Boufflers au Sénégal," *Revue des questions historiques*, XXVI (1880): 280–87; Paul Bonnefon, "Le Chevalier de Boufflers au Sénégal. Lettres et documents inédits," *Mercure de France*, LXXXVI (July–August 1910); and the circumscribed edition of letters sent to Senegal by the Chevalier de Boufflers (*Lettres d'Afrique à Madame de Sabran*, edited, with a preface, notes, and dossier by François Bessire [Arles: Actes Sud, 1998]), notable for its scholarly apparatus.

Bibliographic References

For Boufflers's family history and the record of his formative years, the works of Gaston Maugras remain indispensable: *La Cour de Lunéville au XVIIIe siècle. Les Marquises de Boufflers et du Châtelet, Voltaire, Devau, Saint-Lambert, etc.* (Paris: Plon, Nourrit et Cie, 1904); *Dernières années de la cour de Lunéville, Madame de Boufflers, ses enfants et ses amis* (Paris: Plon, Nourrit et Cie, 1906); *La Marquise de Boufflers et son fils, le chevalier de Boufflers* (Paris: Plon, Nourrit et Cie, 1907).

Though it is over a century old, Nesta H. Webster's *The Chevalier de Boufflers: A Romance of the French Revolution* (New York: E. Dutton, 1916), is still the most successful biography of the Chevalier; she has been paraphrased by Joseph Callewaert in *La Comtesse de Sabran et le Chevalier de Boufflers* (Paris: Perrin, 1990).

Even though it is explicitly reductive, the most informed historical and literary essay on Boufflers is the one cited above, *Le Chevalier de Boufflers et son temps*, by Grangeat.

For Mme de Sabran's biography, see the testimony of Elzéar de Sabran, "Notice sur Madame la Comtesse de Sabran depuis Marquise de Boufflers," in Alex Sokalski and Susan L. Carrell, "Les souvenirs d'un fils: documents inédits sur la Comtesse de Sabran," *Studies on Voltaire and the Eighteenth Century*, no. 302 (Oxford: The Voltaire Foundation-University of Oxford, 1992); the portrait by Lucien Perey, "La jeunesse de Mme de Sabran," in *Figures du temps passé, dix-huitième siècle* (Paris: Lévy, 1990); and Gaston Maugras and Pierre de Croze-Lemercier, *Delphine de Sabran, Marquise de Custine* (Paris: Plon, Nourrit et Cie, 1912).

ON THE COMTE DE SÉGUR

Works

In the Comte de Ségur's vast historical and literary production, I have limited myself to mentioning those works that I have utilized in tracing his portrait.

Mémoires ou Souvenirs et Anecdotes par M. le Comte de Ségur, 3 vol. (Paris: Alexis Eymery, 1824–1826).

Extraits de Lettres écrites d'Amérique par le Comte de Ségur, colonel en second du régiment de Soissonnais à la Comtesse de Ségur, dame de Madame Victoire (1782–1783), in *Deux Français aux États-Unis et dans la Nouvelle Espagne en 1782, Journal de Voyage du Prince de Broglie et Lettres du Comte de Ségur*, edited by the Duc de Broglie (Paris: Société des Bibliophiles français, Mélanges par la société des Bibliophiles français, Pièce no 6, Imprimerie Lahure, 1903).

Crispin Duègne, comédie, en trois actes et en prose; *Caius-Marcius Coriolan, tragédie, en cinq actes et en vers*; *Le Sourd et le Bègue, proverbe en un acte, en prose* ("À quelque chose malheur est bon" [Every cloud has a silver lining]).

L'Enlèvement, comédie-proverbe en un acte, en prose ("Chat échaudé craint l'eau froide" [A scalded cat fears cold water]).

L'Homme Inconsidéré, comédie en un acte, en prose, in *Recueil des pièces de l'Hermitage* (St. Petersburg: s.l., s.d., 1788–1789). *Théâtre de l'Hermitage de Catherine II*, 2 vol. (Paris: Buisson, Year VII of the Republic [1799]), published at the initiative of Ségur.

Contes, fables, chanson et vers (Paris: Buisson, 1801).

Galerie morale et politique, 2 vol. (Paris: Alexis Eymery, 1824–1828).

Bibliographic References

Leon Apt, *Louis-Philippe de Ségur: An Intellectual in a Revolutionary Age* (The Hague: Martinus Nijhoff, 1969).

Gabriel de Broglie, *Ségur sans cérémonie 1757–1805, ou la Gaieté libertine* (Paris: Perrin, 1977).

Sainte-Beuve, "Le Comte de Ségur" (1843), in *Portraits littéraires, texte et notes de Gérald Antoine* (Paris: Robert Laffont, 1993), 597–611.

Pierre de Ségur, *Le Maréchal de Ségur (1724–1801), ministre de la Guerre sous Louis XVI* in

Philippe-Paul de Ségur, *Histoire et Mémoires par le Général Cte Philippe de Ségur*, 7 vol. (Paris: Firmin Didot, 1877).

Pierre de Ségur, "Le Comte Louis Philippe de Ségur (1753–1830)," *Revue des deux mondes, cinquième série*, XLIII (1908).

ON THE COMTE DE VAUDREUIL

Preserved in the National Archives of the Russian Federation (GARF, Moscow), collection no. 728 (Collection of Winter Palace Documents), inventory 2 (French emigration), no. 288, alongside Vaudreuil's correspondence with the Comte d'Artois published by Léonce Pingaud, are letters, notes, and documents by the Enchanter. It would not be until Vaudreuil's departure from France and his *Correspondance intime du Comte de Vaudreuil et du Comte d'Artois pendant l'émigration (1789–1815)*, introduction, notes, and appendix by Léonce Pingaud, 2 vol. (Paris: Plon, Nourrit et Cie, 1889), that there was direct evidence of his manner of thinking and feeling. But by then the Comte was fifty years old and so, in order to reconstruct the brilliant years of his youth, I have largely relied on the testimony of his contemporaries.

Bibliographic References

Le Guide des Amateurs et des Étrangers voyageurs à Paris, vol. II, 542–49; the catalogs of two auctions of his paintings by Le Brun; and the remarkable essay by Colin B. Bailey (in *Patriotic Taste: Collecting Modern Art in Pre-Revolutionary Paris* [New Haven: Yale University Press, 2002], 163–205) bear witness to his passion for contemporary French painting and the confidence of his taste.

On the friendship that tied Vaudreuil to Chamfort, see the lovely biography by Claude Arnaud, *Chamfort* (Paris: Robert Laffont, 1988).

See also *Oeuvres complètes de Chamfort, recueillies et publiées, avec une notice historique sur la vie et les écrits de l'auteur, par R. Auguis*, 5 vol. (Paris: Chaumerot Jeune, 1824–1825).

Pierre-Louis Ginguené, "Notice sur la vie de Chamfort," in *Oeuvres de Chamfort. Recueillies et publiées par un de ses Amis*, 4 vol. (Paris: Chez le Directeur de l'Imprimerie des Sciences et des Arts, Year III de la République [1794]), vol. I.

Chamfortiana ou Recueil choisi d'anecdotes piquantes et de traits d'esprit de Chamfort, with a "Note on his life and works" (Paris: Marchands de Nouveautés, De l'Imprimerie de Delance, Year IX [1800]).

Maurice Pellisson, *Chamfort. Étude sur sa vie, son caractère et ses écrits* (Paris: Lecène, Oudin et Cie, 1895).

Jean Dagen, Preface to *Chamfort, Maximes, Pensées, Caractères* (Paris: Flammarion, 1968).

Sylvain Ménant, "Chamfort: naissance d'un moraliste," *Cahiers de l'Association internationale des études françaises*, XXX, 1 (1978), 29th Congrès de l'AIEF.

Laurent Loty, "Forme brève et pessimisme. Le cas de Chamfort," in *"La Licorne," XXI: Brièveté et écriture, Actes du Colloque international de Poitiers sur la forme brève*, under the direction of Pierre Testud, November 1991.

Cyril Le Meur, *Les Moralistes français et la Politique à la fin du XVIIIe siècle* (Paris: Honoré Champion, 2002).

Index

Chambre to the Dauphine. Once she became Queen, Marie-Antoinette appointed her as first *Femme de Chambre*. Her husband (1749–1797) was in the service of the Comtesse d'Artois and *Officier de la Chambre* to the Dauphine, and her father-in-law, Pierre-Dominique Berthollet, was secretary and librarian to Queen Marie-Antoinette from 1778. Despite their attachment and loyalty to the royal family, the Campans shared the reformist hopes of 1789, and the brother of Mme Campan, Edmond Genêt, who replaced the Comte de Ségur in the ambassadorship to St. Petersburg, did not hide his Girondist sympathies. After Thermidor, while remaining loyal to the dead Queen and determined to defend her memory, Mme Campan adapted herself pragmatically to the changing times. Driven by financial necessity, she founded at Saint-Germaine-en-Laye, a school for the young daughters of the nobility who had survived the Terror, as well as for those of the new class in power, beginning with the sisters of the First Consul. Appointed by Napoleon as superintendent of the academy of the Légion d'Honneur at Écouen, Mme Campan paid for the favor that she had enjoyed under the Empire with the hostility of Louis XVIII and the daughter of Marie-Antoinette, the Duchesse d'Angoulême. It was in this climate of ostracism and calumny that Mme Campan would continue to work at her memoirs, which she had begun during the Revolution; in them she laid out her self-defense, but without deciding to publish. They finally appeared two years after her death, 84, 85, 272, 279, 281

GENLIS, Charles-Alexis, Comte de, *see* BRÛLART, Charles-Alexis

GENLIS, Mme de, *see* SAINT-AUBIN, Stéphanie-Félicité Ducrest de

GEOFFRIN, Marie-Thérèse –, Marquise Philippe Charles d'Estampes de La Ferté-Imbault (1731), known as Mme de La Ferté-Imbault, (1715–1791), she led a celebrated salon, 254

GEORGE III, George William Frederick, Prince of Wales and then King of the United Kingdom of Great Britain and Ireland, (1738–1820), 19, 20, 53, 54, 123, 261, 348, 382

GEORGE IV, George Augustus Frederick, Prince of Wales and then King of the United Kingdom of Great Britain and Ireland, and of Hanover, (1762–1830), 348, 387

GIBELIN, Victor de, (1771–1853), officer of the company of Gardes Suisses under the command of Besenval, 333

GINGUENÉ, Pierre-Louis, (1748–1816), poet, writer, journalist, Director of Public Instruction under the Directory, member of the institute, founder of the journal *La Décade philosophique, littéraire et politique*, 101, 292, 295–96, 302, 305, 438

GIRARDIN, Sophie-Victoire de –, Marquise de Vassy while widowed, then Mme André Guillaume de Bohm, (1763–1845), daughter of the Marquis Girardin who had buried Rousseau at Ermenonville, she related her experiences during the Revolution in *Les Prisons en 1793, scènes et impressions* (1830), 126

GLUCK, Christoph Willibald von, (1714–1787), composer, 295

GODOLPHIN, Lord Francis, Second Earl of, (1678–1766), British politician, owner of the celebrated Godolphin Arabian stallion, 42

GOETHE, Johann Wolfgang von, (1749–1832), German writer, 31, 147

GONDI, François-Paul de –, Cardinal de Retz, (1616–1679), Coadjutor then

(1724–1816), admiral, contributed to the victory of the English fleet, under the orders of Admiral Rodney over the Franco-Spanish fleet occupying Jamaica at the Battle of Saintes (1782). On August 27, 1783, at the request of the French royalists, he occupied Toulon but was chased off four months later by the Revolutionary troops under the command of Napoleon Bonaparte, 381

HORACE, (65–8 BC), Latin poet, 219

HORTENSE, Queen, *see* BEAUHARNAIS, Hortense de

HOUDETOT, Claude-Constant-César, Comte d', (1724–1806), lieutenant general, husband (1748) of Élisabeth-Françoise-Sophie Lalive de Bellegarde, mistress of the Marquis de Saint-Lambert, who inspired a violent passion in Jean-Jacques Rousseau, 162

HOUDON, Jean-Antoine, (1741–1828), sculptor, 202

HOWARD, Lord Frederick –, Fifth Earl of Carlisle, (1748–1825), statesman, 19

HUME, David, (1711–1776), Scottish philosopher and historian, spent three years in Paris (1763–1766) as secretary to the English Ambassador, where he frequented both philosophers and society salons, 181

HUNTER, Elizabeth, (1762–1849), Anna, (1766–1859), Catherine, (1773–1860), daughters of Doctor William Hunter, physician to Rhode Island's patriot militias, who gave a warm welcome to the French officers accompanying Rochambeau to the garrison at Newport in 1780–1781, 70

ISSEMBOURG D'APPONCOURT, Françoise d'–, Mme François Huguet de Graffigny (or Grafigny) (1712), (1695–1758), born to a family of the minor nobility of Lorraine, abused by her husband, she was left a widow in

1725, and overwhelmed by debt. She frequented the little court at Lunéville and, befriending Saint-Lambert and François-Antoine Devaux (known as Panpan, with whom she maintained an assiduous correspondence for twenty years), she made her literary debut. In 1742, she settled in Paris, joined Mlle Quinault's salon, the Société du Bout du Banc, and found success with *Lettres d'une Péruvienne* (1747), 80

JARENTE D'ORGEVAL, Suzanne-Françoise-Élisabeth de –, Mme Laurent Grimod de La Reynière (1758), (1736–1815), wife of the very rich *Fermier Général and Administrateur des Postes*, brother-in-law of Malesherbes, 315

JAUBERT, Pierre Amédée, (1779–1847), Belgian actor who drew up the lists of prisoners at Saint-Lazare to be sent before the tribunal, 424

JAUCOURT, Arnail-François, Chevalier then Comte and Marquis de, (1757–1852), soldier, representative of the nobility to the Estates General, he fought for a constitutional monarchy. Opposed to the declaration of war of April 20, 1792, and of the excesses of the Revolution, in disagreement with the majority of the assembly, he resigned. Accused of treason and imprisoned at the Abbaye, he escaped the September Massacres thanks to Mme de Staël's intervention with Munel, prosecutor for the commune, and found refuge in England, 363, 365, 366, 367, 369, 373, 380, 433

JEAN DE MANVILLE, Françoise-Éléonore de –, Comtesse de Sabran (1769) then Marquise de Boufflers (1797), (1750–1827), 113, 142, 188–93, 195–205, 207–9, 212, 213, 216, 218–20, 221, 222, 271, 279, 321–23, 355, 359–62, 403, 435, 436

branches of the family. His eldest son, Louis-Philippe (first branch), was the father of Louis-Philippe de Vaudreuil (1724–1802), the Marquis de Vaudreuil. His third son (third branch) was Joseph-Hyacinthe, father of Joseph-Hyacinthe-François de Paule, Comte de Vaudreuil, 270

RIGAUD, Vicomte de Vaudreuil, a nephew of Vaudreuil, belonging to the second branch of the family, 237

RIVAROL, Antoine, known as the Comte de, (1753–1801), writer, author of the famous *Discours sur l'universalité de la langue française* (1784), journalist, author of antirevolutionary epigrams, he emigrated in 1792, 336

RIVIÈRE, Auguste Louis Jean-Baptiste, (1761–1833), copyist and miniaturist, elder brother of Suzanne, wife of Étienne Vigée, brother of Mme Vigée Le Brun, accompanied the artist on her journey across Europe during the Revolution, 295

RIVIÈRE, Suzanne de –, Mme Étienne Vigée, (1764–1811), 294–95

ROBERT, Hubert, (1733–1808), painter, 291, 331, 332, 416

ROBESPIERRE, Maximilien-François-Isidore de, (1758–1794), 4, 345, 379, 404, 409, 410, 418, 420, 421, 425, 427

ROCHAMBEAU, Donatien-Marie-Joseph de Vimeur, Vicomte de, (1750–1813), son of General Rochambeau, he fought under his command during the American War of Independence, and was then named Governor of the Leeward Isles. He returned to Europe to serve under Napoleon and died at the Battle of Leipzig, 69, 72

ROCHAMBEAU, Jean-Baptiste-Donatien de Vimeur, Maréchal de France, Comte de, (1725–1807), he began his military career at the age of sixteen in the War of the Austrian

Succession, then served during the Seven Years' War and, promoted to General, went to fight in America on the side of the rebels. When the Revolution broke out, he received command of the Army of the North and, after the flight to Varennes, refused the position of Minister of War so as not to have to leave the army. He declared himself opposed to the war against Germany, was charged by the Committee of Public Safety, and jailed at the Conciergerie. Thermidor saved him from the guillotine, 67, 69–72, 73, 74, 196, 234, 236, 344, 349, 399, 400–401

ROCHEFORT, Marie-Thérèse, Comtesse de, *see* BRANCAS, Marie-Thérèse de

RODET, Marie-Thérèse –, Mme François Geoffrin (1713), (1699–1777), leader of one of the most celebrated Parisian salons, 254

RODNEY, George Brydges, (1717–1792), English admiral, 348

ROHAN (family), 77, 78, 329

ROHAN-CHABOT, Alexandre-Louis-Auguste, Duc de, (1761–1818), General, deputy for the nobility to the Estates General, he emigrated in 1790 and joined the Army of the Princes, but, in 1792, went to London. Peer of France under the Restoration, 394

ROHAN-CHABOT, Louis-Antoine-Auguste de –, Comte then Duc de Chabot, then Duc de Rohan, (1733–1807), Lieutenant General of the Armies of the King (1781), 68, 387, 396

ROHAN-CHABOT, Marie-Sylvie de –, Mme Charles-Juste de Beauvau-Craon, Princesse de Beauvau (1764), (1729–1807), 23

ROHAN-GUÉMÉNÉE, Charles-Alain-Gabriel de –, Prince de Rohan, Duc de Montbazon and de Bouillon, then Prince de Guéménée, (1764–1836), son of the Prince de Guéménée, 79

Illustration Credits

BENEDETTA CRAVERI is currently a professor of French literature at the University Suor Orsola Benincasa, Naples. She is a corresponding member of Accademia dei Lincei and contributes to *The New York Review of Books* and to the cultural pages of the Italian newspaper *La Repubblica*. Her books include *Madame du Deffand and Her World*, *Mistresses and Queens*, and *The Age of Conversation* (available from New York Review Books). She is married to a French diplomat and in 2017 was awarded the Prix mondial Cino Del Duca by l'Institut de France.

AARON KERNER is a translator, editor, and teacher who lives in Boston.